THE **COMM** SOLUTION

D0132000

COMM⁴ delivers all the key terms and core concepts for the **Speech Communication** course.

Print
+
Online

COMM Online provides the complete narrative from the printed text with additional interactive media and the unique functionality of **StudyBits**—all available on nearly any device!

What is a StudyBit™? Created through a deep investigation of students' challenges and workflows, the StudyBit™ functionality of **COMM Online** enables students of different generations and learning styles to study more effectively by allowing them to learn their way. Here's how they work:

COLLECT WHAT'S IMPORTANT
Create StudyBits as you highlight text, images or take notes!

WEAK
FAIR
STRONG
UNASSIGNED

RATE AND ORGANIZE STUDYBITS
Rate your understanding and use the color-coding to quickly organize your study time and personalize your flashcards and quizzes.

StudyBit™

TRACK/MONITOR PROGRESS
Use Concept Tracker to decide how you'll spend study time and study YOUR way!

85%

PERSONALIZE QUIZZES
Filter by your StudyBits to personalize quizzes or just take chapter quizzes off-the-shelf.

CORRECT
INCORRECT
CORRECT
CORRECT

COMM4

Kathleen S. Verderber, Deanna D. Sellnow,
Rudolph F. Verderber

Vice President, General Manager, 4LTR Press
and the Student Experience: Neil Marquardt

Product Director, 4LTR Press: Steven E. Joos

Product Manager: Laura Redden

Marketing Manager: Sarah Seymour

Content Developer: Patricia Hempel

Product Assistant: Lauren Dame

Content Project Manager: Darrell E. Frye

Manufacturing Planner: Ron Montgomery

Production Service: MPS Limited

Sr. Art Director: Bethany Casey

Interior Designer: Joe Devine/Red Hangar Design

Cover Designer: Lisa Kuhn/Curio Press, LLC

Cover Image: © Rawpixel/Shutterstock.com

Intellectual Property

    Analyst: Alexandra Ricciardi

    Project Manager: Betsy Hathaway

Vice President, General Manager, Humanities,
World Languages: Cheryl Costantini

Product Director: Monica Eckman

Product Manager: Kelli Strieby

Library of Congress Control Number: 2015949182

Student Edition with *COMM Online* Printed Access Card ISBN: 978-1-305-65958-2

Student Edition (book only) ISBN: 978-1-305-65955-1

Cengage Learning
20 Channel Center Street
Boston, MA 02210
USA

Cengage Learning is a leading provider of customized learning solutions with employees residing in nearly 40 different countries and sales in more than 125 countries around the world. Find your local representative at **www.cengage.com**.

Cengage Learning products are represented in Canada by Nelson Education, Ltd.

To learn more about Cengage Learning Solutions, visit **www.cengage.com**

Purchase any of our products at your local college store or at our preferred online store **www.cengagebrain.com**

Printed in the United States of America
Print Number: 01   Print Year: 2015

VERDERBER/SELLNOW/VERDERBER

COMM⁴

Rawpixel/Shutterstock.com

BRIEF CONTENTS

CONTENTS

PART 1
FOUNDATIONS OF COMMUNICATION

Rawpixel/Shutterstock.com

PART 4
PUBLIC SPEAKING

© Nelosa/Shutterstock.com

YOUR FEED-BACK YOUR BOOK

Our research never ends. Continual feedback from you ensures that we keep up with your changing needs.

1 Communication Perspectives

LEARNING OUTCOMES

1-1 Describe the nature of communication

1-2 Explain the communication process

1-3 Identify the characteristics of communication

1-4 Assess messages using the principles of ethical communication

1-5 Develop a personal communication improvement plan

After finishing this chapter go to **PAGE 15** for **STUDY TOOLS.**

Rawpixel/Shutterstock.com

Numerous studies done over the years have shown that for almost any job, employers seek oral communication skills, teamwork skills, and interpersonal abilities (College learning for the new global century, 2007; Hansen & Hansen,(n.d.); Young, 2003). For example, an article on the role of communication in the workplace reported that in engineering, a highly technical field, speaking skills were very important for 72 percent of the employers surveyed (Darling & Dannels, 2003). A survey by the National Association of Colleges and Employers (Hart Research Associates, 2006) reported the top 10 personal qualities and skills that employers seek from college graduates. The number one skill was communication, including face-to-face speaking, presentational speaking, and writing. Other "Top 10" skills, which you will learn about and practice in this course, include teamwork skills (number three), analytical skills (number five), interpersonal skills (number eight), and problem-solving skills (number nine). The employers also said that these very skills are, unfortunately, the ones many new graduates lack (Hart Research Associates, 2010). Taking this course to heart can significantly increase your ability to get a job and be successful in your chosen career.

How effectively you communicate with others is important not only to your career but also to your personal relationships. Your ability to make and keep friends, to be a good family member, to have satisfying intimate relationships, to participate in or lead groups, and to prepare and present speeches depends on your communication skills. During this course, you will learn about the communication process and have an opportunity to practice basic communication skills that will help you improve your relationships.

We begin this chapter by describing the nature of communication and the communication process. From there, we will discuss several principles of communication and five tenets of ethical communication. Finally, we explain how to develop a personal communication improvement plan to hone your skills based on what you learn throughout the semester.

1-1 THE NATURE OF COMMUNICATION

Communication is a complex process through which we express, interpret, and coordinate messages with others to create shared meaning, meet social goals, manage personal identity, and carry out our relationships. At its core, communication is about messages.

Messages are the verbal utterances, visual images, and nonverbal behaviors used to convey thoughts and feelings. We refer to the process of creating messages as **encoding** and the process of interpreting them as **decoding**. So when the toddler points to her bottle and cries out "Ba-ba," her message (consisting of a nonverbal gesture—pointing—and a verbal utterance—"Ba-ba") expresses her desire to have her father hand her the bottle of milk she sees on the table. How her father responds, however, depends on how he decodes it. He might respond by handing her the bottle or by saying, "Sorry, cutie, the bottle is empty." Or he may just look at her with a puzzled expression on his face. Either response is also a message. **Feedback** is a reaction and response to a message that indicates how the message was interpreted.

1-1a Canned Plans and Scripts

How do we form and interpret messages? We do so, in part, based on our canned plans and scripts. A **canned plan** is a "mental library" of scripts each of us draws from to create messages based on what worked for us or others in the past (Berger, 1997). A **script** is an actual text of what to say and do in a specific situation. We have canned plans and scripts for a wide variety of typical interactions, such as greeting people, making small talk, giving advice, complimenting or criticizing someone, or persuading others.

communication the process through which we express, interpret, and coordinate messages with others

messages the verbal utterances, visual images, and nonverbal behaviors used to convey thoughts and feelings

encoding the process of putting our thoughts and feelings into words and nonverbal behaviors

decoding the process of interpreting another's message

feedback reactions and responses to messages

canned plan a "mental library" of scripts each of us draws from to create messages based on what worked for us in the past or that we have heard or used numerous times in similar situations

script an actual text of what to say and do in a specific situation

Great apes are known for their complex communication system and for their ability to learn sign language to communicate with humans. Here a teacher works and communicates with a chimpanzee. Both use scripts to communicate.

Terrace, H.S./Animals Animals

We develop canned plans and scripts from our own previous experiences and by observing what appears to work for other people (even fictitious people we see on TV or in movies) (Pajares, Prestin, Chen, & Nabi, 2009). We draw on scripts from our canned plans as we form a message and usually customize what we say based on the person and the situation. For example, you might have several canned "greeting" plan scripts to draw from when addressing a close friend, a parent, a supervisor, or a stranger.

The point is that we don't usually start from scratch to form messages. Instead, we recognize what type of message we want to form, search our mental canned plan library for an appropriate script, and then customize it to fit the unique parts of the current situation. All of this mental choosing happens in nanoseconds and somewhat automatically. We also use our canned plans and scripts when we interpret messages from others.

Obviously, the larger your canned plan library and the more scripts you have for each canned plan, the more likely you will be to form appropriate and effective messages, as well as to understand and respond appropriately to the messages of others.

1-1b Communication Contexts

According to noted German philosopher Jürgen Habermas, the ideal communication situation is impossible to achieve, but considering its contexts as we communicate can move us closer to that goal (Littlejohn & Foss, 2011). The context in which a message is embedded affects the expectations of the participants, the meaning these participants derive, and their subsequent behavior. The **communication context** is made up of the physical, social, historical, psychological, and cultural situations that surround a communication event.

The **physical context** includes the location of a communication encounter, the environmental conditions surrounding it (temperature, lighting, noise level), and the physical proximity of participants to each other. Increasingly, however, communication occurs via smartphones and over the Internet. And while e-communication allows us to interact at a distance, our ability to share meaning may be affected by the media we use. For instance, when you telephone a friend, you lose nonverbal cues such as posture, gestures, eye contact, and facial expressions that are part of a face-to-face message. Without these cues, you have less information on which to base your interpretation of your friend's message. E-mail and text messages are missing even more of the nonverbal cues that help us interpret messages accurately.

The **social context** is the nature of the relationship that already exists between the participants. The better you know someone and the better relationship you have with him or her, the more likely you are to accurately interpret the messages.

The **historical context** is the background provided by previous communication between the participants. For instance, suppose Chas texts Anna saying he will pick up the draft of the report they had left for their manager. When Anna sees Chas at lunch later that day, she asks, "Did you get it?" Another person listening to the conversation would have no idea what "it" is. Yet Chas may well reply, "It's on my desk." Anna and Chas understand one another because of their earlier exchange.

communication context the physical, social, historical, psychological, and cultural situations that surround a communication event

physical context the location of a communication encounter, the environmental conditions surrounding it (temperature, lighting, noise level), and the physical proximity of participants to each other

social context the nature of the relationship that exists between participants

historical context the background provided by previous communication episodes between the participants that influence understandings in the current encounter

The **psychological context** includes the moods and feelings each person brings to the communication encounter. For instance, suppose Corinne is under a great deal of stress. While she is studying for an exam, a friend stops by and asks her to take a break to go to the gym. Corinne, who is normally good-natured, may respond with irritation, which her friend may misinterpret as Corinne being mad at him.

The **cultural context** includes the beliefs, values, orientations, underlying assumptions, and rituals that belong to a specific culture (Samovar, Porter, & McDaniel, 2010). Everyone is part of one or more cultural groups (e.g., ethnicity, religion, age, gender, sexual orientation, physical ability). When two people from different cultures interact, misunderstandings may occur because of their different cultural values, beliefs, orientations, and rituals.

1-1c Communication Settings

The setting in which communication occurs also affects how we form and interpret messages. **Communication settings** differ based on the number of participants and the level of formality in the interactions (Littlejohn & Foss, 2011). These settings are intrapersonal, interpersonal, small group, public, and mass.

Intrapersonal communication refers to the interactions that occur in our minds when we are talking to ourselves. We usually don't verbalize our intrapersonal communication. When you think about what you'll do later today or when you send yourself e-mail reminders, you are communicating intrapersonally. Much of our intrapersonal communication occurs subconsciously (Kellerman, 1992). When you drive to school every day "without thinking" about each turn you make along the way, you are communicating intrapersonally on a subconscious level. The study of intrapersonal communication often focuses on its role in shaping self-perceptions and in managing communication apprehension—that is, the fear associated with communicating with others (Richmond & McCroskey, 1997). In this book, our study of intrapersonal communication focuses on self-talk as a means to improve self-concept and self-esteem and, ultimately, communication competence in a variety of situations.

Interpersonal communication is characterized by informal interaction between two people who have an identifiable relationship with each other (Knapp & Daly, 2002). Talking to a friend between classes, visiting on the phone with your mother, and texting or chatting online with your brother are all examples of interpersonal communication. In chapters 7 and 8, we will study how interpersonal communication helps us develop, maintain, improve, and end interpersonal relationships.

Small-group communication typically involves three to 20 people who come together to communicate with one another (Beebe & Masterson, 2006; Hirokawa, Cathcart, Samovar, & Henman, 2003). Examples of small groups include a family, a group of friends, a group of classmates working on a project, and a workplace management team. Small-group communication can occur in face-to-face settings as well as online through electronic mailing lists, discussion boards, virtual meetings, and blogs. In chapters 9 and 10, our study of small groups focuses on the characteristics of effective groups, ethical and effective communication in groups, leadership, problem-solving, conflict, and group presentations.

Public communication is delivered to audiences of more than 20 people. Examples include public speeches, presentations, and forums we may experience in person or via mediated or technology-driven channels. For example, when a president delivers the State of the Union address, some people may be in attendance on location, others watch on TV or the Internet, and still others view it later in the form of televised broadcast snippets, digital recordings, or Internet video. The Internet is also becoming the medium of choice for posting job ads and résumés, for advertising and buying products, and for political activism. In Part IV, our study of public communication focuses on preparing, practicing, and delivering effective oral presentations in both face-to-face and virtual environments.

Mass communication is delivered by individuals

---

psychological context the moods and feelings each person brings to a communication encounter

cultural context the beliefs, values, orientations, underlying assumptions, and rituals that belong to a specific culture

communication setting the different communication environments within which people interact, characterized by the number of participants and the extent to which the interaction is formal or informal

intrapersonal communication the interactions that occur in our minds when we are talking to ourselves

interpersonal communication informal interaction between two people who have an identifiable relationship with each other

small-group communication three to 20 people who come together for the specific purpose of solving a problem or arriving at a decision

public communication one participant, the speaker, delivers a message to a group of more than 20 people

mass communication communication that is delivered by individuals and entities through mass media to large segments of the population at the same time

Intrapersonal Communication

Interpersonal Communication

Small-Group Communication

Public Communication

Mass Communication

and entities through mass media to large segments of the population at the same time. Some examples include newspaper and magazine articles and advertisements, as well as radio and television programs and advertisements.

communication process a complex set of three different and interrelated activities intended to result in shared meaning

message production the steps you take when you encode a message

THE COMMUNICATION PROCESS

The **communication process** is a complex set of three different and interrelated activities intended to result in shared meaning (Burleson, 2009). Three activities are message production, message interpretation, and interaction coordination.

First, **message production** is what we do when we *encode* a message. We begin by forming goals based on our understanding of the situation and our values, ethics, and needs. Based on these goals, we recall an effective canned plan script and adapt it to the current situation.

Second, **message interpretation** is what we do when we *decode* a message. We read or listen to someone's words, observe their nonverbal behavior, and take note of other visuals. Then we interpret the message based on the canned plan scripts we remember that seem similar. Based on this interpretation, we prepare a feedback message.

Interaction coordination consists of the behavioral adjustments each participant makes in an attempt to create shared meaning (Burgoon et al., 2002).

Shared meaning occurs when the receiver's interpretation is similar to what the speaker intended. We can usually gauge the extent to which shared meaning is achieved by the sender's response to the feedback message. For example, Sarah says to Nick, "I dropped my phone and it broke." Nick replies, "Cool, now you can get a Droid." Sarah responds, "No, you don't understand, I can't afford to buy a new phone." Sarah's response to Nick's feedback message lets Nick know he misunderstood her. The extent to which we achieve shared meaning can be affected by the channels we use and by the interference/noise that compete with our messages.

1-2a Channels

Channels are both the route traveled by the message and the means of transportation. Face-to-face communication has three basic channels: verbal symbols, nonverbal cues, and visual images. Technologically mediated communication uses these same channels, though nonverbal cues such as movements, touch, and gestures are represented by visual symbols like **emoticons** (textual images that symbolize the sender's mood, emotion, or facial expressions) and **acronyms** (abbreviations that stand

lightwavemedia/Shutterstock.com

Messages are not always interpreted as the sender expects, which can be clarified by feedback.

in for common phrases). For example, in a face-to-face interaction, Barry might express his frustration about a poor grade verbally by noting why he thought the grade was unfair, visually by showing the assignment along with the grading criteria for it, and nonverbally by raising his voice and shaking his fist. In an online interaction, however, he might need to insert a frowning-face emoticon (☹) or the acronym "POed" to represent those nonverbal behaviors.

With so many technology-driven channels available for communicating today, we must now thoughtfully select the best channel for our purpose, audience, and situation. We can do so by considering media richness and synchronicity.

Media richness refers to how much and what kinds of information can be transmitted via a particular channel. Face-to-face is the richest channel because we can hear the verbal message content and observe the nonverbal cues to interpret its meaning. Sometimes, however, communicating face-to-face is either impossible or not a good use of time. The less information offered via a given channel, the leaner it is. The leaner the channel, the greater the chances are for misunderstanding. For example, texts and Twitter messages are lean because they use as few characters as possible whereas videoconferencing channels such as Skype and FaceTime are richer because we can observe nonverbal cues almost as much as in a face-to-face setting.

Synchronicity is the extent to which a channel allows for immediate feedback. Synchronous channels allow communication to occur in "real time" and asynchronous channels allow for "lag time." Synchronous channels allow for immediate feedback to clarify potential misunderstandings whereas asynchronous channels provide time to carefully craft and revise our messages (Condon & Cech, 2010). Generally, you should use a rich channel if your message is complicated, difficult, or controversial. It is also usually a good idea to use a synchronous channel in these cases. You might choose an asynchronous channel, however, if you could benefit from having extra time to carefully organize and word your message. On the other hand, use a lean channel when you merely want to convey simple and emotionally neutral information. Figure 1.1 illustrates the continuum of communication channels available today.

1-2b Interference/Noise

Interference or **noise** is any stimulus that interferes with the process of achieving shared meaning. Noise can be physical or psychological. **Physical noise** is any external sight

message interpretation the steps you take when you decode a message

interaction coordination the behavioral adjustments each participant makes in an attempt to create shared meaning

channel the route traveled by the message and the means of transportation

emoticons textual images that symbolize the sender's mood, emotion, or facial expressions

acronyms abbreviations that stand in for common phrases

media richness the amount and kinds of media transmitted via a particular channel

synchronicity the extent to which a channel allows for immediate feedback

interference (noise) any stimulus that interferes with the process of sharing meaning

physical noise any external sight or sound that detracts from a message

FIGURE 1.1 CONTINUUM OF COMMUNICATION CHANNELS

ASYNCHRONOUS					SYNCHRONOUS	
Bulk letters	Posted letters	Facebook	**Interactive chat**	**Telephone**	Skype	**Face-to-Face**
Posters	E-mail	Twitter			iChat	
E-mail spam	Text messages	Other social media websites			Other video conferencing	

LEAN	RICH
LOW SOCIAL PRESENCE	**HIGH SOCIAL PRESENCE**

or sound that distracts us from the message. For example, when someone enters the room, a cell phone goes off, or someone near us is texting while a speaker is talking, we might be distracted from the message. Or, when communicating online, we might be distracted when we get a Facebook or Twitter notification. **Psychological noise** refers to the thoughts and feelings we experience that compete with the sender's message for our attention. So when we daydream about what we have to do at work or feel offended when a speaker uses foul language, we are being distracted by psychological noise. That's why it is a good practice to close social media sites and power off smart phones while engaged in important face-to-face or online conferences, meetings, or classroom discussions.

1-2c A Model of the Communication Process

In summary, let's look at a graphic model of a message exchange between two people presented in Figure 1.2. The process begins when one person, who we will call Andy, is motivated to share his thoughts with another person, Taylor. Andy reviews the communication situation, including the communication context, and sorts through the scripts in his canned plan library to find one he thinks will be appropriate. Based on this script, he encodes a customized message and shares it with Taylor.

Taylor decodes the message using her understanding of the situation and matching it to scripts in her canned plan library. She might misinterpret Andy's intended meaning because she is distracted by physical or psychological interference/noise, or because her scripts don't match Andy's. Taylor encodes a feedback message using a script from her canned plan library as a guide. She then shares her feedback message and Andy decodes it. If Taylor understood what Andy was saying, he will extend the conversation. If, on the other hand, Andy believes Taylor misunderstood his meaning, he will try to clarify what he meant before extending the conversation. Finally, the communication process is not linear. In other words, both Andy and Taylor simultaneously encode and decode verbal and nonverbal messages throughout the message exchange.

psychological noise
thoughts and feelings we experience that compete with a sender's message for our attention

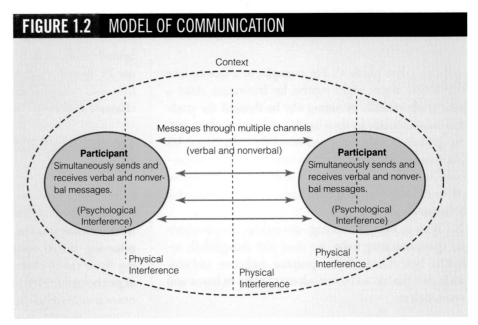

FIGURE 1.2 MODEL OF COMMUNICATION

Modern Mourning

Mourning is a universal human communication process of celebrating the life of someone while grieving his or her death. Mourning rituals and traditions vary by culture and religion and change over time. So it is not surprising that mourning in the United States in the 21st century is adapting past practices to modern life.

Web sites such as Legacy.com, MyDeathSpace.com, and Memory-Of.com facilitate the creation of these interactive online memorials. Users can create slide shows to "talk" about their deceased loved one and mourners can "visit" with the departed and connect with other mourners. T-shirts have become a new type of mourning clothes, often featuring pictures of the deceased. This is particularly common when commemorating a young person or a violent death. Another sign of mourning in the 21st century is the use of decals on cars and bikes. Decals are visual markers that can

Jeff Lueders/Shutterstock.com

not only memorialize a loved one who died but can also connect mourners to others who have suffered a similar loss.

1-3 CHARACTERISTICS OF COMMUNICATION

Several communication characteristics provide a foundation for practicing and improving communication skills. In this section, we discuss eight of them.

1-3a Communication Has Purpose

Whenever we communicate, we have a purpose for doing so. The purpose may be serious or trivial, and we may or may not be aware of it at the time. There are five basic purposes for communication.

1. We communicate to develop and maintain our sense of self. Through our interactions, we learn who we are and what we are good at.

2. We communicate to meet our social needs. Just as we need food, water, and shelter, we also need contact with other people.

3. We communicate to develop and maintain relationships. We communicate not only to meet simple social needs but also to develop relationships.

4. We communicate to exchange information. We exchange information through observation, reading, and direct communication with others, whether face-to-face, via text messaging, or online.

5. We communicate to influence others. We may communicate to try to convince friends to go to a particular restaurant or to see a certain movie, encourage a supervisor to alter the work schedule, or talk an instructor into changing a grade.

1-3b Communication Is Continuous

We are always sending and interpreting messages. Even silence communicates if another person infers meaning from it. Why? Because our nonverbal behavior represents reactions to our environment and to the people around us. If we are cold, we might shiver; if we are hot or nervous, we might perspire; if we are bored, happy, or confused, our nonverbal language will probably show it.

1-3c Communication Is Irreversible

Once an exchange takes place, we can never go back in time and erase the communication. We might be able to repair damage we have done, but the message has been communicated. When you participate in an online discussion or leave a post on a blog, you are leaving an electronic "footprint" that others can follow and read. E-mails, IMs, and text messages are not always completely private either. Once you push the "send" button, not only can't you take it back, but you have little control over who the receiver might forward it to or how it might be used publicly.

1-3d Communication Is Situated

When we say that communication is *situated* we mean that it occurs within a specific communication setting that affects how the messages are produced, interpreted, and coordinated (Burleson, 2009). The interpretation of the statement "I love you" varies depending on the setting. During a candlelit anniversary dinner, it may be interpreted as a statement of romantic feelings. If a mother says it as she greets her daughter, it may be interpreted as motherly love. If it is made in response to a joke delivered by someone in a group of friends gathered to watch a football game, it may be interpreted as a complement for being clever. So what is said and what is meant depends on the situation.

index a measure of the emotional temperature of our relationship at the time

trust the extent to which partners rely on, depend on, and have faith that their partners will not intentionally do anything to harm them

control the degree to which one participant in the communication encounter is perceived to be more dominant or powerful

1-3e Communication Is Indexical

How we communicate is also an **index** or measure of the emotional temperature of our relationship at the time. For instance, when they are getting into the car to leave for a holiday, Laura says to Darryl, "I remembered to bring the map." She is not just reporting information. Through her tone of voice and other nonverbal cues, she is also communicating something about the relationship, such as, "You can always depend on me" or "You never remember to think of these things."

A message exchange can also signal the level of trust, control, and intimacy in a relationship (Millar & Rogers, 1987).

Trust is the extent to which partners rely on, depend on, and have faith that their partners will not intentionally do anything to harm them. For instance, Mark says, "I'll do the final edits and turn in the paper." Sandy replies, "Never mind, I'll do it so that it won't be late." Sandy's response may signal that she doesn't trust Mark to get the group's paper in on time.

Control is the degree to which partners believe themselves to be "in charge" in the relationship. When Tom says to Sue, "I know you're concerned about the budget, but I'll see to it that we have enough money to cover everything," through his words, tone of voice, and nonverbal behavior, he is signaling that he is "in charge" of the finances. In turn, Sue may respond by either verbally responding or nonverbally showing that she agrees with him or by challenging him and

This couple's position suggests trust and intimacy in their relationship.

Vlad Teodor/Shutterstock.com

asserting her desire to control the budget. In other words, control is communicated with either complementary or symmetrical feedback. **Complementary feedback** signals agreement about who is in control, whereas **symmetrical feedback** signals disagreement. If Sue says, "Great, I'm glad you're looking after it," her feedback complements his message. But if Sue responds, "Wait a minute, you're the one who overdrew our checking account last month," she is challenging his control with a symmetrical response. Relational control is not negotiated in a single exchange, but through many message exchanges over time. The point, however, is that control is negotiated through communication.

Intimacy is the degree of emotional closeness, acceptance, and disclosure in a relationship. When Cody asks Madison what she is thinking about, and Madison begins to pour out her problems, she is revealing the degree of intimacy she feels in the relationship. Or, should she reply, "Oh I'm not really thinking about anything important. Did you hear the news this morning about . . . ," her subject change signals that the relationship is not intimate enough to share her problems.

1-3f Communication Messages Vary in Conscious Thought

Recall that creating shared meaning involves encoding and decoding verbal messages, nonverbal cues, and even visual images. Our messages may (1) occur spontaneously, (2) be based on a "script," or (3) be carefully constructed.

Many messages are **spontaneous expressions**, spoken without much conscious thought. For example, when you burn your finger, you may blurt out, "Ouch!" When something goes right, you may break into a broad smile. Some messages are *scripted* and drawn from our canned plan libraries. Finally, some are **constructed messages** that are formed carefully and thoughtfully when our known scripts are inadequate for the situation.

1-3g Communication Is Guided by Cultural Norms

Culture is a system of shared beliefs, values, symbols, and behaviors. How messages are formed and interpreted depends on the cultural background of the participants. We need to be mindful of our communication behavior as we interact with others from different cultures, so we don't unintentionally communicate in ways that are culturally inappropriate or insensitive.

The United States has become more culturally diverse than ever before. According to the U.S. Census Bureau (Humes, Jones, & Ramirez, 2011), using data from the 2010 census, people of Latin and Asian decent constituted 16.3 percent and 5.6 percent, respectively, of the total U.S. population. African Americans make up about 13 percent of the U.S. population, and another 2.9 percent regards itself as multiracial. These four groups account for nearly 49 percent of the total U.S. population. The cultural influences of all these groups are profoundly changing our nation's demographics.

According to Samovar, Porter, and McDaniel (2007), "a number of cultural components are particularly relevant to the student of intercultural communication. These include (1) perception, (2) patterns of cognition, (3) verbal behaviors, (4) nonverbal behaviors, and (5) the influence of context" (p. 13). Because cultural concerns permeate all of communication, each chapter of this book points out when certain concepts and skills may be viewed differently by members of various cultural groups.

1-4 COMMUNICATION AND ETHICS

Can people depend on you to tell the truth? Do you do what you say you will do? Can people count on you to be respectful? In any encounter, we choose whether to behave in a way others view as ethical. **Ethics** is a set of moral principles that may be held by a society, a group, or an individual. An ethical standard does not tell us exactly what to do in any given situation, but it can tell us what general principles to consider when deciding how to behave.

1-4a Ethical Principles

Every field of study—from psychology and biology to sociology and history—has a set of ethical principles designed to guide the practice of that field.

Communication is no exception. Every time we communicate, we

complementary feedback a message that signals agreement about who is in control

symmetrical feedback a message that signals disagreement about who is in control

intimacy the degree of emotional closeness, acceptance, and disclosure in a relationship

spontaneous expressions messages spoken without much conscious thought

constructed messages messages that are formed carefully and thoughtfully when our known scripts are inadequate for the situation

culture a system of shared beliefs, values, symbols, and behaviors

ethics a set of moral principles that may be held by a society, a group, or an individual

make choices with ethical implications. The general principles that guide ethical communication include:

1. Ethical communicators are honest. We should not intentionally try to deceive others.

2. Ethical communicators act with integrity. Integrity is maintaining consistency between what we say we believe and what we do. The person who says "Do what I say, not what I do" lacks integrity, while the person who "practices what he or she preaches" acts with integrity. Integrity is basically the opposite of hypocrisy.

3. Ethical communicators behave fairly. A fair person is impartial. To be fair to someone is to gather all of the relevant facts, consider only circumstances relevant to the decision at hand, and not be swayed by prejudice or irrelevancies. For example, if two siblings are fighting, their mother exercises fairness if she allows both children to explain "their side" before she decides what to do.

4. Ethical communicators demonstrate respect. Respect is showing regard for others, their points of view, and their rights. We demonstrate respect through listening and understanding others' points of view, even when they differ from our own.

bright side messages
messages that are ethical and appropriate
dark side messages
messages that are not ethical and/or appropriate

5. Ethical communicators are responsible. Responsible communicators recognize the power of words. Our messages can hurt others and their reputations. So we act responsibly when we refrain from gossiping, spreading rumors, bullying, and so forth.

1-4b Bright Side and Dark Side Messages

Interpersonal communication scholars, Spitzberg and Cupach (2011) came up with metaphors to characterize the differences between ethical/appropriate and unethical/inappropriate communication. They label messages that are both ethical and appropriate as **bright side messages**. In contrast, **dark side messages** are unethical and/or inappropriate. "Hard dark side" messages are somewhat ethical and unethical because they are honest, but also potentially damaging to the relationship. "Easy dark side" messages are somewhat ethical and unethical because they are dishonest in order to maintain a good relationship. Finally, "evil dark side" messages are both disrespectful and damaging to the relationship (see Figure 1.3).

Let's use Liz as an example. She just spent a fortune having her hair cut and colored and asks her good friend, Pat, "Do you like my new hairstyle?" Pat, who doesn't really like the new look, could respond to Liz in one of the ways shown in Figure 1.3, below.

As you can see, relationships may benefit from bright, hard, and easy side responses depending on the situation. But dark side responses damage people and relationships.

FIGURE 1.3 UNDERSTANDING DARK SIDE MESSAGES

Ethical

Appropriate		Inappropriate
Bright side response: "Liz, it doesn't matter what I think. I can see that you really like how it looks and that makes me happy." (*This response is ethical and appropriate. It is both honest and respectful.*)		**Hard dark side response:** "Wow Liz, it's a dramatic change. I liked your hair long and I'd always admired the red highlights you had. But I'm sure it will grow on me." (*This response is honest but could hurt Liz's feelings and damage the relationship.*)
Easy dark side response: "It looks great." (*This response is dishonest but doesn't hurt Liz's feelings.*)		**Evil dark side response:** "It doesn't matter what you do to your hair, you're still fat and ugly." (*This response is unethical and inappropriate. It is hurtful and damaging to Liz's feelings and the relationship*)

Unethical

1-5 INCREASING YOUR COMMUNICATION COMPETENCE

When we communicate effectively and ethically, it feels good. And when we experience the opposite, we may get frustrated and even angry. So let's look at what it means to be a competent communicator, how communication anxiety can affect competence, and how to develop and use your own communication improvement plan to improve the chances for success in your interactions with others.

1-5a Communication Competence

Communication competence is the impression that communicative behavior is both appropriate and effective in a given situation (Spitzberg, 2000). Communication is *effective* when it achieves its goals and *appropriate* when it conforms to what is expected in a situation. Competence is a judgment people make about others. Our goal is to communicate in ways that increase the likelihood that others will judge us as competent.

Communication competence is achieved through personal motivation, knowledge acquisition, and skills practice (Spitzberg, 2000). Motivation is important because we will be able to improve our communication only if we are *motivated*—that is, if we want to improve. Knowledge is important because we must know what to do to increase competence. The more knowledge we have about how to behave in a given situation, the more likely we are to convey competence. Skill is important because we must act in ways that are consistent with our communication knowledge. The more skills we have, the more likely we are to structure our messages effectively and appropriately.

In addition to motivation, knowledge, and skills, credibility and social ease also influence whether others perceive us to be competent communicators. **Credibility** is a perception of a speaker's knowledge, trustworthiness, and warmth. Listeners are more likely to be attentive to and influenced by speakers they perceive as credible. **Social ease** means managing communication apprehension so we do not appear nervous or anxious. To be perceived as a competent communicator, we must speak in ways that convey confidence and poise. Communicators that appear apprehensive are not likely to be regarded as competent, despite their motivation or knowledge.

1-5b Communication Apprehension

Communication apprehension is "the fear or anxiety associated with real or anticipated communication with others" (McCroskey, 1977, p. 78). Although most people think of public speaking anxiety when they hear the term *communication apprehension* (CA), there are actually four different types of CA. These are traitlike CA, audience-based CA, situational CA, and context-based CA. People who experience *traitlike communication apprehension* feel anxious in most speaking situations. About 20 percent of all people experience traitlike CA (Richmond & McCroskey, 1997). People who experience *audience-based communication apprehension* feel anxious about speaking only with a certain person or group of people. *Situational communication apprehension* is a short-lived feeling of anxiety that occurs during a specific encounter—for example, during a job interview. Finally, *context-based communication apprehension* is anxiety only in a particular situation—for example, when speaking to a large group of people. All these forms of communication apprehension can be managed effectively in

> **communication competence** the impression that communicative behavior is both appropriate and effective in a given situation
>
> **credibility** a perception of a speaker's knowledge, trustworthiness, and warmth
>
> **social ease** communicating without appearing to be anxious or nervous
>
> **communication apprehension** the fear or anxiety associated with real or anticipated communication with others

Many people may experience trait-based apprehension and feel nervous when faced with making small talk in social situations

ways that help convey social ease. Throughout this book, we offer strategies for managing communication apprehension in various settings.

The combination of motivation, knowledge, skills, perceived credibility, and social ease make up competent communication. The goal of this book is to help you become a competent communicator in interpersonal, group, and public speaking situations.

1-5c Communication Improvement Plans

A communication improvement plan consists of setting a new goal to resolve a communication problem, identifying procedures to reach the goal, and determining a way to measure progress.

Before you can write a goal statement, you must first analyze your current communication skills repertoire. After you read each chapter and practice the skills described, select one or two skills to work on. Then write down your plan in four steps.

1. Identify the problem. For example: "*Problem: Even though some of the members of my class project group have not produced the work they promised, I haven't spoken up because I'm not very good at describing my feelings.*"

2. State the specific goal. A specific goal identifies a measurable outcome. For example, to deal with the problem just identified, you might write: "*Goal: To describe my disappointment to other group members about their failure to meet deadlines.*"

3. Outline a specific procedure for reaching the goal. To develop a plan for reaching your goal, first consult the chapter that covers the skill you wish to hone. Then translate the general steps recommended in the chapter to your specific situation. For example: "*Procedure:* I will practice the steps of describing feelings. (1) I will identify the specific feeling I am experiencing. (2) I will encode the emotion I am feeling accurately. (3) I will include what has triggered the feeling. (4) I will own the feeling as mine. (5) I will then put that procedure into operation when I am talking with my group members."

4. Devise a method for measuring progress. A good method points to minimum requirements for determining positive progress. For example: "*Test for Making Progress Toward Goal Achievement:* I will have made progress each time I describe my feelings to my group members about missed deadlines."

Figure 1.4 provides another example of a communication improvement plan, this one relating to a public speaking problem.

FIGURE 1.4 SAMPLE COMMUNICATION IMPROVEMENT PLAN

Problem: When I speak in class or in the student senate, I often find myself burying my head in my notes or looking at the ceiling or walls.

Goal: To look at people more directly when I'm giving a speech.

Procedure: I will take the time to practice oral presentations aloud in my room.

(1) I will stand up just as I do in class.

(2) I will pretend various objects in the room are people, and I will consciously attempt to look at those objects as I am talking.

(3) When giving a speech, I will try to be aware of when I am looking at my audience and when I am not.

Test for Achieving Goal: I will have achieved this goal when I am maintaining eye contact with my audience most of the time.

Quick Quiz

T F 1. A participant in a communication interaction can either be the sender or receiver of a message.

T F 2. The context of a message is the organizational aspect of the message.

T F 3. Meaning shared in a communication interaction can be affected by the physical context in which the message is delivered.

T F 4. Competence is the perception by others that our communication behavior is appropriate as well as effective.

T F 5. When you show regard or consideration for others and their ideas, even if you don't agree with them, you are demonstrating the ethical standard of fairness.

6. What are the three sub-processes that must be performed to achieve shared meaning?

   a. message production, message interpretation, and interaction coordination

   b. nonverbal coding, acronym depiction, and feeling coordination

   c. canned plan access, spontaneous construction, and symmetrical feedback

   d. recipient selection, message production, interaction method

   e. channel selection, feedback decoding, response construction

7. An example of intrapersonal communication is

   a. chatting around the dinner table with your family and friends.

   b. recounting a past experience during a speech to an audience.

   c. thinking to yourself about what you are going to make for dinner that evening.

   d. texting a message to a friend.

   e. entering into a discussion in a chatroom.

8. Why do we communicate?

   a. to meet our social needs

   b. to develop and maintain our sense of self

   c. to develop relationships

   d. to exchange information and influence others

   e. All of these answers are correct.

9. Which of the following is NOT one of the guidelines for ethical communication?

   a. Ethical communicators are truthful and honest.

   b. Ethical communicators act spontaneously.

   c. Ethical communicators behave fairly.

   d. Ethical communicators demonstrate respect.

   e. Ethical communicators are responsible.

10. If you feel anxious about speaking with a certain person or group of people, you are experiencing

   a. situational communication apprehension.

   b. audience-based communication apprehension.

   c. traitlike communication apprehension.

   d. general communication apprehension.

   e. context-based communication apprehension.

Answers: 1.T, 2.F, 3.T, 4.T, 5.F, 6.A, 7.C, 8.E, 9.B, 10.B

2 Perception of Self and Others

LEARNING OUTCOMES

2-1 Describe the perception process

2-2 Explain how self-perception is formed and maintained

2-3 Employ communication strategies to improve self-perceptions

2-4 Examine how we form perceptions of others

2-5 Employ strategies to improve perceptions of others

After finishing this chapter go to **PAGE 29** for **STUDY TOOLS.**

Social perception—who we believe ourselves and others to be—influences how we communicate. To explain how, we begin this chapter by reviewing the basics of sensory perception. Then we explore how social perception influences self-concept and self-esteem and how these self-perceptions in turn influence communication. From there we offer suggestions for improving self-perceptions, explain how and why we perceive others as we do, and offer guidelines for improving our perceptions of others.

2-1 THE PERCEPTION PROCESS

Perception is the process of selectively attending and assigning meaning to information (Gibson, 1966). At times, our perceptions of the world, other people, and ourselves agree with the perceptions of others. At other times, our perceptions are significantly different from the perceptions of other people. For each of us, however, our perception becomes our reality. What one person sees, hears, and interprets is real and considered true to that person. Another person may see, hear, and interpret something entirely different from the same situation and also

social perception who we believe ourselves and others to be

perception the process of selectively attending and assigning meaning to information

regard his or her different perception as real and true. When our perceptions differ from those with whom we interact, sharing meaning becomes more challenging. So how does perception work? Essentially, the brain selects some of the information it receives from the senses (sensory stimuli), organizes the information, and then interprets it.

2-1a Attention and Selection

Although we are constantly exposed to a barrage of sensory stimuli, we focus our attention on relatively little of it. Just think about how many TV channels you watch regularly compared to the number of channels offered. Or consider how many Web sites pop up when you do an Internet search. Can you imagine visiting all of them? Because we cannot focus on everything we see and hear all the time, we choose what stimuli to concentrate on based on our needs, interests, and expectations.

How many emails do you actually read compared to the number you immediately dump into the trash? Why?

© pio3/Shutterstock.com

NEEDS We choose to pay attention to information that meets our biological and psychological needs. When you go to class, how well you pay attention usually depends on whether you believe the information is relevant.

Your brain communicates intrapersonally by asking such questions as "Will what I learn here help me in school, in the work world, or in my personal life?"

INTERESTS We are likely to pay attention to information that piques our interest. For instance, when we hear or see a news story about a crisis event or natural disaster, we are more likely to pay attention when it is happening in our local community.

EXPECTATIONS Finally, we are likely to see what we expect to see and miss what violates our expectations. Take a quick look at the phrases in the triangles in Figure 2.1. If you have never seen these triangles, you probably read "Paris in the springtime," "Once in a lifetime," and "Bird in the hand." But if you reexamine the words, you will see that what you perceived was not exactly what is written. Do you now see the repeated words? They are easy to miss because we don't *expect* to see the words repeated.

2-1b Organization

Through the process of attention and selection, we reduce the number of stimuli our brains must process. Still, the number of stimuli we attend to at any moment is substantial. So our brains organize these stimuli using the principles of simplicity and pattern.

FIGURE 2.1 EXPECTATIONS AND PERCEPTION

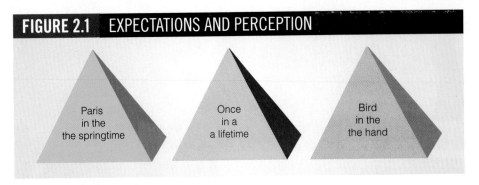

Paris
in the
the springtime

Once
in a
a lifetime

Bird
in the
the hand

your ability to interpret these numbers depends on your familiarity with the patterns. A French person may not recognize *631 7348* as a phone number since the pattern for phone numbers in France is: *0x xx xx xx xx.*

SIMPLICITY If the stimuli we attend to are complex, the brain simplifies them into some commonly recognized form. Based on a quick look at what someone is wearing, how she is standing, and the expression on her face, we may perceive her as a business executive, a doctor, or a soccer mom. We simplify the verbal messages we receive in a similar way. For example, after an hour-long performance review in which his boss described four of Tony's strengths and two areas for improvement, Tony might say to Jerry, his coworker, "Well, I'd better shape up or I'm going to get fired!"

PATTERN The brain also makes sense of complex stimuli by relating them to things it already recognizes. For example, when you see a crowd of people, instead of perceiving each individual, you may focus on sex and "see" men and women. Alternatively, you may focus on age and "see" children, teens, and adults.

2-1c Interpretation

As the brain selects and organizes information, it also assigns meaning to it. Look at these three sets of numbers. What are they?

A. 631 7348

B. 285 37 5632

C. 4632 7364 2596 2174

If you are used to seeing similar sets of numbers every day, you might interpret A as a telephone number, B as a Social Security number, and C as a credit card number. But

2-1d Dual Processing

You may be thinking, "Hey, I don't go through all of these steps. I just automatically 'understand' what's going on." If so, you are right. Most of the perceptual processing we do happens subconsciously (Baumeister, 2005). This **automatic processing** is a fast, top-down subconscious approach of making sense of what we are encountering. In other words, we use **heuristics**, which are our short-cut rules of thumb for understanding how to perceive something based on past experience with similar stimuli. Consider, for example, sitting at a red light. When it turns green, you go. You probably don't consciously think about taking your foot off the brake and applying it to the gas pedal.

But what happens when we encounter things that are out of the realm of our normal experiences or expectations? Then we must exert conscious effort to make sense of what is going on. **Conscious processing** is a slow, deliberative approach where we examine and reflect about the stimuli. Remember when you were first learning to drive? It took a lot of concentration to figure out what was happening on the road and how you were supposed to react. You probably thought carefully about doing things like taking your foot off the brake and applying it to the gas pedal when the light turned green.

Whether we engage in automatic or conscious processing, perception influences and is influenced by communication in a number of ways. The rest of this chapter is devoted to how we form our perceptions of self and others and the role communication plays in each.

2-2 PERCEPTION OF SELF

Self-perception is the overall view we have of ourselves, which includes both self-concept and self-esteem. **Self-concept** is the perception we have of our skills, abilities, knowledge, competencies, and personality traits (Weiten, Dunn, & Hammer, 2012). **Self-esteem** is the evaluation we make about our personal worthiness based on our self-concept (Hewitt, 2009). In this section, we explain how self-concept and self-esteem are formed.

2-2a Self-Concept

How do we decide what our skills, abilities, competencies, and personality traits are? We do so based on the interpretations we make about our personal experiences and how others react and respond to us.

Our personal experiences are critical to forming our self-concept. We cannot know if we are competent at something until we've tried doing it, and we cannot discover our personality traits until we uncover them through experience. We place a great deal of emphasis on our first experiences with particular phenomena (Bee & Boyd, 2011). When we have a positive first experience, we are likely to believe we possess the competencies and personality traits associated with that experience. So if Sonya discovers at an early age that she does well on math problems and exams, she is likely to incorporate "competent mathematician" into her self-concept. If Sonya continues to excel at math throughout her life, that part of her self-concept will be reinforced and maintained.

Similarly, when our first experience is negative, we are likely to conclude we do not possess that particular skill or trait. For instance, if you get anxious and draw a blank while giving a speech for the first time, you might conclude that you are a poor public speaker. Even when a negative first experience is not repeated, however, it is likely to take more than one contradictory additional experience to change our original perception. So even if you succeed the second time you give a speech, it will probably take several more positive public speaking experiences for you to change your original conclusion about not being a good public speaker.

Our self-concept is also shaped by how others react and respond to us in two important ways (Weiten, Dunn, & Hammer, 2012). First, we use other people's comments to validate, reinforce, or alter our perceptions of who we think we are. For example, if during a brainstorming session, one of your coworkers says, "You're really a creative thinker," you may decide this comment fits your image of who you are, thus reinforcing your self-concept as someone who can think "outside the box."

Second, the feedback we receive from others may reveal abilities and personality characteristics we had never before associated with ourselves. For example, after Michael receives several compliments about being good with children, he decides to pursue a career in early childhood education. The feedback (compliments) helped him recognize his natural ability to connect with preschoolers.

Alanna perceives that she has strength (self-concept), and evaluates that strength is a positive competency, giving her high self-esteem.

Not all reactions and responses we receive have the same effect on our self-concept. For instance, reactions and responses coming from someone we respect or someone we are close to tend to be more powerful (Aron, Mashek, & Aron, 2004; Rayner, 2001). This is especially important in families. Since self-concept begins to form early in life, information we receive from our family deeply shapes our self-concept (Bee & Boyd, 2011). Thus, one major ethical responsibility of family members is to notice and comment on traits and abilities that help develop accurate and positive self-concepts in other family members. When Jeff's dad compliments him for keeping his bedroom clean because he is "so organized" or Carla's brother tells her she did a great job on her science project because she is "really smart," they are encouraging positive self-concepts.

As we interact with others, we also form an **ideal self-concept**, which is what we would like to be. For example, although Jim may know he is not naturally athletic, in his ideal self-concept he wants to be. So he plays on an intramural basketball team, works out at the gym daily, and regularly runs in local 5k and 10k races.

2-2b Self-Esteem

Self-concept and self-esteem are two different but related components of self-perception. Whereas self-concept is our perception of our competencies and personality traits, self-esteem is our positive or negative evaluation of

> **ideal self-concept**
> competencies and personality traits we would like to have

those competencies and traits. So self-esteem is not just our perception of how well or poorly we do things (self-concept), but also the importance we place on what we do well or poorly (Mruk, 2006). For instance, Eduardo believes he is an excellent piano player, a faithful friend, and good with kids. But if he doesn't believe that these competencies and traits are valuable to have, then he will have low self-esteem. It takes both the perception of having a competency or personality trait and a belief that it is valuable to produce high self-esteem (Mruk, 2006). When we use our skills to achieve worthwhile endeavors, we raise our self-esteem. When we are unsuccessful in doing so, and/or when we use them in unworthy endeavors, we lower our self-esteem.

As is the case with self-concept, self-esteem depends not only on what each individual views as worthwhile but also on the ideas, morals, and values of the family and cultural group(s) to which the individual belongs. So if Eduardo comes from a family where athletic success is valued but artistic talents are not, if he hangs out with friends who don't appreciate his piano playing, and if he lives in a society where rock guitarists (not piano players) are the superstars, then his piano-playing ability may not raise his self-esteem and might actually lower it.

We've already noted that families are critically important to developing one's self-concept, but they are even more central to developing positive self-esteem. For example, when Jeff's dad pointed out that Jeff's room is always tidy, he also said he was proud of Jeff, which raised Jeff's self-esteem about being organized. And when Carla's brother said she did a great job on her science project, he reinforced the value their family places on being smart, which raised her self-esteem about that attribute of her self-concept. Unfortunately, in some families, negative messages repeatedly sent can create an inaccurate self-concept and damage self-esteem. Communicating blame, name-calling, and constantly pointing out shortcomings are particularly damaging to self-esteem and some people never fully overcome the damage done to them by members of their families.

Our self-esteem can affect the types of relationships we form and with whom. Individuals with high self-esteem tend to form relationships with others who reinforce their positive self-perception; similarly, individuals with low self-esteem tend to form relationships with those who reinforce their negative self-perception (Fiore, 2010). This phenomenon plays out in unfortunate ways when a person perpetually goes from one abusive relationship to another (Engel, 2005).

Bullying and cyberbullying, which are aggressive behaviors designed to intimidate others, also damage self-esteem. Children who are just forming their self-concepts and self-esteem, and adolescents whose self-concepts and self-esteem are in transition, are particularly sensitive to bullying messages. The effects of bullying can have long-lasting effects on self-esteem. In fact, many years after childhood bullying incidents, victims may still have inaccurate self-perceptions (Hinduja & Patchin, 2010).

2-2c Cultural Norms and Self-Perceptions

Cultural norms play a critical role in shaping both our self-concept and self-esteem (Becker et al., 2014). Two important ways they do so are in terms of independence/interdependence and masculinity/femininity.

Media attention on cyberbullying has increased awareness about the seriousness of the effects on children. More than "kids being kids," cyberbullying has effects such as dropping out of school and even suicide.

© Sylvie Bouchard/Shutterstock.com

In individualist cultures, such as Western Europe and the United States, people tend to form and value independent self-perceptions. In collectivist cultures, such as Japan and China, people form and value interdependent self-perceptions (Becker et al., 2014). **Independent self-perceptions** are based on the belief that traits and abilities are internal to the person and are universally applicable to all situations. The goal for people with independent self-perceptions is to demonstrate their abilities, competencies, characteristics, and personalities during interactions with others. For example, if you have an independent self-concept and believe that one of your competencies is your ability to persuade others, you gain self-esteem by demonstrating your skill, convincing others, and having others praise you for it.

Interdependent self-perceptions are based on the belief that traits and abilities are specific to a particular context or relationship. The goal of people with interdependent self-perceptions is to maintain or enhance the relationship by demonstrating the appropriate abilities and personality characteristics for the situation. People with interdependent self-perceptions don't think, "I'm really persuasive," but rather, "When I am with my friends I am able to convince them to do what is good for all of us. When I am with my father I do what he believes is best for the good of our family." High self-esteem comes from knowing when to be persuasive and when to be compliant.

Cultural norms also play a role in shaping self-perception around masculinity and femininity. In the dominant culture of the United States, for instance, many people continue to expect boys to behave in "masculine" ways and girls to behave in "feminine" ways (Wood, 2007). In the past, boys in the United States were taught to base their self-esteem on their achievements, status, and income, and girls learned that their culture valued their appearance and their relationship skills. So boys and girls developed high or low self-esteem based on how well they met these criteria (Wood, 2007).

Today these cultural norms about "appropriate" characteristics and behaviors for males and females are becoming less rigid, but they do still exist and are promoted incessantly in popular culture and entertainment media. Consider just about any television sitcom (e.g., *Two and a Half Men* and even *Modern Family*). Such programs continue to portray women as the "natural" caregivers for the family, and when men attempt to perform a caregiver behavior, they often make a mess of the situation.

Some people are intimately involved in more than one cultural group. If one of the cultures encourages interdependent and/or gendered self-perceptions and the other encourages independent and/or gender neutral self-perceptions, these people may develop both types of self-perception and actually switch "cultural frames" based on the cultural group they are interacting within at a given time. They are more likely to do this well when they see themselves as part of and appreciate the strengths of both cultures (Benet-Martínez & Haritatos, 2005).

2-2d Accuracy and Distortion of Self-Perceptions

The accuracy of our self-concept and self-esteem depends on the accuracy of our perceptions of our own experiences and observations, as well as how we interpret others' reactions and responses to us. All of us experience successes and failures, and all of us hear praise and criticism. Since our perceptions are more likely than our true abilities to influence our behavior accurate self-perception is critical to competent communication. Self-perception may suffer from **incongruence** when there is a gap between self-perception and reality. For example, Sean may actually possess all of the competencies and personality traits needed for effective leadership, but if he doesn't perceive himself to have these skills and characteristics, he won't step forward when leadership is needed. Unfortunately, individuals tend to reinforce these incongruent self-perceptions by behaving in ways that conform to them rather than attempting to break free from them.

If we are overly attentive to successful experiences and positive responses, our self-perception may become inflated. We tend to describe such individuals as "arrogant," "pompous," "haughty," or "snobbish." On the other hand, if we dwell on our failures and not our successes, remember only the criticism we receive, or focus on how we don't measure up to our ideal self-concept, we may have a deflated self-perception. We tend to describe such individuals as "depressed," "despondent," "sullen," or "gloomy." Neither the person with the inflated

independent self-perceptions perceptions based on the belief that traits and abilities are internal to the person and are universally applicable to all situations

interdependent self-perceptions perceptions based on the belief that traits and abilities are specific to a particular context or relationship

incongruence a gap between self-perception and reality

If Paul expects people to ignore him at his new school, he is less likely to try to engage them—ultimately ending up spending the whole day not talking to anyone new.

Sometimes a self-fulfilling prophecy is other-imposed and is based on what others say about us. When teachers act as if their students are bright, students buy into this expectation and learn more as a result. Likewise, when teachers act as if students are not bright, students may "live down" to these imposed prophecies and fail to achieve. A good example takes place in the popular book *Harry Potter and the Order of the Phoenix*. A prophecy was made that suggested Harry Potter would vanquish the Dark Lord (Voldemort). So the Dark Lord sets out to kill Harry Potter. Dumbledore explains to Harry that the prophecy is true only because the Dark Lord believes it. Still, because the Dark Lord will not rest until he kills Harry, it becomes inevitable that Harry will, in fact, have to kill Voldemort (or vice versa).

nor deflated self-perception accurately reflects who they are. These incongruent and distorted self-perceptions are magnified through self-fulfilling prophecies, filtering messages, and media images.

SELF-FULFILLING PROPHECIES A **self-fulfilling prophecy** is an inaccurate perception of a skill, characteristic, or situation that leads to behaviors that perpetuate that false perception as *true* (Merton, 1968). Self-fulfilling prophesies may be self-created or other-imposed.

Self-created prophecies are predictions you make about yourself. For example, when people expect rejection, they are more likely to behave in ways that lead others to reject them (Downey, Freitas, Michaelis, & Khouri, 2004). By contrast, if Stefan sees himself as quite social and able to get to know people easily, he looks forward to attending a friend's party and, just as he predicted, makes several new acquaintances and enjoys himself.

> **self-fulfilling prophecy**
> an inaccurate perception of a skill, characteristic, or situation that leads to behaviors that perpetuate that false perception as true

FILTERING MESSAGES Our self-perceptions can also become distorted through the way we filter what others say to us. We tend to pay attention to messages that reinforce our self-perception, and downplay or ignore messages that contradict this image. For example, suppose Tien prepares an agenda for her study group. Someone comments that Tien is a good organizer. If Tien spent her childhood hearing how disorganized she was, she may downplay or even ignore this comment. If, however, Tien thinks she is good at organizing, she will pay attention to the compliment and may even reinforce it by responding, "Thanks, I AM a pretty organized person. I learned it from my mom."

MEDIA IMAGES Another way self-perception can become distorted is through our interpretation of what we see on television, in the movies, and in popular magazines. Social cognitive learning theory suggests that we strive to copy the characteristics and behaviors of the characters portrayed as perfect examples or "ideal types" (Bandura, 1977). Persistent media messages of violence, promiscuity, use of profanity, bulked-up males, and pencil-thin females have all been linked to distorted self-perceptions among viewers. One particularly disturbing study found that before television was widely introduced on the Pacific island of Fiji, only 3 percent of girls reported vomiting to lose weight or being unhappy with their body image. Three years after the introduction of television, that percentage had risen to 15 percent, and an alarming 74 percent reported thinking of themselves as too big or too fat (Becker, 2004). Unfortunately, distorted body image perceptions lead to low self-esteem and, sometimes, to self-destructive behaviors such as anorexia and bulimia.

2-3 SELF-PERCEPTION AND COMMUNICATION

Self-perception influences how we talk to ourselves, how we talk about ourselves with others, how we talk about others to ourselves, the self we present to others, and our ability to communicate with others.

Self-talk (or intrapersonal communication) is the internal conversations we have with ourselves in our thoughts. People who have a positive self-perception are more likely to engage in positive self-talk, such as "I know I can do it" or "I did a really good job." People who have a negative self-perception are more likely to engage in negative self-talk, such as "There's no way I can do that" or "I really blew it." Not surprisingly, a high level of speech anxiety (the fear of public speaking) is often rooted in negative self-talk.

Self-perception also influences how we talk about ourselves with others. If we have a positive self-perception, we are likely to convey a positive attitude and take credit for our successes. If we have a negative self-perception, we are likely to convey a negative attitude and

downplay our accomplishments. Some research suggests that the Internet can influence how we communicate about ourselves with others in unique ways. Some Internet discussion groups, for example, are designed to be online journals where the user engages in reflection and introspection. These users are actually communicating with themselves while imagining a reader. On the Internet, people can be more aware of themselves and less aware of the people to whom they are talking (Shedletsky & Aitken, 2004).

Self-perception also influences how we talk about others to ourselves. First, the more accurate our self-perception is, the more likely we are to perceive others accurately. Second, the more positive our self-perception is, the more likely we are to see others favorably. Studies show that people who accept themselves as they are tend to be more accepting of others; similarly, those with a negative self-perception are more likely to be critical of others. Third, our own personal characteristics influence the types of characteristics we are likely to perceive in others. For example, people who are secure tend to see others as equally secure. If you recall that we respond to the world as we perceive it to be (and not necessarily as it is), you can readily see how negative self-perception can account for misunderstandings and communication breakdowns.

Our self-perceptions are the complete picture

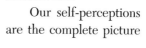

self-talk the internal conversation we have with ourselves in our thoughts

Six social constructions, one woman, all real.

Born This Way?

From the moment she burst onto the pop music scene in 2009, Lady Gaga has been synonymous with outrageous performances and heavily stylized celebrity personas. For Lady Gaga, her "behind-the-scenes self" appears to be just as constructed as her public celebrity persona. At the same time, however, she consistently frames this self as "real" in her songs and media appearances. Her celebrity persona is completely rooted in the idea that she is being her true self, even though that self is glamorous, constructed, extreme, over-the-top, and all the things that we already associate with her public image. Like all personas, what you see is constructed, but it is not necessarily "fake" or "inauthentic."

Gaga's "real" self remains self-consciously constructed in her physical appearance and how she behaves in public, but it is not intended to be an act or something distinct from her "authentic" self. Her constant message is that individuals should be themselves no matter what, even if that self does not fit into dominant social expectations. Indeed, Gaga further supported her message after being lambasted in the popular media for gaining weight. She posted images of herself online in just her underwear—no

make-up, no wigs, no platform shoes—along with the caption "Bulimia and anorexia since I was 15." The photos became the first in a series of posts by Gaga and her fans supporting a "body revolution" of self-acceptance and rejection of media-imposed ideals. In some ways, this would seem to contradict her well-constructed media image, but in fact it functions as another persona, consistent with her presentation of public and private self, icon of outsiders, supporter of real self-image.

Source: Haiken, M. (2012, September 26). Lady Gaga puts bulimia and body image on the table in a big way. Forbes. Retrieved from http://www.forbes.com/sites/melaniehaiken/2012/09/26/lady-gaga-puts-bulimia-and-body-image-on-the-table-in-a-big-way.

---

of how we view ourselves. When we communicate with others, however, most of us share only the parts we believe are appropriate to the situation. This phenomenon is known as the **social construction of self**. For example, Damon presents his "manager self" at work where he is a serious, task-oriented leader. When he is with his good friends, however, he is laid back, jovial, and more than happy to follow what the group wants to do. Which is the "real" Damon? Both are. Social networking sites such as Facebook have added a new twist to the social construction of self because once we have posted information on our page, others can co-opt our identity and actually reconstruct us in ways we never intended to do.

How effective we are at constructing different social selves depends on how actively we self-monitor. **Self-monitoring** is the internal process of being aware of how we are coming across to others and adjusting our behavior accordingly. It involves being sensitive to other people's feedback and using that information to determine how we will respond (Rose & Kim, 2011). If you have ever been in a situation where you made a remark and did not get the response you expected, you may have thought to yourself, "Ooh, I wish I hadn't said that. I wonder how to fix it." This is an example of self-monitoring. Some people are naturally high self-monitors, constantly aware of how they are coming across to others. But even low self-monitors are likely to self-monitor when they are in a new situation or relationship.

social construction of self the phenomenon of sharing different aspects of our self-concept based on the situation and people involved

self-monitoring the internal process of being aware of how we are coming across to others and adjusting our behavior accordingly

We all use self-monitoring to determine which "self" we choose to display in different situations and with different people.

2-3a Changing Self-Perceptions

Self-concept and self-esteem are fairly enduring characteristics, but they can be changed. Comments that contradict your current self-perception may lead you to slowly change it. Certain situations, such as experiencing a profound change in your social environment, can expedite this process. When children begin school or go to sleep-away camp; when teens start part-time jobs; when young adults go to college; or when people begin or end jobs or relationships, become parents, or grieve the loss of someone they love, they are more likely to absorb messages that contradict their current self-perceptions.

Therapy and self-help techniques can help alter our self-concept and improve our self-esteem. In fact, noted psychologist Christopher Mruk (2013) points out that anyone can improve their negative self-concept and self-esteem through hard work and practice.

So why is this important to communication? Because our self-perception affects who we choose to form relationships with, how we interact with others, and how comfortable we feel when we are called on to share our opinions or present a speech. Essentially, improving self-perception improves how we interact with others, and improving how we interact with others improves self-perception.

(2-4) PERCEPTION OF OTHERS

Now that we have a basic understanding of self-perception, let's look at how we perceive others and the role communication plays in that process. When we meet someone for the first time, we may ask ourselves questions such as "What is this person like?" or "What is this person likely to do, and why?" We might wonder whether we have anything in common, whether he or she will like us, whether we will get along, and whether we will enjoy the experience or feel uncomfortable. The natural reaction to such feelings is to say and do things that will reduce these uncertainties (Littlejohn & Foss, 2011).

2-4a Uncertainty Reduction

Uncertainty reduction (Berger & Bradac, 1982) is a communication theory that explains how individuals monitor their social environment in order to know more about themselves and others (Littlejohn & Foss, 2011). When people interact, they look for information to help them understand who their partner is and predict what their partner is likely to do. As we reduce uncertainty, we usually become more comfortable communicating (Guerrero, Andersen, & Afifi, 2007). To reduce uncertainty, we form impressions and make judgments about others as we interact with them.

FORMING IMPRESSIONS We engage in a variety of processes to form our perceptions about others. Researchers call these processes **impression formation**. Three of the most important ways we form impressions are based on physical appearance, perceived personality, and assumed similarity.

MAKING ATTRIBUTIONS At the center of our quest to reduce uncertainty is the need to predict how others will behave. By its nature, predicting something depends on understanding the cause and effect relationship between two things. When we see someone acting a certain way, we try to figure out why. Then we use this explanation to predict how that person will act in similar situations in the future. **Attributions** are reasons we give for our own and others' behavior. For instance, suppose a coworker with whom you had a noon lunch date has not arrived by 12:30. How do you explain her tardiness? One way you might explain it is to make a **situational attribution**, a reason that is beyond your coworker's control. You might assume, for instance, that your coworker must have had an accident on the way to the restaurant. On the other hand, you may make a **dispositional attribution**, attributing behavior to a cause that is under your coworker's control. In this case, you may perceive your coworker to be forgetful, self-absorbed, or insensitive to others. In any case, your attribution reduces your uncertainty by answering the question, "Why is my coworker late?" But the type of attribution you make influences how you interact with your coworker once she shows up. If you believe it is not her fault, you are likely to be concerned, understanding, and supportive. On the other hand, if you made a dispositional attribution, you are likely to be annoyed or hurt.

uncertainty reduction communication theory that explains how individuals monitor their social environment to know more about themselves and others

impression formation processes we use to form perceptions of others

attributions reasons we give for our own and others' behavior

situational attribution attributing behavior to a cause that is beyond someone's control

dispositional attribution attributing behavior to a cause that is under someone's control

Forming Impressions

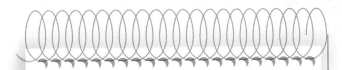

☐ **Physical appearance**
The first thing we notice about other people is how they look. Although it may seem superficial, we form these first impressions very quickly. In fact, one study found that we assess how attractive, likeable, trustworthy, competent, and aggressive we think people are after looking at their faces for only 100 milliseconds (Willis & Todorov, 2006).

☐ **Implicit personality theory**
We also form impressions based on assumptions we make about another's personality. **Implicit personality theory** is our tendency to assume that two or more personality characteristics go together. So if we see someone displaying one trait, we assume she has the other traits we associate with it. For example, if you meet someone who is multilingual you might assume she is also intelligent. Or if you meet someone who volunteers at a homeless shelter, you might assume that he is compassionate.

☐ **Assumed similarity**
We also form impressions about others by assuming that someone who shares one characteristic with us also shares others. Researchers call this **assumed similarity**. We assume someone is similar to us in a variety of ways until we get information that contradicts this assumption. For instance, when Ian attended a campaign event for a city council candidate who belonged to his political party, he expected the candidate's views on locating a new prison in the city to be the same as his. Ian was pleased to hear that the candidate agreed with his viewpoint, but he was shocked to hear the candidate's racist reasoning.

implicit personality theory the tendency to assume that two or more personality characteristics go together

assumed similarity assuming someone is similar to us in a variety of ways until we get information that contradicts this assumption

social presence the sense of being "there" with another person in a particular moment in time

2-4b Mediated Communication and Social Presence

Have you ever "talked back" to someone on the TV or radio or "coached" your favorite team while watching a televised game? If so, you perceived yourself as in some way "present" with those on the screen, even though you knew they could not actually see or hear you. **Social presence** is the sense of being "there" with another person in a particular moment in time. Social presence is also the extent to which you believe you can sense what another person is thinking and feeling and the extent to which you believe your partner also knows that you are "there." When we interact face-to-face, we are fully aware of the social presence of one another.

When we interact with others through a mediated channel, however, social presence is filtered through technology. So instead of experiencing another's physical presence, we experience their "mediated presence." In other words, we sense that someone is immediately available to us in a particular moment—even if they are not (Biocca & Harms, 2002). Experiencing someone's social presence is easier through some mediated channels (such as phone calls and text messages) than others (e-mails, blogs, and Facebook posts). When we communicate through mediated channels, we usually realize that our partner is not really physically present; however, when we communicate through richer and more synchronous channels, we are more likely to perceive others as socially present. For example, when we read an e-mail message, we may be able to conjure up a mental image of the person that wrote it, but we don't generally perceive them to be present with us as we read. In fact, the time stamp may indicate that the message was written hours, days, or weeks earlier. However, when we Skype with someone, we experience them as more socially present since we can talk back and forth and interpret nonverbal cues to understand their emotional tone.

Refer back to Figure 1-2 in chapter 1, which displays common forms of social media by degrees of richness, synchronicity, and social presence. Notice the position of face-to-face communication along the right side of the continuum and how mediated messages demonstrate a lower social presence as you scan farther and farther to the left.

2-4c Inaccurate and Distorted Perceptions of Others

As we work to reduce uncertainty, we also must be careful to reduce perceptual inaccuracies. Because perception is a complex process, we use shortcuts to help us focus

An Alabama monument dedicated to the 1965 Selma to Montgomery voting rights march. Prior to the enactment of the Voting Rights Act later that year, many African Americans in the South experienced discrimination when they were prevented from exercising the voting rights guaranteed by the 14th and 15th Amendments to the U.S. Constitution.

attention, interpret information, and make predictions about others. Selective perceptions, faulty attributions, forced consistency, and prejudice are shortcuts that can lead to perceptual inaccuracies.

Selective perception is the perceptual distortion that arises from paying attention only to what we expect to see or hear and ignoring what we don't expect. For instance, if Lily sees Mason as a man with whom she would like to develop a strong relationship, she will tend to see the positive side of Mason's personality and ignore the negative side. Similarly, if Artrell thinks that his landlord is mean and unfair, he may ignore any acts of kindness or generosity offered by the landlord.

Forced consistency is the inaccurate attempt to make several perceptions about another person agree with each other. It arises from our need to eliminate contradictions. Imagine that Leah does not like her coworker, Jill. If Jill supplies some information Leah missed on a form, Leah is likely to perceive Jill's behavior as interference, even if Jill's intention was to be helpful. If Leah likes Jill, however, she might perceive the very same behavior as helpful—even if Jill's intention was to interfere. In each case, the perception of "supplying missing information" is shaped by the need for consistency. It is consistent to regard someone we like as doing favors for us. It is inconsistent to regard people we don't like as doing favors for us. However, consistent perceptions of others are not necessarily accurate.

Prejudice is judging a person based on the characteristics of a group to which the person belongs without regard to how the person may vary from the group characteristic (Dovidio & Gaertner, 2010). Prejudices are based on **stereotypes**, which are exaggerated or oversimplified generalizations used to describe a group. A professor may see a student's spiked purple hair and numerous tattoos and assume the student is a rebel who will defy authority, slack off on classroom assignments, and seek attention. In reality, this person may be a polite, quiet, serious honor student who aspires to go to graduate school. Prejudice can lead to **discrimination**, which is acting differently toward a person based on prejudice (Dovidio & Gaertner, 2010). Prejudice deals with perception and attitudes, while discrimination involves actions. For instance, when Laura meets Wasif and learns that he is Muslim, she may use her knowledge of women's roles in Islamic countries to inform her perception of Wasif and conclude that he is a chauvinist without really talking to him. This is prejudice. If based on this prejudice she refuses to be in a class project group with him, she would be discriminating. Wasif may actually be a feminist, but Laura's use of the perceptual shortcut may prevent her from getting to know Wasif for the person he really is, and she may have cost herself the opportunity of working with the best student in class.

selective perception the perceptual distortion that arises from paying attention only to what we expect to see or hear and ignoring what we don't expect

forced consistency the inaccurate attempt to make several perceptions about another person agree with each other

prejudice judging a person based on the characteristics of a group to which the person belongs without regard to how the person may vary from the group characteristic

stereotypes exaggerated or oversimplified generalizations used to describe a group

discrimination acting differently toward a person based on prejudice

Racism, **ethnocentrism**, **sexism**, **heterosexism**, **ageism**, and **ableism** are various forms of prejudice in which members of one group believe that the behaviors and characteristics of their group are inherently superior to those of another group. All people can be prejudiced and act on their prejudices by discriminating against others. Nevertheless, "prejudices of groups with power are farther reaching in their consequences than others" (Sampson, 1999, p. 131). Because such attitudes can be deeply ingrained and are often subtle, it is easy to overlook behaviors we engage in that in some way meet this definition. Prejudicial perceptions may be unintentional, or they may seem insignificant or innocuous, but even seemingly unimportant prejudices rob others of their humanity and severely impede competent communication.

2-5 COMMUNICATION AND PERCEPTION OF OTHERS

Because perceptions of others influence how we communicate, improving perceptual accuracy is an important element of competent communication. We offer the following guidelines to improve your perceptions of others and their messages.

1. Question the accuracy of your perceptions. Questioning accuracy begins by saying, "I know what I think I saw, heard, tasted, smelled, or felt, but I could be wrong. What other information should I be aware of?" By accepting the possibility that you have overlooked something, you will stop automatic processing and begin to consciously search out information that should increase your accuracy.

2. Choose to use conscious processing as you get to know people. When you mindfully pay attention to someone, you are more likely to understand that person's uniqueness. Doing so can increase the accuracy of your perceptions.

3. Seek more information to verify perceptions. If your perception is based on only one or two pieces of information, try to collect additional information. Note that your perception is tentative—that is, subject to change. The best way to get additional information about people is to talk with them. It's OK to be unsure about how to treat someone from another group. But rather than letting your uncertainty cause you to make mistakes, talk with the person and tell him you want to be respectful. Then ask him for the information you need to become more comfortable about interacting appropriately and respectfully with him.

4. Realize that your perceptions of a person will change over time. People often base their opinions, assumptions, and behaviors on perceptions that are outdated. So when you encounter someone you haven't seen for a while, let the person's current behavior rather than her past actions or reputation inform your perceptions. For example, a former classmate who was wild in high school may well have changed and become a mature, responsible adult.

5. Seek clarification respectfully by perception checking. One way to assess the accuracy of a perception is to verbalize it and see whether others agree with what you see, hear, and interpret. A **perception check** is a message that reflects your understanding of the meaning of another person's behavior. It is a process of describing what you have seen and heard and then asking for feedback from the other person. A perception check consists of three parts. First, in a non-evaluative way, describe what you observe. Second, offer two possible interpretations. Third, ask for clarification.

Let's look at an example. Isabel's boyfriend, Liam, has not responded to her texts all day and was very quiet at dinner the night before. Isabel has jumped to the conclusion that Liam is going to break up with her. Rather than use this assumption and cause a defensive reaction when she does talk to Liam, Isabel could employ a perception-checking message—something like this:

> *"When you didn't respond to my texts today"* (nonjudgmental description of the observed behavior), *"I thought you were mad at me"* (first interpretation), *"or maybe you were really busy at work"* (second interpretation). *"Is everything ok? Is it something else?"* (request for clarification).

Perception checking is simply a tool to respectfully check for understanding of another's behavior without assuming your interpretation is correct.

racism, ethnocentrism, sexism, heterosexism, ageism, and ableism various form of prejudice in which members of one group believe that the behaviors and characteristics of their group are inherently superior to those of another group

perception check a message that reflects your understanding of the meaning of another person's behavior

LOCATED IN TEXTBOOK

☐ Tear-out Chapter Review cards at the end of the book

☐ Review with the Quick Quiz below

☐ Review Key Term flashcards and create your own cards

☐ Track your knowledge and understanding of key concepts in communication

☐ Complete practice and graded quizzes to prepare for tests

☐ Complete interactive content within COMM4 Online

☐ View the chapter highlight boxes for COMM4 Online

Quick Quiz

T F 1. The process of selectively attending to information and assigning meaning to it is called perception.

T F 2. A person's culture has a strong influence on the self-perception process.

T F 3. Self-created prophecies are predictions that you make about other people.

T F 4. Implicit personality theories are assumptions about which physical characteristics and personality traits or behaviors are associated with each other.

T F 5. A reality check is a message that reflects your understanding of the meaning of another person's nonverbal communication.

6. The phenomenon of presenting different aspects of self-concept based on the social context (people and situations involved) is called

   a. social construction.
   b. self-concept.
   c. personality.
   d. temperament.
   e. persona.

7. Suppose you expect to be rejected when you ask someone out and then behave in ways that lead the person to reject you. This would be an example of

   a. high self-esteem.
   b. incongruence.

   c. a self-fulfilling prophecy.
   d. filtering messages.
   e. a perception.

8. The process of monitoring the social environment to learn more about self and others is called

   a. observing others.
   b. uncertainty reduction.
   c. the halo effect.
   d. stereotyping.
   e. social construction.

9. If you grew up hearing that you were a "slow learner" and then a professor praised you for being a quick study, you might downplay the comment, not really hear it, or discount it entirely. This is an example of

   a. incongruence.
   b. filtering messages.
   c. poor self-perception.
   d. delayed reaction.
   e. a self-fulfilling prophecy.

10. Which of the following is performed during a perception check?

   a. watching the behavior of another person
   b. describing the behavior
   c. considering what the behavior means
   d. putting your interpretation into words
   e. all of the above

Answers: 1.T, 2.T, 3.F, 4.T, 5.F, 6.A, 7.C, 8.B, 9.B, 10.E

3 Intercultural Communication

After finishing this chapter go to **PAGE 42** for **STUDY TOOLS.**

LEARNING OUTCOMES

3-1 Define culture and the role of communication in it

3-2 Explain the relationship between dominant and co-cultures

3-3 Understand the seven dimensions in which cultures differ

3-4 Describe the inherent barriers in intercultural communication and the methods to develop competent intercultural communication

© Maciej Czekajewski/Shutterstock.com

Because culture has a profound impact on perception and communication, in this chapter we examine the relationship between culture and communication. We begin by explaining some basic concepts of culture and several ways cultures are unique. We end by proposing how to improve intercultural communication competence.

3-1 CULTURE AND COMMUNICATION

culture the system of shared values, beliefs, attitudes, and norms that guides what is considered appropriate among an identifiable group of people

values the commonly accepted standards of what is considered right and wrong, good and evil, fair and unfair, etc.

ideal values values that members of a culture profess to hold

real values values that guide actual behavior

intercultural communication interactions that occur between people whose cultures are so different that the communication between them is altered

Culture is the system of shared values, beliefs, attitudes, and norms that guides what is considered appropriate among an identifiable group of people (Samovar, Porter, & McDaniel, 2012). In a real sense, culture is a way of life. It's the structure of taken-for-granted *rules* for how and why we believe and behave as we do.

At the heart of any culture are its values. **Values** are the commonly accepted standards of what is considered right and wrong, good and evil, fair and unfair, just and unjust, and so on. Cultures have both ideal and real values. **Ideal values** are the ones that members profess to hold, whereas **real values** are the ones that guide actual behavior. For example, the United States Constitution professes equal rights and opportunities for all (ideal value), yet some people are treated unfairly based on sex, race, ethnicity, age, disability, or sexual orientation (real value in action).

Intercultural communication refers to the interactions that occur between people whose cultures are so different that the communication between them is altered (Samovar, Porter, & McDaniel, 2012). To become effective intercultural communicators, we must begin by understanding what a culture is, then identifying how cultures differ from one another, and finally realizing how those differences influence communication.

We do not need to visit other countries to meet people of different cultures. The United States is a multicultural society. Our population includes not only recent immigrants from other countries, but also descendents

of earlier immigrants and of native peoples. So understanding how communication varies among cultural groups can help us as we interact with the people we encounter every day right here in the United States.

Because each of us is so familiar with our own customs, norms, and values, we may feel anxious when they are disrupted. We call this psychological discomfort when engaging in a new cultural situation **culture shock** (Klyukanov, 2005). We are likely to feel culture shock most profoundly when thrust into an unfamiliar culture through travel, business, or studying abroad. In the film *Lost in Translation*, for example, Bill Murray's character struggles with culture shock while filming a commercial on location in Japan. Culture shock can also occur when interacting with others within our own country. For instance, city-dwellers may experience culture shock when visiting a small, rural town, or vice versa.

Culture is both transmitted and modified through communication. In Western cultures, for example, most people eat using forks, knives, spoons, individual plates, and bowls. In many Eastern cultures, people may eat with chopsticks. In some countries, people use bread as a utensil, and in others, people use their fingers and share a common bowl. All of these dining rituals are culturally based and taught by one generation to the next through communication.

Communication is also the mechanism through which culture is modified. For example, several generations ago most American children were taught to show respect by addressing adult family friends using a title and last name (e.g., Mr. Jones, Miss Smith). Today, children often address adult family friends by their first names.

DOMINANT CULTURES, CO-CULTURES, AND CULTURAL IDENTITY

Dominant culture refers to the learned system of norms held by the majority group of empowered people in a society. The dominant culture of the United States has evolved over time. It once strictly reflected and privileged the values of white, Western European, English-speaking, Protestant, heterosexual men. Before the 1960s, people immigrating to the United States were expected to embrace and adapt to this dominant culture in place of the culture of their native country. Immigrants

> **culture shock** psychological discomfort when engaging in a new cultural situation
>
> **dominant culture** the learned system of norms held by the majority group of empowered people in a society

Traditional South Asian wedding ceremonies are one example of how cultures differ. Ceremonies can last for days and are highly intricate. For example, the bride always sits on the right side of the groom (a place reserved for acquaintances) until they exchange their vows, when she sits on the left, becoming the Vamangi, or one-who-sits-on-the-left, signifying the couple's unity.

many people also identify with one or more co-cultures. A **co-culture** is a group consisting of a smaller number of people who hold common values, beliefs, attitudes, and customs that differ from those of the dominant culture.

Co-culture also influences communication. For example, co-cultural group members sometimes **code switch**, altering their linguistic and nonverbal patterns to conform to the dominant culture or co-culture depending on the topic and participants involved (MacSwan, 2013). So Linh may speak Vietnamese and defer to her older relatives while conversing at the dinner table. She may speak English and question her teachers openly during class discussions at school. And she may speak a mixture of Vietnamese and English (as well as slang and other accepted in-group jargon) when hanging out with friends. If you are familiar with the movie *Windtalkers*, you might know that the film is based on the real-life role Navajo code switchers played in Saipan during World War II (Jackson, 2004).

Cultural identity is the part of our self-concept that is based on how closely we associate with both the dominant culture and various co-cultures (Ting-Toomey & Chung, 2012). For example, you may be proud to be a third-generation Polish-American who embraces the co-culture of your heritage through communication patterns, religion, food choices, and so on. Or you might identify more with the dominant American culture and rarely think about being Polish. If the dominant culture stigmatizes your co-culture, you might downplay this part of your identity to fit into the dominant culture. Conversely, you may choose to identify even more closely with the co-culture and become a vocal activist for it.

Some of the co-cultures that exist in the United States today are formed around shared beliefs and values related to, for example, race, ethnicity, sex and gender, sexual orientation, religion, socioeconomic status, age or generation, and disability.

3-2a Race

Traditionally, the term *race* was used to classify people based on biological characteristics (e.g., skin and eye color, hair texture, body shape). However, today the use of the word "race" has become problematic and some scholars prefer to use the term "populations" instead (Waples & Gaggiotti, 2006). Nevertheless, people do experience the social effects of *perceived race* and form co-cultures based on similar experiences with respect to it (Rhodes et al., 2010).

co-culture a group consisting of a smaller number of people who hold common values, beliefs, attitudes, and customs that differ from those of the dominant culture

code switch altering linguistic and nonverbal patterns to conform to the dominant or co-culture

cultural identity the part of our self-concept that is based on how closely we associate with both the dominant culture and various co-cultures

even changed their names to sound more "American." They were expected to learn English quickly and use it instead of other languages. Since the 1960s, however, dominant American culture has slowly begun to respect and honor the diversity of cultures that co-exist here.

In addition to embracing the dominant American culture, then,

communicate in feminine ways. If you have ever heard someone tell an outspoken young girl to "hush up and act like a lady," or a weeping boy to "buck up and act like a man," you have witnessed young people *learning gender* based on their sex. Obviously, people differ in the extent to which they identify with these gendered co-cultures, and those who do not strongly identify with them may not behave in accord with expectations at all.

3-2d Sexual Orientation

The dominant American culture has historically valued and privileged heterosexuality. People who deviated from the heterosexual norm were severely mistreated. Although laws that reflect a change in attitude toward sexuality are gaining popularity, people who are not heterosexual still face discrimination, as well as legal and physical threats. Thus, co-cultures exist across the country based on the collective experiences of those who embrace a sexual orientation that is not heterosexual. Although many people are working hard to modify the dominant American culture with regard to sexual orientation, and some progress has been made, much remains to be done.

3-2b Ethnicity

Ethnicity refers to a shared cultural heritage that is learned rather than inherited. The degree to which people identify with their ethnicity can vary greatly. For example, Maria and Juan are both Mexican Americans. Juan, who immigrated with his parents to the United States, identifies more with his ethnic heritage than does Maria, who is a fourth-generation Mexican American.

Native language (or first) is the language of one's ethnic heritage and is typically the language a person learns from birth. Native language obviously influences communication. Even after learning English, many immigrants choose to speak their native language at home and to live in close proximity to others from their home country. Although the United States is considered an English-speaking country, Spanish is the second most common language spoken here and is the primary language spoken at home by 38.3 million people in the United States (U.S. Census Bureau, 2010).

3-2c Sex and Gender

In the dominant American culture, **sex** (which consists of biologically determined physical traits) and **gender** (which consists of the learned roles and communication patterns deemed "appropriate" for males and females in the dominant culture) tend to be intertwined. In other words, the dominant American culture expects men to communicate in masculine ways and women to

3-2e Religion

A **religion** is a belief system with a set of rituals and ethical standards based on a common perception of what is sacred or holy. Although the dominant culture in the United States values religious freedom, historically it has reflected monotheistic Judeo-Christian values and practices. However, many religious co-cultures exist harmoniously across the country today. Unfortunately, some people in the United States have become prejudiced against Muslims based on a misunderstanding that

ethnicity a classification of people based on combinations of shared characteristics such as nationality, geographic origin, language, religion, ancestral customs, and tradition

native language the language of one's ethnic heritage; typically the language learned at birth

sex biologically determined physical traits

gender the learned roles and communication patterns deemed "appropriate" for males and females in the dominant culture

religion a belief system with a set of rituals and ethical standards based on a common perception of what is sacred or holy

inaccurately equates Muslims with Al-Qaeda, the militant group responsible for the 9/11 terrorist attacks and, more recently, ISIS, the Islamic State of Iraq and Syria, which promotes extreme violence and mass killings in the name of its extremist religious ideology. These terrorist groups, however, are not representative of Muslim religious views. About 23 percent (1.6 billion people) of the world's population is Muslim, and among the core values of this religion are peace, mercy, and forgiveness (DeSilver, 2013).

3-2f Socioeconomic Status (SES)

Socioeconomic status (SES) is the position of a person or family in the power hierarchy of a society based on income, education, and occupation. SES is typically divided into three categories: high, middle, and low. Most Americans identify with the middle class even though they may really be members of a higher or lower class (U.S. Department of Commerce, 2010). People develop co-cultures that reinforce distinct values, rituals, and communication practices based on SES. Although not true in all cases, parents in low-SES groups tend to emphasize obedience, acceptance of what others think, and hesitancy in expressing desires to authority figures. Middle-class parents tend to emphasize intellectual curiosity. And, in terms of nonverbal communication, people of high SES backgrounds tend to perform more disengagement cues (e.g., doodling) and fewer engagement cues (e.g., head nods, laughs) than people from low SES backgrounds (Bornstein & Bradley, 2003; Kraus & Keltner, 2009). Finally, SES is at the heart of the American dream. Unfortunately, however, recent reports suggest that "the widening gap between the rich and poor is eroding the American dream" (Lynch, 2013).

3-2g Age/Generation

People born and raised in the same generation may identify with a co-culture distinct to it. Although not all people identify with their generational co-culture, generally speaking, people who grew up during the Great Depression tend to be frugal, and those who grew up during World War II tend to value sacrifice of self for cause and country. Baby Boomers who came of age during the turbulent 1960s are likely to question authority. Many Generation Xers, who grew up as *latch-key kids* (with parents at work when they got home from school), are likely to be self-sufficient and adaptable. Millennials (a.k.a. Generation Y and Generation NeXt), who grew up during the 1990s and came of age after 9/11, have never known life without computers, became aware of the realities of school and world violence at an early age, and experienced globalization. They tend to be adept at using technology to multitask, are cautious about safety issues, and appreciate diversity (Pew Research Center, 2007). Finally, Generation Z (a.k.a. the Internet Generation or Digital Natives) were born after 1997. They have never known a world without instant access to information via Internet searches on computers and smartphones, nor access to others via text messaging and social media sites like Facebook. They are adept at multitasking as well as learning and using new technologies (Prensky, 2001; Wallis, 2006).

When people from different generations interact, their co-cultural orientations can cause communication challenges. For example, when people from earlier generations interact with people who came of age after the 1960s, different expectations about how to demonstrate respect might cause misunderstandings and even conflict.

© Anton Oparin/Shutterstock.com

Striving to demonstrate respect for all people is one way to work toward intercultural harmony.

socioeconomic status (SES)
the position of a person or family in the power hierarchy of a society based on income, education, and occupation

3-2h Disability

A **disability** is any physical, emotional, mental, or cognitive impairment that impacts how a person functions in society. A disability co-culture is a group of people who share a distinct set of shared values, beliefs, and attitudes based on their common experiences of living with a disability.

Recently, a number of feature films and documentaries have been produced to help people who do not live with a disability to both understand and respect various disability co-cultures. For example, in 2010 HBO produced a film about the real life of Temple Grandin, a professor of animal science who improved the ethical treatment of animals, and who is also autistic. *Music Within* tells the story of what two Vietnam veterans did to help get the Americans with Disabilities Act passed, and *Front of the Class* focuses on the true story of a boy with Tourette syndrome who grew up to become a gifted teacher. Such films help to break through misinformed stereotypes and prejudiced thinking about the value and human potential of people who live with a disability.

3-3 HOW CULTURES DIFFER

Understanding how cultures differ becomes critical when we interact with people whose cultural norms differ from ours, because it helps us empathize and adapt our communication patterns accordingly (Kim, 2001; 2005). Consequently, we end up demonstrating the ethical principles of respect and integrity.

Understanding to which cultural groups people identify with can be challenging. The early work of Edward T. Hall and, more recently, Gerard Henrik (Geert) Hofstede give us a way to understand how cultures are similar to and different from one another and to understand how these cultural variations may affect communication. Based on their work, we offer several dimensions for consideration: (1) individualism/collectivism, (2) context, (3) chronemics, (4) uncertainty avoidance, (5) power distance, (6) masculinity/femininity, and (7) long-term/short-term orientation.

3-3a Individualism/Collectivism

Cultures differ in the extent to which individualism or collectivism is valued. Highly **individualistic cultures** value personal rights and responsibilities, privacy, voicing one's opinion, freedom, innovation, and self-expression (Andersen, Hecht, Hoobler, & Smallwood,

© Diego Cervo/Shutterstock.com

2003). People in highly individualistic cultures place primary value on the self and personal achievement. Competition is considered both desirable and useful, and the interests of others are considered primarily as they affect personal interests. Cultures in the United States, Australia, Canada, and Northern and Western European countries are considered to be highly individualistic.

In contrast, highly **collectivist cultures** value community, collaboration, shared interests, harmony, the public good, and avoiding embarrassment (Andersen et al., 2003). Highly collectivist cultures place primary value on the interests of the group and group harmony. Decisions are shaped by what is considered best for the group, regardless of whether they serve an individual's personal interests. Maintaining harmony and cooperation is valued over competition and personal achievement. A variety of cultures throughout South and Central America, East and Southeast Asia, and Africa are considered to be highly collectivist.

Individualism and collectivism influence many aspects of communication (Samovar, Porter, & McDaniel, 2012). First, individualism and collectivism affect self-concept and self-esteem. People in individualist cultures form independent self-concepts and base their self-esteem on individual accomplishments. People in collectivist cultures

---

disability any physical, emotional, mental, or cognitive impairment that impacts how a person functions in society

individualistic cultures cultures that value personal rights and responsibilities, privacy, voicing one's opinion, freedom, innovation, and self-expression

collectivist cultures cultures that value community, collaboration, shared interests, harmony, the public good, and avoiding embarrassment form interdependent self-concepts and base their self-esteem on how well they work in a group.

Second, emphasis on the individual leads members of highly individualistic cultures to be assertive and confront conflict directly, whereas members of highly collectivist cultures are more likely to engage in collaboration or to avoid conflict. In the United States, assertiveness and argumentation are skills used in personal relationships, small group situations, politics, and business. In Japan, a highly collectivist culture, common business practices are based on an elaborate process called *nemawashii* (a term that also means "binding the roots of a plant before pulling it out"). To maintain harmony and avoid confrontational argument, any subject that might cause conflict should be discussed among individuals before the group meets to ensure that interactions during the meeting will not seem rude or impolite (Samovar, Porter, & McDaniel, 2012).

Finally, individualism and collectivism influence how people make group decisions. In highly collectivist cultures, group members strive for consensus and may sacrifice optimal outcomes for the sake of group harmony. In highly individualistic cultures, optimal outcomes are paramount, even at the expense of disharmony. Groups consisting of members who come from both highly individualistic and highly collectivist cultures may experience difficulties because of these different cultural values related to individualism and collectivism.

3-3b Context

Another cultural distinction that affects intercultural communication is the extent to which members rely on contextual cues to convey the meaning of a message (Hall, 1976; Schein, 2010). In **low-context cultures**, speakers use words to convey most of the meaning. In low-context cultures such as those of the United States, Germany, and Scandinavia speakers are expected to say exactly what they mean and get to the point. In **high-context cultures**, much of the speaker's

message is conveyed indirectly and can be accurately interpreted only by referring to unwritten cultural rules and subtle nonverbal behaviors. So in high-context cultures such as those of American Indian, Latin American, and Asian communities, verbal messages are ambiguous and understood by "reading between the lines" (Chen & Starosta, 1998).

Effective communication between members of high- and low-context cultures can be challenging. When low-context communicators interact with high-context communicators, they should be mindful that building a good relationship first is important for long-term effectiveness. Also, nonverbal messages and gestures will probably be more important than what is actually said. When high-context communicators interact with low-context communicators, they should recognize that the verbal message should be taken at face value and direct questions, assertions, and observations are not meant to be offensive. Finally, they need to recognize that low-context communicators might not notice or understand indirect contextual cues.

3-3c Chronemics

Chronemics is the study of how the perception of time differs among cultures (Hall, 1976). **Monochronic cultures** view time as a series of small units that occur sequentially. Monochronic cultures value punctuality, uninterrupted task completion, meeting deadlines, following plans, and doing things one at a time. The dominant culture of the United States values a monochronic orientation to time.

Polychronic cultures, for example, Latin American, Arab, and Southern European cultures, view time as a continuous flow. Thus, appointment times and schedules are perceived as approximate and fluid. People who abide by a polychronic orientation to time are comfortable doing several things at once, having a flexible schedule or none at all, and disregarding deadlines to satisfy other needs (Chen & Starosta, 1998). Interruptions are not perceived as annoying but as natural occurrences.

Differences in time orientation can make intercultural communication challenging. In polychronic cultures, relationships are more important than schedules. So when Dante, who is polychronic, shows up for a noon lunch with Sean at 12:47 because a coworker had needed some help, he doesn't perceive this as a problem. But Sean, who is monochronic, is annoyed because Dante arrived so "late," and quickly moves the discussion to the business they need to complete. Sean's attitude and immediate discussion of business seems rude to Dante.

low-context cultures cultures in which speakers use words to convey most of the meaning; verbal messages are direct, specific, and detailed

high-context cultures cultures in which much of a speaker's message is understood from the context

chronemics the study of how the perception of time differs among cultures.

monochronic cultures cultures that view time as a series of small units that occur sequentially

polychronic cultures cultures that view time as a continuous flow

Needing to control unpredictable events may create systems of formal rules and stems from high uncertainty avoidance.

© klublu/Shutterstock.com

3-3d Uncertainty Avoidance

Cultures differ in their attitudes toward **uncertainty avoidance**, which is the extent to which people desire to predict what is going to happen. **Low uncertainty-avoidance cultures** such as those of the United States, Sweden, and Denmark tolerate uncertainty and are less driven to control unpredictable people, relationships, or events. People tend to accept unpredictability, tolerate the unusual, prize creative initiative, take risks, and think there should be as few rules as possible.

High uncertainty-avoidance cultures such as those of Germany, Portugal, Greece, Peru, and Belgium have a low tolerance for uncertainty and a high need to control unpredictable people, relationships, or events. These cultures often create systems of formal rules as a way to provide more security and reduce risk. They also tend to be less tolerant of people or groups with deviant ideas or behaviors. People in these cultures often experience anxiety when confronted with unpredictable people, relationships, or situations (Samovar, Porter, & McDaniel, 2012).

How our culture teaches us to view uncertainty impacts communication. People from high uncertainty-avoidance cultures tend to value and use precise language to be more certain of what a person's message means. Students from high uncertainty-avoidance cultures would probably ask a lot of questions about school assignments and would probably welcome a specific checklist of the exact criteria by which an assignment would be graded. By contrast, students from low uncertainty-avoidance cultures might be annoyed if given such a specific list of rules, viewing them as a barrier to creativity.

Uncertainty avoidance also influences how people communicate in new and developing relationships. People from high uncertainty-avoidance cultures tend to be wary of strangers and may not seek out new relationships with people they perceive as different and, thus, unpredictable. They might prefer meeting people through friends and family. And in the early stages of a developing relationship, they might guard their privacy and refrain from self-disclosure. People from low uncertainty-avoidance cultures, on the other hand, are likely to initiate new relationships with people who seem unusual and unique, and might enjoy the excitement of disclosing personal information as a way to get to know one another earlier in the relationship.

3-3e Power Distance

Power distance is the extent to which members of a culture expect and accept that power will be equally or unequally shared. In **high power-distance cultures**, unequal distribution of power is accepted by both high and low power holders. Although no culture distributes power equally, people in high power-distance cultures (like many countries in the Middle East, Malaysia, Guatemala, Venezuela, and Singapore) view unequal power distribution as normal.

In **low power-distance cultures**, members prefer power to be more equally distributed. In the cultures of Austria, Finland, Denmark, Norway, and the United States, inequalities in power and status are muted. People know that some individuals have more clout, authority, and influence, but lower-ranking people are not in awe of or more respectful toward people in higher positions of power. Even though power differences exist, people value democracy and egalitarian behavior.

Our cultural beliefs about power distance

uncertainty avoidance the extent to which people desire to predict what is going to happen

low uncertainty-avoidance cultures cultures that tolerate uncertainty and are less driven to control unpredictable people, relationships, or events

high uncertainty-avoidance cultures cultures with a low tolerance for uncertainty and a high need to control unpredictable people, relationships, or events

power distance the extent to which members of a culture expect and accept that power will be equally or unequally shared

high power-distance cultures cultures that view unequal power distribution as normal

low power-distance cultures cultures in which members prefer power to be more equally distributed

naturally affect how we interact with others in authority positions. If you are a student or employee living in a high power-distance culture, you are not likely to argue with your teacher, supervisor, or boss. Rather, you will probably do what is ordered without question. In contrast, if you come from a low power-distance culture where status differences are muted, you might be more comfortable questioning or even arguing with those in authority.

3-3f Masculinity/Femininity

Cultures differ in how strongly they value traditional gender role distinctions. In highly **masculine cultures**, men and women are expected to adhere to traditional gender roles and behaviors. These cultures also value masculine roles more highly than feminine ones. If you come from a highly masculine culture (like those of Mexico, Italy, and Japan), you are likely to expect men to act in assertive and dominant ways and to expect women to be nurturing, caring, and service-oriented. You are likely to feel uncomfortable when you encounter people who don't meet these expectations. You are also likely to view masculine behaviors as more valuable, regardless of your sex. As a result, even though women are not supposed to enact such behaviors, you are likely to value the traditionally masculine characteristics of performance, ambition, assertiveness, competitiveness, and material success enacted by men more than you value traditionally feminine traits such as service, nurturing, relationships, and helping behaviors enacted by women embracing traditional gender roles and behaviors (Hofstede, 2000).

In highly **feminine cultures**, people assume a variety of roles and are valued for doing so regardless of sex. In feminine cultures (like those of Sweden, Norway, and Denmark), both men and women are accustomed to being nurturing, caring, and service oriented and value those traits as much as performance, ambition, and competitiveness depending on the circumstances of a situation (Hofstede, 1998).

Whether you come from a highly masculine or feminine culture influences how you communicate with others. People from masculine cultures have strict definitions of what are appropriate behaviors for males and females and are rewarded for adhering to them. Men in these cultures tend to be unprepared to engage in nurturing and caring behaviors and women tend to be unprepared to be assertive or to argue persuasively. Both women and men in feminine cultures learn to nurture, empathize, assert, and argue, and are rewarded for doing so.

3-3g Long-Term/Short-Term Orientation

Long-term and short-term orientations deal with how a culture values patience in arriving at rewards in the future or immediately in the here and now. **Short-term oriented cultures** tend to value rewards in the here and now and, thus, emphasize quick results, fulfilling social obligations, and getting to the bottom line efficiently. People in cultures with a short-term orientation, such as those found in the United States, Pakistan, Russia, Canada, Norway, and the United Kingdom, tend to determine what result

© Svetlanamiku/Shutterstock.com

masculine cultures cultures in which men and women are expected to adhere to traditional gender roles

feminine cultures cultures in which people assume a variety of roles and are valued for doing so regardless of sex

short-term oriented cultures cultures that tend to value static rewards in the here and now and emphasizes quick results

is desired at the outset of an experience and then do whatever it takes to achieve it. People in short-term oriented cultures also value keeping leisure time distinctly separate from working time. **Long-term oriented cultures**, such as those of China, Japan, Hong Kong, and Taiwan, emphasize potential future rewards that will be realized after slow and steady perseverance toward achieving a mutually acceptable result. Adaptability and honoring relationships are more important than quickly achieving the bottom line. And leisure time is not expected to be separate from working time.

Misunderstandings may arise when people from cultures with a long-term orientation interact with people from cultures with a short-term orientation. One of your authors experienced this on a business trip to Shanghai, China. Coming from a short-term oriented culture, when her hosts began discussing business ideas at dinner, she lightheartedly said, "No talking business at the dinner table." While this remark would have been quite appropriate in the United States, where a short-term orientation values leisure time as separate from working time, her hosts politely reminded her that they always talk business at the dinner table.

© Rawpixel/Shutterstock.com

Respecting other cultures is one way to avoid ethnocentricity and to experience different cultures than your own.

3-4 DEVELOPING INTERCULTURAL COMMUNICATION COMPETENCE

We can develop intercultural communication competence by first acknowledging potential barriers and then by employing several strategies to overcome them.

3-4a Potential Barriers

Several of the most common barriers to effective intercultural communication include anxiety, assuming similarity or difference, ethnocentrism, stereotyping, incompatible communication codes, and incompatible norms and values.

ANXIETY It is normal to feel some level of discomfort when entering a cultural setting with unfamiliar norms and customs. Most people experience fear, dislike, and distrust when first interacting with someone from a different culture (Luckmann, 1999).

ASSUMED SIMILARITY OR DIFFERENCE When we cross into an unfamiliar cultural environment, we might

assume that the norms that apply to our culture will also apply in the new one. When traveling internationally from the United States, for example, many people expect to eat their familiar hamburgers and fries and to be provided with rapid service when ordering. Likewise, they may be annoyed when shops and restaurants close during the early afternoon in countries that observe the custom of a siesta.

It can be just as great a mistake to assume that *everything* about an unfamiliar culture will be different. For example, a Mexican-American student from California studying at a small private college in Vermont may assume that everyone is different from her. However, her *quinceañera* party is very similar to Jewish bat/bar mitzvah celebrations and confirmation parties, all three celebrating coming of age.

ETHNOCENTRISM Ethnocentrism is the belief that one's own culture is superior to others. The stereotype of the tourist in the host country, loudly complaining about how much better everything is back home, is the classic example of ethnocentrism. Ethnocentrism exists in every culture to some degree (Haviland, 1993) and can occur in co-cultures, as well. An ethnocentric view of the world leads to attitudes of superiority and messages that are condescending in content and tone.

STEREOTYPING Recall that stereotyping is a perceptual shortcut in which people assume that everyone in a cultural group is the same. When we interact based on stereotypes, we risk engaging in inaccurate

long-term oriented cultures cultures that emphasize potential future rewards that will eventually be realized after slow and steady perseverance toward achieving a mutually acceptable result

ethnocentrism the belief that one's own culture is superior to others

and even unethical communication that is likely to damage our relationships.

INCOMPATIBLE COMMUNICATION CODES When others speak a different language than we do, it is easy to see that we have incompatible communication codes. But even when people speak the same language, cultural variations can result from belonging to different co-cultures. For example, people from Great Britain take a "lift" to reach a higher floor and eat "chips" with their fish. Americans ride an "elevator" and eat "French fries" with their burgers. Within the United States, many Midwesterners drink "pop" rather than "soda." Cocultural groups will often purposefully develop in-group codes that are easily understood by co-culture members but are unintelligible to those from the outside.

INCOMPATIBLE NORMS AND VALUES Sometimes what is considered normal or highly valued in one culture is offensive in another. To the Vietnamese, dog meat is considered a delicacy. Many Americans might find the practice of eating dog meat disgusting but think nothing of eating beef. However, practicing Hindus may not eat beef because the cow is sacred to their religion. Different norms and values can cause serious problems when communicating unless we are aware of and respect differences.

3-4b Competent Communication Strategies

Unfortunately, there is no "silver bullet" strategy for communicating effectively across cultures. However, competent intercultural communicators work to overcome potential cultural barriers by acquiring accurate information about other cultures' values and practices, adopting an appropriate attitude, and developing culture-centered skills.

ACQUIRE ACCURATE KNOWLEDGE The more we know about other cultures before we attempt to interact with people in them, the more likely we are to be competent intercultural communicators (Neuliep, 2006). There are several ways to learn about other cultures.

1. Formal study. You can learn about other cultures by reading books, periodicals, and Web sites about them. You can read personal accounts and

© Aysezgicmeli/Shutterstock.com

ethnographic research studies, take courses, and interview members of the group.

2. Observation. You can learn about a culture or co-culture by watching as members interact with each other. We call this form of watching **nonparticipant observation**. As you watch, you can notice how certain values, rituals, and communication styles are similar to and different from your own.

3. Immersion. You can learn a great deal about another culture by actively participating in it. When you live or work with people whose cultural assumptions are different from yours, you not only acquire obvious cultural information, you also learn nuances that escape passive observers and are not accessible through formal study alone. We call this form of immersion **participant observation**. One reason study-abroad programs often include home stays is to ensure that students become immersed in the culture of the host country.

ADOPT AN APPROPRIATE ATTITUDE We must be willing to try and must have a genuine desire to succeed when communicating across cultures. We must be willing to adapt rather than expect the other person to adjust to our communication style. We can begin to adopt an appropriate attitude by tolerating ambiguity, being open-minded, and acting altruistically.

1. Tolerate ambiguity. Communicating with strangers usually creates uncertainty; when the stranger also comes from a different culture, we often become even more anxious about what he or she will expect of us. When communicating, we must be prepared to tolerate a high degree of uncertainty about the other person and to tolerate it for a long time. If you enter an intercultural interaction believing that it is OK to be unsure about how to proceed, you are likely to pay closer attention to the feedback you receive. You can then work to adjust your communication to demonstrate respect and to achieve mutual understanding.

nonparticipant observation learning about a culture or co-culture by watching as members interact with each other

participant observation learning about a culture or co-culture by living or working with people whose cultural assumptions are different from yours

2. Be open-minded. Open-minded people are aware of their own cultural norms and values and recognize that other people's norms and values may be different, but not wrong. Resist the impulse to judge the values of other cultures in terms of your own culture. Also avoid jumping to conclusions about what you think others mean by something they say or do. Instead, seek to learn from those you interact with by assuming their intentions are honorable and asking sincere questions about what they say and do differently and why.

3. Be altruistic. Altruism is a display of genuine and unselfish concern for the welfare of others. The opposite of altruism is **egocentricity**, a selfish interest in one's own needs to the exclusion of everything else. Egocentric people focus on themselves, whereas altruistic people focus on others. Altruistic communicators do not neglect their own needs, but they recognize that for a conversation to be successful, both parties must be able to contribute what they want and take what they need from the exchange. One way to demonstrate this is to learn some basic phrases in the language of your peer's culture and try to use them when possible. When people hear you say "please" and "thank you" in their native language, even if your pronunciation is imperfect, they are likely to perceive you as respectful and are likely to engage more openly with you as a result.

DEVELOP CULTURE-CENTERED SKILLS To be effective in intercultural situations, you may need to adapt the basic communication skills you learn in this course to a particular culture. Three very useful skills are listening, empathy, and flexibility.

1. Practice listening. There are cultural differences in how people value and engage in listening. In the dominant culture of the United States, people listen closely for concrete facts and information and often ask questions while listening. In other cultures, such as those in Japan, Finland, and Sweden, listeners are more reserved and do not ask as many questions (Samovar, Porter, & McDaniel, 2012). Many cultures in East Asian countries value listening more than speaking.

2. Practice intercultural empathy. Intercultural empathy means imaginatively placing yourself in the other person's cultural world and attempting to experience what he or she is experiencing (Ting-Toomey et al., 2000). Conveying intercultural empathy demonstrates that we sincerely respect the other person and his or her cultural norms even though those norms may not be upheld in our culture. Try to honor the practices of the host culture. If you are in an East Asian country, for example, try to use chopsticks rather than asking for a knife and fork.

3. Develop flexibility. Flexibility is the ability to adjust your communication to fit the other person and the situation. With flexibility, you can use a wide variety of communication skills during an interaction and modify your behavior within and across situations. Being flexible means analyzing a situation, making good decisions about how to communicate in that situation, and then modifying your communication when necessary as you go along.

> **altruism** a display of genuine and unselfish concern for the welfare of others
>
> **egocentricity** a selfish interest in one's own needs to the exclusion of everything else
>
> **intercultural empathy** imaginatively placing yourself in another person's cultural world and attempting to experience what he or she is experiencing
>
> **flexibility** the ability to adjust your communication to fit the other person and the situation

Practice Makes...for Smoother Communication

When visiting with college students at Shanghai University, one of your authors asked each student his or her name. Although each student first introduced himself or herself with an "English" name, the author also asked students to offer their Chinese names, which she repeated back to them. When the students heard her make this genuine attempt to honor them and their given Chinese names, they began to trust her and opened up more during the classroom discussion. People who make a sincere effort to listen attentively and respond in an other-centered way find the most success when interacting with people from cultures that differ from their own.

STUDY TOOLS 3

LOCATED IN TEXTBOOK

☐ Tear-out Chapter Review cards at the end of the book

☐ Review with the Quick Quiz below

LOCATED ON COMM 4 ONLINE AT CENGAGEBRAIN.COM:

☐ Review Key Term flashcards and create your own cards

☐ Track your knowledge and understanding of key concepts in communication

☐ Complete practice and graded quizzes to prepare for tests

☐ Complete interactive content within COMM4 Online

☐ View the chapter highlight boxes for COMM4 Online

Quick Quiz

T F 1. Intercultural communication can be defined as the psychological discomfort of adjusting to a new cultural situation.

T F 2. Once immigrants to the United States have learned English, they often speak it at home so they can learn to better fit in with their neighbors.

T F 3. People who come from high uncertainty-avoidance cultures have a high tolerance for unpredictable people, relationships, and events.

T F 4. People from masculine cultures expect that individuals will assume a variety of roles depending on the circumstances and their own choices, regardless of sex; they do not have any sex-role expectations.

T F 5. An ethnocentric view of the world leads to attitudes of superiority and messages that are directly and subtly condescending in content and tone.

6. Which of the following is not one of the major contributors to co-cultures in U.S. society today, as listed by the text?

a. gender
b. ethnicity
c. race
d. political beliefs
e. sexual orientation

7. Which of the following is the most obvious influence of ethnicity on communication?

a. the foods you prefer
b. your religion
c. the language of your original country
d. traditions handed down from your ancestors
e. distinguishable physical characteristics

8. Based on the discussion in the text, when parents place emphasis on intellectual curiosity, they are likely to be associated with which social class?

a. upper class
b. lower class
c. elite
d. middle class
e. impoverished

9. Geert Hofstede identified major dimensions of culture that affect communication. Which of the following is NOT one of them?

a. individualism-collectivism
b. religious beliefs
c. uncertainty avoidance
d. power distance
e. masculinity-femininity

10. In cultures characterized by _____, inequalities in power, status, and rank are underplayed and muted.

a. high power distance
b. low power distance
c. masculinity
d. femininity
e. individualism

Answers: 1.F, 2.F, 3.F, 4.F, 5.T, 6.D, 7.C, 8.D, 9.B, 10.B

YOUR
FEEDBACK
MATTERS.

4 Verbal Messages

© Gustavo Frazao/Shutterstock.com

LEARNING OUTCOMES

4-1 Define a language, a dialect, and an idiolect

4-2 List the characteristics of language

4-3 Compose effective verbal messages based on semantic, pragmatic, and sociolinguistic meanings

After finishing this chapter go to **PAGE 53** for **STUDY TOOLS.**

In this chapter, you'll learn many reasons why people can interpret the same message in a wide variety of ways, which can lead to serious misunderstandings that affect our relationships. We begin by explaining the nature of language. Then we describe the relationship between language and meaning and offer suggestions for improving your ability to communicate both face-to-face and online.

4-1 THE NATURE OF LANGUAGE

When you hear the word "language," what comes to mind? If you're like most people, you probably think of English, Spanish, French, Chinese, Hindi, Swahili, and so forth. While each language is certainly different from the others in some ways, their purposes and fundamentals are the same.

In terms of purposes, we use language to label, compare, and define. So when we label some music as hip hop, we do so to differentiate it from other musical genres such as rock, pop, country, and classical. We also use language to compare and judge things as better or worse. Television programs such as *What Not to Wear* and *American Idol* are based on this very principle. We also use language to discuss and learn from the experiences of others. We might do so by taking a course, attending a lecture, visiting with a friend, watching a TV program, or surfing the Internet.

In terms of fundamentals, all languages are based on the exchange of utterances. An **utterance** is a complete unit of talk bounded by the speaker's silence (Arnoff & Rees-Miller, 2001). "Silence" can be either literal (e.g., during a face-to-face or telephone conversation) or figurative (e.g., waiting for a response to a text message). Exchanging utterances is known as **turn-taking**. With these purposes and fundamentals in mind, let's turn now to a more specific discussion about what a language is and what its characteristics are.

4-1a What Is a Language?

A **language** is a system of symbols used by people to communicate. Verbal languages communicate thoughts and feelings. Each verbal language consists of a **lexicon**, a collection of words and expressions; a **phonology**, sounds

---

utterance a complete unit of talk bounded by the speaker's literal or figurative silence

turn-taking the exchange of utterances

language a system of symbols used by people to communicate

lexicon the collection of words and expressions in a language

phonology the sounds used to pronounce words

WORDS HAVE POWER

used to pronounce words; and **syntax and grammar**, rules for combining words to form sentences.

All people who understand a particular language are part of a **language community**. For example, most of the people who live in Australia, Scotland, Ireland, Canada, India, and the United States, belong to the English language community. The five largest language communities in the world are Chinese, Spanish, English, Arabic, and Hindi (Lewis, 2009).

If all people in a particular language community knew all the words, pronounced them the same way, and used the same rules of grammar and syntax, communication would be easy. Unfortunately, this is not the case. The English spoken in England is not the same as the English spoken in the United States. And the English spoken in Boston is not the same as the English spoken in Biloxi, Mississippi, or in Fargo, North Dakota.

Languages are really collections of dialects. A **dialect** is a unique form of a more general language spoken by a specific culture or co-culture (O'Grady, Archibald, Aronoff, & Rees-Miller, 2001). These smaller groups that speak a common dialect are known as **speech communities**.

No one dialect is better or worse than another. Each simply uses different lexicons, phonologies, grammars, and syntaxes. However, some dialects are *perceived* to be "better" than others because they are spoken by the power elite of a language community. This dialect tends to be promoted as the "proper" form.

As is demonstrated in the cases of the former Yugoslavia and China, what is called a *language* and what is called a *dialect* is usually rooted in politics. When Yugoslavia was a country, its official language (Serbian-Croatian) consisted of many similar dialects among various regions. Since the collapse of Yugoslavia in the 1990s, however, each region is now a separate country and many of these regional dialects are considered the official languages of each country. Serbian is spoken in Serbia, Croatian in Croatia, Bosnian in Bosnia, and Montenegrin in Montenegro (Cvetkovic, 2009).

On the other hand, the official language of China is Chinese and all literate people use this same written symbol system. Thus, people from one part of the country can easily read compositions written by someone in other parts of the country. But the written symbols do not have commonly shared pronunciations. So although the regional tongues of Mandarin, Wu, Cantonese, and Min are dialects of Chinese, speakers of one dialect often can't understand someone speaking another (Wright, 2010).

In addition to language and dialect, each of us uses our own personal symbol system called an

syntax and grammar rules for combining words to form sentences and larger units of expression

language community all people who can speak or understand a particular language

dialect a unique form of a more general language spoken by a specific culture or co-culture

speech communities smaller groups that speak a common dialect

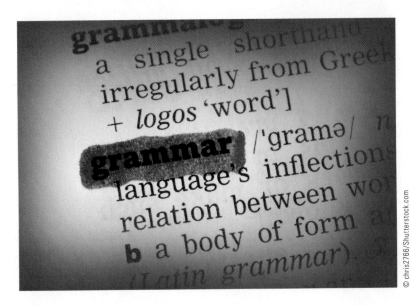

idiolect, which includes our active vocabularies and our unique pronunciations, grammar, and syntax (Higginbotham, 2006). We may have words in our personal lexicon that are understood by very few people as well as words understood by large numbers of people. Likewise, we may pronounce some words or use grammar or syntax in idiosyncratic ways. Those with whom we talk frequently understand our idiolect best.

4-2 CHARACTERISTICS OF LANGUAGE

Sharing meaning can be difficult because we speak different languages and use different dialects and idiolects than those with whom we are communicating. Sharing meaning can also be difficult because language is arbitrary, abstract, and constantly changing.

4-2a Language Is Arbitrary

In any language, the **words** used to represent things are arbitrary symbols. There is not necessarily a literal connection between a word and the thing it

represents. For a word to have meaning, it must be recognized by members of the language or speech community as standing for a particular object, idea, or feeling. The word *dog* is nothing more than three letters used together unless members of a community agree that it stands for a certain four-legged animal. Different language communities use different word symbols to represent the same phenomenon. In Spanish, for instance, *el perro* represents the same thing that *dog* represents in English. Different speech communities within a language community may also use different words to represent the same phenomenon. For example, the storage compartment of an automobile is called a *trunk* in the United States and a *boot* in England.

4-2b Language Is Abstract

Not only is language arbitrary, but it is also abstract. For example, in the United States, the word *pet* is commonly understood to be an animal kept for companionship. Still, if Rema refers simply to her "pet," Margi may think of a dog, cat, snake, bird, or hamster. Even if Rema specifically mentions her cat, Margi still might think of cats of various breeds, sizes, colors, and temperaments.

4-2c Language Changes over Time

New words are constantly being invented and existing words abandoned or assigned new meanings. Just think, for example, of the words that have been invented to represent new technologies, such as *texting*, *Googling*,

idiolect our own personal symbol system that includes our active vocabularies and our unique pronunciations, grammar, and syntax

words arbitrarily chosen symbols used to represent thoughts and feelings

The characteristics of language demonstrate why sharing meaning can be challenging.

cyberbullying, sexting, tweeting, retweeting, netiquette, webinar, emoticon, and *blogging.* Some of the new words most recently added to English dictionaries include *vanity sizing* (the deliberate undersizing of clothes), *twirt* (flirt via Twitter), *mankle* (the male ankle), and *cougar* (an older woman in a romantic relationship with a younger man). Did you know that the *Oxford English Dictionary* now also includes *OMG, LOL,* and <3 as actual words?

Some words become obsolete because the thing they represent is no longer used. For example, today we use *photocopiers* and *computers* to make multiple copies of print documents rather than *mimeographs* (low-cost printing presses) and *stencils.* We record audio and video data using *smartphones* rather than using *tape recorders, cassette tapes,* and *videotapes.* And we take notes on *iPads* and *laptops* rather than on pads of paper.

Sometimes the meanings of existing words change. For example, in the United States, *gay* once meant *happy* and only that. Today, its more common usage references one's sexual orientation. In some communities, *bad* might mean *not good,* in others it might mean *naughty,* and in others it might mean *really great* (e.g., "That movie was really bad."). And language can change when aspects of multiple languages blend together. For instance, phrases in *Tex-Mex* and *Spanglish* both blend English and Spanish, and we don't think twice about children going to *kindergarten,* a word introduced into the United States by German immigrants.

4-3 THE RELATIONSHIP BETWEEN LANGUAGE AND MEANING

On the surface, the relationship between language and meaning seems pretty simple. If we select words and structure them using the grammar and syntax rules of a language community, people in that language community should understand what we mean when we say them. As you undoubtedly know, however, communicating verbally is much more complicated than that. Therefore, in this section we focus specifically on the relationship between language and meaning in terms of semantics (meanings derived from the words themselves), pragmatics (meanings derived from the conversational context), and sociolinguistics (meanings derived from social and cultural contexts).

© Stuart Miles/Shutterstock.com

4-3a Semantics

Semantic meaning is derived from the words themselves and how they are arranged into sentences. Although we learn new words every day, our ability to express our thoughts and feelings and to understand others is limited by the size and accuracy of our vocabulary.

Identifying the meaning of a word is tricky because words have two types of meanings. **Denotation** is the explicit meaning found in the dictionary of a language community. However, different dictionaries may define words in slightly different ways and many words have multiple denotative definitions. For instance, the *Random House Dictionary of the English Language* lists 23 definitions for the word *great.* Not only that, the lexicon of our personal idiolect rarely corresponds precisely to the definitions found in formal dictionary definitions. So when your friend says your performance was *great,* he might mean it was very good, exceptional, powerful, or that it lasted a long time. All are denotative dictionary definitions of *great.*

Connotation is the implicit additional meaning we associate with a word. For example, think of the different meanings people might associate with the word *family* based on their experiences growing up. To one person, a "family" may connote a safe place where one is loved unconditionally. To another, it might connote a dangerous place where people must fend for and protect themselves. Word denotation and connotation are important because the only message that counts is the message that is understood, regardless of whether it is the one you intended.

semantic meaning meaning derived from the words themselves and how they are arranged into sentences

denotation the explicit meaning of a word found in the dictionary of a language community

connotation the implicit additional meaning we associate with a word

Semantic meaning is based on both the words themselves and how they are combined into meaningful phrases, sentences, and larger units of expression For example, you might communicate the same message by saying:

"When he went to the pound, he adopted a three-pound puppy."

"He went to the pound and adopted a three-pound puppy."

"Upon arriving at the pound, he adopted a three-pound puppy."

© Vudhikrai/Shutterstock.com

Improving Semantics

1. **Use specific language.** **Specific language** refers to precise words that clarify semantic meaning by narrowing what is understood from a general category to a particular item or group within that category. For example, saying "a banged-up Honda Civic" is more specific than saying "a car."

2. **Use concrete language.** **Concrete language** clarifies semantic meaning by appealing to the senses (e.g., seeing, hearing, feeling, tasting, smelling). Instead of saying Jill "speaks in a weird way," we might say Jill "mumbles," "whispers," "blusters," or "drones."

3. **Use familiar language.** We also need to use words our receivers will understand. For example, we should use jargon and slang only when we are certain the meaning will be clear or by defining it clearly the first time we use it. Overusing and misusing abbreviations and acronyms can also hinder understanding.

4. **Use descriptive details and examples.** Sometimes semantic meaning can be improved by using descriptive details or examples. Suppose Lucy says, "Rashad is very loyal." Since the meaning of *loyal* (faithful to an idea, person, company, and so on) is abstract, Lucy might add, "I mean, he never criticizes friends behind their backs." By following up the abstract concept of loyalty with an example, Lucy clarifies what she means as it applies to Rashad.

5. **Demonstrate linguistic sensitivity.** **Linguistic sensitivity** is achieved by using language that is inclusive and demonstrates respect for others.

    Inclusive language does not use words that apply only to one sex, race, or other group as though they represent everyone. In the past, English speakers used the masculine pronoun *he* to represent all humans regardless of sex. This approach is not inclusive because it excludes half of the population. For example, use plurals or both male and female pronouns rather than saying, "When *a person* shops, *he* should have a clear idea of what *he* wants to buy," say "When *people* shop, *they* should have a clear idea of what *they* want to buy."

    To be inclusive, we also need to avoid words that indicate a sex, race, age, or other group distinction. For example, rather than say *fireman, mailman, stewardess,* or *mankind,* say *firefighter, postal carrier, server,* and *humankind.*

    Demonstrating linguistic sensitivity also means avoiding potentially offensive humor, profanity, and vulgarity. Dirty jokes and racist, sexist, or other "-ist" remarks may not be intended to be offensive, but if someone perceives them to be offensive, then that person will likely lose sight of your intended meaning and focus on the offensive remark instead. The same thing can happen when you pepper your message with profanity and vulgar expressions. Listeners may be offended and focus on those words rather than on the semantic meaning of your intended message.

These three sentences use slightly different syntax and grammar to convey the same semantic meaning. But notice how the semantic meaning can change through subtle modification:

"He, the 3 pound adopted puppy, went to the pound."

Now the semantic meaning is that an adopted three-pound premature canine went to the place where unclaimed animals are kept. Next consider how the semantic meaning can change based on its position in a sentence. The word *pound* is used twice in each sentence, but in one instance it signifies a unit of weight, and in the other it signifies a place.

GUIDELINES FOR IMPROVING SEMANTICS To improve semantics, choose words and arrange them in ways that both improve clarity and demonstrate respect. You can do so by using specific, concrete, and familiar words; by embellishing them with descriptive details and examples; and by demonstrating linguistic sensitivity. In terms of clarity, compare the language used in the following two descriptions of the same incident:

"Some nut almost got me a while ago."

"About 1:00 p.m. last Saturday afternoon, an older man in a banged-up Honda Civic ran through the red light at Calhoun and Clifton and came within inches of hitting my car while I was in the intersection waiting to turn left."

© Rick Lord/Shutterstock.com

In the second description, the speaker used specific, concrete language, as well as descriptive details and examples, to improve semantic clarity.

4-3b Pragmatics

Pragmatic meaning comes from understanding a message related to its conversational context. Whereas semantic meaning focuses on what the *words* mean (Korta & Perry, 2008), pragmatic meaning focuses on what *people* mean. So, pragmatic meaning changes across speakers and situations.

A **speech act** is the utterance of a verbal message and what it implies about how the listener should respond. In other words, when we *speak*, we *do*. Although our speech acts are usually explicit, what we are doing is often implied. To discover pragmatic meaning, we ask ourselves, "What is the speaker *doing* by saying these words to me right now?" For example, if I say, "Karen, pass me the bowl of potatoes," I have directly ordered Karen to pick up the bowl of potatoes and hand them to me. Instead, suppose I ask, "Karen, would you mind passing me the potatoes?" At the semantic level, this question appears to give Karen a choice. At the pragmatic level, however, what I am doing is the same. I am directing her to pass the bowl of potatoes to me. As you can see, then, we can accomplish the same pragmatic goal with either a direct/explicit or indirect/implicit speech act.

What is meant by a speech act also depends on the context. Let's look at a simple example.

specific language precise words that clarify semantic meaning by narrowing what is understood from a general category to a particular item or group within it

concrete language words that clarify semantic meaning by appealing to the senses

linguistic sensitivity inclusive word choices that demonstrate respect for others

inclusive language use of words that do not apply only to one sex, race, or other group

pragmatic meaning understanding a message related to its conversational context

speech act the utterance of a verbal message and what it implies about how the listener should respond

A doctor asking "How are you feeling" is a speech act—his words invite you to explain your ailment or reason for visiting the doctor's office.

Mainstream Media: Rumor Mill or Reliable Source?

The tabloids that line the checkout aisles claim to bring us the latest juicy details about the private lives of our favorite celebrities. Headlines pasted over photos of famous women like Angelina Jolie, Jennifer Aniston, Beyonce, Taylor Swift, and Catherine, Duchess of Cambridge (Kate Middleton) often proclaim: "I'm having a baby!," "Yes, I'm pregnant!," or "Countdown to baby!" Yet more often than not, the featured celebrity isn't pregnant (though Kate has now actually delivered two babies). We're usually not surprised, however, when the actual story turns out to be very different from what aroused our curiosity on the cover.

Though we may expect sensationalized stories in tabloids there is increasing concern about the "tabloidization of the mainstream press." Tabloidization is a word coined in the 1980s to represent the ongoing "decline in traditional journalistic standards" (Bird, 2008). As news media try to stay viable, "tabloid-style news" is becoming more commonplace in mainstream outlets, as well (Uberti, 2014). Celebrity stories were once largely confined to the tabloids, but in this hyper-competitive media market, the so-called "serious" news outlets now spend more time reporting on celebrity

© Thinglass/Shutterstock.com

deeds and misdeeds than in the past, and articles and stories in general focus more on rumors and innuendos. For example, mainstream media frequently "report" stories that appear in tabloids without confirming the information reported in the original article ("The Star reports that Jen is pregnant"). Given this trend toward blurring facts with fiction, how do you think we should approach mainstream media stories and why?

When Harry's car wouldn't start one morning, he made three phone calls:

Phone Call 1:

Harry: The car won't start.
Katie: Sorry about that. I'll just take the bus.

Phone Call 2:

Harry: The car won't start.
AAA Customer Service Representative: Where is the car, sir? I'll send a tow truck right away.

Phone Call 3:

Harry: The car won't start.
Previous owner who recently sold the car to Harry: Wow, that never happened to me. But I told you I was selling the car "as is."

In all three cases, the verbal utterance and the semantic meaning of Harry's message is the same. In terms of pragmatic meaning, however, Harry performed three different speech acts. What he was *doing* when he was talking to Katie was different from what he was *doing* when he was talking with the AAA customer service representative and different still from what he was *doing* when he made the statement to the person who sold him the car. He expressed his feelings by apologizing to Katie and implied that Katie should understand and release him from his obligation to take her to school. With the AAA representative, Harry's speech act was a request for assistance. When Harry called the previous owner of the car, he was complaining and implying that the previous owner should accept responsibility. In each case, Harry used the same words and syntax, but performed three different speech acts.

The feedback from each person illustrates that each understood Harry's pragmatic meaning. Katie's response

Guidelines for Improving Pragmatics

We understand pragmatic meaning based on an assumption that both partners want to achieve mutual understanding (Grice, 1975). With this in mind, we suggest the following guidelines.

1. Tell the truth. This guideline seems pretty self-explanatory. Say only what you believe to be true based on evidence to support your position. Sometimes we tell partial truths and rationalize that we are "protecting" our listeners or ourselves. For example, when your friend asks you what you think of her new boyfriend, you may offer a noncommittal response that masks your immediate dislike for the guy. You might say, "Well, he certainly appears to like you." Your friend may interpret your remark as approval rather than an attempt to spare her feelings. Obviously, this makes it more difficult to correctly understand what you truly believe. You can tell the truth by adding a comment about something you don't particularly like about him.

2. Include all the information needed to fully answer the question and refrain from adding irrelevant information. For instance, when Sam is getting ready to leave for work, he asks Randy where he parked the car. If Randy responds with, "You just wouldn't believe the trouble I had finding a parking space . . ." followed by a five-minute monologue about trying to find a parking space after midnight, he would be providing too much irrelevant information.

3. Relate what you say to the topic being discussed. Link your messages to the purpose of the conversation and interpret the messages of others in line with the topic at hand. For example, Barry asks, "Who's going to pick up Mom from work today?" His brother answers, "I've got a big test tomorrow." Barry assumes that his brother's remark is relevant to the topic at hand and interprets it as, "I can't. I have to study." Barry was able to correctly understand the pragmatic meaning of his brother's answer because he assumed that it was relevant to figuring out how to get their mother home.

4. Acknowledge when your message violates a guideline. When you violate one of these guidelines, you should tell your partner that you are breaking it. Doing so will help your partner interpret what you are saying accurately. For example:

▸ If you violate guideline #1, you might say "I don't know if this is true, but my sister said. . . ."

▸ If you violate guideline #2, you might say "I realize this is a bit off topic but…"

▸ If you violate guideline #3, you might say "This may be beside the point, but. . . ."

5. Assume the best first. At times, you or your partner may intentionally break one of these guidelines and not signal beforehand. In these instances, rather than take offense, employ perception checking in an attempt to come to mutual understanding.

showed that she understood she would need to find another way to get to school. The AAA representative expected the call to be about car trouble so she responded by asking where the car was located. The previous owner also understood Harry's speech act when he responded by refusing to accept responsibility for the problem.

Sometimes the media use the principles of pragmatics to get the attention of and even mislead us about what the facts are in a given situation. For example, some tabloids do so to entice potential readers to buy magazines. The practice is even being adopted by mainstream media outlets today.

4-3c Sociolinguistics

Sociolinguistic meaning varies according to the norms of a particular culture or co-culture. Sociolinguistic misunderstandings occur when we interact with someone who operates using different norms regarding how words are combined, how and when to say what to whom, and verbal style.

First, cultures have norms that assign meaning to specific words and combinations of words that may be different

> **sociolinguistic meaning**
> meaning that varies according to the norms of a particular culture or co-culture

The saying "his head was in the clouds" could be confusing to non-native speakers of English, since it is used to say a person is daydreaming and has nothing to do with clouds.

your Japanese friend by saying, "Miki, this is the *best* miso soup I have ever tasted." To Miki, however, your compliment might sound insincere because in Japanese culture the language of compliments is more humble. So she might reply, "Oh, it's nice of you to say that, but I am sure that you have had better miso soup at sushi restaurants in the city." Similarly, midwesterners often smile and say "Hi" to strangers on the street as a sign of being friendly. In China, acknowledging a stranger in this way typically assumes an unwarranted familiarity and is likely to be considered rude.

Third, preferred verbal style differs from culture to culture, particularly in terms of how direct or indirect one ought to be (Ting-Toomey & Chung, 2005). A **direct verbal style** is characterized by language that openly states the speaker's intention in a straightforward and unambiguous way. An **indirect verbal style** is characterized by language that masks the speaker's true intentions in a roundabout and ambiguous way. Consider the following example of how these different styles can create communication challenges.

Jorge and Kevin are roommates at college. They come from the same hometown as Sam, who lives across the hall and owns a car. Thanksgiving is fast approaching and both Jorge and Kevin need to find a ride home. One night while watching a football game in Sam's room, the following conversation occurs:

from their semantic meaning. For example, in English we associate the word *pretty* with women and *handsome* with men, even though both refer to physical beauty. So choosing to say "She is a pretty woman" sends a different message than saying "She is a handsome woman" (Chaika, 2008). All cultures also use **idioms**, which are expressions whose meanings are different from the literal meanings associated with the words used in them. So imagine how confusing it is to someone learning English when we say, "That test was *a piece of cake*" or "That test was a real killer."

Second, cultures develop different norms about what is appropriate to say to whom, by whom, when, and about what. For example, the "appropriate" way to compliment others and accept compliments can vary from culture to culture. In the dominant culture of the United States, you might compliment

Jorge (to Sam): "Are you driving home for Thanksgiving?" [Maybe he'll give me a ride.]

Sam: "Yep." [If he wanted a ride he'd ask.]

Kevin: "Well, I'd like a ride home."

Sam: "Sure, no problem."

Jorge: "Are you taking anyone else?" [I wonder if he still has room for me.]

Sam: "Nope. I'm leaving after my last class on Tuesday and not coming back until late Sunday evening." [I guess Jorge already has a ride home.]

Jorge: "Well, enjoy Thanksgiving!" [If he wanted to give me a ride I gave him plenty of opportunities to offer. I guess I'll take the bus.]

In this conversation, Jorge used an indirect style he learned from his parents and relatives, who are all from Nicaragua. His questions were meant to prompt

idioms expressions whose meanings are different from the literal meanings associated with the words used in them

direct verbal style language that openly states the speaker's intention in a straightforward and unambiguous way

indirect verbal style language that masks the speaker's true intentions in a roundabout and ambiguous way

Guidelines for Improving Sociolinguistics

1. **Develop intercultural competence.** The more you learn about other cultures, the better you will be able to convey and interpret messages when communicating with those whose sociolinguistic verbal styles differ from yours.

2. **Practice mindfulness. Mindfulness** is the practice of paying attention to what is happening at any given moment during a conversation (Langer & Moldoveanu, 2000). If we are mindful when we interact with others, we will constantly attend to how our cultural norms, idioms, scripts, and verbal styles are similar to and different from our conversational partners'.

3. **Respect and adapt to the sociolinguistic practices of others.** The old saying, "When in Rome, do as the Romans do" captures the essence of this guideline. For example, if you are invited to your Indonesian-American friend's home for the weekend, you should adapt your verbal style to that of

© g-stockstudio/Shutterstock.com

your hosts. Or if you are from a low-context culture and are talking with someone from a high-context culture, be sensitive to the indirect meanings in their verbal messages. If you are fluent in more than one language or dialect, you can even codeswitch and converse in the language or use the dialect of your conversational partner.

Sam to offer him a ride home. But Sam, whose family is from New York, used a direct style and completely missed Jorge's intent. As a result, Jorge rode the bus even though Sam would have gladly given him a ride if their preferred verbal styles had not gotten in the way of mutual understanding.

> **mindfulness** paying attention to what is happening at any given moment during a conversation

---

STUDY TOOLS 4

LOCATED IN TEXTBOOK

☐ Tear-out Chapter Review cards at the end of the book

☐ Review with the Quick Quiz below

LOCATED ON COMM 4 ONLINE AT CENGAGEBRAIN.COM:

☐ Review Key Term flashcards and create your own cards

☐ Track your knowledge and understanding of key concepts in communication

☐ Complete practice and graded quizzes to prepare for tests

☐ Complete interactive content within COMM4 Online

☐ View the chapter highlight boxes for COMM4 Online

Quick Quiz

T F 1. Waiting for a response to an e-mail is an example of silence.

T F 2. If you are confused when your friend asks you to put something in the boot, it is because you are not from the same language community.

T F 3. We can improve our messages by choosing words that make our meaning clear and language that makes our implicit intent known and demonstrates sensitivity.

T F 4. Inclusive sensitivity means choosing language and symbols that are adapted to the needs, interests, knowledge, and attitudes of the listeners and avoiding language that alienates them.

T F 5. Saying, "Kalpana, would you text Daphne and see if she is bringing a salad?" is an example of an idiolect.

6. What term or terms clarify meaning by narrowing what is understood from a general category to a particular item or group within that category?

   a. general responses
   b. correct words
   c. specific language
   d. descriptive words
   e. metaphors

7. Your friend says, "My mom told me my room smells like gym socks. I think she wants me to clean it." Your friend's mom is using

   a. concrete language.
   b. specific language.
   c. a dialect.
   d. sociolinguistics.
   e. pragmatics.

8. Saying "Ralphie borrowed my phone" instead of, "Ralphie took my phone" is choosing a word based on

   a. sociolinguistics.
   b. denotation.
   c. connotation.
   d. pragmatics.
   e. idiolects.

9. Which of the following is an example of an idiolect?

   a. You say "Ouch!" when you stub your toe.
   b. Your dad says "out of the frying pan into the fire" when your sister gets a new (apparently not great) boyfriend.
   c. Your best friend says "Geesh-a-la-momma!" when excited or surprised.
   d. Your teacher instructs the class to "hit the books" after passing back a low-scoring test.
   e. All of the above.

10. Which of the following is NOT an example of linguistic sensitivity?

   a. If you are an industrial engineer and are talking to the teenager who cuts your grass, you use jargon to help him understand what it is that you do.
   b. If you are communicating with someone whose vocabulary is not as vast as yours, you adjust your words accordingly without talking down to the person.
   c. You're visiting with your grandmother and avoid using slang because she won't understand what you are saying.
   d. You see a police car speed down your street and say, "Wow, I wonder where that police officer is heading in such a hurry!"
   e. During class, you refrain from using offensive language that you normally use when hanging out with friends.

Answers: 1. T, 2. F, 3. T, 4. F, 5. T, 6. C, 7. A, 8. C, 9. E, 10. A

YOUR FEED-BACK YOUR BOOK

Our research never ends. Continual feedback from you ensures that we keep up with your changing needs.

5 Nonverbal Messages

LEARNING OUTCOMES

5-1 Identify characteristics of nonverbal communication

5-2 Identify the different types of nonverbal communication

5-3 Employ strategies to improve your nonverbal communication

After finishing this chapter go to **PAGE 65** for **STUDY TOOLS.**

Communication exchanges are more than verbal messages, such as those covered in chapter 4. Communication exchanges are also rich in nonverbal communication. **Nonverbal communication** consists of all the messages we send in ways that transcend spoken or written words (Knapp, Hall, & Horgan, 2014). More specifically, **nonverbal messages** are cues we send with our body, voice, space, time, and appearance to support, modify, contradict, or even replace a verbal message.

Nonverbal messages play an important role in communication. In fact, research suggests that 65–90 percent of meaning comes from the nonverbal messages we use to communicate in face-to-face interactions (Burgoon & Bacue, 2003; Littlejohn & Foss, 2009). In other words, the meaning we assign to any utterance is based on our interpretation of both the verbal message and the nonverbal messages that accompany it. Interpreting nonverbal messages accurately is critical to understanding and responding appropriately to what others are "saying."

The widespread use of social media (e.g., e-mail, Facebook, texting Twitter, Instagram, and smartphone technology) emphasizes the important role of nonverbal messages. Because these modes force us to rely only on words, (Yuasa, Saito, & Mukawa, 2011) we often use emoticons, all capital letters, and acronyms such as LOL to communicate the nonverbal messages we would employ in face-to-face communication.

We begin this chapter by briefly describing the characteristics of nonverbal communication. Next, we identify the types of nonverbal messages we use to communicate with others. Finally, we offer suggestions for improving nonverbal communication as both senders and receivers.

nonverbal communication
all the messages we send in ways that transcend spoken or written words

nonverbal messages
cues we send with our body, voice, space, time, and appearance to support, modify, contradict, or even replace a verbal message

CHARACTERISTICS OF NONVERBAL COMMUNICATION

We use nonverbal messages to emphasize, substitute for, or contradict a verbal message. We also use nonverbal messages to cue a sender to continue, repeat, elaborate, or finish what he or she is saying. And nonverbal messages can convey a particular image of ourselves to others through our choice of clothing, grooming, jewelry, and body art. Even when we don't consciously choose to do so, our nonverbal messages give people an impression of who we are. The challenge of conveying and interpreting nonverbal messages accurately is rooted in four fundamental characteristics.

1. Nonverbal communication is *inevitable.* The phrase "We cannot NOT communicate" (Watzlawick, Bavelas, & Jackson, 1967) captures the essence of this characteristic. If you are in the presence of someone else, your nonverbal messages (whether intentional or not) are communicating. When Austin yawns and stares off into the distance during class, his classmates may notice this behavior and assign meaning to it. One classmate may interpret it as a sign of boredom, another might see it as a sign of fatigue, and yet another may view it as a message of disrespect. Meanwhile, Austin may be oblivious to all of the messages his behavior is sending.

2. Nonverbal communication is the primary conveyer of emotions. We interpret how others feel about what they are communicating based almost entirely on their nonverbal messages. In fact, some research suggests that an overwhelming 93 percent of the emotional meaning of messages is conveyed nonverbally (Mehrabian, 1972). So, when Janelle frowns, clenches her fists, and forcefully says, "I am NOT angry!" her friend ignores the verbal message and believes the contradicting nonverbal messages, which communicate that Janelle is actually very angry.

3. Nonverbal communication is *multi-channeled.* We perceive meaning from a combination of different nonverbal behaviors including, for example, posture, gestures, facial expressions, vocal pitch and rate, and appearance. So, when Anna observes her daughter Mimi's failure to sustain eye contact, her bowed head, and her repetitive toe-stubbing in the dirt, she may decide that Mimi is lying when she says she did not hit her brother. The fact that nonverbal communication is multi-channeled is one reason people are more likely to believe nonverbal communication when nonverbal behaviors contradict the verbal message (Burgoon, Blair, & Strom, 2008).

4. Nonverbal communication is *ambiguous.* Very few nonverbal messages mean the same thing to everyone. The meaning of one nonverbal behavior can vary based on culture, sex, gender, and even context or situation. For example, in the dominant American culture, direct eye contact tends to be understood as a sign of respect. That's why parents often tell their children, "Look at me when I'm talking to you." In some cultures, however, direct eye contact from a listener might be interpreted as disrespectful. Not only can the meaning of nonverbal messages vary among different cultures, but the meaning of the same nonverbal message also can differ based on the situation. For example, a furrowed brow might convey Byron's confusion when he did not understand his professor's explanation of the assignment, or Monica's anger when she discovered she did not get the internship she had worked so hard for, or Max's disgust when he was dissecting a frog during biology lab.

5-2 TYPES OF NONVERBAL COMMUNICATION

We use various types of nonverbal messages to communicate. These include the use of body (kinesics), voice (paralanguage/vocalics), space (proxemics), time (chronemics), and appearance.

5-2a Use of Body: Kinesics

Kinesics is the technical name for what and how body motions communicate (Birdwhistell, 1970). We may use gestures, eye contact, facial expression, posture, and touch.

GESTURES Gestures are the movements of our hands, arms, and fingers to accompany or replace a verbal message. **Emblems** are gestures that substitute entirely for a word or words. For example, when you raise your finger and place it vertically across your lips, it signifies "Be quiet." Other gestures, called **illustrators**, clarify a verbal message. When you say "about this high" or "nearly this round," your

listeners expect to see a gesture accompanying your verbal description. Sometimes, these gestures augment the verbal message by conveying the emotional stance of the sender. Still other gestures, called **adaptors**, are unconscious responses to physical or psychological needs. For example, you may scratch an itch, adjust your glasses, or rub your hands together when they are cold. You do not mean to communicate a message with these gestures, but others may notice and attach meaning to them.

The use and meaning of gestures can vary greatly across cultures. For example, the American hand sign for "OK" has an obscene sexual meaning in some European countries, means "worthless" in France, is a symbol for money in Japan, and stands for "I'll kill you" in Tunisia (Axtell, 1998). Similarly, in the dominant American culture, people nod their heads to communicate "I am listening to you." In some parts of India, however, they shift their heads from side to side to demonstrate they are listening. When communicating with people who come from different cultures, be especially careful about the gestures you use; their meaning is not necessarily universal.

EYE CONTACT The technical term for **eye contact** is oculesics. It has to do with how and how much we look at others when communicating. Eye contact can signal that you are paying attention and that you respect the person you are speaking with, as well as a variety of different emotions. Intense eye contact may be an attempt to dominate (Pearson, West, & Turner, 1995). That's why we sometimes say things like "if looks could kill" when we see someone glare at someone else.

What is considered appropriate eye contact varies across cultures. Studies show that in Western cultures, talkers hold eye contact about 40 percent of the time and listeners nearly 70 percent of the time (Knapp, Hall, & Horgan, 2014). In Western cultures people also generally maintain more eye contact when discussing topics they are comfortable with, when they are genuinely interested in what another person is saying, and when they are trying to persuade others. Conversely, they tend to avoid eye contact when discussing

© Hyunsuss/Shutterstock.com

kinesics the interpretation of what and how body motions communicate

gestures movements of our hands, arms, and fingers to replace or accompany a verbal message

emblems gestures that substitute entirely for a word or words

illustrators gestures that clarify a verbal message

adaptors unconscious responses to physical or psychological needs

eye contact (oculesics) how and how much we look at others when communicating

topics that make them feel uncomfortable, when they aren't interested in the topic or the person talking, or when they are embarrassed, ashamed, or trying to hide something.

A majority of people in the United States and other Western cultures expect those with whom they are communicating to "look them in the eye." But direct eye contact is not universally considered appropriate (Samovar, Porter, & McDaniel, 2009). For instance, in Japan, prolonged eye contact is considered rude, disrespectful, and threatening. Similarly, in China and Indonesia, too much direct eye contact is a sign of bad manners. In many Middle Eastern countries, people tend to use continuous and direct eye contact with others to demonstrate keen interest.

Various co-cultural groups within the United States use eye contact differently, as well. For instance, African Americans tend to use more continuous eye contact than European Americans when they are speaking, but less when they are listening (Samovar, Porter, & McDaniel, 2012). Native Americans tend to avoid eye contact when communicating with superiors as a sign of respect for their authority. And women tend to use more eye contact during conversations than men do (Santilli & Miller, 2011).

FACIAL EXPRESSION Facial expression is using facial muscles to communicate. Facial expressions are especially important in conveying the six basic emotions of happiness, sadness, surprise, fear, anger, and disgust. For example, we may furrow our brows and squint our eyes when we are confused, or purse our lips and raise one eyebrow to convey skepticism. Facial expressions are so important for communicating emotional intent that we often use emoticons to represent emotions when texting, sending e-mail, or posting comments on Facebook (Walther & Parks, 2002).

Unlike gestures and eye contact, many facial expressions mean something similar across cultures (Samovar, Porter, McDaniel, & Roy, 2012). For instance, a slight raising of the eyebrow communicates recognition and wrinkling one's nose conveys repulsion (Martin & Nakayama, 2006). However, whether or not doing so is appropriate

may vary across cultures and co-cultures. For instance, in some cultures, people downplay facial expressions like frowning and smiling; whereas members of other cultures amplify emotional meaning through facial expressions.

POSTURE Posture is how we position and move our body. Posture can communicate attentiveness, respect, and dominance. **Body orientation** refers to how we position our body in relation to other people. *Direct body orientation* is when two people face each other squarely; *indirect body orientation* is when two people sit or stand side-by-side. In many situations, direct body orientation signals attentiveness and respect. In a job interview, for example, we are likely to sit up straight and face the interviewer directly because we want to communicate interest, attentiveness, and respect. **Body movement** is changing body position. It can be motivated (movement that helps clarify meaning) or unmotivated (movement that distracts listeners from the point being made). When making a speech, an upright stance and squared

> **facial expression** arranging facial muscles to communicate emotions or provide feedback
>
> **posture** how we position and move our body
>
> **body orientation** how we position our body in relation to other people
>
> **body movement** changing body position

© Konstantin Chagin/Shutterstock.com
© Viktor Gladkov/Shutterstock.com

Direct body orientation.

Indirect body orientation.

shoulders communicates poise and confidence. Taking a few steps to the left or right can signal a transition from one main point to the next, but pacing actually distracts listeners from the message.

TOUCH **Haptics** is the technical term for what and how touch communicates. We may pat, hug, slap, kiss, pinch, stroke, hold, or embrace others.

There are three types of touch: spontaneous touch, ritualized touch, and task-related touch. *Spontaneous touch* is automatic and subconscious. Patting someone on the back after learning that he or she has won an award is an example of spontaneous touch. *Ritualized touch* is scripted rather than spontaneous. Handshakes high-fives, and fist bumps are examples of ritualized touch. *Task-related touch* is used to perform a certain unemotional function. For instance, a doctor may touch a patient during a physical examination or a personal trainer may touch a client during a gym workout.

Some people like to touch and be touched; other people do not. Touching behavior that seems innocuous to one person may be perceived as overly intimate or threatening to another. Moreover, the touch that is considered appropriate in private may embarrass a person when done in public.

Touching behavior is highly correlated with culture (Gudykunst & Kim, 1997). In some cultures, frequent touching is considered normal; in other cultures, it is considered inappropriate. Some countries in South and Central America, as well as many in southern Europe, encourage contact and engage in frequent touching (Neuliep, 2006). In many Arabic countries, for example, two grown men walking down the street holding hands is a sign of friendship. In the United States, however, it might be interpreted as a sign of an intimate relationship. Because the United States is a country of immigrants, however, the degree of touching behavior considered appropriate varies widely from individual to individual based on family heritage and norms.

5-2b Use of Voice: Paralanguage

Paralanguage (also known as *vocalics*) is the voiced part of a spoken message that goes beyond the actual words. Six vocal characteristics of paralanguage are pitch, volume, rate, voice quality, intonation, and vocalized pauses.

PITCH **Pitch** is the highness or lowness of vocal tone. We raise and lower our pitch to emphasize ideas and emotion, as well as to signal a question. We sometimes raise our pitch when feeling nervous or afraid. We may lower our pitch to convey peacefulness or sadness (as in a speech given at a funeral) or when we are trying to be forceful.

VOLUME **Volume** is the loudness or softness of vocal tone. Whereas some people have booming voices that carry long distances, others are normally soft-spoken. Regardless of our normal volume level, however, we also tend to vary our volume depending on the situation, the topic of discussion, and emotional intent. For example,

haptics the interpretation of what and how touch communicates

paralanguage (vocalics) the voiced part of a spoken message that goes beyond the actual words

pitch the highness or lowness of vocal tone

volume the loudness or softness of vocal tone

we might talk more loudly when we wish to be heard in noisy settings and when we are angry. We might speak more softly when we are being reflective or romantic. There are also some cultural variations in the meanings attached to volume. For example, Arabs tend to speak with a great deal of volume to convey strength and sincerity; whereas soft voices are preferred in Britain, Japan, and Thailand (Samovar, Porter, & McDaniel, 2012).

RATE Rate is the speed at which a person speaks. Most people in the USA naturally speak between 100 and 200 words per minute. People tend to talk more rapidly when they are happy, frightened, nervous, or excited and more slowly when they are problem-solving out loud or are trying to emphasize a point. People who speak too slowly run the risk of boring listeners, and those who speak too quickly may not be intelligible.

VOICE QUALITY (TIMBRE) Voice quality (or timbre) is the sound of a person's voice that distinguishes it from others. Voice quality may be breathy (Marilyn Monroe or Kathleen Turner), strident (Joan Rivers or Marge Simpson), throaty (Nick Nolte or Jack Nicholson), or nasal (Fran Drescher in *The Nanny*). Although each person's voice has a distinct quality, too much breathiness can make people sound frail, too much stridence can make them seem overly tense, too much throatiness can make them seem cold and unsympathetic, and too much nasality can make them sound immature or unintelligent.

INTONATION Intonation is the variety, melody, or inflection in one's voice. Voices that use very little or no intonation are described as monotone and tend to bore listeners. If you've ever seen the movie *Ferris Bueller's Day Off*, you may recall the teacher (played by Ben Stein) who is portrayed as boring via a monotone voice as he questions the class: "Anyone? Anyone? Bueller? Bueller?" Other voices that use a lot of intonation may be perceived as ditzy, singsongy, or childish. People prefer to listen to voices that use a moderate amount of intonation.

VOCALIZED PAUSES Vocalized pauses are extraneous sounds or words that interrupt fluent speech. They are essentially "place markers" designed to fill in momentary gaps while we search for the right word or idea. The most common vocalized pauses that creep into our speech include "uh," "er," "well," "OK," "you know," and "like."

Occasional vocalized pauses are generally ignored by listeners. However, when used excessively, vocalized pauses can give others the impression that we are unsure of ourselves or that our ideas are not well thought out. Sometimes speakers use so many vocalized pauses that listeners are distracted by them to the point of not being able to concentrate on the meaning of the message.

5-2c Use of Space: Proxemics

Proxemics refers to how space and distance communicate (Hall, 1968). We communicate via proxemics through our use of personal space, territorial space, and acoustic space.

PERSONAL SPACE Personal space is the distance we try to maintain when interacting with others. How much space we perceive as appropriate depends on our individual preference, the nature of the relationship, and our cultural norms. With these variations in mind, the amount of personal space we view as appropriate generally decreases as the intimacy of our relationship increases. For example, in the dominant U.S. culture, four distinct distances are generally perceived as appropriate and comfortable, depending on the context and relationship. *Intimate distance* is defined as up to 18 inches and is appropriate for private conversations between close friends. *Personal distance*, from 18 inches to 4 feet, is the space in which casual conversation occurs. *Social distance*, from 4 to 12 feet, is where impersonal business such as a job interview is conducted. *Public distance* is anything more than 12 feet (Hall, 1968). Figure 5.1 illustrates the concept of personal space.

When "outsiders" violate our personal space, we tend to become uncomfortable. For instance, in a sparsely populated movie theater, people tend to leave one or more seats

rate the speed at which a person speaks

voice quality (timbre) the sound of a person's voice that distinguishes it from others

intonation the variety, melody, or inflection in one's voice

vocalized pauses extraneous sounds or words that interrupt fluent speech

proxemics the study of how space and distance communicate

personal space the distance we try to maintain when we interact with other people

FIGURE 5.1 PERSONAL SPACE

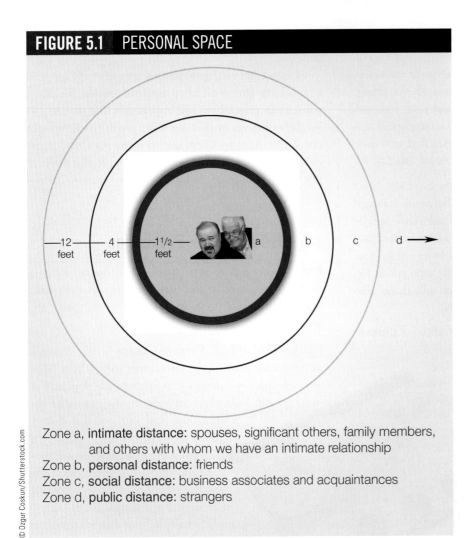

Zone a, **intimate distance:** spouses, significant others, family members, and others with whom we have an intimate relationship

Zone b, **personal distance:** friends

Zone c, **social distance:** business associates and acquaintances

Zone d, **public distance:** strangers

empty between themselves and others they do not know. If a stranger sits right next to us in such a setting, we are likely to feel uncomfortable and may even move to another seat. We will accept intrusions into our personal space only in certain settings and then only when all involved follow the unwritten rules. For example, we tend to tolerate being packed into a crowded elevator or subway by following unwritten rules, such as standing rigidly, looking at the floor or above the door, and not making eye contact with others.

TERRITORIAL SPACE Territorial space is the physical space over which we claim ownership. As with personal space, we expect others to respect our territory and may feel annoyed or even violated when they do not. we do not realize how we are claiming or "marking" our territory. For example, Graham may have subconsciously marked "his chair" in the family room and others just "know" not to sit in it when Graham is around. Other times we mark our territory quite consciously. For example, by using locks, signs, and fences.

Territorial space can also communicate status. To clarify, higher-status people generally claim larger and more prestigious territory (Knapp, Hall, & Horgan, 2014). In business, for example, the supervisor is likely to have the largest and nicest office in the unit.

We often use artifacts—or objects—to mark our territory. We display things on our desks and in our offices and homes, not just for their function but also because they communicate about our territory in some way. For example, we use artifacts to signal what we expect to happen in the space. The chairs and couch in your living room may approximate a circle that invites people to sit down and talk. Classroom seating may be arranged in auditorium style to discourage conversation. A manager's office with a chair facing the manager across the desk encourages formal conversation and signals status. It says, "Let's talk business—I'm the boss and you're the employee." A manager's office with a chair placed at the side of her desk encourages more informal conversation. It says, "Don't be nervous—let's just chat."

ACOUSTIC SPACE Acoustic space is the area over which our voice can be comfortably heard. Competent communicators protect acoustic space by adjusting the volume of our voices to be easily heard by our conversational partners and not overheard by others. Loud cell phone conversations occurring in public places violate acoustic space. With the invention of Bluetooth technology, this problem has become even more pronounced. This is why some communities have ordinances prohibiting cell phone use in restaurants, hospitals, and theaters.

territorial space the physical space over which we claim ownership

acoustic space the area over which your voice can be comfortably heard

The New Age of Old Body Art

Did you know that every culture has used body art to signal status, to mark a special occasion, or just to make a fashion statement (American Museum of Natural History, 1999)? There are many different types of body art, all stemming from ancient practices and adapted to modern definitions of status, ritual, and beauty.

▶ Body painting is a temporary means of creating a different identity or celebrating a particular occasion. For centuries, Eastern cultures have used henna to dye hands and other body parts to celebrate rites of passage such as marriages. Today, women use cosmetics, sports fans decorate their faces and bodies before big games, and children have their faces painted at community festivals.

▶ Piercing has a long history. Some tribal cultures had a rite of passage calling for a person to hang from large piercings in the limbs or body trunk, other societies used piercings as a sign of slavery, and still others viewed them as signs of beauty or royalty (Schurman, n.d.). Today piercing is voluntary and ranges from nose, ear, and genital piercing to stretching and gauging.

▶ Scarification is the deliberate and controlled cutting or burning of the skin to create a pattern or picture. Scarification has been widely practiced in Africa, where facial scars identify a person's ethnic group or family or can just be an individual statement of beauty. Today, scarification may be part of a fraternity or gang initiation rite; cutting is also sometimes used to escape from feeling trapped in an intolerable psychological and emotional situation (Jacobs, 2005). Such application is generally considered unacceptable by U.S. society.

© mariiamanger/Shutterstock.com

▶ Tattooing is the oldest form of body art; tattooed mummies have been found in various parts of the world. Tattoos are permanent alterations to the body using inks or dyes, and they are symbolic in nature. Historically, tattoos have been used to mark people who were considered property or inferior in some other way, such as African American slaves or Jews and other "undesirables" in World War II concentration camps. Today, tattoos are losing their outsider status. Celebrities, soccer moms, corporate executives, star athletes, and high school students sport tattoos as statements of individuality and personal aesthetic.

▶ Shaping, another type of body art, is altering the silhouette or shape of the body based on a culturally validated aesthetic (Australian Museum, 2009). Cranial shaping, neck stretching, foot binding, and corsetry have been practiced in various cultures at various times. The Spanx undergarments that many women wear today have their origins in body shaping.

5-2d Use of Time: Chronemics

Recall from chapter 3 that chronemics is how we interpret the use of time; it is largely based on cultural norms. Just as cultures tend to be more monochronic or polychronic, so too are individuals. If your approach to time is different from those with whom you are interacting, your behavior could be viewed as inappropriate and put strains on your relationship.

5-2e Physical Appearance

Physical appearance is how we look to others and is one of the first things others notice and judge. American society places so much emphasis on physical appearance that entire industries are devoted to it. Options for changing

physical appearance
how we look to others

our physical appearance range from surgical procedures to weight loss programs and products to cosmetics and clothing lines.

Today, more than ever, people use clothing choices, body art, and other personal grooming to communicate who they are and what they stand for. Likewise, when we meet new people, we are likely to form our first impression of them based on how they are dressed and groomed. Thus, we can influence how others are likely to perceive us by our clothing and grooming choices. For example, Marcus, a successful sales representative, typically wears dress slacks and a collared shirt to the office, a suit and tie when giving a formal presentation, and a graphic T-shirt and jeans when hanging out with friends. Body art (such as piercings and tattoos) has become quite popular in the United States today. Although body art can be an important means of self-expression, we often make choices about how much of it to display based on the situation and how others are likely to judge us based on it. For example, when Tiffany is at work she dresses conservatively and covers the tattoo on her arm by wearing long-sleeved blouses. But on evenings and weekends, she does not.

5-2f Mediated Communication and Media Richness

Media richness refers to how much and what kinds of information can be transmitted via a particular channel. Media richness theory suggests that some media are better suited than others for communicating the meaning of different types of messages (Daft & Lengel, 1984). Face-to-face is generally the richest channel and the standard against which other channels are measured. When we communicate face-to-face, we not only hear the verbal message content, but we also observe the nonverbal cues and physical context to interpret a speaker's meaning. We can touch each other, hear pitch, and interact spatially. Sometimes, however, communicating face-to-face is either impossible or not a good use of time. Other times, we may want time to carefully compose and revise our message, as well as time to carefully ponder the feedback we receive, even at the expense of physical interaction.

Although mediated channels allow us to communicate across distances, they often cannot do so as richly as in face-to-face interaction. The

> **media richness** how much and what kinds of information can be transmitted via a particular channel

less information offered via a given channel, the leaner it is. The leaner the channel, the greater the chances become for misunderstanding. For example, text messages are very lean since they do not include nonverbal cues and context information and because they use as few characters as possible to convey a single message. On the other hand, videoconferencing channels such as Skype are richer than text messaging because we can observe nonverbal cues and contextual information almost as much as in a face-to-face setting. However, sending a composed email may offer more benefits than calling a person. The situation dictates the proper channel for mediated communication. Chapter 6 offers guidelines on how to choose the best channel.

5-3 GUIDELINES FOR IMPROVING NONVERBAL COMMUNICATION

Because nonverbal messages are inevitable, multi-channeled, ambiguous, and sometimes unintentional, interpreting them accurately can be tricky. Add to this the fact that the meaning of any nonverbal behavior can vary by situation, and culture, and the reasons we so often misinterpret the behavior of others become clear. The following guidelines can help improve the likelihood that your nonverbal messages will be perceived accurately and that you will accurately interpret the nonverbal messages of others.

5-3a Sending Nonverbal Messages

1. Consciously monitor your nonverbal messages. Try to be more consciously aware of the nonverbal messages you send through your use of body, voice, space, time, and appearance. If you have difficulty doing this, ask a friend to point them out to you.

2. Intentionally align your nonverbal messages with your purpose. When nonverbal messages contradict verbal messages, people are more likely to believe the nonverbal messages, so it is important to align your nonverbal messages with your purpose. For instance, if you want to be persuasive, you should use direct eye contact, a serious facial expression, an upright posture, a commanding vocal tone with no vocalized pauses, and professional clothing and grooming. If you want to be supportive and convey empathy, you might use less direct eye contact, a more relaxed facial expression, a softer voice, a nonthreatening touch, and a lean inward toward your partner.

3. Adapt your nonverbal messages to the situation. Just as you make language choices to suit different situations, you should vary your nonverbal messages depending on the circumstances. Assess what the situation calls for. For example, you would not dress the same way for a wedding as you would for a workout.

4. Reduce or eliminate distracting nonverbal messages. Fidgeting, tapping your fingers on a table, pacing, mumbling, using lots of pauses, and checking your phone often for texts and e-mails can distract others from the message you are trying to convey. Make a conscious effort to learn which distracting nonverbal messages have become habits and work to eliminate them from your communication with others.

5-3b Interpreting Nonverbal Messages

1. Remember that the same nonverbal message may mean different things to different people. Most nonverbal messages have multiple meanings that vary from person to person, culture to culture, and even situation to situation. Just because you fidget when you are bored doesn't mean that others are bored when they fidget. What you perceive as an angry vocal tone might not be intended as such by the person talking. So always try to consider multiple interpretations of the nonverbal messages you receive and seek clarification, particularly when your first interpretation is negative. This guideline becomes even more important when interpreting messages sent via social media and technology. For example,

when Larissa read her brother's text, "CALL ME!", rather than jump to any conclusions, she interpreted his meaning as urgent and stepped into the hallway to call him right away to seek clarification rather than waiting until later.

2. Consider each nonverbal message in context. Because any one nonverbal message can mean different things in different contexts, take the time to consider how it is intended in a given situation. Also realize that you might not understand all the details of the situation. For example, if you see a classmate sleeping during your speech, you might interpret the nonverbal message as boredom or disrespect. What the message might be communicating, however, is utter exhaustion because your classmate just finished back-to-back 12-hour shifts at work while trying to keep up with homework for a full load of courses.

3. Pay attention to the multiple nonverbal messages being sent and their relationship to the verbal message. In any one interaction, you are likely to receive simultaneous messages from a person's appearance, eye contact, facial expressions, gestures, posture, voice, and use of space and touch. By considering *all* nonverbal messages together with the verbal message, you are more likely to interpret others' messages accurately.

4. Use perception checking. The skill of perception checking lets you see if your interpretation of another person's message is accurate. By describing the nonverbal message you notice, sharing two possible interpretations of it, and asking for clarification, you can get confirmation or correction of your interpretation.

Quick Quiz

T F 1. Studies show that talkers hold eye contact about 70 percent of the time and listeners only 40 percent of the time.

T F 2. While talking quietly to a friend at a restaurant, you realize you have attracted the attention of other diners. You need to adjust your rate to decrease your territorial space.

T F 3. Nonverbal messages convey as much as 65 percent of the meaning in face-to-face interactions.

T F 4. Some societies used body painting as a sign of slavery.

T F 5. Fidgeting, tapping your fingers on a table, pacing, mumbling, and using vocal interferences and adaptors can hinder another person's interpretation of your message.

6. Which of the following is NOT a characteristic of nonverbal communication?
   a. It is continuous.
   b. It is multi-channeled.
   c. It is intentional.
   d. It is unintentional.
   e. It is unambiguous.

7. Gestures that augment a verbal message are called
   a. emphasizers.
   b. illustrators.
   c. emblems.
   d. symbols.
   e. adaptors.

8. Which of the following is an interrupter of fluent speech?
   a. the variety or melody, or inflections in one's voice
   b. pauses like "uh," "er," and "um"
   c. the loudness or softness of a person's tone
   d. too much stridence in a person's voice
   e. the speed at which a person speaks

9. Your boss asks you to lead a meeting regarding a new client and tells you he has booked the conference room and arranged for the projector to be on hand. Your boss is
   a. giving you permission to increase your acoustic space.
   b. using artifacts to indicate he would like a visual presentation.
   c. demonstrating his ownership of the space.
   d. using task-related touch to show the conference room.
   e. using posture to indicate he isn't very interested in what happens.

10. In interpreting nonverbal messages, you should
   a. consider the situation before making assumptions.
   b. not assume that another person will interpret a particular behavior the same way you do.
   c. pay attention to the relationship of the verbal message and the multiple nonverbal cues being sent.
   d. check in with someone else to see if your interpretation of what you think you are seeing is accurate or inaccurate.
   e. All of the above.

YOUR FEED-BACK YOUR BOOK

Our research never ends. Continual feedback from you ensures that we keep up with your changing needs.

6 Listening

After finishing this chapter go to **PAGE 78** for **STUDY TOOLS.**

LEARNING OUTCOMES

6-1 Define listening

6-2 Identify the three challenges of listening

6-3 Practice the steps involved in active listening

6-4 Employ strategies to respond effectively in different situations

Are you a good listener? Or do you occasionally find yourself jumping to conclusions before hearing others out, particularly when you're under pressure? We shouldn't underestimate the importance of listening; it can provide clarification, help us understand and remember material, improve our personal and professional relationships, and increase our ability to evaluate information effectively (Weger Jr., et al., 2014). In fact, survey after survey reports that listening is one of the most important skills employers seek in job candidates and the skills they are least effective at performing (e.g., Galagan, 2013; Mumford, 2007; National Association of Colleges and Employers, 2012; Pomeroy, 2007). So the skills you learn and apply from this chapter will set you apart in ways that will benefit you both personally and professionally.

We begin this chapter with a discussion of what listening is and some of the challenges we must overcome to listen effectively. Then we describe the steps involved in the active listening process and propose some specific guidelines you can follow to improve your listening skills during each step. Finally, we suggest strategies for responding appropriately in different listening situations.

6-1 WHAT IS LISTENING?

People sometimes make the mistake of thinking listening and hearing are the same, but they're not. Hearing is a physiological process. **Listening**, on the other hand, consists of complex affective, cognitive, and behavioral processes. Affective processes are those that motivate us to attend to a message. Cognitive processes include understanding and interpreting its meaning (Imhof, 2010) and behavioral processes are those related to responding with verbal and nonverbal feedback (Bodie, et al., 2012). Listening is important because studies show that, even when we factor in the use of technology such as social media and e-mail, as well as cell phone texting, listening is still "the most widely used daily communication activity" (Janusik & Wolvin, 2009, p. 115). Not only that, even when we try to listen carefully, most of us remember only about half of what we heard shortly after and less than 25 percent two days later (International Listening Association, 2003).

listening the process of receiving, constructing meaning from, and responding to spoken and/or nonverbal messages

We choose to listen for various reasons depending on the situation. For example, sometimes we listen to learn about something new. Other times we might listen to provide support as others work through their feelings about an emotionally charged experience. Still other times, we listen to make discerning inferences beyond the surface message by "listening between the lines," so to speak. And sometimes we listen not only to understand but also to evaluate and assign worth to a message. To become effective listeners, we must first consciously overcome three key challenges.

© muzsy/Shutterstock.com

6-2 CHALLENGES TO EFFECTIVE LISTENING

The three challenges to effective listening are rooted in listening apprehension, preferred listening style, and processing approach.

6-2a Listening Apprehension

Listening apprehension is the anxiety we feel about listening. Listening apprehension may increase when we worry about misinterpreting the message, or when we are concerned about how the message may affect us psychologically (Brownell, 2006). For example, if you are in an important meeting or job training session, you may worry about trying to absorb all the important technical information needed to do your job well. Or you might feel anxiety when the material you need to absorb is difficult or confusing. Likewise, your anxiety may increase when you feel ill, tired, or stressed about something else going on in your life. Listening apprehension makes it difficult to focus on the message.

> **Listening apprehension** the anxiety felt about listening

6-2b Listening Style

Listening style is our favored and usually unconscious approach to listening (Watson, Barker, & Weaver, 1995). Each of us favors one of four listening styles. However, we also may change our listening style based on the situation and our goals for the interaction (Gearhart, Denham, & Bodie, 2014).

Content-oriented listeners focus on and evaluate the facts and evidence. Content-oriented listeners appreciate details and enjoy processing complex messages that may include a good deal of technical information. Content-oriented listeners are likely to ask questions to get even more information.

People-oriented listeners focus on the feelings their conversational partners may have about what they are saying. For example, people-oriented listeners tend to notice whether their partners are pleased or upset and will encourage them to continue speaking based on nonverbal cues like head nods, eye contact, and smiles.

Action-oriented listeners focus on the ultimate point the speaker is trying to make. Action-oriented listeners tend to get frustrated when ideas are disorganized and when people ramble. Action-oriented listeners also often anticipate what the speaker is going to say and may even finish the speaker's sentences.

Finally, **time-oriented listeners** prefer brief and hurried conversations and often use nonverbal and verbal cues to signal that their partner needs to be more concise. Time-oriented listeners may tell others exactly how much time they have to listen, interrupt when feeling time pressures, regularly check the time on their smart phones, during a conversation, and may even nod their heads rapidly to encourage others to pick up the pace.

Each of these styles has advantages and disadvantages. Content-oriented listeners are likely to understand and remember

Visiting a doctor can create apprehension and negatively affect listening. Does visiting the doctor make you anxious? Why or why not?

© Monkey Business Images/Shutterstock.com

details but may miss the overall point of the message and be unaware of the speaker's feelings. People-oriented listeners are likely to understand how the speaker feels, empathize, and offer comfort and support. However, they might become so focused on the speaker's feelings that they miss important details or fail to evaluate the facts offered as evidence. Action-oriented listeners may notice inconsistencies but, because they tend to anticipate what will be said rather than hearing the speaker out, may miss important details. Finally, time-oriented listeners are prone to only partially listen to messages while also thinking about their time constraints; thus, they might miss important details and be insensitive to their partner's emotional needs.

Preferred listening style may also be influenced by cultural and co-cultural identity. For example, women who identify with the feminine co-culture are more likely to describe themselves as person-oriented. Similarly, men who identify with the masculine co-culture are more likely to be time-oriented (Salisbury & Chen, 2007). People from collectivist cultures, where maintaining group harmony is highly valued, are more likely to have a people-oriented listening style; conversely, people from individualistic cultures often have an action-oriented listening style (Kiewitz, Weaver, Brosius, & Weimann, 1997). People from high-context cultures tend to favor a person-oriented listening style; people from low-context cultures tend to prefer an action-oriented style (Harris, 2003).

6-2c Processing Approach

We process information in two ways—passively or actively. **Passive listening** is the habitual and unconscious process of receiving messages. When we listen passively,

listening style our favored and usually unconscious approach to listening

content-oriented listeners focus on and evaluate the facts and evidence

people-oriented listeners focus on the feelings their conversational partners may have about what they're saying

action-oriented listeners focus on the ultimate point the speaker is trying to make

time-oriented listeners prefer brief and hurried conversations and use nonverbal and verbal cues to signal that their partner needs to be more concise

passive listening the habitual and unconscious process of receiving messages

Presidential Debates, Freedom of Speech, and Democratic Discourse

Political debates are, ideally, moments of civil discourse intended to enhance a listener's understanding of a topic or viewpoint. However, debates in the most recent presidential election mattered more for what they revealed about the continuing decline of civil discourse in political culture.

There are several examples of crowd noise moving the dialogue away from policy, such as the cheers that erupted when reporter Brian Williams asked Texas Governor Rick Perry about "the 234 executions of death row inmates over which Perry has presided" (Greenwald, 2011). Though the cheers were clearly an instance of partisan support for Perry's position on the death penalty, many criticized this response as inappropriate, saying it shut down any meaningful public conversation about this difficult issue.

The candidates themselves also used emotionally charged language during the debates and cut one another off mid-sentence. In their second debate, former Massachusetts Governor Mitt Romney and President Barack Obama both found themselves reprimanding the other, Obama saying at one point, "I'm used to being interrupted" as Romney attempted to take the floor. At another point in the debate, Romney held off the president by saying, "You'll get your chance in a moment. I'm still speaking." These demonstrations of control became the object of media attention, rather than the policies the candidates were discussing. How do these interruptions and power struggles impact how we hear the candidates?

One research study showed that, in debates that are less than civil, viewers are less likely

© Win McNamee/Staff/Getty Images News/Getty Images

to remember the actual arguments underlying the positions than in more civil debates (Mutz, Reeves, & Wise, 2003). The National Institute for Civil Discourse, a bipartisan organization chaired by former presidents George H. W. Bush and Bill Clinton, suggests that the decline of civil discourse in politics and the media's focus on the loudest and most extreme voices over rational and substantive debate "impairs the development of sound policy, making government less effective" and ignores "the multiplicity of opinions and approaches" needed to address the complex political problems facing our nation. Indeed, Mitt Romney's "binders full of women," a phrase from the second debate to which the Internet and media gave full coverage (both mocking and serious), will be remembered much longer than his concern over cutting Medicare or drive to cut taxes.

we are on automatic pilot. We may attend only to certain parts of a message and assume the rest. We tend to listen passively when we aren't really interested or when we are multitasking. By contrast, **active listening** is the deliberate and conscious process of attending to, understanding, remembering, evaluating, and responding to messages. Active listening requires practice. The rest of this chapter focuses on helping you become a better active listener.

6-3 ACTIVE LISTENING

Active listening is a complex process made up of five steps: attending, understanding, remembering, evaluating, and responding to the messages we receive.

active listening the deliberate and conscious process of attending to, understanding, remembering, evaluating, and responding to messages

6-3a Attending

Active listening begins with attending. **Attending** is the process of willfully perceiving and focusing on a message (O'Shaughnessey, 2003). Poor listeners have difficulty exercising control over what they attend to, often letting their minds drift to thoughts unrelated to the topic. One reason for this is that people typically speak at a rate of about 120–150 words per minute, but our brains can process between 400 and 800 words per minute (Wolvin & Coakley, 1996). This means we usually assume we know what a speaker is going to say before he or she finishes saying it. So our minds have lots of time to wander from the message. Not only does the gap between speaking and processing create opportunities for inattention, but research suggests that, thanks in part to the Internet, smart phones, and other technologies, our attention spans continue to get shorter and shorter (Dukette & Cornish, 2009). Consider your own experiences. Do you ever find yourself daydreaming or checking Facebook during class or when participating in an online conference or meeting?

The first step to becoming a good active listener, then, is to train ourselves to focus on or attend to what people are saying regardless of potential distractions. Let's consider three techniques for doing so:

1. Get physically ready to listen. Good listeners create a physical environment that reduces potential distractions and adopt a listening posture. For example, you might turn off background music, your cell phone, and irrelevant websites on your computer so you won't be tempted to turn your attention to them when you are trying to listen. You can also adopt a listening posture by sitting upright in your chair, leaning slightly forward, and looking directly at the person speaking in the room or on the computer screen.

2. Resist mental distractions. Work consciously to block out wandering thoughts that might come from a visual distraction (e.g., a classmate who enters the room while the professor is lecturing), an auditory distraction (e.g., coworkers chatting beside you while your supervisor is giving instructions), or a physical distraction (e.g., wondering what you'll eat for lunch because your stomach is growling).

3. Hear the person out. Far too often, we stop listening because we disagree with something they say, we assume we know what they are going to say, or we become offended by an example or word used. To be effective at attending, we need to train ourselves not to mentally argue with the speaker and to stay focused on the message.

6-3b Understanding

Understanding is accurately interpreting a message. Let's discuss four strategies to improve listening to understand:

1. Identify the main point. As you listen ask yourself, "What does the speaker want me to understand?" and "What is the point being made?" In addition to the surface message, you might also need to consider the pragmatic meaning couched within it. For example, when Makayla, who is running for city council, asks Joanna what she thinks about the plans for the new arts center and begins to talk about some of its pros and cons, Joanna understands that, beneath the surface, Makayla is also attempting to persuade Joanna to vote for her.

2. Ask questions. A **question** is an interrogative word, phrase, or sentence designed to get additional information or details. Suppose Chris says to you, "I am totally frustrated. Would you stop at the store on the way home and buy me some more paper?" You may be a bit confused by his request and need more information to understand. Yet if you simply respond, "What do you mean?" Chris—who is already frustrated—may become defensive. Instead, you might think about what type of information you need and form a question to meet that need. To increase your understanding, you can ask one of these three types of questions:

▶ *To get details:* "What kind of paper and how much should I get?"

▶ *To clarify word meanings:* "What do you mean by *frustrated*?"

▶ *To clarify feelings:* "What's frustrating you?"

3. Paraphrase. Paraphrasing is the process of putting a message into your own words. For example, during an argument with her sister, Midori paraphrased what she thought she heard her sister saying: "I think I hear you saying that I'm trying to act like I'm better than you when I talk about my work so much." Paraphrases may focus on content, on feelings, or on both. A **content paraphrase** focuses on the denotative meaning of the message. In the example, "when I talk about my work so much" is a

---

attending the process of willfully perceiving and focusing on a message

understanding the process of accurately interpreting a message

question an interrogative word, phrase, or sentence designed to get additional information or details

paraphrasing the process of putting your interpretation of a message into words

content paraphrase a paraphrase that focuses on the denotative meaning of the message

By paraphrasing, you give the speaker a chance to verify your understanding.

content paraphrase. A **feelings paraphrase** focuses on the emotions attached to the message. The second part of the example ("you feel that I'm trying to act like I'm better than you") is a feelings paraphrase.

By paraphrasing, you give the speaker a chance to verify your understanding. The longer and more complex the message, the more important it is to paraphrase. When the speaker appears to be emotional or when the speaker is not using his or her native language, paraphrasing is essential to understanding.

To paraphrase effectively, (1) listen carefully to the message, (2) notice what images and feelings you have experienced from the message, (3) determine what the message means to you, and (4) create a message that conveys these images or feelings.

4. Empathize. Empathy is intellectually identifying with or vicariously experiencing the feelings or attitudes of another. Three approaches are empathic responsiveness, perspective taking, and sympathetic responsiveness (Gearhart et al., 2014).

▶ **Empathic responsiveness** occurs when we experience an emotional response parallel to another person's actual or anticipated display of emotion. For instance, when Jackson tells Janis that he is in real trouble financially, and Janis senses the stress and anxiety that Jackson is feeling, we would say that Janis has demonstrated empathic responsiveness.

▶ **Perspective taking** occurs when we use everything we know about the sender and his or her circumstances to understand their feelings. For example, suppose that Jackson tells Janis that he is in serious financial trouble. Janis, who has known Jackson since grade school, understands that Jackson was raised by parents who were very frugal and paid their bills on time. Because of what she knows about Jackson, Janis understands that Jackson must be very worried about his rising debts.

▶ **Sympathetic responsiveness** is feeling concern, compassion, or sorrow for another's situation. Sympathy differs from the other two approaches. Rather than attempting to experience the feelings of the other, we translate our intellectual understanding of what the speaker has experienced into feelings of concern, compassion, and sorrow for that person. In our previous example, Janis has sympathy for Jackson when she understands that Jackson is embarrassed and worried, but instead of trying to feel those same emotions herself, she feels concern and compassion for her friend.

How well we empathize also depends on how observant we are of others' behavior and how clearly we read their nonverbal messages. To improve these skills, develop the habit of silently posing two questions to yourself: "What emotions do I believe the person is experiencing right now?" and "On what cues from the person am I basing this conclusion?"

To further increase the accuracy of reading emotions, we can also use perception checking. This is especially helpful when the other person's culture is different from ours. Let's consider an example. Atsuko, who was raised in rural Japan and is now studying at a university in Rhode Island, may feel embarrassed when her professor publicly compliments her work. Her friend Meredith might notice Atsuko's reddened cheeks and downcast eyes and comment, "Atsuko, I noticed that you looked down when Professor Shank praised you. Did the compliment embarrass you, make you feel uncomfortable, or was it something else?"

feelings paraphrase a paraphrase that emotions attached to the message captures the

empathy the ability to identify with or vicariously experience another's feelings or attitudes

empathic responsiveness occurs when we experience an emotional response parallel to another person's actual or anticipated display of emotion

perspective taking occurs when we use everything we know about a sender and his or her circumstances to understand their feelings

sympathetic responsiveness feeling concern, compassion, or sorrow for another's situation

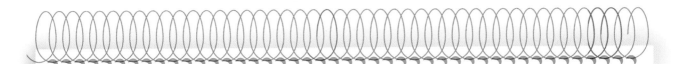

Three techniques to improve our ability to remember information

1. **Repeat the information.** Repetition—saying something aloud or mentally rehearsing it two, three, or four times—helps store information in long-term memory. So when you are introduced to a stranger named Jon McNeil, if you mentally think, "Jon McNeil, Jon McNeil, Jon McNeil" you increase the chances that you will remember his name. Likewise, when a person gives you directions to "go two blocks east, turn left, turn right at the next light, and it's the second apartment building on the right," you should immediately repeat the directions to yourself to help remember them.

2. **Construct mnemonics.** A **mnemonic device** associates a special word or very short statement with new and longer information. One of the most common mnemonic techniques is to form a word with the first letters of a list of items you are trying to remember. For example, a popular mnemonic for the five Great Lakes is HOMES (*Huron, Ontario, Michigan, Erie, Superior*). Most beginning music students learn the mnemonic "*every good boy does fine*" for the notes on the lines of the treble clef (E, G, B, D, F) and the word *face* (F, A, C, E) for the notes on the spaces.

3. **Take notes.** Although note taking may not be an appropriate way to remember information when engaged in casual interpersonal encounters, it is a powerful tool for increasing recall during lectures, business meetings, and briefing sessions. Note taking provides a written record that you can go back to later. It also allows you to take an active role in the listening process (Dunkel & Pialorsi, 2005; Titsworth, 2004).

6-3c Remembering

Remembering is being able to retain and recall information later. Several things can make remembering difficult. For example, we filter out information that doesn't fit our listening style, our listening anxiety prevents us from recalling what we have heard, we engage in passive listening, we practice selective listening and remember only what supports our position, and we fall victim to the primacy-recency effect of remembering only what is said at the beginning and end of a message. Let's look at three techniques to improve our ability to remember information.

What constitutes "good notes" varies depending on the situation. Useful notes may consist of a brief list of main points or key ideas plus a few of the most significant details. Or they may be a short summary of the entire concept (a type of paraphrase). For lengthy and detailed information, however, good notes are likely to consist of a brief outline, including the overall idea, the main points, and key developmental material.

6-3d Evaluating

Evaluating is the process of critically analyzing a message to determine its truthfulness, utility, and trustworthiness. This may involve ascertaining the accuracy of facts, the

repetition saying something aloud or mentally rehearsing it two, three, or more times

mnemonic device associates a special word or very short statement with new and longer information

remembering being able to retain and recall information later

evaluating the process of critically analyzing a message

Dale Carnegie's Tips for Talking and Listening

Dale Carnegie's best-selling book, *How to Win Friends and Influence People*, was first published in 1936. During its more than 75 years on the market, it has sold over 15 million copies, and it remains one of the most influential self-help communication guides available today. Dale Carnegie Training, a communication leadership program Carnegie founded in 1912, also continues to flourish worldwide with offices in over 80 countries. Carnegie's advice on public speaking, leadership, teambuilding, interpersonal communication, and human relations has trained more than 8 million people worldwide and includes over 400 *Fortune* 500 companies on its client list.

Carnegie's advice for winning friends and influencing people can be summarized in the form of six key principles:

1. *Become genuinely interested in other people.*

2. *Smile.*

3. *Remember that a person's name is to that person the sweetest and most important sound in any language.*

4. *Be a good listener. Encourage others to talk about themselves.*

5. *Talk in terms of the other person's interests.*

6. *Make the other person feel important—and do it sincerely.*

(Carnegie, 1936, pp. 110–111)

He elaborates on principle number 4—be a good listener—in this way:

> *If you want to know how to make people shun you and laugh at you behind your back and even despise you, here is the recipe: Never listen to anyone for long. Talk incessantly about yourself. If you have an idea while the other person is talking, don't wait for him or her to finish: bust right in and interrupt in the middle of a sentence.*
>
> *If you aspire to be a good conversationalist, be an attentive listener. Ask questions that other persons will enjoy answering. Encourage them to talk about themselves and their accomplishments.*
>
> *Remember that the people you are talking to are a hundred times more interested in themselves and their wants and problems than they are in you and your problems.... Think of that the next time you start a conversation (pp. 95–96).*

Do you think—as some do—that effective listening as described by Carnegie is becoming a "lost art"? Why or why not?

© marekuliasz/Shutterstock.com

---

amount and type of evidence used, and how a position relates to your personal values. Here are some strategies for evaluating messages effectively:

1. Separate facts from inferences. Facts are statements whose accuracy can be verified as true. If a statement is offered as a fact, you need to determine if it is true. Doing so often requires asking questions that probe the evidence. For example, if Raoul says, "It's going to rain tomorrow," you might ask, "Oh, did you see the weather report this morning?" **Inferences** are assertions based on the facts presented. When a speaker makes an inference, you need to determine whether the inference is valid. You can ask: (1) What are the facts that support this inference? (2) Is this information really central to the inference? (3) Is there other information that would contradict this inference? For example, if someone says, "Better watch it—Katie's in a really bad mood today. Did you catch the look on her face?" you should stop and ask yourself if Katie *is* really in a bad mood. The support for this inference is her facial expression. Is this inference accurate? Is Katie's expression one of anger, unhappiness,

facts statements whose accuracy can be verified as true

inferences assertions based on the facts presented

© Rawpixel/Shutterstock.com

or something else? Is the look on her face enough to conclude that she's in a bad mood? Is there anything else about Katie's behavior that could lead us to believe that she's not in a bad mood? Separating facts from inferences is important because inferences may be false, even if they are based on verifiable facts.

2. Probe for information. Sometimes we need to encourage speakers to delve deeper into a topic in order to truly evaluate the message critically. For example, suppose that Jerrod's prospective landlord asked him to sign a lease. Before signing it, Jerrod should probe for more information. He might ask about the term of the lease and the consequences for breaking the lease early. He might also ask about a deposit and what he will need to do to get the deposit back when the lease is up. He may have noticed inconsistencies between the rental ad on Craigslist and something the landlord says. In that case he might say, "Your ad said that utilities would be paid by the landlord, but just now you said the tenant pays the utility bill. Which one is correct?" With questions like these, Jerrod is probing to accurately evaluate the message.

6-3e Responding

Responding is providing feedback. When we respond to a friend or family member who appears emotionally upset, to a colleague's ideas, or to a public speech, we need to do so in ways that demonstrate respect for the speaker even when we disagree with him or her.

 LISTENING RESPONSE STRATEGIES

Regardless of the situation, we want to respond in ways that demonstrate respect as well as clarity. We can do so by providing appropriate nonverbal feedback cues while the speaker is talking and verbal feedback only after the speaker has finished. **Nonverbal feedback cues** are the signals we use to illustrate that we are attending to and understanding the message. Nodding, smiling, laughing, head cocking, frowning, and eyebrow furrowing are examples. We should give verbal feedback only after the speaker has finished. Next we offer some specific strategies when our goal in responding is to provide emotional support, constructive criticism, and formal constructive speech critiques.

EMOTIONAL SUPPORT RESPONSE STRATEGIES Sometimes the appropriate response is to reassure, encourage, soothe, console, or cheer up. **Supportive responses** create an environment that encourages the other person to talk about and make sense of a distressing situation. Supporting does not mean making false statements or telling someone only what he or she wants to hear. Figure 6.1 summarizes research-based guidelines for forming supportive messages (Burleson, 2010).

CONSTRUCTIVE CRITICISM RESPONSE STRATEGIES When we cannot agree with what a speaker has said, our messages will be most effective if they clearly demonstrate respect. Figure 6.2 provides some guidelines to help demonstrate respect when disagreeing with or critiquing others.

responding the process of providing feedback

nonverbal feedback cues verbal and nonverbal signals used to indicate to the speaker that you are attending to and understanding the message

supportive responses create an environment that encourages another to talk about and make sense of a distressing situation.

FIGURE 6.1 GUIDELINES FOR SUPPORTIVE RESPONSES

Guideline	Example
1. Clearly state that your aim is to help.	*I'd like to help you, what can I do?*
2. Express acceptance or affection; do not condemn or criticize.	*I understand that you just can't seem to accept this.*
3. Demonstrate care, concern, and interest in the speaker's situation; do not give a lengthy recount of a similar situation.	*What are you planning to do now? OR Gosh, tell me more! What happened then?*
4. Indicate that you are available to listen and support the speaker without intruding.	*I know that we've not been that close, but sometimes it helps to have someone to listen and I'd like to do that for you.*
5. State that you are an ally.	*I'm with you on this. OR Well, I'm on your side. This isn't right.*
6. Acknowledge the speaker's feelings and situation, and express your sincere sympathy.	*I'm so sorry to see you feeling so bad. I can see that you're devastated by what has happened.*
7. Assure the speaker that his or her feelings are legitimate; do not tell the speaker how to feel or to ignore those feelings.	*Hey, it's OK, man. With all that has happened to you, you have a right to be angry.*
8. Use prompting comments to encourage elaboration.	*Uh-huh, yeah. OR I see. How did you feel about that? OR Tell me more.*

© Cengage Learning

FIGURE 6.2 GUIDELINES FOR CRITIQUING OTHERS

Guideline	Example
1. Use "I" language to clearly own the comments you make. Do not ascribe them to others.	*Carla, I really like the way you cited the references for your opening quotation.*
2. Use specific language and specific examples to point out areas of disagreement and areas for improvement.	*I can't agree to this plan because I cannot afford a 15% reduction in my personnel budget. I could probably live with a 10% decrease.*
3. Find a point to agree with or something positive to say before expressing your disagreement or offering a negative critique.	*I really appreciate what you have to say on this topic and agree that we need to support our coworkers who need after-school care for their children. I wonder, though, if we should brainstorm additional potential solutions before settling on one.*

© Cengage Learning

FORMAL CONSTRUCTIVE SPEECH CRITIQUE STRATEGIES The goals when providing a formal constructive speech critique are to be respectful, honest, and helpful. To do so, use "I" language, be specific, use examples, and identify what the speaker did well before offering suggestions for improvement. Good speech critiques also address content, structure, and delivery—as well as the construction and integration of presentational aids if used.

▶ When critiquing content, comment on the appropriateness of the speech for that particular audience and the use of facts and inferences, the logic of the arguments, and the evidence used to support ideas.

▶ When critiquing structure, focus on the introduction (attention catcher, thesis statement, main point preview), organizational pattern of main points, transitions, and concluding remarks.

▶ When critiquing delivery, comment on the use of voice (intelligible, conversational expressive), and use of body (attire, poise, eye contact, facial expressions, gestures).

▶ When critiquing presentational aids, talk about construction (large, neat colorful, visual symbol system) and integration (concealed, revealed, and referenced during the speech).

Figure 6.3 provides examples of ineffective and effective speech critique statements.

FIGURE 6.3 EXAMPLES OF EFFECTIVE AND INEFFECTIVE SPEECH CRITIQUES

	Ineffective Critique	Effective Critique
Content	The sources you cited are too old.	I noticed you relied heavily on Johnson's 1969 essay about global warming. For me, your argument would be more compelling if you cited research that has been published in the last five years.
Structure	You were really hard to follow.	I really appreciate what you had to say on this topic. I would have been able to follow your main points better if I had heard clear transitions between each one. Transitions would have helped me notice the switch from one topic to the next.
Delivery	You talk too fast!	I was fascinated by the evidence you offered to support the first main point. It would have been even more compelling for me if you had spoken just a bit more slowly while explaining that information. That would have given me time to understand the material more fully before we moved on to the next main point.
Presentational Aids	Your PowerPoint was ugly.	The content you chose to put on your PowerPoint presentation really highlighted what you were saying. I would have had an easier time reading the slides if the text were shorter and the background was a dark color with light text, or a light color with dark text. This would have made your point even clearer to me.

© Cengage Learning

STUDY TOOLS 6

LOCATED IN TEXTBOOK

- ☐ Tear-out Chapter Review cards at the end of the book
- ☐ Review with the Quick Quiz

LOCATED ON COMM 4 ONLINE AT CENGAGEBRAIN.COM:

- ☐ Review Key Term flashcards and create your own cards
- ☐ Track your knowledge and understanding of key concepts in communication
- ☐ Complete practice and graded quizzes to prepare for tests
- ☐ Complete interactive content within COMM4 Online
- ☐ View the chapter highlight boxes for COMM4 Online

Quick Quiz

T F 1. A biology professor is leading an advanced team as they work on some genetic coding. When one student explains a problem with the experiment, the professor quickly grasps the student's meaning and finishes her sentence for her with enthusiasm. This professor is an action-oriented listener.

T F 2. The five steps in the active listening process are: attending, understanding, remembering, evaluating, and responding.

T F 3. Studies show that our brains can process between 400 and 800 words per minute, which gives us the ability to listen effectively while at the same time we rehearse what we are going to say in response.

T F 4. Empathy is putting into words the ideas or feelings you have perceived from the message.

T F 5. A mnemonic device is any artificial technique used as a memory aid.

6. The process of receiving, constructing meaning from, and responding to spoken and/or nonverbal messages is

   a. remembering.   c. attending.
   b. understanding.   d. evaluating.
   e. listening.

7. Ansel's puppy has been missing all day, and he is very upset, worried, and constantly trying to find her. When he tells you about this, which is the appropriate response?

   a. You express concern for the puppy and offer to do whatever you can to help track her down.
   b. You look at your watch and tell Ansel you can't help, you have a casserole in the oven.
   c. You want to verify the fact that the puppy is missing so you ask if your friend is telling the truth.
   d. You think to yourself, "Wow, Ansel doesn't even care that I have a basketball game. He's a bad friend."
   e. You say, "Oh man, good luck with that."

8. During the response phase, which of the following should NOT occur?

   a. You offer supportive phrases that encourage a person to feel less stressed.
   b. You laugh at your friend's explanation of a humorous but slightly embarrassing event.
   c. You change the subject as soon as your sister finishes speaking.
   d. You offer suggestions for changing a presentation when a colleague requests help.
   e. Your mom insists that squid is shellfish, and you explain that you understand how it's tricky, but the squid is not a shellfish.

9. The process of selecting and focusing on specific stimuli from the countless ones that we receive is called

   a. listening.   b. attending.
   c. understanding.   d. remembering.
   e. evaluating.

10. _____ is the process of decoding a message so that the meaning accurately reflects that intended by the speaker.

    a. Listening
    b. Attending
    c. Understanding
    d. Empathizing
    e. Responding

Answers: 1. T, 2. T, 3. F, 4. F, 5. F, 6. E, 7. A, 8. C, 9. B, 10. C

7 Interpersonal Relationships

LEARNING OUTCOMES

7-1 Identify the major types of relationships

7-2 Explain how disclosure and feedback affect relationships

7-3 Examine levels of communication at various stages in relationships

7-4 Examine how technology and social media influence interpersonal relationships

7-5 Identify the sources of tension in relationships

After finishing this chapter go to **PAGE 93** for **STUDY TOOLS.**

Bettmann/Corbis

interpersonal communication
all the interactions that occur between two people to help start, build, maintain, and sometimes end or redefine the relationship

interpersonal relationship
a relationship that is defined by sets of expectations two people have for each other based on their previous interactions

healthy relationship a relationship in which the interactions are satisfying and beneficial to all those involved

acquaintances people we know by name and talk with when the opportunity arises, but with whom our interactions are largely impersonal

Interpersonal communication is all the interactions that occur between two people to help start, build, maintain, and sometimes end or redefine our interpersonal relationships. Interpersonal relationships are defined by the sets of expectations two people have for each other based on their previous interactions (Littlejohn & Foss, 2011). We form interpersonal relationships as we communicate overtly and covertly through face-to-face and online interactions. Interpersonal relationships help satisfy our innate human need to feel connected with others and run the gamut from impersonal acquaintances to intimate friends. Regardless of the level of intimacy, we want to be involved in healthy relationships that are satisfying and beneficial to all those involved. How we communicate is central to achieving that goal.

We begin this chapter by describing three types of interpersonal relationships and providing guidelines for healthy communication in each of them. Next, we explain the role of disclosure in the stages of relationship life cycles. Finally, we offer guidelines for managing the dialectical tensions that exist in any interpersonal relationship.

7-1 TYPES OF RELATIONSHIPS

We communicate differently based on the level of intimacy we feel toward our partner. Moving on a continuum from impersonal to personal, we can classify our relationships as acquaintances, friends, and intimates.

7-1a Acquaintances

Acquaintances are people we know by name, but with whom our interactions are limited. For example, we may be acquaintances with those living in the same neighborhood, apartment building, or residence hall. We may also be acquaintances with

classmates or co-workers. Thus, Whitney and Paige, who meet in calculus class, may talk with each other about class-related issues but make no effort to share personal ideas or to see each other outside of class. Most conversations with acquaintances can be defined as **impersonal communication**, which is essentially interchangeable chit-chat (Beebe, Beebe, & Ivy, 2013). In other words, we may talk about the same thing—for instance, the weather—with the grocery clerk, the sales associate, the bank teller, and the restaurant server. If you have an online social networking profile on Facebook, Twitter, or LinkedIn, many of your online "friends" are probably acquaintances if your online conversations with them are primarily surface-level ones.

Our goals when communicating with acquaintances are usually to reduce uncertainty and maintain face. We attempt to reduce uncertainty by seeking information that may reveal similar beliefs, attitudes, and values (Berger, 1987). In doing so, however, we may say or do something that offends the other person or is taken the wrong way. So our second goal is to help one another save face. **Saving face** is the process of attempting to

maintain a positive self-image in a relational situation (Ting-Toomey, 2004, 2005).

ACQUAINTANCESHIP GUIDELINES To meet other people and develop acquaintance relationships, it helps to be good at starting and developing conversations. The following guidelines can help you develop scripts to become more competent in doing so:

▶ **Initiate a conversation** by introducing yourself, referring to the physical context, referring to your thoughts or feelings, referring to another person, or making a joke. For example:

Whitney: "Do you think it's hot in here, or is it just me? By the way, I'm Whitney."

▶ **Make your comments relevant** to what has previously been said before you change subjects:

Paige: "My name's Paige. Yes, I'm burning up. I wonder if the air conditioner is broken. Do you know if this class meets for 75 or 90 minutes today?"

impersonal communication interchangeable polite chit-chat involving no or very little personal disclosure

saving face the process of attempting to maintain a positive self-image in a relational situation

▶ **Develop an other-centered focus** by asking questions, listening carefully, and following up on what has been said. For example:

Whitney: "I'm pretty sure it's only a 75-minute session. Have you ever taken a class from this professor?"
Paige: "Yeah, I took algebra from her."
Whitney: "What was she like?"
Paige: "She was pretty good. Her tests were hard, but they were fair. I learned a lot."
Whitney: "Did she offer study guides?"
Paige: "Yes, and we had what she called 'algebra Jeopardy' review sessions. That worked well for me."
Whitney: "Sounds like I'm going to like this class and this instructor!"

▶ **Engage in appropriate turn-taking** by balancing talking with listening and not interrupting. In his best-selling book, *How to Win Friends and Influence People,* Dale Carnegie (1936) put it this way: "Listen first and let them finish. Do not resist, defend or debate. This only raises barriers. . . . Remember that the people you are talking to are a hundred times more interested in themselves and their wants and problems than they are in you and your problems" (pp. 98, 127).

▶ **Be polite.** Consider how your conversational partner will feel about what you say and work to phrase your comments in a way that allows your partner to save face. For example:

friends people with whom we have voluntarily negotiated more personal relationships

Whitney: "I wish I wouldn't have signed up for this section that meets right at noon. I'm famished. Here, do you want some M&Ms?"
Paige: "No thanks."
Whitney: "Are you sure? I don't mind sharing. A little sugar never hurt anyone."
Paige: "I'm diabetic."
Whitney: "Oh, I'm so sorry. I'll save these for later."

7-1b Friends

Over time, some acquaintances become friends. **Friends** are people with whom we have voluntarily negotiated more personal relationships (Canary, Cody, & Manusov, 2008). For example, Whitney and Paige, who are acquaintances, may decide to get together after class to work out at the gym. If they find that they enjoy each other's company, they may continue to meet outside of class and eventually become friends.

We often refer to friends according to the context in which we interact with them. For example, we may have tennis friends, office friends, or neighborhood friends. These context friendships may fade if the context changes. For instance, our friendship with a person at the office may fade if one of us takes a job with a different company.

FRIENDSHIP GUIDELINES Several key communication behaviors will help you maintain your friendships whether you live close to one another or are separated by a distance and can only communicate remotely via e-mail, Facebook, Skype, or mobile phone (Walther, 2011).

▶ **Initiation.** Be proactive about setting up times to spend together. Friendship is not likely to form or endure between people who rarely interact.

▶ **Responsiveness.** Each person must listen. Ask questions and then focus on listening and responding to what they say.

▶ **Self-disclosure.** Although acquaintances can be maintained by conversations that discuss surface issues, friendships are based on the exchange of more personal information, opinions, and feelings. For example, after Paige and Whitney start to spend more time together outside of class, they might have this conversation:

Blend Images/Shutterstock.com

Paige: "Can I tell you something and trust you to keep it between us?"

Whitney: "Of course."

Paige: "Well, you know I've been seeing David for a while now."

Whitney: "Yeah, he seems like a nice guy."

Paige: "Well, the other night we got into a little fight and he pushed me onto the couch. I actually have a bruise here on my arm from it."

▶ **Emotional support.** Provide comfort and support when needed. When your friends are hurting, they need you to support them by clarifying your supportive intentions, confirming their feelings, helping them make sense of what has happened, and giving advice (Burleson, 2009).

Whitney: "Oh, no. I'm here to help in any way I can."

Paige: "He said he was sorry and I believe him, but I just don't feel comfortable around him now."

Whitney: "I understand. I'm not sure I would feel comfortable either. Is there anything I can do?"

Paige: "No, not really. I guess I just wanted someone to confirm that I'm not overreacting."

Whitney: "Well, I don't think you're overreacting at all. Please let me know what I can do to help, OK?"

Paige: "OK. I'm so lucky to have you for a friend."

wavebreakmedia/Shutterstock.com

▶ **Conflict management.** Friends will sometimes disagree about ideas or behaviors. Healthy friendships handle these disagreements effectively through conversation.

Whitney: "Maybe you should talk to a campus counselor about this."

Paige: "No, I don't want to make a big deal out of it."

Whitney: "Paige, you got a bruise. That seems like a big deal to me."

Paige: "Actually, I bruise really easily. I don't want to see a counselor. Maybe I shouldn't have even told you about it."

Whitney: "Oh, Paige. I'm so glad you did and I totally respect your decision. If anything like this happens again, though, will you please talk to someone?"

Paige: "OK, if something happens again, I promise I will."

7-1c Intimates

Intimates are those close personal friends with whom we share a high degree of interdependence, commitment, disclosure, understanding, affection, and trust. We may have countless acquaintances and many friends, but we are likely to have only a few truly intimate relationships. Unfortunately, the percentage of Americans who identify having even just one intimate relationship beyond family members declined from 80 percent in 1985 to 57 percent in 2006 (McPherson, Smith-Lovin, & Brashears, 2006). Today most Americans report having no more than two intimate friends, including family members (Bryner, 2011). In fact, according to a recent University of Oxford study, even though we may have hundreds of "Facebook friends," the number of truly close friends is still very small (Saramki et al., 2014). This dramatic decline is particularly troubling given that intimate relationships are the most important predictor of life satisfaction and emotional well-being (Moore, 2003; Peterson, 2006).

Intimate relationships can be platonic or romantic. A **platonic relationship** is one in which the partners are not sexually attracted to each other or do not

intimates people with whom we share a high degree of interdependence, commitment, disclosure, understanding, affection, and trust

platonic relationship an intimate relationship in which the partners are not sexually attracted to each other or do not act on an attraction they feel

Who Are You IRL?

Throughout history—in life, literature, and the media—people hoping to find love have solicited help from others. Today we've expanded our search for love to online dating services, but advanced technologies don't eliminate the need some of us have to seek outside help in expressing ourselves. A quick Internet search produces several results promising online dating success, and personal coaching for online dating is also on the rise. Online services such as Dating-Profile.com, ProfileHelper.com, and E-Cyrano.com help singles write their profiles for a fee. Dating coaches claim their services are not aimed at helping clients lie but, rather, to more effectively communicate their true, in-real-life (IRL) identities in a virtual dating world.

Opinions vary on the ethics of using such ghostwriting services on dating profile sites. One Match.com user says hiring someone to help write her profile would obscure who she truly is. "I'm not a person who is put together or always knows the right thing to say," she says. "I would feel like if I went out on a date with someone, I would have to be what they read instead of myself" (Alsever, 2007). Another online dater sings the praises of ProfileHelper.com, where he learned to be more specific and inquisitive when communicating on online dating sites (Alsever, 2007). In his case, a profile-writing coach stressed basic communication principles that helped him more accurately convey the kind of person he is, pinpointing the types of

mtkang/Shutterstock.com

things he enjoys, and what he is looking for in a potential partner.

However you feel about profile-writing coaches, most would agree that communication on online dating sites is tricky. An article in *Skeptic* explores the pros and cons of self-disclosing when dating online (King, Austin-Oden, & Lohr, 2009): On one hand, information presented online is easy to manipulate and control, so people can present themselves in any way they like—even if what they present isn't 100 percent accurate. On the other hand, the relative anonymity of online communication "accelerates intimacy through increased openness about aspects of the self." When what we disclose about ourselves is true, self-disclosure is an important step in making a successful relationship.

---

act on an attraction they feel. If you're familiar with the television series *Parks and Recreation*, the relationship between Leslie and Ron is platonic, but they are also intimate friends. Conversely, a **romantic relationship** is one in which the partners acknowledge their sexual attraction to one another.

Regardless of whether the relationship is platonic or romantic, both partners must trust each other for it to become and remain intimate. **Trust** is placing confidence in another in a way that almost always involves some risk. As we share private information and feelings, we monitor how well our partner keeps our confidence. If our partner keeps our confidence, we share more and the relationship becomes more intimate. If our partner proves untrustworthy, we share less and, as a result, over time intimacy decreases. When there is a severe breach of trust, we may even abruptly end the relationship altogether.

CULTURAL AND CO-CULTURAL INFLUENCES ON INTIMACY Research suggests that intimate relationships are based on four types of interactions. The first comes from physical touch, which may include holding

romantic relationship an intimate relationship in which the partners act on their sexual attraction

trust placing confidence in another in a way that almost always involves some risk

hands, hugging, being held, kissing, and engaging in sexual relations. The second comes from the intellectual sharing of important ideas and opinions. The third comes from sharing important feelings. The final type comes from participating in shared activities. Such activities can include anything from working together on the job or on a class project to participating on a sports team or in a civic club, getting together regularly for coffee or lunch, going to a movie or dinner, or going shopping.

Our cultural identity may influence which type of interactions we are most likely to engage in. For example, women who identify with the feminine co-culture tend to be more willing to share their thoughts and feelings than men (Dindia, 2009). Men who identify with the masculine co-culture may prefer participating in shared activities (Dindia & Canary, 2006). Of course, since masculine and feminine co-cultural norms are socialized, these generalizations may not be true for all men or for all women. Frankly, recent research suggests that such differences are increasingly becoming less prominent in the United States.

Intimacy development norms also vary across cultures. In collectivist cultures such as China, Taiwan, and Japan, for example, people do not typically reach out to acquaintances until properly introduced and then take care to keep private information about close friends and family to themselves. In individualistic cultures such as the United States, people are likely to share more private information and personal feelings with acquaintances (Lustig & Koester, 2013). As with gender differences, however, such cultural differences are becoming increasingly less pronounced as the world becomes more connected through travel, media, and technology (Hatfield & Rapson, 2006).

INTIMACY GUIDELINES The following guidelines can help you establish and maintain affection, understanding, trust, and commitment in your intimate relationships

▶ **Be dependable** so your partner learns that he or she can rely on you. Of course, nobody is perfect. But striving to be dependable will provide a foundation for understanding when something does come up.

▶ **Be responsive** in meeting your partner's needs. At times, this will require you to put their needs before your own.

wallybird/Shutterstock.com

Some cultures are careful to keep personal information private, which may seem overly secretive to more open cultures.

▶ **Be collaborative** in managing conflict. Doing so includes saying you're sorry for something you've done or said, agreeing to disagree, and letting go of the need to be "right."

▶ **Be faithful** by maintaining your partner's confidential information and by abiding by sexual or other exclusivity agreements between you and your partner.

▶ **Be transparent** by honestly sharing your ideas and feelings with your partner.

▶ **Be willing** to put your relationship first. This is not to say you should give up all other activities and relationships. However, you should strive for a balance between doing things together and doing things apart (Baxter & Montgomery, 1996).

 7-2

DISCLOSURE IN RELATIONSHIP LIFE CYCLES

Relationships are not something we *have*, but rather are something we *make* as we communicate with others (Parks, 2007). Even though no two relationships develop in exactly the same way, all relationships tend to move through identifiable and overlapping phases of coming together and coming apart (Knapp & Vangelisti, 2009). This moving back and forth among the phases is known as the **relationship life cycle**.

How we move among the phases depends on how we communicate with one another (Duck, 2007). We do so through **disclosure**, which is the process of revealing confidential information, and feedback, which includes the verbal and nonverbal responses to such information. Disclosure can come in the form of **self-disclosure**, which is the confidential information we deliberately choose to share about ourselves, and **other-disclosure**, which is the confidential information shared about someone by a third party (Petronio, 2002). **Social penetration theory** describes the different kinds of self-disclosure we use in our relationships, and the **Johari window** explains how these various forms of disclosure and feedback operate in them. Knowing these processes can help us make wise disclosure decisions depending on relationship type and life cycle stage.

7-2a Social Penetration

Not all self-disclosure is equally revealing. In other words, some messages reveal more about our thoughts and feelings than others. Irwin Altman and Dalmas Taylor (1973; 1987) conceptualized a model of self-disclosure based on the breadth and depth of information shared. *Breadth* has to do with the range of different subjects you discuss with your partner. *Depth* has to do with the quality of information shared, which can range from relatively impersonal and "safe" to very confidential and "risky." For example, when Whitney and Paige first met, the breadth of subjects they discussed focused on their families, hometowns, and things they were learning in class. As their relationship became more intimate they added subjects about career ambitions, feelings about people they were dating, and feelings about their own relationship. The depth of disclosure also deepened. For example, in addition to sharing impersonal information, such as how many siblings they each have, they also disclosed characteristics they liked and did not like about their brothers and sisters. Discussions about

their hometowns became deeper as they shared personal stories about positive and negative experiences they had growing up. And discussions about class grew to include opinions each had about whether what they were learning would help them achieve their career goals. Paige and Whitney's social penetration model is illustrated in Figure 7.1.

7-2b The Johari Window

Relational closeness depends on appropriate self-disclosure along with appropriate feedback and other-disclosure. One way to understand the nature of disclosure and feedback in interpersonal relationships is through the Johari window. The Johari window, named after its two originators, Joe Luft and Harry Ingham (1970), consists of four panes that comprise all information about you. You and your partner each know some (but not all) of this information (see Figure 7.2).

THE OPEN PANE The "open" pane represents the information about you that both you and your partner know. It might include mundane information that you share with most people, such as your college major, but it also may include information that you disclose to relatively few people. Similarly, it could include simple observations that your partner has made, such as how you doodle when you're bored, or more serious ones such as how you behave when you're angry.

THE SECRET PANE The "secret" pane contains everything you know about yourself but your partner does

---

relationship life cycle moving back and forth among the relationship phases

disclosure the process of revealing confidential information

self-disclosure the confidential information we deliberately choose to share about ourselves

other-disclosure the confidential information shared about someone by a third party

social penetration theory describes the different kinds of self-disclosure we use in our relationships

Johari window a tool for examining the relationship between disclosure and feedback in the relationship

FIGURE 7.1 SOCIAL PENETRATION MODEL

Families

Hometowns

Feelings about our relationship

Classes

Dating partners

Career ambitions

FIGURE 7.2 THE JOHARI WINDOW

	Known to self	Not known to self
Known to others	Open	Blind
Not known to others	Secret	Unknown

not yet know. As you share secret information through self-disclosure, that information moves into the open pane. For example, suppose you were once engaged to be married but your partner broke the engagement. You may not want to share this part of your history with casual acquaintances, so it will be in the secret pane of your window in many of your relationships. But when you disclose this fact to an intimate friend, it moves into the open pane with this person. As you disclose information, the secret pane becomes smaller and the open pane grows larger.

THE BLIND PANE The "blind" pane contains information your partner knows about you that you don't realize about yourself. They may have discovered it by observing you or from other-disclosure shared by a mutual friend or acquaintance. Information moves from the blind pane to the open pane through feedback. The open pane becomes larger and the blind pane becomes smaller.

THE UNKNOWN PANE The "unknown" pane contains information that neither you nor your partner knows about you. Obviously, you cannot develop a list of this information. So how do we know that it exists?

Well, because periodically we discover it. If, for instance, you have never tried zip lining, then nobody knows whether you'll like it or not. Once you try it, you gain information about yourself that becomes part of the secret pane, which you can move to the open pane through disclosure. Also, once you have tried it, others who observe your flight will have information about your performance that you may not know unless they give you feedback.

7-3 STAGES OF RELATIONSHIPS

Every relationship develops and changes with time. We can describe these changes as coming together, staying together, and coming apart (Dindia, 2003; Knapp & Vangelisti, 2005). Our relationships move among these stages based on the *information* we share and our *interpretation* of it (Duck, 2007).

7-3a Coming Together: Beginning and Developing Relationships

The stages of coming together focus on beginning and developing relationships. Communication focuses on reducing uncertainty as we try to understand how our partner sees the world. Noted interpersonal communication scholar Steve Duck (1999) conceived the Relationship Filtering Model to explain the process that relationships go through in the beginning stages. According to the model, when we first meet someone we assume he or she is similar to us until his/her words or actions tell us otherwise. We begin by communicating very generally about noncontroversial topics and asking questions about surface information such as hometowns and hobbies. Then, we make inferences about the person's general attitudes, values, and ways of thinking. If we decide we have enough in common, we will choose to develop the relationship by disclosing more.

Let's look again at Whitney and Paige. They decided to become college roommates and are a bit nervous about it. To reduce uncertainty, they get to know

Yuri Arcurs/Shutterstock.com

well. They spend time together, get to know each other well, and consider themselves to be intimate friends. By second semester, they hug each other when they return from spring break, share clothes, and do each other's hair.

Of course, cultural norms also affect how people engage in physical contact in relationships. In some cultures, for instance, male friends who are not romantic partners may hold hands in public or kiss to greet one another. In contrast, for orthodox Jews and observant Muslim women, touching men is abhorred.

each other better through disclosure and feedback. They talk about favorite hobbies, foods, movies, and music. As they learn more about each other, they find that although Whitney is majoring in fine arts and Paige is pre-med, both are passionate environmentalists and vegetarians. As they learn more, they begin to relax and find that although they have many differences, they like and respect each other. Over the semester, life in the room they share begins to take on a predictable pattern. When one of them is stressing over a class project, the other often goes to the library or to the lounge to give her space.

Relationships can begin in face-to-face or online environments. Online communication may present a potentially less difficult way to meet others than traditional face-to-face interactions. The initial interaction can occur in the comfort of our own home and at our own pace. We need not be concerned about physical appearance, and we can more precisely select what we are going to say (Ward & Tracy, 2004).

As the relationship develops, we continue coming together by disclosing more and engaging in more physical contact (Duck & McMahan, 2012). Through disclosure and feedback, we identify and capitalize on similarities and tolerate or negotiate differences. Physical contact may involve sitting closer together, leaning toward each other, and engaging in more eye contact and touch. Such physical behaviors may or may not involve romantic feelings. Even platonic friends increase physical contact with each other as the relationship develops, for example, through hugs, high-fives, and fist bumps. Let's say the relationship between Whitney and Paige is working out

As a relationship develops, partners will feel psychologically closer as well (Duck, 1999). If we share no common interests, attitudes, or ways of interpreting the world, we are not likely to develop a deeper relationship. Think about the people you met during your first weeks on campus. Which ones did not become your friends and why? Most likely, you gathered information that reduced uncertainty, but what you learned was that they did not share enough common interests or attitudes to warrant developing a relationship. Finally, many people engage in coming together via social media and some report achieving more closeness in their online relationships than in equivalent face-to-face ones (Brooks, 2011).

RELATIONAL MAINTENANCE Once a relationship has developed, we employ communication strategies to maintain it. **Relational maintenance** consists of those communication strategies used to keep a relationship operating smoothly and satisfactorily (Dindia, 2009). Researchers have catalogued many relational maintenance strategies (Rusbult, Olsen, Davis, & Hannon, 2004). Some of them include prosocial behaviors (e.g., being friendly and polite), observing ceremonial occasions (e.g., birthdays, anniversaries, regular "date nights"). For example, Paige and Whitney celebrate one another's birthdays by going bowling and then to dinner at a favorite restaurant. Paige also tries not to be overtly critical when Whitney strews papers around while working on a big project, knowing that Whitney will tidy things up when she is finished. Instead, Paige admires Whitney for having such a serious work ethic.

Other strategies include spending time together (both with one another and with mutual friends), communicating honestly and frequently about both deep and everyday topics, and offering words and actions

relational maintenance
communication strategies used to keep a relationship operating smoothly and satisfactorily

that demonstrate affection and respect for one another. Whitney and Paige, for example, gave each other "best friend" status on their Facebook pages, decided to join some of the same clubs, and even visited each other's hometowns to meet each other's families and high school friends.

Partners also **sacrifice** by putting their needs or desires on hold to attend to the needs of their partner or the relationship. For example, when Whitney was ill, Paige sacrificed a date in order to stay home and take care of her sick roommate. Because all relationships involve give and take, being willing to do what is best for the other person or for the relationship itself can help maintain it.

Finally, because conflict is inevitable in developed relationships, we may do or say things that hurt our partner. If not handled properly, such transgressions can harm the relationship and move it to a less intimate level. By forgiving minor transgressions, we can keep a relationship at the desired level of closeness. For example, Whitney and Paige each have little habits that annoy the other, but they choose not to let these annoyances get in the way of a good friendship.

7-3b Coming Apart: Declining and Dissolving Relationships

When one or both partners fail to engage actively in relational maintenance strategies, the relationship may begin to come apart and could eventually end altogether. Relationships between acquaintances, casual friends, co-workers, and neighbors are more likely to end than highly developed ones (Parks, 2007). The communication in declining relationships is marked by four stages: circumscribing, stagnating, avoiding, and terminating.

CIRCUMSCRIBING The first sign that a relationship is coming apart is known as the **circumscribing stage**, which is where communication decreases in both quantity and quality. Rather than discuss a disagreement, for example, both parties ignore it outwardly even if it troubles them inside. Even though Whitney and Paige were close during their first two years of college, they drifted apart as they each met people with more aligned personal and professional interests. They found they had less and less to talk about when they were together, so they started spending less time with each other.

Relational maintenance includes prosocial behaviors such as celebrating birthdays.

Hannamariah/Shutterstock.com

STAGNATING If circumscribing continues, it may eventually lead to the **stagnating stage**, which is when partners just go through the motions of interacting without enthusiasm or emotion. When employees reach this stage, we say they have "job burnout." Because Whitney and Paige share a dorm room, they continue to engage in the routines they had developed for studying, cleaning, and eating. But they now do so in silence, neither of them wanting to make the effort to initiate a conversation about meaningless topics.

AVOIDING When a relationship that has stagnated becomes too painful, partners move into the **avoiding stage** by creating physical distance between themselves and by making excuses not to do things together. The overriding tone is usually not marked by hostility but by indifference. When Whitney tells Paige she is moving into an apartment with other friends, Paige responds with "Whatever."

TERMINATING Of course, not all relationships end. However, when partners decide the relationship is no longer worth trying to maintain, they have reached the **terminating stage**. People give many reasons for terminating relationships, including poor communication, lack of fulfillment, differing lifestyles and interests, rejection, outside interference, absence of rewards, and boredom (Cupach and Metts, 1986). These attempts to

sacrifice putting one's needs or desires on hold to attend to the needs of one's partner or the relationship

circumscribing stage relationship stage during which communication decreases in both quantity and quality

stagnating stage relationship stage during which partners just go through the motions of interacting with each other routinely without enthusiasm or emotion

avoiding stage relationship stage during which partners create physical distance by making excuses not to do things with the other person in the relationship

terminating stage relationship stage in which partners no longer interact with each other

When partners decide a relationship is no longer worth maintaining, they have reached the terminating stage.

relationship transformation. Romantic relationships may transform into friendships, best friends may become casual friends, and even marriages may continue on friendly terms or as a type of business relationship where child-rearing practices and expenses are coordinated (Parks, 2007). After Whitney and Paige graduate, their friendship may be transformed into that of acquaintances who enjoy seeing each other at reunions.

7-4 MEDIATED COMMUNICATION AND INTERPERSONAL RELATIONSHIPS

explain why the relationship failed are called **grave-dressing** (Duck & McMahan, 2012).

Unfortunately, partners sometimes look for reasons to blame each other rather than trying to find equitable ways to bring the relationship to an acceptable conclusion. They do so by using strategies of manipulation, withdrawal, and avoidance. Manipulation involves being indirect and failing to take any responsibility for ending the relationship. Manipulators may purposely sabotage the relationship in hopes that the other person will break it off. Withdrawal and avoidance, also unsuitable strategies, are passive approaches that lead to the slow and often painful death of the relationship.

The most competent way to end a relationship is to be direct, open, and honest. If two people have had a satisfying and close relationship, they owe it to themselves and to each other to be forthright and fair about terminating. Although some people terminate their romantic relationships via text message, it is more respectful to do so in person. For example, when DeMarcus decided to break up with his girlfriend, Larissa, he thought about just ignoring her e-mails and texts hoping she would "get the hint." Instead he invited her to coffee and explained his feelings honestly and respectfully. To his surprise, she thanked him for telling her in person rather than via text like her last boyfriend.

Even when partners agree that their relationship in its current form is over, they may continue to interact and influence each other through a different type of relationship. This is called

grave-dressing attempts to explain why a relationship failed

relationship transformation the process of changing a relationship from one level of intimacy to another

Almost all of us have met someone online, used the Internet to keep connected to a friend or loved one who lives far away, or used e-mail and text messaging to "converse" with friends and family. Internet technology and social media have changed how we build and maintain our relationships in several important ways:

▸ People can begin friendships and even meet their soul mates online. Sometimes these relationships stem from shared interests, such as online gaming or forums for specific hobbies like home-brewing beer or practicing martial arts.

▸ Our online partners usually respond to our verbal messages rather than our physical appearance or nonverbal cues. As a result, we are more likely to develop "pure relationships" based on mutual interests unconstrained by pressures to maintain the social order. This increases the likelihood that we will form relationships that cross boundaries of race, class, and sex (Baym & Ledbetter, 2009; Clark, 1998; Giddens, 1993; Mesch & Talmud, 2006; Rawlins, 1992).

▸ Social media makes it very easy to stay connected and maintain our existing relationships. When we are temporarily separated from our friends and loved ones, we can still be together in cyberspace. In addition, we can communicate with our partners whenever it is convenient for us, regardless of the time.

▸ Meeting people online can sometimes be riskier than meeting in person since we don't know whether the "cyber-self" being presented is an accurate reflection of who the person really is. On the other

Lasse Kristensen/Shutterstock.com

that many of us find self-disclosure and feedback easier online (McKenna et al., 2002). In addition, one study found that Americans reported being more honest with family members online than they are in face-to-face encounters (Rainie, Lenhart, Fox, Spooner, & Horrigan, 2000). As we interact online, we also develop new "rites of passage" that signal important relationship transitions. For example, giving your partner the passwords to your social networking pages and e-mail accounts might signal a deepening bond of trust (Gershon, 2010).

We also use digital technology to maintain relationships. Most of our ongoing relationships are characterized by **media multiplexity**, which simply means that we use more than one medium to maintain our relationships. Interestingly, research has found that closer relationships use more media (Haythornthwaite, 2005). Although we are likely to e-mail or call our coworkers, we are more likely to also text and video chat with close friends and family members. We also maintain our relationships using social networking sites (SNS) like Facebook (Gilbert, Karahalois, & Sandvig, 2008; Golder, Wilkinson, & Huberman, 2007).

Finally, not only do we begin, develop, and maintain our relationships online, but we also often use mediated technology to disengage from relationships. Just as we distance ourselves physically in face-to-face relationships, digitally connected partners signal a desire to disengage by exchanging fewer e-mails, texts, and phone calls. For example, Brian began letting phone calls from Ruth go to voice mail rather than picking up. He also began ignoring her e-mails and texts. Ruth, who was not ready to let go of the relationship, began checking Brian's Facebook page more frequently to figure out why he wasn't responding to her messages. Some research suggests that young adults today choose to "break up" using technology rather than by having a face-to-face conversation even though they believe such behavior is inappropriate (Gershon, 2010).

hand, online relationships can also be less risky because we can get to know people at a distance before meeting face-to-face.

When people meet online, they don't experience what we traditionally call interpersonal communication. Rather, they experience **hyperpersonal communication**, which differs from face-to-face interaction in that senders have a greater capacity to strategically manage their self-presentation because nonverbal and relevant contextual cues are more limited (Walther, 1996). As you would expect, they "put their best foot forward." So, hyperpersonal communication receivers are left to fill in the blanks. They do this by assuming that their partner is similar to them and by using implicit personality theory. Thus, partners who begin their relationships online seem to like each other more than partners who first meet face-to-face (Walther, 1996).

TECHNOLOGY AND THE RELATIONSHIP CYCLE

Relationships that begin online show a predictable pattern of adding additional media as they develop, each bringing more nonverbal and contextual cues into play. Partners who meet in an online group, like a class blog, may begin to exchange private e-mails, exchange pictures, then make phone calls, conduct video chats, and finally arrange face-to-face meetings. In one study, over 50 percent of the people who met online had followed this progression through to a face-to-face meeting (McKenna, Green, & Gleason, 2002).

Relationships that begin in face-to-face settings may also use digital technology and social media as the relationship develops. Research suggests, in fact,

hyperpersonal communication online interaction in which senders have a greater capacity to strategically manage their self-presentation because nonverbal and relevant contextual cues are more limited

media multiplexity using more than one medium to maintain relationships

7-5 DIALECTICS IN INTERPERSONAL RELATIONSHIPS

Have you ever felt ambivalent about a relationship? On the one hand, you really wanted to become close to someone, but at the same time you wanted your "space." Or have you met someone who seemed a bit too nosy yet you really wanted to get to know them? Have you ever enjoyed the stability of a long-term relationship, but at the same time longed for the same excitement as when you first met? If so, you were experiencing what scholars call a relational dialectic. A **dialectic** is a tension between conflicting forces. **Relational dialectics** are the competing psychological tensions that exist in any relationship. At any one time, one or both people may be aware of these tensions. Let's take a look at some specific relational dialectics and then discuss some ways to manage these inevitable tensions effectively.

dialectic a tension between conflicting forces

relational dialectics the competing psychological tensions in a relationship

autonomy the desire to do things independent of one's partner

connection the desire to do things and make decisions with one's partner

openness the desire to share intimate ideas and feelings with one's partner

closedness the desire to maintain one's privacy in a relationship

novelty originality, freshness, and uniqueness in a relationship

predictability consistency, reliability, and dependability in a relationship

7-5a Relational Dialectics

Three dialectics common to most relationships are the tugs between autonomy and connection, openness and closedness, and novelty and predictability (Baxter & Montgomery, 1996; Baxter & Braithwaite, 2009; Baxter, 2011). How these tensions are dealt with can alter the stage and life cycle of a relationship.

AUTONOMY/CONNECTION Autonomy is the desire to do things independent of our partner. **Connection** is the desire to link our actions and decisions with our partner. Joel and Shelly have been dating for about a year. At this point in their relationship, Shelly wants to spend most of her free time with Joel and enjoys talking with him before acting or making decisions. Joel, however, has begun to feel stifled. Still he doesn't want to hurt Shelly's feelings or ruin the closeness of their relationship. Shelly is happy with their relationship and doesn't even realize there is any tension. If Joel begins to act autonomously, he may relieve his own tension but at the same time create tension in the relationship.

Bloom Design/Shutterstock.com

OPENNESS/CLOSEDNESS Openness is the desire to share intimate ideas and feelings whereas **closedness** is the desire to maintain privacy. Suppose Joel believes it is important to disclose his intimate feelings to Shelly, and he expects her to do the same. Shelly is a more private person and does disclose to Joel, but not as much as he would like. These differences in preferred levels of self-disclosure are a dialectical tension in their relationship.

NOVELTY/PREDICTABILITY Novelty is the desire for originality, freshness, and uniqueness in our own or our partner's behavior or in the relationship. **Predictability** is the desire for consistency, reliability, and dependability. People experience tension between their desires for novelty and predictability. Because Shelly and Joel have been dating for over a year, much of the uncertainty is gone from their relationship. But they do not want to eliminate uncertainty altogether. With no uncertainty at all, a relationship becomes so predictable and so routine that it is boring. Although Shelly and Joel know each other well, can predict much about each other, and have quite a few routines in their relationship, they also want to be surprised and have new experiences together. Shelly may shock Joel by spontaneously breaking into their favorite song in the middle of the mall. Joel might surprise Shelly by taking her on a "mystery date."

Although our example of Shelly and Joel is an intimate relationship, dialectical tensions exist in all relationships—and they are always in flux. Sometimes these dialectical tensions are active and in the foreground; at other times they are in the background. Nevertheless, when we experience them, they influence the nature of our relationship.

7-5b Managing Dialectical Tensions

How do people satisfy opposing needs at the same time? Four strategies for doing so include temporal selection, topical segmentation, neutralization, and reframing.

Temporal selection is the strategy of choosing one desire and ignoring the other for the time being. Perhaps you and a friend realize that you have spent too much time apart lately (autonomy), so you make a conscious decision to pursue connection. You plan several activities together for a few weeks and then begin to feel that you are spending too much time together. As a result, you start cancelling dates. Seesawing back and forth like this is one way to temporarily manage a relational dialectic.

Topical segmentation is the strategy of choosing certain topics to satisfy one desire and other topics to satisfy the opposite desire. You and your mom may practice openness by sharing your opinions and feelings about certain topics such as school, work, and politics but maintain privacy concerning your sex lives. This segmentation satisfies your needs for balance in the openness/closedness dialectic.

Neutralization is the strategy of compromising between the desires of one person and the desires of the other. Neutralization partially meets the needs of both people but does not fully meet the needs of either. A couple might pursue a moderate level of novelty and spontaneity in their lives, which satisfies both of them. The amount of novelty in the relationship may be less than what one person would ideally want and more than what the other would normally desire, but they have reached a middle point comfortable to both.

Reframing is the strategy of changing your perception about the opposing desires so they no longer seem quite so

Nicoleta Ionescu/Shutterstock.com

contradictory. Maybe you are tense because you perceive that you are more open and your partner is more closed. You might decide to discuss this issue and in doing so begin to realize the times you have also held back (closedness) and you partner was open. After the conversation, you see yourselves as more similar than different on this dialectic. You have reframed your perception of the tension.

In most cases when we are developing, maintaining, or trying to repair a deteriorating relationship, it helps to openly talk with our partner about the tensions we are feeling and come to an agreement about how to manage the dialectic going forward. Sometimes however, partners will be unable to resolve the tensions. In these instances, the relationship may deteriorate or end.

> **temporal selection** the strategy of choosing one desire and ignoring its opposite for a while
>
> **topical segmentation** the strategy of choosing certain topics with which to satisfy one dialectical tension and other topics for its opposite
>
> **neutralization** the strategy of compromising between the desires of the two partners
>
> **reframing** the strategy of changing one's perception about the level of tension

STUDY TOOLS 7

LOCATED IN TEXTBOOK

☐ Tear-out Chapter Review cards at the end of the book

☐ Review with the Quick Quiz on next page

LOCATED ON COMM 4 ONLINE AT CENGAGEBRAIN.COM:

☐ Review Key Term flashcards and create your own cards

☐ Track your knowledge and understanding of key concepts in communication

☐ Complete practice and graded quizzes to prepare for tests

☐ Complete interactive content within COMM4 Online

☐ View the chapter highlight boxes for COMM4 Online

Quick Quiz

T F 1. Sometimes a relationship may deteriorate simply because the partners are not vigilant in doing what is necessary to maintain the relationship at its current level.

T F 2. Decreased communication is an initial sign of relationship decline.

T F 3. Autonomy is the desire to link your actions and decisions with your partner.

T F 4. Originality, freshness, and uniqueness in your own or your partner's behavior or in the relationship is referred to as novelty.

T F 5. Topical segmentation is the strategy of compromising between the desires of one person and the desires of the other.

6. A relationship with people whom you share a high degree of commitment, trust, interdependence, and disclosure is called
   a. platonic.
   b. intimate.
   c. romantic.
   d. impersonal.
   e. professional.

7. An intimate relationship in which the partners are not sexually attracted to each other or do not act on an attraction they feel is called
   a. platonic.
   b. intimate.
   c. romantic.
   d. impersonal.
   e. professional.

8. The Johari window is a tool for examining the
   a. relationship between disclosure and feedback in a relationship.
   b. level of trust in an intimate relationship.
   c. gender difference in communication styles.
   d. strength of a close friendship.
   e. life cycle of a relationship.

9. When romantic relationships turn into friendships, best friends become casual friends, and marriages continue on friendly or business-like terms because of shared values on child-rearing, this is an example of
   a. relationship maintenance.
   b. relationship connection.
   c. relational dialectics.
   d. relationship transformation.
   e. None of the above is correct.

10. Which of the following is a strategy in managing dialectical tensions in relationships?
   a. choosing one desire and ignoring the other for the time being
   b. compromising between the desires of one person and the desires of the other person
   c. changing your perception about the level of tension in the relationship
   d. choosing certain topics to satisfy one desire and other topics to satisfy the opposite desire
   e. All of the above are strategies in managing tensions in relationships.

Answers: 1. T, 2. T, 3. F, 4. T, 5. F, 6. B, 7. A, 8. A, 9. D, 10. E

ONE APPROACH.
70 UNIQUE SOLUTIONS.

www.cengage.com/4ltrpress

8 Interpersonal Communication

LEARNING OUTCOMES

8-1 Compose effective emotional support messages

8-2 Practice direct and indirect strategies for managing privacy and disclosure

8-3 Express your personal desires and expectations assertively

8-4 Manage interpersonal conflict by using an appropriate conflict management style

After finishing this chapter go to **PAGE 107** for **STUDY TOOLS.**

© Andrey Armyagov/Shutterstock.com

In the last chapter, you learned about how we begin, maintain, and end relationships and the dialectical tensions that pull partners between competing desires. As you and your partner interact, you create the communication climate—the overall emotional tone of your relationship—through the messages you exchange (Cissna & Seiberg, 1995). A positive communication climate is one where partners feel valued and supported. We use confirming communication messages to convey that we care about our partner (Dailey, 2006). We can say "you're important to me" and "you matter to me" verbally through skillfully wording our messages. At the same time, we need to avoid disconfirming communication messages, which signal a lack of regard for our partner. In this chapter, we look at how to create confirming messages when we want to (1) respond to a partner who is experiencing emotional distress, (2) share or keep private some of our personal information, (3) express a personal desire or expectation, and (4) resolve a conflict.

8-1 PROVIDING EMOTIONAL SUPPORT

Can you recall a time when you were emotionally distraught? Perhaps someone close to you died unexpectedly, or a romantic partner dumped you, or someone you trusted betrayed you, or a supervisor treated you unfairly. If so, you probably appreciated the emotional support you received from some friends and family members. You can also probably recall times when you've comforted others when they were feeling distressed. **Comforting** is helping others feel better about themselves, their behavior, or their situation by creating a safe space to express their thoughts and feelings. Comforting also helps those doing the comforting by improving self-esteem and their relationship with the person being comforted.

Many people believe that women expect, need, and provide more emotional support than men. However, a growing body of research suggests that both men and women value emotional support from their partners in a variety of relationships, including same-sex friendships, opposite-sex friendships, romantic relationships, and sibling relationships (Burleson, 2003). Providing

emotional support is also generally valued across cultural and co-cultural groups (Burleson, 2003).

8-1a Comforting Guidelines

The following guidelines can help you succeed when providing emotional support.

1. Clarify supportive intentions. When people are experiencing emotional turmoil, they may have trouble trusting the motives of those who want to help. You can clarify your supportive intentions by openly stating that your goal is to help. Notice how David does this:

David: *(noticing Paul sitting in his cubicle with his head in his lap and his hands over his head):* Paul, is everything OK?

Paul: *(sitting up and looking miserable and then defiant):* Like you should care. Yeah, everything is fine.

David: Paul, I do care. You've been working for me for five years. You're one of our best technicians. So if something is going on, I'd like to help, even if all I can do is listen. So what's up?

2. Buffer potential face threats. Face is the perception we want others to have of our worth (Ting-Toomey & Chung, 2012). **Positive face needs** are the desires we have to be appreciated, liked, and valued. **Negative face needs** are the desires we have to be independent and self-sufficient. The very act of providing comfort can threaten your partner's face needs. So effective comforting messages must be buffered to address the other person's positive and negative face needs. When David says to Paul, "You're one of our best technicians," he attends to Paul's positive face need to be valued. When David says that all he can do is listen, he attends to Paul's negative face need for independence.

communication climate the overall emotional tone of your relationship

positive communication climate communication climate in which partners feel valued and supported

confirming communication messages messages that convey that we care about our partner

disconfirming communication messages messages that signal a lack of regard for our partner

comforting helping people feel better about themselves, their behavior, or their situation by creating a safe conversational space where they can express their feelings and work out a plan for the future

face the perception we want others to have of our worth

positive face needs the desire to be appreciated, liked, and honored

negative face needs the desire to be free from imposition and intrusion

© Nikki Zalewski/Shutterstock.com

3. Use other-centered messages. Other-centered messages encourage those feeling emotional distress to talk about what happened and how they feel about it. These messages can come in the form of questions or prods (e.g., uh-huh, wow, I see, go on, tell me more) encouraging others to elaborate. Other-centered messages are the most highly valued type of comforting message among most cultural and co-cultural groups (Burleson, 2003).

4. Reframe the situation. We might **reframe the situation** by offering ideas, observations, information, or explanations that help our partner understand the situation in a different light. To reframe the situation, Abe might remind Travis that he has been putting in many hours of overtime at work and ask Travis if he thinks the heavy work schedule might be cutting into his study time. Or he might suggest that Travis seek help at the tutoring center, a resource many of their mutual friends found helpful. In each case, Abe has provided

> For example, imagine that Travis returns from class and tells his roommate, Abe, "Well, I'm flunking calculus. It doesn't matter how much I study, I just can't get it. I might as well just drop out of school before I flunk out completely. I can ask for a full-time schedule at work and not torture myself with school anymore."

new observations and information that can help Travis reframe the situation.

5. Give advice. We can also **give advice** by presenting relevant suggestions for resolving a problem or situation. You should not give advice, however, until your supportive intentions have been understood, you have attended to your partner's face needs, and you have sustained an other-centered conversation for some time. Even then, always ask permission before offering advice and always acknowledge that your advice is only one suggestion and it's ok if they choose not to follow it.

MANAGING PRIVACY AND DISCLOSURE

As you recall from chapter 7, people in relationships experience dialectical tensions, one of which is the tension between openness and closedness. When we want more openness, we disclose confidential information and feelings. When we want more closedness, we manage privacy to limit what others know about us.

Communication **Privacy Management Theory** describes the decision-making process we go through as we choose whether or not to disclose confidential information about ourselves (self-disclosure) or about others (other-disclosure) (Petronio, 2013). The concept of *privacy* assumes that people *own* their personal information and have the right to control it by determining whether or not to communicate it (Petronio, 2002).

If your partner has your permission to share some of your personal information, then disclosing it to others is unlikely to affect your relationship. However, if you have not given your partner permission to disclose certain information and you expect it to remain between the two of you, then disclosure is likely to damage your relationship.

other-centered messages comforting messages that encourage relational partners to talk about and elaborate on what happened and how they feel about it

reframe the situation offering ideas, observations, information, or alternative explanations that might help a relational partner understand a situation in a different light

give advice presenting relevant suggestions that a person can use to resolve a situation

privacy management theory maintaining confidential or secret information to enhance autonomy or minimize vulnerability

Controlling who has access to your personal information is becoming more complicated with our ever-increasing use of technology. For example, search engines such as Google routinely track our searches. A bug in Apple software recently allowed people to access photos stored on others' personal cell phones (Bilton, 2012). And whenever we post something to a Facebook page, that comment or image can quickly become viral if a friend decides to comment on it or tag it for another network of friends to see. Remember that information posted on the Web has no expiration date. So before you post, you should consider whether the information is something you are comfortable sharing not only with your friends and your friends' friends, but also to potential employers and strangers today and in the future.

Effective communicators choose to disclose or withhold information and feelings based on their relational motive, the situation, and a careful risk–benefit analysis. For example, we may disclose information or feelings to a classmate in an attempt to get to know her better, to a therapist in an attempt to sort out personal issues, or to a coworker we mentor in an attempt to help him make an informed life choice.

One of the most important criteria we use to decide whether to disclose information or keep it private is the risk–benefit analysis. That is, we weigh the advantages we might gain by disclosing or maintaining private information against the disadvantages of doing so. Common benefits of disclosing include building a relationship, coping with stress, and emotional or psychological catharsis. Common benefits of maintaining privacy include control and independence. The risks of disclosing include loss of control, vulnerability, and embarrassment. Risks of maintaining privacy include social isolation and being misunderstood.

8-2a Effects of Disclosure and Privacy on Relationships

Privacy and disclosure decisions affect relationships in three major ways. They affect intimacy level, reciprocity expectations, and information co-ownership.

INTIMACY Because disclosure is the mechanism for increasing intimacy, you might think people move in a clear-cut way toward deeper disclosure as relationships develop. However, people actually move back and forth between periods of choosing to disclose and choosing to maintain privacy (Altman, 1993). We may choose privacy over disclosure to protect the other person's feelings, avoid unnecessary conflict, protect the relationship, or re-establish a boundary of independence (Petronio, 2013).

Social Media Sting

Many young professionals have felt the sting of social media coming back to bite them. More and more, people lose jobs due to inappropriate content posted on public social media sites. Sharing a photo on Facebook with friends may lead to a coworker accidentally sharing the photo with your boss—and you getting fired. This happened to a teacher in Georgia after she shared a photo of herself drinking alcohol on a vacation (Warren, 2011).

As employers become more and more savvy, they are also willing to check out potential employees' social media presence before hiring them. It takes only a simple search to find someone's Facebook page (and all the mischievous wall posts and photos ever tagged), Twitter account (with all the tweets and retweets purposefully and mistakenly sent), and any other public social media profile.

Though some states prohibit employers to require employees to provide access to their personal social media accounts, it is still important to check your posts,

evaluate who sees and shares your activity, and to curate any older content that may show you in an unfavorable light to employers. Despite the laws, employers may still check to see what you do in your spare time.

For example, disclosing an infidelity to a romantic partner may do irreparable damage to the relationship, whereas opting for privacy may actually preserve intimacy (Hendrick, 1981) and avoid conflict (Roloff & Ifert, 2000).

RECIPROCITY Whether your disclosure is matched by similar disclosure from your partner also can affect your relationship. Although you may expect immediate reciprocity, research suggests that there can be a long time lag after one person discloses before the other reciprocates (Dindia, 2000).

INFORMATION CO-OWNERSHIP A third way disclosure and privacy can affect relationships has to do with how partners treat the private information they know about one another. When we disclose private information, the person with whom we share it becomes a co-owner. If a partner shares that confidential information without permission, it is likely to damage the relationship—at least temporarily.

As we rely more and more on technology to develop and maintain relationships, the lines between what is public and what is private are blurring (Kleinman, 2007). For example, we may use mobile phones and Bluetooth technology to carry on even the most private conversations in public spaces. Similarly, when we e-mail a friend, we can't be sure that friend won't forward the message to others. The same problem exists on social networking sites. Once we post information, it is there for others to take and share with anyone.

8-2b Disclosure Guidelines

The following guidelines can help you make wise decisions regarding disclosure when sharing personal information, sharing feelings, and providing feedback.

SHARING PERSONAL INFORMATION When sharing personal information, use the following five strategies:

> **describing feelings** naming the emotions you are feeling without judging them

1. Self-disclose the kind of information you want others to disclose to you. You can determine whether certain information is appropriate to disclose by asking yourself whether you would feel comfortable if the other person were to share similar information with you.

2. Self-disclose private information only when doing so represents an acceptable risk. Some risk is inherent in any self-disclosure. The better you know your partner, the more likely a difficult self-disclosure will be well received.

3. Move gradually to deeper levels of self-disclosure. Because receiving self-disclosure can be as threatening as giving it, most people become uncomfortable when the level of disclosure exceeds their expectations. So we should disclose surface information early in a relationship and more personal information after it has become more intimate (Petronio, 2013).

4. Continue self-disclosing only if it is reciprocated. Although a self-disclosure may not be immediately reciprocated, when it is clearly not being returned you should consider limiting additional self-disclosure. Failure to reciprocate suggests that your partner does not feel comfortable with that level of intimacy.

5. Reserve very personal self-disclosure for ongoing intimate relationships. Disclosures about intimate matters are appropriate in close, well-established relationships. Making intimate self-disclosures before a bond of trust is established risks alienating the other person.

SHARING PERSONAL FEELINGS At the heart of intimate self-disclosure is sharing personal feelings. Doing so demonstrates a bond of trust. Effective communicators share by **describing feelings**. Doing so teaches others how to treat us by explaining how what has happened affects us. For example, if you tell Connor that you enjoy it when he visits you, this description of your feelings should encourage him to visit you again. Likewise, when you tell Charlotte that it bothers you when she borrows your iPad without asking, she may be more likely to ask the next time. To practice describing feelings, follow these three guidelines:

1. Identify what *triggered* the feeling. What did someone specifically say or do?

2. Identify the *specific emotion* you feel as a result. If what you are feeling is similar to anger, try to be more specific. Are you annoyed, betrayed, cheated, crushed, disturbed, furious, outraged, or shocked?

3. Frame your response as an "I" statement. "I" statements help neutralize the impact of an emotional description because they do not imply blame. Be careful, however, not to couch a blaming statement as an "I" statement. For example, "I feel like you don't respect me" is actually a blaming statement because it doesn't let the other person know how you feel (e.g., hurt, angry, betrayed) about what happened.

These two examples describe feelings effectively:

"Thank you for the compliment [trigger]; I [the person having the feeling] feel gratified [the specific feeling] that you noticed my efforts."

"I [the person having the feeling] feel hurt and unappreciated [the specific feelings] when you criticize my cooking after I've worked all afternoon to prepare this meal [trigger]."

PROVIDING PERSONAL FEEDBACK The following three guidelines can help you provide feedback effectively:

1. Describe the specific behavior. As when sharing feelings, be descriptive rather than evaluative and specific rather than vague. Statements like "You're so mean" and "You're a real friend" are ineffective because they are evaluative and vague.

Instead, describe the specific behavior(s) without commenting on appropriateness. What led you to conclude someone was *mean*? Was it something the person said or did? If so, what? Once you identify the specific behaviors, actions, or messages that led to your conclusion, you can share that information as feedback. For example, rather than saying, "You're so mean," you could be more specific by saying, "You called me a liar in front of the team knowing I have no way to prove that I told the truth."

2. Praise positive behavior. Praise is describing the specific positive behavior and its effect on others. Praise is not the same as flattery. When we flatter someone, we use insincere compliments to ingratiate ourselves to that person. Praise compliments are sincere.

To praise effectively, identify the specific behavior you want to reinforce and then describe any positive feelings you or others experienced as a result.

So if your sister, who tends to be forgetful, remembers your birthday, saying something to her like "Thanks for the birthday card; I really appreciate that you remembered my birthday" describes the specific behavior you want to reinforce and the effect it had on you.

3. Give constructive criticism. Although the word *criticize* can mean

judgment, constructive criticism does not condemn but is based on empathy and a sincere desire to help someone understand the impact of his or her behavior. Use the following strategies when providing constructive criticism:

▶ *Ask for permission.* A person who has agreed to hear constructive criticism is more likely to be receptive to it than someone who was not accorded the respect of being asked beforehand.

▶ *Describe the behavior and its consequences precisely.* Your objective description allows the other person to maintain face while receiving accurate feedback about the damaging behavior. For example, DeShawn asks, "What did you think of the visuals I used when I delivered my report?" If you reply, "They weren't very effective," you would be too general and evaluative to be helpful. In contrast, you might say, "Well, the small font size on the first two made it hard for me to read." Notice this constructive criticism does not attack DeShawn's competence. Instead, it describes the font size and its consequences and, in so doing, enables DeShawn to see how to improve.

▶ *Preface constructive criticism with an affirming statement.* Remember, even constructive criticism threatens the innate human need to be liked and admired. So preface constructive criticism with statements that validate your respect for the other person. You could begin your feedback to DeShawn by saying, "First, the chart showing how much energy we waste helped me see just how much we could improve. And the bold colors you

praise describing the specific positive behaviors or accomplishments of another and the effect that behavior has on others

Praise reinforces a specific positive behavior in another person.

© lofoto/Shutterstock.com

used really helped me focus on the main problems. I think using a larger font size on the first two PowerPoint slides would have made it easier for me to see from the back of the room."

▶ *When appropriate, suggest how the person can change the behavior.* Because the goal of constructive criticism is to help, you can do so by providing suggestions that might lead to positive change. In responding to DeShawn's request for feedback, you might also add, "In my communication class, I learned that most people in a small audience should be able to read 18-point font or larger. You might want to give that a try." By including a positive suggestion, you not only help the person by providing useful information, you also show that your intentions are respectful.

8-2c Communication Privacy Management Guidelines

Because reciprocity is a way to develop a relationship, maintaining privacy without damaging the relationship can be difficult. We offer three indirect strategies and one direct strategy you can use when being pressed to disclose something you do not want to share.

INDIRECT STRATEGIES You may choose to maintain privacy by changing the subject, masking your feelings, or practicing strategic ambiguity.

▶ **Change the subject.** Observant partners will recognize changing the subject as a signal that you don't want to disclose.

▶ **Mask feelings.** If you decide that sharing your personal feelings is too risky, you might mask your emotions. For example, Alita masks her feelings of betrayal and embarrassment by laughing along with the others as Manny tells a joke at her expense. On occasion, masking feelings can be an effective strategy. Regularly masking our feelings, however, can create

> For example, as Pat and Eric leave economics class, Pat says to Eric, "I got an 83 on the test, how about you?" If Eric doesn't want to share his grade, he might redirect the conversation by saying, "Hey, that's a B. Good going. Did you finish the homework for calculus?"

health problems, many of which are stress related. We also run the risk of damaging our relationships because our partners won't really know or understand us.

▶ **Practice strategic ambiguity.** You can sometimes be intentionally ambiguous to avoid embarrassment to you or your partner. So when Pat asks Eric about his grade on the test, Eric might respond, "I'm not sure. I got a few tests back this week."

DIRECT STRATEGY Changing the subject, masking feelings, and using strategic ambiguity are indirect ways to maintain privacy and generally work in one-time situations. But these strategies will eventually damage your relationships if used repeatedly. So you might decide to use a more direct approach. *Establishing a* **personal boundary** is a direct approach for responding to people who expect you to disclose information or feelings you prefer to keep private.

To establish a personal boundary, begin by recognizing why you choose not to share the information. For example, when Pat asks Eric about the grade he received on the economics test, Eric may tell Pat he feels uncomfortable sharing. Then identify your privacy policy that guided this decision. Eric, who has been teased for getting good grades, has developed a rule that he does not disclose the grades he receives. Next, preface your personal boundary statement with an apology or other face-saving statement. Eric might tell Pat that he values the fact that Pat is interested in Eric's achievement. Finally, form an "I"-centered message that briefly establishes a boundary. For example, Eric might reply to Pat's question like this:

personal boundary
The way we respond to others who expect disclosure of personal information or feelings we wish to keep private

When we mask our feelings too often we can damage relationships.

© Yevhen Vitte/Shutterstock.com

"I'm sorry. I know that everyone's different, and I don't mean to be rude, but I'm not comfortable sharing my grades. It's been my policy not to ask other people about their grades or to discuss my own ever since getting teased about grades when I was a kid. I value you and our friendship and hope my policy doesn't offend you."

Phrasing his response this way lets Pat know that Eric's decision is based on a personal boundary rule rather than an indication of his trust in Pat or their relationship.

8-3 EXPRESSING DESIRES AND EXPECTATIONS

Even two people in a mutually satisfying, intimate relationship have different needs, desires, and expectations (Alberti & Emmons, 2008). How they choose to express them to their partner will affect the relationship's communication climate. Let's look at four such communication styles and how each can affect the climate of a relationship.

8-3a Passive Communication Style

A **passive communication style** is submitting to another's demands while concealing one's own desires and expectations. For example, Aaron and Katie routinely go to the gym at 10 a.m. on Saturday mornings. However, Aaron's Friday work schedule has recently changed and now he doesn't get home until 3 a.m. on Saturdays. Aaron behaves passively if he doesn't say anything to Katie and drags himself out of bed even though he'd much rather sleep. We tend to choose a passive approach when we value our relationship with the other person more than we value asserting our own particular need. If used habitually, however, passive communication will eventually damage the relationship because we will begin to resent our partner as we continually ignore our own needs, desires, and expectations.

8-3b Aggressive Communication Style

An **aggressive communication style** is attacking another person's self-concept and/or expressing personal hostility in order to inflict psychological pain (Rancer & Avtgis, 2006). Verbally aggressive messages disregard a partner's right to

be treated with dignity and respect. Examples of aggressive communication range from yelling, badgering, and name calling to sarcasm, put-downs, and taunting. Suppose Aaron continues to meet Katie at the gym on Saturdays at 10 a.m. without telling her about his work schedule change. If Katie suggests they meet at 8 a.m. next week, Aaron may explode and aggressively reply, "No way! We always do what you want when you want. I'm sick of it. You are so selfish and inconsiderate. In fact, I don't care if I ever work out on Saturday again!" Katie, who has no context for understanding this aggressive outburst, may be startled, hurt, and confused. People may use verbal aggression when they perceive themselves to be powerful, do not value the other person, lack emotional control, or feel defensive. Studies have found that verbally aggressive messages can lead to less satisfying relationships, family violence, divorce, and loss of credibility (Hample, 2003). The term **cyberbullying** describes the increasingly prevalent use of technology to convey verbally aggressive messages (Kleinman, 2007).

8-3c Passive-Aggressive Communication Style

A **passive-aggressive communication style** is expressing hostility indirectly. For example, you may say yes when you want to say no or complain about others behind their backs. For example, suppose Aaron apologizes for his outburst and then tells Katie about his work schedule change. Although Katie claims to accept the apology and

passive communication style when one does not express personal preferences or defend their rights to others

aggressive communication style when one belligerently or violently confronts others with preferences, feelings, needs, or rights with little regard for the preferences or rights of the other

cyberbullying increasingly prevalent use of technology to convey verbally aggressive messages

passive-aggressive communication style when one submits to others' demands and conceals their own preferences while indirectly expressing hostility toward their partner

tells Aaron "It's no big deal," the next week she doesn't call him and instead goes alone to the gym. When Aaron shows up and asks for an explanation, Katie shrugs her shoulders and says, "Well I thought you said you were sick of always doing things 'my way.'" Over time, passive-aggressive behavior damages relationships because it undercuts mutual respect.

8-3d Assertive Communication Style

An **assertive communication style** uses messages that describe personal needs, rights, desires, and expectations honestly and directly in ways that also demonstrate respect and value for you, your partner, and the relationship.

An effective assertive message (1) describes the behavior or event as objectively as possible, (2) proposes your interpretation of it, (3) names the feeling you have as a result, (4) identifies potential consequences for you, your partner, or others, and (5) suggests your intentions regarding how you will act and/or what you expect in the future. For example, Aaron could have assertively responded to Katie's suggestion to go to the gym at 8 a.m. like this:

"I understand that you want to work out at 8 a.m. starting next week (description). I am guessing you want more time to run errands, do chores, or study (interpretation). But the thought of working out at 8 a.m. frustrates me (feeling) because my work schedule changed and I don't even get home until 3 a.m. I can't imagine having the energy to exercise at 8 a.m. (consequence). But I really like working out together and would like to keep doing so on Saturdays. So maybe we could start at 9 a.m. instead, or you could start earlier and I could join you at 9 a.m. (intention)."

Notice how Aaron honestly and directly communicates his desires in confirming ways that demonstrate respect for Katie and his relationship with her.

assertive communication style when one expresses personal preferences and defends his or her rights to others while respecting the preferences and rights of their partner

interpersonal conflict an expressed struggle between two interdependent people who perceive incompatible goals, scarce resources, and interference from the other in achieving their goals

8-3e Cultural and Co-Cultural Considerations

Assertiveness is typically valued in individualistic cultures, such as in the United States, where direct communication is preferred. However, this style is not necessarily the norm across the world (Holt & DeVore, 2005). For example, collectivist cultures such as China and Japan, which value accord and harmony, may tend to prefer passive behavior (Samovar, Porter, & McDaniel, 2012). In fact, those who abide by traditional collectivist norms may even find what North Americans interpret as appropriate assertive communication to be rude and insensitive (Alberti & Emmons, 2008).

Co-cultural groups within the United States may also prefer different communication styles. For example, females who have been socialized to embrace feminine gender norms are likely to use passive or passive-aggressive communication styles (Hess & Hagen, 2006). Numerous books and workshops exist to help women learn to replace passive and passive-aggressive communication styles with assertive ones. Similarly, males who embrace masculine gender norms tend to use aggressive communication styles and likewise benefit from replacing them with assertive styles.

Although differences exist across cultures and co-cultures, the distinctions are becoming less dramatic. Nevertheless, when talking with people whose cultural or co-cultural norms differ from your own, you may need to observe their behavior and their responses to your statements before you can be sure about how best to communicate your needs, rights, desires, and expectations.

8-4 MANAGING INTERPERSONAL CONFLICT

Interpersonal conflict is an expressed struggle between two interdependent people who perceive incompatible goals, scarce resources, and interference from the other in achieving their goals (Wilmot & Hocker, 2010). Let's untangle this definition. To be an *expressed struggle*, both people

© Ostill/Shutterstock.com

must be aware of the disagreement. To be *interdependent*, achieving a satisfactory outcome for each person depends on the actions of the other. By *perceived incompatible goals* we mean that both people believe they have something to lose if the other person gets his/her way. *Perceived scarce resources* assumes that there isn't enough of something to go around and *perceived interference* is the belief that the other person is forcing us to do or not to do something. For example, when sixteen-year-old Darla's mother (interdependence) told her she should not waste money (scarce resources) on a tattoo (perceived interference), she claimed that Darla would regret having the tatoo when she grew up (perceived incompatible goals)—resulting in an argument (expressed struggle). In conflicts such as this, participants have choices about how they communicate with each other to manage and, hopefully, resolve the situation.

Conflict is not necessarily a bad thing. In fact, conflict is a natural part of interpersonal relationships and, when managed effectively, can actually strengthen them (Cupach & Canary, 1997). When managed ineffectively, however, conflict can hurt people and relationships (Brake, Walker, & Walker, 1995). The consequences of poorly managed conflict can be particularly devastating when communicating across cultures (Ting-Toomey, 2006). In this section, we discuss five conflict management styles and how to skillfully initiate and respond to conflict situations that arise in your relationships. These five styles are avoiding, accommodating, competing, compromising, and collaborating (Thomas, 1976; Thomas & Kilmann, 1978; Thomas, 1992). Figure 8.1 is a visual representation of these styles as they relate to assertiveness and cooperativeness.

8-4a Avoiding (Lose–Lose)

Avoiding involves physically or psychologically removing yourself from the conflict. It is both unassertive and uncooperative and is typically characterized as a lose–lose approach. Avoiding may be appropriate when hot tempers need to cool down or when either the issue or the relationship isn't important to us. For instance, imagine Eduardo and Justina get into an argument about their financial situation. Eduardo may say, "I don't want to talk about this" and walk out the door. Or he may psychologically withdraw by simply ignoring Justina. We risk damaging our relationships when avoidance becomes a habit because it doesn't deal with or resolve the conflict; instead, avoidance usually makes the conflict more difficult to deal with later on.

8-4b Accommodating (Lose–Win)

Accommodating is satisfying the needs or accepting the opinions of our partner while neglecting our own needs or

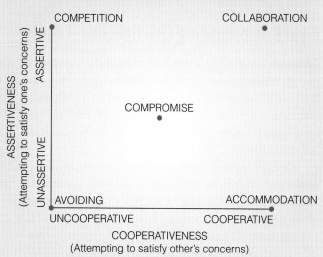

FIGURE 8.1 CONFLICT MANAGEMENT STYLES

opinions. It is unassertive and cooperative and is typically characterized as a lose–win approach. Accommodating may be appropriate when the issue is not important to us, but the relationship is. For instance, Anthony doesn't particularly enjoy romantic movies but knows Marianne has her heart set on seeing *The Vow*. He suggests going to see it because he doesn't really care which movie they see and he wants to please her because he values his relationship with her.

8-4c Competing (Win–Lose)

Competing is satisfying our own needs or desires with little or no concern for others' desires or for our relationships. It is assertive and uncooperative and is typically characterized as a win–lose approach. Competing may be appropriate when quick and decisive action must be taken to ensure your own or another's welfare or safety. For example, Prabhakar knows that, statistically speaking, the likelihood of death or serious injury increases dramatically if one does not wear a helmet when riding a motorcycle. So he insists that his sister wear one when she rides with him.

If one partner uses competing and the other responds by avoiding or accommodating, the conflict may seem to have resolved even though it has not. And if both partners engage in competing, the conflict is likely to escalate. Finally, although competing may result in getting your way, when you use it

avoiding physically or psychologically removing oneself from the conflict

accommodating managing conflict by satisfying others' needs or accepting others' ideas while neglecting our own

competing satisfying our own needs or with little or no concern for others' needs or for the harm it may do to our relationships

repeatedly it will usually hurt your partner and damage the relationship.

8-4d Compromising (Partial Lose–Lose)

Compromising occurs when each partner gives up part of what they desire to satisfy part of what their partner wants. It is partially assertive and cooperative and is typically characterized as a partial lose–lose approach. Neither partner is completely satisfied, but it seems to be the best solution either can hope for.

Compromising may be appropriate when the issue is moderately important, when there are time constraints, when doing so will buy credits for future negotiations, and when attempts at collaborating have not been successful. For example, if Heather and Zachary need to meet outside of class to complete a class project but both have busy schedules, they may compromise to meet at a time that isn't ideal for either of them but which they can both live with.

8-4e Collaborating (Win–Win)

Collaborating occurs when people work through the problem together to discover a mutually acceptable solution. It is assertive and cooperative and is typically characterized as a win–win approach. Collaborating may be appropriate when the issue is too important for a compromise, when the relationship is important, and when we want to come up with a creative solution to a problem. We collaborate by discussing the issues, describing feelings, and identifying the characteristics of a solution that will satisfy everyone. For example, Fadi really wants to vacation alone with Aliana, but Aliana wants to invite their friends, Greg and Shelly. Aliana may explain how she thinks that vacationing with friends would lower the cost of the trip. Fadi may describe his desire to have "alone time" with Aliana. As they discuss their vacation goals, they arrive at a plan that meets both of their needs. For example, they may decide to vacation alone, but camp rather than stay in hotels

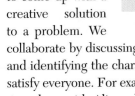

compromising managing conflict by giving up part of what you want to provide at least some satisfaction for both parties

collaborating managing conflict by fully addressing the needs and issues of each party and arriving at a solution that is mutually satisfying

to lower their expenses. Or they may share a condo with their friends, but schedule alone time each day.

8-4f Collaboration Guidelines

Follow these guidelines when using collaboration to resolve a conflict:

▶ **Identify and own the problem.** "Hi, I'm trying to study and I need your help."

▶ **Describe the problem in terms of behavior, consequences, and feelings.** "When I hear your music, I listen to it instead of studying, and then I get frustrated and behind schedule."

▶ **Refrain from blaming or accusing.** "I know you aren't trying to ruin my study time and are just enjoying your music."

▶ **Find common ground.** "I would guess that you have had times when you became distracted from something you needed to do, so I'm hoping that you can help me out by lowering the volume a bit."

▶ **Mentally rehearse so that you can state your request briefly.**

It is more difficult to collaborate when you have to respond to a conflict that someone initiates in a confrontational manner. But you can shape the conversation toward collaboration by following these guidelines:

▶ **Disengage.** Avoid a defensive response by emotionally disengaging. Remember, your partner has a problem and you want to help.

▶ **Respond with genuine concern.** Sometimes your partner needs to vent before being ready to problem solve: "I can see that you're angry. Tell me about it."

▶ **Paraphrase and ask questions.** "Is it the volume of my music or the type of music that is making it difficult for you to study?"

▶ **Seek common ground.** "I can understand that you would be upset about losing precious study time."

▶ **Ask for alternative solutions.** "Can you give me a couple of ideas about how we could resolve this so your study is more effective?"

Collaboration may be appropriate when we want to come up with a creative solution to a problem.

STUDY TOOLS 8

LOCATED IN TEXTBOOK

☐ Tear-out Chapter Review cards at the end of the book

☐ Review with the Quick Quiz below

LOCATED ON COMM 4 ONLINE AT CENGAGEBRAIN.COM:

☐ Review Key Term flashcards and create your own cards

☐ Track your knowledge and understanding of key concepts in communication

☐ Complete practice and graded quizzes to prepare for tests

☐ Complete interactive content within COMM4 Online

☐ View the chapter highlight boxes for COMM4 Online

Quick Quiz

T F 1. Negative face needs are the desires to be free from imposition and intrusion.

T F 2. The use of technology to develop and maintain relationships is impacting people's decisions about what to disclose and what to keep private.

T F 3. In a crowded line, your friend accidentally bumps into a man's wife. The man proceeds to yell at your friend for being inconsiderate. The man has an assertive communication style.

T F 4. When sharing personal feelings, it is most appropriate to begin with the "trigger" and follow with a "feeling."

T F 5. Flattery is described as disclosing a specific positive behavior or accomplishment of another person and the effect that behavior has on others.

6. _____ means helping people feel better about themselves, their behavior, or their situation by creating a safe conversational space where they can express their feelings and work out a plan for the future.

    a. Encouraging

    b. Buffering

    c. Advising

    d. Welcoming

    e. Comforting

7. Which of the following is considered a direct communication strategy that you can use when being pressed to disclose something that you are not comfortable sharing?

    a. giving a vague answer

    b. changing the subject

    c. masking your feelings

    d. telling a white lie

    e. setting a boundary

8. A straight-faced poker player whose expression is impossible to decipher has become a master of

    a. self-disclosure.

    b. rapport-talk.

    c. report-talk.

    d. masking feelings.

    e. managing privacy.

9. A(n) _____ person has the skill to stand up for himself or herself in interpersonally effective ways.

    a. passive

    b. assertive

    c. aggressive

    d. accommodating

    e. passive-aggressive

10. When people submit to others' demands even when it is inconvenient, against their best interests, or violates their rights, it is considered

    a. passive behavior.

    b. passive-aggressive behavior.

    c. assertive behavior.

    d. aggressive behavior.

    e. assertive-aggressive behavior.

Answers: 1.T, 2.T, 3.F, 4.F, 5.F, 6.E, 7.E, 8.D, 9.B, 10.A

9 Communicating in Groups

LEARNING OUTCOMES

9-1 Identify different types of groups

9-2 Analyze the characteristics of healthy groups

9-3 Understand how groups develop

9-4 Describe the nature of conflict in groups

After finishing this chapter go to **PAGE 121** for **STUDY TOOLS.**

© xuanhuongho/Shutterstock.com

group a collection of about three to 20 people who interact and attempt to influence each other to accomplish a common purpose

group communication all the verbal and nonverbal messages shared among members of the group

We all belong to many formal and informal groups. Although each group has different purposes one thing all groups have in common is that their effectiveness depends on communication. In fact, year after year, surveys conducted by the National Association of Colleges and Employers report "the ability to work well in groups" is one of the top ten skills sought in college graduates. Unfortunately, however, very few students actually graduate from college with any formal training in how to communicate effectively in groups.

In this chapter and the one that follows, we discuss how groups function and how to communicate most effectively within them. We begin by defining the nature and types of different groups, as well as some of the communication challenges you are likely to face when interacting in each of them. Then we describe key characteristics of healthy groups and the stages of development groups often follow over the course of their existence. We end this chapter with a discussion about conflict in groups and provide guidelines for managing conflict effectively.

9-1 THE NATURE AND TYPES OF GROUPS

Take a moment to think about the groups of people you interact with consistently. Examples may range from student clubs to friendship groups to family groups to study groups to online networking groups. What makes each of these a group rather than a mere assembly of people? A **group** is a collection of about three to 20 people who feel a sense of belonging and attempt to influence each other to accomplish a common purpose. **Group communication**, which consists of all the verbal and nonverbal messages shared among members, is what makes participating in groups a positive or negative experience. Let's look at some of the most common group types and the role communication plays in them.

9-1a Families

A **family** is a group of intimates who, through their communication, generate a sense of home, group identity, history, and future (Segrin & Flora, 2014). Families can be nuclear (consisting of two parents who live together with their biological or adopted children), single parent (consisting of one adult living with his or her children), extended (consisting of a parent or parents and children living with grandparents, cousins, aunts and uncles, or other relatives), blended (consisting of committed or married adults living with the children of their previous marriages and relationships as well as perhaps the children of their union), as well as unrelated by either blood or marriage (Galvin, Braithwaite, & Bylund, 2015).

Research suggests that families typically function using one of four family communication patterns (Koerner & Fitzpatrick, 2006). In *protective families*, issues are not discussed and are decided solely by the family authority figure. In the movie *The Sound of Music*, prior to Maria's arrival, the Von Trapp family exemplified this family dynamic. In *consensual families*, all members engage in conversation about an issue but a family authority figure still makes the final decision. Many television sitcoms from the 1950s, '60s, and '70s, such as

Father Knows Best, Leave It to Beaver, and *The Brady Bunch*, portray families with a benevolent and self-sacrificing father filling this role. In *pluralistic families*, all members engage in conversation about an issue and everyone participates in the decision making. These families may have formal family meetings to decide important family issues. The popular 1980s television sitcom *Full House*, in which three men raised children together, operated as a pluralistic family. Finally, in *laissez-faire families*, members may converse about an issue, but each member makes his or her own decision and is responsible for its consequences. The cartoon family portrayed on *The Simpsons* tends to function this way.

We initially learn how to communicate in groups based on how our family members communicated with each other while we were growing up. Healthy family communication builds self-concept and self-esteem through messages of (1) praise (e.g., "awesome job on that painting"), (2) acceptance (e.g., "whether you decide to go to college or get a full-time job, just know that we support you"), and (3) love (e.g., "I love you no matter what"). Unfortunately, however, not all families engage in healthy communication.

> **family** a group of intimates who through their communication generate a sense of home and group identity, history, and future

9-1b Social Groups

social group a group consisting of friends who have a genuine concern about each other's welfare and enjoy spending time together

support group a group consisting of people who come together to provide encouragement, honest feedback, and a safe environment for expressing deeply personal feelings about a problem common to the members

interest group a group consisting of individuals who come together because they share a common hobby, or activity

A **social group** is composed of people who genuinely care about each other's welfare and enjoy spending time together. Most of us belong to more than one social group. You may have had a group of friends you were close to in high school, a group of buddies you were close to when you served in the military, or a group of friends you play golf or softball with regularly. Sometimes people who work together evolve into a social group when they begin to get together for social activities outside of work. Popular TV programs such as *New Girl*, *Unbreakable Kimmy Schmidt*, and *Big Bang Theory* provide examples of social groups.

Because social groups fill our needs to be accepted and to belong, communication in these groups should (1) encourage quieter members to participate in conversations ("Hey Jules, you haven't had a chance to catch us up on how your Dad is doing"); (2) protect members from playful harassment ("Hey Jenna, back off, you've been picking on Pam all evening"); and (3) provide opportunities for friends to disclose problems and receive support ("Hey, Zach, I heard that your sister was in a bad accident. How's she doing?").

9-1c Support Groups

A **support group** is composed of people who come together to provide encouragement, honest feedback, and a safe environment for expressing deeply personal feelings about a problem common to the members. Support groups include addiction recovery groups such as AA (Alcoholics Anonymous), grief counseling support groups, survivor or caregiver support groups, and abuse recovery groups such as the ASCA (Adult Survivors of Child Abuse). Until recently, support groups only met face-to-face, but today thousands of online support groups also connect people who have never met face-to-face.

Support group members need to feel safe in disclosing highly personal information. So members need to make sure that their messages follow guidelines for comforting (see chapter 8), which include clarifying supportive intentions, buffering face threats, using other-centered language, framing, and selectively offering advice.

9-1d Interest Groups

An **interest group** is composed of individuals who come together because they share a common interest, hobby, or activity. These groups may be formal with defined goals and tasks (such as a 4-H club or community theater troupe) or they may be informal (like a neighborhood book or gardening club). They may be part of a larger organization like La Raza, the Urban League, or the Houston Area Apple Users Group. Some interest groups are externally focused on a common political or social issue and adopt an agenda to achieve change. MADD (Mothers Against Drunk Driving) is an example. Other interest groups are internally focused on increasing members' skills or knowledge. Toastmasters, for instance, helps its members improve their public speaking skills. Some interest groups meet online. Meetup.com is an Internet site that helps people find others who share their interests.

Because interest group members share some passion, all members ought to have an opportunity to communicate their expertise by (1) encouraging members to share

We learn group communication skills based on how our family members communicated with each other in our formative years.

Social Support Groups Thrive Online

Online outlets for co-cultural groups can be a good thing (Pascoe, 2008). One example is the vast online community of gay, lesbian, bisexual, and transgendered (GLBT) teenagers. These teens, who can have a difficult time finding friends or dates in their physical communities, can easily find other GLBT teenagers online on sites like the It Gets Better project (http://www.itgetsbetter.org). The site was originally created by syndicated columnist and author Dan Savage in response to a rash of bullying-related suicides among GLBT youth. It Gets Better provides a place where GLBT youth and adults and their friends can come together to share their stories without judgment and find support from other members, showing that the Internet can be a place where healthy groups can be created.

© LEE SNIDER PHOTO IMAGES/Shutterstock.com

success stories ("I'm really glad that Brian was able to get Ace Hardware to donate all the bathroom fixtures for our project. Brian, can you tell us what you said and did?") and (2) allowing all members to highlight what they know without demeaning the knowledge or opinions of others ("I really liked hearing Brian's story and I'd like to know how other people approach getting donations.").

9-1e Service Groups

A **service group** is composed of individuals who come together to perform hands-on charitable works or to raise money to help organizations that perform such work. Service groups may be local affiliates of larger secular or religious organizations like Lions Club International, the Red Cross, the Salvation Army, and Habitat for Humanity. Other service groups are local and function independently. Examples include small soup kitchens and community beautification groups.

Because service groups are both voluntary and task-oriented, they need to be dedicated to the task as well as sensitive to the emotional needs of members. So communication should (1) be clear about individual tasks, roles, and responsibilities ("Jim, as I recall, you agreed to work on patching the roof"); (2) encourage and praise member accomplishments ("I was really impressed with how sensitive you were when you said no to her"); and (3) be polite ("Mary, thank you so much for pitching in to stuff envelopes today. I could not have finished the job without your help.")

9-1f Work Groups

A **work group** is a collection of three or more people formed to complete a task. A **work group team** is a subset of a work group where members also hold themselves mutually accountable. Examples of work group teams include class project groups (established to create a joint presentation, paper, or other learning project) and workplace teams (established as needed to perform specific activities in the workplace). Effective work group teams have an appropriate number of members with diverse skills and viewpoints, clearly defined goals, and explicit roles and rules for members (Katzenbach & Smith, 2003).

What is the best size for a work group team? In general, the ideal size for most work group teams is five to seven members (Myers and Anderson, 2008). However, the best size is the smallest number of people capable of effectively achieving the goal (Beebe and Masterson, 2014). As the size of the group increases, discussion time also increases. Smaller groups can make decisions more quickly than larger ones. If the goals and issues are complex, however, a group with more members is more likely to have the breadth of information, knowledge, and skills needed to make high-quality decisions.

Effective work group teams also consist of people who offer different but relevant knowledge and skills (Valacich, George,

service group a group consisting of individuals who come together to perform hands-on charitable works or to raise money to help organizations that perform such work

work group a collection of three or more people formed to solve a problem

work group team a subset of a work group where members also hold themselves mutually accountable

CrossFit is an organization for people interested in developing broad, general, and inclusive fitness through high-intensity workouts. These groups meet in smaller gyms called "boxes" all over the world.

© Kjetil Kolbjørnsrud/Shutterstock.com

motivate the group to work toward achieving it (Johnson & Johnson, 2003). Effective work group team goals meet four important criteria (see box "Effective Work Group Team Goals").

Work group teams should develop explicit member roles and rules (Katz & Koenig, 2001). Because the goals of work group teams are typically quite challenging, all members must understand and perform their specific roles for the group to succeed (LaFasto & Larson, 2001). These roles and rules are always discussed and sometimes even written down in a formal or informal contract.

Most work group team communication focuses on task-related issues and should (1) update other members on the status of individual efforts ("I thought you all should know that I will

Nonamaker, & Vogel, 1994). A **heterogeneous group** is usually better than a **homogeneous group**. In homogeneous groups, members are likely to know the same things and come at the problem from the same perspective; consequently, they are likely to overlook some important information or take shortcuts in the problem-solving process. In contrast, heterogeneous groups are more likely to have diverse information, perspectives, and values; consequently, they tend to thoroughly discuss issues before reaching a decision. For example, a medical group composed of seven nurses who are all young white females would be considered a homogeneous group; a medical group composed of nurses, doctors, nutritionists, and physical therapists of different ages, races, and sexes would be considered a heterogeneous group. The heterogeneous medical group would probably make a more comprehensive decision about a patient's care than the homogeneous group of nurses.

WORK GROUP TEAM GOALS What are the elements of an effective work group team goal? An effective **work group team goal** is a clearly stated objective desired by enough members to

heterogeneous group a group in which various demographics, levels of knowledge, attitudes, and interests are represented

homogeneous group a group in which members have a great deal of similarity

work group team goal a future state of affairs desired by enough members to motivate the group to work toward its achievement

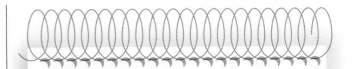

Effective Work Group Team Goals

1. **Effective goals are specific.** For example, the crew at a local fast-food restaurant set the specific goal: "During the next quarter, the crew will increase profitability by reducing food costs by 1 percent. They will do so by throwing away less food due to precooking."

2. **Effective goals serve a common purpose.** Achieving one goal must not prevent achieving another. For the fast-food crew, all members must believe that reducing the amount of precooked food on hand will not hinder their current level of service.

3. **Effective goals are challenging.** Achieving them will require hard work and team effort.

4. **Effective goals are shared.** People tend to support things they help create. So group members who participate in setting the goals are likely to exert high effort to achieve them as well.

be about two days late with that feasibility report because the person providing me with the cost data is on vacation"); (2) appropriately credit the contributions of other team members ("Today I am presenting the conclusions, but Len did the initial research and Mavis did the quantitative analysis that led to them"); (3) keep the discussion focused on the task ("Georgia, let's talk more about your party after the meeting, ok?"); and (4) seek collaboration to resolve conflicts ("Felicia, I'm stuck and I really need your help").

9-1g Virtual Groups

Until recently, group communication occurred almost exclusively in face-to-face settings. A **virtual group** is a group whose members "meet" via technological media from different physical locations. We can interact with our families, social friendship groups, support groups, interest groups, service groups, and work group teams from different physical locations through e-mail, teleconferences, and videoconferences; online social networks such as LinkedIn, Facebook, Instagram, and

FIGURE 9.1	TYPES OF VIRTUAL GROUPS
Type of Group	**Description**
Computer conferences (threaded discussions)	Asynchronous virtual forums in which comments related to an issue are organized by topic and available for all group members to read and comment upon
Online social networks	Internet sites that focus on building social relationships among people who share interests, activities, and backgrounds
Teleconferences	Multiperson telephone meetings using telephone conferencing technology
Video chats	Synchronous informal meetings using personal computer video capabilities
Videoconferences	Synchronous formal meetings using video conferencing technology provided at various sites

Twitter; and other technologies (Timmerman & Scott, 2006). We can also use technology to form groups without ever meeting other members in person.

Because these technologies have changed the communication landscape, and are continuing to do so, research about how communication functions in them is still in its youth. We do know, however, that while effective **virtual group communication** follows the same fundamental principles as effective communication in face-to-face groups it is also unique in several ways. Technology makes virtual group communication possible (1) at the same time and location, (2) at the same time but from different locations, (3) at different times but from the same location, and (4) at different times and from different locations (Becker-Beck, Wintermantel, & Borg, 2005). Teleconferences and videoconferences are examples of virtual group communication taking place in **real time**, which means at the same time. Communication in videoconferences most closely resembles group communication in face-to-face settings because participants can interact using both verbal and nonverbal messages. By contrast, virtual group communication that occurs on social networking sites, blogs, and Web sites takes place at the same location (on a particular Internet page) but not necessarily at the same time. Virtual group communication that occurs via e-mail typically occurs at different times; a group member can send a message and wait hours or days before getting a reply.

9-1h Mediated Communication and Virtual Groups

Have you ever participated in a threaded online discussion? Perhaps you have done so as part of a course requirement or as part of a work team. Or have you ever held a three-way telephone conversation with your friends to decide where to go on a Friday night? If so, you have been part of a virtual group. There are several types of virtual groups, as illustrated in Figure 9.1.

Virtual groups and virtual group meetings have become popular for a number of reasons. First, members need not be physically present to communicate. Before these technologies, group members had to meet face-to-face to exchange information or make a decision. But today, group members can interact while in different cities, states, and countries. Second, asynchronous virtual

virtual group a group whose members "meet" via technological media from different physical locations

virtual group communication communication that occurs in virtual groups

real time at the same time

groups allow people to participate across time. Busy people often struggle to find a meeting time that works with everyone's schedule. So a group can "meet" and communicate using a threaded discussion instead. Third, virtual meetings can save money. Before these technologies, meeting participants often had to travel to a meeting site, which can be expensive. Because virtual group meetings can be conducted over the phone or Internet, meeting costs can be reduced for both participants and hosts.

These benefits also come with potential costs. For example, research has found that communication problems can impact both task and relationship outcomes (Andres, 2002). Face-to-face groups are often more dedicated to task (Olsen & Teasley, 1996), and the rich communication environment leads to more effective interactions and results than virtual teams. Face-to-face groups are also better at maintenance functions. They are more cohesive (Huang, Wei, Watson, & Tan, 2003), have stronger social ties (Warkentin, Sayeed, & Hightower, 1997), and are more dedicated to other team members (Olsen & Teasley, 1996).

Because the use of virtual groups is becoming increasingly common in both education and industry, improving virtual group communication can increase work quality and member satisfaction. We offer several guidelines for doing so.

1. Use the richest form of technology available. While e-mails and threaded discussions allow people the freedom to communicate at their own convenience, these technologies also convey the fewest social nonverbal cues. When possible, try to meet via videoconference to both see and hear the other group members.

2. Make sure all members are both equipped and trained to use the technology. Don't assume that all members know how to use the technology or are aware of all of its capabilities. Although this is crucial for virtual work groups and teams, it is equally important for any group that chooses to meet online.

3. Create opportunities for group members to become acquainted, develop and maintain social bonds, and build trust. Just as members of face-to-face groups take time to socialize and get to know one another, so should members of groups take time to do so when meeting virtually.

What are some specific communication strategies you should follow when meeting virtually?

4. Develop ground rules. Because misunderstandings can abound when communicating via technology, virtual groups will operate most effectively when rules for communicating are set up at the outset. These rules are often referred to as **netiquette**. They may include, for example, being courteous and respectful, being attentive and focused (e.g., not checking e-mail during the meeting), using emoticons and imogees, keeping messages short, and being patient with new users (Shoemaker-Galloway, 2007).

5. Create regular opportunities to evaluate the technology and use of it. Regularly scheduled surveys of group members can identify emerging problems some members may be experiencing in order to correct them before they undermine the group's goals.

Now that we have illustrated some different types of groups and the role communication plays in them, let's turn to a discussion of the similarities among healthy groups regardless of type.

9-2 CHARACTERISTICS OF HEALTHY GROUPS

Healthy groups are formed around a constructive purpose and are characterized by ethical goals, interdependence, cohesiveness, productive norms, accountability, and synergy.

9-2a Healthy Groups Have Ethical Goals

Sometimes the actual goal of a group is unethical; other times, fulfilling the goal would require some or all group members to behave in unethical ways. For example,

netiquette etiquette rules users follow when communicating over computer networks

healthy group a group formed around a constructive purpose and characterized by ethical goals, interdependence, cohesiveness, productive norms, accountability, and synergy

criminal gangs can be highly effective but unethical groups. They may make lots of money, but at the expense of society at large and often by risking the welfare of members. By contrast, healthy groups have goals that benefit both members and the larger society. Fulfilling these goals may require sacrifice and hard work, but accomplishing them does not depend on illegal or unethical behavior.

9-2b Healthy Groups Are Interdependent

In **interdependent groups**, members rely on each other's skills and knowledge to accomplish the ultimate group goal(s). One concrete way to understand interdependence is to observe a musical group—a symphony orchestra, for instance. One reason the music we hear is so beautiful is not only because the various instruments sound different but because the parts in the musical score for each instrument are well-balanced with each other. If any of the musicians did not perform their part well, the beautiful sound would be compromised. Likewise, in any group, if one person tries to do all the work, or if anyone performs poorly,

or if everyone does the same task while others are left unattended, then that group is not interdependent and will consequently be ineffective.

9-2c Healthy Groups Are Cohesive

Cohesiveness is the force that brings group members closer together (Eisenberg, 2007). In a highly cohesive group, members genuinely respect each other and work cooperatively to reach the group's goals (Evans & Dion, 1991). Because cohesiveness is such an important characteristic of healthy groups, many newly formed groups often engage in **team-building activities** designed to build rapport and develop trust among members (Midura

> **interdependent group** a group in which members rely on each other's skills and knowledge to accomplish the group goals
>
> **cohesiveness** the force that brings group members closer together
>
> **team-building activities** activities designed to build rapport and develop trust among members

---

Trigger Warning: Tumblr and "Pro-Ana" Diarists

A thriving "pro-ana" (promoting anorexia nervosa) scene exists on some popular social media sites such as Tumblr, driven in large part by the diary format that allows users to track weight loss, post diet tips, and share images and quotes that provide "thinspiration" for themselves and others striving to achieve their "ultimate goal weight" (Gregoire, 2012). Although initially these sites may seem to provide a positive environment, posts often encourage people to develop and continue dangerous behaviors.

Many young women stumble on to these sites while searching for "fitspo" or fit-inspiration images. What they see on "thinspo" pages may turn some away, but others flock to the so-called supportive community. They Skype, exchange texts, and e-mail to encourage each other not to binge. They've co-opted second-wave feminist terms to describe their "lifestyle choice." According to body image expert Jess Weiner, this desire for connectivity sustains thinspo blogs—but the danger comes from forming a community around hatred and shame of your body (Gregoire, 2012).

Some sites, like Facebook, are working to establish guidelines to report and flag encouragement of

disordered-eating and unhealthy lifestyle choices. *Vogue Italia* pulled photos of popular model Karlie Kloss from its Web site when the images began to appear on pro-ana sites. But the television show *Skins* continues to feature the pro-ana poster girl, Cassie, whose character is described as a starry-eyed, anorexic, pill-popping teen (Gregoire, 2012).

While awareness of eating disorders is on the rise, and much media is paying attention to how women and men are portrayed, there is still an easily accessible "support" community for disorders that was not there before the Internet. It is a community founded on unhealthy group communication that can trigger bad habits and relapses in participants.

Some companies build group cohesion through adventure team-building activities, such as high-ropes courses, hiking, or white-water rafting.

& Glover, 2005). Research suggests that five factors help foster cohesiveness in groups (Balgopal, Ephross, & Vassil, 1986; Widmer & Williams, 1991; Wilson, 2005). First, members are attracted to its purpose. Daniel, for example, joined the local Lions Club because he was attracted to its community service mission. Second, groups are generally more cohesive when membership is voluntary. If Daniel had joined the Lions Club because he felt obligated to do so, cohesiveness would have suffered. Third, members feel safe expressing themselves even when they disagree with others. Fourth, members support, encourage, and provide positive feedback to each other. Finally, members perceive the group

norms expectations for the way group members are to behave

ground rules prescribed behaviors designed to help a group meet its goals and conduct its conversations

accountability group members being held responsible for adhering to the group norms and working toward the group's goal

to be achieving its goals and celebrate their accomplishments. For example, when the local chapter of the Lions Club surpassed its previous fundraising record for the annual Journey for Sight 5K Community Run, the group celebrated the accomplishment with a picnic in the park.

9-2d Healthy Groups Develop and Abide by Productive Norms

Norms are expectations about the way group members are to behave. Healthy groups develop norms that help them achieve their goals (Shimanoff, 1992) and foster cohesiveness (Levine, 2013). Norms can be developed through formal discussions or informal group processes (Johnson & Johnson, 2003). Some groups choose to formulate explicit **ground rules**, prescribed behaviors designed to help the group meet its goals and conduct its conversations. These may include sticking to the agenda, refraining from interrupting others, making brief comments rather than lengthy monologues, expecting everyone to participate, focusing on issues rather than personalities, and sharing decision making.

In most groups, however, norms evolve informally. When we join a new group, we act in ways that were considered appropriate in the groups we participated in previously. When members of our new group respond positively to our actions, an informal norm is established. For example, suppose Daniel and two others show up late for a Lions Club meeting. If the latecomers are greeted with disapproving glares, then Daniel and the others will learn that this group has an on-time norm. A group may never actually discuss informal norms, but members understand what they are, follow them, and educate new members about them.

9-2e Healthy Groups Are Accountable

Accountability means all group members are held responsible for adhering to the group norms and working toward the group's goal. This means a group will penalize a member who violates a group norm. The severity of the penalty depends on the importance of the norm, the extent of the violation, and the status of the person who violated it. Violating a norm that is central to a group's performance or cohesiveness will generally receive a harsher penalty than violating a norm that is less central. In addition, violations by newcomers to the group are generally punished less severely than violations by veteran group members. As a new Lions Club member, for example, Daniel's "penalty" for arriving late was merely a stern look from the others. Group members who have achieved higher status in the group also tend to receive more lenient penalties—or even escape them altogether.

Being accountable can also mean changing counterproductive norms. For example, suppose a few folks spend more time socializing than seriously discussing community service issues at the Lions Club meetings. If the group does not effectively control this behavior, then it could become a counterproductive group norm. As a result, work toward the group's goals could be delayed, set aside, or perhaps even forgotten. If counterproductive behavior continues for several meetings and becomes a norm, it will be very difficult (though not impossible) to change.

What can a group member do to try to change a norm? You can help your group change a counterproductive norm by (1) observing the norm and its outcome, (2) describing the results of the norm to the group, and (3) soliciting opinions of other group members (Renz & Greg, 2000). For instance, Daniel observed that every Lions Club meeting began 15–20 minutes late and that this was making it necessary to schedule additional meetings. When members express their frustration about holding extra meetings, he could bring up his observations and the consequences and ask the group for their reaction.

9-2f Healthy Groups Are Synergetic

The old saying "two heads are better than one" captures an important characteristic of healthy groups. **Synergy** is the multiplying force of a group of individuals working together that results in a combined effort greater than any of the parts (Henman, 2003). For instance, the sports record books are filled with "no-name teams" that have won major championships over opponents with more talented players. A healthy group can develop a collective intelligence and a dynamic energy that translate into an outcome that exceeds what even a highly talented individual could produce. When a group has ethical goals and is interdependent, cohesive, and held accountable to productive norms, the group is well on its way toward achieving synergy.

 9-3 # STAGES OF GROUP DEVELOPMENT

Just as interpersonal relationships go through identifiable life cycles, so too do groups move through overlapping stages of development. Although numerous models have been proposed to describe these stages, psychologist, Bruce Tuckman's (1965) model has been widely accepted because it identifies central issues facing a group at each stage. In this section, we describe each of these stages and the nature of communication during each one.

9-3a Forming

Forming is the initial stage of group development characterized by orientation, testing, and dependence. Members try to understand precisely what the goal is, what role they will play in reaching the goal, and what the other group members are like. As the goal becomes clearer, members assess how their skills, talents, and abilities might be used in accomplishing it. Group interactions are typically polite and tentative as members become acquainted with each other and find their place in the group. Any real disagreements between people often remain unacknowledged during this stage because members want to be perceived as flexible and likable. During the forming stage, you should communicate a positive attitude; refrain from making abrasive or disagreeable comments; self-disclose appropriately benign information and feelings; and demonstrate open-minded and genuine interest in others (White, 2009).

9-3b Storming

As members figure out the goal and become comfortable with each other, they begin to express their honest opinions and vie for power and position. This signals the beginning of the second stage. The **storming** stage is characterized by conflict and power plays as members seek to have their ideas accepted and to find their place within the group's power structure. The politeness exhibited during forming may be replaced by pointedly aggressive exchanges between some members. While storming, members may also take sides and form coalitions. Although storming occurs in all groups, some groups manage it better than others. When storming is severe, it can threaten the group's survival. However, if a group does not storm, it may experience **groupthink**, a deterioration of mental efficiency, reality testing, and moral judgment that results from in-group pressure to conform (Janis, 1982). To avoid groupthink, members need to communicate in ways that encourage constructive disagreement,

> **synergy** the multiplying force of a group working together that results in a combined effort greater than any of the parts
>
> **forming** the initial stage of group development characterized by orientation, testing, and dependence
>
> **storming** the stage of group development characterized by conflict and power plays as members seek to have their ideas accepted and to find their place within the group's power structure
>
> **groupthink** a deterioration of mental efficiency, reality testing, and moral judgment that results from in-group pressure to conform

"Today's theme is 'Getting Beyond Group Think'."

© Cartoonresource/Shutterstock.com

avoid name-calling and inflammatory language, and use active listening skills with an emphasis on paraphrasing and honest questioning (White, 2009).

9-3c Norming

Norming is characterized by increased cohesion, collaboration, emerging trust among members, and motivation to achieve the group goal. Having expressed honest opinions, resolved major differences, and sorted out specific roles, members become loyal to each other and to the group goal. During this stage, members come to appreciate their differences, strengthen their relationships, and freely express their ideas and opinions. Members accept the norms established by the group

and provide positive and constructive feedback to each other.

9-3d Performing

Performing is characterized by harmony, productivity, problem solving, and shared leadership. During this stage, the group capitalizes on the skills, knowledge, and abilities of all members to work toward achieving its goal; conversations are focused on sharing task-related information and problem solving. Groups cannot achieve their full potential in this stage unless they have successfully resolved storming conflicts and developed productive norms.

9-3e Adjourning and Transforming

Adjourning is characterized by celebrating goal accomplishment and disengagement. The group usually engages in some type of formal or informal celebration during which they recognize their accomplishment and the role each member played. Sometimes the group will formally disband but a few members will continue to interact interpersonally with one another. Other times, rather than adjourn and disband, the group will engage in **transforming** and continue to exist with a new goal. The new goal will inevitably cause the members to revisit the earlier stages of group development, but the

norming the stage of group development during which the group solidifies its rules for behavior, resulting in greater trust and motivation to achieve the group goal

performing the stage of group development when the skills, knowledge, and abilities of all members are combined to overcome obstacles and meet goals successfully

adjourning the stage of group development in which members assign meaning to what they have done and determine how to end or maintain interpersonal relations they have developed

transforming the stage of group development that occurs when a group continues to exist with a new goal

cohesion, trust, and norms developed earlier are likely to help the group move quickly and more smoothly through them.

9-4 CONFLICT IN GROUPS

Just as conflict is inevitable in interpersonal relationships, so is it to be expected in group interactions (Bradley, et al., 2012). As we discussed earlier, groups that experience no conflict are likely to engage in groupthink. Groups that experience conflict but fail to manage it effectively are likely to stall out and never achieve their goal (Nussbaum, Singer, Rosas, Castillo, Flies, Lara, & Sommers, 1999). Conflict can be directed toward other members (interpersonal conflict) or ideas (issues) or both (Li & Hambrick, 2005; Wilmot & Hocker, 2007). Let's look at three types of conflict that will inevitably occur during group interactions and reveal some communication strategies you can employ to manage the disagreements effectively.

9-4a Pseudo-Conflict

Pseudo-conflict occurs when group members who actually agree about something believe they disagree due to poor communication. Since *pseudo* means *fake*, the perceived conflict is essentially a misperception. To manage or resolve pseudo-conflict, employ the effective listening, perception-checking, and paraphrasing skills we discussed in chapters 6, 7, and 8. This will reveal misinterpretations and result in a moment of revelation that you are actually on the same page after all.

9-4b Issue-Related Group Conflict

Issue-related group conflict occurs when two or more group members' goals, ideas, or opinions about the topic are incompatible. One major advantage of collaboration is the synergy that occurs as a result of expressing diverse points

Penalties for breaking norms keep the group functioning well.

© ostil/Shutterstock.com

of view. So issue-related conflict is actually a good thing when handled appropriately. To manage issue-related conflict effectively, begin by clarifying your position and the position of the other group member using perception-checking and paraphrasing skills. Then, as we discussed in chapter 8, express your position using assertive communication supported with facts rather than opinions or feelings. Finally, make the conflict a group discussion by asking others for input; if possible, postpone making a final decision until later. This will provide time to conduct additional research to make an informed decision as well as for tensions among members to subside.

pseudo-conflict conflict that occurs when group members who actually agree about something believe they disagree due to poor communication

issue-related group conflict conflict that occurs when two or more group members' goals, ideas, or opinions about the topic are incompatible

personality-related group conflict conflict that occurs when two or more group members become defensive because they feel like they are being attacked

9-4c Personality-Related Group Conflict

Personality-related group conflict occurs when two or more group members become defensive because they feel like they are being attacked. Typically, personality-related conflicts are rooted in a power struggle (Sell, Lovaglia, Mannix, Samuelson, & Wilson, 2004).

Personality-related conflicts sometimes emerge from poorly managed issue-related conflict. For example, Jack thought the group should do something fun to celebrate the end of finals. Jill thought they should do a service project to give something back to the community before everyone headed home for the summer.

What began as an issue-related conflict turned sour as Jill exclaimed, "Jack, all you ever think about is yourself. You are so self-centered!" and Jack retorted with, "You are such a downer, Jill. You don't even know HOW to have fun. That's why you end up sitting alone in your room so much!"

Factions emerged and, ultimately, some group members sided with Jill and others with Jack. The group ended up doing nothing to mark the successful completion of the semester. Had the group handled the issue-related conflict effectively, they could probably have done something both fun *and* useful. Instead, they did neither and departed feeling frustrated and dissatisfied.

To manage personality-related conflict effectively, try to turn the conflict into an issue-related problem to be solved rather than a conflict someone must win. Develop rules that allow for differences of opinion. Be descriptive rather than evaluative. Use "I" language and perception-checking. Finally, if the conflict isn't central to the group's goal, agree to disagree and move on.

9-4d Culture and Conflict

People who belong to different cultural and co-cultural groups tend to abide by unique communication norms. When managing conflict in groups, keep in mind that cultural differences may exist. For instance, people who identify with individualistic cultural norms tend to use direct verbal methods to manage conflict, whereas those who identify with collectivist norms tend to use indirect nonverbal methods (Ting-Toomey & Chung, 2012). Knowing that cultural differences may exist can help you select communication strategies both for managing group conflict effectively and for interpreting the messages of others accurately.

9-4e Virtual Groups and Conflict

Managing conflict effectively in virtual groups poses an additional set of challenges because it can be more difficult to catch the subtle meanings of group members' messages. This is due, in part, to the fact that most technology channels reduce our ability to send and receive nonverbal messages, particularly emotional and relational cues. Although most of us use emoticons and acronyms to represent missing nonverbal cues, a smiley face can be offered sincerely or sarcastically and it can be difficult for the receiver to perceive the difference. Unfortunately, conflict goes unresolved more often in virtual groups than in face-to-face groups because in most virtual settings we cannot see the nonverbal reactions of frustration that are visible when interacting in person (Bordia, DiFonzo, & Chang, 1999). However, when communication is effective, the bonds among virtual group members can be even stronger than those in face-to-face groups (Jiang, Bazarova, & Hancock, 2011; Wang, Walther, & Hancock, 2009).

To manage potential conflict effectively in virtual groups, then, work to overcome the limitations of virtual communication by making a conscious effort to communicate both what you *think* and how you *feel* about a topic. You can do so most clearly in your verbal messages, although emoticons and acronyms can also help when used deliberately to aid communication.

© Rommel Canlas/Shutterstock.com

LOCATED IN TEXTBOOK

☐ Tear-out Chapter Review cards at the end of the book

☐ Review with the Quick Quiz below

LOCATED ON COMM 4 ONLINE AT CENGAGEBRAIN.COM:

☐ Review Key Term flashcards and create your own cards

☐ Track your knowledge and understanding of key concepts in communication

☐ Complete practice and graded quizzes to prepare for tests

☐ Complete interactive content within COMM4 Online

☐ View the chapter highlight boxes for COMM4 Online

Quick Quiz

T F 1. In the norming stage, group members may take sides and form coalitions.

T F 2. The use of paraphrasing and honest questioning helps a group avoid groupthink.

T F 3. A nuclear family consists of two parents who live together with their biological or adoptive children.

T F 4. Studies show that group meetings must be face-to-face to be effective.

T F 5. Habitat for Humanity is an example of an interest group.

6. A _____ group is one in which various demographics, levels of knowledge, attitudes, and interests are represented.
   a. homogeneous
   b. heterogeneous
   c. cohesive
   d. problem-solving
   e. synergistic

7. All of the following are factors leading to cohesiveness in groups except
   a. attractiveness of the group's purpose.
   b. commitment to specific ground rules.
   c. voluntary membership.
   d. feeling free to share opinions.
   e. celebration of accomplishments.

8. The stage of group development during which the group clarifies its goals and determines the roles each member will have in the group power structure is called
   a. forming.
   b. storming.
   c. norming.
   d. performing.
   e. adjourning.

9. Which is the correct sequence in the stages of group development model?
   a. forming, norming, storming, performing, adjourning, transforming
   b. storming, transforming, forming, norming, performing, adjourning
   c. forming, performing, transforming, norming, storming, adjourning
   d. norming, transforming, forming, storming, performing, adjourning
   e. None of these is correct.

10. In _____ families, members may converse about an issue, but each member makes his or her own decision and is responsible for its consequences.
   a. laissez-faire
   b. consensual
   c. protective
   d. pluralistic
   e. progressive

Answers: 1. F, 2. T, 3. T, 4. F, 5. F, 6. B, 7. B, 8. B, 9. E, 10. A

10 Group Leadership and Problem Solving

LEARNING OUTCOMES

10-1 Understand how leadership functions in teams

10-2 Describe how to run effective meetings

10-3 List the six steps of systematic problem solving

10-4 Know the various methods for communicating group solutions

10-5 Evaluate group effectiveness using provided guidelines

After finishing this chapter go to **PAGE 137** for **STUDY TOOLS.**

When group meetings are ineffective, it is easy to point the finger at the leader. But the responsibility for any "waste of time" lies not with one person; instead, it is part of the complex nature of making decisions in groups. Although working in groups can have its disadvantages, it is the preferred approach in business and industry today (Levi, 2014; Northouse, 2013; Williams, 2013). Business leaders realize that when groups work effectively to solve problems, they generate greater breadth and depth of ideas, promote positive group morale, and increase productivity. This chapter focuses on effective leadership and problem solving in groups. We begin by discussing what effective group leadership means and the responsibilities of every group member in achieving it. Then we illustrate how shared leadership and effective communication plays out before, during, and after group meetings. From there we turn our attention specifically to problem solving and take you through a systematic problem-solving process. Finally, we propose methods for communicating your results with others and evaluating group effectiveness.

10-1 LEADERSHIP

Leadership is a process "whereby an individual influences a group of individuals to achieve a common goal" (Northouse, 2013, p. 5). When we think of leadership, we usually think of a person who is in charge (Gardner, 2011). Today, however, we understand leadership as a set of communication functions performed by any group member at various times based on each one's unique strengths and expertise (Fairhurst, 2011; Frey & Sunwulf,

2005). So, although a group may have a **formal leader**, a person designated or elected to oversee the group process, a series of **informal emergent leaders**, members who help lead the group to achieve different leadership functions, make for effective leadership in groups.

Shared leadership functions are the sets of roles you and other members perform to facilitate the work of the group and help maintain harmonious relationships among members. A **role** is a specific communication behavior that group members perform to address the needs of the group at a given point in time. When

these roles are performed effectively, the group functions smoothly. The three sets of shared leadership functions can be categorized as task, maintenance, and procedural roles.

10-1a Task Roles

Task leadership roles help the group acquire, process, or apply information that contributes directly to completing a task or goal.

▶ **Givers**: Information or opinion givers provide content for the discussion. People who perform this role are well informed on the content of the task and share what they know with the group. Your ability to assume this role depends on your command of high-quality information that the group needs to complete its task. "Well, the articles I read seem to agree that . . ." and "Based on how my sorority raised money for the Ronald McDonald House, we could . . ." are statements typical of information and opinion givers.

▶ **Seekers**: Information or opinion seekers probe others for their ideas and opinions during group meetings. Typical comments by information and opinion seekers include "Before going further, what information do we have about how raising fees is likely to affect membership?" or "How do other members of the group feel about this idea?"

▶ **Analyzers**: Information or opinion analyzers help the group scrutinize the content and the reasoning of discussions. They may question what is being said and help members understand the hidden assumptions in their statements. Information or opinion analyzers make statements such as "Enrique, you seem to be generalizing from only one instance. Can you give us some others?"

leadership a process whereby an individual influences a group of individuals to achieve a common goal

formal leader a person designated or elected to facilitate the group process

informal emergent leaders members who help lead the group to achieve different leadership functions

shared leadership functions the sets of roles that group members perform to facilitate the work of the group and help maintain harmonious relationships between members

role a specific communication behavior that group members perform

task leadership roles sets of behaviors that help a group acquire, process, or apply information that contributes directly to completing a task or goal

10-1b Maintenance Roles

Maintenance leadership roles are the sets of behaviors that help the group develop and maintain cohesion, commitment, and positive working relationships.

- **Supporters** encourage others to give opinions through positive body language or encouraging words. When someone contributes an idea or opinion, supporters may smile, nod, or vigorously shake their heads. They might also say things like "Good point, Ming," "I really like that idea, Paolo," or "It's obvious you've really done your homework, Janelle."

- **Interpreters** use their knowledge about the different social, cultural, and gender orientations of group members to help group members understand each other (Jensen & Chilberg, 1991). For example, an interpreter might say privately, "Paul, Lin Chou is Chinese, so when she says that she will think about your plan she might mean that she does not support your ideas, but she doesn't want to embarrass you in front of the others."

- **Harmonizers** intervene when conflict is threatening to harm group cohesiveness or a relationship between specific group members by speaking to the group with positive and calming words. Harmonizers are likely to make statements such as "Tom, Jack, hold it a second. I know you're on opposite sides of this, but let's see where you might have some agreement" or "Cool it, everybody, we're coming up with some good stuff; let's not lose our momentum by name-calling."

- **Mediators** are impartial arbiters who guide the discussion to help find a mutually acceptable resolution. Mediators do this by maintaining their own neutrality, keeping the discussion focused on issues and not personalities, helping to identify areas of common ground, and using paraphrasing and perception checking.

maintenance leadership roles sets of behaviors that help a group develop and maintain cohesion, commitment, and positive working relationships

procedural leadership roles sets of behaviors that provide logistical support, keep the group focused on the task, and record the group's accomplishments and decisions

- **Tension relievers** recognize when group members are stressed or tired and intervene to relieve the stress and reenergize the group, usually through humor. We know that humor "facilitates communication, builds relationships, reduces stress, provides perspective, and promotes attending and energizes" (Martin, Kuiper, Olinger, & Dance, 1993, p. 89). Fortune 500 companies such as General Electric, AT&T, Lockheed, and IBM all emphasize the value of workplace humor in their training programs. People who are effective in this leadership role might tell a joke, kid around, or tell a lighthearted story. A single well-placed one-liner can get a laugh, break the tension, and jolt the group out of its lethargy. Although the tension reliever momentarily distracts the group from its task, this action helps the group remain cohesive.

10-1c Procedural Roles

Procedural leadership roles provide logistical support, keep the group focused on the task, and record the group's accomplishments and decisions.

- **Logistics coordinators** arrange for appropriate spaces for group meetings, procure the supplies and equipment needed, and manage other details to meet the group's physical needs. The logistics coordinator's leadership role is usually carried out behind the scenes, but it is crucial to a group's success.

- **Expediters** keep track of the group's objectives and help move the group through the agenda. When the group strays, expediters make statements like "I'm enjoying this, but I can't quite see what it has to do with resolving the issue" or "Let's see, aren't we still trying to find out whether these are the only criteria that we should be considering?"

- **Gatekeepers** manage the flow of conversation so that all members have an opportunity to participate. If one or two members begin to dominate the conversation, the gatekeeper acknowledges this and invites other group members to participate. Gatekeepers also notice nonverbal signals that indicate that a member wishes to speak. The gatekeeper is the one who sees that Juanita is on the edge of her chair, eager to comment, and says,

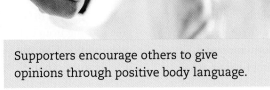

© Andresr/Shutterstock.com

Supporters encourage others to give opinions through positive body language.

Gatekeepers manage the flow of conversation.

"We haven't heard from Juanita, and she seems to have something she wants to say."

▶ **Recorders** take careful notes of group decisions and the evidence upon which they are based, sometimes called *minutes*. Recorders usually distribute edited copies of their notes to group members prior to the next meeting.

10-1d Shared Leadership Responsibilities

For shared leadership to work, all members must do their part. We propose five key shared leadership responsibilities (see Figure 10.1) that all members must abide by for the group to function effectively.

1. Be committed to the group goal. Being committed to the group goal means finding a way to align your expertise with the agreed-upon goal of the group. In addition to demonstrating responsibility, being committed to the group goal conveys both integrity and respect.

2. Keep discussions on track. It is every member's responsibility to keep the discussion on track by offering only comments that are relevant and by gently reminding others to stay focused if the discussion starts to get off track. It is unproductive to talk about personal issues during the team's work time. Moreover, it is unethical to try to get the discussion off track because you disagree with what is being said.

3. Complete individual assignments on time. One potential advantage of group work is that tasks can be divided among members.

However, each member is responsible for completing his or her tasks thoroughly and on time.

4. Encourage input from all members. All too often, quiet members are overshadowed by extroverts. If you are an extrovert, you have a special responsibility to refrain from dominating the discussion and to ask others for their opinions. If you tend to be an introvert, make a conscious effort to express yourself. You might jot down what you want to say to encourage yourself to speak up.

5. Manage conflict among members. As you learned in chapter 9, all small groups experience some *conflict*—disagreements or clashes among ideas, principles, or people. If managed appropriately, conflict can actually be beneficial to the group goal by stimulating thinking, fostering open communication, encouraging diverse opinions, and enlarging members' understanding of the issues (de Wit, Greer, & Jehn, 2012). So do your part to manage pseudo-conflict, issue-related conflict, and personality-related conflict effectively when it arises.

Now that we have a clear understanding of effective leadership in groups, let's turn our attention to one of the most common group communication workplace events—meetings.

FIGURE 10.1 FIVE KEY LEADERSHIP RESPONSIBILITIES

Be committed to the group goal.

Keep the discussion on track.

Complete individual assignments.

Encourage input from all members.

Manage conflict among members.

EFFECTIVE MEETINGS

We all participate regularly in meetings, sometimes as leaders and other times as participants. Yet, few people are skilled at doing so effectively. In fact, recent research from the Harvard Business School and the London School of Economics reports that business managers spend more than 18 hours of their workweek in meetings. What is particularly troubling, however, is that they say 25–50% of these meetings are a waste of time (Bailey, 2013). To ensure that your meetings are not a waste of time, let's look at several guidelines for meeting leaders and meeting participants.

10-2a Guidelines for Meeting Leaders

Most of us will be responsible for convening a group meeting at some point in our lives. Whether you are the designated formal leader for a class project or a task force at work or simply substituting for your manager at the monthly department meeting, you need to know how to effectively plan for, facilitate, and follow up after meetings.

© Natalia Siverina/Shutterstock.com

BEFORE THE MEETING Meeting leaders should follow these guidelines before the meeting begins.

1. Prepare and distribute an agenda. An **agenda** is an organized outline of the information and decision items to be covered during a meeting. It is a road map that lets the members know the purpose of the meeting and what they are expected to accomplish as a result of attending. Agenda items should move the group toward its goals. You can identify the items for your agenda by

▸ reviewing your notes and the formal minutes of the previous meeting;

▸ clarifying what the group decided to accomplish between meetings; and

▸ identifying what decisions the group expected to make in this next session.

Then you can structure the agenda into information items and decision items. In other words, you can have members report on their assignments (information items), then make decisions and determine next steps.

> **agenda** an organized outline of the information and decision items that will be covered during a meeting

It is critical to distribute the agenda at least 24 hours before the meeting so that members have time to prepare. You can e-mail the agenda, post it to the group's Web page, or hand-deliver it. None of us likes to come to a meeting and be embarrassed because we forgot to complete an assignment or be called on to make decisions about something we have not had time to think about. As the meeting leader, you are responsible for providing the information members need to come prepared. Figure 10.2 shows an agenda for a group meeting to decide which one of three courses to offer over the Internet next semester.

2. Decide who should attend the meeting. In most cases, all group members will attend meetings. Today, very often some or all members might meet virtually via teleconferencing or videoconferencing platforms.

3. Manage meeting logistics. You may choose to carry out this role or ask another group member to do so. But even if you delegate, it remains your responsibility to confirm that the meeting arrangements are made and appropriate. As a general rule, meetings should be shorter than 90 minutes, or have breaks scheduled every 90 minutes to reduce fatigue.

Face-to-face meetings need:

▸ an appropriately sized room based on the number of people attending,

▸ necessary equipment to be available and operational,

▸ a table set up to encourage interaction (usually with chairs around it).

Remote meetings need:

▸ technology for remote interface that is available and operational.

4. Speak with each participant prior to the meeting. As the leader, you need to understand members' positions and personal goals. Time spent discussing issues in advance allows you to anticipate conflicts that might emerge during the meeting and plan how to manage them effectively if they do.

DURING THE MEETING Meeting leaders should follow these guidelines as the meeting proceeds.

1. Review and modify the agenda. Begin the meeting by reviewing the agenda and modifying it based on members' suggestions. Reviewing the agenda ensures

FIGURE 10.2 AGENDA FOR INTERNET COURSE COMMITTEE

March 1, 2016

To: Campus computer discussion group

From: Janelle Smith

Re: Agenda for discussion group meeting

Meeting Date: March 8, 2016

Place: Student Union, Conference Room A

Time: 3:00 p.m. to 4:30 p.m.

Meeting objectives

☐ We will familiarize ourselves with each of three courses that have been proposed for Internet-based delivery next semester.

☐ We will evaluate each course against the criteria we developed last month.

☐ We will use a consensus decision process to determine which of the three courses to offer.

Agenda for group discussion

☐ Review and discussion of Philosophy 141 (Report by Justin)

☐ Review and discussion of Art History 336 (Report by Marique)

☐ Review and discussion of Communication 235 (Report by Kathryn)

Consensus-building discussion and decision

☐ Which proposals fit the criteria?

☐ Are there non-criteria-related factors to consider?

☐ Which proposal is more acceptable to all members?

Discussion of next steps and task assignments

Set date of next meeting

that the group will be working on items that are still relevant and gives members a chance to provide input into what will be discussed.

2. Monitor member interaction. If other group members are assuming the task-related, maintenance, and procedural leadership functions, you need do nothing. But when there is a need for a particular role and no one is assuming it, you should do so. For example, if you notice that some people are talking more than their fair share and no one is trying to draw out quieter members, you should assume the gatekeeper role and invite reluctant members to comment. Similarly, if a discussion becomes too heated, you may need to take on the role of harmonizer or tension reliever.

3. Monitor the time. Although another group member may serve as expediter, it is ultimately your responsibility to make sure the group stays on schedule.

4. Praise in public and reprimand in private. Meetings provide an excellent opportunity to praise individuals

or the entire group for jobs well done. Being recognized among one's peers often boosts self-esteem and group morale. Conversely, criticizing individuals or the entire group during a meeting has the opposite effect. The humiliation of public criticism can deflate self-esteem, group morale, and motivation.

5. Check periodically to see if the group is ready to make a decision. You should listen carefully for agreement among members and move the group into its formal decision-making process when the discussion is no longer adding insight.

6. Implement the group's decision rules. You are responsible for executing the decision-making rule the group has agreed to use. If the group is deciding by consensus, for example, you must make sure all members feel they can support the chosen alternative. If the group is deciding by majority rule, you call for the vote and tally the results.

7. Summarize decisions and assignments. You should summarize what has been and is left to accomplish, as well as assignments tasked to various members.

8. Set the next meeting. Clarify when future meetings will take place if necessary.

AFTER THE MEETING Leaders should follow these guidelines after the meeting is over.

1. Review the meeting outcomes and process. A good leader learns how to be more effective by reflecting on how well the meeting went. Did the meeting accomplish its goals? Was group cohesion improved or damaged in the process? What will you do differently next time to improve the experience?

2. Prepare and distribute a meeting summary. Although some groups have a designated recorder, many groups rely on their leader to take notes of the discussion. If your group has a designated recorder, be sure to review the minutes and compare them to your notes before they are distributed. Summaries are most useful when they are distributed within two or three days of the meeting when everyone's memories are still fresh.

3. Repair damaged relationships. If any heated debate occurred during the meeting, some members may have left angry or hurt. You should help repair relationships by seeking out these participants and talking with them. Through empathic listening, you can soothe hurt feelings and spark a recommitment to the group.

4. Conduct informal progress reports. When participants have been assigned specific task responsibilities, you should periodically check to see if they have encountered any problems in completing those tasks and how you might help them.

10-2b Guidelines for Meeting Participants

Just as there are guidelines for effective meeting leaders to follow before, during, and after meetings, there are also guidelines for meeting participants.

BEFORE THE MEETING Too often people think of group meetings as a "happening" that requires attendance but no preparation. Countless times we have observed people arriving at a meeting unprepared even though they come carrying packets of material they received in advance. Here are some important preparation guidelines for meeting participants.

1. Study the agenda. Consider the meeting's purpose and determine what you need to do to be prepared. If you had an assignment, make sure you are ready to report on it.

2. Study the minutes. If this is one in a series of meetings, read the minutes and your own notes from the previous meeting. This should prepare you for the next meeting.

Informal progress reports can help ensure that responsibilities are fulfilled and that problems are solved quickly.

© OPOLJA/Shutterstock.com

3. Do your homework. Read the material distributed prior to the meeting and inform yourself about each agenda item. Bring any materials to the meeting that may help the group accomplish its objectives.

4. List questions. Make a list of questions related to any agenda items that you would like to have answered during the meeting.

5. Plan to play a leadership role. Consider which leadership functions and roles you are best at and decide what you will do to enact them during the meeting.

DURING THE MEETING Go into the meeting planning to be a full participant.

1. Listen attentively. Concentrate on what others say so you can complement, supplement, or counter what is presented.

2. Stay focused. Keep your comments focused on the specific agenda item under discussion. If others get off the subject, do what you can to get the discussion back on track.

3. Ask questions. Honest questions help stimulate discussion and build ideas.

4. Take notes. Even if someone else is responsible for providing the official minutes, you'll need notes to remember what occurred and any tasks you agreed to take on after the meeting.

5. Play devil's advocate. When you think an idea has not been fully discussed or tested, be willing to voice disagreement or encourage further discussion.

6. Monitor your contributions. Make sure that you are neither dominating the discussion nor abdicating your responsibility to share insights and opinions.

AFTER THE MEETING When meetings end, too often people leave and forget about what took place until they arrive at the next meeting. Instead:

1. Review and summarize your notes. Do this soon after the meeting while the discussion is still fresh in your mind. Make sure your notes include what you need to do before the next meeting.

2. Evaluate your effectiveness. How effective were you in helping the group move toward achieving its goals? Where were you strong? Where were you weak? What should you do next time to improve, and how? For example, if you didn't speak up as much as you would have liked to, perhaps you'll decide to write down questions or topics when you think of them to use as notes to encourage you to speak up next time.

3. Review decisions. Make notes about what your role was in making decisions. Did you do all that you could have done? If not, what will you do differently next time, why, and how?

4. Communicate progress. Inform others who need to know about information conveyed and decisions made in the meeting.

5. Complete your tasks. Make sure you complete all assignments you agreed to take on in the meeting.

6. Review minutes. Compare the official meeting minutes to your own notes and report any discrepancies to the member who prepared them.

Sometimes the goal of a workplace meeting is to regroup and refocus as we perform the regular duties assigned to us. Other times, however, we will meet as part of a work group team charged with a specific problem-solving challenge. In these situations, we will be most successful if we work through the problem using a systematic problem-solving process.

10-3 SYSTEMATIC PROBLEM SOLVING

When a work group team is charged with tackling a problem together, members may use an orderly series of steps or a less-structured spiral pattern in which they refine, accept, reject, modify, and combine ideas, then circle back to the previous discussion as they go along.

Whether the deliberations are linear or spiral, groups that arrive at high-quality decisions accomplish the six tasks that make up what is known as the Systematic Problem-Solving Process. This process, first described by John Dewey in 1933 and since revised by others, remains a tried and true approach to individual or group problem solving (Duch, Groh, & Allen, 2001; Edens, 2000; Levin, 2001; Weiten, Dunn, & Hammer, 2011).

10-3a Step One: Identify and Define the Problem

The first step is to identify the problem and define it in a way that all group members understand and agree with. Even when a group is commissioned by an outside agency that provides a description of the problem, the group still needs to understand precisely what is at issue and needs to be resolved. Many times, what appears to be a problem is only a symptom of a problem; if the group focuses on solutions that eliminate only a symptom, the underlying problem will remain. For example, let's say that a group's budget crisis stems from a recession-related membership drop. How does the group know that the inability to fund the budget is the problem and not just a symptom of the problem? What if their membership drop has some other cause? If that is the case, then cutting the budget may be a temporary fix but will not solve the problem. One way to see if you have uncovered the root cause or real problem is to ask, "If we solve this problem, are we confident that the consequences of the problem will not recur?" If we cut the budget, are we confident that we won't need to make additional cuts later? If not, then we probably need to look further for the root problem. We will need to look more closely at causes for the drop in membership and other ways besides dues for funding the budget. The real problem may be how to fund the budget.

Once your group agrees about the nature of the root problem, you will want to draft a **problem definition**, which is a formal written statement describing the problem. An effective problem definition is stated as a question of fact, value, or policy; it contains only one central idea; and it uses specific, precise, and concrete language. **Questions of fact** ask

> **problem definition** a formal written statement describing a problem
>
> **question of fact** a question asked to determine what is true or to what extent something is true

Review and summarize notes soon after a meeting has ended.

© Yuri Arcurs/Shutterstock.com

the group to determine what is true or to what extent something is true. "What percentage of our projected expenses can be covered with our existing revenue?" is a question of fact. **Questions of value** ask the group to determine or judge whether something is right, moral, good, or just. Questions of value often contain words such as *good, reliable, effective,* or *worthy*—for instance, "What is the most effective way to recruit new members?" **Questions of policy** concern what course of action should be taken or what rules should be adopted to solve a problem—for example, "Should we sponsor an annual fund-raising event with the local Public Relations Society of America chapter to help fund our budget?" After some discussion, the student chapter decided that the problem they needed to solve was a policy question that could be best stated: "How can we increase our revenues to meet our budget in the current economic conditions?"

10-3b Step Two: Analyze the Problem

Problem analysis involves finding out as much as possible about the problem. Most groups begin this process with each member sharing information he or she already knows about the problem. Then members determine which additional questions they need to answer and search for additional information to answer them. Some members may be assigned to conduct library or online research about the problem, others may interview experts, and still others may conduct surveys to gather information from particular target groups. The information gathered by group members should help the group answer key questions about the nature of the problem such as those listed in Figure 10.3.

During the information gathering and analysis step, group members should be encouraged to share information that is new or contradicts the sentiments or preferences expressed in the group. A group that is willing to consider new and unexpected information will

| FIGURE 10.3 | QUESTIONS TO GUIDE PROBLEM ANALYSIS |

- ☐ What are the symptoms of this problem?
- ☐ What are the causes of this problem?
- ☐ What have others who have faced this problem done?
- ☐ How successful have they been with the solutions they attempted?
- ☐ How is our situation similar to and different from theirs?
- ☐ Does this problem consist of several smaller problems? If so, what are their symptoms, causes, previously tried solutions, and so forth?
- ☐ What would be the consequences of doing nothing?
- ☐ What would be the consequences of trying something and having it fail?

more deeply analyze the problem and, therefore, will likely come to a more effective solution.

10-3c Step Three: Determine Criteria for Judging Solutions

Criteria are standards used for judging the merits of proposed solutions—a blueprint for evaluating them. Research suggests that when groups develop criteria before they think about specific solutions, they are more likely to come to a decision that all members can accept (Young, Wood, Phillips, & Pedersen, 2007). Without clear criteria, group members may argue for their preferred solution without regard to whether it will adequately address the problem and whether it is feasible. Figure 10.4 provides a list of questions that can help a group think about the types of criteria that a solution might need to meet.

Once you've agreed on the list of solution criteria, the group needs to prioritize the list. Although rank ordering the list from most to least important may be unwieldy and counterproductive, it is probably useful to agree which criteria are major (must meet) and which are minor (would like to meet).

VALUE

FACT

POLICY

© Vadim Georgiev/Shutterstock.com

question of value a question asked to determine or judge whether something is right, moral, good, or just

question of policy a question asked to determine what course of action should be taken or what rules should be adopted to solve a problem

criteria standards or measures used for judging the merits of proposed solutions

FIGURE 10.4 QUESTIONS TO GUIDE DISCUSSION OF SOLUTION CRITERIA

- [ ] What are the quantitative and qualitative measures of success that a solution must be able to demonstrate?
- [ ] Are there resource constraints that a good solution must meet (costs, time, personnel)?
- [ ] Is solution simplicity a factor?
- [ ] What risks are unacceptable?
- [ ] Is ease of implementation a consideration?
- [ ] Is it important that no constituency be unfairly harmed or advantaged by a solution?

© Konstantin Chagin/Shutterstock.com

10-3d Step Four: Identify Alternative Solutions

Ending up with a good solution depends on having a wide variety of possible solutions to choose from. Therefore, one of the most important activities of problem solving is coming up with solution ideas. Many groups fail to generate solution ideas because they criticize the first ideas expressed; this discourages members from taking the risk to put their ideas out for the group to consider. One way to encourage everyone's ideas is to use the technique of brainstorming. **Brainstorming** is an uncritical, non-evaluative process of generating possible solutions by being creative, suspending judgment, and combining or adapting ideas. During a brainstorming session, members offer ideas without censoring themselves. Other members may build on ideas that have been presented, combine two or more ideas, or even offer off-the-wall thoughts.

10-3e Step Five: Evaluate Solutions and Decide

After generating potential solutions, the group must find the one or ones that will best solve the problem. To do this, consider each solution as it meets the criteria and eliminate solutions that do not meet them adequately. Once each potential solution has been thoroughly evaluated based on the criteria, the group must select the best one(s).

Decision making is the process of choosing among alternatives. Sometimes your group will make the decision. Other times, your group may present the results of your work to someone else who will then make the final decision. Five methods are commonly used to reach a group decision.

1. The expert opinion method. Once the group has eliminated those alternatives that do not meet the criteria, the group asks the member who has the most expertise to make the final choice. Obviously, this method is quick and useful if one member is much more knowledgeable about the issues or has a greater stake in the implementation of the decision.

2. The average group opinion method. In this approach, each group member ranks each of the alternatives that meet all the criteria. Their rankings are then averaged, and the alternative receiving the highest average becomes the choice. This method is useful for routine decisions or when a decision needs to be made quickly. It can also be used as an intermediate straw poll so the group can eliminate low-scoring alternatives before moving to a different process for making the final decision.

3. The majority rule method. In this method, the group votes on each alternative, and the one that receives a majority of votes is selected. Although this method is considered democratic, it can create problems. If the majority voting for an alternative is slight, then nearly as many members oppose the choice as support it. If these minority members strongly object to the choice, they may sabotage implementation of the solution either actively or passively.

4. The unanimous decision method. In this method, the group must continue deliberation until every member of the group believes that the same solution is the best. As you would expect, it is very difficult and time-consuming to arrive at a

brainstorming an uncritical, non-evaluative process of generating possible solutions by being creative, suspending judgment, and combining or adapting ideas

decision making the process of choosing among alternatives

truly unanimous decision. When a group reaches unanimity, however, each member is likely to be committed to selling the decision to others and helping to implement it.

5. The consensus method. This method is an alternative to the unanimous decision method. In consensus, the group continues deliberation until all members of the group find an acceptable solution, one they can support and are committed to helping implement. Some group members may believe there is a better solution than the one chosen, but all can live with the chosen solution. Arriving at consensus, although easier than reaching unanimity, is still difficult. Although the majority rule method is widely used, the consensus method is a wise investment if the group needs everyone's support to implement the decision successfully.

Sometimes a group will choose only one solution. But frequently a group will decide on a multi-pronged approach that combines two or three of the acceptable solutions.

10-3f Step Six: Implement the Agreed-Upon Solution and Assess It

Finally, the group may be responsible for implementing the agreed-upon solution or, if the group is presenting the solution to others for implementation, making recommendations for how the solution should be implemented. The group has already considered implementation in terms of selecting a solution but now must fill in the details. What tasks are required by the solution(s)? Who will carry out these tasks? What is a reasonable time frame for implementation generally and for each of the tasks specifically? Because the agreed-upon solution may or may not prove effective, the group should determine a point at which they will revisit and assess its success.

deliverables tangible or intangible products of work that must be provided to someone else

written brief a very short document that describes a problem, background, process, decision, and rationale so that a reader can quickly understand and evaluate a group's product

comprehensive report a written document that provides a detailed review of the problem-solving process used to arrive at a recommendation

executive summary a one-page synopsis of a comprehensive report

Doing so builds in an opportunity to revise or replace the solution if warranted.

10-4 COMMUNICATING GROUP SOLUTIONS

Once a group has completed its deliberations, it is usually expected to communicate its results. **Deliverables** are tangible or intangible products of your work that must be provided to someone else. Although some deliverables are objects, typically the deliverables from problem-solving groups are communications of the information gathered, analyses, decisions, and recommendations. These kinds of intangible deliverables can be communicated in written formats, oral formats, or virtual formats.

10-4a Written Formats

1. A **written brief** is a very short document that describes the problem, background, process, decision, and rationale so that the reader can quickly understand and evaluate the group's product. Most briefs are one or two pages long. When preparing a brief, begin by describing your group's task. What problem were you attempting to solve and why? Then briefly provide the background information the reader will need to evaluate whether the group has adequately studied the problem. Present solution steps and timelines for implementation as bullet points so the reader can quickly understand what is being proposed. Close with a sentence or very short paragraph that describes how the recommendation will solve the problem, as well as any potential side effects.

2. A **comprehensive report** is a written document that provides a detailed review of the problem-solving process used to arrive at the recommendation. A comprehensive report is usually organized into sections that parallel the problem-solving process.

Because comprehensive reports can be very long, they usually include an executive summary. An **executive summary** is a one-page synopsis of the report. This summary contains enough information to acquaint readers

WoW Problem Solving

For some, mention of games like *World of Warcraft* might conjure up a stereotypical image of a teenage boy typing away at his computer alone. But role-playing games are actually social interactions that encourage successful group problem solving.

World of Warcraft (WoW) is a popular MMORPG (massively multiplayer online role-playing game). *World of Warcraft* is played online and players communicate with one another using text or voice chat programs. To advance in the game, players must work with others to defeat monsters, find treasure, and gain experience (Newman, 2007).

In a *BusinessWeek* Online article, researcher John Seely Brown and business consultant John Hagel (2009) argue that many aspects of *WoW* encourage group problem solving and can even be applied as innovative workplace strategies. They claim that *WoW* creates opportunities for teams to self-organize around challenging performance targets; provides opportunities to develop tacit knowledge without neglecting the exchange of broader knowledge; and encourages frequent and rigorous performance feedback.

Based on these benefits, some MMORPGs are actually being developed for a range of "real-life" applications. For example, the Bill and Melinda Gates Foundation recently awarded a $3 million grant to the MIT Education Arcade to develop games that help high school students learn math and biology. The games enable self-directed and collaborative learning experiences, where the players take on the roles of scientists, engineers, and mathematicians.

---

with the highlights of the full document without reading it. Usually, it contains a statement of the problem, some background information, a description of any alternatives, and the major conclusions.

10-4b Oral Formats

1. An **oral brief** is essentially a summary of a written brief delivered to an audience by a group member. An oral brief can typically be delivered in less than 10 minutes.

2. An **oral report** is similar to a comprehensive report. It provides a more detailed review of a group's problem-solving process. Oral reports can range from 30 to 60 minutes.

3. A **symposium** is a set of prepared oral reports delivered sequentially by group members before a gathering of people who are interested in the group's work. A symposium may be organized so that each person's speech focuses on one step of the problem-solving process, or it may be organized so that each speaker covers all of the steps in the problem-solving process as they relate to one of several issues or recommendations that the group worked on or made. In a symposium, the speakers usually sit together at the front of the room. One member acts as moderator, offering the introductory and concluding remarks and providing transitions between speakers. When introduced by the moderator, each speaker may stand and walk to a central spot, usually a lectern. Speakers who use a computerized slideshow should coordinate their slides so that there are seamless transitions between speakers. Symposia often conclude with a question-and-answer session facilitated by the moderator, who directs one or more of the members to answer based on their expertise. Questions can be directed to individuals or to the group as a whole.

4. A **panel discussion** is a structured problem-solving discussion held by a group in front of an audience. One member serves as moderator, introducing the topic and providing structure by asking a series of planned questions that panelists answer. Their answers and the interaction among them provide the supporting evidence. A well-planned panel discussion seems spontaneous and interactive but requires careful planning and rehearsal to ensure that all relevant information is presented and that all speakers are afforded equal speaking time. After the formal discussion, the audience

oral brief a summary of a written brief delivered to an audience by a group member

oral report a detailed review of a group's problem-solving process delivered to an audience by one or more group members

symposium a set of prepared oral reports delivered sequentially by group members before a gathering of people who are interested in the group's work

panel discussion a structured problem-solving discussion held by a group in front of an audience

A set-up like this may be useful for larger meetings or symposia, where one person speaks at a time either giving a report or part of a report.

is often encouraged to question the participants. Perhaps you've seen or heard a panel of experts discuss a topic on a radio or television talk show like *SportsCenter* or *The Doctors*.

10-4c Virtual Formats

1. A **remote access report (RAR)** is a computer-mediated audiovisual presentation of the group's process and outcome that others can receive electronically. One or more group members prepare the RAR with slideshow software to provide a visual overview of the group's process, decisions, and recommendations. Effective RARs typically consist of no more than 15 to 20 slides. Slides are titled and content is presented in outline format or with bullet-point phrases or key words (rather than complete sentences or paragraphs), as well as through visual representations of important information. RARs may be self-running so that the slides automatically forward after a certain number of seconds, but it is better to let the viewer choose the pace and control when the next slide appears. RARs

> **remote access report (RAR)** a computer-mediated audiovisual presentation of a group's process and outcome that others can receive electronically
>
> **streaming video** a recording that is sent in compressed form over the Internet
>
> **group dynamics** the way a group interacts to achieve its goal

can be silent or narrated. When narrated, a voice-over accompanies each slide, providing additional or explanatory information.

2. A **streaming video** is a recording that is sent in compressed form over the Internet. You are probably familiar with streaming video from popular Web sites such as YouTube. Streaming videos are a great way to distribute oral briefs, but they also can be used to distribute recordings of oral reports, symposia, or panel presentations. Streaming videos are useful when everyone who needs to know the results of the group's work cannot meet at one time or in one place.

10-5 EVALUATING GROUP EFFECTIVENESS

As with any communication skill, group communication can improve over time based on practice, reflective assessment, and revision. In this section, we offer some guidelines for evaluating the group communication process and a group presentation.

10-5a Group Dynamics

Group dynamics is the way a group interacts to achieve its goal. Effective groups periodically stop to evaluate how their interactions affect what they are accomplishing and how members perceive themselves and others. At times you may be asked to provide a formal evaluation of the group dynamics of a class project group or other work team. One way you might evaluate members is to describe how each member performed his or her specific tasks and how well his or her communication contributed to the cohesiveness, problem solving, and conflict resolution processes in the group. Figure 10.5 is one example you can use for evaluating class project group member participation. Alternatively, in a class project group, members could prepare a "reflective thinking process paper," which details in paragraph form what each member did well and could improve upon as well as a self-analysis of their own contributions and what they could do to improve.

Like the performance evaluations business managers make of employees, these evaluations document the efforts of group members. They can be submitted to the instructor, just as they would be submitted to a supervisor. In business, these documents provide a basis for determining promotion, merit pay, and salary adjustments. In the classroom, they can provide a basis for determining one portion of each member's grade.

FIGURE 10.5 GROUP DYNAMICS EVALUATION FORM

Meeting Date: _____

Your name: _____

Directions

After each required group meeting, provide ethical critiques for both your group members and yourself. Rate each individual on his or her performance in the group. Justify the rating with specific examples. As you rate each member, consider the following:

☐ committed to the group goal

☐ fulfills individual assignments

☐ manages interpersonal conflicts

☐ encourages group participation

☐ helps keep the discussion on track

Yourself _____

Circle overall individual rating

| 0 | 1 | 2 | 3 | 4 | 5 | 6 | 7 |

(poor)   (met requirements)   (excellent)

Tasks accomplished:

Tasks assigned:

Ethical critique:

Group member _____

Circle overall individual rating

| 0 | 1 | 2 | 3 | 4 | 5 | 6 | 7 |

(poor)   (met requirements)   (excellent)

Tasks accomplished:

Tasks assigned:

Ethical critique:

Group member _____

Circle overall individual rating

| 0 | 1 | 2 | 3 | 4 | 5 | 6 | 7 |

(poor)   (met requirements)   (excellent)

Tasks accomplished:

Tasks assigned:

Ethical critique:

Group member _____

Circle overall individual rating

| 0 | 1 | 2 | 3 | 4 | 5 | 6 | 7 |

(poor)   (met requirements)   (excellent)

Tasks accomplished:

Tasks assigned:

Ethical critique:

Group member _____

Circle overall individual rating

| 0 | 1 | 2 | 3 | 4 | 5 | 6 | 7 |

(poor)   (met requirements)   (excellent)

Tasks accomplished:

Tasks assigned:

Ethical critique:

10-5b Group Presentations

Effective group presentations depend on quality individual presentations as well as overall group performance. So evaluations of group presentations should consist of both an individual and a group component (see Figure 10.6). And, if you are serious about improving your individual presentation skills, you will also evaluate yourself to discover areas where you can improve (see Figure 10.7).

FIGURE 10.6 SAMPLE EVALUATION FORM FOR GROUP PRESENTATIONS

Group Member Name: _____   Critic (your name): _____

Directions: Evaluate the effectiveness of each group member according to each of the following criteria for effective presentations individually and as a group.

Rating Scale:

Circle overall individual rating

0   1   2   3   4   5   6   7

(poor)   (met requirements)   (excellent)

_____

Individual Performance Critique

_____   **Content (Breadth and depth and listener relevance)**

(rating)   **Critique (Provide a rationale for the rating you gave):**

_____   **Structure (Macrostructure and microstructure/language)**

(rating)   **Critique (Provide a rationale for the rating you gave):**

_____   **Delivery (Use of voice and use of body)**

(rating)   **Critique (Provide a rationale for the rating you gave):**

Group Performance Critique

_____   **Content (Thematic? Focused? Thorough? Construction of presentational aids?)**

(rating)   **Critique (Provide a rationale for the rating you gave):**

_____   **Structure (Balanced? Transitions/Flow? Attention Getter/Clincher?)**

(rating)   **Critique (Provide a rationale for the rating you gave):**

_____   **Delivery (Teamwork? Cooperation? Fluency? Use of aids?)**

(rating)   **Critique (Provide a rationale for the rating you gave):**

Overall Comments:

FIGURE 10.7 SAMPLE SELF-CRITIQUE FORM FOR GROUP PRESENTATIONS

Directions: Complete the items below with regard to your presentation in the group symposium.

1. In terms of content, I did the following things well in my oral presentation:
   a.
   b.

2. In terms of structure, I did the following things well in my oral presentation:
   a.
   b.

3. In terms of delivery, I did the following things well in my oral presentation:
   a.
   b.
   c.

4. If I could do my portion of the oral presentation over again, I would do the following things differently:
   a.
   b.

5. In terms of my role as a group member, I am most proud of how I:

6. In terms of my role as a group member, I am least proud of how I:

7. Overall, I would give myself a grade of _____ for the group speech because:

LOCATED IN TEXTBOOK

☐ Tear-out Chapter Review cards at the end of the book

☐ Review with the Quick Quiz below

LOCATED ON COMM 4 ONLINE AT CENGAGEBRAIN.COM:

☐ Review Key Term flashcards and create your own cards

☐ Track your knowledge and understanding of key concepts in communication

☐ Complete practice and graded quizzes to prepare for tests

☐ Complete interactive content within COMM4 Online

☐ View the chapter highlight boxes for COMM4 Online

Quick Quiz

T F 1. Criteria are standards or measures that provide the blueprint for how a group will evaluate the virtues of each alternative solution.

T F 2. Leadership is the set of roles performed to facilitate group work and to maintain relationships among members.

T F 3. A tension reliever's main role is to momentarily distract the group from its task, which helps break monotony or tension within the group.

T F 4. An oral brief is similar to a comprehensive report, whereas an oral report is a summary of a written brief delivered to an audience by a group member.

T F 5. Panel discussions require careful planning and rehearsal to ensure that all relevant information is presented and that each speaker is afforded equal speaking time.

6. According to the problem-solving method, a process of identifying an alternative solution can be reached through

  a. analyzing.
  b. defining.
  c. developing criteria.
  d. evaluation.
  e. brainstorming.

7. In which decision-making method does a group continue deliberations until every member of the group believes that the same solution is best?

  a. the average group opinion method
  b. the unanimous decision method

  c. the majority rule method
  d. the expert opinion method
  e. None of these is correct.

8. _____ are neutral and impartial arbiters who guide discussions, whereas _____ intervene in the group's discussion when conflict is threatening group cohesiveness.

  a. Tension relievers; interpreters
  b. Interpreters; mediators
  c. Mediators; harmonizers
  d. Harmonizers; mediators
  e. Supporters; mediators

9. Which procedural role do you play when you ensure that everyone has an opportunity to speak and be heard?

  a. gatekeeper
  b. encourager
  c. harmonizer
  d. peacekeeper
  e. initiator

10. When running a meeting, be sure to complete each of the following tasks except

  a. modifying the agenda based on members' suggestions.
  b. monitoring the roles that members assume.
  c. encouraging conflict and arguments among group members to elicit everyone's true feelings.
  d. implementing the group's decision rules.
  e. periodically checking to see if the group is ready to make a decision.

Answers: 1.T, 2.F, 3.T, 4.F, 5.T, 6.E, 7.B, 8.C, 9.A, 10.C

11 Topic Selection and Development

LEARNING OUTCOMES

11-1 Determine a speech topic and goal that is appropriate for the rhetorical situation

11-2 Locate and evaluate information sources

11-3 Identify and evaluate different types of evidence

11-4 Record information and sources

11-5 Cite sources effectively in your speeches

After finishing this chapter go to **PAGE 155** for **STUDY TOOLS.**

Developing effective public speaking skills is empowering. Whether giving a "job talk" speech during an interview, presenting oral reports and proposals, responding to questions, or training other workers, you will spend a good portion of your work life in activities that require effective public speaking skills. This chapter focuses on the first steps in effective speechmaking: (1) selecting a specific speech goal that is adapted to the rhetorical situation and (2) gathering and evaluating information to develop your speech.

11-1 THE RHETORICAL SITUATION

As Figure 11.1 illustrates, the **rhetorical situation** is a state in which you (and your knowledge and intentions), the audience (and their knowledge and expectations), and the occasion (and the constraints of it) overlap. Effective speakers address all three of these components throughout the speech preparation and presentation process. Lloyd Bitzer (1968), coined the term **exigence** as *the reason the speech needs to be given.* And because the audience is a critical component of the rhetorical situation, your specific speech goal

rhetorical situation a state in which you, the audience, and the occasion overlap

exigence the reason the speech needs to be given

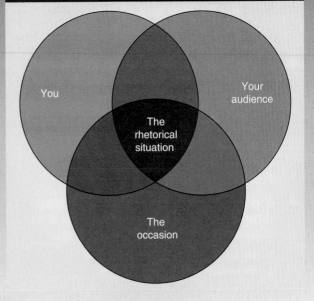

FIGURE 11.1 THE RHETORICAL SITUATION

You

Your audience

The rhetorical situation

The occasion

must be based on **audience analysis**, the study of the intended audience for your speech, and **audience adaptation**, the process of tailoring your speech to their needs, interests, and expectations. Audience analysis and adaptation is rooted in what communication scholars refer to as **uncertainty reduction theory**, which explains the processes we go through to get to know strangers (Berger & Calabrese, 1975; Knobloch & McAninch, 2014). Although effective speakers adapt their speech to the audience throughout the speech preparation and presentation process, they begin doing so at the point of determining a specific speech goal.

ACTION STEPS

Action Step 1
Select a specific speech goal that is adapted to the rhetorical situation

Action Step 2
Gather and evaluate information to develop your speech

To determine a specific speech goal that is adapted to the rhetorical situation, begin by identifying several subjects and topics that interest you. A **subject** is a broad area of knowledge, such as contemporary cinema, renewable energy, computer technology, or Middle Eastern politics. A **topic** is a narrow, specific aspect of a subject. Ultimately, a good speech is one that interests you, is adapted to address the needs, interests, and expectations of the audience, and is appropriate for the occasion.

11-1a Analyze the Audience

Because addressing the specific needs and expectations of your intended audience is integral to the rhetorical situation, you need to examine who they are by collecting both **demographic** and subject-related data. This information will help you

audience analysis the study of the intended audience for your speech

audience adaptation the process of tailoring your speech to the needs, interests, and expectations of your audience

uncertainty reduction theory explains the processes we go through to get to know strangers

subject a broad area of knowledge

topic some specific aspect of a subject

demographics the statistical characteristics of a specific group of people

Select a Specific Speech Goal That Is Adapted to the Rhetorical Situation

select and tailor your topic and goal to meet their needs, interests, and expectations.

DEMOGRAPHIC DATA Helpful demographic information includes each audience member's approximate age, education level, sex, income, occupation, race, ethnicity, religion, geographic uniqueness, and first language. Figure 11.2 presents a list of questions that may help uncover important demographic information about your audience.

SUBJECT-RELATED DATA You also want to collect subject-related audience disposition data, including: their level of knowledge, initial level of interest in, and attitude toward the potential topics you are considering. Once you know this information, you can use a process of elimination to choose a topic and goal that will offer some new information, insight, or perspective for them.

survey an examination of people to gather information about their ideas and opinions

DATA-GATHERING METHODS You can use several different methods to gather data about your audience.

1. Conduct a survey. Although it is not always possible, the most direct way to collect audience data is to survey them. A **survey** is a direct examination of people to gather information about their ideas and opinions. Some surveys are done as interviews, others as written questionnaires. The four most common types of questions used in a survey are two-sided, multiple-response, scaled, and open-ended. *Two-sided questions* force respondents to choose between two answers (e.g., yes/no, for/against). *Multiple-response questions* give respondents several alternatives from which to choose. *Scaled questions* measure the direction of intensity of respondents' feelings or attitudes toward something (e.g., on a scale from 1 to 5, with 5 being "very likely," . . .). *Open-ended questions* encourage respondents to elaborate on their opinions without forcing them to answer in a predetermined way. Figure 11.3 gives examples of each type.

2. Observe informally. If you are familiar with the members of your audience (as you are with members of your class audience), you can learn a lot through informal observation. For instance, after being in class for even a couple of sessions, you should be able to estimate the approximate age or age range of the class as well as the ratio of men to women. As you

---

FIGURE 11.2 AUDIENCE ANALYSIS QUESTIONS

Age: What is the average age range of the people in your audience?

Educational Level: What percentage of your audience has a high school, college, or postgraduate education?

Sex: What percentage of your audience is male? Female?

Occupation: Is a majority of your audience from a single occupational group, industry, or major? Or do they come from a variety of occupations, industries, or majors?

Socioeconomic Status: What percentage of your audience comes from high-, middle-, or low-income families?

Race: Are most members of your audience of the same race, or is there a mixture of races represented?

Ethnicity: What cultural and co-cultural groups do your audience members identify with?

Religion: What religious traditions are represented?

Geographic Uniqueness: Are audience members from the same state, city, or neighborhood?

Language: What language (if any) is spoken by all audience members? What are the most common primary languages?

FIGURE 11.3 SAMPLE SURVEY QUESTIONS

Two-Sided Question
Are you ☐ a man ☐ a woman?

Multiple-Response Question
Which is the highest educational level you have completed?

☐ Less than high school ☐ High school
☐ Attended college ☐ Associate's degree
☐ Bachelor's degree ☐ Master's degree
☐ Doctorate ☐ Postdoctorate

Scaled Question
How much do you know about Islam?

1   2   3   4   5
nothing   detailed knowledge

Open-Ended Question
What do you think about labor unions?

listen to your classmates talk, you will learn more about their interest in, knowledge of, and attitudes about many issues.

3. Question a representative. When you are invited to speak to a group you are unfamiliar with, ask your contact person for demographic and subject-related audience data.

4. Make educated guesses. If you can't get information in any other way, you can make educated guesses based on indirect data such as the general makeup of the people who live in a certain community, belong to a certain organization, or are likely to attend a speech of this nature.

11-1b Ethical Use of Audience Data

Once you have collected audience data, you can use it to tailor your speech to your audience's interests, needs, and expectations. But adapting to your audience also means creating a speech that all audience members can

relate to. So you will want to avoid two potential pitfalls: marginalizing and stereotyping.

Marginalizing is the practice of ignoring the values, needs, interests, and subject-specific knowledge of some audience members, leaving them to feel excluded.

Stereotyping is assuming all members of a group have similar knowledge, behaviors, or beliefs simply because they belong to that group. To avoid stereotyping based on demographic data, you also need to collect subject-related data from your audience.

You also can reduce your chances of marginalizing or stereotyping by identifying and acknowledging the diversity represented in your audience. **Audience diversity** is the range of demographic characteristics and subject-specific differences represented in an audience.

11-1c Examine the Occasion

The **occasion** is the expected purpose for the speech and the setting where it will be given. Answers to several questions about the occasion should guide you when selecting your topic and throughout the speech-making process.

1. What is the intended purpose of the speech? In other words, why does the audience think this speech is being given? At a Sunday church service, the congregation expects the minister's sermon to have a religious theme. At a national sales meeting, the field representatives expect to hear about new products. For your classroom speeches, a major expectation is that your speech will meet the assignment criteria.

marginalizing ignoring the values, needs, interests, and subject-specific knowledge of some audience members

stereotyping assuming all members of a group have similar knowledge levels, behaviors, or beliefs simply because they belong to that group

audience diversity the range of demographic characteristics and subject-specific differences represented in an audience

occasion the expected purpose and setting for the speech

© Halfpoint/Shutterstock.com

Analyze Your Audience

1. Decide on the audience characteristics (demographic and subject-related data) you want to research to adapt your topic and speech effectively.
2. Choose a method for gathering audience information.
3. Collect the data.

2. What is the expected length? Time limits for classroom speeches are usually quite short, so choose a topic that is narrow enough to be covered in the brief time allotted. For example, "Three Major Causes of the Declining Honeybee Population" could probably be covered in a five-minute speech; however, "A History of Human Impact on the Environment" could not. Speakers who speak for more or less than the allotted time can seriously interfere with event programming and lose the respect of both their hosts and their audience.

3. Where will the speech be given? Rooms vary in size, shape, lighting, and seating arrangements. Some are a single level, some have stages or platforms, and some have tiered seating. The space affects the speech. For example, in a long, narrow room, you may have to speak loudly to be heard in the back row. If you are speaking in an auditorium to a large group of people, you will need to speak loudly and perhaps use a microphone. You will also need to use large gestures and presentational aids that can be seen and heard easily in all parts of the room. The brightness of the room and the availability of shades may affect the kinds of visual aids you can use. So you will want to know and consider the layout of the room as you plan your speech. At times, you might request that the room be changed or rearranged so that the space is better suited to your needs.

4. When will the speech be given? A speech given early in the morning requires a different approach from one given right after lunch or in the evening. If a speech is scheduled after a meal, for example, the audience may be lethargic, mellow, or even on the verge of sleep. So you may want to plan more material that gains and regains their interest throughout the speech. Similarly, where you are placed on the schedule of events should influence your speech planning. For example, if you are first, you may need to "warm up" the audience and be prepared to deal with the distraction of latecomers entering the room while you are speaking. If you speak later in the program, you will need to integrate attention-catching material to keep the interest of a weary audience.

5. What equipment is necessary and available? Would you like to use a microphone, lectern, flip chart, smartboard, computer and LCD projector, or Internet during your speech? If so, check with your host to make sure that the equipment can be made available to you. In some cases, the unavailability of equipment may limit your topic choice. Regardless of the arrangements that have been made, however, experienced speakers expect that something may go wrong and always prepare a backup plan. For example, although computer slide shows can be very effective, technological glitches can sometimes interfere with their use. So it's a good idea to bring handouts as a backup.

Large auditorium?

OR

Small conference room?

© Ferenc Szelepcsenyi/Shutterstock.com

© Nataliya Ostapenko/Shutterstock.com

ACTION STEP 1b

Analyze the Occasion

Hold a conversation with the person who arranged for you to speak and get answers to the following questions:

1. **What is the intended purpose of the speech?**
   _____

2. **What is the expected length for the speech?**
   _____

3. **Where will the speech be given and to how many people?**
   _____

4. **When will the speech be given?**
   _____

5. **What equipment is necessary to give the speech?**
   _____

Write a short paragraph discussing which aspects of the occasion are most important to consider for your speech and why.

_____

_____

_____

_____

 11-2 SELECTING A SPEECH TOPIC

Good speech topics come from subject areas that you have some knowledge about and interest in. To some extent, your analysis of the audience and your topic selection will occur simultaneously.

11-2a Subjects

You can identify subjects by listing those that (1) you think are important and (2) you know something about. Subjects may be related to careers that interest you, your major area of study, special skills or competencies you have or admire, your hobbies, or even your social, economic, or political interests. So if your major is marketing, favorite hobbies are skateboarding and snowboarding, and special concerns are substance abuse and childhood obesity, then these are *subjects* from which you can identify potential speech topics.

Figure 11.4 contains a list of subjects that Holly identified as she began thinking about her upcoming speech. She chose to organize her subject areas under three headings: (1) career interests, (2) hobbies, and (3) issues of concern.

11-2b Brainstorm and Concept Map

Because a topic is a specific aspect of a subject, you can identify many topics related to one subject. Two methods for identifying topics are brainstorming and concept mapping.

As you recall from chapter 10, *brainstorming* is an uncritical, nonevaluative process of generating associated ideas. When you brainstorm, you list as many ideas as you can think of without evaluating them. Holly, for example, decided she wanted to give a speech on the subject of social networking. By brainstorming, she came up with a list of potential topics that included the history of social networking, future trends in social networking, comparisons of popular social networking sites, the downside of social networking, and the social impacts of online social networks.

Concept mapping is a visual means of exploring connections between a subject and related ideas

> **concept mapping** a visual means of exploring connections between a subject and related ideas

---

FIGURE 11.4 HOLLY'S SUBJECT LISTS

Career Interests	Hobbies	Issues of Concern
• Teacher	• Social Networking	• Endangered Birds
• Web Site Designer	• Rowing	• Child Pornography Online
• Information Systems Specialist	• Big Brothers/Big Sisters Organizations	• Personal Privacy and the Internet
• Technology Trainer	• Birding	• Water Pollution
• Public Relations	• Photography	• Global Warming/Climate Change

FIGURE 11.5 HOLLY'S ENDANGERED BIRDS CONCEPT MAP

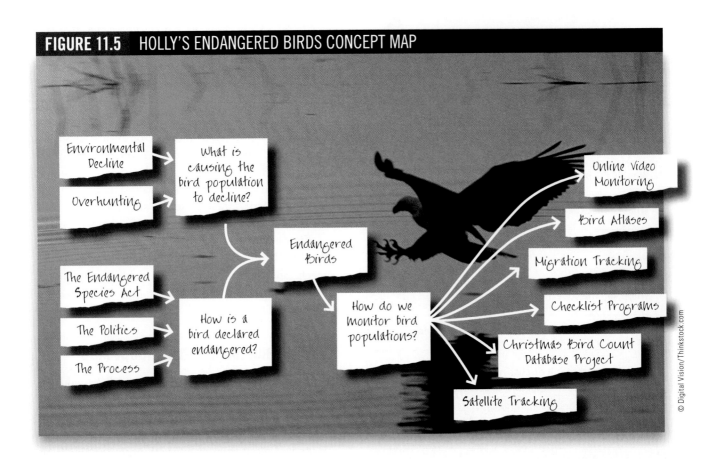

(Callison, 2001). To generate connections, you might ask yourself questions about your subject, focusing on who, what, where, when, and how. In Figure 11.5, you can see Holly's concept map on the subject of endangered birds.

11-2c Select a Topic

As you review your topic list, compare each to your audience profile. Are any topics too simple or too difficult for this audience's knowledge base? If so, eliminate those topics. Are some topics likely to bore the audience and you can't think of any way to pique their interest? Eliminate those as well. How might the audience's age range, ethnicity, and other demographic characteristics mesh with each topic? By asking these and similar questions, you will be able to identify topics that are appropriate for the audience. Also consider the occasion. Are some topics inappropriate for the intended purpose? Are some too broad to cover adequately in the time allotted? Would any require equipment that cannot be made available where you will be speaking? Answers to these kinds of questions help identify topics appropriate to the occasion. Finally, the topics that remain should be appropriate for the rhetorical situation.

Choose one that you would enjoy preparing and sharing with the audience.

ACTION STEP 1c

Brainstorm and Concept Map for Topics

1. **Develop a subject list.**
   a. **Divide a sheet of paper into three columns. Label column 1 "career interests," column 2 "hobbies," and column 3 "issues of concern."**
   b. **Working on one column at a time, identify subjects that interest you. Try to identify at least three subjects in each column.**
   c. **Place a check mark next to one subject in each column you might enjoy speaking about.**
   d. **Keep these lists for future use in choosing a topic for an assigned speech.**
2. **For each subject you checked, brainstorm a list of potential speech topics related to it.**
3. **Then, for each subject you checked, develop a concept map to identify potential speech topics.**

Select a Topic

Use your responses to Action Steps 1a, 1b, and 1c to complete this step.

1. Write each of the topics that you checked in Action Step 1c on the lines below:

_____

_____

_____

_____

2. Using the information you compiled in Action Step 1a (audience analysis), compare each topic to your audience profile. Draw a line through topics that seem less appropriate for your audience.

3. Using the information you compiled in Action Step 1b (analysis of the occasion), compare the remaining topics to the expectations of the occasion. Draw a line through topics that seem less suited to the occasion.

4. From the remaining topics, choose one that you would find enjoyable preparing and sharing in your speech.

11-3 WRITING A SPEECH GOAL STATEMENT

Once you have chosen your topic, you are ready to identify the general goal of your speech and then to write your specific goal statement tailored to the audience and occasion.

11-3a Understanding General and Specific Speech Goals

The **general goal** is the overall intent of the speech. Most speeches intend to entertain, inform, or persuade, even though each type can include elements of the others. Consider the following examples. Jimmy Kimmel's opening monologue on *Jimmy Kimmel Live* is generally intended to entertain, even though it may include persuasive material. Presidential campaign speeches are intended to persuade, even though they also include informative material. The general goal is usually dictated by the occasion. (In this course, your instructor is likely to specify it.)

FIGURE 11.6 IINFORMATIVE AND PERSUASIVE SPEECH GOALS

Informative Goals

Increasing Understanding: I want my audience to understand the three basic forms of a mystery story.

Increasing Knowledge: I want my audience to learn how to light a fire without a match.

Increasing Appreciation: I want my audience to appreciate the intricacies of spiderweb designs.

Persuasive Goals

Reinforce Belief : I want my audience to maintain its belief in drug-free sports.

Change Belief: I want my audience to believe that SUVs are environmentally destructive.

Motivation to Act: I want my audience to join Amnesty International.

Whereas the general goal is typically determined by the occasion, the **specific goal** (or specific purpose) is a single statement that identifies the desired response a speaker wants from the audience. For a speech about vanishing honeybees, for instance, you might state a specific goal as, "I want my audience to understand the four reasons honeybees are vanishing" if your general goal is to inform. If your general goal is to persuade, you might state as your specific goal, "I want my audience to donate money to *Honeybee Advocacy International,* a group trying to solve the problem and stop the crisis." Figure 11.6 offers additional examples of informative and persuasive speech goals.

11-3b Phrasing a Specific Goal Statement

A specific speech goal statement must be carefully crafted because it lays the foundation for organizing your speech. The following guidelines can help you create a specific goal statement.

1. Write a first draft of your specific speech goal statement. Julia, who has been concerned with and is knowledgeable about the subject of illiteracy, drafts the following: "I want my audience to understand the effects of illiteracy." Julia's draft is a complete sentence, and it specifies the response she wants from the audience: *to understand* the effects of illiteracy. Thus, she is planning to give an informative speech.

> **general goal** the overall intent of the speech
>
> **specific goal** a single statement of the exact response the speaker wants from the audience

2. Make sure the goal statement contains only one central idea. Suppose Julia had written: "I want the audience to understand the nature of illiteracy and innumeracy." This would need to be revised because it includes two distinct ideas: illiteracy and innumeracy. It would be difficult to adequately address both within one speech. If your goal statement includes the word *and*, you probably have more than one idea and need to narrow your focus.

3. Revise the statement until it clearly articulates the desired audience response. The draft "I want my audience to understand illiteracy" is a good start, but it is fairly broad. Julia narrows the statement to: "I want my audience to understand three effects of illiteracy." This version is more specific but still does not clearly capture her intention, so she revises it again to: "I would like the audience to understand three effects of illiteracy in the workplace." Now the goal is limited by Julia's focus not only on the specific number of effects but also on a specific situation.

> **secondary research** the process of locating information discovered by other people
>
> **primary research** the process of collecting data about your topic directly in the real world
>
> **credentials** your experiences or education that qualifies you to speak with authority on a subject

ACTION STEP 1e

Write a Specific Speech Goal Statement

General speech goal

_____

1. Write a draft of your specific speech goal, using a complete sentence that specifies the type of response you want from the audience: *to learn about, to understand,* or *to appreciate* the topic.

2. Review the specific goal statement. If it contains more than one idea, select one and redraft your specific goal statement.

Write your revised specific speech goal statement:

_____

_____

_____

11-4 LOCATING AND EVALUATING INFORMATION SOURCES

How can you quickly find the best information related to your specific speech goal? You can start by assessing your own knowledge and experience. Then you can move to **secondary research**, which is the process of locating information discovered by other people. This includes doing Internet and library searches for relevant books, articles, general references, and Web sites. If the information you find from secondary sources doesn't answer all your questions, you may need to conduct **primary research**, which is the process of collecting data about your topic directly from the real world.

11-4a Personal Knowledge and Experience

Because you will be speaking on a topic you know something about, you can include examples from your personal experiences. For instance, a saxophone player knows how to select and care for a reed. Likewise, entrepreneurs know the key features of a business plan, and dieticians have a wealth of information about healthy diets. So Diane, a skilled long-distance runner, can draw from her own knowledge and experience to develop her speech on "How to Train for a Marathon." If you have personal knowledge and experience about the topic, however, you should also share your **credentials**—your experiences or education that qualifies you to speak with authority on a subject. For Diane, establishing her credentials means briefly mentioning her training and expertise as a long-distance runner before she launches into her speech about training for a marathon.

ACTION STEP 2

Gather and Evaluate Information to Develop Your Speech

To use the most effective information to support your speech goal, you must be able to locate and evaluate appropriate sources, identify and select relevant information, and cite information and sources appropriately during your speech.

© Protasov AN/Shutterstock.com

11-4b Secondary Research

Even if you are an expert on your topic, you may need to do secondary research as you adapt the information for your intended audience. To conduct secondary research, you'll need to know how to locate sources, what types of sources you can draw from, and how to skim and evaluate them.

LOCATING SOURCES Begin by locating potential sources. Today we usually start searching for potential sources online. Because there is so much material available on the Internet, we can quickly access many sources from which to collect general facts about a topic, as well as quickly identify some of the outlets that tend to publish material on it. We can also locate relevant material found on personal and commercial Web sites, blogs, and discussion boards, as well as original content created by people on sites such as YouTube.

You can also do online library searches to locate secondary sources about your topic. Some of these materials will be available digitally. Others may require you to visit a library to pick up hard copies. When you locate a source that is not available digitally or in your local library, you may be able to get it through interlibrary loan.

Visiting the library can prove helpful when you get stuck trying to locate information for your speech. Although you can ask librarians for help online via an "ask the librarian" link, visiting with them face-to-face affords you their undivided attention until you are satisfied with the sources they've helped you locate. Librarians are free resources, experts who can demystify thorny research problems. Helping you is their job, so you're not imposing on them when you seek their advice.

TYPES OF SOURCES You'll want to draw from a variety of source types. You can find pertinent information in encyclopedias, books, articles in academic journals and magazines, newspapers, statistical sources, biographies, quotation books and Web sites, and government documents.

1. Encyclopedias Encyclopedia entries can serve as a good starting point by providing an overview acquainting you with the basic terminology associated with a topic. But because encyclopedias provide only overviews, they should never be the only source you rely on. General encyclopedias contain short articles about a wide variety of subjects. In addition, specialized encyclopedias focus on areas such as art, history, religion, philosophy, and science.

2. Books If your topic has been around for awhile, books have probably been written about it. Although books are excellent sources of in-depth material about a topic, keep in mind that most of the information in a book is likely to be at least two years old by the time it is published. So books are not a good resource if you're looking for the latest information on a topic.

3. Articles Articles may contain more current or highly specialized information on your topic than a book. They are published in **periodicals**—magazines and journals that appear at regular intervals. The information in periodical articles is often more current than that published in books because many periodicals are published weekly, biweekly, or monthly. So a periodical article is likely to be a better source if a topic is one that's "in the news." Four frequently available periodical databases are InfoTrac College Edition, InfoTrac University Library, Periodical Abstract, and EBSCO.

4. Newspapers Newspaper articles are excellent sources of facts about and interpretations of both contemporary and historical issues and provide information about local issues and perspectives. Keep in mind, however, that most authors of newspaper articles are journalists who are not experts themselves on the topics they write about. Therefore, it is best not to rely solely on newspaper articles for your speech. Today, most newspapers are available online, which makes them very accessible.

5. Statistical Sources Statistical sources present numerical information on a wide variety of subjects. When you need facts about demography, continents, heads of state, weather, or similar subjects, access one of the many single-volume sources that report such data.

6. Biographies When you need an account of a person's life, from thumbnail sketches to reasonably complete essays, you can use a biographical reference source. Although you can access some biographical information online, you will find information of more depth and breadth by reading full-length biographies and by consulting biographical references such as *Who's Who in America* and *International Who's Who*.

7. Quotation Books and Web Sites A good quotation can be especially provocative as well

periodicals magazines and journals that appear at regular intervals

To Wikipedia or Not to Wikipedia?

Wikipedia is one of the top ten Web sites used worldwide, offering over 18 million articles in 285 different languages; the English language section alone features 4.5 million articles (Cohen, 2011; Kirkpatrick, 2011) Nonetheless, hoaxes and other incidents have spurred a "credibility" backlash against the site. U.S. courts have begun ruling that Wikipedia cannot be used as legal evidence, and in October 2011, Wikipedia member Sven Manguard reported the community was facing a huge backlog of editorial work with over 250,000 articles lacking even a single citation to support them (Manguard, 2011). Though Wikipedia and its community plan to take steps to address the problem and ensure more quality content in the future, these sorts of issues have led many educators to discourage their students from using Wikipedia as a research tool. Some schools have even banned access to it completely. Even Wikipedia founder Jimmy Wales cautions against relying on the site as a primary source (Helm, 2005).

But some educators argue that to simply dismiss Wikipedia as a "bad" source misses the opportunity for

students to think critically about how to do authoritative research. Many university librarians suggest that instead of simply banning Wikipedia's use, today's college students need to be taught to develop information literacy skills that will help them navigate an increasingly complex information environment. For example, instead of uncritically accepting a Wikipedia entry as "fact," students should, at the very least, verify the information by clicking on the sources in the "Notes" section at the end of an entry to see if it comes from a primary and trusted source.

---

as informative, and there are times you want to use a quotation from a respected person. *Bartlett's Familiar Quotations* is a popular source of quotes from historical as well as contemporary figures. But many other collections of quotations are also available.

8. Government Documents

If your topic is related to public policy, government documents may provide useful information. The *Federal Register* publishes daily regulations and

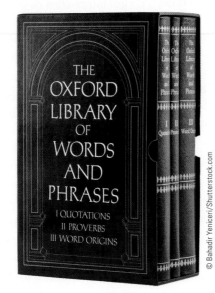

legal notices issued by the executive branch of the United States and all federal agencies. The *Monthly Catalog of United States Government Publications* covers publications of all branches of the federal government.

SKIM SOURCES Because your search of secondary sources is likely to uncover far more information than you can use, skim sources to determine whether or not to read them in full. **Skimming** is a method of rapidly viewing a work to determine what is covered and how.

As you skim an article, think about whether it really presents information on the area of the topic you are exploring and whether it contains any documented statistics, examples, meaningful visuals, or quotable opinions. Many journal articles are printed with an **abstract**—a short paragraph summarizing the research findings—which may make it easier for you to determine if you can use the information in your speech.

skimming rapidly viewing a work to determine what is covered and how

abstract a short paragraph summarizing the research findings

As you skim a book, read the table of contents carefully, look at the index, and review the headings and visuals in pertinent chapters, asking the same questions as you would for a magazine article. A few minutes spent skimming will save you hours of time.

EVALUATE SOURCES The validity, accuracy, and reliability of secondary sources vary widely. **Valid sources** report factual information that can be counted on to be true. Tabloid magazines and tabloid newspapers are generally considered less valid sources for information on celebrities than mainline news organizations that use "fact-checkers" before publishing an article. **Accurate sources** present information that often includes a balanced discussion of controversial ideas. For example, the *Congressional Record* provides an accurate account of what each member of the U.S. Congress has said on the House or Senate floor. A newspaper account of a member's speech, however, may only report part of what was said and may distort the remark by taking it out of context. **Reliable sources** are those with a history of presenting accurate information. For example, the *Bureau of Labor Statistics* is an accurate source for information about U.S. employment. A union newsletter, on the other hand, may sometimes report accurate information about employment trends and at other times may report only information that supports its case. Four criteria can help you assess the validity, accuracy, and reliability of sources.

Authority. The first test of a source is the expertise of its author and/or the reputation of the publishing or sponsoring organization. When an author is listed, you can check the author's credentials through biographical references or by seeing if the author has a home page listing professional qualifications. Use the electronic periodical indexes or check the Library of Congress to see what else the author has published in the field.

On the Internet, you will sometimes find information that is anonymous or credited to someone whose background is not clear. In these cases, your ability to trust the information depends on evaluating the qualifications of the sponsoring organization. URLs ending in .gov (governmental), .edu (educational), and .org are noncommercial sites with institutional publishers. The domain name .com indicates that the Web site sponsor is a for-profit organization. If you do not know whether you can trust the sources, do not use the information.

Objectivity. Although all authors have a viewpoint, be wary of information that seems excessively slanted. Documents that have been published by business, government, or public interest groups should be carefully

There are specific criteria to help you evaluate the reliability of your sources.

scrutinized for obvious biases or good public relations fronts. To evaluate the potential biases in articles and books, read the preface or identify the thesis statement. These often reveal the author's point of view. When evaluating a Web site with which you are unfamiliar, look for its purpose. Most home pages contain a purpose or mission statement (sometimes in a link called "About"). Armed with this information, you are in a better position to recognize potential biases in the information.

Currency. In general, newer information is more accurate than older information (unless, for example, you are documenting a historical event). So when evaluating your sources, unless your speech covers a historical event, be sure to consult the latest information you can find. One of the reasons for using Web-based sources is that they can provide more up-to-date information than printed sources. But just because a source is found online does not mean that the information is timely. To determine how current the information is, you will need to find out when the book was published, the article was written, the study was conducted, or the article was placed on the Web or revised. Web page dates are usually listed at the end of the article. If there are no dates listed, you have no way of judging how current the information is.

Relevance. During your research, you will likely come across a great deal of interesting information. Whether that information is appropriate for your speech is another matter. Relevant information is directly related to your topic and supports your main points, making

valid sources sources that report factual information that can be counted on to be true

accurate sources sources that present information that often includes a balanced discussion of controversial ideas

reliable sources sources with a history of presenting accurate information

your speech easier to follow and understand. Irrelevant information will only confuse listeners, so you should avoid using it no matter how interesting it is.

11-4c Primary Research

When there is little secondary research available on your topic or on a main idea you want to develop in your speech, or when you wonder whether what you are reading about is true in a particular setting, consider doing primary research. Recall that *primary research* is conducting your own study in the real world. But keep in mind that primary research is much more labor intensive and time consuming than secondary research—and, in the professional world, much more costly. You can conduct fieldwork observations, surveys, interviews, original artifact or document examinations, or experiments.

FIELDWORK OBSERVATIONS You might choose to learn about a group of people and their practices by conducting **fieldwork observations**, which is a method focused on careful observation of people or groups of people while immersed in their community. You can conduct fieldwork as a *participant observer* by engaging in interactions and activities with the people you are studying, or as a *non-participant observer* by observing but not engaging with them. If, for instance, you are planning to talk about how social service agencies help the homeless find shelter and job training, or the process involved in adopting a pet, you can learn more by visiting or even volunteering for a period of time at a homeless shelter or humane society. By focusing on specific behaviors and taking notes on your observations, you will have a record of specifics that you can use in your speech.

SURVEYS Recall that a survey is an examination to get information about peoples' ideas and opinions. Surveys may be conducted in person, over the phone, via the Internet, or in writing.

INTERVIEWS Like media reporters, you may get some of your best information from an **interview**—a planned, structured conversation where one person asks questions and another answers them. The Appendix at the end of this book provides information and guidelines for conducting effective interviews.

ORIGINAL ARTIFACT OR DOCUMENT EXAMINATIONS Sometimes the information you need has not been published. Rather, it may exist in an original unpublished source, such as an ancient manuscript, a diary, personal correspondence, or company files. Or you may need to view an object to get the information you need, such as a geographic feature, a building, a monument, or an artifact in a museum.

EXPERIMENTS You can design an experiment to test a **hypothesis**, which is an educated guess about a cause-and-effect relationship between two or more things. Then you can report the results of your experiment in your speech. Keep in mind that experiments take time, and you must understand the principles of the scientific process to be able to trust the results of a formal experiment. However, sometimes you can conduct an informal experiment to test the results of a study you learn about elsewhere.

11-5 IDENTIFYING AND CITING INFORMATION

Once you have collected a variety of sources, you need to identify different types of information or evidence to use in your speech. These include factual statements, expert opinions, and elaborations. You may find the information written in narrative form or presented as a graphic in visual form.

© a katz/Shutterstock.com

Volunteering is not only rewarding but is also a good way to get first-hand experiences in various subject areas.

---

fieldwork observations a research method focused on careful observations of people or groups of people while immersed in their community

interview a planned, structured conversation where one person asks questions and another answers them

hypothesis an educated guess about a cause-and-effect relationship between two or more things

11-5a Factual Statements

Factual statements are those that can be verified. *A recent study confirmed that preschoolers watch an average of 28 hours of television a week* and *The microprocessor, which was invented by Ted Hoff at Intel in 1971, made the creation of personal computers possible* are both statements of fact that can be verified. One way to verify whether a statement is accurate is to check it against other sources on the same subject. Never use information that is not carefully documented unless you have corroborating sources. Factual statements may come in the form of statistics or examples.

STATISTICS **Statistics** are numerical facts. *Only five of every ten local citizens voted in the last election* or *The national unemployment rate for March 2010 was 9.7 percent* can provide impressive support for a point, but when statistics are poorly used in a speech, they may be boring and, in some instances, downright deceiving. Here are some ethical guidelines for using statistics:

▶ Use only statistics you can verify to be reliable and valid. Taking statistics from only the most reliable sources and double-checking any startling statistics with another source will guard against the use of faulty statistics.

▶ Use only recent statistics so your audience will not be misled.

▶ Use statistics comparatively. You can show growth, decline, gain, or loss by comparing two numbers. For example, *according to the U.S. Department of Labor, the national unemployment rate for March 2010 was 9.7 percent.* This statistic is more meaningful when you also mention that this figure has held steady for three months or when you compare it to 8.5 percent in March 2009 and to 5.1 percent in March 2008.

▶ Use statistics sparingly. A few pertinent numbers are far more effective than a battery of statistics.

▶ Remember that statistics can be biased. Mark Twain once said there are three kinds of lies: "lies, damned lies, and statistics." Not all statistics are lies, of course, but consider the source of statistics you'd like to use, what that source may have been trying to prove with these data, and how the data were collected and interpreted. So statistics, like other types of information, must be thoughtfully evaluated and cross-checked for validity, accuracy, and reliability (Frances, 1994).

EXAMPLES **Examples** are specific instances that illustrate or explain a general factual statement. One or two short examples like the following can provide concrete detail that makes a general statement more meaningful to the audience:

One way a company increases its power is to buy out another company. Recently, Delta bought out Northwest and thereby became the world's largest airline company.

> **factual statements** statements that can be verified
>
> **statistics** numerical facts
>
> **examples** specific instances that illustrate or explain a general factual statement
>
> **expert opinions** interpretations and judgments made by authorities in a particular subject area

11-5b Expert Opinions

Expert opinions are interpretations and judgments made by authorities in a particular subject area. They can help explain what facts

Experts can help explain what facts mean or put them into perspective.

© Lisa F. Young/Shutterstock.com

mean or put them into perspective. *Watching 28 hours of television a week is far too much for young children, but may be OK for adults* and *Having a FireWire port on your computer is absolutely necessary* are opinions. Whether they are expert opinions depends on who made the statements. An **expert** is a person who has mastered a specific subject, usually through long-term study, and who is recognized by other people in the field as being a knowledgeable and trustworthy authority. When you use expert opinions in your speech, remember to cite their credentials.

11-5c Elaborations

Both factual information and expert opinions can be elaborated upon through anecdotes and narratives, comparisons and contrasts, or quotable explanations and opinions.

ANECDOTES AND NARRATIVES Anecdotes are brief, often amusing stories; **narratives** are accounts, personal experiences, tales, or lengthier stories. Because holding audience interest is important and because audience attention is likely to be captured by a story, anecdotes and narratives are worth looking for or creating. The key to using them is to be sure the point of the story directly addresses the point you are making in your speech. Good anecdotes and narratives may be humorous, sentimental, suspenseful, or dramatic.

COMPARISONS AND CONTRASTS One of the best ways to give meaning to new ideas or facts is through comparison and contrast. **Comparisons** illuminate a point by showing similarities, whereas **contrasts** highlight differences. Although comparisons and contrasts may be literal, like comparing and contrasting the murder rates in different countries or during different eras, they may also be figurative.

▶ *Figurative comparison:* "In short, living without health insurance is as much of a risk as having uncontrolled diabetes or driving without a safety belt" (Nelson, 2006, p. 24).

expert a person who has mastered a specific subject, usually through long-term study

anecdotes brief, often amusing stories

narratives accounts, personal experiences, tales, or lengthier stories

comparisons illuminate a point by showing similarities

contrasts illuminate a point by highlighting difference

plagiarism the unethical act of representing a published author's work as your own

annotated bibliography a preliminary record of the relevant sources you find as you conduct your research

▶ *Figurative contrast:* "If this morning you had bacon and eggs for breakfast, I think it illustrates the difference. The eggs represented 'participation' on the part of the chicken. The bacon represented 'total commitment' on the part of the pig!" (Durst, 1989, p. 325).

QUOTATIONS At times, information you find will be so well stated that you want to quote it directly in your speech. Because the audience is interested in listening to your ideas and arguments, you should avoid using quotations that are too long or too numerous. But when you find that an author or expert has worded an idea especially well, quote it directly and then verbally acknowledge the person who said or wrote it. Using quotations or close paraphrases without acknowledging their source is **plagiarism**, the unethical act of representing another person's work as your own.

11-5d Seek Information from Multiple Cultural Perspectives

With many topics, the way we perceive facts as well as the opinions we hold are influenced by our cultural background. Therefore, it is important to seek information from a variety of cultural perspectives by drawing from sources with different cultural orientations and by interviewing experts with diverse cultural backgrounds. For example, when Carrie was preparing her speech on proficiency testing in grade schools, she purposefully searched for articles written by noted Hispanic, Asian-American, African-American, and European-American authors. In addition, she interviewed two local school superintendents—one from an urban district and another from a suburban district. Doing so boosted Carrie's confidence that her speech would accurately reflect multiple sides of the debate on proficiency testing.

11-5e Record Information

As you find information to use in your speech, you need to record it accurately and keep a careful account of your sources so you can cite them appropriately during your speech. How should you keep track of the information you plan to use? One way is to compile an annotated bibliography of the sources you believe are relevant and create a research card for each individual item of information you plan to cite in the speech.

ANNOTATED BIBLIOGRAPHY An **annotated bibliography** is a preliminary record of the relevant sources you find as you conduct your research. Each entry in an annotated bibliography includes a short summary of information in that source. You can compile an annotated bibliography on your computer as you work. When you identify the exact information you want to use in the speech, you can edit your bibliography to create your speech reference list. A good annotated bibliography for speech planning includes:

▶ A complete bibliographic citation for each source based on the type of source (such as book, article, or Web site) and the style guide (such as APA or MLA) you are using;

▶ Two or three sentences summarizing the information in the source;

▶ Two or three sentences explaining how the source is related to your speech topic; and

▶ Any direct quotations you might want to include verbatim in your speech.

RESEARCH CARDS **Research cards** are individual three-by-five-inch or four-by-six-inch index cards or electronic facsimiles that record one piece of information relevant to your speech along with a key word or main idea and the bibliographic information identifying where you found it. Recording each piece of information using a key word or main idea identifier on a unique research card allows you to easily find, arrange, and rearrange individual pieces of information as you prepare your speech.

As your stack of research cards grows, you can sort the material and place each item under the heading to which it is related. Figure 11.7 shows a sample research card.

ACTION STEP 2b

Prepare Research Cards: Record Facts, Opinions, and Elaborations

The goal of this step is to review the source material you identified in Action Step 2a and to record specific items of information that you might wish to use in your speech.

1. Carefully read all print and electronic sources (including Web site material) you have identified and evaluated as appropriate sources for your speech. Review your notes and any tapes from interviews and observations.

2. As you read an item (fact, opinion, example, illustration, statistic, anecdote, narrative, comparison/contrast, quotation, definition, or description) that you think might be useful in your speech, record it on a research card or on the appropriate electronic note card form available on the *COMM3* CourseMate site. If you are using an article from a periodical that you read online, use the periodical research card form.

11-5f Cite Sources

Whenever you use information that is not your own, you need to acknowledge the source of it. Specifically mentioning sources during your speeches not only helps the audience evaluate them but also enhances their perception of you as knowledgeable. Frankly, failure to cite sources constitutes plagiarism. Just as you would provide internal citations or footnotes in a written document, you must provide oral footnotes during your speech. **Oral footnotes** are references to an

---

FIGURE 11.7 SAMPLE RESEARCH CARD

Topic: Fracking

Key Term/Main Idea: Health Issues

Theo Colborn, president of The Endocrine Disruption Exchange in Paonia, Colorado, believes that some drilling and fracking additives that can end up in produced water are neurotoxic; among these are 2-buxtoxyethanol. "If you compare [such chemicals] with the health problems the people have," Colborn says, "they match up."

Brown, V. J. (February 2007). Industry issues: Putting the heat on gas. Environmental Health Perspectives (U.S. National Institue of Environmental Health Sciences), 115, p. 2.

---

research cards individual cards or facsimiles that record one piece of relevant information for your speech

oral footnotes references to an original source, made at the point in the speech where information from that source is presented

Cite Sources

On the back of each research card, write a short phrase that you can use in your speech as an oral footnote.

original source, made at the point in the speech where information from that source is presented. The key to preparing oral footnotes is to include enough information for listeners to access the sources themselves and to offer enough credentials to enhance the credibility of the information you are citing. Figure 11.8 has some examples.

FIGURE 11.8 ORAL FOOTNOTES

"Thomas Friedman, noted columnist for *The New York Times*, stated in his book *The World Is Flat* . . ."

"In an interview with *New Republic* magazine, Governor Chris Christie stated . . ."

"According to an article in last week's *Time* magazine, the average college graduate . . ."

"In the latest Gallup poll cited in the February 10 issue of *The New York Times* online . . ."

"But to get the complete picture, we have to look at the statistics. According to the *2012 Statistical Abstracts*, the level of production for the European Economic Community fell from . . ."

"During the Indo-U.S. Strategic Dialogue in Afghanistan in 2012, Secretary of State John Kerry stated . . ."

LOCATED ON COMM 4 ONLINE AT CENGAGEBRAIN.COM:

☐ Review Key Term flashcards and create your own cards

☐ Track your knowledge and understanding of key concepts in communication

☐ Complete practice and graded quizzes to prepare for tests

☐ Complete interactive content within COMM4 Online

☐ View the chapter highlight boxes for COMM4 Online

LOCATED IN TEXTBOOK

☐ Tear-out Chapter Review cards at the end of the book

☐ Review with the Quick Quiz below

Quick Quiz

T   F   1. A well-worded specific goal statement should always contain three central ideas.

T   F   2. Experience and education that qualify you to speak with authority on a subject are called credentials.

T   F   3. Encyclopedias are excellent sources of facts about and interpretations of both contemporary and historical issues.

T   F   4. Primary research is much more labor intensive and costly than secondary research.

T   F   5. Footnotes can be written or oral.

6. A _____ is a broad area of expertise about something such as movies, cognitive psychology, or computer technology.

   a. subject
   b. talking point
   c. topic
   d. main idea
   e. bullet point

7. Demographic information of an audience member includes

   a. occupation, income, and education.
   b. gender and age.
   c. race and language.
   d. ethnicity and religion.
   e. All of these are correct.

8. Each of the following questions should be asked about the speech occasion to help with speech planning beforehand except

   a. What are the special expectations for the speech?
   b. Will a meal be served before the speech?
   c. What is the appropriate length for the speech?
   d. How large will the audience be?
   e. Where will the speech be given?

9. Although _____ are excellent sources of in-depth material about a topic, most of the information is likely to be at least two years old at the time of publishing.

   a. statistical sources
   b. encyclopedias
   c. periodicals
   d. books
   e. government documents

10. When presenting information in a speech that you've learned from a secondary source, it is crucial to _____ or you could be accused of _____.

   a. tell the truth; ethical behavior
   b. cite sources; plagiarism
   c. fabricate statistics; lying
   d. read your full bibliography during the speech; being sloppy
   e. show confidence; concept mapping

Answers: 1.F, 2.T, 3.F, 4.T, 5.T, 6.A, 7.E, 8.B, 9.D, 10.B

12 Organizing Your Speech

LEARNING OUTCOMES

12-1 Develop your speech body using an appropriate main point pattern

12-2 Create an effective speech introduction

12-3 Construct an effective conclusion

12-4 Compile a formal speech outline and reference list

After finishing this chapter go to **PAGE 175** for **STUDY TOOLS.**

We have all heard speeches packed with interesting information and delivered in ways that hold our attention, but find it difficult to recall the speaker's main ideas, afterward. So we may listen to a speech and find that, even though we have been entertained, the speaker's words have no lasting impact on us.

Well-constructed speeches have impact. When a speech is over, we must remember not only the opening joke or a random story, but we must also remember the main ideas. In this chapter, we describe the third of the five speech plan action steps: organizing ideas into a well-structured outline.

Organizing, the process of arranging your speech material, is guided by what you learned from your audience analysis. To turn your ideas into a well-organized outline, begin by developing the body, then the introduction, and finally the conclusion.

ACTION STEPS

Action Step 3
Organize ideas into a well-structured outline

12-1 DEVELOP THE BODY

Once you have completed the first two action steps (identified your general and specific speech goal and assembled a body of information on your topic), you are ready to plan the body of your speech by (a) identifying and arranging the main points; (b) crafting them into a well-phrased thesis statement; (c) developing each main point with appropriate supporting material

organizing the process of arranging your speech material

(evidence and reasoning); and (d) creating transitions to move smoothly from one main point to the next.

12-1a Identify Main Points

Begin by identifying two to four main point ideas that will help you achieve your speech goal. You will then develop each main idea with supporting material. In fact, the difference between a 5-minute speech and a 25-minute speech with the same speech goal is not the number of main points, but the extent to which each one is developed with supporting material.

For some goals, determining the main points is easy. For example, if your goal is to teach your audience how to create a Web site, your main points will likely be the steps involved in developing a very basic one. Most times, however, identifying main points is more complex. How can you identify the main ideas when they aren't obvious? First, begin by listing the ideas you believe relate to your specific goal. You will probably find it easy to list as many as nine or more. Second, eliminate ideas that you believe this audience already understands. Third, eliminate any ideas that might be too complicated or too broad for this audience to comprehend in the time allotted. Fourth, check to see if some of the ideas can be grouped together under a broader theme. Finally, from the ideas that remain, choose two to four that will help you accomplish your specific speech goal.

Let's look at how Katie used these steps to identify the main points for her speech to inform her classmates of the growing problem of Adderall use among college students. To begin, Katie listed ideas she had discovered while doing her research.

▶ What is a prescription drug?

▶ What is Adderall?

▶ What are the ingredients in Adderall?

▶ How is Adderall made?

▶ What is the history of Adderall?

▶ Who takes Adderall?

▶ Why is it prescribed?

▶ What are its benefits?

▶ What are its risks?

▶ How many college students take Adderall without a prescription?

▶ What are the demographics of college students who take Adderall without a prescription?

▶ Why do college students who don't have a prescription take it (perceived benefits)?

▶ What are the benefit myths?

▶ What are the actual results and/or consequences of taking Adderrall without a prescription?

Second, Katie eliminated the idea "what is a prescription drug" because she knew her audience already understood this. Third, Katie noticed that several of the ideas seemed to be related. What Adderall is, why it is prescribed, who takes it, and the risks and benefits seemed to go together. How many people take it, demographics, and perceived benefits of college students who take Adderall without a prescription also seemed to be related. And benefit myths and actual results/consequences could be grouped together. Fourth, Katie decided the ingredients, history, and how Adderall is made were too broad to cover adequately in the time she was allotted for the speech and

FIGURE 12.1 KATIE'S SPEECH FRAMEWORK

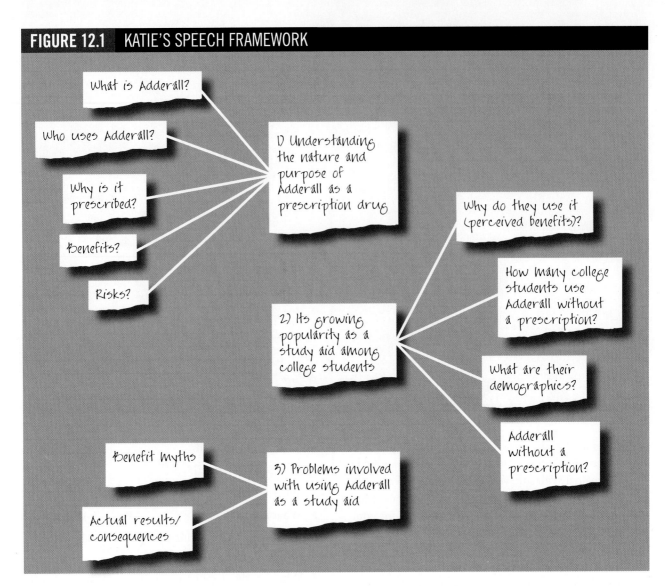

were not directly related to her goal. Finally, Katie decided her main points would be: (1) understanding the nature and purpose of Adderall as a prescription drug; (2) its growing popularity as a study aid among college students; and (3) problems involved with using Adderall without a prescription. These main points became the framework for the body of Katie's speech. When she finished her analysis and synthesis, Katie's list looked like Figure 12.1.

12-1b Word Main Points

Once you have identified your two to four main points, you can begin to shape each into a clear sentence. Let's look at how Katie did this.

Recall that Katie's main point ideas are understanding the nature and purpose of Adderall as a prescription drug, its

preparation outline the first draft of organizing the main aids and supporting material into a speech outline

growing popularity as a study aid among college students, and the risks involved in doing so. Suppose she wrote her first draft of main points as follows:

  I. What exactly is Adderall, and why is it prescribed?

 II. College student use

III. Risks

Some people refer to this first version of wording main points as a **preparation outline**. It provides a draft of main points but doesn't do so in the form of a completed sentence. Katie might clarify her main points like this:

  I. What exactly is Adderall?

 II. An increasing number of American college students are using Adderall.

III. Abusing Adderall is risky.

Study these statements. Do they seem a bit vague? Let's consider Katie's draft statements more carefully. Her three main points are complete sentences, which is good. To assure herself that she has achieved the best wording, Katie next applies two test questions to them.

1. Is the relationship between each main point and the speech goal clearly specified? Katie's first main point statement doesn't indicate what purposes Adderall serves as a prescription medicine. So she could improve this statement by saying:

> *What exactly is Adderall, and what is it prescribed for?*

Similarly, she can improve the second main point statement by saying:

> *Adderall abuse is becoming increasingly popular among American college students.*

The third point might be redrafted to state:

> *Abusing Adderall as a study aid is dangerous.*

2. Are the main points parallel in structure? Parallel structure means the main points follow the same structural pattern. Parallel structure is not a requirement, but

ACTION STEP 3a

Choose Main Points

The goal of this activity is to help you determine two to four main ideas or main points that you can use as the framework for your speech.

1. **List all the ideas you have found that relate to the specific goal of your speech.**

   _____

   _____

   _____

   _____

2. **If you have trouble limiting the number, do the following:**
   a. **Draw a line through each idea that you believe the audience already understands, that you have no supporting information for, or that just seems too complicated.**
   b. **Combine ideas that can be grouped together under a single heading.**
3. **From the ideas that remain, choose the two to four you will use as main points in your speech.**

ACTION STEP 3b

Write a Thesis Statement

The goal of this activity is to use your specific goals and the main points you have identified to develop a well-worded thesis statement for your speech.

1. **Write the general and specific goals you developed in chapter 11 with Action Step 1e.**
2. **List the main points you determined in Action Step 3a.**
3. **Now write a complete sentence that combines your specific goal with your main point ideas.**

it can help the audience recognize main points when you deliver your speech. So, Katie made one more small adjustment:

I. *First, what exactly is Adderall, and why is it prescribed?*

II. *Second, a growing number of American college students are using Adderall.*

III. *Third, abusing Adderall as a study aid is dangerous.*

Parallelism can be achieved in many ways. Katie used numbering: "first . . . second . . . third." Another way is to start each sentence with an active verb. Suppose Adam wants his audience to understand the steps involved in writing an effective job application cover letter. He wrote the following first draft of his main points:

I. Format the heading elements correctly.

II. The body of the letter should be three paragraphs long.

III. When concluding, use "sincerely" or "regards."

IV. Then you need to proofread the letter carefully.

Adam then revised his main points to make them parallel in structure by using active verbs (italicized):

I. *Format* the heading elements correctly.

II. *Organize* the body into three paragraphs.

III. *Conclude* the letter with "sincerely" or "regards."

IV. *Proofread* the letter carefully.

12-1c Select a Main Point Pattern

A speech can be organized in many different ways. Although speeches may use many different organizational patterns, four fundamental patterns are time (a.k.a. sequential or chronological) order, narrative order, topical order, and logical reasons order.

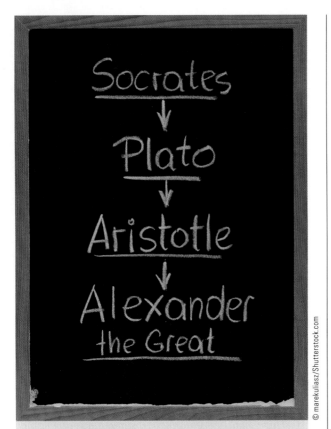

Time or chronological order is one pattern that can be used in organizing a speech.

1. Time order, sometimes called *sequential order* or *chronological order*, arranges main points in sequence or by steps in a process. When you explain how to do something, how to make something, how something works, or how something happened, you will use time order. Adam's speech on the steps in writing a job application and cover letter followed a time order pattern. Let's look at another example.

Specific Goal: I want the audience to understand the four steps involved in developing a personal network.

I. First, analyze your current networking potential.

II. Second, position yourself in places for opportunity.

III. Third, advertise yourself.

IV. Fourth, follow up on contacts.

2. Narrative order conveys ideas through a story or series of stories. Narrative order is rooted in narrative theory, which suggests that one important way people communicate is through storytelling. We use stories to teach and learn, to entertain, and to make sense of the world around us (Fisher, 1987). While a narrative may be presented in chronological order, it may also use a series of flashbacks or flash forwards to increase the dramatic effect. Each main point may be an event in a single story or each main point may be a different story that illustrates the thesis. Lonna shared her story about having anorexia to help listeners understand the impact of the condition on someone's life.

Specific Goal: I want my audience to understand how anorexia nervosa affects the lives of its victims and their loved ones.

I. First, let's talk about a typical day for me as a recovering anorexic.

II. Second, let's focus on a historical account about how I became anorexic.

III. Finally, let's discuss an inspirational story about two people who basically saved my life.

3. Topical order arranges the main points using some logical relationship among them. Main points might progress from general to specific, least to most important, most to least familiar, and so forth.

Specific Goal: I want the audience to understand three proven methods of ridding our bodies of harmful toxins.

I. One proven method for ridding our bodies of harmful toxins is reducing our intake of animal products.

II. A second proven method for ridding our bodies of harmful toxins is eating more natural whole foods.

III. A third proven method for ridding our bodies of harmful toxins is keeping well hydrated.

4. Logical reasons order structures the main points according to reasons for accepting the thesis as desirable or true. Logical reasons order is usually used when your goal is to persuade.

Specific Goal: I want the audience to donate money to the United Way.

I. When you donate to the United Way, your one donation can be divided among many charities.

II. When you donate to the United Way, you can stipulate which charities you wish to support.

time (sequential or chronological) order an organizational pattern that arranges the main points by a chronological sequence or by steps in a process

narrative order an organizational pattern that dramatizes the thesis using a story or series of stories that includes characters, settings, and a plot

topical order an organizational pattern that structures the main points using some logical relationship among them

logical reasons order an organizational pattern that structures the main points as reasons for accepting the thesis as desirable or true

12-1d Write the Thesis Statement

A **thesis statement** is a one- or two-sentence summary that incorporates your general and specific goals and previews the main points of your speech. Katie crafted the following thesis statement for her speech on Adderall: "Off-label Adderall use by college students is growing in popularity among college students. To clarify, let's discuss the nature and purpose of Adderall as a prescription drug, its growing popularity as a study aid among college students, and problems associated with using Adderall as a study aid." Review Figure 12.1 for several additional examples.

12-1e Outline the Speech Body

Once you have identified each main point, ordered them according to an appropriate main point pattern, and constructed your thesis statement, you are ready to develop the speech body. A good way to do so is to construct an outline. An **outline** is a written framework of the sequential and hierarchical relationships among ideas in the speech. In most speeches, three levels of hierarchy are all you will need: main points (numbered with Roman numerals), subpoints that support a main point (ordered under each main point with capital letters), and sometimes sub-subpoints (numbered under the relevant subpoint with Arabic numbers). Figure 12.2 shows the general form of most speech outlines. Notice that it proposes between two and four main points and offers at least two subpoints under each main point.

12-1f Develop Main Points

You develop each main point with subpoints and supporting material. **Subpoints** are statements that elaborate on a main point. A main point may have two, three, or even more subpoints depending on the complexity of it. Subpoints are developed further through **supporting material**— evidence you gathered through secondary and primary research along with reasoning you use

Logical reasons order is usually used when your goal is to persuade your audience of something.

III. When you donate to the United Way, you know that a high percentage of your donation will go directly to the charities you've selected.

These four organizational patterns are the most basic ones. In Chapters 16 and 17, you will be introduced to several additional patterns for structuring the main points of informative and persuasive speeches.

ACTION STEP 3c

Outline the Main Points

The goal of this activity is to help you phrase and order your main points.

1. Write your thesis statement (Action Step 3b).
2. Using the thesis statement you wrote in Action Step 3b, underline the two to four main points for your speech.
3. Review the main points as a group.
   a. Is the relationship of each main point statement to the goal statement clearly specified? If not, revise.
   b. Are the main points parallel in structure? If not, revise.
4. Choose an organizational pattern for your main points.
5. Write your main points down in this order. Place a "I." before the main point you will make first, a "II." before your second point, and so on.

thesis statement a one- or two-sentence summary of your speech that states your general and specific goals and previews the main points

outline a written framework of the sequential and hierarchical relationships among ideas in a speech

subpoints statements that elaborate on a main point

supporting material developmental material you gathered through secondary and primary research

Raise a Glass: Giving a Toast

© DUSAN ZIDAR/Shutterstock.com

While a celebratory toast may not seem like the place for a prepared and structured speech, most experts suggest it's best to prepare your remarks ahead of time. This will give you a chance to gather your thoughts and help you manage your nerves when you actually give the toast. Practicing aloud in advance will also help you to sound more natural and conversational because you are less likely to simply read it.

When considering how to structure your toast, begin by writing down your thoughts about the subject of the toast. From this brainstorming list, you can begin to structure your speech by pairing your research with your personal experience and your personal knowledge. A toast should focus on the personal. At a wedding, for example, humorous or heartfelt anecdotes about the couple can be a great way to personalize the speech and keep your audience interested. In fact, including a joke or a poignant memory about the bride or groom can be an effective way to start your toast and set the tone for the entire speech. Most experts recommend keeping such personal anecdotes positive rather than embarrassing. Be mindful of your audience, as it's unlikely that Grandma wants to hear a raunchy story about the bride's single days. Choosing an appropriate anecdote can help you structure the entire speech, as the emotions brought out in the anecdote can set up the well-wishes you use to end your toast. You can end with your own words or turn to popular quotations that exemplify the positive emotions you've expressed during your toast.

FIGURE 12.2 GENERAL FORM FOR A SPEECH OUTLINE

I. Main point one
  A. Subpoint A for main point one
    1. Sub-subpoint one (optional)
    2. Sub-subpoint two (optional)
  B. Subpoint B for main point one
II. Main point two
  A. Subpoint A for main point two
    1. Sub-subpoint one (optional)
    2. Sub-subpoint two (optional)
  B. Subpoint B for main point two
III. Main point three
  A. Subpoint A for main point three
    1. Sub-subpoint one (optional)
    2. Sub-subpoint two (optional)
  B. Subpoint B for main point three
    . . . and so on.

ACTION STEP 3d

Identify and Outline Subpoints

The goal of this activity is to help you develop and outline your subpoints. Complete the following steps for each of your main points.

1. List the main point.
2. Using your research cards or annotated bibliography, list the key information related to that main point.
3. Analyze that information and cross out items that seem less relevant or don't fit.
4. Look for items that seem related and can be grouped under a broader heading.
5. Try to group information until you have between two and four supporting points for the main point.
6. Write those supporting subpoints in full sentences.
7. Repeat this process for all main points.
8. Write an outline using Roman numerals for main points, capital letters for supporting points, and Arabic numbers for material related to supporting points.

to link it to the main point it supports. You can identify subpoints by sorting through the research you compiled in your annotated bibliography and/or on research cards to find evidence (e.g., definitions, examples, facts statistics, stories). Then, look for relationships between and among ideas. As you analyze, you can draw lines connecting items of information that fit together logically, cross out information that seems less important or doesn't really fit, and combine similar ideas using different language. One subpoint in each main point should be a **listener relevance link**, a piece of information that alerts listeners to why the main point is relevant to them.

12-1g Create Transitions

Transitions are words, phrases, or sentences that show the relationship between the two ideas. Good transitions are certainly important in writing, but they are crucial in public speaking. If listeners get lost or think they have missed something, they cannot go back and check as they can when reading. Transitions can come in the form of section transitions or signposts.

SECTION TRANSITIONS Section transitions are complete sentences that show the relationship between and bridge major parts of the speech. They typically summarize what has just been said in one main point and preview the one coming up next. Essentially, section transitions are the "glue" that links the main points of your speech together.

For example, suppose Adam just finished his introduction on creating a cover letter and is now ready to launch into his main points. Before stating his first main point, he might say, "Creating a good cover letter is a process that has four steps. Now, let's consider the first one." When his listeners hear this transition, they are signaled to listen to and remember the first main point. When he finishes his first main point, he will use another section transition to signal that he is finished speaking about the first main point and is moving on to the second main point:

© Regien Paassen/Shutterstock.com

"Now that we understand what is involved in creating the heading elements, let's move on to discuss what to include in the body of the letter."

Section transitions are important for two reasons. First, they help the audience follow the organization of ideas in the speech. Second, they help audience members remember information.

SIGNPOSTS Signposts are words or phrases that connect pieces of supporting material to the main point or sub point they address. Sometimes signposts number ideas: *first, second, third,* and *fourth.* Sometimes they help the audience focus on a key idea: *foremost, most important,* or *above all.* Signposts can also be used to introduce an explanation: *to illustrate, for example, in other words, essentially,* or *to clarify.* Signposts can also signal that a lengthy anecdote, or even the speech itself, is coming to an end: *in short, finally, in conclusion,* or *to summarize.* Just as section transitions serve as the glue that holds your big-picture main points together, signposts connect your subpoints and supporting material together within each main point.

listener relevance link a piece of information that alerts listeners to why the main point is related to them or why they should care about the topic or point

transitions words, phrases, or sentences that show the relationship between or bridge ideas

section transition a complete sentence that shows the relationship between or bridges major parts of a speech

signposts short word or phrase transitions that connect pieces of supporting material to the main point or subpoint they address

12-2 DEVELOPING THE INTRODUCTION

Once you have developed the speech body, you need to decide how to introduce it. Because the introduction is so important to success, develop two or three different introductions and then select the one that seems best for your specific goal and the audience you will be addressing. An introduction is generally about 10 percent of the length of the entire speech, so for a five-minute speech (approximately 750 words), an introduction of about 30 seconds (approximately 60–85 words) is appropriate.

An effective introduction achieves four primary goals: (1) it gets the audience's attention, (2) it establishes listener relevance, (3) it begins to establish speaker credibility, and (4) it states the thesis (speech goal and main point preview).

12-2a Get Attention

An audience's physical presence does not guarantee people will actually listen to your speech. Your first goal, then, is to create an opening that will win your listeners' attention by arousing their curiosity and motivating them to want to know more about your topic. Let's look at several strategies for getting attention: startling statements, questions, stories, jokes, personal references, quotations, action, and suspense.

STARTLING STATEMENTS A **startling statement** is a shocking expression or example. Chris used this startling statement to get his listeners' attention for his speech about how automobile emissions contribute to global warming:

Look around. Each one of you is sitting next to a killer. That's right. You are sitting next to a cold-blooded killer. Before you think about jumping up and running out of this room, let me explain. Everyone who drives an automobile is a killer of the environment. Every time you turn the key to your ignition, you are helping to destroy our precious surroundings.

QUESTIONS Questions are requests for information that encourage the audience to think about something related to your topic. Questions can be *rhetorical* or *direct*. A **rhetorical question** is one that doesn't require an overt response. Notice how a student began her speech on counterfeiting with three short, rhetorical questions:

What would you do with this $20 bill if I gave it to you? Would you take your friend to a movie? Or would you treat yourself to pizza and drinks? Well, if you did either of these things, you could get in big trouble—this bill is counterfeit!

Notice that the speaker didn't ask the question to find out what her audience members would actually do with the money, but to set up the speech on counterfeiting.

Unlike a rhetorical question, a **direct question** seeks an overt response from the audience. It might be a "yea" or "nay" or a show of hands. For example, here's how author and motivational speaker Harvey MacKay started his commencement address at the University of Southern California in 2009:

Let me start by asking all of you in the audience this question: How many people talk to themselves? Please raise your hands. I count approximately 50 percent. To the other 50 percent who didn't raise your hands, I can just hear you now, saying to yourself: "Who me? I don't talk to myself!"

Well I think all of you will be talking to yourself about the day's events on your way home this evening. This is an unforgettable moment among many fine hours you will have in your career and life. (Mackay, 2009)

Direct questions get audience attention because they require a physical response. However, getting listeners to actually comply with your request can also pose a challenge.

STORIES A **story** is an account of something that has happened (actual) or could happen (hypothetical). Most people enjoy a well-told story, so it makes a good attention getter. One drawback is that stories can sometimes take more time to tell than is appropriate for the length of your speech. Use a story only if it is short or if you

startling statement a shocking expression or example used to arouse an audience's interest

questions requests for information that encourage an audience to think about something related to your topic

rhetorical question a question that doesn't require an overt response from an audience

direct question a question that demands an overt response from an audience

story an account of something that has happened or could happen

can abbreviate it so that it is just right for your speech length.

JOKES A **joke** is an anecdote or a piece of wordplay designed to make people laugh. A joke can be used to get attention when it meets the *three R's test:* It must be realistic, relevant, and repeatable (Humes, 1988). In other words, the joke can't be too far-fetched, unrelated to the speech purpose, or potentially offensive to some listeners. In his speech about being a person of integrity, for example, Joel Osteen offered this joke to get attention:

> *A kindergarten teacher asked one of her students what she was drawing a picture of. The little girl said, "I'm drawing a picture of God." The teacher replied, "Oh honey, nobody knows what God looks like." Without missing a beat, the little girl replied, "They will in a minute . . ."* (Osteen, 2012)

© Oksana Kuzmina/Shutterstock.com

PERSONAL REFERENCES A **personal reference** is a brief account of something that happened to you or a hypothetical situation that listeners can imagine themselves in. In addition to getting attention, a personal reference can engage listeners as active participants. A personal reference like the one that follows is suitable for a speech of any length:

> *Were you panting when you got to the top of those four flights of stairs this morning? I'll bet there were a few of you who vowed you're never going to take a class on the top floor of this building again. But did you ever stop to think that maybe the problem isn't that this class is on the top floor? It just might be that you are not getting enough exercise.*

QUOTATIONS A **quotation** is a comment made by and attributed to someone other than the speaker. A particularly vivid or thought-provoking quotation can make an excellent introduction as long as it relates to your topic.

ACTION An **action** is an attention-getting act designed to highlight and arouse interest in your topic. You can perform an action yourself, just as Juan did when he split a stack of boards with his hand to get attention for his speech on karate, or you can ask volunteers from the audience to perform the action. For example, Cindria used three audience members to participate in breaking a piñata to create interest in her speech

on the history of the piñata. If you choose to use audience members, consider soliciting participants ahead of time to avoid the possibility of having no volunteers when you ask for them during your speech. Finally, you can ask your entire audience to perform some action related to your speech topic. If you'd like to ask your whole audience to perform an action, realistically assess whether what you are asking is something your audience is likely to comply with.

SUSPENSE To create **suspense**, word your attention-getter so that what is described generates uncertainty or mystery and excites the audience. When your audience wonders, "What is she leading up to?" you have created suspense. A suspenseful opening is especially valuable when your audience is not particularly interested in hearing about your topic. Consider this suspenseful introduction from Midori's speech:

> *It costs the United States more than $116 billion per year. It has cost the loss of more jobs than a recession. It accounts for nearly 100,000 deaths a year. I'm not talking about drug abuse—the problem is alcoholism. Today I want to show you how we can avoid this inhumane killer by abstaining from alcohol.*

By putting the problem, alcoholism, near the end of her suspenseful comments, Midori encourages the audience to try to anticipate her topic. And because the audience may well be thinking the problem is drugs, the revelation that the answer is alcoholism is likely to be that much more effective.

12-2b Establish Relevance

Even if you successfully get your listeners' attention, to *keep* their attention you will need to motivate them to listen to your speech. You can do this by offering a clear listener relevance link in

joke an anecdote or a piece of wordplay designed to be funny and make people laugh

personal reference a brief account of something that happened to you or a hypothetical situation that listeners can imagine themselves in

quotation a comment made by and attributed to someone other than the speaker

action an act designed to highlight and arouse interest in a topic

suspense wording your attention-getter so that it generates uncertainty and excites the audience

the introduction. Recall that a listener relevance link is a statement of how and why your speech relates to or might affect your audience. Sometimes your attention-getting statement will serve this function, but if it doesn't, you will need to provide a personal connection between your topic and your audience. Notice how Tiffany created a listener relevance link for her speech about being a vegetarian by asking her audience to consider the topic in relation to their own lives:

> Although a diet rich in eggs and meat was once the norm in this country, more and more of us are choosing a vegetarian lifestyle to help lower blood pressure, reduce cholesterol, and even help prevent the onset of some diseases.

When creating a listener relevance link, answer these questions: Why should my listeners care about what I'm saying? In what way(s) might they benefit from hearing about it? How might my speech address my listeners' needs or desires for such things as health, wealth, well-being, self-esteem, success, and so forth?

12-2c Establish Credibility

If someone hasn't formally introduced you, audience members are going to wonder who you are and why they should pay attention to what you say. So another goal of the introduction is to begin to build your credibility. **Credibility** is the perception your audience has about your competence and character. You want to provide some indication that you are an authority on the subject and that you care about the audience and the occasion. Remember, though, that your goal is to highlight that you are a credible speaker on this topic, one who respects the audience and occasion, not that you are *the* or even *a* final authority on the subject.

12-2d State the Thesis

Because audiences want to know what the speech is going to be about, it's important to state your thesis. After Miguel gained the audience's attention and established relevance and credibility, he introduced his thesis, "In the next five minutes, I'd like to explain to you that romantic love consists of three elements: passion, intimacy, and commitment."

Stating main points in the introduction is necessary unless you have some special reason for not revealing the details of the thesis. For instance, after

credibility the perception your audience has about your competence and character

getting the attention of his audience, Miguel might say, "In the next five minutes, I'd like to explain the three aspects of romantic love," a statement that specifies the number of main points but leaves specifics for transition statements immediately preceding the main points. In a commencement address at Stanford University, Steve Jobs stated the main points in his introduction in this way: "Today I want to tell you three stories from my life. That's it. No big deal. Just three stories" (Jobs, 2005).

12-3 DEVELOPING THE CONCLUSION

Shakespeare once said, "All's well that ends well." Effective conclusions heighten the impact of a good speech by summarizing the main ideas and leaving the audience with a vivid impression. Even though the conclusion is a relatively short part of the speech—seldom more than 5 percent (35 to 40 words for a five-minute speech)—your conclusion should be carefully planned. As with your speech introduction, prepare two or three conclusions and then choose the one you believe will be the most effective with your audience.

12-3a Summarize Goal and Main Points

An effective speech conclusion includes an abbreviated restatement of your goal and main points. An appropriate summary for an informative speech on how to improve your grades might be "So I hope you now understand [informative goal] that three techniques to help improve your grades are to attend classes regularly, to develop a positive attitude toward the course, and to study systematically [main points]." A short ending for a persuasive speech on why you should exercise might be "So you should exercise for at least 30 minutes each day [persuasive goal] to improve your appearance as well as your physical and mental health [main points]."

12-3b Clinch

Although a good summary helps the audience remember your main points, a good clincher leaves the audience with a vivid impression. A **clincher** is a short memorable statement that provides a sense of closure by driving home the importance of your speech in a memorable way. If you can, try to devise a clincher that refers back to the introductory comments in some way. Two effective strategies for clinching are using vivid imagery and appealing to action.

VIVID IMAGERY To develop vivid imagery, you can use any of the devices we discussed for getting attention (startling statement, question, story, joke, personal reference, quotation, action, or suspense). For example, in Tiffany's speech about being a vegetarian, she referred back to the personal reference she had made in her introduction about a vegetarian Thanksgiving meal:

> So now you know why I made the choice to become a vegetarian and how this choice affects my life today. As a vegetarian, I've discovered a world of food I never knew existed. Believe me, I am salivating just thinking about the meal I have planned for this Thanksgiving: fennel and blood orange salad; followed by baked polenta layered with tomato, Fontina, and Gorgonzola cheeses; an acorn squash tart; marinated tofu; and with what else but pumpkin pie for dessert!

Sounds good, doesn't it? Clinchers with vivid imagery are effective because they leave listeners with a picture imprinted in their minds.

APPEAL TO ACTION The appeal to action is a common clincher for persuasive speeches. The **appeal to action** describes the behavior that you want your listeners to follow after they have heard your arguments.

Notice how Matthew Cossolotto, president and founder of Study Abroad Alumni International, concludes his speech on global awareness and responsibility with a strong appeal to action:

> So, yes, you should have this re-entry program. Yes, you should network and explore international career opportunities. That's all good.

> But I also encourage you to Globalize Your Locality. I urge you to Think Global. . . . Act Global. . . . Be Global.

> This is an urgent call to action . . . for you and other study abroad alumni . . . to help us reduce the global awareness deficit.

> You can do so by becoming involved with SAAI . . . and other organizations such as the National Council for International Visitors, Sister Cities, or Rotary International.

> You can speak to local schools and community organizations about your study abroad experience and the need for more global awareness.

> When you studied abroad, I'm sure you were told many times that you would be serving as unofficial ambassadors of the United States . . . your campus . . . and even your community back home.

> Now that you're home again, I hope you'll become ambassadors for the value of the study abroad experience and for the need for greater international awareness.

> In wrapping up . . . I'd like to leave you with this image . . . just picture in your mind's eye that iconic photograph of planet earth. I'm sure you've seen it. Taken over four decades ago . . . in December 1968 . . . on the Apollo 8 mission to the moon.

> The photograph—dubbed Earthrise—shows our small, blue planet rising above a desolate lunar landscape. This photo was a true watershed in human history . . . marking the first time earthlings . . . fellow global citizens had traveled outside earth's orbit and looked back on our lonely planet.

> The widespread publication of Earthrise had a lot to do with launching the worldwide environmental movement. It's no accident that the first Earth Day—on April 22, 1970—took place so soon after the publication of this remarkable photograph.

> We're all privileged to inhabit this same planet—truly an island in space. And voices to the contrary notwithstanding . . . whether we

clincher a one- or two-sentence statement that provides a sense of closure by driving home the importance of your speech in a memorable way

appeal to action describes the behavior you want your listeners to follow after they have heard your arguments

Create Speech Conclusions

The goal of this activity is to help you create choices for how you will conclude your speech.

1. For the speech body you outlined earlier, write three different conclusions that review important points you want the audience to remember and leave the audience with a vivid impression.
2. Which do you believe is the best? Why?
3. Write that conclusion in outline form.

want to admit it or not . . . we are all, undeniably and by definition, citizens of the world.

The only question is: will we accept the responsibilities of global citizenship?

Your future . . . and perhaps the survival of the planet . . . just may depend on how many of us answer yes to that question. (Cossolotto, 2009)

12-4 COMPILING THE REFERENCE LIST AND FORMAL OUTLINE

Regardless of the type or length of your speech, you'll want to prepare a list of the sources you use in it. This list will enable you to direct audience members to the specific source of any information you used and allow you to quickly find the information at a later date. The two standard methods of organizing source lists are (1) alphabetically by author's last name or (2) by content category, with items listed alphabetically by author within each category. For speeches with a short list, the first method is efficient. But for long speeches with a lengthy source list, it is helpful to group sources by content categories.

Many formal bibliographic style formats can be used (e.g., MLA, APA, Chicago, CBE). The "correct" form differs by professional or academic discipline. Check to see if your instructor has a preference about which style you use for this class. Figure 12.3 gives examples of Modern Language Association (MLA) and American Psychological Association (APA) citations for the most commonly used sources.

12-4a Reviewing the Outline

At this point, it is time to put all parts of your outline together in complete formal outline form. Use this checklist to complete the final review of your outline.

1. **Have I used a standard set of symbols to indicate structure?** Main points are indicated by Roman numerals, major subpoints by capital letters, sub-subpoints by Arabic numerals, and further subdivisions by lowercase letters.

2. **Have I written main points and major subpoints as complete sentences?** Complete sentences help you to see (1) whether each main point actually develops your speech goal and (2) whether the wording makes your intended point.

3. **Do main points and major subpoints each contain a single idea?** This guideline ensures that the development of each part of the speech will be relevant to the point. Thus, rather than:

Organically produced food is good for the environment and good for animals and good for you.

Divide the sentence so that each part is stated separately:

I. Organically produced food is good for the environment.

II. Organically produced food is good for animals.

III. Organically produced food is good for you.

4. **Does each major subpoint relate to or support its major point?** This principle, called subordination,

Compile a List of Sources

The goal of this activity is to help you record the list of sources you used in the speech.

1. Review your research cards and/or annotated bibliography, separating those with information you used in your speech from those you did not use.
2. List the sources of information used in the speech by copying the bibliographic information recorded into a "references" or "works cited" list using the format required by your instructor.
3. Arrange your entries alphabetically by the last name of the first author.

FIGURE 12.3 EXAMPLES OF MLA AND APA CITATION FORMS FOR SPEECH SOURCES

	MLA Style	APA Style
Book	Jones, Phillip March. *Points of Departure: Roadside Memorial Polaroids*. Lexington, KY: The Jargon Society, 2011.	Jones, P. M. (2011). *Points of departure: Roadside memorial polaroids*. Lexington, KY: The Jargon Society.
Academic Journal	Von Burg, Ron. "Decades Away or *The Day After Tomorrow*?: Rhetoric, Film, and the Global Warming Debate." *Critical Studies in Media Communication*, 29.1(2012):7–26.	Von Burg, R. (2012). Decades away or *The Day After Tomorrow?*:Rhetoric, film, and the global warming debate. *Critical Studies in Media Communication, 29*(1) 7–26.
Magazine	Abrahamson, Rachel Paula. "Destroyed by Plastic Surgery." *US Weekly*, 19 March, 2012: 54–55.	Abrahamson, R. P. (2012, March 19). Destroyed by plastic surgery. *US Weekly, 892*, 54–55.
Web Site	"Supplier Responsibility at Apple." Apple.com. n.d. Web. 01 June 2012.	Apple. (n.d.). Supplier responsibility at Apple. Retrieved from http://www.apple.com/supplierresponsibility/
Blog Post	Ramsey, G. "UK Hoops Dominates SEC Awards." Cat Scratches: The Official Blog of UK Athletics. ukathletics.com. 29 February 2012. Web. 01 June 2012.	Ramsey, G. (2012, February 29). UK hoops dominates SEC awards [Web blog post]. Retrieved from http://www.ukathletics.com /blog/2012/02/uk-hoops-dominates-sec-awards.html
Movie	*The Iron Lady*. Dir. Phyllida Lloyd. Prod. Damien Jones. Pathe, 2011. DVD.	Jones, D. (Producer), & Lloyd, P. (Director). (2011). *The iron lady* [Motion picture]. United Kingdom: Pathe.
Online Video	"Barry Schwartz: The Paradox of Choice." TEDtalks. *YouTube*. 2007. Web. 01 June 2012.	TEDtalksDirector. (2007, January 16). *Barry Schwartz: The paradox of choice* [Video file]. Retrieved from http://www.youtube.com /watch?v=VO6XEQIsCoM

ensures that you don't wander off point and confuse your audience. For example:

I. *Proper equipment is necessary for successful play.*

   A. *Good gym shoes are needed for maneuverability.*

   B. *Padded gloves will help protect your hands.*

   C. *A lively ball provides sufficient bounce.*

   D. *A good attitude doesn't hurt either.*

Notice that the main point deals with equipment. Subpoints A, B, and C (shoes, gloves, and ball) all relate to the main point. But D, attitude, is not equipment and should appear under some other main point, if at all.

5. Are potential subpoint elaborations indicated? Recall that subpoint elaborations help build the speech. Because you don't know how long it might take you to discuss these elaborations, you should include more than you are likely to use. During rehearsals, you may discuss each a different way.

Now that we have considered the various parts of an outline, let us put them together for a final look. The complete outline for Katie's speech on Adderall illustrates the principles in practice.

Speech Outline

Using and Abusing Adderall: What's the Big Deal?

by Katie Anthony
University of Kentucky

General goal:

I want to inform my audience.

Specific goal:

I would like the audience to understand the uses and abuses of Adderall by college students.

Thesis statement:

I want to inform you about the growing problem of off-label Adderall usage by college students, explaining the nature and legal uses of Adderall, its growing popularity as a study aid for college students, and the problems associated with abusing Adderall.

Introduction

I. Attention getter: Raise your hand if anyone you know has taken the drug Adderall. Keep your hand raised if the person you know to be taking Adderall is doing so without a prescription for the drug. — *Attention getter*

II. Listener relevance: The illegal use of stimulants like Adderall among college students has increased dramatically over the past decade. The latest National Study on Drug Use and Health found that nearly 7 percent of full-time college students reported using Adderall without a prescription. So if you know ten people who are in college, it is likely that you know someone who is abusing Adderall. — *Listener relevance*

III. Speaker credibility: I became interested in this topic my freshman year when my roommate received a call from her mother telling her that her best friend, who was a sophomore at a different college, had died suddenly from an Adderall-induced heart attack. Because I had several friends who were also using Adderall without a prescription but who thought it was safe to do so, I began to read all I could about the drug, its use, and its risks. Not only have I become versed in the written information on Adderall, but I have also interviewed several faculty here who are studying the problem, and I have become an undergraduate research assistant helping one faculty member to collect data on this problem. Today, I want to share with you some of what I have learned. — *Speaker credibility*

IV. Thesis statement: Specifically, I want to inform you about the growing problem of off-label Adderall usage by college students, explaining the nature and legal uses of Adderall, its growing popularity as a study aid for college students, and the problems associated with abusing Adderall. — *Thesis statement*

Body

I. Adderall is a psychostimulant prescribed to treat three conditions.

Listener relevance link: Understanding the intended medical uses of the drug Adderall may help you understand why the drug is so widely abused by collegians.

Listener relevance link

A. Adderall, the brand name for amphetamine-dextroamphetamine, is a psychostimulant, one of a class of drugs intended to promote concentration, suppress hyperactivity, and promote healthy social experiences for patients (Willis, 2001).

   1. Adderall stimulates the central nervous system by increasing the amount of dopamine and norepinephrine in the brain. These chemicals are neurotransmitters that help the brain send signals between nerve cells (Daley, 2004, April 20).

   2. Mentally, Adderall brings about a temporary improvement in alertness, wakefulness, endurance, and motivation.

   3. Physically, it can increase heart rate and blood pressure and decrease perceived need for food or sleep.

B. Adderall is prescribed for the medical treatment of attention deficit/hyperactivity disorder (ADHD) in children and adults as well as for narcolepsy and clinical depression.

   1. ADHD is a neurobehavioral developmental disorder characterized by problems of attention coupled with hyperactivity.

      a. Since the mid-1990s, there has been a documented increase in the number of American children diagnosed and treated for ADHD (McCabe, Teter, & Boyd, 2004).

      b. According to the *Diagnostic and Statistical Manual of Mental Disorders* (2000), symptoms must be present for at least six months for diagnosis and symptoms must be excessive for medicinal treatment.

      c. The drugs Ritalin and Dexedrine are also used to treat ADHD. Adderall, however, remains the most widely prescribed of these drugs (Willis, 2001).

      d. According to the Centers for Disease Control, approximately 4.4 million American children have been diagnosed with ADHD, and over 2.5 million of those patients have been prescribed medicine to treat the condition (2005).

   2. Adderall is also prescribed to treat narcolepsy, which occurs when the brain can't normally regulate cycles of sleep and waking.

      a. Sufferers of narcolepsy experience excessive daytime sleepiness that results in episodes of suddenly falling asleep.

      b. A chronic sleep disorder, narcolepsy affects between 50,000 and 2.4 million Americans. (National Heart, Lung, and Blood Institute, 2008).

   3. Adderall can also be used to treat clinical depression.

      a. Clinical depression is a disorder characterized by low mood, a loss of interest in normal activities, and low self-esteem.

    b. According to the National Institute of Mental Health, 9.5% of the adult population—that is nearly 1.8 million American adults suffer from clinical depression.

Now that we understand the basic properties and medical uses of the drug Adderall, let's assess the increasing level of abuse of the drug by college students. ▶ Transition

II. Unfortunately, Adderall has become popular among college students, who use it as a study aid and for recreational purposes.

    Listener relevance link: As college students, we need to be aware of what students believe about Adderall and why they are abusing it. ▶ Listener relevance link

  A. College students who don't suffer ADHD, narcolepsy, or depression will take it with no prescription because they believe that it will improve their focus and concentration, allowing them to perform better on academic tasks (Teter, McCabe, Crandford, Boyd, & Gunthrie, 2005).

    1. Adderall abuse among college students occurs especially at stressful times of the semester when students get little sleep.

      a. DeSantis, Webb, and Noar (2008) found that 72 percent of the students they surveyed reported using the drug to stay awake so that they could study longer when they had many assignments due.

      b. Katherine Stump, a Georgetown University student, reported in the school newspaper: "During finals week here at Georgetown, campus turns into an Adderall drug den. Everyone from a cappella singers to newspaper writers become addicts, while anyone with a prescription and an understanding of the free market becomes an instant pusherman" (Jaffe, 2006, January 1).

      c. Collegians report using the drug frequently during stressful times of the semester. One student said, "I use it every time I have a major paper due" (Daley, 2004, April 20).

  B. Students also use Adderall for purposes other than academic ones.

    1. A survey of undergraduate and graduate students revealed that students engage in Adderall abuse for partying at a frequency just slightly less than taking the drug for academic purposes (Prudhomme White, Becker-Blease, & Grace-Bishop, 2006).

    2. DeSantis, Webb, and Noar (2007) report that students take the drug for its energizing effects. Other students report taking the drug to make them more social and outgoing at parties.

    3. Some college students, especially women, report using the drug for its use as an appetite suppressant for dieting purposes (Daley, 2004, April 20).

Now that we understand that Adderall abuse is prevalent on university campuses among students, it is important to understand the detrimental effects that can accompany the illegal use of Adderall. ▶ Transition

III. Whether students acknowledge the dangers or not, there are great risks involved in illegally using Adderall.

    Listener relevance link: As we have now discussed the pervasiveness of Adderall abuse, statistically, it is likely that several of you have used this substance without a prescription to either enhance your academic performance ▶ Listener relevance link or your social outings. Thus, it is important that we all recognize the adverse effects that result from taking Adderall without a prescription.

A. Adderall abuse can cause negative health effects for individuals not diagnosed with ADHD (Daley, 2004, April 20).

   1. Adderall is reported to cause a heightened risk for heart problems when used inappropriately. Problems include sudden heart attack or stroke, sudden death in individuals with heart conditions, and increased blood pressure and heart rate (FDA, 2010).

   2. Adderall abuse also can result in a myriad of mental problems, including manifestation of bipolar disorder, an increase of aggressive thoughts, and a heightened risk for psychosis similar to schizophrenia (FDA, 2010).

B. Adderall is highly addictive.

   1. Adderall is an amphetamine, and while amphetamines were once used to treat a variety of ailments including obesity in the 1950s and 1960s, the drugs began to be much more closely regulated once their addictive nature was realized (Daley, 2004, April 20).

   2. Adderall has similar properties to cocaine, and, as a result, abuse of the drug can lead to substance dependence (FDA, 2010).

C. Though clear risks are associated with the illegal use of Adderall, unlike other drugs, collegians do not view the inappropriate use of Adderall as harmful or illegal.

   1. College students typically view stimulant abuse as morally acceptable and physically harmless. In a 2010 study, DeSantis and Hane found that students were quick to justify their stimulant abuse by claiming its use was fine in moderation.

   2. The *Kentucky Kernel*, the student newspaper at the University of Kentucky, published an editorial of a student who flippantly described the use of Adderall among college students. He states, "If you want to abuse ice cream, amphetamines or alcohol, then there are going to be serious problems; however, let's not pretend a person using Adderall twice a semester to help them study is in any way likely to die a horrible death or suffer terrible side effects" (Riley, 2010, May 3).

   3. In a study assessing the attitudes of college students toward the inappropriate use of stimulants, the authors found that "the majority of students who reported misuse or abuse were not concerned about the misuse and abuse of prescription stimulants, and a number of students thought that they should be more readily available (Prudhomme White, Becker-Blease, & Grace-Bishop, 2006, p. 265).

Conclusion

I. Restatement of thesis: Adderall is a prescription stimulant that is increasingly being abused by college students primarily as a study aid.

    Restatement of thesis

II. Main point review: We have examined today what the drug Adderall is, its growing popularity among college students especially as a study aid, and the risks associated with using the drug illegally.

    Main point review

III. Clincher: The next time you or a friend considers taking Adderall as a study aid, think again. The potential harm that the drug could cause to your body is not worth even a perfect grade point average.

    Clincher

References

American Psychiatric Association. (2000). *Diagnostic and statistical manual of mental disorders*. Arlington, VA: Author.

Centers for Disease Control and Prevention. (2005, September 2). *Morbidity and Mortality Weekly Report (MMWR)*. Retrieved from http://www.cdc.gov

Daley, B. (2004, April 20). Perspective: Miracle drug? Adderall is prescribed for individuals with ADD and ADHD; for nonprescribed users there can be some serious risks. *Daily Pennsylvanian*. Retrieved from http://www.vpul.upenn.edu

DeSantis, A. D., & Hane, A. C. (2010). "Adderall is definitely not a drug": Justifications for the illegal use of ADHD stimulants. *Substance Use & Misuse, 45*, 31–46.

DeSantis, A. D., Webb, E. M., & Noar, S. M. (2008). Illicit use of prescription ADHD medications on a college campus: A multimethodological approach. *Journal of American College Health, 57*, 315–324.

Food and Drug Administration. (2010). *Drugs @ FDS: FDA approved drug products*. Retrieved from http://www.accessdata.fda.gov

National Heart, Blood, and Lung Institute (2008). "What is narcolepsy?" *National Heart, Blood, and Lung Institute Diseases and Conditions Index*. Retrieved from http://www.nhlbi.nih.gov/health/dci/Diseases/nar/nar_what.html

Jaffe, H. (2006, January 1). ADD and abusing Adderall. *The Washingtonian*. Retrieved from http://www.washingtonian.com

McCabe, S. E., Teter, C. J., & Boyd, C. J. (2004). The use, misuse and diversion of prescription stimulants among middle and high school students. *Substance Use and Misuse, 39*, 1095–1116.

Prudhomme White, B., Becker-Blease, K. A., & Grace-Bishop, K. (2006). Stimulant medication use, misuse, and abuse in an undergraduate and graduate student sample. *Journal of American College Health, 54*, 261–268.

Riley, T. (2010, May 3). Prescription drug abuse is a personal choice. *Kentucky Kernel*. Retrieved from http://kykernel.com

Substance Abuse and Mental Health Services Administration, Office of Applied Studies. (2009, April 7). *The NSDUH report: Nonmedical use of Adderall among full-time college students*. Rockville, MD.

Teter, J. C., McCabe, S. E., Crandford, J. A., Boyd, C. J., & Gunthrie, S. K. (2005). Prevalence and motives for illicit use of prescription stimulants in an undergraduate student sample. *Journal of American College Health, 53*, 253–262.

Willis, F. (2001). Attention deficit disorder. *Modern Drug Discovery, 4*, 84–86.

LOCATED IN TEXTBOOK

☐ Tear-out Chapter Review cards at the end of the book

☐ Review with the Quick Quiz below

LOCATED ON COMM 4 ONLINE AT CENGAGEBRAIN.COM:

☐ Review Key Term flashcards and create your own cards

☐ Track your knowledge and understanding of key concepts in communication

☐ Complete practice and graded quizzes to prepare for tests

☐ Complete interactive content within COMM4 Online

☐ View the chapter highlight boxes for COMM4 Online

Quick Quiz

T   F   1. A speech should always be organized according to sequential order.

T   F   2. A direct question seeks a mental response from the audience, whereas a rhetorical question demands an overt response from the audience.

T   F   3. A clincher is a restatement of your speech's goal and summary of the main points.

T   F   4. If your speech is particularly short, it would be appropriate to list your sources alphabetically, by authors' last name.

T   F   5. Startling statements, rhetorical questions, quotations, and personal references can all be used to state the thesis.

6. A plot, characters, and settings to dramatize the thesis are used in which organizational pattern?

   a. topic order
   b. logical reasons order
   c. story order
   d. narrative order
   e. time order

7. Which of the following is NOT a technique used to get your audience's attention?

   a. personal references
   b. startling statements
   c. stories
   d. suspense
   e. signposts

8. _____ is used in a speech when the main points are the rationale or proof that support the thesis.

   a. A thesis statement
   b. Logical reasons order
   c. Time order
   d. Topic order
   e. Persuasive order

9. In the conclusion of a speech, you should

   a. summarize the main points.
   b. read the sources compiled from the bibliographic information recorded on research note cards for the audience.
   c. get the audience's attention.
   d. introduce the thesis.
   e. establish credibility.

10. In the final review of the outline before you move into adaptation and rehearsal, you should ask yourself all of these questions EXCEPT

   a. Have I used a standard set of symbols to indicate structure?
   b. Have I written main points and major subdivisions as complete sentences?
   c. Do main points and major subdivisions each contain multiple ideas to hold the audience's attention?
   d. Does the outline include no more than one-third the total number of words anticipated in the speech?
   e. Are potential subdivision elaborations indicated?

Answers: 1.F, 2.F, 3.F, 4.T, 5.F, 6.D, 7.E, 8.B, 9.A, 10.C

13 Presentational Aids

LEARNING OUTCOMES

13-1 Identify several reasons for incorporating presentational aids into your speech

13-2 Describe the different types of presentational aids

13-3 Choose appropriate presentational aids

13-4 Prepare effective presentational aids

13-5 Display presentational aids professionally

After finishing this chapter go to **PAGE 185** for **STUDY TOOLS.**

© Maxim Blinkov/Shutterstock.com

We live in an era when the written, oral, visual, and digital modes of communicating are merging. Whether it is a TV news program, your professor's lecture, or a motivational speech, audiences have come to expect messages to be enhanced with presentational aids. This means that as you prepare your speech, you will need to decide which presentational aids will enhance your verbal message and motivate your audience to both pay attention to and remember it. In fact, presentational aids have become so important to public speeches that they are essentially a form of supporting material you should be looking for when conducting your research. Ultimately, you might use them to get attention in the introduction, to support a main point in the body, or to clinch the conclusion.

A **presentational aid** is any visual, audio, audiovisual, or other sensory material used to enhance a verbal message. **Visual aids** enhance a speech by allowing audience members to see what you are describing or explaining. Examples of visual aids include actual objects, models, photographs, drawings and diagrams, maps, charts, and graphs. **Audio aids** enhance a verbal message through sound. Some examples include musical clips from CDs and iTunes, recorded clips from conversations, interviews, famous speeches, and recordings of nature sounds like bird calls and whale songs. **Audiovisual aids** enhance a speech using a combination of sight and sound. Examples of audiovisual aids include clips from movies and television, YouTube videos, and podcasts, as well as other events or observations captured on video. Other sensory aids include materials that enhance your ideas by appealing to smell, touch, or taste. For example, a speaker can enhance the verbal description of the fragrance of a particular perfume by allowing audience members to smell it, and the flavor of a particular entrée by allowing audience members to taste it.

presentational aid any visual, audio, audiovisual, or other sensory material used to enhance a verbal message

visual aids presentational aids that enhance a speech by allowing audience members to see what you are describing or explaining

audio aids presentational aids that enhance a verbal message through sound

audiovisual aids presentational aids that enhance a verbal message through a combination of sight and sound

ACTION STEPS

Action Step 4
Identify, prepare, and use appropriate presentational aids

13-1 BENEFITS OF PRESENTATIONAL AIDS

Research documents several benefits for using presentational aids. First, they get audience attention by dramatizing the verbal message. Second, they help audiences understand and remember information (Garcia-Retamero & Cokely, 2013). Third, they allow you to address the diverse learning style preferences of your audience (Rogers, 2013). Fourth, they increase persuasive appeal (Krauss, 2012). In fact, some research suggests that speakers who use presentational aids are almost two times more likely to convince listeners than those who do not (Hanke, 1998). Finally, using presentational aids may help you feel more competent and confident (Campbell, 2015).

Today, presentational aids are usually developed into computerized slide shows using presentation software such as PowerPoint, MediaPro, Adobe Acrobat, or Photodex and projected onto a large screen via a computer and projector. These programs allow you to embed audio and audiovisual links from local files and the Internet, which makes it fairly simple to create effective multimedia presentations. Whether you are creating multimedia presentations or developing simpler presentational aids, the purpose is the same: to enhance your message without overpowering it. Speakers who violate this purpose end up with "death by PowerPoint," a situation where the audience is overwhelmed by the aids and the message gets lost. In this chapter, we describe various types of presentational aids, criteria to consider when choosing and preparing them, and methods for displaying them during your speech.

13-2 TYPES OF PRESENTATIONAL AIDS

Presentational aids range from those that are readily available from existing sources to those that are custom produced for a specific speech.

13-2a Visual Aids

Visual aids enhance your verbal message by allowing listeners to see what you are describing or explaining. They include actual objects and models, photographs, drawings and diagrams, maps, charts, and graphs.

ACTUAL OBJECTS Actual objects are inanimate or animate physical samples of the idea you are communicating. Inanimate objects make good visual aids if they are (1) large enough to be seen by all audience members, (2) small enough to transport to the speech site, (3) simple enough to understand visually, and (4) safe. A volleyball or a Muslim prayer rug would be appropriate in size for most classroom audiences. An iPhone or Droid might be OK if the goal is to show what a smartphone looks like, but it might be too small if you want to demonstrate how to use any of the phone's specialized functions. A smart board or Mondopad would work better for this purpose.

On occasion, *you* can be an effective visual aid. For instance, you can demonstrate the motions involved in a golf swing; or you can use your clothing to illustrate the traditional attire of a particular country. Sometimes it can be appropriate to use another person as a visual aid, such as when Jenny used a friend to demonstrate the Heimlich maneuver. Animals can also be effective visual aids. For example, Josh used his AKC Obedience Champion dog to demonstrate the basics of dog training. But keep in mind that some animals placed in unfamiliar settings can become difficult to control and then distract audience members from your message.

MODELS When an actual object is too large or too small for the room where you'll be speaking, too complex to understand visually, or potentially unsafe or uncontrollable, a model of it can be an effective visual aid. A **model** is a three-dimensional scaled-down or scaled-up version of an actual object that may also be simplified to aid understanding. In a speech on the physics of bridge construction, a scale model of a suspension bridge would be an effective visual aid.

PHOTOGRAPHS If an exact reproduction of material is needed, enlarged photographs can be excellent visual aids. In a speech on smart weapons, enlarged before-and-after photos of target sites would be effective in helping the audience understand the pinpoint accuracy of these weapons. When choosing photographs, be sure that the image is large enough for the audience to see, that the object of interest in the photo is clearly identified, and, ideally, that the object is in the foreground. For example, if you are giving a speech about your grandmother and show a photo of her with her college graduating class, you might circle her image or use an LED pointer to highlight her image among her classmates in the photo.

SIMPLE DRAWINGS AND DIAGRAMS Simple drawings and **diagrams** (a type of drawing that shows how the whole relates to its parts) are easy to prepare and can be effective because you can choose how much detail to include. To make sure your drawings or diagrams look professional, prepare them using a basic computer software program or use finished pieces you find in a book, an article, or on the Internet. If you do this, however, be sure to credit the source during your speech to enhance your credibility and avoid plagiarism. Andria's diagram of the human body and its pressure points, for example, worked well to clarify her message visually (see Figure 13.1).

MAPS Simple maps allow you to orient audiences to landmarks (mountains, rivers, and lakes), states, cities, land routes, weather systems, and so on. As with drawings and diagrams, include only the details that are relevant to your purpose (Figure 13.2).

CHARTS A **chart** is a graphic representation that distills a lot of information and presents it in an easily interpreted visual format. Flow charts, organizational

© WilleeCole/Shutterstock.com

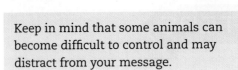
Keep in mind that some animals can become difficult to control and may distract from your message.

actual objects inanimate or animate physical samples of the idea being communicated

model a three-dimensional scaled-down or scaled-up version of an actual object

diagram a type of drawing that shows how the whole relates to its parts

chart a graphic representation that distills a lot of information into an easily interpreted visual format

FIGURE 13.1   SAMPLE DIAGRAM

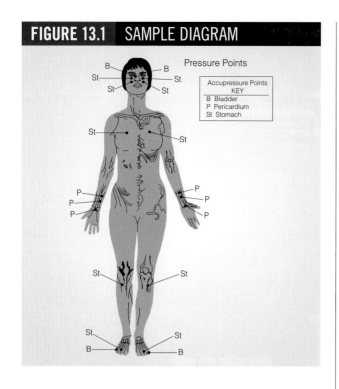

charts, and pie charts are the most common. A **flow chart** uses symbols and connecting lines to diagram the progression through a complicated process. Tim used a flow chart to help listeners move through the sequence of steps to assess their weight (Figure 13.3) An **organizational chart** shows the structure of an organization in terms of rank and chain of command. The chart in Figure 13.4 illustrates the organization of a student union board. A **pie chart** shows the relationships among parts of a single unit. Ideally, pie charts have two to five "slices," or wedges—more than eight wedges clutter a pie chart. If your chart includes too many wedges, use another kind of chart unless you can consolidate several of the less important wedges into the category of "other," as Kirk did to show the percentage of total calories that should come from the various components of food (see Figure 13.5).

GRAPHS A **graph** presents numerical information. Bar graphs and line graphs are the most common forms of graphs.

A **bar graph** uses vertical or horizontal bars to show relationships between two or more variables. For instance, Jacqueline used a bar graph to compare the amounts of caffeine found in one serving each of brewed coffee, instant coffee, tea, cocoa, and cola (see Figure 13.6).

A **line graph** indicates the changes in one or more variables over time. In a speech on the population of the United States, for example, the line graph in Figure 13.7 helps by showing the population increase, in millions, from 1810 to 2010.

13-2b   Audio Aids

Audio aids enhance a verbal message through sound. They are especially useful when it is difficult, if not impossible, to describe a sound in words. For example, in David's speech about the

flow chart a chart that uses symbols and connecting lines to diagram the progression through a complicated process

organizational chart a chart that shows the structure of an organization in terms of rank and chain of command

pie chart a chart that shows the relationships among parts of a single unit

graph a diagram that presents numerical information

bar graph a graph that uses vertical or horizontal bars to show relationships between two or more variables

line graph a graph that indicates the changes in one or more variables over time

FIGURE 13.2   SAMPLE MAP

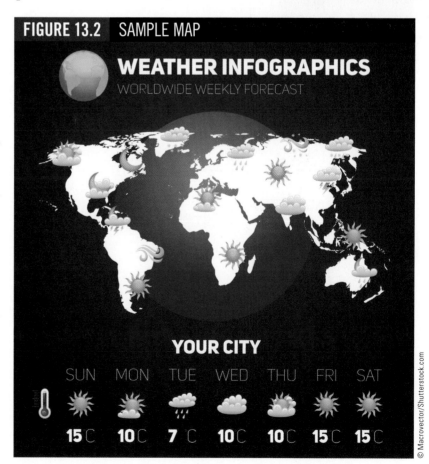

FIGURE 13.3 SAMPLE FLOW CHART

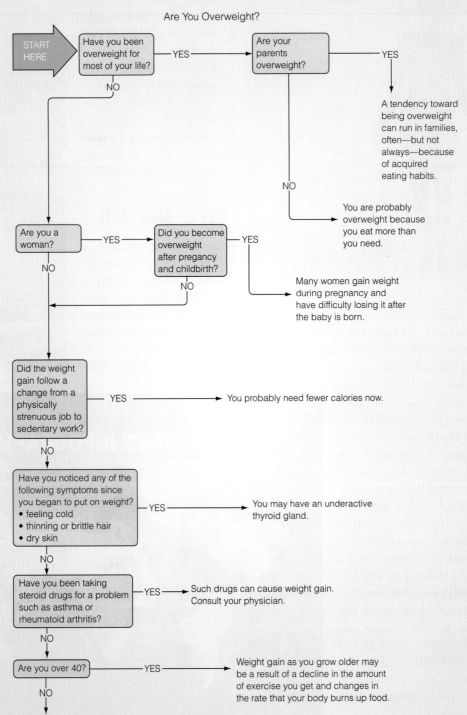

Are You Overweight?

START HERE → Have you been overweight for most of your life? — YES → Are your parents overweight? — YES → A tendency toward being overweight can run in families, often—but not always—because of acquired eating habits.

NO

Are your parents overweight? — NO → You are probably overweight because you eat more than you need.

Are you a woman? — YES → Did you become overweight after pregancy and childbirth? — YES → Many women gain weight during pregnancy and have difficulty losing it after the baby is born.

NO

NO

Did the weight gain follow a change from a physically strenuous job to sedentary work? — YES → You probably need fewer calories now.

NO

Have you noticed any of the following symptoms since you began to put on weight?
• feeling cold
• thinning or brittle hair
• dry skin
— YES → You may have an underactive thyroid gland.

NO

Have you been taking steroid drugs for a problem such as asthma or rheumatoid arthritis? — YES → Such drugs can cause weight gain. Consult your physician.

NO

Are you over 40? — YES → Weight gain as you grow older may be a result of a decline in the amount of exercise you get and changes in the rate that your body burns up food.

NO

If you are unable to make a diagnosis from this chart, your excess weight is probably due only to overeating.
If, after a month of dieting, you fail to lose weight, consult your physician.

FIGURE 13.4 SAMPLE ORGANIZATIONAL CHART

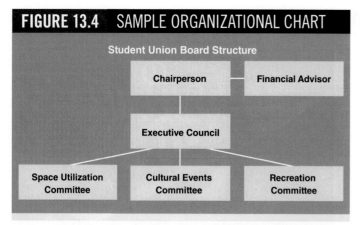

FIGURE 13.5 SAMPLE PIE CHART

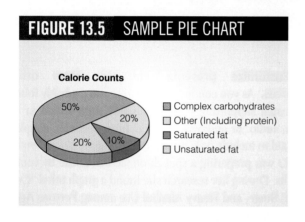

FIGURE 13.6 SAMPLE BAR GRAPH

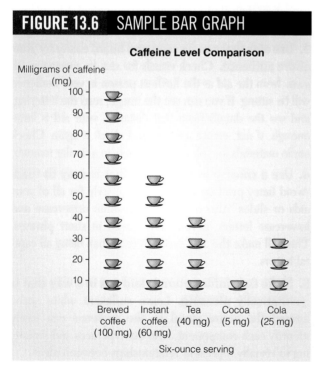

FIGURE 13.7 SAMPLE LINE GRAPH

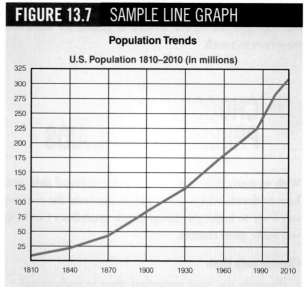

from sources such as famous speeches, radio programs, interviews, and recordings of music or environmental sounds. Chas wrote a song and used a snippet from it as an attention catcher and clincher in his speech. He later posted a link to it on his Facebook page, which he also referenced in his speech in case anyone would like to hear it in its entirety later. Before using an audio aid, make sure you have enough time to present it (it should take no more than about 5 percent of your speaking time) and that you have access to a quality sound system.

13-2c Audiovisual Aids

Audiovisual aids enhance a verbal message using a combination of sight and sound. You can use short clips from films and videos that are relatively easy to access on Internet sites such as YouTube. For example, in his speech about the use of robots in automobile production, Chad, who worked as a technician at the local Ford plant, showed a 20-second video clip of a car being painted in a robotic paint booth. As with audio aids, your audiovisual aid should take no more than 5 percent of your speaking time.

13-2d Other Sensory Aids

Depending on your topic, other sensory aids that appeal to smell, touch, or taste may effectively enhance your speech. For example, a speech about making perfume might benefit from allowing your audience to smell scented swatches as you describe the ingredients used to

three types of trumpet mutes and how they alter the trumpet's sound, he played his trumpet so that listeners could hear what he meant. If you can't or don't want to make your own sounds, you can use recorded excerpts

make the scents. In a speech about Braille, Javier handed out copies of his outline written in Braille for audience members to touch.

© ra2studio/Shutterstock.com

13-3 CHOOSING PRESENTATIONAL AIDS

With so many different types of presentational aids, you have to decide which ones will best illustrate the content you want to highlight. Some simple guidelines can help you make good choices.

Choose aids that:

▸ illustrate the most important ideas to understand and remember.

▸ clarify complex ideas that are difficult to explain verbally.

▸ are appropriate for the size of the audience.

▸ make dull information and details more interesting.

▸ you will feel comfortable using and transporting to the speech site.

▸ enhance rather than overwhelm the verbal message.

▸ you have the time and money to prepare.

▸ demonstrate cultural sensitivity and do not offend members of your audience.

13-4 PREPARING PRESENTATIONAL AIDS

However simple your presentational aids, you still need to produce them carefully. You may need to find or create charts, graphs, diagrams, maps, or drawings. You may need to search for and prepare photographs. You may look for audio or audiovisual snippets and then convert them into a format you can embed into your computerized slide show to use at your speech site.

The goal is to prepare professional-looking presentational aids that will enhance your perceived competence, credibility, and character in addition to clarifying your message and making it more memorable. Prepare your presentational aids with the following guidelines in mind.

1. Limit the reading required of the audience. The audience should be listening to you, not reading the presentational aid. So use key words and short phrases rather than complete sentences.

2. Customize presentational aids from other sources. As you conducted research, you probably found potential supporting material already represented in visual, audio, or audiovisual form. In these cases, simplify the aid to include only relevant information. For example, Jia Li was preparing a speech on alcohol abuse by young adults. During her research she found a graph titled "Current, Binge, and Heavy Alcohol Use among Persons Aged 12 or Older by Age." Since this graph presented more information than Jia Li needed, she simplified it to include only the information regarding young adults aged 16 to 29.

3. Use aids that can be seen and heard easily by your entire audience. Check visuals for size by moving as far away from the aid as the farthest person in your audience will be sitting. If you can see the image, read the lettering, and see the details from that distance, your aid is large enough; if not, create another and check it again. Check audio materials for volume and quality in a similar manner.

4. Use a consistent print style that is easy to read. Avoid fancy print styles and use one style for all of your aids or slides. Also be sure to combine uppercase and lowercase letters in your aids—even in short phrases. This will make the aids easier to read than using all capital letters.

5. Make sure information is laid out in a way that is aesthetically pleasing. Leave sufficient white space around the entire visual so the audience can easily identify each component. Also use typefaces and indenting to visually represent relationships between ideas.

6. Use pictures or other visual symbols on all visual aids. To truly enhance a verbal message, a presentational aid should consist of more than just words (Booher, 2003). Even something as simple as a relevant piece of clip art can make the verbal message more memorable. Of course, clip art can be overdone, so don't let your message be overpowered by unnecessary pictures or animations.

7. Use color strategically. Although black and white can work well for your visual aids, consider using color strategically to emphasize points. Here are some suggestions for doing so:

▶ Use the same background color and theme for all the slides on your computerized slide show.

▶ Use the same color to show similarities between ideas, and use opposite colors (on a color wheel) to show differences.

▶ Use bright colors, such as red, to highlight important information. Be sure to avoid using red and green together, however, because audience members who are color-blind may not be able to distinguish between them.

▶ Use dark colors for lettering on a white background and a light color for lettering on black or deep blue backgrounds.

▶ Use no more than two or three colors on any presentational aid that is not a photograph or video clip.

▶ Pretend you are your audience. Sit as far away as they will be sitting, and evaluate the colors you have chosen for their readability and appeal.

Let's see if we can put all of these principles to work. Figure 13.8 contains a lot of important information, but notice how unpleasant it is to the eye. As you can see, this visual aid ignores all the principles we've discussed. However, with some thoughtful simplification, this speaker could produce the visual aid shown in Figure 13.9, which sharpens the focus by emphasizing the key words (*reduce, reuse, recycle*), highlighting the major details, and adding clip art for a professional touch.

FIGURE 13.9   AN EFFECTIVE VISUAL AID

The Three R's of Recycling

Reduce Waste

Reuse
cloth towels
dishes
glass bottles

Recycle
collect
sort
deliver

© Joe Belanger/Shutterstock.com

13-5 DISPLAYING PRESENTATIONAL AIDS

Once you have decided on the specific presentational aids for your speech, you will need to choose how to display them. As with choosing and preparing aids, your goal is to display them using a method that is professional looking and sounding to enhance your ethos, as well as your verbal message. Speakers can choose from the following methods for displaying presentational aids.

13-5a Posters

One easy method for displaying simple drawings, charts, maps, photos, and graphs is by mounting them on stiff cardboard or foam core. Then the visual can be placed on an easel when it is referred to during the speech. Because posters tend to be fairly small, use them only with smaller audiences (30 people or fewer). Many professional conferences include poster sessions where scholars explain their research using a poster as a presentational aid.

13-5b Whiteboards or Chalkboards

Writing on a whiteboard or chalkboard is appropriate only for very short items of information that can be written in a few seconds. Nevertheless, being able to use a whiteboard or chalkboard effectively should be a part of any speaker's repertoire.

FIGURE 13.8   AN INEFFECTIVE VISUAL AID

I WANT YOU TO REMEMBER THE THREE R'S OF RECYCLING

Reduce the amount of waste people produce, like over packing or using material that won't recycle.

Reuse by relying on cloth towels rather than paper towels, earthenware dishes rather than paper or plastic, and glass bottles rather than aluminum cans.

Recycle by collecting recyclable products, sorting them correctly, and getting them to the appropriate recycling agency.

Whiteboards or chalkboards should be written on prior to speaking or during a break in speaking. Otherwise, the visual is likely to be either illegible or partly obscured by your body as you write. Or you may end up talking to the board instead of to the audience. Should you need to draw or write on the board while you are talking, you should practice beforehand. If you are right-handed, stand to the right of what you are drawing. Try to face at least part of the audience while you work. Although it may seem awkward at first, your effort will allow you to maintain contact with your audience and allow them to see what you are doing while you are doing it.

Such "chalk talks" are easy to prepare, but they are the most likely to result in damage to speaker credibility. It is the rare individual who can develop well-crafted visual aids on a whiteboard or chalkboard. More often, they signal a lack of preparation.

© Olivier Le Moal/Shutterstock.com

13-5c Flip Charts

A **flip chart**, a large pad of paper mounted on an easel, can be an effective way to present visual aids. Flip charts (and easels) are available in many sizes. For a presentation to four or five people, a small tabletop version works well; for a larger audience, use a pad (30″ × 40″).

As with whiteboards and chalkboards, you should prepare flip charts prior to giving the speech. In some situations, you may write down some information before the speech begins and then add information while speaking.

13-5d Handouts

At times it may be useful for each member of the audience to have a personal copy of the visual aid. In these situations, you can prepare a **handout** (material printed on sheets of paper). The benefit is that everyone in the audience can have a copy to refer to and take with them after the speech. The drawback is that distributing handouts can distract audience members from you and your message.

Before you decide to use handouts, carefully consider why they would be better than some other method. Handouts are effective for information you want listeners to refer

flip chart a large pad of paper mounted on an easel

handout material printed on sheets of paper to be distributed to an audience

to after the speech, such as a set of steps to follow later, useful telephone numbers and addresses, or mathematical formulas.

If you decide to use handouts, distribute them at the end of the speech. If you want to refer to information on the handout during the speech, create another visual aid to use while discussing the information during your speech.

13-5e Document Cameras

Another simple way to project drawings, charts, photos, and graphs is by using a document camera, such as an Elmo. If you choose this method, be sure to transfer drawings, charts, photos, and graphs from original sources onto a sheet of 8½″ × 11″ piece of paper so you can display them smoothly and professionally.

13-5f Computers, CD/DVD Players, and LCD Projectors

Most people today prefer to present audio recordings, audiovisual recordings, and computerized slide shows using a computer and projector. However, you should always prepare back-up aids to use if the equipment fails. Also, to ensure that audience members focus their attention on you when you're not talking about one of your slides or clips, insert blank screens between slides, press the "B" key on your computer or press the "mute" key on your projector remote to display blank screens.

ACTION STEP 4a

Identify Presentational Aids

The goal of this activity is to help you decide which visual aids you will use in your speech.

1. **Identify the key ideas you could emphasize with a presentational aid to increase audience interest, understanding, or retention.**

2. **For each idea you have identified, list the type of presentational aid you think would be most appropriate to develop and use.**

3. **For each idea you plan to enhance with an aid, decide on the method you will use to display it.**

4. **Write a brief paragraph describing why you chose the types of presentational aids and display methods that you did. Be sure to consider how your choices will affect your preparation time and the audience's perception of your credibility.**

Ignite: The Power(Point) of eXtreme Audience Adaptation

Ignite is a global event, organized by volunteers, where participants are given five minutes to speak about their ideas and personal or professional passions, accompanied by 20 slides. Ignite asks speakers, "If you had five minutes on stage, what would you say? What if you only had 20 slides and they rotated automatically after 15 seconds?" ("What Is Ignite?" n.d.). Ignite challenges speakers to engage in what could be called extreme audience adaptation, sharing information in a timely and relevant manner so that audiences can easily comprehend it.

Speeches at Ignite events range from "Fighting Dirty in Scrabble" and "Causal Inference Is Hard" to "How I Learned to Appreciate Dance: Being Married to a Ballerina," "Geek Generation," and "How to Buy a Car Without Getting Screwed" ("Ignite Seattle 7," 2009; Guzman, 2009). The emphasis on extreme brevity as a way to share ideas is reflected in Ignite Seattle's tagline: "Enlighten us, but make it quick," and reveals the importance of well-designed visual aids to successful public speaking (*Ignite Seattle,* n.d.). Since Ignite presenters are given just 20 slides, each slide must be carefully crafted to concisely and creatively express an idea in only a few seconds. Part of Ignite's success has been its ability to adapt to the interests of its

© iStockphoto.com/Blend_Images

various audiences. For example, cocreator Brady Forrest attempts to balance the gender of the speakers and to keep topics only moderately tech-oriented so that more audience members can relate to them (Guzman, 2009). Ignite presentations are even finding their way into college classrooms. Tailoring assignments to Ignite's short presentation style helps students develop as speakers by honing their ability to analyze and distill research into its most important points as well as becoming comfortable with creating and delivering presentations using digital media.

STUDY TOOLS 13

LOCATED IN TEXTBOOK

☐ Tear-out Chapter Review cards at the end of the book

☐ Review with the Quick Quiz below

LOCATED ON COMM 4 ONLINE AT CENGAGEBRAIN.COM:

☐ Review Key Term flashcards and create your own cards

☐ Track your knowledge and understanding of key concepts in communication

☐ Complete practice and graded quizzes to prepare for tests

☐ Complete interactive content within COMM4 Online

☐ View the chapter highlight boxes for COMM4 Online

Quick Quiz

T F 1. Bringing a goat to a presentation about the benefits of goat farming is an appropriate use of an actual object.

T F 2. Giving a speech on the length of color wavelengths and the resulting brightness to the human eye would benefit greatly from visual aids.

T F 3. It is okay to use green text on a red background for visual aids.

T F 4. Whiteboards are the best way to impress your audience with technical diagrams that you draw from memory.

T F 5. For an audience of 80 people, a large flip chart is an appropriate visual aid.

6. Which of the following is NOT one of the benefits of using presentational aids?

a. They clarify and dramatize the verbal message.
b. They help audiences remember information.
c. They allow you to narrow down who you appeal to.
d. They increase personal appeal.
e. They make you feel more confident.

7. To help her audience determine the correct course of action for their sick family members, Yolanda should use a

a. decision map.
b. flow chart.
c. video clip from *Grey's Anatomy* or *E.R.*
d. bar chart.
e. pie graph.

8. A speech about the history of the Ohio River at Cincinnati, with a particular focus on buildings then and now, would benefit from

a. your watercolor drawings of today's stadiums.
b. models of the bridges and highways crossing the river.
c. a piece of concrete from when one building was demolished.
d. a bar chart showing construction activity along the river from 1890 to today.
e. photographs of buildings no longer standing.

9. Your company has recently hired a new CEO, who is preparing a speech. He sends you the speech, which includes a list of new department heads and who they report to, to evaluate the need for visual aids. You would do well to suggest

a. a flow chart to guide employees to the right boss.
b. an organizational chart that visually illustrates who reports to whom.
c. that all the department heads stand on stage in front of their employees.
d. a pie chart of employees, department heads, and other members of the company.
e. All of these would be helpful.

10. In a speech about a group of children who suffer from a rare congenital heart defect, which of the following presentational aids would be the most effective to explain the effect of the disease on the heart itself?

a. a photograph
b. an actual object
c. a model
d. a diagram
e. a simple drawing

Answers: 1. F, 2. T, 3. F, 4. F, 5. F, 6. C, 7. B, 8. E, 9. B, 10. D

ONE APPROACH.
70 UNIQUE SOLUTIONS.

14 Language

LEARNING OUTCOMES

14-1 Explain how oral style differs from written style

14-2 Use appropriate language in your speeches

14-3 Choose clear and specific language that helps the audience understand and remember your ideas

14-4 Choose vivid language that helps the audience see and experience your ideas

After finishing this chapter go to **PAGE 198** for **STUDY TOOLS**.

Recall from chapter 11 that audience adaptation is the process of tailoring your speech to your specific audience. In this chapter, we turn our focus to tailoring your language and oral style to the audience.

We begin by clarifying how oral style differs from written style, as well as how the formal oral style we use in public speeches differs from the informal oral style we use in conversations with friends and family. Then we review several aspects of semantic, pragmatic, and sociolinguistic word meanings we introduced in chapter 4 as they relate specifically to public speaking.

14-1 ORAL STYLE

Oral style refers to how we convey messages through the spoken word. An effective oral style differs quite a bit from written style, though when giving a speech your oral style is still more formal than everyday talk. Your goal is to adapt your language to your purpose, the audience, and the occasion. For example, when you are speaking to a small audience of colleagues at a business meeting, your language will be more formal than when conversing with a friend at dinner—but not as formal as when you are speaking to an audience of 100 or more at a professional conference or workshop. Still, even in a formal public speaking situation, you must *establish a relationship* with your listeners. Although your oral style is slightly more formal than in everyday

> **oral style** the manner in which one conveys messages through the spoken word

conversations, it should still reflect a personal tone that encourages listeners to perceive you to be *having a conversation with them*. Four primary characteristics distinguish an effective oral style from an effective written style.

1. An effective oral style tends toward short sentences and familiar language. Because listeners expect to grasp your main ideas while they listen, work to ensure your words are ones that your audience is likely to understand without looking up definitions. Likewise, opt for short, simple sentences rather than

ACTION STEPS

Action Step 5
Practice oral language and delivery style

complex ones that require additional time for audience members to decipher. We certainly live in a digital age where live public speeches can be recorded and even posted online to be heard multiple times. Even when watching a recorded public speech, however, listeners should not be required to press "pause" to look up word meanings or to press "reverse" to replay complex sentences.

2. An effective oral style features plural personal pronouns. Using personal pronouns such as *we, us,* and *our* creates a sense of relationship with the audience. It demonstrates respect for the audience as participants in the rhetorical situation. Remember your goal is to create a perception of conversing *with* your audience rather than presenting *to* or *in front of* them. Personal pronouns help foster that perception.

3. An effective oral style features descriptive words and phrases that appeal to the ear in ways that sustain listener interest and promote retention. By using colorful adjectives and adverbs that appeal to the senses, as well as rhetorical figures of speech (to be discussed later in this chapter), you will capture the interest of your audience to pay attention and motivate them to stay focused on it throughout.

4. An effective oral style incorporates clear macro structural elements (e.g., main point preview, section transitions, and signposts as discussed in chapter 12). Unless your public speech is being recorded and posted for additional viewing, listeners will hear it only once. Consequently, you need to intentionally articulate a preview of your main points so listeners can conceptualize the framework for your main ideas at the outset. Similarly, you need to provide section transitions that verbally signal when you are moving from one major idea to the next, as well as signposts such as *first, second, third,* and *fourth* to help listeners follow your train of thought as the speech progresses.

Now that you have a sense of the nature of oral style as it differs from written style, let's examine some specific language choices to consider as you practice and revise your speeches. These include speaking appropriately, clearly, and vividly.

SPEAKING APPROPRIATELY

Speaking appropriately means using language that adapts to the needs, interests, knowledge, and attitudes of your audience and avoiding language

> **speaking appropriately** using language that adapts to the needs, interests, knowledge, and attitudes of the audience

Listeners pay attention to and are interested in ideas that have a personal impact.

that might alienate anyone. In the communication field, we use the term **verbal immediacy** to describe language used to reduce the psychological distance between you and your audience (Witt, Wheeless, & Allen, 2004). In other words, speaking appropriately means making language choices that enhance a sense of connection between you and your audience members. Speaking appropriately demonstrates that we respect others, even those who differ from us. If we speak inappropriately, on the other hand, we are likely to offend some listeners, and from that moment on, offended audience members are likely to stop listening. Speaking appropriately during a speech means highlighting the relevance of your topic to the interests and needs of audience members, establishing common ground and speaker credibility, demonstrating linguistic sensitivity, and adapting to cultural diversity.

14-2a Relevance

Your first challenge is to help the audience see the relevance of your topic. Listeners pay attention to and are interested in ideas that they perceive as personally relevant (when they can answer the question, "What does this have to do with me?"); they are bored when they don't see how the speech relates to them. You can help the audience perceive your speech as

verbal immediacy language used to reduce the psychological distance between you and your audience

timeliness how the information can be used now

proximity information in relation to listeners' personal space

relevant by highlighting its timeliness, proximity, and personal impact.

ESTABLISH TIMELINESS Listeners are more likely to be interested in information they perceive as **timely**—they want to know how they can use the information *now*. For example, in a speech about the hazards of talking on the phone or texting while driving, J. J. quickly established the topic's relevance in his introduction:

> *Most of us in this room, as many as 90 percent in fact, are a danger to society. Why? Because we talk or text on our cell phones while driving. Although driving while phoning (DWP) seems harmless, a recent study conducted by the Nationwide Mutual Insurance Company reports that DWP is the most common cause of accidents today—even more common than driving under the influence (DUI)! Did you know that when you talk on the phone when you're driving—even if you do so on a hands-free set— you're four times more likely to get into a serious crash than if you're not doing so? So texting while driving is not the only problem. So is talking on the phone. So this issue is far from harmless and is one each of us should take seriously.*

ESTABLISH PROXIMITY Your listeners are more likely to be interested in information that has **proximity**, a relationship to their personal "space." Psychologically, we pay more attention to information that is related to our "territory"—to our family, our neighborhood, or our city, state, or country. You have probably heard speakers say something like this: "Let me bring this closer to home by showing you . . ." and then make their point by using a local example. As you review the supporting material you collect for your speech, look for statistics and examples that have proximity for your audience. For example, J. J. shared a story reported in the local paper of a young mother who was killed while texting and driving.

DEMONSTRATE PERSONAL IMPACT Finally, your audiences are more likely to be interested when you present information that can have a serious physical, economic, or psychological impact. For example, notice how your classmates' attention picks up when your instructor mentions that what she says next "will definitely be on the test." Your instructor understands that this "economic" impact (not paying attention can "cost") is enough to refocus most students' attention on what is being said. To drive home his point, J. J. introduced John, his high school friend, who is now paralyzed and a wheelchair user because he crashed into another car while texting.

14-2b Common Ground

Common ground is the background, knowledge, attitudes, experiences, and philosophies that you share with your audience. You should use audience analysis to identify areas of similarity, then use plural personal pronouns, rhetorical questions, and common experiences to help establish common ground.

USE PERSONAL PRONOUNS As we've already mentioned, one simple way to establish common ground is to use *plural personal pronouns: we, us,* and *our.* You can easily replace "I" and "you" language in the macrostructural elements of your speech. In your thesis statement, for example, you can say "let's discuss . . ." rather than "I will inform you . . ." and in your section transitions, you can say "Now that we all have a clearer understanding of . . . ," rather than, "Now that I've explained . . ." and so on. For his Meckles Diverticulum speech, Josh suggested Nathan introduce his thesis and preview using "we" language this way: "In the next few minutes, let's explore the symptoms, diagnosis, and treatment of a fairly unkown defect in the small intestine known as a Meckel's Diverticulum."

ASK RHETORICAL QUESTIONS Recall that a *rhetorical question* is one whose answer is obvious to audience members and to which they are not expected to reply. Rhetorical questions create common ground by alluding to information that is shared by the audience and the speaker. They are often used in speech introductions but can also be effective as transitions and in other parts of the speech. For instance, notice how this transition, phrased as a rhetorical question, creates common ground:

> *When watching a particularly violent TV program, have you ever asked yourself, "Did they really need to be this graphic to make the point?"*

DRAW FROM COMMON EXPERIENCES You can also develop common ground by sharing personal experiences, examples, and illustrations that embody what you and the audience have in common. For instance, in a speech about the effects of television violence, you might allude to a common viewing experience:

> *Remember how sometimes at a key moment when you're watching a really frightening scene*

in a movie, you may quickly shut your eyes? I vividly remember closing my eyes over and over again during the scariest scenes in The Shining, The Blair Witch Project, *and* Halloween.

Rhetorical questions create common ground by touching on shared experiences of the audience and the speaker.

14-2c Speaker Credibility

Credibility is the confidence an audience places in the truthfulness of what a speaker says. Some people are widely known experts in a particular area and don't need to adapt their remarks to establish their credibility. However, most of us—even if we are given a formal introduction to acquaint the audience with our credentials—will still need to adapt our remarks to demonstrate our knowledge and expertise.

You can verbally share your formal education, special study, demonstrated skill, and personal examples and stories. You can also share high-quality examples and illustrations from external sources you discovered through research. Determining what is "high-quality" material can sometimes be difficult, particularly with the wide range of source materials available on the Internet.

14-2d Linguistic Sensitivity

Recall from chapter 4 that we demonstrate *linguistic sensitivity* by choosing words that are respectful of others and by avoiding potentially offensive language. Just as this is crucial to effective interpersonal and group communication, so is it imperative in public speaking situations. To demonstrate linguistic sensitivity, avoid using generic language, nonparallel language, potentially offensive humor, and profanity or vulgarity.

GENERIC LANGUAGE **Generic language** uses words that apply only to one sex, race, or other co-cultural group as though they represent everyone. In the past, English speakers used the masculine pronoun

> **common ground** the background, knowledge, attitudes, experiences, and philosophies a speaker shares with an audience
>
> **generic language** words used that apply to one co-cultural group as though they represent everyone

Where Have All the Experts Gone?

From editing a Wikipedia entry or writing a book review on Amazon.com to creating a blog about any topic imaginable, more of us are becoming "prosumers" in that we not only consume Web content but share in producing it as well.

However, critics argue that this "collective intelligence" has diluted true expertise without any sense of distinction between facts and opinions or recognition of the validity of a piece of information. Digital theorist Jaron Lanier (2006) says, "[Y]ou get to include all sorts of material without committing to anything. You can be superficially interesting without having to worry about the possibility of being wrong."

The problem is not the broadening of the knowledge base to include more perspectives, but the fact that certain voices, both online and off, are using their place in the public sphere to act as experts despite having little claim to such a title. For example, media watchdog group Media Matters reported that during the height of the debt-ceiling debate in July 2011, only 4.1 percent of the 1,258 guests on Fox, CNN, and MSNBC news programs were actually economists "with an advanced degree in economics" or who have served as an "economics professor at a college or university level." Cable news programs have the ability to reach a large number of people and frame our knowledge about current events. The lack of actual experts hinders rather than helps our understanding of issues; and in the case of the debt-ceiling issue, it resulted in much of the public adopting beliefs that differed from those of most economists (Feldman, 2011).

---

he to stand for all humans regardless of sex. This example of generic language excludes 50 percent of the audience. The best way to avoid using generic language in public speeches is to use plurals: "When we shop, we should have a clear idea of what we want to buy" (Stewart, Cooper, Stewart, & Friedley, 2003).

NONPARALLEL LANGUAGE Nonparallel language results when terms are changed because of the sex, race, or other group characteristics of the individual. Two common forms of nonparallelism are marking and irrelevant association.

Marking is the *addition* of sex, race, age, or other group designations to a description. For instance, a doctor is a person with a medical degree who is licensed to practice medicine. Notice the difference between the following two sentences:

> *Jones is a good doctor.*
>
> *Jones is a good Hispanic doctor.*

In the second sentence, the marker "Hispanic" has nothing to do with doctoring. Marking is inappropriate because it trivializes the subject's role by introducing an irrelevant characteristic (Treinen & Warren, 2001). The speaker may intend to praise Jones, but listeners may interpret the sentence as saying that Jones is a good doctor for a Hispanic person (or a woman or an old person) but not as good as a white doctor (or a male doctor or a young doctor).

A second form of nonparallelism is **irrelevant association**, which is when one person's relationship to another is emphasized, even though that relationship is irrelevant to the point. For example, introducing a speaker as "Gladys Thompson, whose husband is CEO of Acme Inc., is the chairperson for this year's United Way campaign" is inappropriate. Mentioning her husband's status implies that Gladys Thompson is chairperson because of her *husband's* accomplishments, not her own.

OFFENSIVE HUMOR Dirty jokes and racist, sexist, or other "-ist" remarks may not be intended to be offensive, but if some listeners are offended, you will have lost verbal immediacy. To be most effective with your formal public speeches, avoid humorous comments or jokes that may be offensive to some listeners. Being inclusive means demonstrating respect for all listeners. As a general rule, when in doubt, leave it out.

PROFANITY AND VULGARITY Appropriate language avoids profanity and vulgar expressions. Fifty years ago, a child was punished for saying "hell" or "damn," and adults used profanity and vulgarity only in rare situations

---

nonparallel language
words that are changed because of the sex, race, or other group characteristics of the individual

marking the addition of sex, race, age, or other group designations to a description

irrelevant association
emphasizing one person's relationship to another when doing so is not necessary to make the point

to express strong emotions. Today, "casual swearing"—profanity injected into regular conversation—is an epidemic in some language communities, including college campuses (Lehman & DuFrene, 2010).

As a result, some of us have become desensitized to them. However, when giving a public speech, we need to remember that some peple in our audience may still be offended by swearing. People who casually pepper their formal speeches with profanity and vulgar expressions are often perceived as abrasive and lacking in character, maturity, intelligence, manners, and emotional control (O'Connor, 2000).

14-2e Cultural Diversity

Language rules and expectations vary from culture to culture. When you address an audience composed of people from ethnic and language groups different from your own, you should make extra effort to ensure that you are being understood. When the first language spoken by audience members is different from yours, they may not be able to understand what you are saying because you may speak with an accent, mispronounce words, choose inappropriate words, and misuse idioms. Speaking in a second language can make you anxious and self-conscious. But most audience members are more tolerant of mistakes made by a second-language speaker than they are of those made by a native speaker.

Nevertheless, when speaking in a second language, you can help your audience by speaking more slowly and articulating as clearly as you can. By slowing your speaking rate, you give yourself additional time to pronounce difficult sounds and choose words whose meanings you know.

© Undrey/Shutterstock.com

You also give your listeners additional time to adjust their ears so that they can more easily process what you are saying. You can also use visual aids to reinforce key terms and concepts as you move through the speech. Doing so assures listeners that they've understood you correctly.

One of the best ways to improve when you are giving a speech in a second language is to practice the speech in front of friends who are native speakers. Ask them to take note of words and phrases that you mispronounce or misuse. Then they can work with you to correct the pronunciation or choose other words that better express your idea. Also keep in mind that the more you practice speaking the language, the more comfortable you will become with it.

14-3 SPEAKING CLEARLY

Speaking clearly means using words that convey your meaning precisely. Remember from our discussion in chapter 4 that words are arbitrarily chosen symbols to represent our thoughts and feelings (Saeid, 2003). In communication studies, we often simply say the *word* is NOT the *thing*. In their influential book, *The Meaning of Meaning: A Study of the Influence of Language upon Thought and the Science of Symbolism*, I. A. Richards and C. K. Ogden (1923) clarify this idea using the semantic triangle. As depicted in Figure 14.1, a "referent" is the *thing* or object we refer to with a word, which is the "symbol" we use to refer to it. Our audience then attaches meaning to that symbol, which is what Richards and Ogden label the "thought of referent." For example, when you hear the word *dog*, what image forms in your mind? Do you visualize a poodle? A sheepdog? A mutt? There is so much variation in what the word *dog* conjures in our minds because the word *dog* is not the actual animal. The word is a symbol you use to represent the animal. So if you use the word *dog* in a speech, each member of your audience may picture something different. Because the *word* is not the *thing*, as a public speaker you should use words that most closely match the thing or idea you want your audience to see or understand. By doing so, your meaning is more likely to be understood as you intended. Let's review four strategies for improving clarity that are crucial for effective public speakers: use specific language, choose familiar terms, provide details and examples, and limit vocalized pauses.

> **speaking clearly** using words that convey your meaning precisely

Pretentious Words

A plumber e-mailed a government agency, saying he found that hydrochloric acid quickly opened drainpipes, but he wasn't sure whether it was a good thing to use.

A scientist at the agency replied, "The efficacy of hydrochloric acid is indisputable, but the corrosive residue is incompatible with metallic permanence."

The plumber wrote back thanking him for the assurance that hydrochloric acid was all right.

Disturbed by this, the scientist showed the e-mail to his boss, another scientist, who then e-mailed the plumber: "We cannot assume responsibility for the production of toxic and noxious residue with hydrochloric acid and suggest you use an alternative procedure."

The plumber e-mailed back that he agreed. Hydrochloric acid worked fine.

Greatly disturbed by this misunderstanding, the scientists took their problem to the top boss. She wrote to the plumber: "Don't use hydrochloric acid. It eats the hell out of pipes."

FIGURE 14.1 THE SEMANTIC TRIANGLE

Thought of referent

Symbol   Referent

14-3a Specific Language

Specific language refers to using precise words that clarify meaning by narrowing what is understood from a general category to a particular item or group within that category. For instance, if in her speech Nevah refers to a "blue-collar worker," you might picture any number of occupations that fall within this broad category. If, instead, she uses the term "construction worker," the number of possible images you can picture is reduced. Now you select your image from the subcategory of construction worker, and your meaning is likely to be closer to the one Nevah intended. If she is even more specific, she may say "bulldozer operator." Now you are even clearer on the specific occupation.

Choosing specific language is easier when you have a large working vocabulary. As a speaker, the larger your vocabulary, the more choices you have from which to select the word you want. As a listener, the larger your vocabulary, the more likely you are to understand the words used by others. Some speakers think that to be effective they must impress their audience with their extensive vocabularies. As a result, instead of looking for specific and precise words, they use words that appear pompous, affected, or stilted. Speaking precisely and specifically does not mean speaking obscurely. The box on this page illustrates the problem with pretentious words.

As a general rule, use a more complex word *only* when you believe that it is the very best word for a specific context. Let's suppose you wanted to use a more precise or specific word for *building*. Using the guideline

specific language words that narrow what is understood from a general category to a particular item or group within it

© Auremar/Shutterstock.com

of familiarity, you might select *house, apartment, high-rise,* or *skyscraper,* but you would avoid *edifice.* Each of the other choices is more precise or more specific, but *edifice* is neither more precise nor more specific, and in addition to being less commonly understood, it will be perceived as affected or stilted.

14-3b Familiar Terms

Using familiar terms is just as important as using specific words. Avoid jargon, slang, abbreviations, and acronyms unless (1) you define them clearly the first time they are used and (2) using them is central to your speech goal.

Jargon is the unique technical terminology of a trade or profession that is not generally understood by outsiders. We might forget that people who are not in our same line of work or who do not have the same hobbies may not understand the jargon that seems such a part of our daily communication. In short, limit your use of jargon in formal speeches and always define jargon in simple terms the first time you use it.

Slang refers to nonstandard vocabulary and nonstandard definitions assigned to words by a social group or co-culture. For example, today the word *wicked,* which has a standard definition denoting something wrong or immoral, can mean quite the opposite in some social groups and co-cultures (Rader, 2007). You should generally avoid slang in your public speeches not only because you risk being misunderstood but also because the use of slang doesn't sound professional and can hurt your credibility.

Overusing and misusing abbreviations and acronyms can also hinder clarity. Even if you think the abbreviation or acronym is common, always define it the first time you use it in the speech to ensure intelligibility. For example, in his speech about stock car racing, Jared initially refers to the sport's sanctioning organization by its full name and then provides the acronym: "National Association for Stock Car Auto Racing, or NASCAR." Providing the full and abbreviated forms of the name will ensure clarity for all listeners.

14-3c Details and Examples

Sometimes the word we use may not have a precise synonym. In these situations, clarity can be achieved by adding details or examples. Saying "He lives in a really big house," for instance, can be clarified by adding, "He lives in a fourteen-room Tudor mansion on a six-acre estate."

14-3d Vocalized Pauses

Vocalized pauses are unnecessary words interjected into sentences to fill moments of silence. Words commonly used for this purpose are "like," "you know," "really," and "basically," as well as "um" and "uh." We sometimes refer to vocalized pauses as "verbal garbage" because they do not serve a meaningful purpose and actually distract audience members from the message. Although a few vocalized pauses typically don't hinder clarity, practicing your speech aloud will help you eliminate them.

14-4 SPEAKING VIVIDLY

Speaking vividly is one effective way to maintain your audience's interest and help them remember what you say. **Vivid language** is full of life—vigorous, bright, and intense. For example, a mediocre football announcer might say, "Jackson made a great catch," but a better commentator's vivid account might be, "Jackson stretched for the ball and grasped it in both hands, struggling to keep both feet in bounds, and successfully made the touchdown as he crashed into the reporters." The words *stretched, grasped, struggling,* and *crashed* paint a vivid verbal picture of the action. You can make your ideas come to life by using sensory language and by using rhetorical figures and structures of speech.

14-4a Sensory Language

Sensory language appeals to the senses of seeing, hearing, tasting, smelling, and feeling. Vivid sensory language begins with vivid thought. You are much more likely to express yourself vividly if you can physically or psychologically

jargon the unique technical terminology of a trade or profession

slang informal, nonstandard vocabulary and definitions assigned to words by a social group or subculture

vocalized pauses unnecessary words interjected to fill moments of silence

vivid language words that are full of life

sensory language words that appeal to seeing, hearing, tasting, smelling, and feeling

sense the meanings you are trying to convey. If you feel the "bite of the wind" or "the sting of freezing rain," or if you hear and smell "the thick, juicy sirloin steaks sizzling on the grill," you will be able to describe these sensations. Does the cake "taste good"? Or do your taste buds "quiver with the sweet double-chocolate icing and velvety feel of the rich, moist cake"?

To develop vivid sensory language, begin by considering how you can re-create what something, someone, or some place *looks like.* Consider, too, how you can help listeners imagine how something *sounds.* How can you use language to convey the way something *feels* (textures, shapes, temperatures)? How can language re-create a sense of how something *tastes* or *smells*? To achieve this in your speech, use colorful descriptors. They make your ideas more concrete and can arouse emotions. They invite listeners to imagine details. Here's an example about downhill skiing:

> Sight: *As you climb the hill, the bright winter sunshine glistening on the snow is blinding.*

> Touch and feel: *Just before you take off, you gently slip your goggles over your eyes. They are bitterly cold and sting your nose for a moment.*

> Taste: *You start the descent and, as you gradually pick up speed, the taste of air and ice and snow in your mouth invigorates you.*

> Sound: *An odd silence fills the air. You hear nothing but the swish of your skis against the snow beneath your feet. At last, you arrive at the bottom of the slope. Reality hits as you hear the hustle and bustle of other skiers and instructors directing them to their next session.*

> Smell and feel: *You enter the warming house. As your fingers thaw in the warm air, the aroma from the wood stove in the corner comforts you as you ready yourself to drift off into sleep.*

By using colorful descriptors that appeal to the senses, you arouse and maintain listener interest and make your ideas more memorable.

14-4b Rhetorical Figures and Structures of Speech

Rhetorical figures of speech make striking comparisons between things that are not obviously alike. Doing so helps listeners visualize or internalize what you are saying. **Rhetorical structures of speech** combine ideas in a particular way. Either of these devices can make your speech more memorable—as long as they aren't overused. Let's look at some examples.

A **simile** is a direct comparison of dissimilar things using the words *like* or *as.* Clichés such as "He walks like a duck" and "She's as busy as a bee" are similes. If you've seen the movie *Forrest Gump,* you might recall Forrest's use of the simile: "Life is like a box of chocolates. You never know what you're going to get." Similes can be effective because they make ideas more vivid in listeners' minds. But they should be used sparingly or they lose their appeal. Clichés should be avoided because their predictability reduces their effectiveness.

A **metaphor** is an implied comparison between two unlike things, expressed without using *like* or *as.* Instead of saying that one thing is *like* another, a metaphor says that one thing *is* another. Thus, problem cars are "lemons," and the leaky roof is a "sieve." Metaphors can be effective because they make an abstract concept more concrete, strengthen an important point, or heighten emotions. Dan used a metaphor to help explain the complex concept of bioluminescence. He described it as "a miniature flashlight that fireflies turn on and off at will."

An **analogy** is an extended metaphor. Sometimes, you can develop a story from a metaphor that makes a concept more vivid. If you were to describe a family member as the "black sheep in the barnyard," that's a metaphor. If you went on to talk about the other members of the family as different animals on the farm and the roles ascribed to them, you would be extending the metaphor into an analogy. Analogies can be effective for holding your speech together in a creative and vivid way. Analogies are particularly useful to highlight the similarities between a complex or unfamiliar concept and a familiar one.

Alliteration is the repetition of consonant sounds at the beginning of words that are near one another. Tongue twisters

© Big Pants Production/Shutterstock.com

such as "Sally sells seashells by the seashore" use alliteration. In her speech about the history of jelly beans, Sharla used alliteration when she said, "And today there are more than fifty fabulous fruity flavors from which to choose." Used sparingly, alliteration can catch listeners' attention and make the speech memorable. But overuse can hurt the message because listeners might focus on the technique rather than the content of your message.

Assonance is the repetition of vowel sounds in a phrase or phrases. "How now brown cow" is a common example. Sometimes the words rhyme, but they don't have to. As with alliteration, assonance can make your speech more memorable as long as it's not overused.

Onomatopoeia is the use of words that sound like the things they stand for, such as "buzz," "hiss," "crack," and "plop." In the speech about skiing, the "swish" of the skis is an example of onomatopoeia.

Personification attributes human qualities to a concept or an inanimate object. When Madison talked about her truck, "Big Red," as her trusted friend and companion, she used personification. Likewise, when Rick talked about flowers dancing on the front lawn, he used personification.

Repetition is restating words, phrases, or sentences for emphasis. Martin Luther King Jr.'s "I Have a Dream" speech is a classic example, as is Winston Churchill's 1940 address to the House of Commons, which notes, "We shall fight on the beaches, we shall fight on the landing grounds, we shall fight in the fields . . . . we shall never surrender."

In his 2013 State of the Union address, U.S. President Barack Obama stepped away from his prepared text to use repetition when discussing gun control, making an emotional point.

Antithesis is combining contrasting ideas in the same sentence, as when John F. Kennedy said, "My fellow Americans, ask not what your country can do for you; ask what you can do for your country." Likewise, astronaut Neil Armstrong used antithesis when he first stepped on the moon: "That's one small step for [a] man, one giant leap for mankind." Speeches that offer antithesis in the concluding remarks are often very memorable.

ACTION | STEP 5a

Adapt Oral Language and Style

The goal of this activity is to help you plan how you will adapt your language and style to the specific audience.

Write your thesis statement:

_____

_____

_____

Review the audience analysis that you completed in Action Steps 1 through 4. Now verbally adapt to your audience by answering the following questions:

1. **How can I adapt my language to foster verbal immediacy with this audience?**

2. **How can I adapt my language choices to demonstrate respect for this audience?**

3. **Where can I adapt my language to be most intelligible for this audience?**

4. **How can I use sensory language and rhetorical figures of speech to make my ideas more vivid for this audience?**

---

assonance the repetition of vowel sounds in a phrase or phrases

onomatopoeia the use of words that sound like the things they stand for

personification attributing human qualities to a concept or an inanimate object

repetition restating words, phrases, or sentences for emphasis

antithesis combining contrasting ideas in the same sentence

STUDY TOOLS 14

LOCATED IN TEXTBOOK

☐ Tear-out Chapter Review cards at the end of the book

☐ Review with the Quick Quiz below

LOCATED ON COMM 4 ONLINE AT CENGAGEBRAIN.COM:

☐ Review Key Term flashcards and create your own cards

☐ Track your knowledge and understanding of key concepts in communication

☐ Complete practice and graded quizzes to prepare for tests

☐ Complete interactive content within COMM4 Online

☐ View the chapter highlight boxes for COMM4 Online

Quick Quiz

T F 1. The skill of audience adaptation involves both verbally and visually preparing presentational aids that facilitate audience understanding.

T F 2. In order to be timely, you must adapt the information in your speech so that audience members view it as important to them.

T F 3. Saying that Bryony is an excellent female architect is an example of marking.

T F 4. Palani notes in a speech that human traffickers often use containers to run their illegal trade. This is specific language.

T F 5. When you are speaking in a second language, audience members are less likely to tolerate your mistakes.

6. When you are choosing the supporting material for your speech, it's important to select materials that
   a. are relevant to the audience.
   b. are not offensive to the audience.
   c. establish common ground between you and the audience.
   d. maintain or develop credibility.
   e. accomplish all of these things.

7. A speech that includes information about the audience's neighborhood or town is establishing
   a. relevance.
   b. timeliness.
   c. proximity.
   d. personal impact.
   e. credibility.

8. Which is NOT one of the five guidelines that can aid in adapting the information of your speech so that the audience can more easily understand it?
   a. avoiding jargon
   b. using precise words
   c. limiting words like "um" and "like"
   d. using rhetorical structures of speech
   e. using technical language where necessary

9. Millie begins her speech by saying, "I've decided to talk today about volcanoes and their impact on Hawaiians. I'll tell you about native Hawaiian culture and how volcanoes have influenced that culture." Millie needs to
   a. use personal pronouns.
   b. ask rhetorical questions.
   c. speak Hawaiian.
   d. increase her verbal immediacy.
   e. use a visual aid.

10. A fashion design professor giving a lecture describes coated denim as having a strong conviction and strength of character. She is using
    a. a simile.
    b. a metaphor.
    c. alliteration.
    d. personification.
    e. onomatopoeia.

Answers: 1.T, 2.F, 3.T, 4.F, 5.F, 6.E, 7.C, 8.E, 9.A, 10.D

LEARNING YOUR WAY

Go to **www.cengagebrain.com**
to access **MIS Online!**

 Follow us at
www.facebook.com/4ltrpress

15 Delivery

LEARNING OUTCOMES

15-1 Employ strategies to effectively manage public speaking apprehension

15-2 Identify the characteristics of an effective delivery style

15-3 Use your voice to convey effective delivery style

15-4 Use your body to convey effective delivery style

15-5 Select an appropriate delivery method for your speeches

15-6 Engage in productive rehearsals

15-7 Adapt appropriately as you deliver your speech

15-8 Evaluate speech effectiveness

After finishing this chapter go to **PAGE 224** for **STUDY TOOLS.**

The difference between a good speech and a great speech is often how well it is delivered. In fact, research suggests that listeners are often influenced more by speech delivery than content (Decker, 1992; Gardner, 2003; Towler, 2003). Although a speaker's delivery alone cannot compensate for a poorly researched, developed, or organized speech, a well-delivered speech can really capture an audience.

In the last chapter, we focused on one aspect of the fifth action step: oral language style. In this chapter, we turn our attention to the other aspect: delivery style. We begin by discussing public speaking anxiety and ways to manage it effectively. Then we explain how to use your voice and body effectively, as well as three common methods for delivering a speech. We then introduce a process designed to make your practice sessions productive and some delivery guidelines to consider while giving the actual speech. Finally, we offer several criteria you can use to evaluate your speeches and apply that criteria to a sample student speech.

ACTION STEPS

Action Step 5
Practice oral language and delivery style

15-1 PUBLIC SPEAKING APPREHENSION

Most of us feel some fear about public speaking. In fact, according to the National Institute of Mental Health, as many as 75 percent of us suffer from some public speaking anxiety (Fear of Public Speaking Statistics, 2013). Did you know,

for example, that award-winning actors Meryl Streep, Kim Basinger, and Harrison Ford; singer Barbra Streisand, singer/actor Donny Osmond; professional football player Ricky Williams; and evangelists Billy Graham and Joel Olsteen all experience a fear of public speaking? In spite of their fear, they are all effective public speakers.

Public speaking apprehension is the level of fear we experience when anticipating or actually speaking to an audience. Fortunately, we can benefit from the results of a good deal of research about managing public speaking apprehension effectively. We say *manage* because having some fear actually makes us better speakers. Just as an adrenaline boost helps athletes, musicians, and actors perform better, it can also help us deliver better public speeches (Kelly, Duran, & Stewart, 1990; Motley, 1997; Phillips, 1977).

What if they laugh at me?

© Addimage/Shutterstock.com

15-1a Symptoms and Causes

The symptoms of public speaking apprehension vary from individual to individual and range from mild to debilitating. Symptoms can be cognitive, physical, or emotional. Cognitive symptoms stem from negative self-talk (e.g., "I'm going to blow it" or "I just know I'll make a fool of myself"), which is also the most common cause of speech apprehension (Richmond & McCroskey, 2000). Physical symptoms may be stomach upset (or butterflies), flushed skin, sweating, shaking, light-headedness, rapid or pounding heartbeats, stuttering, and vocalized pauses ("like," "you know," "ah," "um," and so on). Emotional symptoms include feeling anxious, worried, or upset.

In addition to negative self-talk, previous experience, modeling, and negative

> **public speaking apprehension** the level of fear we experience when anticipating or actually speaking to an audience

reinforcement can also cause public speaking apprehension. Previous experience has to do with being socialized to fear public speaking as a result of modeling and negative reinforcement (Richmond & McCroskey, 2000). Modeling has to do with observing how your friends and family members react to speaking in public. If they tend to be quiet and reserved and avoid public speaking, your fears may stem from modeling. Negative reinforcement concerns how others have responded to your public speaking endeavors. If you experienced negative reactions, you might be more apprehensive about speaking in public than if you had been praised for your efforts (Motley, 1997).

Luckily, our apprehension gradually decreases for most of us as we speak. Researchers have identified three phases we proceed through: anticipation, confrontation, and adaptation (Behnke & Carlile, 1971). Figure 15.1 illustrates these phases. The **anticipation phase** is the anxiety we experience before giving the speech, both while preparing it and waiting to speak. The **confrontation phase** is the surge of anxiety we feel as we begin delivering the speech. The **adaptation phase** is the period during which our anxiety level gradually decreases. It typically begins about one minute into the presentation and tends to level off after about five minutes (Beatty & Behnke, 1991).

15-1b Management Techniques

We propose five techniques to help manage apprehension effectively: communication orientation, visualization, systematic desensitization, cognitive restructuring, and public speaking skills training.

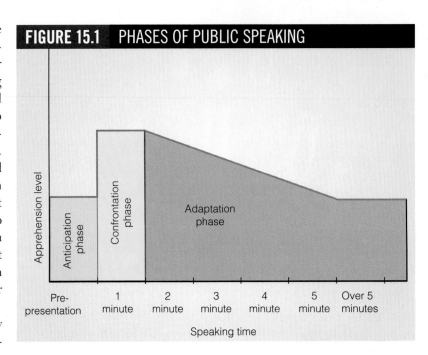

FIGURE 15.1   PHASES OF PUBLIC SPEAKING

anticipation phase anxiety we experience before giving a speech

confrontation phase the surge of anxiety we experience when we begin delivering a speech

adaptation phase the period during a speech when our anxiety gradually decreases

performance orientation believing we must impress a hypercritical audience with our knowledge and delivery

communication orientation seeing a speech situation as an opportunity to talk with a number of people about a topic that is important to the speaker and to them

visualization a method to reduce apprehension by developing a mental picture of yourself giving a masterful speech

systematic desensitization a method to reduce apprehension by gradually visualizing and then engaging in more frightening speaking events while remaining in a relaxed state

COMMUNICATION ORIENTATION MOTIVATION Communication orientation motivation (COM) techniques reduce anxiety by helping us adopt a *communication* rather than *performance* orientation toward speeches (Motley, 1997). When we have a **performance orientation**, we believe we must *impress* a hypercritical audience with our knowledge and delivery. On the other hand, when we have a **communication orientation**, we focus on talking with our audience about an important topic and *getting a message across to them*—not about how they might be judging our performance.

VISUALIZATION Visualization helps us reduce anxiety by developing a mental picture of ourselves giving a masterful speech. If we visualize ourselves going through an entire speech-making process successfully, we are more likely to be successful when we actually deliver the speech (Ayres & Hopf, 1990; Ayres, Hopf, & Ayres, 1994).

SYSTEMATIC DESENSITIZATION Systematic desensitization can help reduce anxiety by gradually visualizing and engaging in increasingly more frightening speaking events while remaining in a relaxed state. The process starts with consciously tensing and then relaxing muscle groups to learn how to recognize the difference between the two states. Then, while in a relaxed state, you first imagine yourself and then engage in successively more stressful situations—for example, researching a speech topic in the library, practicing the speech out loud to a roommate, and finally giving a speech. The ultimate goal of systematic desensitization is to transfer the calm feelings we attain while visualizing to the actual speaking event. Calmness on command—it works.

COGNITIVE RESTRUCTURING Cognitive restructuring helps reduce anxiety by replacing anxiety-arousing negative self-talk with anxiety-reducing positive self-talk through a four-step process.

1. Identify your fears. Write down all the fears that come to mind when you know you must give a speech.

2. Determine whether or not these fears are rational. Most of your fears about public speaking are irrational because public speaking is not life threatening.

3. Develop positive coping statements to replace each negative self-talk statement. There is no list of coping statements that will work for everyone. Psychologist Richard Heimberg of the State University of New York at Albany reminds his clients that most listeners don't notice or even care if the clients do what they're afraid of doing when giving a speech. Ultimately, he asks them, "Can you cope with the one or two people who [notice or criticize or] get upset?"

4. Incorporate positive coping statements into your life so they become second nature. You can do this by writing your statements down and reading them aloud to yourself each day, as well as before you give a speech. The more you repeat your coping statements, the more natural they will become (see Figure 15.2).

PUBLIC SPEAKING SKILLS TRAINING Public speaking skills training is systematically practicing the skills involved in preparing and delivering an effective public speech. Skills training is based on the assumption that some public speaking anxiety is caused by not knowing how to be successful. So if we learn the skills associated with effective speech making (e.g., audience analysis, topic selection and development, organization, oral language, and delivery style), then we will be less anxious (Kelly, Phillips, & Keaten, 1995).

15-2 EFFECTIVE DELIVERY STYLE

Think about one of the best speakers you have ever heard. What made them stand out in your mind? In all likelihood, how the speaker delivered the speech had a lot to do with it. **Delivery** is how a message is communicated

FIGURE 15.2 COGNITIVE RESTRUCTURING

Beth decided to try cognitive restructuring to reduce her anxiety about giving speeches in front of her classmates. Here are the positive statements she developed to counter her negative self-talk:

Negative self-talk

1. I'm afraid I'll stumble over my words and look foolish.
2. I'm afraid everyone will be able to tell that I am nervous.
3. I'm afraid my voice will crack.
4. I'm afraid I'll sound boring.

Positive coping statements

1. Even if I stumble, I will have succeeded as long as I get my message across.
2. They probably won't be able to tell I'm nervous, but as long as I focus on getting my message across, that's what matters.
3. Even if my voice cracks, as long as I keep going and focus on getting my message across, I'll succeed at what matters most.
4. I won't sound bored if I focus on how important this message is to me and to my audience. I don't have to do somersaults to keep their attention, because my topic is relevant to them.

orally and visually through the use of voice and body. So we achieve effective delivery by adapting the types of nonverbal communication introduced in chapter 5 to a public speaking situation. An effective public speaking delivery style is both conversational and animated.

15-2a Conversational

You have probably heard ineffective speakers whose delivery was overly dramatic and affected or stiff and mechanical. In contrast, effective delivery is **conversational.** The audience perceives you as *talking with* them and not performing *in front of* or *reading to* them. The hallmark of a conversational style is spontaneity. **Spontaneity** is the ability to sound natural—as though you are really thinking about the ideas and getting them across to your audience—no matter how many times you've practiced.

cognitive restructuring replacing anxiety-arousing negative self-talk with anxiety-reducing positive self-talk

public speaking skills training the systematic teaching of the skills associated with preparing and delivering an effective public speech, with the intention of improving speaking competence and thereby reducing public speaking apprehension

delivery how a message is communicated orally and visually through the use of voice and body

conversational style presenting a speech so that your audience feels you are talking with them

spontaneity a naturalness that seems unrehearsed and unmemorized

15-2b Animated

Have you ever been bored by a professor reading a well-structured lecture while looking at the lecture notes rather than the students and making few gestures other than turning the pages? Even a well-written speech given by an expert can bore an audience unless its delivery is **animated**, that is, lively and dynamic.

How can we sound conversational and animated at the same time? The secret is to focus on conveying the passion we feel about the topic through our voice and body. When we are passionate about sharing something with someone, almost all of us become more animated in our delivery. Our goal is to duplicate this level of liveliness when we deliver our speeches. The next two sections focus more closely on how we can use our voice and our body to achieve effective conversational and animated delivery.

If you don't speak intelligibly, you may sound like you are talking with your mouth full!

15-3 USE OF VOICE

Recall from chapter 5 that your *voice* is the sound you produce using your vocal organs. How your voice sounds depends on its pitch, volume, rate, and quality. As a public speaker, you can achieve a conversational and animated delivery style by varying your pitch, volume, rate, and quality in ways that make you more intelligible and expressive.

15-3a Intelligibility

To be **intelligible** means to be understandable. All of us have experienced situations in which we couldn't understand what was being said because the speaker was talking too softly or too quickly. If you practice your speech using appropriate pitch, volume, rate, and vocal quality, you can improve the likelihood that you will be intelligible to your audience.

Most of us speak at a pitch that is appropriate for us and intelligible to listeners. However, some people naturally have voices that are higher or lower in register or become accustomed to talking in tones that are either above or below their natural pitch. Speaking at an appropriate pitch is particularly important if your audience includes people who have hearing loss because they may find it difficult to hear a pitch that is too high or too low.

Appropriate volume is key to intelligibility. You must speak loudly enough, with or without a microphone, to be heard easily by the audience members in the back of the room but not so loudly as to cause discomfort to listeners seated in the front. You can also vary your volume to emphasize important information. For example, you may speak louder when you introduce each main point or when imploring listeners to take action. When recording a speech to post online, you want to be heard easily, but not sound as though you are shouting.

The rate at which you speak can also influence intelligibility. Speaking too slowly gives your listeners time to let their minds wander after they've processed an idea. Speaking too quickly, especially when sharing complex ideas and arguments, may not give listeners enough time to process the information completely. Because nervousness may cause you to speak more quickly than normal, monitor your rate and adjust if you are speaking more quickly than normal.

In addition to vocal characteristics, articulation, pronunciation, and accent can affect intelligibility. **Articulation** is using the tongue, palate, teeth, jaws, and lips to shape vocalized sounds that combine to produce a word. Many of us suffer from minor articulation and **pronunciation** problems such as adding an extra sound ("athalete" for *athlete*), leaving out a sound ("libary" for *library*), transposing sounds ("revalent" for *relevant*), and distorting sounds ("troof" for *truth*).

Accent is the inflection, tone, and speech habits typical of native speakers of a language. When you

animated lively and dynamic

intelligible understandable

articulation using the tongue, palate, teeth, jaw movement, and lips to shape vocalized sounds that combine to produce a word

pronunciation the form and accent of various syllables of a word

accent the inflection, tone, and speech habits typical of the native speakers of a language

misarticulate or speak with a heavy accent during a conversation, your listeners can ask you to repeat yourself until they understand you. But in a speech setting, audience members are unlikely to interrupt to ask you to repeat something. If your accent is "thick" or very different from that of most of your audience, practice pronouncing key words so that you are easily understood, speak slowly to allow your audience members more time to process your message, and consider using visual aids to reinforce key terms, concepts, and important points.

15-3b Vocal Expression

Vocal expression is achieved by changing your pitch, volume, and rate; stressing certain words; and using pauses strategically. Doing so clarifies the emotional intent of your message and helps animate your delivery. Generally, speeding up your rate, raising your pitch, or increasing your volume reinforces emotions such as joy, enthusiasm, excitement, anticipation, and a sense of urgency or fear. Slowing down your rate, lowering your pitch, or decreasing your volume can communicate resolution, peacefulness, remorse, disgust, or sadness.

A total lack of vocal expression produces a **monotone**—a voice in which the pitch, volume, and rate remain constant, with no word, idea, or sentence differing significantly in sound from any other. Although few people speak in a true monotone, many severely limit themselves by using only two or three pitch levels and relatively unchanging volume and rate when giving public speeches. An actual or near monotone not only lulls an audience to sleep but, more importantly, diminishes the chances

of audience understanding. For instance, if the sentence "Congress should pass laws limiting the sale of pornography" is presented in a monotone, listeners will be uncertain whether the speaker is concerned with *who* should be taking action, what Congress should *do*, or *what* the laws should be.

Pauses, moments of silence strategically used to enhance meaning, can also mark important ideas. If you use one or more sentences in your speech to express an important idea, pause before each sentence to signal that something important is coming or pause afterward to allow the idea to sink in. Pausing one or more times within a sentence can also add impact. Nick included several short pauses within and a long pause after his sentence "Our government has no compassion (*pause*), no empathy (*pause*), and no regard for human feeling" (*longer pause*).

15-4 USE OF BODY

Because your audience can see as well as hear you, how you use your body also contributes to how conversational and animated your audience perceives you to be. Body language elements that affect speech delivery include appearance, posture, poise, eye contact, facial expressions, gestures, and movement.

15-4a Appearance

Some speakers think that what they wear doesn't or shouldn't affect the success of their speech. But unless your audience cannot see you because you are doing a voiced-over slideshow, studies show that a neatly groomed and professional appearance sends important messages about a public speaker's commitment to the topic and occasion, as well as about the speaker's credibility (ethos) (Bates, 1992; Hammer, 2000; Howlett, Pine, Chaill, Orakcioglu, & Fletcher, 2015; Morgan, 2013; Sellnow & Treinen, 2004). Three guidelines can help you decide how to dress for your speech.

1. Consider the audience and occasion. Dress a bit more formally than you expect members of your audience to dress. If you dress too formally, your audience is

© R. Gino Santa Maria/Shutterstock.com

vocal expression the contrasts in pitch, volume, rate, and quality that affect the meaning an audience gets from the sentences you speak

monotone a voice in which the pitch, volume, and rate remain constant, with no word, idea, or sentence differing significantly from any other

pauses moments of silence strategically used to enhance meaning

likely to perceive you to be untrustworthy and insincere; if you dress too casually, your audience may view you as uncommitted to your topic or disrespectful of them or the occasion.

2. Consider your topic and purpose. In general, the more serious your topic, the more formally you should dress. For example, if your topic is AIDS and you are trying to convince your audience to be tested for HIV, you will want to look like someone who is an authority by dressing the part. But if your topic is yoga and you are trying to convince your audience to take a yoga class at the new campus recreation center, you might dress more casually.

3. Avoid extremes. Your attire shouldn't detract from your speech. Avoid gaudy jewelry, over- or undersized clothing, and sexually suggestive attire. Remember: You want your audience to focus on your message, so your appearance should be neutral.

15-4b Posture

Recall from chapter 5 that *posture is* how you hold your body. When giving a public speech, an upright stance and squared shoulders communicate a sense of confidence. Speakers who slouch may be perceived as lacking self-confidence and not caring about the topic, audience, and occasion.

15-4c Poise

Poise is a graceful and controlled use of the body

poise graceful and controlled use of the body

that gives the impression that you are self-assured, calm, and dignified. Mannerisms that convey nervousness, such as swaying from side to side, drumming fingers on the lectern, taking off or putting on glasses, jiggling pocket change, smacking the tongue, licking the lips, or scratching the nose, hand, or arm should be noted during practice sessions and avoided during the speech.

15-4d Eye Contact

When giving a formal presentation, effective *eye contact* involves looking at people in all parts of an audience throughout the speech. As long as you are looking at someone (those in front of you, in the left rear of the room, in the right center of the room, and so on) and not at your notes or the ceiling, floor, or window, everyone in the audience will perceive you as having good eye contact with them. Generally, you should look at your audience at least 90 percent of the time, glancing at your notes (even if they are on your PowerPoint or Prezi slides) only when you need a quick reference point. Maintaining eye contact is important for several reasons.

1. Maintaining eye contact helps audiences concentrate on the speech. If you do not look at audience members while you talk, they are unlikely to maintain eye contact with you. This break in mutual eye contact reduces a sense of conversational delivery and often decreases concentration on the message.

2. Maintaining eye contact bolsters ethos. Just as you are likely to be skeptical of people who do not look you in

If you expect your audience to dress like this . . .

the eye as they converse, so too audiences will be skeptical of speakers who do not look at them. In the dominant American culture, eye contact is perceived as a sign of sincerity. Speakers who fail to maintain eye contact with audiences are almost always perceived as ill at ease and often as insincere or dishonest (Levine, Asada, & Park, 2006).

3. Maintaining eye contact helps you gauge the audience's reaction to your ideas. Because communication is two way, audience members communicate with you while you are speaking to them. In conversation, the audience's response is likely to be both verbal and nonverbal. In public speaking, the audience's response is likely to occur only through nonverbal cues. Bored audience members might yawn, look out the window, slouch in their chairs, and even sleep. Confused audience members might look puzzled by furrowing their brows or shaking their head. Audience members who understand or agree with something you say might nod their heads. By monitoring your audience's behavior, you can adjust by becoming more animated, offering additional examples, or moving more quickly through a point.

When speaking to large audiences of 100 or more people, you must create a *sense* of looking listeners in the eye even though you actually cannot. This process is called **audience contact**. You can create audience contact by mentally dividing your audience into small groups. Then, tracing the letter Z with your gaze, talk for four to six seconds with each group as you move through your speech. When speaking virtually via web conferencing software using a computer screen and camera, be sure to look into the camera as you speak rather than at your image or their image(s) on the screen. When you look into the camera, your audience will perceive you as having eye contact with them.

15-4e Facial Expressions

Recall from chapter 5 that *facial expression* is the arrangement of facial muscles to express emotions. For public speakers, effective facial expressions can convey **nonverbal immediacy** by communicating that you are personable and likable. They can also help animate your speech. Speakers who do not vary their facial expressions during their speech but instead wear a deadpan expression, perpetual grin, or permanent scowl tend to be perceived as boring, insincere, or stern. To assess whether you are using effective facial expressions during your

© Warren Goldswain/Shutterstock.com

Dress like this.

speech, practice delivering it to yourself in a mirror or record your rehearsal and evaluate your facial expressions as you watch it.

15-4f Gestures

As we discussed in chapter 5, *gestures* are the movements of your hands, arms, and fingers. You can use gestures when delivering speeches to describe or emphasize what you are saying, refer to presentational aids, or clarify structure. For example, as Aaron began to speak about the advantages of smart phone apps, he said, "on one hand" and lifted his right hand face up. When he got to the disadvantages, he lifted his left hand face up as he said, "on the other hand." Recall from chapter 5, however, that certain gestures mean different things in different cultures.

Some people who are nervous when giving a speech clasp their hands behind their backs, bury them in their pockets, or grip the lectern. Unable to pry their hands free gracefully, they wiggle their elbows or appear stiff, which can distract listeners from the message.

As with facial expressions, effective gestures must appear spontaneous and natural even though they are carefully planned and practiced. When you practice and then deliver your speech, leave your hands free so that you will be available to gesture as you normally do.

15-4g Movement

Recall that *movement* refers to changing your body position. During your speech, it is important to engage only in **motivated movement**, movement with a specific purpose such as emphasizing an important idea, referencing a presentational aid, or clarifying structure. To emphasize a particular point, you might move closer to the audience. To create a feeling of intimacy before telling a personal story, you might walk out from behind a lectern and sit down on a chair placed at the edge of the stage. Each time you begin a new main point, you might take a few steps to one side of the stage or the other. To use motivated movement effectively, you need to practice when and how you will move so you can do so in a way that appears spontaneous and natural while remaining "open" to the audience (not turning your back to them).

audience contact when speaking to large audiences, create a sense of looking listeners in the eye even though you actually cannot

nonverbal immediacy communicating through body language that you are personable and likeable

motivated movement movement with a specific purpose

Avoid unmotivated movement such as bobbing, weaving, shifting from foot to foot, or pacing from one side of the room to the other; unplanned movements distract the audience from your message. Because many unplanned movements result from nervousness, you can minimize them by paying mindful attention to your body as you speak. At the beginning of your speech, stand up tall on both feet. If you find yourself fidgeting, readjust and position your body with your weight equally distributed on both feet.

15-5 DELIVERY METHODS

Speeches vary in the amount of content preparation and practice you do ahead of time. The three most common delivery methods are impromptu, scripted, and extemporaneous.

15-5a Impromptu Speeches

An **impromptu speech** is one that is delivered with only seconds or minutes of advance notice for preparation and is usually presented without referring to notes of any kind. Because impromptu speakers must quickly gather their thoughts just before and while they speak, carefully organizing and developing ideas can be challenging. As a result, they may leave out important information or confuse audience members. Delivery can suffer as speakers often use "ahs," "ums," "like," and "you know" to buy time as they scramble to collect their thoughts. That's why the more opportunities you have to organize and deliver your thoughts using an impromptu method, the better you'll become at doing so.

Common situations that require the impromptu method include employment and performance review interviews, business meetings, classes, social ceremonies, and speaking to the media. In each situation, having practiced organizing ideas quickly and conveying them intelligibly and expressively will bolster your ethos and help you succeed.

You can improve your impromptu performances by practicing mock impromptu speeches. For example, if you are taking a class in which the professor calls on students at random to answer questions, you can prepare by anticipating the questions that might be asked on the readings for the day and practice giving your answers aloud. Over time, you will become more adept at organizing your ideas and thinking on your feet.

15-5b Scripted Speeches

At the other extreme, a **scripted speech** is one that is prepared by creating a complete written manuscript and then delivered by reading from or memorizing a written copy. Obviously, effective scripted speeches take a great deal of time to prepare because both an outline and a word-for-word transcript must be prepared, practiced, and delivered in a way that sounds both conversational and animated. When you memorize a scripted speech, you face the increased anxiety of forgetting your lines. When you read a scripted speech, you must become adept at looking at the script with your peripheral vision so that you don't appear to be reading and sound conversational and animated.

Because of the time and skill required to effectively prepare and deliver a scripted speech, they are usually reserved for important occasions that have important consequences. Political speeches, keynote addresses at conventions, commencement addresses, and CEO remarks at annual stockholder meetings are examples of occasions when a scripted speech might be appropriate and worth the extra effort.

15-5c Extemporaneous Speeches

Most speeches, whether in the workplace, in the community, or in class, are delivered extemporaneously. An

impromptu speech a speech that is delivered with only seconds or minutes to prepare

scripted speech a speech that is prepared by creating a complete written manuscript and delivered by rote memory or by reading a written copy

© wellphoto/Shutterstock.com

critique, and prepare assignments critiquing themselves or each other.

Technology also makes it possible to speak publicly to multiple audiences across the country and around the world. For example, a speech posted to YouTube could reach an audience far beyond the classroom. Although public speaking certainly still occurs in traditional face-to-face settings, it is no longer limited by place and time—far from it!

President Franklin Delano Roosevelt (FDR) is credited as one of the first public figures to capitalize on the benefits of technology to break through the *place* limitation to reach a wider audience. Throughout his presidency in the 1930s and 1940s, FDR delivered *fireside chats*, weekly radio addresses about important issues facing the country (Mankowski & Jose, 2012). These speeches could be heard by anyone who chose to tune in. U.S. presidents have been offering weekly addresses ever since! In fact, today President Obama even posts weekly addresses on YouTube and the White House Web site (Obama, *Your Weekly Address*).

Perhaps one of the most significant examples of technology overcoming the limitation of *time* comes from Martin Luther King, Jr. Over 200,000 people were at the political rally in Washington, D.C., on August 28, 1963, to hear his famous "I Have a Dream" speech live and in person. More than 50 years later, we can join the 200,000 who made up that first audience to hear him deliver this powerful oration by clicking on any number of Web sites where it is archived. In fact, a quick *Google* search of "I Have a Dream speech" yields more than 37,400,000 hits.

The benefits of overcoming *place* and *time* barriers also come with some new challenges, particularly regarding *audience analysis and adaptation*. While many fundamentals of effective public speaking remain true, today speakers must also adapt to multiple audiences and to some unique demands of a mediated platform.

To reach multiple audiences successfully, we must consider not just those who are informed about the topic and issue, but also those who may not be informed, may be apathetic, and perhaps may even be hostile toward it. Those who have analyzed Dr. King's speech, for instance, claim he did so by using the rhetorical

extemporaneous speech is researched and planned ahead of time, but the exact wording is not scripted and will vary somewhat from presentation to presentation. When speaking extemporaneously, you refer to speaking notes reminding you of key ideas, structure, and delivery cues as you speak. Some speakers today use their computerized slideshows as speaking notes. If you choose to do so, however, be careful not to include too many words on any given slide, which will ultimately distract listeners from focusing on you as you speak.

Extemporaneous speeches are the easiest to give effectively. Unlike impromptu speeches, when speaking extemporaneously you can prepare your thoughts ahead of time and have notes to prompt you. Unlike scripted speeches, extemporaneous speeches do not require as lengthy a preparation process to be effective.

15-5d Delivering Speeches through Mediated Technology

When great orators like Plato, Aristotle, and Cicero engaged in public speaking to conduct business, debate public issues, and gain and maintain power, the communication event occurred in real time with both the speaker and audience physically present. Thanks to technology, however, public speeches today may be delivered in both face-to-face and virtual environments. Technology also makes it possible to record public speeches and watch them again and again. A professor can record and upload a speech to the class Web site. Later, students can watch,

> **extemporaneous speech**
> a speech that is researched and planned ahead of time, although the exact wording is not scripted and will vary from presentation to presentation

Politics, Politicians, and Public Speech Delivery

In political speeches, it is not always *what* you say that resonates with audiences, but *how* you say it. Politicians are often criticized for exhibiting an overly rehearsed speaking style that leaves audiences believing that the speaker is simply saying what he or she thinks we want to hear.

On the other hand, New Jersey governor Chris Christie is often celebrated for using a blunt and straightforward speaking style that contrasts with the scripted style exhibited by many politicians. He is well known for routinely using words like "stupid," "crap," and "insane" in news briefings, town hall meetings, and even more formal political speeches (Barron, 2011). Christie supporters champion his spirited style as evidence of his real commitment to his goals of political reform and his rejection of political pandering. In an era when Americans are increasingly frustrated with Washington political bickering, Christie's straightforward style seems like a welcome alternative.

However, not everyone is a fan of Christie's frank and confrontational style. Some critics suggest that his combative delivery style makes him come off as a bully; others worry that Christie's tendency to allow his emotions get the better of him during his public speeches does not fit with the need for rational and measured debate within the political realm. But his supporters say it is exactly this heartfelt and authentic expression of his ideas that makes Christie appealing as a politician.

© Fliegenwulf/Shutterstock.com

---

devices common to the black preacher style, and at the same time, transcending the typical Civil Rights–era speeches that were aimed at supportive audiences. In the first half of the speech, King addressed his remarks to the assembled throng, but he then moved from addressing the grievances of black Americans to focus on the bedrock of American values. Linking civil rights to the American Dream appealed not only to the audience present on the Washington Mall, but also to the millions of noncommitted Americans who watched the speech on TV. Today, more than 50 years later, it continues to resonate as representing American values and the American dream.

Technology today brings with it a challenge to address mediated audiences that we intentionally target, as was the case with King. However, because speeches today may be easily uploaded to Web sites like YouTube with or without our permission and then quickly go viral, we also must always be cognizant of possible audiences we never intended to target. Not doing so can result in devastating consequences. For example, in 2011 Texas governor and then–GOP presidential hopeful Rick Perry discovered this when a speech he delivered to a group of supporters in New Hampshire went viral. Blog posts and newspaper editorials blamed his giggling and rambling remarks on being "drunk" or "drugged" (Camia, 2011).

GUIDELINES FOR PUBLIC SPEAKING IN A VIRTUAL WORLD The benefits of mediated public speaking to overcome *place* and *time* barriers can be traced to FDR's fireside chats in the 1930s. However, the unique challenges it poses are only beginning to surface. So, the following list of guidelines provides a starting point that will inevitably grow as we learn more about the role technology and digital media play in effective public speaking.

© wavebreakmedia/Shutterstock.com

1. Adapt your speech to address multiple audiences. Assume that any speech you give may be recorded and made available to those who are not in your immediate target audience. Always consider how you might adapt your content, structure, and delivery to accurately and respectfully address uninformed, apathetic, and oppositional audiences who may view your speech virtually.

2. Adapt your speech to account for unintended audiences. Don't say anything to one specific audience that you would not want broadcast to a wider audience. With just a few clicks of a smartphone, an audience member can record a video and post it online. So make sure your content, language, and humorous anecdotes are accurate and respectful.

3. Choose presentational aids carefully. Make sure the visuals and audiovisuals you use can be easily viewed and heard in an online format. Also, be sure to explain them so that those who only have audio access or who view them on a small smartphone screen can understand the information on them.

4. Become proficient with technology. Consult with communication technology experts at your university, college, place of business, or professional organization to learn how to use the technologies effectively. Consider taking a course or seminar devoted to developing these competencies.

5. Employ the fundamentals of effective public speaking. Although this might seem to go without saying, be sure to adhere to the strategies of effective public speaking even when delivering your speech online to mediated audiences. In other words, use an attention getter to pique curiosity, thesis statement with preview to frame what is to come, and transitions to help your audience follow along. Use accurate, clear, and vivid language, and employ verbal and nonverbal techniques that are intelligible, conversational, and animated.

15-6 REHEARSALS

Rehearsing is the process of repeatedly practicing your speech aloud. A speech that is not practiced out loud is likely to be far less effective than it would have been had you given yourself sufficient time to revise, evaluate, and mull over all aspects of the speech (Anderson 2013). Figure 15.3 provides a useful timetable for preparing a classroom speech.

In this section, we describe how to rehearse effectively by preparing speaking notes, handling presentational aids, and recording, analyzing, and refining delivery.

FIGURE 15.3 — TIMETABLE FOR PREPARING A SPEECH

8 days before	Select topic; begin research
7 days before	Continue research
6 days before	Outline body of speech
5 days before	Work on introduction and conclusion
4 days before	Finish outline; find additional material if needed; have all presentational aids completed
3 days before	First rehearsal session
2 days before	Second rehearsal session
1 day before	Third rehearsal section
Due date	Deliver speech

15-6a Preparing Speaking Notes

Prior to your first rehearsal session, prepare a draft of your speaking notes. **Speaking notes** are a keyword outline of your speech including hard-to-remember information or quotations and delivery cues. The best notes contain the fewest words possible written in lettering large enough to be seen instantly at a distance.

To develop your notes, begin by reducing your speech outline to an abbreviated outline of key phrases and words. Then, if there are details you must cite exactly accurately—such as a specific example, a quotation, or a set of statistics—add these in the appropriate spots. You might also put these on a separate card as a "Quotation Card" to refer to when delivering direct quotations during the speech, which is what Alyssa did (see Figure 15.4). Next, indicate exactly where you plan to share presentational aids. Finally, incorporate delivery cues indicating where you want to use your voice and body to enhance intelligibility or expressiveness. For example, indicate where you want to pause, gesture, or make a motivated movement. Capitalize or underline words you want to stress. Use slash marks (///) to remind yourself to pause. Use an upward-pointing arrow to remind yourself to increase rate or volume.

For a 3- to 5-minute speech, you should need no more than three 3 × 5-inch note cards to record your speaking notes. For longer speeches, you might need one card for the introduction, one for each main point, and one for the conclusion. If your speech contains a particularly important and long

> **rehearsing** practicing the presentation of your speech aloud
>
> **speaking notes** key word outline of the speech including hard-to-remember information or quotations

FIGURE 15.4 ALYSSA'S SPEAKING NOTES

NOTE CARD 1: Introduction
PLANT FEET . . . DIRECT EYE CONTACT . . . POISE/ETHOS!
   I. Famous Indian peace activist Mahatma Gandhi: 'We must become
      the change we seek in the world.' Tall order . . . We can make a
      difference right here in Lexington, KY
  II. Think for a moment . . . child/homework, neighbor/leaves,
     stranger/groceries . . . It's easy for college students like us to
     get involved.
III. I volunteer at LRM and reaped benefits (Slide 1)
IV. Benefits volunteering
    a. get acquainted
    b. responsibility & privilege
    c. résumé-building skills
BLANK SLIDE, WALK RIGHT, EYE C. Let's begin by explaining the
ways volunteering can help us connect to our local community.

NOTE CARD 2: Body
  I. GREAT WAY to become acquainted ☺ ☺
    LR: Comforts of home . . . unfamiliar city . . . volunteering . . . easy and
    quick way . . .
    Natalie Cunningham-May 2nd (Q. CARD #1) Social issues and conditions
    Acc. to a 1991 article published in the J. of Prevention and Intervention
    in the Community by Cohen, Mowbray, Gillette, and Thompson raise
    awareness . . .
    My experience at LRM (SLIDES 2 & 3)
    BLANK SLIDE, WALK LEFT, EYE C. Not only is volunteering important
    . . . familiar and social issues . . . FRANKLY . . . dem society . . .
  II. Civic responsibility AND privilege . . . LR. We benefit college . . . give back.
    I agree with Wilson and Musick who said in their 1997 article in Social
    Forces active participation or deprived. (SLIDES 4 & 5)
    Also a privilege . . . make a difference . . . feel good . . . self-
    actualization (SLIDE #6)

NOTE CARD 3: Body & Conclusion
BLANK SLIDE, WALK RIGHT, EYE C: privilege & responsibility . . .
  résumé-building . . .
III. Life skills
    Article "Employability Credentials: A Key to Successful Youth
    Transition to Work" by I. Charner—1988 issue of the Journal of Career
    Development . . . (Q. CARD #2)
    Laura Hatfield . . . leadership, teamwork, and listening skills Andrea
    Stockelman, volunteer (SLIDE #7) (Q. CARD #3) MY RÉSUMÉ
    (SLIDE #8)
    BLANK SLIDE, WALK TO CENTER, EYE C: Today, we've discussed . . .
    get acquainted, responsibility & privilege, résumé-building life skills
    help after grad.
    CL: So, I'm hoping the next time you recall . . . not distant past. Instead,
    I hope you'll be thinking about how you ARE being the change you seek
    in the world by volunteering right here //in Lexington///right now!
    PAUSE, EYE CONTACT, POISE, NOD ☺

Quotation Card
#1: 'My first group of students needed rides to all the various volunteer
    sites b/c they had no idea where things were in the city. It was
    really easy for the students who lived on campus to remain ignorant
    of their city, but while volunteering they become acquainted with
    Lexington and the important issues going on here.'
#2: 'Employers rely on credentials to certify that a young person
    will become a valuable employee. Credentials that document the
    experiences and employability skills, knowledge, and attitude.'
#3: 'I learned that there was a lot more that went into preparing food
    for the homeless than I ever thought possible. It was neat to be a
    part of that process.'

quotation or a complicated set of statistics, you can record this information in detail on a separate card. Speakers who use computerized slideshows often use the "notes" feature on the program for their speaking notes.

Use your notes during practice sessions as you will when you actually give the speech. If you will use a lectern, set the notes on the speaker's stand or, alternatively, hold them in one hand and refer to them only when needed. How important is it to construct good speaking notes? Speakers often find that the act of making the notes is so effective in helping cement ideas in the mind that during practice, or later during the speech itself, they rarely refer to them at all.

15-6b Handling Presentational Aids

Some speakers think that once they have prepared good presentational aids, they will have no trouble using them in the speech. However, many speeches with good aids have become a shambles because the aids were not well handled. You can avoid problems by following these guidelines:

1. Carefully plan when to use presentational aids. Indicate in your speaking notes exactly when you will reveal and conceal each aid. Practice introducing and using your aids until you can use them comfortably and smoothly.

2. Consider audience needs carefully. As you practice, eliminate any presentational aid that does not contribute directly to the audience's attention to, understanding of, or retention of the key ideas in the speech.

3. Position presentational aids and equipment before beginning your speech. Make sure your aids and equipment are where you want them and that everything is ready and in working order. Test electronic equipment to make sure everything works and that excerpts are cued correctly.

4. Reveal a presentational aid only when talking about it. Because presentational aids will draw audience attention, practice sharing them only when you are talking about them, then conceal them when they are no longer the focus of attention.

Because a single presentational aid may contain several bits of information, practice revealing only the portion you are currently discussing. On computerized slideshows, you can do so by using the "custom animation" feature to allow only one item to appear at a time. You can also strike the "B" key for a black screen when you aren't directly referencing the aid and insert blank slides where ideas in your speech are not being supplemented with something on the slideshow.

5. Display presentational aids so that everyone in the audience can see and hear them. The inability to see or hear an aid is frustrating. If possible, practice in the space where you will give your speech so you can adjust equipment accordingly. If you cannot practice in the space ahead of time, then arrive early enough on the day of the presentation to practice quickly with the equipment you will use.

6. Reference the presentational aid during the speech. Because you already know what you want your audience to see in a visual aid, tell your audience what to look for, explain the various elements in it, and interpret figures, symbols, and percentages. For an audio or audiovisual aid, point out what you want your audience to listen for before you play the excerpt. When showing a visual or audiovisual aid, use the "turn-touch-talk" technique.

▶ When you display the visual, walk to the screen—that's where everyone will look anyway. Slightly turn to the visual and touch it—that is, point to it with an arm gesture or a pointer if necessary. Then, with your back to the screen and your body still facing the audience at a slight forty-five-degree angle, talk to your audience about it.

▶ When you finish making your comments, return to the lectern or your speaking position and conceal the aid.

If possible, practice in the space where you will give your speech to check any equipment or materials and to understand the room layout.

© Pressmaster/Shutterstock.com

First Practice

Your initial rehearsal should include the following steps:

1. Record (audio and video) your practice session. You may also want to have a friend sit in on it.

2. Read through your complete sentence outline once or twice to refresh your memory. Then put the outline out of sight and practice the speech using only your speaking notes.

3. Make the practice as similar to the speech situation as possible, including using the presentational aids you've prepared. Stand up and face your imaginary audience. Pretend that the chairs, lamps, books, and other objects in your practice room are people.

4. Write down the time that you begin or start the stopwatch on your smartphone.

5. Begin speaking. Regardless of what happens, keep going until you have presented your entire speech. If you goof, make a repair as you would have to do if you were actually delivering the speech to an audience.

---

7. Talk to your audience, not to the presentational aid. Although you will want to acknowledge the presentational aid by looking at it occasionally, it is important to maintain eye contact with your audience as much as possible. As you practice, resist the urge to stare at or read from your presentational aid.

8. Resist the temptation to pass objects through the audience. People look at, read, handle, and think about whatever they hold in their hands. While they are so occupied, they are not likely to be listening to you. If you have handouts or objects to distribute, do so after the speech rather than during it.

15-6c Rehearsing and Refining Delivery

As with any other activity, effective speech delivery requires practice. Each practice round should consist of: (a) practicing aloud, (b) analyzing and making adjustments, and (c) practicing aloud again. The more of these practice rounds you have, the better your speech will be. During each practice round, evaluate your language choices, as well as your use of voice, body, and presentational aids. Do so until your speech delivery appears spontaneous and is both conversational and animated. Let's look at how you can proceed through several practice rounds.

ANALYSIS Watch and listen to the recorded performance while reviewing your complete outline. How did it go? Did you leave out any key ideas? Did you talk too long on any one point and not long enough on another? Did you clarify each of your points? Did you adapt to your anticipated audience? (If you had a friend or relative watch and listen to your practice, have him or her help with your analysis.) Were your speaking notes effective? How well did you do with your presentational aids? Make any necessary changes before your second rehearsal.

SECOND PRACTICE ROUND Repeat the six steps outlined for the first rehearsal. By practicing a second time right after your analysis, you are more likely to make the kind of adjustments that begin to improve the speech.

ADDITIONAL PRACTICES ROUNDS After you have completed one full practice round—consisting of two practices and the analysis in between them—put the speech away until that night or the next day. Although you should rehearse the speech at least a couple more times, you will not benefit if you cram all the practices into one long rehearsal time. You may find that a final practice right before you go to bed will be very helpful; while you are sleeping, your subconscious will continue to work on the speech. As a result, you are likely to find significant improvement in delivery when you practice again the next day.

15-7 ADAPTING WHILE DELIVERING THE SPEECH

Even when you've practiced your speech to the point that you know it inside and out, you must be prepared to adapt to your audience and possibly change course a bit as you give your speech. Remember that your primary goal as a public speaker is to generate shared understanding with your listeners, so pay attention to the audience's feedback as you speak and adjust accordingly. Here are six tips to guide you.

© Losevsky Pavel/Shutterstock.com

1. Be aware of and respond to audience feedback. As you make eye contact with members of your audience, notice how they react to what you say. For instance, if you see quizzical looks on the faces of several listeners, you may need to explain a particular point in a different way. On the other hand, if you see listeners nodding impatiently, recognize that you don't need to belabor your point and move on. If you notice that many audience members look bored, try to rekindle their interest by showing emotional expression in your delivery.

2. Be prepared to use alternative developmental material. Your ability to adjust to your audience's needs depends on how much additional alternative information you have to share. If you have prepared only one example, you wouldn't be ready if your audience is confused and needs another. If you have prepared only one definition for a term, you may be unable to rephrase an additional definition if needed.

3. Stop your watch or write down the time you finish. Compute the length of the speech. Correct yourself when you misspeak. Every speaker makes mistakes. They stumble over words, mispronounce terms, forget information, and mishandle presentational aids. It's normal. What's important is what you do when you make that mistake. If you stumble over a phrase or mispronounce a word, correct yourself and move on. Don't make a big deal of it by laughing, rolling your eyes, or in other ways drawing unnecessary attention to it. If you suddenly remember that you forgot to provide some information, consider how important it is for your audience to have that information. If what you forgot to say will make it difficult for your audience to understand a point that comes later, figure out how and when to provide the information later in your speech. Usually, however, information we forgot to share is not critical to the audience's understanding and it's better to leave it out and move on.

4. Adapt to unexpected events. Maintain your composure if something unexpected happens, such as a cell phone ringing or someone entering the room while you're speaking. Simply pause until the disruption ceases and then move on. If the disruption causes you to lose your train of thought or has distracted the audience, take a deep breath, look at your speaking notes, and continue your speech at a point slightly before the interruption occurred. This will allow both you and your

© Robert Kneschke/Shutterstock.com

conclusions beyond what you have said. Whenever you answer a question, be honest about what you know and don't know. If an audience member asks a question you don't know the answer to, admit it by saying something like, "That's an excellent question. I'm not sure of the answer, but I would be happy to follow up on it later if you're interested." Then move on to the next question. If someone asks you to state an opinion about a matter you haven't thought much about, it's okay to say, "You know, I don't think I have given that enough thought to have a valid opinion."

Be sure to monitor how much time you have to answer questions. When the time is nearly up, mention that you'll entertain one more question to warn listeners that the question-and-answer period is almost over. You might also suggest that you'll be happy to talk more with individuals one on one later—this provides your more reserved listeners an opportunity to follow up with you.

audience to refocus on your speech. You might acknowledge that you are backtracking by saying something like, "Let's back up a bit and remember where we were . . ."

5. Adapt to unexpected audience reactions. Sometimes, you'll encounter listeners who disagree strongly with your message. They might show their disagreement by being inattentive, heckling you belligerently, or rolling their eyes when you try to make eye contact with them. If these behaviors are limited to one or only a few members of your audience, ignore them and focus on the rest of your listeners. If, however, you find that your audience analysis was inaccurate and that the majority of your audience is hostile to what you are saying, try to anticipate and address their concerns. You might begin by acknowledging their feedback and then try to convince your audience to suspend their judgment while they listen. For example, you could say something like, "I can see that most of you don't agree with my first point. But let me ask you to put aside your initial reaction and think along with me on this next point. Even if we end up disagreeing, at least you will understand my position."

6. Handle questions respectfully. It is rare for audience members to interrupt speakers with questions during a speech. But if you are interrupted, be prepared to deal respectfully with the question. If the question is directly related to understanding the point you are making, answer it immediately. If it is not, acknowledge the question, indicate that you will answer it later, and then do so.

In most professional settings, you will be expected to answer questions when you've finished your speech. Some people will ask you to clarify information. Some will ask you for an opinion or to draw

15-8 EVALUATING SPEECHES

In addition to learning to prepare and present speeches, you are learning to evaluate (critically analyze) the speeches you hear. From an educational standpoint, critical analysis of speeches provides the speaker with an analysis of where the speech went right and where it went wrong; it also gives you, the critic, insight into the methods that you can incorporate or avoid in your own speeches. In this section, we look at some general criteria for evaluating public speeches.

If a speech has good content that is adapted to the audience, is clearly organized, and is delivered well, it is likely to achieve its goal. Thus, you can evaluate any speech by answering questions that relate to the basics of content, structure, and delivery. Figure 15.5 is a speech critique checklist. You can use this checklist to analyze your first speech during your rehearsal period and to critique sample student speeches at the end of this chapter as well as speeches delivered by your classmates and others.

FIGURE 15.5 SPEECH CRITIQUE CHECKLIST

Check all items that were accomplished effectively.

Content

- [ ] 1. Was the goal of the speech clear?
- [ ] 2. Did the speaker offer breadth and depth to support each main point?
- [ ] 3. Did the speaker use high-quality information and sources?
- [ ] 4. Did the speaker provide appropriate listener relevance links?
- [ ] 5. Were presentational aids appropriate?

Structure

- [ ] 6. Did the introduction gain attention, establish relevance and listener relevance, and lead into the speech using a thesis with main point preview?
- [ ] 7. Were the main points clear, parallel, and in meaningful complete sentences?
- [ ] 8. Did section transitions lead smoothly from one point to another?
- [ ] 9. Was the language appropriate, accurate, clear, and vivid?
- [ ] 10. Did the conclusion tie the speech together by summarizing the goal and main points and providing a clincher?

Delivery

- [ ] 11. Did the speaker appear and sound conversational?
- [ ] 12. Did the speaker appear and sound animated?
- [ ] 13. Was the speaker intelligible?
- [ ] 14. Was the speaker vocally expressive?
- [ ] 15. Was the speaker's appearance appropriate?
- [ ] 16. Did the speaker have good posture and poise?
- [ ] 17. Did the speaker look directly at and throughout the audience at least 90% of the time?
- [ ] 18. Did the speaker have good facial expressions?
- [ ] 19. Were the speaker's gestures and movement appropriate?
- [ ] 20. Did the speaker handle the presentational aids effectively?

Based on these criteria, evaluate the speech as (check one):

- [ ] excellent
- [ ] good
- [ ] satisfactory
- [ ] fair
- [ ] poor

ACTION STEP 5a

Rehearse Your Speech

The goal of this activity is to rehearse your speech, analyze it, and rehearse it again. One complete rehearsal includes a practice, an analysis, and a second practice.

1. Find a place where you can be alone to practice your speech. Follow the six points for the first practice round explained earlier.
2. Review your outline as you watch and listen to the recording and then answer the following questions.

Are you satisfied with how well . . .

the introduction got attention and led into the speech? _____

main points were clearly stated? _____

and well developed? _____

material was adapted to the audience? _____

section transitions were used? _____

the conclusion summarized the main points? _____

and left the speech on a high note? _____

Presentational aids were used? _____

Ideas were expressed vividly? _____

and clearly? _____

Sounded conversational throughout? _____

Sounded animated? _____

Sounded intelligible? _____

Used effective gestures and movement? _____

Used effective eye contact? _____

Facial expression? _____

Posture? _____

Appearance? _____

List the three most important changes you will make in your next practice session:

One: _____

Two: _____

Three: _____

3. Go through the six steps outlined for the first practice again.

Then assess: Did you achieve the goals you set for the second practice?

_____

Reevaluate the speech using the checklist and continue to practice until you are satisfied with all parts of your presentation.

Sample Informative Speech

Read the speech adaptation plan developed by Alyssa Grace Millner in preparing her speech on volunteering and civic engagement. Then read the transcript of Alyssa's speech, using the speech critique checklist from Figure 15.5 to help you evaluate her speech.

Adaptation Plan

1. **Key aspects of audience.** The majority of listeners know what volunteering is in a general sense, but they probably don't know the ways it can benefit them as college students.

2. **Establishing and maintaining common ground.** I'll use personal pronouns throughout the speech, as well as specific examples about volunteering from volunteers right here in Lexington.

3. **Building and maintaining interest.** I'll insert listener-relevant links in the introduction and for each main point that point out how volunteering is directly related to improving the lives of college students in some way.

4. **Building credibility.** I will point out right away that I volunteer and that I've done a good deal of research on it. I'll insert examples of my own experiences throughout the speech, as well as cite credible research to support my claims.

5. **Audience attitudes.** Some may be indifferent, but according to the research I've found, most will probably be open to the idea of volunteering. They might not know how easy it can be to get started though.

6. **Adapting to audiences from different cultures and language communities.** Although most of my classmates are U.S. citizens, there are a couple of international students in the class. So, when I talk about volunteering being a civic responsibility, I'll make sure to talk about how all of us are reaping the benefits of a U.S. education; that's why we are all responsible for giving back in some way. I'll talk about it as an ethical responsibility.

7. **Use presentational aids.** I will show photographs of people engaged in volunteer work throughout the speech. I think this will make my ideas very concrete for the audience and will enhance pathos (emotional appeal). I'll also show some graphs about homelessness in Lexington and the percentage of college students who believe in volunteering. I think these will bolster my ethos as the audience will see I've done research. Finally, I'll show my résumé with elements highlighted that I've been able to include because I've volunteered. I think this will drive home my point about the future benefits for college students who volunteer while still in school.

Speech Outline
College Student Volunteering and Civic Engagement

by Alyssa Grace Milner

© wavebreakmedia/Shutterstock.com

General goal:

I want to inform my audience.

Specific goal:

I want my audience to realize the benefits of volunteering in Lexington while we are still students at the University of Kentucky.

Introduction

I. The famous Indian peace activist and spiritual leader Mahatma Gandhi is known for saying "We must become the change we seek in the world." That sounds at first like an awfully tall order, but today I'd like to show you how each of us can do just that and make a difference right here in Lexington, Kentucky. | ▶ *Attention getter*

II. Think for a moment of a time in your life when you did something kind for someone else. Maybe you helped a child do homework, or a neighbor rake leaves, or even a stranger get groceries from the store to the car. Do you remember how that made you feel? Well, that feeling can be a normal part of your week when you choose to be a volunteer. And for college students like us, it's easy to get involved as volunteers in our local community. | ▶ *Listener relevance link*

III. Personally, I volunteer at the Lexington Rescue Mission and have reaped many benefits by doing so. *(Show slide 1: picture of me volunteering at the Mission)* I've also done extensive research on volunteering and civic engagement. | ▶ *Speaker credibility*

IV. So, let's spend the next few minutes discussing the benefits volunteering can have for us as college students by focusing on how volunteering helps us get acquainted with the local community, why civic engagement is the responsibility of every one of us, and what volunteering can do to teach us new skills and build our résumés. | ▶ *Thesis statement with main point preview*

Let's begin by explaining the ways volunteering can connect each of us to our local community. | ▶ *Transition*

Body

I. Volunteering is a great way to become acquainted with a community beyond the university campus.

Most college students move away from the comforts of home to a new and unfamiliar city. Not knowing what there is to do or even how to get around can be overwhelming and isolating. Volunteering is an easy way to quickly become familiar with and begin to feel a part of this new city in addition to the campus community. | ▶ *Listener relevance link*

A. Volunteering allows you to learn your way around town.

    1. In an interview I had with Natalie Cunningham, the volunteer coordinator of the Lexington Rescue Mission, she said, "I've been working with students for several years now. While every group is different, one lingering trend is each group's unawareness of their city. It is easy for the students who live on campus to stay in their 'on-campus bubble'. Volunteering allows students to become acquainted with Lexington and the important issues facing their new home" (personal communication, January 2, 2013).

    2. It seems like a silly thing, but knowing your way around town starts to make any city feel like home. Volunteering gets you out into the local area and helps you begin to get acquainted with new people and places.

B. Volunteering can also open your eyes to local social issues and conditions.

    1. Many nonprofit organizations strive to raise awareness of important social issues, things like hunger and homelessness (Norris Center, 2013).

    2. The second time I showed up to volunteer at the Lexington Rescue Mission, I served food to the homeless. *(Show slide 2: group of volunteers in the kitchen)*

        a. I served soup and hung out with other volunteers and local homeless people. One of the "veteran" volunteers explained to me that Lexington has approximately 3,000 homeless people. *(Show slide 3: homelessness statistics in Lexington)*

        b. I was shocked to learn that we had such a large number of men, women, and children without a regular place to sleep. I wouldn't have known about this problem or the organizations working to end homelessness if I hadn't been a volunteer.

Not only is volunteering important because it helps us become familiar with a town and its social issues; frankly, as members of a democratic society, volunteering is our civic responsibility. ▶ Transition

II. Giving back to the community through volunteer work is our civic responsibility and a privilege.

Each of us in this room—whether as U.S. citizens or international students— are reaping the benefits of earning college degrees in this democratic society. With that benefit comes the responsibility and privilege of giving back. ▶ Listener relevance link

A. Volunteering is our civic responsibility.

    1. Grant (2012) explains that, without active participation in the local community, civil society becomes deprived.

    2. I agree. Giving back by volunteering helps the community in so many ways. *(Show slides 4 and 5: volunteers sorting clothes at the mission and then volunteers playing cards with people served at the shelter)*

B. Volunteering is also a privilege. Making a difference by volunteering ends up making us feel better about ourselves and our role in the world we live in.

    1. In fact, according to the Bureau of Labor Statistics, about 25 percent of the U.S. population volunteered in 2014. What is troubling,

however, is that on 18.7 percent of people aged 20–24 volunteered that year (Volunteering in the United States, 2014). *(Show slide 6: bar graph of demographic comparisons)*

2. This seems odd in light of the study of first-year college students done by the Higher Education Research Institute published in January 2009 that revealed that 69.7 percent of students believe it is *essential or very important* to volunteer in order to help people in need (Pryor et al., 2009).

Certainly, the privilege of giving back as volunteers is our civic responsibility and helps our local community, but we can also reap valuable résumé-building life skills by volunteering. ▶ Transition

III. Volunteering helps teach us new skills.

These new skills and talents can actually make us more marketable for better jobs once we graduate. ▶ Listener relevance link

A. Being a consistent volunteer at a nonprofit organization while attending college can strengthen your résumé.

1. Educational credentials are not enough to ensure college graduates are ready for the workforce. They also need credentials that document their experiences and employability skills (Tomlinson, 2008). They can be a pathway to getting a job (Spera, Ghertner, Nerino, & DiTommaso, 2013).

2. Laura Hatfield, director of the Center for Community Outreach at the University of Kentucky, points out that volunteers can include leadership, teamwork, and listening skills on their résumés because they can document the experiences where they had to use them effectively in the real world.

3. Andrea Stockelman, another volunteer at the Lexington Rescue Mission, explained some of the new skills she picked up with volunteering. She said, "I learned that there was a lot more that went into preparing food for the homeless than I ever thought possible. It was neat to be a part of that process" (personal communication, April 28, 2010). *(Show slide 7: photo of Andrea preparing food)*

B. Volunteering at the Lexington Rescue Mission taught me new skills that bolstered my résumé. *(Show slide 8: résumé with skills highlighted)*

1. I learned to coordinate the schedules of other volunteers.

2. I also practiced important people skills such as teamwork, empathy, conflict management, and listening.

Conclusion

I. Today we've discussed why volunteering is beneficial to college students by focusing on how volunteering can connect us quickly and easily to our local community, why it's both our responsibility and a privilege to do so, and how volunteering will benefit us after we graduate. ▶ Thesis restatement with main point summary

II. So, I'm hoping the next time you recall a time you really enjoyed making a difference by helping someone, that memory won't come from the distant past. Instead, I hope you'll be thinking about how you are being the change you seek in the world by volunteering right here in Lexington right now. ▶ Clincher

References

Charner, I. (1988). Employability credentials: A key to successful youth transition to work. *Journal of Career Development, 15*(1), 30–40.

Cohen, E., Mowbray, C. T., Gillette, V., & Thompson, E. (1991). Religious organizations and housing development. *Journal of Prevention and Intervention in the Community, 10*(1), 169–185.

Corporation for National and Community Service. (2006). *College students helping America.* Washington, DC: Author.

Grant, A. (2012). Giving time, time after time: Work design and sustained employee participation in corporate volunteering. *Academy of Management Review,* amr-2010.

Norris Center (2013, January 2). *Center for student involvement: Volunteer opportunities.* Northwestern University. Retrieved from: http://norris.northwestern.edu/csi/community/volunteer-opportunities/

Pryor, J. H., Hurtado, S., DeAngelo, L., Sharkness, J., Romero, L., Korn, W. S., & Tran, S. (2009). *The American freshman: National norms for fall 2008.* Los Angeles, CA: Higher Education Research Institute.

Spera, C., Ghertner, R., Nerion, A., & DiTommaso, A. (2013). *Volunteering as a pathway to employment: Does volunteering increase odds of finding a job for the out of work?* Washington, DC: Corporation for National and Community Service.

Tomlinson, M. (2008). The degree is not enough: Students' perceptions of the role of higher education for graduate work and employability. *British Journal of Sociology of Education, 29*(1), 49-61. Doi: 10.1080/01425690701737457

United States Bureau of Labor Statistics. (2015, February 25). *Economic news release: Volunteering in the United States, 2014.* Retrieved from: http://www.bls.gov/news.release/volun.nr0.htm

Wilson, J., & Musick, M. A. (1997). Work and volunteering: The long arm of the job. *Social Forces, 76*(1), 251–272.

Speech and Analysis

The famous Indian peace activist and spiritual leader Mahatma Gandhi is known for saying "We must become the change we seek in the world." That sounds at first like an awfully tall order, but today I'd like to show you how each of us can do just that and make a difference right here in Lexington, Kentucky. Think for a moment of a time in your life when you did something kind for someone else. Maybe you helped a child do homework, or a neighbor rake leaves, or even a stranger get groceries from the store to the car. Do you remember how that made you feel? Well, that feeling can be a normal part of your week when you choose to be a volunteer. And for college students like us, it's easy to get involved as volunteers in our local community. Personally, I volunteer at the Lexington Rescue Mission and have reaped many benefits by doing so. *(Show slide 1: picture of me volunteering at the Mission)* I've also done extensive research on volunteering and civic engagement. So, let's spend the next few minutes discussing the benefits volunteering can have for us as college students by focusing on how volunteering helps us get acquainted with the local community, why civic engagement is the responsibility of every citizen, and what volunteering can do to teach us new skills and build our résumés. Let's begin by explaining the ways volunteering can connect each of us to our local community.

Analysis

Notice how Alyssa uses a famous quotation to get the attention of her audience in a way that also piques interest about the topic.

Here, Alyssa establishes listener relevance by pointing out that helping others makes us feel good and that volunteering can be easy.

Alyssa mentions that she volunteers, which bolsters ethos and establishes her credibility to speak on the topic.

Notice how Alyssa's thesis with main point preview gives us a sense of the organizational framework for her ideas.

Volunteering is a great way to become acquainted with a community beyond the university campus. Most college students move away from the comforts of home to a new and unfamiliar city. Not knowing what there is to do or even how to get around can be overwhelming and isolating. Volunteering is an easy way to quickly become familiar with and begin to feel a part of this new city in addition to the campus community.

Volunteering allows you to learn your way around town. In an interview I had with Natalie Cunningham, the volunteer coordinator of the Lexington Rescue Mission, she said, "I've been working with students for several years now. While every group is different, one lingering trend is each group's unawareness of their city. It is easy for the students who live on campus to stay in their 'on-campus bubble'. Volunteering allows students to become acquainted with Lexington and the important issues facing their new home." It seems like a silly thing, but knowing your way around town starts to make any city feel like home. Volunteering gets you out into the local area and helps you begin to get acquainted with new people and places.

Volunteering can also open your eyes to local social issues and conditions. According to Cohen, Mowbray, Gillette, and Thompson, many nonprofit organizations strive to raise awareness of important social issues, things like hunger and homelessness. The second time I showed up to volunteer at the Lexington Rescue Mission, I served food to the homeless. *(Show slide 2: group of volunteers in the kitchen)* I served soup and hung out with other volunteers and local homeless people. One of the "veteran" volunteers explained to me that Lexington has approximately 3,000 homeless people. *(Show slide 3: homelessness statistics in Lexington)* I was shocked to learn that we had such a large number of men, women, and children without a regular place to sleep. I wouldn't have known about this problem or the organizations working to end homelessness if I hadn't been a volunteer. Not only is volunteering important because it helps us become familiar with a town and its social issues; frankly, as members of a democratic society, volunteering is our civic responsibility.

Giving back to the community through volunteer work is our civic responsibility and a privilege. Each of us in this room—whether as U.S. citizens or international students—are reaping the benefits of earning college degrees in this democratic society. With that benefit comes the responsibility and privilege of giving back. Volunteering is our civic responsibility. In a 2012 article published in the *Academy of Management Review*, Grant explains that, without active participation in the local community, civil society becomes deprived. I agree. Giving back by volunteering helps the community in so many ways. *(Show slides 4 and 5: volunteers sorting clothes at the mission and then volunteers playing cards with people served at the shelter)*

Volunteering is also a privilege. Making a difference by volunteering ends up making us feel better about ourselves and our role in the world around us. In fact, according to the Bureau of Labor Statistics, about 25 percent of the US population volunteered in 2014. What is troubling, however, is that only 18.7 percent of people aged 20-24 volunteered that year. I say this because volunteering, according to a 2013 article published by the Corporation for National and Community Service, can be a pathway to getting a job after graduating. *(Show slide 6: bar graph showing demographics)* This seems odd in light of a study done by the Higher Education Research Institute published in January of 2009 that shows that a whopping 69.7 percent of first-year college students believe it is essential or very important to volunteer to help

Again, as Alyssa introduces the first main point, she encourages us to tune in because we all know how overwhelming and isolating it can feel when we move to a new place.

Quoting the volunteer coordinator is a great piece of developmental material that encourages us to trust Alyssa's message. (Note that interviews are not included in the reference section but are cited in the text of the outline.)

Alyssa intersperses actual photos of herself and others volunteering throughout the speech. Doing so enhances her verbal message but doesn't replace it. The photos also provide pathos, making her ideas more emotionally compelling.

Here and throughout the speech, notice how Alyssa uses effective section transitions to tie the point she is concluding into the next point to come. This makes her speech flow smoothly so listeners can follow her train of thought. It also bolsters her ethos because she sounds prepared.

Alyssa's careful audience analysis reveals itself here as she reminds her audience that even those who are not American citizens are benefiting as students in our educational system, and thus have a responsibility to give back in some way.

Alyssa's choice to include national statistics of college student volunteers boosts her credibility and provides listener relevance by reinforcing that college students are doing this kind of work, want to do this kind of work, and feel good about doing this kind of work.

people in need. Certainly, the privilege of giving back as volunteers is our civic responsibility and helps our local community, but we can also reap valuable résumé-building life skills by volunteering.

Volunteering helps teach us new skills. These new skills and talents can actually make us more marketable for better jobs once we graduate. Being a consistent volunteer at a nonprofit organization while attending college can strengthen your résumé. According to Charmer, in the *Journal of Career Development*, "Employers rely on credentials to certify that a young person will become a valuable employee. Credentials that document the experiences and employability skills, knowledge, and attitude." Laura Hatfield, director of the Center for Community Outreach at the University of Kentucky, points out that volunteers can include leadership, teamwork, and listening skills on their résumés because they can document the experiences where they had to use them effectively in the real world. Andrea Stockelman, another volunteer at the Lexington Rescue Mission, explained some of the new skills she picked up with volunteering. She said, "I learned that there was a lot more that went into preparing food for the homeless than I ever thought possible. It was neat to be a part of that process." *(Show slide 7: photo of Andrea preparing food)*

Volunteering at the Lexington Rescue Mission taught me new skills that bolstered my résumé. *(Show slide 8: résumé with skills highlighted)* I learned to coordinate the schedules of other volunteers. I also practiced important people skills such as teamwork, empathy, conflict management, and listening.

Today we've discussed why volunteering is beneficial to college students by focusing on how volunteering can connect us quickly and easily to our local community, why it's both our responsibility and privilege to do so, and how volunteering will benefit us after we graduate. So, I'm hoping the next time you recall a time you really enjoyed making a difference by helping someone, that memory won't come from the distant past. Instead, I hope you'll be thinking about how you are being the change you seek in the world by volunteering right here in Lexington right now.

▶ Students want to know how to market themselves to get good jobs. This main point will help maintain listener interest at a point when minds might tend to wander.

▶ By preparing a quotation from another volunteer, Alyssa insinuates that we don't have to take her word alone.

▶ This very clear thesis restatement with main point summary signals a sense of closure.

▶ Notice how Alyssa incorporates her opening quotation into her clincher, providing a sense of closure without saying "thank you." This lets listeners know that the speech is complete in a unique and memorable way.

LOCATED IN TEXTBOOK

☐ Tear-out Chapter Review cards at the end of the book

☐ Review with the Quick Quiz below

LOCATED ON COMM 4 ONLINE AT CENGAGEBRAIN.COM:

☐ Review Key Term flashcards and create your own cards

☐ Track your knowledge and understanding of key concepts in communication

☐ Complete practice and graded quizzes to prepare for tests

☐ Complete interactive content within COMM4 Online

☐ View the chapter highlight boxes for COMM4 Online

Quick Quiz

T F 1. The symptoms of public speaking apprehension can be physical, emotional, or cognitive.

T F 2. Research has shown that being nervous or in a state of tension can help you do your best.

T F 3. Cognitive restructuring is transferring the calm feelings we attain while visualizing to the actual speaking event.

T F 4. A pause is the total lack of vocal expressiveness.

T F 5. You should show a visual aid only when talking about it.

6. How your voice sounds depends on its
   a. tone, pitch, quality, and rate.
   b. pitch, volume, rate, and quality.
   c. quality, volume, clarity, and tone.
   d. clarity, pitch, rate, and quality.
   e. volume, quality, clarity, and tone.

7. The position or bearing of your body while giving a speech is called
   a. articulation.
   b. gestures.
   c. posture.
   d. movement.
   e. poise.

8. The hallmark of a conversational style is
   a. poise.
   b. vocal expressiveness.
   c. spontaneity.
   d. fluency.
   e. eye contact.

9. Speeches that are researched and planned ahead of time, although the exact wording is not scripted and will vary from presentation to presentation, are called
   a. impromptu.
   b. scripted.
   c. extemporaneous.
   d. practiced.
   e. spontaneous.

10. When handling your presentational aids, what is the most important thing to consider?
    a. that you share the aid only when you are talking about it
    b. that you indicate on your outline exactly when you plan on revealing and concealing the presentational aid
    c. that you direct your attention to the audience, not the aid
    d. that you practice repeatedly the handling of your aid
    e. that you display your aid so everyone can see or hear it

Answers: 1.T, 2.T, 3.F, 4.F, 5.T, 6.B, 7.C, 8.C, 9.C, 10.D

YOUR FEEDBACK MATTERS.

16 Informative Speaking

After finishing this chapter go to **PAGE 242** for **STUDY TOOLS.**

LEARNING OUTCOMES

16-1 Identify the characteristics of effective informative speaking

16-2 Employ methods of informing in your speeches

16-3 Create both process and expository informative speeches

An **informative speech** is one whose goal is to explain or describe facts, truths, and principles in a way that stimulates interest, facilitates understanding, and increases the likelihood of remembering. In short, informative speeches are designed to educate audiences. Informative speeches answer questions about a topic, such as those beginning with who, when, what, where, how, and how to. For example, your informative speech might describe who popular singer-songwriter Adele is, define Scientology, compare and contrast the similarities and differences between Twitter and Facebook, tell the story of golf professional Rory McIlroy's rise to fame, or demonstrate how to create and post a video on a Web site like YouTube. Informative speaking differs from other speech forms (such as speaking to persuade, to entertain, or to celebrate) in that your goal is simply to achieve mutual understanding about an object, person, place, process, event, idea, concept, or issue.

In this chapter, we discuss five distinguishing characteristics of informative speeches and five methods of informing. Then, we discuss two common types of informative speeches (process and expository speeches) and provide an example of an informative speech.

16-1 CHARACTERISTICS OF EFFECTIVE INFORMATIVE SPEAKING

informative speech a speech whose goal is to explain or describe facts, truths, and principles in a way that increases understanding

Effective informative speeches are intellectually stimulating, relevant, creative, memorable, and address diverse learning styles.

16-1a Intellectually Stimulating

Your audience will perceive information to be **intellectually stimulating** when it is new to them and when it is explained in a way that piques their curiosity and interest. By *new*, we mean information that most of your audience is unfamiliar with or fresh insights into a topic with which they are already familiar.

If your audience is unfamiliar with your topic, you should consider how you might tap their natural curiosity. Imagine you are an anthropology major who is interested in prehistoric humans, which is not an interest

shared by most members of your audience. You know that in 1991, the 5,300-year-old remains of a man, now called Ötzi, were found surprisingly well preserved in an ice field in the mountains between Austria and Italy. Even though the discovery was big news at the time, your audience today probably doesn't know much about it. You can draw on their natural curiosity, however, as you present "Unraveling the Mystery of the Iceman," describing scientists' efforts to understand who Ötzi was and what happened to him ("Ötzi, the Ice Man," n.d.).

If your audience is familiar with your topic, you will need to identify new insight about it. Begin by asking yourself, "What things about my topic do listeners probably not know?" Answer the question by addressing depth and breadth. *Depth* involves going into more detail than people's general knowledge of the topic. If you've ever watched programs on the Food Network, that's what they do. Most people know basic recipes, but these programs show new ways to cook the same foods. *Breadth* involves looking at how your topic relates to associated topics. Trace considered breadth when he informed his audience about Type 1 diabetes. He discussed not only the physical and emotional effects of the disease on a diabetic person, but also the emotional and relational effects on family and friends, as well as the financial implications for society.

16-1b Relevant

As you prepare an informative speech, don't assume your listeners will recognize how the information is relevant to them. Remember to incorporate *listener relevance links* throughout the speech. As you prepare each main point, ask and answer the question: How would knowing this information make my listeners happier, healthier, wealthier, wiser, and so forth?

16-1c Creative

Your audience will perceive your information to be **creative** when it yields innovative ideas. You may not ordinarily consider yourself to be creative, but that may be because you have never recognized or fully developed your own innovative ideas. Creativity comes from doing good research, taking time, and practicing productive thinking.

Creative informative speeches begin with *good research*. The more you learn about a topic, the more you will have to work with to develop it creatively.

The creative process also requires time to mull over ideas. Rarely do creative ideas come when we are in a time crunch. Instead, they are likely to

intellectually stimulating information that is new to audience members and piques interest

creative using information in a way that yields innovative ideas and insights

Creative ideas are likely to come when we least expect them.

come when we least expect it—when we're driving our car, preparing for bed, or daydreaming.

For the creative process to work, you also have to *think productively*. **Productive thinking** occurs when we contemplate something from a variety of perspectives. Then, with numerous ideas to choose from, we can select the ones that are best suited to our particular audience. In the article "A Theory about Genius," Michael Michalko (1998) describes several tactics for becoming better at productive thinking. They include:

1. Rethink a problem, issue, or topic from many perspectives. Albert Einstein actually came up with the theory of relativity this way. As you brainstorm, try to think about a possible topic as it might be perceived by many different groups and co-cultural groups. Then as you conduct research, try to find sources that represent a variety of viewpoints and perspectives, as well.

2. Make your thoughts visible by sketching drawings, diagrams, and graphs. Galileo revolutionized science by doing this. Try concept mapping as you generate topics and approaches to them.

3. Set regular goals to produce *something*. The great NHL hockey player, Wayne Gretzky, put it this way: "You miss every shot you don't take." So take some shots! Thomas Edison actually set a goal to produce an invention every 10 days.

productive thinking
contemplating something from a variety of perspectives

J. S. Bach wrote one cantata per week. And T. S. Eliot's many drafts of *The Waste Land* eventually became a masterpiece. Don't let writer's block keep you from drafting an initial outline. You need to start somewhere. Getting ideas out of your head and onto paper or a computer screen gives you something to work with and revise. After all, you can't edit air.

4. Combine and recombine ideas, images, and thoughts in different ways. The Austrian monk, Gregor Mendel, combined mathematics and biology to come up with the laws of heredity, which still ground the modern science of genetics today. Jennifer's list of possible speech topics included gardening, something she loved to do, and the issue of rising college tuition costs. She put the two ideas together and came up with the idea of doing an informative speech about how to use gardening (services, produce, and products) to raise money to help pay for college. To nurture creative thinking about transnational celebrity activism in global politics, Anne Marie not only conducted an extensive library search on several databases, but she also researched the topic by reading celebrity gossip magazines and visiting the Web sites of celebrities known for practicing it. After learning about what people like Angelina Jolie, Matt Damon, George Clooney, Madonna, and others were doing, she gave herself time to let what she had discovered percolate for a few days and even sketched a concept map to visualize links among her material. Ultimately, she was able to make the topic more interesting for her audience.

16-1d Memorable

If your speech is really informative, your audience will hear a lot of new information but will need help remembering what is most important. Emphasizing your specific goal, main points, and key facts are good starting points. Figure 16.1 summarizes several memory-enhancing techniques you might use.

16-1e Learning Styles

Because audience members differ in how they prefer to learn, we are most successful when we address diverse learning styles. You can appeal to people who prefer to learn through the feeling dimension by providing concrete, vivid images, examples, stories, and testimonials. Address the watching dimension by using visual aids. Address the thinking dimension by including definitions,

FIGURE 16.1 TECHNIQUES FOR MAKING INFORMATIVE SPEECHES MEMORABLE

Technique	Use	Example
Presentational aids	To provide audience members with a visual, audio, or audiovisual conceptualization of important information	A diagram of the process of making ethanol
Repetition	To give the audience a second or third chance to retain important information by repeating or paraphrasing it	"The first dimension of romantic love is passion; that is, it can't really be romantic love if there is no sexual attraction."
Transitions	To help the audience understand the relationship between the ideas, including primary and supporting information	"So the three characteristics of romantic love are passion, intimacy, and commitment. Now let's consider five ways to keep love alive."
Humor and other emotional anecdotes	To create an emotional memory link to important ideas	"True love is like a pair of socks, you have to have two, and they've got to match. So you and your partner need to be mutually committed and compatible."
Mnemonics and acronyms	To provide an easily remembered memory prompt for a series or a list	"You can remember the four criteria for evaluating a diamond as the four Cs: carat, clarity, cut, and color."

explanations, and statistics. Address the doing dimension by encouraging your listeners to do something during the speech or afterward. In his speech about what it is like to do a tour of duty as a soldier in Iraq, Ray addressed diverse learning styles by sharing stories of his own experiences (feeling), showing visual aids of the places he had been and the equipment he used (watching), explaining why the days were structured as they were (thinking), and asking his audience to respond silently to four questions every soldier must answer "yes" to (doing).

 ## 16-2 METHODS OF INFORMING

We can inform through description, definition, comparison and contrast, narration, and demonstration. Let's look at each of these methods more closely.

16-2a Description

Description is a method used to create an accurate, vivid, verbal picture of an object, geographic feature, setting, event, person, or image. This method usually answers an overarching *who*, *what*, or *where* question. Descriptions are, of course, easier if you have a presentational aid, but vivid verbal descriptions can also create informative mental pictures. To describe something effectively, you can explain its size, shape, weight, color, composition, age, condition, and spatial organization.

You can describe size subjectively as large or small and objectively by noting specific numerical measurements. For example, you can describe New York City subjectively as the largest city in the United States or more objectively as home to more than 8 million people with more than 26,000 people per square mile.

You can describe shape by reference to common geometric forms like round, triangular, oblong, spherical, conical, cylindrical, or rectangular, or by reference to common objects such as a book or a milk carton. For example, the Lower Peninsula of Michigan is often described as being shaped like a left-hand mitten. Shape is made more vivid by using adjectives, such as *smooth* or *jagged*.

You can describe weight subjectively as heavy or light and objectively by pounds and ounces or kilograms, grams, and milligrams. As with size, you can clarify weight with comparisons. For example, you can describe a Humvee (Hummer) objectively as weighing about 7,600 pounds, or subjectively as about as much as three Honda Civics.

You can describe color by coupling a basic color (such as black, white, red, or yellow) with a common object. For instance, instead of describing something as puce or ochre, you might describe the object as "eggplant purple" or "lime green."

You can describe the composition of something by indicating what it is made of, such as by saying

description method of informing used to create an accurate, vivid, verbal picture of an object, geographic feature, setting, person, event, or image

the building was made of brick, concrete, or wood. Sometimes you might be clearer by describing what it looks like rather than what it is. For example, you might say something looks metallic, even if it is made of plastic rather than metal.

You can also describe something by its age and condition. For example, describing a city as ancient, historic, and well kept produces different mental pictures than describing a city as old and war torn.

Finally, you can describe spatial organization going from top to bottom, left to right, outer to inner, and so on. A description of the Sistine Chapel, for example, might go from the floor to the ceiling, while a description of a NASCAR automobile might go from the body to the engine to the interior.

© Valentyn Volkov/Shutterstock.com

"Eggplant purple" is more descriptive than just purple.

16-2b Definition

Definition is a method that explains the meaning of something. There are four ways to define something.

First, you can define a word or idea by classifying it and differentiating it from similar words or ideas. For example, in a speech on veganism, you might use information from the Vegan Society's Web site (www.vegansociety.com). "A vegan is a vegetarian who is seeking a lifestyle free from animal products for the benefit of people, animals, and the environment. Vegans eat a plant-based diet free from all animal products including milk, eggs, and honey. Vegans also don't wear leather, wool, or silk and avoid other animal-based products."

Second, you can define a word by explaining its derivation or history. For instance, the word *vegan* is made from the beginning and end of the word *vegetarian* and was coined in the United Kingdom in 1944, when the Vegan Society was founded.

definition a method of informing that explains the meaning of something

synonym a word that has the same or similar meaning

antonym a word that has the opposite meaning

comparison and contrast a method of informing that explains something by focusing on how it is similar and different from other things

narration a method of informing that explains something by recounting events or stories

Third, you can define a word by explaining its use or function. For example, in vegan recipes, you can use tofu or tempeh to replace meat and use almond milk or soy milk to replace cow's milk.

The fourth, and perhaps quickest way to define something, is by using a familiar synonym or antonym. A **synonym** is a word that has the same or a similar meaning; an **antonym** is a word that has the opposite meaning. So you could define *vegan* by comparing it to the word *vegetarian*, which is a synonym with a similar although not identical meaning, or to the word *carnivore*, which is an antonym.

16-2c Comparison and Contrast

Comparison and **contrast** is a method that focuses on how something is similar to and different from other things. For example, in a speech on veganism, you might tell your audience how vegans are similar to and different from other types of vegetarians. You can point out that like vegetarians, vegans don't eat meat. In contrast, semi-vegetarians eat fish or poultry. Like lacto vegetarians, vegans don't eat eggs, but unlike this group and lacto-ovo vegetarians, vegans don't use dairy products. So of all vegetarians, vegans have the most restrictive diet. Because comparisons and contrasts can be figurative or literal, you can use metaphors and analogies as well as make direct comparisons.

16-2d Narration

Narration is a method that recounts an autobiographical or biographical event, myth, or other story. Narratives usually have four parts. First, the narrative orients listeners by describing when and where the event took place and introducing important characters. Second, the narrative explains the sequence of events that led to a complication or problem. Third, the narrative discusses how the complication or problem affected the key characters. Finally, the narrative recounts how the complication or problem was solved. The characteristics of a good narrative include a strong story line; use of descriptive language and detail that enhance the plot, people, setting, and events; effective use of dialogue; pacing that builds suspense; and a strong voice (Baerwald, n.d.).

Narratives can be presented in a first-, second-, or third-person voice. A first person narrative reports what you experienced or observed personally, using the pronouns *I*, *me*, and *my*: "Let me tell you about the first time I tried to water-ski." In a second person narrative, you place your audience at the scene by using pronouns *you* and *your*: "Imagine that you just got off the plane in Hong Kong. You look at the signs, but can't read a thing. Which way is the terminal?" Finally, in a third person narrative, you describe what has happened, is happening, or will happen to other people by using pronouns like *he*, *she*, *his*, *her*, and *they*: "When the students arrived in Venice for their study-abroad experience, the first thing they saw was the Rialto bridge."

16-2e Demonstration

Demonstration is a method that shows how something is done, displays the stages of a process, or depicts how something works. Demonstrations range from very simple with a few easy-to-follow steps (such as how to iron a shirt) to very complex (such as explaining how a nuclear reactor works). Regardless of whether the topic is simple or complex, effective demonstrations require expertise, developing a hierarchy of steps, and using vivid language and presentational aids.

In a demonstration, your experience with what you are demonstrating is critical. Expertise gives you the necessary background to supplement bare-bones instructions with personally lived experiences. Why are TV cooking shows so popular? Because the chef doesn't just read the recipe and do what it says. Rather, while performing each step, the chef shares tips that aren't mentioned in any cookbook. It is the chef's experience that allows him or her to say that one egg will work as well as two, or how to tell if the cake is really done.

In a demonstration, you organize the steps from first to last so that your audience will be able to remember the sequence of actions accurately. Suppose you want to demonstrate the steps in using a touch-screen voting machine. If you present 14 separate points, your audience is unlikely to remember them. However, if you group them under a few headings (I. Get ready to vote; II. Vote; III. Review your choices; and IV. Cast your ballot), chances are much higher that your audience will be able to remember most of the items.

Although you could explain a process with only words, most demonstrations show the audience the process or parts of the process. That's one reason why TV shows like *What Not to Wear* and *Flip This House* are so popular. If what you are explaining is relatively simple, you can demonstrate the entire process from start to finish. However, if the process is lengthy or complex, you may choose to pre-prepare the material for some of the steps. Although you will show all stages in the process, you will not need to take the time for every single step as the audience watches. For example, many of the ingredients used by TV chefs are already cut up, measured, and separated into little bowls.

Effective demonstrations require practice. Remember that under the pressure of speaking to an audience, even the simplest task can become difficult. (Have you ever tried to thread a needle with 25 people watching you?) As you practice, you will want to consider the size of your audience and the configuration of the room. Be sure that all of the audience will be able to see what you are doing.

© npine/Shutterstock.com

16-3 COMMON INFORMATIVE PATTERNS

Two of the most common patterns for organizing informative speech ideas are process patterns and expository patterns.

demonstration a method of informing that explains something by showing how it is done, by displaying the stages of a process, or by depicting how something works

FIGURE 16.2 PROCESS SPEECH TOPICS

How to do it	How to make it	How it works
select running shoes	compost bin	3-D movies
apply for a loan	rope knots	stem cell reproduction
bouldering	lefse	solar energy

16-3a Process Speeches

The goal of a **process speech** is to demonstrate how something is done, is made, or works. Effective process speeches require you to carefully delineate the steps and the order in which they occur. These steps typically become the main points and explanations of each step become the subpoints. Process speeches rely heavily on the demonstration method of informing.

Although some process speeches require you to demonstrate, others are not suited to demonstrations. For these, you can use visual or audiovisual aids to help the audience see the steps in the process. In a speech on remodeling a kitchen, for example, it would not be practical to demonstrate the process; however, you could greatly enhance the verbal description by showing pictures before, during, and after the remodeling. Figure 16.2 offers some examples of topic ideas for process speeches.

16-3b Expository Speeches

The goal of an **expository speech** is to provide carefully researched, in-depth knowledge about a complex topic. For example, "understanding the health care debate," "the origins and classification of nursery rhymes," "the sociobiological theory of child abuse," and "viewing rap as poetry" are all topics on which you could give an interesting expository speech. Lengthy expository speeches are known as *lectures*.

All expository speeches require speakers to draw from an extensive research base, choose an organizational pattern best suited to the material and specific speech goal, and use a variety of informative methods (e.g., descriptions, definitions, comparisons and contrasts, narration, and short demonstrations) to sustain the audience's attention and help them understand the material presented.

process speech an informative speech that demonstrates how something is done, is made, or works

expository speech an informative presentation that provides carefully researched, in-depth knowledge about a complex topic

Expository speeches include speeches that explain a political, economic, social, religious, or ethical issue; forces of history; a theory, principle, or law; and a creative work.

EXPOSITION OF POLITICAL, ECONOMIC, SOCIAL, RELIGIOUS, OR ETHICAL ISSUES In an expository speech, you have the opportunity to help the audience understand the background or context of an issue, including the forces that gave rise to and continue to affect it. You may also present the various positions held about the issue and the reasoning behind these positions. Finally, you may discuss various ways that have been presented for resolving the issue.

The general goal of an expository speech is to inform, not to persuade. So you will want to present all sides of controversial issues, without advocating which side is better. You will also want to make sure that the sources you draw from are respected experts and are objective in what they report. Finally, you will want to present complex issues in a straightforward manner that helps your audience understand them, while refraining from oversimplifying knotty issues. Figure 16.3 provides examples of topic ideas for an expository speech about a political, economic, social, religious, or ethical issue.

For example, while researching a speech on fracking—the controversial method for extracting natural gas deposits—you need to be careful to consult articles and experts on all sides of this issue and fairly represent and incorporate their views in your outline. You should discuss not only the technology that is used but also the controversies that surround its use. If time is limited, you might discuss just one or two of these issues, but you should at least inform the audience of others.

EXPOSITION OF HISTORICAL EVENTS AND FORCES It has been said that those who don't understand history may be destined to repeat it. So an expositional speech about historical events and forces can be fascinating for its own sake, but it can also be relevant for what is happening today. Unfortunately, some people think history is boring. So you have an obligation to seek out stories and narratives that can enliven your speech. And you will want to analyze the events you describe and their impact at the time they occurred, as well as the meaning they have today. Figure 16.4 proposes examples of topic ideas for an expository speech about historical events and forces.

EXPOSITION OF A THEORY, PRINCIPLE, OR LAW The way we live is affected by natural and human laws and principles and is explained by various theories. Yet there are many theories, principles, and laws that

FIGURE 16.3   TOPIC IDEAS FOR EXPOSITORY SPEECHES ABOUT POLITICAL, ECONOMIC, SOCIAL, RELIGIOUS, OR ETHICAL ISSUES

global warming	cyber bullying	fracking
teacher accountability	digital remixing	capital punishment
patterns of immigration	right to bear arms	Occupy Wall Street
Sikhism	media bias	cleaning up oil spills
stem cell research	celebrity culture	consequences of Arab Spring

FIGURE 16.4   TOPIC IDEAS FOR EXPOSITORY SPEECHES ABOUT HISTORICAL EVENTS AND FORCES

women's suffrage	the colonization of Africa	Irish immigration
the Olympics	Ghandi and his movement	the Ming Dynasty
the New Madrid earthquake	the Spanish Flu epidemic	the Balfour Declaration
the papacy	the Industrial Revolution	

we do not completely understand—or, at least, we don't understand how they affect us. The main challenge is to find material that explains the theory, law, or principle in language that is understandable to the audience. You will want to search for or create examples and illustrations that demystify complicated concepts and terminology. Using effective examples and comparing unfamiliar ideas with those that the audience already knows are techniques that can help you with this kind of speech. In a speech on the psychological principles of operant conditioning, for example, a speaker can help the audience understand the difference between continuous reinforcement and intermittent reinforcement by providing the following explanation:

When a behavior is reinforced continuously, each time the person performs the behavior, a reward is given, but when the behavior is reinforced intermittently, the reward is not always given when the behavior is displayed. Behavior that is learned by continuous reinforcement disappears quickly when the reward no

Coloring the News: Is the Information Provided by the Media Biased?

The Pew Research Center for the People and the Press (2011) found that 77 percent of Americans across political affiliations think news organizations "tend to favor one side" and 66 percent believe news organizations are politically biased in their reporting. Though many Americans agree that media bias is a problem, there is little consensus about how to determine the nature of such bias or which side it even favors. For example, National Public Radio (NPR) has long been accused of having a liberal bias in its reporting, and some conservative critics have called for an end to federal funding of the organization. Some, like respected journalist Bill Moyers, have defended NPR as an independent news source that practices journalistic objectivity and balanced reporting because they don't take explicit stands on controversial issues like abortion and gay marriage (Moyers & Winship, 2011). Conservative critics, such as Bernard Goldberg (2011), counter that the partiality of NPR and other news organizations is rooted in ideological biases that shape what stories they choose to cover and how they are reported, such as the choice of sources and amount of time given to sources on each

© REDAV/Shutterstock.com

side of an issue. At times, bias may be as subtle as the language used to describe people on different sides of controversial issues. For example, consider how the pragmatics of messages change depending on whether a reporter chooses to label opponents as pro-choice vs. pro-life, pro-choice vs. antiabortion; anti-life vs. antiabortion, or anti-life vs. pro-life. By choosing nonparallel labels to opposing sides, the reporter subtly colors the perceptions of unsophisticated audience members.

---

longer is provided, but behavior that is learned by intermittent reinforcement continues for long periods of time, even when not reinforced. Every day you can see the effects of how a behavior was conditioned. For example, take the behavior of putting a coin in a machine. If the machine is a vending machine, you expect to be rewarded every time you "play." And if the machine doesn't dispense the item, you might wonder if the machine is out of order and "play" just one more coin, or you might bang on the machine. In any case, you are unlikely to put in more than one more coin. But suppose the machine is a slot machine or a machine that dispenses instant-winner lottery tickets. How many coins will you "play" before you stop and conclude that the machine isn't going to give you what you want? Why the difference? Because you were conditioned to a vending machine on a

continuous schedule, but a slot machine or automatic lottery ticket dispenser "rewards" you on an intermittent schedule.

Figure 16.5 provides some examples of topic ideas for an expository speech about a theory, principle, or law.

EXPOSITION OF A CREATIVE WORK Courses in art, theater, music, literature, and film appreciation give students tools by which to recognize the style, historical period, and quality of a particular piece or group of pieces. Yet most of us know very little about how to understand a creative work, so presentations designed to explain creative works like poems, novels, songs, or even famous speeches can be very instructive for audience members.

When developing a speech that explains a creative work, you will want to find information on the work and the artist who created it. You will also want to find sources that educate you about the period in which this

FIGURE 16.5 TOPIC IDEAS FOR EXPOSITORY SPEECHES ABOUT THEORIES, PRINCIPLES, OR LAWS

natural selection	number theory	Maslow's
gravity	the law of	hierarchy of
Murphy's Law	diminishing	needs
the Peter Principle	returns	intelligent design
feminist theory	color theory	social cognitive
Boyle's law	psychoanalytic	theory
	theory	

FIGURE 16.6 TOPIC IDEAS FOR EXPOSITORY SPEECHES ABOUT CREATIVE WORKS

hip-hop music	the love sonnets	the Hunger
Impressionist	of Shakespeare	Games trilogy
painting	Kabuki theater	iconography
salsa dancing	graphic novels	Spike Lee's Mo'
women in	the Martin Luther	Better Blues
cinema	King National	
the films	Memorial	
of Alfred		
Hitchcock		

work was created and inform you about the criteria that critics use to evaluate works of this type. For example, if you wanted to give an expository speech on Freedrick Douglass's Fourth of July Oration given in Rochester, New York in 1852, you might need to orient your audience by first reminding them of who Douglass was. Then you would want to explain the traditional expectations for Fourth of July speakers in the mid-1800s. After this,

you might want to summarize the speech and perhaps share a few memorable quotes. Finally, you would want to discuss how speech critics view the speech and why the speech is considered great.

Figure 16.6 presents examples of topics for expository speeches about creative works. Figure 16.7 is a checklist you can use to analyze any informative speech you rehearse or to critique the speeches of others.

FIGURE 16.7 INFORMATIVE SPEECH EVALUATION CHECKLIST

Process Speech:

☐ How something is done
☐ How something is made
☐ How something works

Expository Speech:

☐ Exposition of political, economic, social, religious, or ethical issue
☐ Exposition of historical events or forces
☐ Exposition of a theory, principle, or law
☐ Exposition of creative work

General Criteria

_____ 1. Was the specific goal clear?
_____ 2. Were the main points developed with breadth and depth of appropriate supporting material?
_____ 3. Was the introduction effective in creating interest and introducing the main points?
_____ 4. Was the speech organized and easy to follow?
_____ 5. Was the language appropriate, clear, and vivid?
_____ 6. Was the conclusion effective in summarizing the main points and providing closure?
_____ 7. Was the vocal delivery intelligible, conversational, and expressive?
_____ 8. Did the body actions appear poised, natural, spontaneous, and appropriate?

Specific Criteria for Process Speeches

_____ 1. Was the introduction clear in previewing the process to be explained?
_____ 2. Was the speech easy to follow and organized in a time order?
_____ 3. Were presentational aids used effectively to clarify the process?
_____ 4. Did the process use a demonstration method effectively?

Specific Criteria for Expository Speeches

_____ 1. Was the specific goal of the speech to provide well-researched information on a complex topic?
_____ 2. Did the speaker effectively use a variety of methods to convey the information?
_____ 3. Did the speaker emphasize the main ideas and important supporting material?
_____ 4. Did the speaker present in-depth, high-quality, appropriately cited information?

Sample Process Speech

This section presents a sample informative speech given by a student, including an adaptation plan, an outline, and a transcript.

Internet Identity Theft: Self-Protection Steps

by Anna Rankin

Read the speech adaptation plan, outline, and transcript of a speech by Anna Rankin. You can also use COMM4 online to identify some of the strengths of Anna's speech by completing an evaluation checklist and preparing a 1–2 page critique identifying what she did well and what she could improve on regarding content, structure, delivery, and presentational aids. You can then compare your answers with those of the authors.

Adaptation Plan

1. **Key aspects of audience.** Most people in my audience are probably aware of identity theft but probably don't know all the steps they can take to protect themselves from becoming victims of it.

2. **Establishing and maintaining common ground.** I will begin my speech by using a hypothetical example placing them as victims of Internet identity theft. Throughout the speech, I will refer to the audience's previous knowledge and experience.

3. **Building and maintaining interest.** I will try to gain interest in the introduction by relating the problem of Internet identity theft to college students. Throughout the speech, I will use common analogies and metaphors to explain the self-protection steps. Finally, I will use a well-designed PowerPoint presentation to capture and maintain attention.

4. **Audience knowledge and sophistication.** Because most of the class is probably not familiar with the actual self-protection steps regarding Internet identity theft, I will focus specifically on them throughout my speech.

5. **Building credibility.** Early in the speech, I will tell the audience how I got interested in Internet identity theft and the research I did to learn about it as a pre-law student.

6. **Audience attitudes.** I will try to address audience apathy by using interesting examples and compelling stories they can easily relate to.

7. **Adapting to audiences from different cultures and language-communities.** I will use visual and audiovisual aids in my PowerPoint presentation to help those listeners from different cultures understand what I'm talking about even though English is not their native language.

8. **Using presentational aids to enhance understanding and memory.** Throughout the speech, I will use color-coded PowerPoint slides with headers to reinforce the steps being discussed.

Outline
Internet Identity Theft

by Anna Rankin

General goal:

To inform

Specific goal:

I want my audience to understand the steps to protect themselves from Internet identity theft.

Introduction

I. Imagine this: You are filing your income tax return after starting your first real job after college. After completing the tedious online forms, you hit the "calculate" button. You are ecstatic when the online filing system says you are due a return of a whopping $2,800! Then, imagine hitting "file" to submit your tax return and you get the error message *"Your tax return has already been processed."* Someone has stolen your identity and pocketed your return.   ▶ *Attention getter*

II. If you think this cannot happen to you, think again! According to the U.S. Government Accountability Office (White, 2012), approximately 642,000 cases of tax-related identity theft were reported in the first nine months of 2012 alone.   ▶ *Listener relevance*

III. Through my research, I discovered that 8.3 million Americans were victims of identity theft in 2005 (FTC, 2007). Identity theft can happen when someone simply digs through your trash for bank statements and most of us now shred such items before discarding them. Recently, however, Internet identity theft is becoming far more prevalent (U.S. Department of Justice, n.d.). An identity thief who accesses your information online can apply for jobs, loans, and credit cards, can receive medical care or prescription drugs, and can make large purchases all under your name (FTC, 2012).   ▶ *Speaker credibility and listener relevance*

IV. Today, let's discuss several simple steps we can all take to prevent Internet identity theft (*Slide 1: Four Steps to Prevent Identity Theft*). These three steps are designed to help prevent phishing, hacking, and pharming.   ▶ *Thesis statement with main point preview*

Body

I. The first step in preventing online identity theft is to protect yourself from phishing (*Slide 2: E-mail Phishing [Photo]*).

    A. Most likely, everyone in this room receives hundreds of e-mail messages every week. Whether it is an update from our college professor or coupons from our favorite retail stores, we are bombarded with e-mails that we do not hesitate to open or reply to.

    B. Phishing is a process through which identity thieves persuade Internet users to provide personal information by posing as legitimate organizations (NCPC, 2013).

        1. Identity thieves might send you an e-mail that appears to be from a legitimate organization.

        2. In it, they will ask you to provide personal information such as your bank account numbers, Social Security number, or personal passwords.

C. One way to prevent phishing is by never providing personal information online without verifying the legitimacy of the sender.

   1. Always contact the organization's customer service number provided to verify the legitimacy of the e-mail.

   2. And make it a standard practices to always provide such information over the phone rather than via e-mail (FTC, 2012).

D. Another way to avoid becoming a victim of identity theft through phishing is never to click on links in e-mails from unknown sources (NCPC, 2013).

   1. Clicking on these links can automatically install software on your computer that re-routes your personal information to the identity thief's personal data collection Web site.

   2. Once the thief or thieves have this information, they can basically "become you" all over the Internet.

Now that we all know what we can do to keep our identity safe through good e-mail practices, let's consider how we can prevent identity theft by surfing the Internet wisely. ▶ Transition

II. The second step we can take to protect ourselves from identity theft is to prevent hacking (*Slide 3: Computer Hacking [Photo]*).

A. Take a moment to think about all the personal and financial information you have stored on your electronic devices. If someone were to gain open access to your computer, or even to your smart phone for that matter, he or she would be able to steal your identity in a few swipes of the keys. ▶ Listener relevance

B. Hacking refers to a process through which an identity thief gains access to your personal computer to view documents, files, and personal information (NCPC, 2013).

C. Here are a few simple steps you can take to protect yourself from becoming a victim of hacking.

   1. The first step is to password-protect all of your accounts and devices, and to get creative with your passwords (FTC, 2012).

      a. Avoid using personal information such as your name, date of birth, address, or other personal information that is easily discovered by others (NCPC, 2013).

      b. Never use words that are found in the dictionary—some hacking programs can quickly attempt every word found in the dictionary to access your information.

      c. Try creating acronyms that you will always remember. For example, the phrase "I graduate from college in 2016" could turn into the password IgFcI2k16—a strong and unique password that you can easily remember (*Slide 4: Unique Password Examples*)!

      d. Finally, avoid sharing too much information on social networking sites. If an identity thief finds out enough about your personal life, they can easily answer those "challenge" questions you use to keep your accounts and devices protected.

2. The second step to protect identity theft from hacking is to be sure you wipe clean any of your electronic devices before selling them or disposing of them (FTC, 2012).

   a. Before you dispose of your laptop or smart phone, eliminate any personal information including saved passwords, photos, web search histories, and contact information.

   b. There are several programs you can use to wipe your hard drive clean. However, the National Crime Protection Council (2005) suggests removing and destroying your computer's hard drive altogether before selling or disposing of your laptop.

So now that we know how to protect our e-mail accounts from phishing and our computers from hacking, let's focus on what we need to do to protect ourselves from the most advanced method of online identity theft. ▶ Transition

III. The third step in protecting ourselves from identity theft is to prevent pharming (*Slide 5: Pharming Web site Dangers [Photo]*).

A. Virtually every day, we engage in online transactions. We may log on to our online banking to make sure we have enough money for dinner with friends, we may purchase a gift for someone using Amazon.com, or we may pay tuition using the online payment system.

B. Pharming, one of the toughest methods of online identity theft to detect, is a process through which criminals hack established websites, such as Amazon.com, and re-route the website to a "poser" website that looks very similar and allows them to gather our personal information during a transaction (NCPC, 2005).

C. Although pharming is the most difficult method of identity theft to detect, there are a few steps we can take to protect ourselves when making online transactions.

   1. First, look for the "lock" icon on your Internet browser's status bar. This lock indicates that the Web site you are on is safe (*Slide 6: Internet Browser Safety Features*).

   2. Next, verify that the Web site is secure by inspecting the URL. A safe Web site URL will begin with https:// instead of http://

   3. Finally, you can purchase encryption software that makes sure any information you send over the Internet is jumbled and unreadable to others.

Conclusion

I. As you can see, the Internet is literally a gold mine for identity thieves when our personal information is not protected. ▶ Thesis restatement

II. Fortunately, we can take steps to protect ourselves from phishing, hacking, and pharming (*Slide 9 [same as slide 1]*). ▶ Main point summary

III. According to a 2011 article in the *New York Times* (Perlroth, 2011), it is extremely difficult to prosecute online identity thieves even though they deserve it. One thing we can do, however, is to put a padlock on our gold-mines so these criminals can't access them in the first place! ▶ Clincher

References

Federal Trade Commission. (2007). FTC releases survey of identity theft in the U.S. study shows 8.3 million victims in 2005. Retrieved from http://www.ftc.gov /opa/2007/11/idtheft.shtm

Federal Trade Commission. (2012). Identity theft. Retrieved from http://www .consumer.ftc.gov/features/feature-0014-identity-theft

Koster, C. (n.d.) Identity theft. Retrieved from the Missouri Attorney General Web site: http://ago.mo.gov/publications/idtheft.htm#header3

National Crime Prevention Council. (2013). Evolving with technology: A comprehensive introduction to cybercrime with links to resources. Retrieved from: http:// www.ncpc.org/topics/fraud-and-identity-theft/evolving-with-technology

Perlroth, N. (2011, December 19). A unit to fight cybercrimes. *The New York Times.* Retrieved from http://query.nytimes.com/

U.S. Department of Justice. (n.d.). Identity theft and fraud. Retrieved from http:// www.justice.gov/criminal/fraud/websites/idtheft.html

White, J. R. (2012). *Identity theft: Total extent of refund fraud using stolen identities is unknown* (GAO Publication No. GAO-13-132T). Washington, DC: U.S. Government Accountability Office. Retrieved from http://www.gao.gov/assets/660/650365.pdf

LOCATED ON COMM 4 ONLINE AT CENGAGEBRAIN.COM:

☐ Review Key Term flashcards and create your own cards

☐ Track your knowledge and understanding of key concepts in communication

☐ Complete practice and graded quizzes to prepare for tests

☐ Complete interactive content within COMM4 Online

☐ View the chapter highlight boxes for COMM4 Online

Quick Quiz

T F 1. Creativity is the result of hard work, not a gift that some people have and some don't.

T F 2. Productive thinking occurs when you are presented with a new idea explained in a way that sparks curiosity and interest.

T F 3. Narrations are presented only in the first- or second-person voice.

T F 4. The goal of an expository speech is to demonstrate how something is done or made, or how it works.

T F 5. Lengthy expository speeches are better known as *lectures*.

6. The characteristics of effective informative speaking include all but the following:
   a. relevant
   b. sensitive
   c. stimulating
   d. creative
   e. memorable

7. _____ thinking occurs when we contemplate something from many different perspectives.
   a. Creative
   b. Productive
   c. Informative
   d. Intellectually stimulating
   e. Outside-the-box

8. You can use visual aids, repetition, transitions, humor, and memory aids to
   a. highlight important information that you want your audience to remember.
   b. encourage productive thinking.
   c. create an informative speech.
   d. describe the specific goal of the speech.
   e. ensure that your main points are stated in parallel language.

9. Of the four ways to define a word or idea, which does your text quote as the quickest?
   a. classifying it
   b. explaining its history
   c. using a synonym
   d. using a comparison
   e. explaining its use or function

10. All of the following are required of an expository speech except
   a. acquiring information from reputable sources.
   b. using a variety of methods to keep the audience's attention.
   c. choosing an organizational pattern that is best suited to the material being presented.
   d. understanding what you are presenting.
   e. believing in what you are presenting.

Answers: 1.T, 2.F, 3.F, 4.F, 5.T, 6.B, 7.B, 8.A, 9.C, 10.E

YOUR FEED- BACK YOUR BOOK

Our research never ends. Continual feedback from you ensures that we keep up with your changing needs.

17 Persuasive Speaking

LEARNING OUTCOMES

17-1 Explain how people listen to and process persuasive messages

17-2 Tailor your persuasive speech goals as propositions aimed at your target audience

17-3 Employ rhetorical strategies of logos to support your persuasive proposition

17-4 Employ rhetorical strategies of ethos to support your persuasive proposition

17-5 Employ rhetorical strategies of pathos to support your persuasive proposition

17-6 Organize your persuasive speeches using an appropriate persuasive speech pattern

After finishing this chapter go to **PAGE 270** for **STUDY TOOLS.**

Whenever we attempt to convince others to agree with our position or behave a certain way, we actually construct and present persuasive messages. How successful we are, however, actually depends on how effectively we employ persuasive strategies in doing so. Persuasion is the word we use to label this process of influencing people's attitudes, beliefs, values, or behaviors. Persuasive speaking is the process of doing so in a public speech. Persuasive messages are pervasive. Whether we are attempting to convince others or others are attempting to convince us, we are constantly involved in influencing or being influenced. Friends convince us to go to a particular movie or eat at a certain restaurant, salespeople persuade us to buy a certain sweater or pair of shoes, and advertisements bombard us whenever we turn on the radio or television, or surf the Internet. It is critical to understand persuasion so we can critically examine and evaluate the persuasive messages we receive from others and can create effective and ethical persuasive messages of our own.

In this chapter, we begin by describing the nature of persuasive messages and how people process them. Then we explain how to form an effective persuasive speech goal and develop it with logos, ethos, and pathos. Finally, we discuss several persuasive speech patterns you can use to organize your speech.

persuasion the process of influencing people's attitudes, beliefs, values, or behaviors

persuasive speaking the process of attempting to influence the attitudes, values, beliefs, or behavior of others in a speech

17-1 THE NATURE OF PERSUASION

Persuasive messages are fundamentally different from informative messages. Whereas the goal of an informative message is to teach, the goal of a persuasive message is to lead. So persuasive speakers are successful only when our audience members are convinced to agree with us, change their behavior, or take action. Persuasive speaking can actually be traced to its roots in ancient Greece, where men used it to debate public issues and make important decisions. Thinkers like Aristotle and Plato used the word **rhetoric** to mean using any and all "available means of persuasion" (Solmsen, 1954). Persuasive speakers do so by developing solid arguments. An argument, in this context, is not synonymous with "quarrel" as we sometimes define it today. Rather, **argument** means articulating a position with the support of logos, ethos, and pathos (Perloff, 2010). **Logos** is a persuasive strategy of constructing logical arguments that support your position. **Ethos** is a persuasive strategy of highlighting your competence, credibility, and good character as a means

to convince others to support your position (Kennedy, 1999). And **pathos** is a persuasive strategy of appealing to emotions in order to convince others to support your position.

17-1a Processing Persuasive Messages

What determines how closely we listen to and how carefully we evaluate the hundreds of persuasive messages we hear each day? Richard Petty and John Cacioppo (1996) developed the elaboration likelihood model (ELM) to explain how we evaluate information before making our decisions.

This dual processing model that we introduced in chapter 2 suggests that we process

rhetoric use of all available means of persuasion

argument articulating a position with the support of logos, ethos, and pathos

logos a persuasive strategy of constructing logical arguments supported with evidence and reasoning

ethos a persuasive strategy of highlighting competence, credibility, and good character

pathos a persuasive strategy of appealing to emotions

persuasive messages in one of two ways. Sometimes we use the "central route" and listen carefully, reflect thoughtfully, and maybe even mentally elaborate on the message before making a decision. When we use the central route, we base our decision primarily on appeals to logic and reasoning (logos). The second way, called the "peripheral route," is a shortcut that relies on simple cues, such as a quick evaluation of the speaker's competence, credibility, and character (ethos), or a gut check about what we feel (pathos) about the message.

We choose a route based on how important we perceive the issue to be for us. When we believe the issue is important, we expend the energy necessary to process it using the central route. When we don't, we take the peripheral route. For example, if you have a serious chronic illness that is expensive to treat, you are more likely to pay attention to and evaluate carefully any proposals to change health care benefits. If you are healthy, you are more likely to quickly agree with suggestions from someone you perceive to be credible or with a proposal that seems compassionate. The ELM also suggests that when we form attitudes as a result of central processing, we are less likely to change our minds than when we base our decisions on peripheral cues.

When you prepare a persuasive speech, you will want to use strategies that address both the central and peripheral routes. In other words, be sure to integrate rhetorical strategies of logos (logic and reasoning) to appeal to audience members using the central route and rhetorical strategies that appeal to both ethos (competence, credibility, and good character) and pathos (emotions) to appeal to audience members using the peripheral route. Ultimately, the most compelling persuasive messages offer appeals to all three: logos, ethos, and pathos. Before doing so, however, you need to form your speech goal as a proposition.

Peripheral

Direct

© viewgene/Shutterstock.com

Persuasive speech goals are stated as propositions. A **proposition** is a declarative sentence that clearly indicates the position you advocate. For example, "I want to convince my audience that pirating copyrighted media (downloading from the Internet) without paying for it is wrong." Notice how a persuasive proposition differs from an information speech goal on the same subject: "I want to inform my audience about the practice of pirating copyrighted media." In the informative speech, you will achieve your goal if the audience understands and remembers what you talk about. In the persuasive speech, however, they must not only understand and remember, but also agree with your position and possibly even take action. The three types of propositions are fact, value, and policy.

17-2a Types of Propositions

A **proposition of fact** is a statement designed to convince your audience that something: (1) did, probably did, probably did not, or did not exist or occur; (2) is, probably is, probably is not, or is not true; or (3) will, probably will, probably will not, or will not occur. Although propositions of fact may or may not be true—both positions are arguable—they are stated as though they are, in fact, true. For example, whether or not Princess Diana's death was an unfortunate car accident or an assassination is debatable. So you could argue a proposition of fact in two ways: "Princess Diana's death was nothing more than a tragic car accident" or "Princess Diana's death was a successful assassination attempt." Examples of propositions of fact concerning the present include "God exists" or "There is no God"; and "Mobile phone use causes brain cancer" or "Mobile phone use does not cause brain cancer." Propositions of fact concerning the future are predictions. For example, "Thanks to the Internet, iPads, and Kindles, paperbound books will eventually cease to exist" and "The New York Yankees will surely win the World Series next year" are propositions of fact concerning the future.

A **proposition of value** is a statement designed to convince your audience that something is good,

FIGURE 17.1 EXAMPLES OF PERSUASIVE SPEECH PROPOSITIONS

Propositions of Fact	Propositions of Value	Propositions of Policy
Mahatma Gandhi was the father of passive resistance.	Mahatma Gandhi was a moral leader.	Mahatma Gandhi should be given a special award for his views on and practices of passive resistance.
Pharmaceutical advertising to consumers increases prescription drug prices.	Advertising of new prescription drugs on TV is better than marketing new drugs directly to doctors.	Pharmaceutical companies should be prohibited from advertising prescription drugs on TV.
Using paper ballots is a reliable method for voting in U.S. elections.	Paper ballots are better than electronic voting machines.	Using paper ballots should be required for U.S. elections.

bad, desirable, undesirable, fair, unfair, moral, immoral, sound, unsound, beneficial, harmful, important, or unimportant (van Eemeren, Garssen, Krabbe, Henkemans, Verheij, & Wagemans, 2014). You can attempt to convince your audience that something has more value than something else, or you can attempt to convince them that something meets valued standards. "Running is a better form of exercise than bicycling" is an example of the former, and "The real value of a college education is that it creates an informed citizenry" is an example of the latter.

A **proposition of policy** is a statement designed to convince your audience that a particular rule, plan, or course of action should be taken. Propositions of policy implore listeners using phrases such as *do it/don't do it*, *should/shouldn't*, and *must/must not*. "All college students should be required to take an oral communication skills course in order to graduate," "The U.S. must stop deep-sea oil drilling," and "We must not text while driving" are propositions of policy. Figure 17.1 provides several examples of how propositions of fact, value, and policy can be developed from the same topic idea.

17-2b Tailoring Propositions to Your Target Audience

Because it is very difficult to convince people to change their minds, what you can hope to accomplish in one speech depends on where your audience stands on your topic. So you'll want to analyze your audience and tailor your proposition based on their initial attitude toward the topic.

Audience members' attitudes can range from highly favorable to strongly opposed and can be visualized on a continuum like the one in Figure 17.2. Even though an audience will include individuals with opinions at nearly every point along the continuum, generally audience members' opinions tend to cluster in one area of it. For instance, most of the audience members represented in Figure 17.2 are "mildly opposed," even though a few people are more highly opposed and a few have favorable opinions. This cluster point represents your **target audience**, the group of people you most want to persuade. Based on your target audience, you can classify your audience's initial attitude toward your topic as "in favor" (already supportive), "no opinion" (uninformed, neutral, or apathetic), or "opposed" (holding an opposite point of view).

OPPOSED It is unrealistic to believe that you will change your target audience's attitude from "opposed" to "in favor" in only one short speech. Instead, seek **incremental change**, that is, attempt to move them only a small degree in your direction, hoping for additional movement later. For example, if your target audience is opposed to the goal "I want to convince my audience that gay marriage should be legalized," you might rephrase it to "I want to convince my audience that committed gay couples should be afforded the same legal protection as committed heterosexual couples through state-recognized civil unions." Then brainstorm potential objections, questions, and criticisms that might arise and shape your speech to address them.

proposition of policy a statement designed to convince the audience that a specific course of action should be taken

target audience the group of people a speaker most wants to persuade

incremental change an attempt to move an audience only a small degree in the speaker's direction

FIGURE 17.2 SAMPLE OPINION CONTINUUM

Highly opposed	Opposed	Mildly opposed	Neither in favor nor opposed	Mildly in favor	In favor	Highly in favor
2	2	11	1	2	2	0

© nasirkhan/Shutterstock.com

NO OPINION If your target audience has no opinion for or against your topic, consider whether they are uninformed, neutral, or apathetic. If they are **uninformed**, that is, they do not know enough about the topic to have formed an opinion, you will need to provide the basic arguments and information needed for them to become informed. For example, if your target audience is uninformed about the topic of gay marriage, you might need to begin by highlighting the legal benefits of marriage in general. If your target audience is **neutral**, that is, they know the basics about your topic but not enough to have formed an opinion, you will want to provide evidence and reasoning illustrating why your position is superior to others. Perhaps your audience knows the legal benefits of marriage in general but needs to understand how committed gay couples who do not have these benefits are disadvantaged. When target audience members have no opinion because they are **apathetic**, that is, indifferent to the topic, you will need to find ways to show how it relates to them or their needs. In other words, you need to provide answers to a question such as, "I'm not gay, so why should I care?" You can do this by including strong listener relevance links for each main point.

IN FAVOR If your target audience is only mildly in favor of your proposal, your task is to reinforce and strengthen their beliefs. Audience members who favor your topic may become further committed to the belief by hearing new reasons and more recent evidence that support it. When your target audience strongly agrees with your position, then you can consider a proposition that moves them to act on it. For example, if the topic is gay marriage and your target audience is in favor of the idea, then your goal may be "I want my audience members to e-mail or write letters to their state representatives urging them to support legislation extending the right to marry to same sex couples." Jeff did so in his speech about exhorbidant course fees for college classes. Since he knew his classmates agreed, he tailored his goal as a proposition of policy to lobby the state legislature, the university's Board of Trustees, and the campus president to stop raising them for two full years.

Once you have identified your topic and tailored your proposition to your target audience, you are ready to develop content by using rhetorical strategies appealing to logos, ethos, and pathos.

17-3 RHETORICAL APPEALS TO LOGOS

Logos strategies are built on logic and reasoning. Stephen Toulmin (1958) developed a three-part model to explain logos-based arguments that has stood the test of time. A solid logos argument consists of a claim, support, and warrant.

The **claim (C)** is the conclusion the speaker wants the audience to agree with. For example, you might *claim:* "Jim's car needs a tune-up." The **support (S)** is the evidence offered as grounds for accepting/agreeing with the claim. You can support a claim with facts, opinions, experiences, and observations. In the car example, we might support our claim with observations that the engine is "missing at slow speeds" and "stalling at stoplights." The **warrant (W)** is the reasoning process that connects the support to the claim. Sometimes the warrant is verbalized and sometimes it is implied. For instance, if you claim that "the car needs a tune-up" on the basis of "missing" and "stalling at stoplights," you might also say "Missing at slow speeds and stalling at lights *are common indications* that a car needs a tune-up." Or you might assume that others see these as signs that a car needs a tune-up. Not knowing whether audience members will make these connections, however, the most effective public speakers verbalize their reasoning warrants.

Using C for claim (conclusion) S for support (reasons and evidence), and W for warrant (explanation of the reasoning process), we can write the reasoning for the proposition in our example in outline form as follows:

C: I want Jim to believe that the car needs a tune-up.
S: I. The engine misses at slow speeds.
S: II. The car stalls at stoplights.
W: (I believe this reasoning is sound because missing and stalling are *major indicators—signs—*of the need for a tune-up.) (The warrant is written in parentheses because it may not be verbalized when the speech is given.)

You can connect your supporting evidence to the claim using one of two different types of reasoning warrants: inductive or deductive. **Inductive reasoning** is arriving at a general conclusion based on several pieces of specific evidence. When we reason inductively, how much our audience agrees with our conclusion depends on the number, quality, and typicality of each piece of evidence we offer. For Jim's car, an inductive argument might look like this:

S: Jim's car is missing at slow speeds.
S: Jim's car is stalling at stoplights.
W: These are common indicators that a car needs a tune-up.
C: Jim's car needs a tune-up.

Deductive reasoning is arguing that if something is true for everything that belongs to a certain class (major premise) and a specific instance is part of that class (minor premise), then we must conclude that what is true for all members of the class must be true in the specific instance (claim). This three-part form of deductive

reasoning is called a **syllogism**. For Jim's car, a deductive syllogism might look like this:

Major Premise: Cars need a tune-up when the engine misses consistently at slow speeds.
Minor Premise: Jim's car is missing at slow speeds.
Claim: Jim's car needs a tune-up.

With this introduction in mind, let's look at some different types of logical arguments.

17-3a Types of Logical Arguments

Although a logical argument *always* includes a claim and support, different types of reasoning warrants can be used to illustrate the relationship between the claim and the support on which it is based. Four common types of logical reasoning arguments are sign, example, analogy, and causation.

ARGUING FROM SIGN You **argue from sign** when you support a claim by providing evidence that certain events that signal the claim have occurred.

The general warrant for reasoning from sign is: When phenomena that usually or always accompany a specific situation occur, then we can expect that specific situation is occurring (or will occur). For example: "Hives and a slight fever are indicators (signs) of an allergic reaction."

Signs should not be confused with causes; signs accompany a phenomenon but do not bring about, lead to, or create the claim. In fact, signs may actually be the effects of the phenomenon. In the allergy example, a rash and fever don't *cause* an allergic reaction; they are indications, or effects, of a reaction.

When arguing from sign, you can make sure your reasoning is valid by answering the following questions.

1. Do these signs always or usually accompany the conclusion drawn?

> **inductive reasoning** arriving at a general conclusion based on several pieces of evidence
>
> **deductive reasoning** arguing that if something is true for everything in a certain class, then it is true for a given item in that class
>
> **syllogism** the three-part form of deductive reasoning
>
> **arguing from sign** supports a claim by citing information that signals the claim

2. Are a sufficient number of signs present?

3. Are contradictory signs in evidence?

If your answer to either of the first two questions is "no" or your answer to the third is "yes," then your reasoning is flawed.

ARGUING FROM EXAMPLE

You **argue from example** when the evidence you use as support are examples of the claim you are making. The warrant for reasoning from example is: "What is true in the examples provided is (or will be) true in general or in other instances."

Suppose you are supporting Juanita Martinez for president of the local neighborhood council. One of your reasons is that "Juanita is electable." You provide several examples of her previous victories to support your claim. She was elected treasurer of her high school junior class, chairperson of her church youth group, and president of her college sorority.

When arguing from example, you can make sure your reasoning is solid by answering the following questions.

1. Are enough examples cited to help listeners understand they are not handpicked?

2. Are the examples typical?

3. Are negative examples accounted for?

If the answer to any of these questions is "no," then your reasoning is flawed.

ARGUING FROM ANALOGY

You **argue from analogy** when you support a claim with a single comparable example that is so significantly similar to the claim as to be strong proof. The general warrant for reasoning from analogy is: "What is true for situation A will also be true in situation B, which is similar to situation A" or "What is true for situation A will be true in all similar situations."

Suppose you wanted to argue that the Cherry Fork Volunteer Fire Department should conduct

Are the subjects being compared similar in every important way?

a raffle to raise money for three portable defibrillator units (claim). You could support the claim with an analogy to a single comparable example like this: The Jefferson City Fire Department, which is very similar to that of Cherry Fork, conducted a raffle and raised enough money to purchase four units.

When arguing from analogy, you can make sure that your reasoning is solid by answering the following questions.

1. Are the subjects being compared similar in every important way? If they are not, then your reasoning is flawed.

2. Are any of the ways in which the subjects are dissimilar important to the conclusion? If so, then your reasoning is flawed.

ARGUING FROM CAUSATION

You **argue from causation** when you support a claim by citing events that always (or almost always) bring about or lead to a predictable effect or set of effects. The general warrant for arguments from cause is: "If A, which is known to bring about B, has been observed, then we can expect B to occur." Let's return to Juanita's election campaign for an example.

In researching Juanita's election campaign, you might discover that (1) she has campaigned intelligently (S) and (2) she has won the endorsement of key community leaders (S). In the past, these two events have usually been associated with victory (W). Thus, Juanita is electable (C).

When arguing from causation, you can make sure that your reasoning is solid by answering the following questions.

1. Are the events alone sufficient to cause the stated effect?

2. Do other events accompanying the cited events actually cause the effect?

3. Is the relationship between the causal events and the effect consistent?

If the answer to any of these questions is "no," then your reasoning is flawed.

arguing from example
supports a claim by providing one or more individual examples

arguing from analogy
supports a claim with a single comparable example that is significantly similar to the subject of the claim

arguing from causation
supports a claim by citing evidence that shows one or more events always or almost always brings about, leads to, creates, or prevents another event or effect

© Liliya Kulianionak/Shutterstock.com

17-3b Reasoning Fallacies

As you develop your arguments, you will want to be sure to avoid **fallacies**, or errors in reasoning. Five common fallacies are hasty generalization, false cause, either/or, straw man, and ad hominem arguments.

1. A **hasty generalization** occurs when a claim is either not supported with evidence or is supported with only one weak example. Enough supporting material must be cited to satisfy the audience that the instances are not isolated or handpicked. For example, someone who argued, "All Akitas are vicious dogs," whose sole piece of evidence was, "My neighbor had an Akita and it bit my best friend's sister," would be guilty of a hasty generalization. It is hasty to generalize about the temperament of a whole breed of dogs based on a single action of one dog. Josh knew a lot of classmates who used or abused drugs like marijuana, Adderall, and anabolic steroids. To make sure he didn't make a hasty generalization that a growing percentage of young adults are doing so throughout the United States, he did an online search for statistics and examples from credible sources such as the National Institute on Drug Abuse (NIDA), National Institute of Health (NIH), and the U.S. Department of Health and Human Services.

2. A **false cause** occurs when the alleged cause fails to produce the effect. The Latin term for this fallacy is *post hoc, ergo propter hoc,* meaning "after this, therefore because of this." Just because two things happen one after the other does not mean that the first necessarily caused the second. An example of a false cause fallacy is when a speaker claims that school violence is caused only by television violence, the Internet, a certain song or musical group, or lack of parental involvement. When one event follows another, there may be no connection at all, or the first event might be just one of many causes that contribute to the second.

3. An **either/or** fallacy occurs by suggesting there are only two alternatives when, in fact, others exist. Many such cases are an oversimplification of a complex issue. For example, when Robert argued that "we'll either have to raise taxes or close the library," he committed an either/or fallacy. He reduced a complex issue to one oversimplified solution when there were many other possible solutions.

4. A **straw man** fallacy occurs when a speaker weakens the opposing position by misrepresenting it in some way and then attacks that weaker (straw man) position. For example, in her speech advocating a seven-day waiting period to purchase handguns, Colleen favored regulation, not prohibition, of gun ownership. Bob argued against that by claiming "It is our constitutional right to bear arms." However, Colleen did not advocate abolishing the right to bear arms. Hence, Bob distorted Colleen's position, making it easier for him to refute.

---

fallacies flawed reasoning

hasty generalization a fallacy that presents a generalization that is either not supported with evidence or is supported with only one weak example

false cause a fallacy that occurs when the alleged cause fails to be related to, or to produce, the effect

either/or a fallacy that occurs when a speaker supports a claim by suggesting there are only two alternatives when, in fact, others exist

straw man a fallacy that occurs when a speaker weakens the opposing position by misrepresenting it in some way and then attacks that weaker (straw person) position

Advertising that features celebrities using a particular product is often guilty of ad hominem reasoning.

5. An **ad hominem** fallacy attacks or praises the person making the argument rather than addressing the argument itself. *Ad hominem* literally means "to the man." For example, if Jamal claims that everyone should buy a Mac computer because Steve Jobs, the founder and former president of Apple Computer, was a genius, he is making an ad hominem argument. Jobs's intelligence isn't really a reason to buy a particular brand of computer. Unfortunately, politicians sometimes resort to ad hominem arguments when they attack their opponent's character rather than their platforms while campaigning for office.

ad hominem a fallacy that occurs when one attacks the person making the argument, rather than the argument itself

goodwill the audience perception that the speaker understands, empathizes with, and is responsive to them

responsive showing that you care about the audience by acknowledging feedback

Bullying in person, over the Internet, and via text messaging is another example of ad hominem attacks that can have dire consequences. TV commercials that feature celebrities using a particular product are often guilty of ad hominem reasoning. For example, Robert De Niro and Jerry Seinfeld have both appeared in American Express commercials, and Gwyneth Paltrow has done ads for Estée Lauder. What makes any of these celebrities experts about the products they are endorsing?

17-4 RHETORICAL APPEALS TO ETHOS

Not everyone will choose the central processing route to make a decision regarding a persuasive proposition. One important cue people use when they process information by the peripheral route is ethos. So, you will also want to demonstrate good character, as well as say and do things to convey competence and credibility.

17-4a Conveying Good Character

We turn again to the ancient Greek philosopher Aristotle (384–322 B.C.E.) who first observed that perceived credibility is dependent on the audience's perception of the speaker's goodwill. Today, we define **goodwill** as a perception the audience forms of a speaker who they believe (1) understands them, (2) empathizes with them, and (3) is responsive to them. When audience members believe in the speaker's goodwill, they are more willing to believe what the speaker says.

One way to demonstrate that you understand your audience is by personalizing your information. Use examples that are directly related to them and their experiences.

You can also empathize with your audience. Empathy is the ability to see the world through the eyes of someone else. Empathizing with the views of the audience doesn't necessarily mean that you accept their views as your own. It does mean that you acknowledge them as valid. For example, consider what spokespersons lead with when responding to a national emergency or crisis event. They begin with "our hearts go out to the victims and their loved ones." In short, they demonstrate empathy.

Finally, you can demonstrate goodwill by being responsive. Speakers who are **responsive** show that they care about the audience by acknowledging feedback, especially subtle negative cues. This feedback may occur during the presentation, but it also may have occurred prior to the speech.

You Too Can Have Six-Pack Abs in Only Three Weeks!

Infomercials (the long, often parodied, television advertisements) permeate U.S. culture today. For example, in 2008 Barack Obama used the infomercial format extensively, culminating in his 30-minute advertisement, which played on seven networks and was watched by 33.55 million viewers (Carter, 2008). Infomercials are television and online programs designed to look like 30- or 60-minute talk shows, but they're actually extended advertisements that focus on a product's extraordinary features and offer testimonials of its effectiveness.

Those extraordinary features have caused infomercials to become sources of entertainment. In 2008 and 2009, the Snuggie— "A blanket with sleeves!"—and a similar product, the Slanket, were frequently referenced in popular culture, from YouTube parodies ("The Cult of Snuggie") to *30 Rock* storylines (with Liz Lemon asserting, "It's not product placement; I just like it!"). When "infomercial king" Billy Mays passed away unexpectedly in June 2009, many were inspired to affectionately celebrate his influence.

Despite the fun we like to have with infomercials, some have come under criticism for making false claims

© new photo/Shutterstock.com

and for encouraging people to purchase items they cannot afford and do not need. For example, in 2002 Guthy-Renker, the largest producer of television infomercials, became the subject of a class-action lawsuit, which claimed Guthy-Renker made exaggerated claims of profitability and promoted an Internet "shopping mall" that was simply a scam ("Timothy D. Naegele & Associates," 2002).

Because advertisements are inherently persuasive, it's important to view them with a critical eye, although certainly not all ads and infomercials make false claims. If you suspect that an infomercial is making questionable claims, be careful before you buy.

17-4b Conveying Competence and Credibility

Not surprisingly, we are more likely to be persuaded when we perceive a speaker to be competent and credible. We propose the following strategies so that your **terminal credibility**, the audience's perception of your expertise at the end of your speech, is greater than your **initial credibility**, their perception of your expertise at the beginning of your speech.

1. Explain your competence. Unless someone has formally introduced you and your qualifications to your audience, your initial credibility will be low, and as you speak, you will need to tell your audience about your expertise. Sending these types of messages during the speech results in your achieving a level of **derived credibility** with your audience. You can interweave comments about your expertise into introductory comments and at appropriate places within the body of the speech.

2. Use evidence from respected sources. You can also increase your derived credibility by using supporting material from well-recognized and respected sources. If you have a choice between using a statistic from a known partisan organization or from a dispassionate professional association, choose the professional association. Likewise, if you can quote a local expert who is well known and respected by your audience or an international scholar with limited name recognition with your audience, use the local expert's opinion.

3. Use nonverbal delivery to enhance your credibility. Your audience assesses your credibility not only from what it hears about you before you begin speaking but also from what it observes by looking at you. Although professional attire enhances credibility in any speaking situation, it is particularly important for persuasive speeches. Persuasive speakers dressed more formally are perceived as more credible than those dressed casually or sloppily (Sellnow & Treinen, 2004).

The audience will also notice how confident you appear as you prepare to address them. From the moment you rise to

> **terminal credibility** perception of a speaker's expertise at the end of the speech
>
> **initial credibility** perception of a speaker's expertise at the beginning of the speech
>
> **derived credibility** perception of a speaker's expertise during the speech

speak, you will want to convey through your nonverbal behavior that you are competent. Plant your feet firmly, glance at your notes, then make eye contact or audience contact with one person or group before taking a breath and beginning to speak. Likewise, pause and establish eye contact upon finishing the speech. Just as pausing and establishing eye contact or audience contact before the speech enhances credibility, doing so upon delivering the closing lines has the same result.

4. Use vocal expression to enhance your credibility. Research shows that credibility is strongly influenced by how you sound. Speaking fluently, using a moderately fast rate, and expressing yourself with conviction makes you appear more intelligent and competent.

17-5 RHETORICAL APPEALS TO PATHOS

We are more likely to be involved with a topic when we have an emotional stake in it. **Emotions** are the buildup of action-specific energy (Petri & Govern, 2012). You can increase audience involvement by evoking negative or positive emotions during your speech (Nabi, 2002).

17-5a Evoking Negative Emotions

Negative emotions are disquieting, so when people experience them, they look for ways to eliminate them. Although you can tap numerous negative emotions, we describe five of the most common and how you might use them in a persuasive speech.

FEAR We experience *fear* when we perceive ourselves to have no control over a situation that threatens us. We may fear physical harm or psychological harm. If you use examples, stories, and statistics that evoke fear in your audience, they will be more motivated to hear how your proposal can eliminate the source of their fear or allow them to escape from it.

GUILT We feel *guilt* when we personally violate a moral, ethical, or religious code that we hold dear. We experience guilt as a gnawing sensation that we have done something wrong. When we feel guilty, we are motivated to "make things right" or to atone for our transgression.

SHAME We feel *shame* when a moral code we violate is revealed to someone we think highly of. The more egregious our

emotions buildup of action-specific energy

behavior or the more we admire the person who finds out, the more shame we experience. When we feel shame, we are motivated to "redeem" ourselves in the eyes of that person. If in your speech you can evoke feelings of shame and then demonstrate how your proposal can either redeem someone after a violation has occurred or prevent feelings of shame, then you can motivate the audience to carefully consider your arguments.

ANGER When we are faced with an obstacle that stands in the way of something we want, we experience *anger*. We may also experience anger when someone demeans us or someone we love. But be cautious: Speakers who choose to evoke anger must not incite listeners to the degree that their reasoning processes are short-circuited.

If you can rouse your audience's anger and then show how your proposal will help them achieve their goals or stop or prevent the demeaning that has occurred, you can motivate them to listen to and really consider your arguments. For example, suppose you want to convince the audience to support a law requiring community notification when a convicted sex offender moves into the neighborhood. You might arouse the audience's anger to get their attention by personalizing the story of Megan Kanka.

She was your little girl, just seven years old, and the light of your world. She had a smile that could bring you to your knees. And she loved puppies. So when that nice man who had moved in down the street invited her in to see his new puppy, she didn't hesitate. But she didn't get to see the puppy, and you didn't ever see her alive again. He beat her, he raped her, and then he strangled her. He packaged her body in an old toy chest and dumped it in a park. Your seven-year-old princess would never dig in a toy chest again or slip down the slide in that park. And that hurts. But what makes you really angry is that she wasn't his first. But you didn't know that. Because no one bothered to tell you that the guy down the street was likely to kill little girls. The cops knew it. But they couldn't tell you. You, the one who was supposed to keep her safe, didn't know. Angry? You bet. Yeah, he's behind bars again, but you still don't know who's living down the street from you. But you can. There is a law before Congress right now that will require active notification of the community when a known sex offender takes up residence, and today I'm going to tell how you can help to get this passed. ("Megan's Law," n.d.)

SADNESS When we fail to achieve a goal or experience a loss, we feel *sadness*. Unlike other negative emotions, we tend to withdraw and become isolated when we feel sad. Because sadness is an unpleasant feeling, we look for ways to end it. Speeches that help us understand and find answers for what has happened can comfort us and help relieve this unpleasant feeling.

17-5b Evoking Positive Emotions

Just as evoking negative emotions can cause audience members to internalize your arguments, so too can you tap *positive emotions*, which are feelings that people enjoy experiencing. We discuss five of them here.

HAPPINESS OR JOY *Happiness* or *joy* is the buildup of positive energy we experience when we accomplish something, when we have a satisfying interaction or relationship, or when we see or possess objects that appeal to us. As a speaker, if you can show how your proposal will lead your audience members to be happy or joyful, then they are likely to listen and to think about your proposal. For example, suppose you want to motivate your audience to attend a couples encounter weekend where they will learn how to "rekindle" their relationship with a partner. If you can remind them about how they felt early in their relationship and then prove that they can reignite those feelings, they may be more motivated to listen.

PRIDE When we experience satisfaction about something we or someone we care about accomplishes, we feel *pride*. "We're number one! We're number one!" is the chant of the crowd feeling pride in the accomplishment of "their" team. Whereas happiness is related to feelings of pleasure, pride is related to feelings of self-worth. If you can demonstrate how

your proposal will help audience members feel good about themselves, they will be more motivated to support your proposition. For example, suppose you want to convince your audience to volunteer to work on the newest Habitat for Humanity house being constructed in your community. You might allude to the pride they will feel when they see people moving into the house they helped to build.

RELIEF When a threatening situation has been alleviated, we feel the positive emotion of *relief*. We relax and put down our guard. As a speaker, you use relief to motivate audience members by combining it with the negative emotion of fear.

HOPE The emotional energy that stems from believing something desirable is likely to happen is called *hope*. Whereas relief causes you to relax and let down your guard, hope energizes you to take action to overcome the situation. Hope empowers. As with relief, hope appeals are usually accompanied by fear appeals. So you can motivate audience members to listen by showing them how your proposal provides a plan for overcoming a difficult situation. For example, if you propose adopting a low-fat diet to reduce the risk of high blood pressure, you can use the same personalization of statistics cited in the example of fear but change the ending to state: "Today, I'm going to convince you to beat the odds by adopting a low-fat diet."

COMPASSION When we feel selfless concern for the suffering of another person and that concern energizes us to try to relieve that suffering, we feel *compassion*. Speakers can evoke audience members' feelings of compassion by vividly describing the suffering endured by someone. The audience will then be motivated to listen to see how the speaker's proposal can end that suffering.

You can evoke negative emotions, positive emotions, or both as a way to encourage listeners to internalize your message. You can do so by telling vivid stories and testimonials, offering startling statistics, using striking presentational aids and provocative language, as well as through an animated and expressive delivery style.

17-6 PERSUASIVE SPEECH PATTERNS

The most common patterns for organizing persuasive speeches include statement of reasons, comparative advantages, criteria satisfaction, refutative, problem–solution, problem–cause–solution, and motivated sequence. In this section, we describe and illustrate each pattern by examining the same topic with slightly different propositions.

17-6a Statement of Reasons

The **statement of reasons pattern** is used to confirm propositions of fact by presenting the best-supported reasons in a meaningful order. For a speech with three reasons or more, place the strongest reason last because this is the reason you believe the audience will find most persuasive. Place the second strongest reason first because you want to start with a significant point. Place the other reasons in between.

Proposition of Fact: The proposed school tax levy is necessary.

I. The income is needed to restore vital programs. [second strongest]

II. The income is needed to give teachers cost of living raises.

III. The income is needed to maintain local control and will save the district from state intervention. [strongest]

statement of reasons pattern used to confirm propositions of fact by presenting best-supported reasons in a meaningful order

comparative advantages pattern attempts to convince that something is of more value than something else

criteria satisfaction pattern seeks audience agreement on criteria that should be considered when they evaluate a particular proposition and then shows how the proposition satisfies those criteria

17-6b Comparative Advantages

The **comparative advantages pattern** attempts to convince others that something has more value than something else. A comparative advantages approach to a school tax proposition might look like this:

Proposition of Value: Passing the school tax levy is better than not passing it. [compares the value of change to the status quo]

I. With new income from a tax levy, schools will be able to reintroduce important programs that had been cut. [advantage 1]

II. New income from a tax levy will provide salaries for teachers and avert a strike. [advantage 2]

III. Income from a tax levy will make it possible to retain local control of our schools, which will be lost to the state if additional local funding is not provided. [advantage 3]

17-6c Criteria Satisfaction

The **criteria satisfaction pattern** seeks agreement on the criteria that should be considered when evaluating a particular proposition and then shows how the proposition satisfies the criteria. A criteria satisfaction pattern is especially useful when your audience is opposed to your proposition, because it approaches the proposition indirectly by first focusing on the criteria that the audience should agree with before introducing the specific solution. A criteria satisfaction organization for the school levy might look like this:

Proposition of Value: Passing a school levy is a good way to fund our schools.

I. We all agree that the funding method we select must meet three criteria:

A. The funding method must provide resources needed to reinstate important programs.

B. The funding method must provide funds to pay teachers.

C. The funding method must generate enough income to maintain local control.

II. Passing a local school tax levy will satisfy each of these criteria.

A. A local levy will allow us to fund important programs again.

B. A local levy will provide revenue for teacher raises.

C. A local levy will generate enough income to maintain local control.

17-6d Refutative

The **refutative pattern** arranges main points according to opposing arguments and then both challenges them and bolsters your own. This pattern is particularly useful when the target audience opposes your position. Begin by acknowledging the merit of opposing arguments and then provide evidence of their flaws. Once listeners understand the flaws, they will be more receptive to the arguments you present to support your proposition. A refutative pattern for the school tax proposition might look like this:

Proposition of Value: A school tax levy is the best way to fund our schools.

I. Opponents of the tax levy argue that the tax increase will fall only on property owners.

   A. Landlords will recoup property taxes in the form of higher rents.

   B. Thus, all people will be affected.

II. Opponents of the tax levy argue that there are fewer students in the school district, so schools should be able to function on the same amount of revenue.

   A. Although there are fewer pupils, costs continue to rise.

      1. Salary costs are increasing.

      2. Energy costs are increasing.

      3. Maintenance costs are increasing.

      4. Costs from unfunded federal and state government mandates are rising.

   B. Although there are fewer pupils, there are many aging school buildings that need replacing or renovating.

III. Opponents of the tax levy argue that parents should be responsible for the excessive cost of educating their children.

   A. Historically, our nation has flourished under a publicly funded educational system.

   B. Parents today are already paying more than previous generations.

      1. Activity fees

      2. Lab fees

      3. Book fees

      4. Transportation fees

   C. Of school-age children today in this district, 42 percent live in families that are below the poverty line and have limited resources.

© Africa Studio/Shutterstock.com

17-6e Problem–Solution

The **problem–solution pattern** explains the nature of a problem and proposes a solution. This organization is particularly effective when the audience is neutral or agrees only that there is a problem but has no opinion about a particular solution. A problem–solution organization for the school tax proposition might look like this:

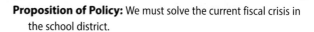

Proposition of Policy: We must solve the current fiscal crisis in the school district.

I. The current funding is insufficient [statement of problem]

   A. The schools have had to cut important programs.

   B. The teachers have not had a cost of living raise in five years.

   C. The state could take over control.

II. The proposed local tax levy will solve these problems. [solution]

   A. The schools will be able ot reinstate important programs.

   B. Teachers will be afforded raises.

   The district will be able to maintain control.

III. We must each do our part to make this happen [call to action]

   A. Vote "yes"

   B. Encourage your friends and neighbors to vote "yes"

> **refutative pattern** arranges main points according to opposing arguments and then both challenges them and bolsters your own
>
> **problem–solution pattern** explains the nature of a particular problem and then proposes a solution

17-6f Problem–Cause–Solution

The **problem–cause–solution pattern** is similar to the problem–solution pattern, but differs from it by adding a main point that reveals the causes of the problem and a solution designed to alleviate those causes. This pattern is particularly useful for addressing seemingly intractable problems that have been dealt with unsuccessfully in the past as a result of treating symptoms rather than underlying causes. A problem–cause–solution organization for the school tax proposition might look like this:

Proposition of Policy: We must solve the current fiscal crisis in the school district.

I. The current funding is insufficient. [statement of problem]

   A. The schools have had to cut programs.

   B. Teachers have not had a cost of living raise in five years.

   C. The state could take over control.

II. We can trace these problems to several key things. [causes]

   A. Government support continues to dwindle.

   B. Operating expenses continue to rise.

III. The proposed local tax levy will address these issues. [solution]

   A. The levy will supplement inadequate government support.

   B. The levy will fill the gap in operating expense needs.

IV. Each one of us is responsible for making sure the tax levy passes [call to action]

   A. Vote "yes."

   B. Encourage your friends and neighbors to vote "yes."

17-6g Motivated Sequence

The **motivated sequence pattern** combines a problem–solution pattern with explicit appeals designed to motivate the audience to act. The motivated sequence pattern is a five-point sequence that replaces the normal introduction-body-conclusion model with (1) an attention step, (2) a need step that fully explains the nature of the problem, (3) a satisfaction step that explains how the proposal solves the problem in a satisfactory manner, (4) a visualization step that provides a personal application of the proposal, and (5) an action appeal step that emphasizes the direction that audience action should take. A motivated sequence pattern for the school tax levy proposition might look like this:

Proposition of Policy: We must solve the current fiscal crisis in the school district.

I. Attention Step: Introduction to the problem.

   A. Comparisons of worldwide test scores in math and sciences show the US continues to lose ground.

   B. I've done extensive research on this problem and today I'm going to convince you to join with me to take actions to stop it.

   C. To do so, we'll start by describing the problem, then explain what we can do to stop it, and finally show you what the future will look like after doing so.

II. Need Step: The local schools are underfunded.

   A. The current funding is insufficient and has resulted in major program cuts.

   B. Excellent teachers are leaving because of stagnant wages.

   C. A threatened state takeover of local schools would lead to more bureaucracy and less learning.

III. Satisfaction Step: The proposed tax levy is large enough to solve these problems.

   A. Programs will be restored.

   B. Qualified teachers will get the needed raises to stay.

   C. We will retain local control.

   D. We can retain pride in our community.

IV. Visualization Step: Imaging the best and the worst.

   A. What it will be like if we pass the levy.

   B. What it will be like if we don't pass the levy.

V. Action Appeal Step: Vote "yes."

   A. If you want to see our schools improve, vote "yes."

   B. Come join me. I'm registered and voting for the levy.

   C. They say it takes a village. Now is our chance. Together we can make a difference for our schools, our kids, and our community.

problem–cause–solution pattern demonstrates that there is a problem caused by specific things that can be alleviated with the proposed solution that addresses the causes

motivated sequence pattern a form of organization that combines the problem–solution pattern with explicit appeals designed to motivate the audience to act

Because motivational patterns are variations of problem–solution patterns, the underlying assumption is similar: When the current means are not solving the problem, a new solution that does solve the problem should be adopted. Figure 17.3 is a checklist that you can use to analyze any persuasive speech you rehearse or to critique the speeches of others.

FIGURE 17.3 PERSUASIVE SPEECH EVALUATION CHECKLIST

You can use this form to critique a persuasive speech to convince that you hear in class. As you listen to the speaker, outline the speech, paying close attention to the reasoning process the speaker uses. Also note the claims and support used in the arguments and identify the types of warrants being used. Then answer the questions that follow.

General Criteria

_____ 1. Was the proposition clear? Could you tell the speaker's position on the issue?

_____ 2. Was the introduction effective in creating interest and involving the audience in the speech?

_____ 3. Was the speech organized using an appropriate persuasive pattern?

_____ 4. Was the language clear, vivid, inclusive, and appropriate?

_____ 5. Was the conclusion effective in summarizing what had been said and mobilizing the audience to act?

_____ 6. Was the speech delivered conversationally and expressively?

_____ 7. Did the speaker establish credibility by demonstrating:

_____ expertise?

_____ personableness?

_____ trustworthiness?

Primary Criteria

_____ 1. Was the specific goal phrased as a proposition (were you clear about the speaker's position on the issue)?

_____ 2. Did the proposition appear to be adapted to the initial attitude of the target audience?

_____ 3. Were emotional appeals used to involve the audience with the topic?

_____ 4. Were the reasons used in the speech

_____ directly related to the proposition?

_____ supported by strong evidence?

_____ persuasive for the particular audience?

_____ 5. Was the evidence [support] used to back the reasons [claims]

_____ from well-respected sources?

_____ recent and/or still valid?

_____ persuasive for this audience?

_____ typical of all evidence that might have been used?

_____ sufficient [enough evidence cited]?

_____ 6. Could you identify the types of arguments that were used?

_____ Did the speaker argue from example?
_____ If so, was it valid?

_____ Did the speaker argue from analogy?
_____ If so, was it valid?

_____ Did the speaker argue from causation?
_____ If so, was it valid?

_____ Did the speaker argue from sign?
_____ If so, was it valid?

_____ 7. Could you identify any fallacies of reasoning in the speech?

_____ hasty generalizations

_____ arguing from false cause

_____ ad hominem attacks

_____ straw person

_____ either-or

_____ 8. Did the speaker demonstrate goodwill?

_____ 9. If the speech called for the audience to take action,

_____ did the speaker describe incentives and relate them to audience needs?

_____ did the speaker acknowledge any costs associated with the action?

_____ 10. Did the speaker use an appropriate persuasive organizational pattern?

_____ statement of reasons

_____ comparative advantages

_____ criteria satisfaction

_____ refutative

_____ problem-solution

_____ problem-cause-solution

_____ motivated sequence

Overall evaluation of the speech (check one):

_____ excellent
_____ good
_____ average
_____ fair
_____ poor

Use the information from this checklist to support your evaluation.

Sample Persuasive Speech

Read the speech adaptation plan developed by Adam Parrish in preparing his speech on cyber-bullying. Then read the transcript of Adam's speech, using the speech critique checklist from Figure 17.3 to help you evaluate his speech.

Adaptation Plan

1. **Target audience initial attitude and background knowledge:** My audience is composed of traditional-aged college students with varying majors and classes. Most are from middle-class backgrounds. The initial attitude about bullying for most will be to agree with me already that it's a bad thing. So I will try to get them to take action. My perception is that my audience knows about cyber-bullying but not the nuances of it.

2. **Organizational framework:** I will organize my speech using a problem-cause-solution framework because my audience already agrees that bullying is bad but may not know what they can and should do to help stop it.

3. **Arguments (logos):** I will demonstrate how widespread (breadth) and harmful (depth of effects) cyber-bullying is and why it persists (causes). Once I've convinced my audience, I will propose solutions that must be taken and cite specifically what we must do to help stop this horrible practice.

4. **Building competence, credibility, and good character (ethos):** I will use credible sources to support my claims and cite them using oral footnotes. I will also offer personal stories to create goodwill.

5. **Creating and maintaining interest (pathos):** I will involve my audience by appealing to several emotions, including guilt, sadness, relief, hope, and compassion.

Speech Outline

Together, We Can Stop Cyber-Bullying

by Adam Parrish

General goal:

To persuade

Specific goal:

To convince my audience to take action to help stop cyber-bullying.

Introduction

I. "I'll miss just being around her." "I didn't want to believe it." "It's such a sad thing." These quotes are from the friends and family of 15-year-old Phoebe Prince, who, on January 14, 2010, committed suicide by hanging herself. Why did this senseless act occur? The answer is simple: Phoebe Prince was bullied to death.

▶ *Attention getter*

II. Many of us know someone who has been bullied in school. Perhaps they were teased in the parking lot or in the locker room. In the past, bullying occurred primarily in and around schools. However, with the advent of new communication technologies such as cell phones with text messaging capability, instant messaging, e-mails, blogs, and social networking sites, bullies can now follow their victims anywhere, even into their own bedrooms. Using electronic communications to tease, harass, threaten, and intimidate another person is called cyber-bullying.

Listener relevance link

III. As a tutor and mentor to young students, I have witnessed cyber-bullying firsthand, and by examining current research, I believe I understand the problem, its causes, and how we can help end cyber-bullying.

Speaker credibility

IV. Cyber-bullying is a devastating form of abuse that must be confronted and stopped.

V. Today, we will examine the widespread and harmful nature of cyber-bullying, discover how and why it persists, and propose some simple solutions that we must engage in to thwart cyber-bullies and comfort their victims.

Thesis statement (stated as a proposition)

Preview

Transition

Let's begin by tackling the problem head on.

Body

I. Cyber-bullying is a pervasive and dangerous behavior.

The problem

Listener relevance link

Many of us have read rude, insensitive, or nasty statements posted about us or someone we care about on social networking sites like Twitter and Facebook. Whether or not those comments were actually intended to hurt another person's feelings, they are perfect examples of cyber-bullying.

A. Cyber-bullying takes place all over the world through a wide array of electronic media.

1. According to Statisticbrain.com, as of 2012, 52 percent of American middle-school students had experienced instances of cyber-bullying ranging from hurtful comments to threats of physical violence (Statisticbrain.com, 2012).

2. According to recent statistics reported by the National Crime Prevention Council, females are just as likely as males to engage in cyber-bullying, although women are twice as likely to be victimized.

3. A 2011 study reported in the journal of *Pediatrics* noted that instances of bullying via text messages have risen significantly since 2006 (Ybarra, Mitchell, & Korchmaros, 2011). And according to an article in the June 2011 issue of *Consumer Reports*, one million young people experienced cyber-bullying on Facebook in 2011 alone.

4. Internet and cell phones are most commonly used by bullies to harass, torment, and threaten young people in North America, Europe, and Asia (National Crime Prevention Council).

5. A particularly disturbing incident occurred in Dallas, Texas, where an overweight student with multiple sclerosis was targeted on a school's social networking page. One message read, "I guess I'll have to wait until you kill yourself, which I hope is not long from now, or I'll have to wait until your disease kills you" (Keith & Martin, 2005, p. 226).

Clearly, cyber-bullying is a widespread problem. What is most disturbing about cyber-bullying, however, is its effects upon victims, bystanders, and perhaps even upon the bullies themselves.

▶ Transition

B. Cyber-bullying can lead to traumatic physical psychological injuries upon its victims.

1. According to a 2012 article in the *Children and Youth Services Review,* 50 percent of the victims of cyber-bullies are also harassed by their attackers in school (Mishna, Khoury-Kassabri, Gadalla, & Daciuk, 2012).

2. For example, the Dallas student with MS had eggs thrown at her car and a bottle of acid thrown at her house (Keith & Martin, 2005).

3. Victims of cyber-bullying experience such severe emotional distress that they often exhibit behavioral problems such as poor grades, skipping school, and receiving detentions and suspensions (Wang, Nansel, Iannotti, 2011).

4. Smith et al. (2008) suggested that even a few instances of cyber-bullying can have these long-lasting and heartbreaking results.

5. What is even more alarming is that victims of cyber-bullying are significantly more likely to carry weapons to school as a result of feeling threatened (Ybarra et al., 2007). Obviously, this could lead to violent, and perhaps even deadly, outcomes for bullies, victims, and even bystanders.

Now that we realize the devastating nature, scope, and effects of cyber-bullying, let's look at its causes.

▶ Transition

II. Cyber-bullying is perpetuated because victims and bystanders do not report their abusers to authorities.

▶ The cause

Think back to a time when you may have seen a friend or loved one being harassed online. Did you report the bully to the network administrator or other authorities? Did you console the victim? I know I didn't. If you are like me, we may unknowingly be enabling future instances of cyber-bullying.

▶ Listener relevance link

A. Cyber-bullies are cowards who attack their victims anonymously.

1. Ybarra et al. (2007) discovered that 13 percent of cyber-bullying victims did not know who was tormenting them.

2. This is an important statistic because, as Keith and Martin (2005) point out, traditional bullying takes place face to face and often ends when students leave school. However, today, students are subjected to bullying in their own homes.

3. Perhaps the anonymous nature of cyber-attacks partially explains why Li (2007) found that nearly 76 percent of victims of cyber-bullying and 75 percent of bystanders never reported instances of bullying to adults.

B. Victims and bystanders who do not report attacks from cyber-bullies can unintentionally enable bullies.

1. According to De Nies, Donaldson, and Netter of ABCNews.com (2010) several of Phoebe Prince's classmates were aware that she was being harassed but did not inform the school's administration.

2. Li (2007) suggested that victims and bystanders often do not believe that adults will actually intervene to stop cyber-bullying.

3. However, ABCNews.com (2010) reports that 41 states have laws against bullying in schools, and 23 of those states target cyber-bullying specifically.

Now that we realize that victims of cyber-bullies desperately need the help of witnesses and bystanders to report their attacks, we should arm ourselves with the information necessary to provide that assistance. ▶ Transition

III. Cyber-bullying must be confronted on national, local, and personal levels. ▶ The solution

Think about the next time you see a friend or loved one being tormented or harassed online. What would you be willing to do to help? ▶ Listener relevance link

A. There should be a comprehensive national law confronting cyber-bullying in schools. According to Stopbullying.gov, at present, there is no federal law that directly addresses bullying. This is simply unacceptable. However, certain statutes currently in state laws could and should be amalgamated to create the strongest protections for victims and the most effective punishments for bullies as possible.

1. According to Limber and Small's (2003) article titled "State Laws and Policies to Address Bullying in Schools," Georgia law requires faculty and staff to be trained on the nature of bullying and what actions to take if they see students being bullied.

2. Furthermore, Connecticut law *requires* school employees to report bullying as part of their hiring contract (Limber & Small, 2003). Washington takes this a step further by protecting employees from any legal action if a reported bully is proven to be innocent (Limber & Small, 2003).

3. When it comes to protecting victims, West Virginia law demands that schools must ensure that a bullied student does not receive additional abuse at the hands of his or her bully (Limber & Small, 2003).

4. Legislating punishment for bullies is difficult. As Limber and Small (2003) noted, zero-tolerance polices often perpetuate violence because at-risk youth (bullies) are removed from all of the benefits of school, which might help make them less abusive.

5. A comprehensive anti-cyber-bullying law should incorporate the best aspects of these state laws and find a way to punish bullies that is both punitive and has the ability to rehabilitate abusers.

B. Local communities must organize and mobilize to attack the problem of cyber-bullying.

1. According to Greene (2006), communities need to support bullying prevention programs by conducting a school-based bullying survey for individual school districts. We can't know how to best protect victims in our community without knowing how they are affected by the problem.

2. It is critical to know this information. As Greene noted, only 3 percent of teachers in the United States perceive bullying to be a problem in their schools (Greene, 2006).

3. Local school districts should create a Coordinating Committee made up of "administrators, teachers, students, parents, school staff, and community partners" to gather bullying data and rally support to confront the problem (Greene, 2006, p. 73).

4. Even if your local school district is unable or unwilling to mobilize behind this dire cause, there are some important actions you can take personally to safeguard those you love against cyber-bullying.

C. Take note of these warning signs that might indicate a friend or loved one is a victim of a cyber-bully.

1. Victims of cyber-bullies often use electronic communication more frequently than do people who are not being bullied.

2. Victims of cyber-bullies have mood swings and difficulty sleeping (Keith & Martin, 2005).

3. Victims of cyber-bullies seem depressed and/or become anxious (Keith & Martin, 2005).

4. Victims of cyber-bullies become withdrawn from social activities and fall behind in scholastic responsibilities (Keith & Martin, 2005).

D. If you see a friend or loved one exhibiting any of these signs, I implore you not to ignore them. Rather, take action. Get involved. Do something to stop it.

1. According to Raskauskas and Stoltz (2007), witnesses of cyber-bullying should inform victims to take the attacks seriously, especially if the bullies threaten violence.

2. Tell victims to report their attacks to police or other authority figures (Raskauskas & Stoltz, 2007).

3. Tell victims to block harmful messages by blocking e-mail accounts and cell phone numbers (Raskauskas & Stoltz, 2007).

4. Tell victims to save copies of attacks and provide them to authorities (Raskauskas & Stoltz, 2007).

5. If you personally know the bully and feel safe confronting him or her, do so! As Raskauskas and Stoltz (2007) noted, bullies will often back down when confronted by peers.

6. By being a good friend and by giving good advice, you can help a victim report his or her attacks from cyber-bullies and take a major step toward eliminating this horrendous problem.

So, you see, we are not helpless to stop the cyber-bulling problem as long as we make the choice NOT to ignore it. ▶ Transition

Conclusion

I. Cyber-bullying is a devastating form of abuse that must be reported to authorities. ▶ Thesis restatement

II. Cyber-bullying is a worldwide problem perpetuated by the silence of both victims and bystanders. By paying attention to certain warning signs, we can empower ourselves to console victims and report their abusers. ▶ Main point summary

III. Today, I implore you to do your part to help stop cyber-bullying. I know that you agree that stopping cyber-bullying must be a priority. First, ▶ Call to action and clincher although other states have cyber-bullying laws in place, ours does not. So I'm asking you to sign this petition that I will forward to our district's state legislators. We need to make our voices heard that we want specific laws passed to stop this horrific practice and to punish those caught doing it. Second, I'm also asking you to be vigilant in noticing signs of cyber-bullying and then taking action. Look for signs that your friend, brother, sister, cousin, boyfriend, girlfriend, or loved one might be a victim of cyber-bullying and then get involved to help stop it! Phoebe Prince showed the warning signs, and she did not deserve to die so senselessly. None of us would ever want to say, "I'll miss just being around her," "I didn't want to believe it," "It's such a sad thing" about our own friends or family members. We must work to ensure that victims are supported and bullies are confronted nationally, locally, and personally. I know that, if we stand together and refuse to be silent, we can and will stop cyber-bullying.

References

Bullying. (2015). National Crime Prevention Council. Retrieved from: http://www.ncpc.org/resources/files/pdf/bullying

Cyber-Bullying Statistics. (2012). Retrieved from http:/www.statisticbrain.com/cyber-bullying-statistics/

De Nies, Y., Donaldson, S., & Netter, S. (2010, January 28). Mean girls: Cyber-bullying blamed for teen suicides. ABCNews.com. Retrieved from http://abcnews.go.com/GMA/Parenting/girls-teen-suicide-calls-attention-cyberbullying/story?id=9685026

Greene, M. B. (2006). Bullying in schools: A plea for measure of human rights. *Journal of Social Issues, 62*(1), 63–79.

Keith, S., & Martin, M. (2005). Cyber-bullying: Creating a culture of respect in the cyber world. *Reclaiming Children and Youth, 13*(4), 224–228.

Li, Q. (2007). New bottle of old wine: A research of cyberbullying in schools. *Computers in Human Behavior, 23,* 1777–1791.

Limber, S. P., & Small, M. A. (2003). State laws and policies to address bullying in schools. *School Psychology Review, 32*(3), 445–455.

Mishna, F., Khoury-Kassabri, M., Gadalla, T., & Daciuk, J. (2012). Risk factors for involvement in cyber bullying: Victims, bullies and bully–victims. *Children and Youth Services Review, 34*(1), 63–70.

Raskauskas, J., & Stoltz, A. D. (2007). Involvement in traditional and electronic bullying among adolescents. *Developmental Psychology, 43*(3), 564–575.

Smith, P. K., Mahdavi, J., Carvalho, M., Fisher, S. Russel, S., & Tippett, N. (2008). Cyberbullying: Its nature and impact in secondary school pupils. *Journal of Child Psychology and Psychiatry, 49*(4), 374–385.

Stopbullying.gov. (2015). U.S. Department of Health and Human Services. Retrieved from: http://www.stopbullying.gov/laws/federal/index.html

That Facebook friend might be 10 years old, and other troubling news. (June 2011). Consumer Reports Online. Retrieved from: http://www.consumerreports.org/cro/magazine-archive/2011/june/electronics-computers/state-of-the-net/facebook-concerns/index.htm

Wang, J., Nansel, T., & Iannotti, R. J. (2011). Cyber and traditional bullying: Differential association with depression. *Journal of Adolescent Health, 48*(4) 415–417.

Ybarra, M. L., Diener-West, M., & Leaf, P. J. (2007). Examining the overlap in Internet harassment and school bullying: Implications for school intervention. *Journal of Adolescent Health, 41,* S42–S50.

Ybarra, M. L., Mitchell, K. J., Wolak, J., & Finkelhor, D. (2006). Examining characteristics and associated distress related to Internet harassment: Findings from the second Youth Internet Safety Survey. *Pediatrics, 118,* 1169–1177.

Ybarra, M. L., Mitchell, K. M., & Korchmaros, J. D. (2011). National trends in exposure to and experiences of violence on the Internet among children. *Pediatrics.* Retrieved from http://pediatrics.aappulications.org/content/early/2011/11/16/peds.2011 -0118.full.pdj+html

Speech and Analysis

"I'll miss just being around her." "I didn't want to believe it." "It's such a sad thing." These quotes are from the friends and family of 15-year-old Phoebe Prince, who, on January 14, 2010, committed suicide by hanging herself. Why did this senseless act occur? The answer is simple. . . . Phoebe Prince was bullied to death.

Many of us know someone who has been bullied in school. Perhaps they were teased in the parking lot or in the locker room. In the past, bullying occurred primarily in school. However, with the advent of new communication technologies such as cell phones, text messaging, instant messaging, blogs, and social networking sites, bullies can now follow and terrorize their victims anywhere, even into their own bedrooms. Using electronic communications to tease, harass, threaten, and intimidate another person is called cyber-bullying.

As a tutor and mentor to young students, I have witnessed cyber-bullying firsthand, and by examining current research, I believe I understand the problem, its causes, and how we can help end cyber-bullying. What I know for sure is that cyber-bullying is a devastating form of abuse that must be confronted on national, local, and personal levels.

Today, we will examine the widespread and harmful nature of cyber-bulling, uncover how and why it persists, and pinpoint some simple solutions we must begin to enact in order to thwart cyber-bullies and comfort their victims. Let's begin by tackling the problem head on.

Many of us have read rude, insensitive, or nasty statements posted about us or someone we care about on social networking sites like Twitter and Facebook. Well, whether or not those comments were actually intended to hurt another person's feelings, if they did hurt their feelings, then they are perfect examples of cyber-bullying.

Cyber-bullying is a pervasive and dangerous behavior. It takes place all over the world and through a wide array of electronic media. According to Statisticbrain.com, as of 2012, 52 percent of American middle-school students had experienced instances of cyber-bullying ranging from hurtful comments to treats of physical violence. Moreover, recent statistics reported by the National Crime Prevention Council reveal that females are just as likely as males to engage in cyber-bullying, but are twice as likely to be victimized.

A 2011 study reported in the journal *Pediatrics* noted that instances of bullying via text messages have risen significantly since 2006. And according to an article in *Consumer Reports,* one million young people experienced cyber-bullying on Facebook in 2011 alone. The problem does not exist in the United States alone.

Li noted that Internet and cell phone technologies have been used by bullies to harass, torment, and threaten young people in North America, Europe, and Asia. However, some of the most horrific attacks happen right here at home.

Analysis

▶ Adam uses quotes from family and friends of cyber-bullying victim Phoebe Prince to get attention and lead into his proposition.

▶ Here, Adam further entices his listeners to pay attention by offering listener relevance that we all can relate to.

▶ Using the vivid term "terrorize," Adam appeals to negative emotions (pathos).

▶ Adam begins to establish ethos by mentioning why he has credibility about this topic. Mentioning that he is a tutor and mentor also conveys goodwill. Listeners are likely to think he must have good character if he volunteers as a tutor and mentor.

▶ Adam does a nice job of previewing his problem-cause-solution organizational framework, but his thesis statement phrased as a proposition is somewhat lost and could be made more overtly here.

▶ Again, Adam's use of a listener relevance link helps keep listeners tuned in and interested in hearing more.

▶ Here Adam bolsters his ethos (and avoids plagiarism) by citing an oral footnote for his statistics.

▶ Although this trend is interesting, it would have been more compelling to use a contemporary statistic.

▶ Notice Adam's word choices (harass, torment, threaten, horrific) to enhance pathos.

According to Keith and Martin, a particularly disturbing incident occurred in Dallas, Texas, where an overweight student with multiple sclerosis was targeted on a school's social networking page. One message read, "I guess I'll have to wait until you kill yourself which I hope is not long from now, or I'll have to wait until your disease kills you." Clearly, cyber-bullying is a worldwide and perverse phenomenon. What is most disturbing about cyber-bullying is its effects upon victims, bystanders, and perhaps even upon bullies themselves.

The use of a real victim in this example creates an emotional appeal.

Cyber-bullying can lead to physical and psychological injuries upon its victims. According to a 2012 article in the *Children and Youth Services Review*, 50 percent of the victims of cyber-bullies are also harassed by their attackers in school. For example, the Dallas student with MS had eggs thrown at her car and a bottle of acid thrown at her house.

This vivid example enhances pathos.

According to a 2011 article published in the *Journal of Adolescent Health*, *Wang and colleagues* reported that victims of cyber-bullying experience such severe emotional distress that they often exhibit behavioral problems such as poor grades, skipping school, and receiving detentions and suspensions. Furthermore, Smith et al. suggested that even a few instances of cyber-bullying can have these long-lasting negative effects.

Now that Adam has established the widespread breadth of the problem, he moves into a discussion about the depth of the effects it can have on victims.

What is even more alarming is that, according to Ybarra and colleagues, victims of cyber-bullying are significantly more likely to carry weapons to school as a result of feeling threatened. Obviously, this could lead to violent outcomes for bullies, victims, and even bystanders (Bullying, 2015, National Crime Prevention Council).

Here Adam helps pique listener interest by pointing out that bystanders can also be hurt if they don't do something to stop this form of terrorism.

Now that we have heard about the nature, scope, and effects of cyber-bullying, let's see if we can discover its causes. Let's think back to a time when we may have seen a friend or loved one being harassed online. Did we report the bully to the network administrator or other authorities? Did we console the victim? I know I didn't. If you are like me, we may unknowingly be enabling future instances of cyber-bullying.

Notice how Adam's transition ties the point he is finishing (problem) to the next point (causes) using inclusive "we" language. This, too, bolsters a sense of goodwill and uses a conversational style that keeps listeners engaged.

Cyber-bullying occurs because of the anonymity offered to bullies by cell phone and Internet technologies, as well as the failure of victims and bystanders to report incidents of cyber-bullying. You see, unlike schoolyard bullies, cyber-bullies can attack their victims anonymously.

Ybarra and colleagues discovered that 13 percent of cyber-bullying victims did not know who was tormenting them. This devastating statistic is important because, as Keith and Martin noted, traditional bullying takes place face to face and often ends when students leave school. However, today, students are subjected to nonstop bullying, even when they are alone in their own homes.

Perhaps the anonymous nature of cyber-attacks partially explains why Li found that nearly 76 percent of victims of cyber-bullying and 75 percent of bystanders never reported instances of bullying to adults. Victims and bystanders who do not report attacks from cyber-bullies can unintentionally enable bullies.

According to De Nies, Donaldson, and Netter of ABCNews.com (2010), several of Phoebe Prince's classmates were aware that she was being harassed but did not inform the school's administration. Li suggested that victims and bystanders often do not believe that adults will actually intervene to stop cyber-bullying. However, ABCNews.com reports that 41 states have laws against bullying in schools, and 23 of those states target cyber-bullying specifically.

Now that we know that victims of cyber-bullies desperately need the help of witnesses and bystanders to report their attacks, we should arm ourselves with the information necessary to provide that assistance. Think about the next time you see a friend or loved one being tormented or harassed online. What would you be willing to do to help?

Cyber-bullying must be confronted on national, local, and personal levels. According to Soptbullying.gov., as of 2015, there is no federal law that directly addresses bullying. This is simply unacceptable. There should be a comprehensive national law confronting cyber-bullying in schools. Certain statutes currently in state laws should be amalgamated to create the strongest protections for victims and the most effective punishments for bullies as possible.

According to Limber and Small's article titled "State Laws and Policies to Address Bullying in Schools," Georgia law requires faculty and staff to be trained on the nature of bullying and what actions to take if they see students being bullied.

Furthermore, Connecticut law *requires* school employees to report bullying as part of their hiring contract. Washington takes this a step further by protecting employees from any legal action if a reported bully is proven to be innocent. When it comes to protecting victims, West Virginia law demands that schools must ensure that a bullied student does not receive additional abuse at the hands of his or her bully.

Legislating punishment for bullies is difficult. As Limber and Small noted, zero-tolerance polices often perpetuate violence because at-risk youth, i.e., bullies, are removed from all of the benefits of school, which might help make them less abusive. A comprehensive anti-cyber-bullying law should incorporate the best aspects of these state laws and find a way to punish bullies that is both punitive and has the ability to rehabilitate abusers. However, for national laws to be effective, local communities need to be supportive.

Local communities must organize and mobilize to attack the problem of cyber-bullying. According to Greene's 2006 article published in the *Journal of Social Issues*, communities need to support bullying prevention programs by conducting a school-based bullying survey for individual school districts. We can't know how to best protect victims in our community without knowing how they are affected by the problem. It is critical to know this information. As Greene noted, only 3 percent of teachers in the United States perceive bullying to be a problem in their schools.

Local school districts should create a Coordinating Committee made up of administrators, teachers, students, parents, school staff, and community partners to gather bullying data and rally support to confront the problem. Even if your local school district is unable or unwilling to mobilize behind this dire cause, there are some important actions you can take personally to safeguard those you love against cyber-bullying.

There are several warning signs that might indicate a friend or loved one is a victim of a cyber-bully. If you see a friend or loved one exhibiting these signs, the decision to get involved can be the difference between life and death.

According to Keith and Martin's article "Cyber-Bullying: Creating a Culture of Respect in a Cyber World," victims of cyber-bullies often use electronic communication more frequently than do people who are not being bullied. Victims of cyber-bullies have mood swings and difficulty sleeping. They seem

▶ Again, Adam does a nice job with his transition.

▶ Notice how Adam gets right to the point about needing to take action on a variety of levels to stop this practice.

▶ Adam gives credence to his policy statement by pointing to several states that have already succeeded in creating such laws.

▶ Here, Adam points to the need for consequences when bullying behavior is exposed.

▶ Adam offers specific action steps that communities ought to take to help stop cyber-bullying.

▶ Here, Adam gets personal, pointing out that each person in the room has an ethical responsibility to help stop cyber-bullying.

depressed and/or become anxious. Victims can also become withdrawn from social activities and fall behind in scholastic responsibilities. If you witness your friends or family members exhibiting these symptoms, there are several ways you can help.

According to Raskauskas and Stoltz's 2007 article in *Developmental Psychology*, witnesses of cyber-bullying should inform victims to take the attacks seriously, especially if the bullies threaten violence. You should tell victims to report their attacks to police or other authorities, to block harmful messages by blocking e-mail accounts and cell phone numbers, and to save copies of attacks and provide them to authorities.

Adam could make this statement more compelling by offering a specific example of what one might tell the police, as well as how to install blockers on e-mail and mobile phones.

If you personally know the bully and feel safe confronting him or her, do so! As Raskauskas and Stoltz noted, bullies will often back down when confronted by peers. By being a good friend and by giving good advice, you can help a victim report his or her attacks from cyber-bullies and take a major step toward eliminating this horrendous problem. So, you see, we are not helpless to stop the cyber-bulling problem as long as we make the choice NOT to ignore it.

To conclude, cyber-bullying is a devastating form of abuse that must be reported to authorities. Cyber-bullying is a worldwide problem perpetuated by the silence of both victims and bystanders. By paying attention to certain warning signs, we can empower ourselves to console victims and report their abusers.

Here, Adam restates his proposition, but his argument could be more comprehensive (beyond just our need to report bullying to the authorities).

Today, I'm imploring you to do your part to help stop cyber-bullying. I know that you agree that stopping cyber-bullying must be a priority. First, although other states have cyber-bullying laws in place, ours does not. So I'm asking you to sign this petition that I will forward to our district's state legislators. We need to make our voices heard that we want specific laws passed to stop this horrific practice and to punish those caught doing it.

Adam reminds listeners of his specific call to action and even asks them to sign a petition. His approach encourages listeners to follow through on his goal—that is—to actuate.

Second, I'm also asking you to be vigilant in noticing signs of cyber-bullying and then taking action. Look for signs that your friend, brother, sister, cousin, boyfriend, girlfriend, or loved one might be a victim of cyber-bullying, and then get involved to help stop it! Phoebe Prince showed the warning signs, and she did not deserve to die so senselessly. None of us would ever want to say, "I'll miss just being around her," "I didn't want to believe it," "It's such a sad thing" about our own friends or family members. We must work to ensure that victims are supported and bullies are confronted nationally, locally, and personally.

Adam does a nice job with his clincher in terms of tying back to the Phoebe story from his attention getter. Doing so appeals to emotions (pathos) in a way that should make his speech very memorable.

I know that, if we stand together and refuse to be silent, we can and will stop cyber-bullying.

LOCATED IN TEXTBOOK

☐ Tear-out Chapter Review cards at the end of the book

☐ Review with the Quick Quiz below

LOCATED ON COMM 4 ONLINE AT CENGAGEBRAIN.COM:

☐ Review Key Term flashcards and create your own cards

☐ Track your knowledge and understanding of key concepts in communication

☐ Complete practice and graded quizzes to prepare for tests

☐ Complete interactive content within COMM4 Online

☐ View the chapter highlight boxes for COMM4 Online

Quick Quiz

T F 1. If your audience is very much opposed to your goal, you should aim to change their attitude from "opposed" to "in favor" by the end of your speech.

T F 2. A proposition of value is a statement designed to convince your audience that they should take a specific course of action.

T F 3. A straw man is a fallacy that occurs when a speaker weakens the opposing position by misrepresenting it in some way, and then attacks that weaker position.

T F 4. An argument is an articulation of a position with the support of logos, ethos, and pathos.

T F 5. The statement of reasons pattern attempts to prove propositions of fact by presenting the best-supported reasons in a meaningful order, placing the strongest reason first because the audience will find it most persuasive.

6. You are arguing by _____ when you cite evidence that one or more events always or almost always brings about, leads to, creates, or prevents a predictable event or set of effects.
   a. examples
   b. analogy
   c. causation
   d. sign
   e. reasoning

7. Which of the following five common errors in reasoning occurs when the alleged cause fails to be related to or to produce the effect?

   a. hasty generalization
   b. ad hominem
   c. either-or
   d. false cause
   e. straw man

8. Speakers demonstrate _____ by showing the audience that they understand and empathize with them.
   a. goodwill
   b. credibility
   c. positive emotions
   d. emotional appeals
   e. responsiveness

9. The _____ pattern is a form of persuasive organization used for arguing a proposition of value when the goal is to prove that something has more value than something else.
   a. statement of reasons
   b. problem solution
   c. comparative advantages
   d. criteria satisfaction
   e. motivated sequence

10. Which of the following patterns for organizing persuasive speeches helps you organize your main points so that you persuade by both challenging opposing arguments and bolstering your own?
   a. statement of reasons
   b. problem-cause-solution
   c. criteria satisfaction
   d. comparative advantages
   e. refutative

Answers: 1.F, 2.F, 3.T, 4.T, 5.F, 6.C, 7.D, 8.A, 9.C, 10.E

APPENDIX Interviewing

LEARNING OUTCOMES

A-1 Discuss how to form and order a series of questions for an interview

A-2 Discuss how to conduct information-gathering interviews

A-3 Examine how to conduct employment interviews

A-4 Discuss interview strategies for job-seekers

A-5 Identify strategies for dealing with news media

Because interviewing is a powerful method of collecting or presenting first-hand information that may be unavailable elsewhere, it is an important communication skill to master. An **interview** is a highly structured conversation in which one person asks questions and another person answers them. By *highly structured*, we mean that the purpose and the questions to be asked are determined ahead of time. Because interviews are highly structured, they can be used to make comparisons. For example, an interviewer may ask two potential employees the same set of questions, compare the answers, and hire the person whose answers fit best with the needs of the organization and responsibilities of the position. Although we have all taken part in interviews, few have learned how to do so effectively—either as the interviewer or the interviewee.

Because the heart of effective interviewing is developing a series of good questions, we begin by describing how to do so. Then we propose some guidelines to follow when engaged in information-gathering, employment, and media interviews.

A-1 THE INTERVIEW PROTOCOL

interview a highly structured conversation in which one person asks questions and another person answers them

interview protocol the list of questions used to elicit desired information from the interviewee

primary questions introductory questions about each major interview topic

The **interview protocol** is the list of questions used to elicit desired information from the interviewee. An effective interviewer always prepares a protocol in advance. How many questions you plan to ask depends on how much time you will have for the interview. Begin by listing the topics you want to cover. Then prioritize them.

Just as the topics in a well-developed speech are structured in an outline with main points, subpoints, and supporting material, an effective interview protocol is structured into primary and secondary questions. The questions should be a mix of open-ended and closed-ended questions, as well as neutral and leading questions. Let's briefly examine each type.

A-1a Primary and Secondary Questions

Primary questions are introductory questions about each major interview topic.

Secondary questions are follow-up questions that probe the interviewee to expand on the answers given to primary questions. The interviewee may not realize how much detail you want or may be purposely evasive. Some follow-up questions probe by simply encouraging the interviewee to continue ("And then?" or "Is there more?"); some probe into a specific detail the person mentioned or failed to mention ("What does 'regionally popular' mean?" and "You didn't mention genre. What role might that play in your decision to offer a contract?"); and some probe into their feelings ("How did it feel when her first record went platinum?").

A-1b Open-ended and Closed-ended Questions

Open-ended questions are broad-based queries that give the interviewee freedom about the specific information, opinions, or feelings that can be divulged. Open-ended questions encourage the interviewee to talk and allow the interviewer an opportunity to listen and observe. Since open-ended questions give respondents more control, interviewers need to intentionally redirect the interviewee to focus on the original purpose (Tengler & Jablin, 1983). For example, in a job interview you might be asked, "What one accomplishment has best prepared you for this job?" In a customer service interview, a representative might ask, "What seems to be the problem?" or "Can you tell me the steps you took when you first set up this product?"

By contrast, **closed-ended questions** are narrowly focused and require very brief (one- or two-word) answers. Closed-ended questions range from those that can be answered yes or no, such as "Have you taken a course in marketing?" to those that require only a short answer, such as "Which of the artists that you have signed have won Grammys?" By asking closed-ended questions, interviewers can control the interview and obtain specific information quickly. But the answers to closed-ended questions cannot reveal the nuances behind responses, nor are they likely to capture the complexity of the story.

A-1c Neutral and Leading Questions

Open-ended and closed-ended questions may also be either neutral or leading. **Neutral questions** do not direct a person's answer. "What can you tell me about your work with Habitat for Humanity?" and "What criteria do you use in deciding whether to offer an artist a contract?" are neutral questions. The neutral question gives the respondent free rein to answer the question without any knowledge of what the interviewer thinks or believes.

By contrast, **leading questions** guide respondents toward providing certain types of information and imply that the interviewer prefers one answer over another. "What do you like about working for Habitat for Humanity?" steers respondents to describe only the positive aspects of their volunteer work. "Having a 'commercial sound' is an important criteria, isn't it?" directs the answer by providing the standard for comparison. In most types of interviews, neutral questions are preferable because they are less likely to create defensiveness in the interviewee.

A good interview protocol will use a combination of open-ended, closed-ended, neutral, and leading questions.

A-2 INFORMATION-GATHERING INTERVIEWS

Interviewing is a valuable method for obtaining information on nearly any topic. Lawyers and police interview witnesses to establish facts; health care providers interview patients to obtain medical histories before making diagnoses; reporters interview sources for their stories; managers interview employees to receive updates on projects; and students interview experts to obtain information for research projects. Once you have prepared a good interview protocol, you need to choose an appropriate person to interview, conduct the interview effectively, and follow up respectfully.

A-2a Choosing the Interviewee

Sometimes the choice of interviewee is obvious, but other times you will need to do research to identify the right person to interview. Suppose your purpose is to learn about how to get a recording contract. You might begin by asking a professor in the music department for the name of a music production agency in the area. Or

secondary questions follow-up questions that probe the interviewee to expand on the answers given to primary questions

open-ended questions broad-based queries that give the interviewee freedom abo u t the specific information, opinions, or feelings that can be divulged

closed-ended questions narrowly focused questions that require very brief (one- or two-word) answers

neutral questions questions that do not direct a person's answer

leading questions questions that guide respondents toward providing certain types of information and imply that the interviewer prefers one answer over another

you could find the name of an agency by searching on-line. Once you find a Web site, you can usually find an "About Us" or "Contact Us" link, which will offer names, titles, e-mail addresses, and phone numbers. You should be able to identify someone appropriate to your purpose from this list.

Once you have identified the person or people to be interviewed, you should make contact to schedule an appointment. Today, it is generally best to do so by both e-mail and telephone. When you contact the interviewee, be sure to clearly state the purpose of the interview, how the interview information will be used, and how long you expect the interview to take. When setting a date and time, suggest several dates and time ranges and ask which would be most convenient for the interviewee. As you conclude, thank the person for agreeing to be interviewed and confirm the date, time, and location you have agreed to for the interview. If you make the appointment more than a few days in advance, call or e-mail the day before the interview to confirm the appointment.

You don't want to bother your interviewee with information you can get elsewhere. So to prepare appropriate protocol questions, do some research on the topic in advance. This includes learning about what the interviewee may have written about the topic and his or her credentials. Interviewees will be more responsive if you appear informed, and being informed will ensure that you ask good questions. For instance, if you are going to interview a music producer, you will want to do preliminary research about what a music producer is and does, whether any general "best practices" exist for signing artists, and whether this particular producer has published any criteria. You can usually do so by carefully reading the information posted on their Web site. Then, during the interview, you can ask about additional criteria, about different criteria, or to expand on how the criteria is used in making judgments.

A-2b Conducting the Interview

To guide you in the process of conducting effective and ethical interviews, we offer this list of best practices.

1. Dress professionally. Dressing professionally conveys that you are serious about the interview and that you respect the interviewee and his or her time.

2. Be prompt. You also demonstrate respect by showing up prepared to begin at the time you have agreed to. Remember to allow enough time for potential traffic and parking problems.

3. Be courteous. Begin by introducing yourself and the purpose of the interview and by thanking the person for taking the time to talk to you. Remember that, although interviewees may enjoy talking about the subject, may be flattered, and may wish to share their knowledge, they most likely have nothing to gain from the interview. So you should let them know you are grateful for their time. Most of all, respect what the interviewee says regardless of what you may think of his or her responses.

4. Ask permission to record. If the interviewee says no, respect his or her wishes and take careful notes instead.

5. Listen carefully. At key points in the interview, paraphrase what the interviewee has said to be sure that you really understand. This will assure the interviewee that you will report the answers truthfully and fairly in your paper, project, or speech.

6. Keep the interview moving. You do not want to rush the person, but you do want to behave responsibly by getting your questions answered during the allotted time.

7. Monitor your nonverbal reactions. Maintain good eye contact with the person. Nod to show understanding, and smile occasionally to maintain the friendliness of the interview. How you look and act is likely to determine whether the person will warm up to you and give you an informative interview.

8. Get permission to quote. Be sure to get permission for exact quotes. Doing so demonstrates that you respect the interviewee and want to report his or her ideas honestly and fairly. Doing so also communicates that you have integrity and strive to act responsibly. You might even offer to let the person see a copy of what you prepare before you share it with others. That way, he or she can double-check the accuracy of direct quotations.

9. Confirm credentials. Before you leave, be sure to confirm your interviewee's professional title and the company or organization he or she represents. To do so is to act responsibly because you will need these details when explaining why you chose to interview this person.

10. End on time. As with arriving promptly, ending the interview when you said you would demonstrates respect for the interviewee and that you act responsibly and with integrity.

11. Thank the interviewee. Thanking the interviewee leads to positive rapport, should you need to follow up later, and demonstrates that you appreciate his or her valuable time. You may even follow up with a short thank-you note after you leave.

A-2c Following Up

Because your interview notes were probably taken in outline or shorthand form, the longer you wait to translate them the more difficult this task will be. So you'll need to sit down with your notes as soon as possible after the interview to make more extensive notes of the information you may want to use later. If you recorded the interview, take some time to **transcribe** the responses by translating them word for word into written form. If at any point you are not sure whether you have accurately transcribed what the person said or meant, telephone or e-mail the interviewee to double-check. When you have completed a draft of your paper, project, or speech outline, you can demonstrate respect for the interviewee and integrity as a reporter by providing him or her with a copy of the product if it is a written paper or report, a link to it if it is an online document, or an invitation to attend if it is a public speech or performance.

 ## A-3 EMPLOYMENT INTERVIEWS

Believe it or not, over the past 50 years, the average amount of time an employee stays with one company or organization has gone from over 23 years to about 4 years (Employee Tenure, 2010; Taylor & Hardy, 2004)! Not only that, but between 15 to 20 million Americans change jobs each year (Bashara, 2006). This means that we spend more time doing employment interviews—both as interviewers and interviewees—than ever before. Employment interviews help interviewers assess which applicants have the knowledge, experience, and skills that best fit the responsibilities of the position and culture of the organization—characteristics and skills that cannot be judged from a résumé. And employment interviews help job-seekers determine whether they would enjoy working for the organization. So let's look at some best practices for both employment interviewers and job-seekers.

A-3a Employment Interviewers

Historically, human resource professionals have conducted most employment interviews on behalf of a firm, but today more and more workplaces are using employees as interviewers. You may have already helped conduct employment interviews, or you may be asked to do so in the near future. As with any interview, you will need to follow some guidelines as you both prepare for and conduct the interview.

PREPARING FOR THE INTERVIEW As with information interviews, you begin employment interviews by doing research—in this case, by familiarizing yourself with the knowledge, skills, and aptitudes someone must have to be successful in the job. It also means studying applicants' résumés, reference letters, and other application materials to narrow the pool of applicants you will actually interview. Before interviewing each applicant, prepare by reviewing their materials again, making notes about topics to address with probing secondary questions.

In most employment interviewing situations, you will see several candidates. It's important to make an interview protocol to make sure that all applicants are asked the same (or very similar) questions about characteristics and skills. Be sure to identify primary questions and secondary questions that will probe knowledge, skills, characteristics, and experiences relevant to the position and the culture of your organization. Using a protocol will also help you avoid questions that violate fair employment practice legislation. The Equal Opportunity Commission has detailed guidelines that spell out which questions are unlawful.

CONDUCTING THE INTERVIEW As with an information-gathering interview, begin with introductions and a question or two designed to establish rapport and to help the interviewee relax. Be sure to greet the applicant warmly, consider your verbal and nonverbal cues, and conclude with a clarification of next steps.

FOLLOWING UP Once you have hired one of the interviewees, be sure to follow up with a short e-mail or letter informing each of the other candidates that the position has been filled. You can do so *respectfully* by thanking each candidate for their interest in the position and taking the time to participate in the interview, reminding them that they were a strong candidate in a strong applicant pool, and wishing them well in their future employment-seeking endeavors.

 ## A-4 JOB-SEEKERS

A **job-seeker** is anyone who is looking for a job or considering a job change. Some may be unemployed and dedicating 100 percent of their time to finding a job. Others may be happily employed and recruited to apply for another position. Still others could be employed, but seeking a more rewarding position.

> **transcribe** translate oral interview responses word for word into written form
> **job-seeker** anyone who is looking for a job or considering a job change

As many employment experts will tell you, "As a rule, the best jobs do *not* go to the best-qualified individuals—they go to the best job seekers" (Graber, 2000). Successful job-seekers are obviously the ones who get the job. To be successful, you need to follow guidelines searching for job openings, as well as when applying and interviewing.

A-4a Locating Job Openings

You have probably been through the hiring process at least once, and perhaps many times. So you know how stressful it can be. You also probably know that sometimes the most difficult part of a job search is simply finding out about job openings. Sometimes openings are easily accessible by searching the Internet, newspaper, career fairs, and career centers. We call this the **visible job market**. Other times, however, job openings are not readily apparent and require you to use other methods to locate and apply for them. We call this the **hidden job market** (Yena, 2011). We focus here on locating jobs in both the visible and hidden job markets by searching published resources (in print and online), using referral services, and networking.

PUBLISHED RESOURCES When employers want to cast a wide net for applicants, they will publish in a variety of outlets that are read most widely by job-seekers. These range from Web sites such as CareerBuilder.com, LinkedIn, HotJobs.com, USAJOBS.gov (dedicated to government jobs), and CollegeJobBank .com (dedicated to recent college graduates), as well as classified sections of online newspapers and newsletters. Some sites allow you to post your résumé online and will forward it to potential employers when your credentials fit their needs. Although employers often use these sites, they also very often publish openings on their own Web sites. So even if you find an announcement posted on another site, you can improve your chances of landing an interview if you actually apply through the company's own Web site (Light, 2011).

REFERRAL SERVICES Some employers like to use referral services to do the initial screening of applicants. Most colleges and universities have an on-site career center that serves this purpose. Your tuition dollars pay for this service, so it's one of the first places you should look. They post and publish local, regional, national, and international openings in a variety of for-profit, nonprofit, and government organizations. In addition to doing initial screenings for employers, career service officers also provide applicants helpful advice about writing cover letters, preparing résumés, selecting references, and doing interviews. Finally, they often facilitate on-campus **career fairs** to help bring potential employers and applicants together to learn about the company and make contacts.

Some employers also have in-house **employee referral programs** that reward current employees for referring strong candidates to the company. If you are interested in working for a particular company, you might seek an opportunity to ask a current employee to recommend you.

NETWORKING Networking is the process of using developing or established relationships to make contacts regarding job openings (in both the visible and hidden job markets). Some research suggests that the majority of jobs are filled via networking (Betty, 2010). Your **network** consists of the people you know, people you meet, and the people who are known to the people you know. These people may include teachers, counselors, your friends, family friends, relatives, service club members, mentors, classmates, colleagues, and even people you meet at sporting events, country clubs, and health clubs. The following two guidelines can help make networking work for you.

1. Reach out to people you know and tell them you are in the job market. Speak up and tell the people you know that you are looking for a job. Bring it up during conversation or intentionally seek them out to let them know. Prepare business cards with your contact information and give them to the people you talk to. In addition to business cards, be prepared to provide people in your network with an **elevator speech**—a 60-second oral summary of the type of job you're seeking and your qualifications for it. Ask people in your network if they know of (1) any job opportunities that might be appropriate and (2) anyone you might contact to help you find such opportunities. Finally, ask them to keep their eyes and ears open about anything that might be of interest to you and to share such information with you.

visible job market easily accessible job opening announcements

hidden job market job openings that are not readily apparent and require alternative methods to locate

career fairs events that bring potential employers and applicants together to foster networking and create awareness about employment opportunities

employee referral programs in-house reward programs for employees who refer strong candidates to the company

networking the process of using developing or established relationships to make contacts regarding job openings

network the people you know, people you meet, and people who are known to the people you know

elevator speech a 60-second oral summary of the type of job you are seeking and your qualifications for it

2. Grow your network. Attend networking events in your area that may be hosted by your college or university career center, the local chamber of commerce, and your alumni association. Join professional and civic organizations. Volunteer. The more people you know, the more people you will have to ask about potential opportunities on the *hidden job market*. You should also join online networking groups such as LinkedIn, Facebook, and Twitter. Remember that the key here is to develop and nurture relationships. People will make a special effort to help you if they believe you are a friend and a good person.

A-4b Preparing Application Materials

Because interviewing is time consuming, most organizations do not interview all the people who apply for a job. Rather, they use a variety of screening devices to eliminate people who don't meet their qualifications. Chief among them are evaluating the qualifications you highlight on your résumé and in your cover letter (Kaplan, 2002). A **résumé** is a summary sheet highlighting your related experience, educational background, skills, and accomplishments. A **cover letter** is a short well-written letter or e-mail expressing your interest in the position and piquing curiosity about why your application materials deserve a closer look. The goal of your cover letter and résumé is to land an interview (Farr, 2009).

Whether you send your application materials electronically or through regular postal mail, the guidelines for preparing them effectively are the same. Before you can begin, you need to know something about the company and about the job requirements so that you can tailor your application materials to highlight how and why you are the best candidate. Today you can learn a lot about an organization by visiting its Web site and reading online material thoroughly. You can also talk to people you know who work or worked there, or acquaintances of employees.

TAILORING YOUR RÉSUMÉ You should tailor your résumé to highlight your skills and experiences related to the position and its responsibilities. There are two types of résumés. In both, you begin by supplying basic contact information (name, address, e-mail, phone number), educational degrees or certificates earned, and career objective. In a **chronological résumé**, you list your job positions and accomplishments in reverse chronological order. Chronological résumés are most appropriate if you have held jobs in the past that are clearly related to the position you are applying for. In a **functional résumé**, you focus on highlighting the skills and experiences you have that qualify you for the

position. You may find a functional résumé best for highlighting your skills and accomplishments if you are changing careers, have a gap in your work history, or have limited formal job experience but have acquired job-related skills in other ways (courses you have taken, clubs you have belonged to, service-learning and volunteer work, etc.).

TAILORING YOUR COVER LETTER Just as you need to tailor your résumé to the position, you should also tailor your cover letter appropriately. Be sure to highlight your qualifications for *a specific job and its responsibilities*. You can learn some of this information in the job description, but you may also need to make inferences about it by visiting the company's Web site and talking to people who are associated with the organization or who are familiar with the type of position described in the advertisement.

Your cover letter should be short—no more than four or five paragraphs. If you prepare your cover letter in the body of an e-mail message, it should be even shorter. These paragraphs should highlight your job-related skills and experiences *using key words that appeared in the posting*. Many employers use software programs that scan e-mails and résumés for job-relevant key words. Using them in your cover letter will increase the likelihood that someone will actually look at your application materials. Use a spell-checker and carefully proofread for errors such programs don't catch. Your cover letter must be 100 percent error free to serve as a catalyst for getting an interview.

TAILORING MATERIALS FOR ONLINE SUBMISSIONS You must also tailor your application materials for a variety of online submission programs. Because you will apply for most jobs online, make sure your materials can be submitted in several formats.

A-4c Conducting the Employment Interview

An **employment interview** is a conversation or set of conversations between a job candidate and a representative or representatives

résumé a summary sheet highlighting your related experience, educational background, skills, and accomplishments

cover letter a short, well-written letter or e-mail expressing your interest in a particular job and piquing curiosity about you as an applicant

chronological résumé a résumé that lists your job positions and accomplishments in reverse chronological order

functional résumé a résumé that focuses on highlighting the skills and experiences that qualify you for the position

employment interview a conversation or set of conversations between a job candidate and a representative or representatives of a hiring organization

of a hiring organization. Your goal is to convince the interviewer that you are the best qualified candidate and the best fit for the position and company. Successful interviewing begins with thorough preparation, then with the actual interview, and finally with appropriate follow up.

PREPARING Once you submit your application materials, you need to prepare for the interview you hope to get. In this section, we offer four suggestions to prepare for a job interview.

1. Do your homework. Although you should have already done extensive research on the position and the organization to prepare your application materials, you should review what you've learned before going to the interview. Be sure you know the organization's products and services, areas of operation, ownership, and financial health. Nothing puts off interviewers more than applicants who arrive at an interview knowing little about the organization. Be sure to look beyond the "Work for Us" or "Frequently Asked Questions" links on the company's Web site. Find more specific information such as pages that target potential investors, report company stock performance, and describe the organization's mission (Slayter, 2006). Likewise, pictures can suggest the type of organizational culture you can expect—formal or informal dress, collaborative or individual work spaces, diversity, and so on. Researching these details will help you decide whether the organization is right for you, as well as help you form questions to ask during the interview.

2. Prepare a self-summary. You should not need to hesitate when an interviewer asks you why you are interested in the job. You should also be prepared to describe your previous accomplishments. Form these statements as personal stories with specific examples that people will remember (Beshara, 2006). Robin Ryan (2000), one of the nation's foremost career authorities, advises job-seekers to prepare a 60-second general statement they can share with a potential employer. She advises job-seekers to identify which aspects of their training and experience would be most valued by a potential employer. She suggests making a five-point agenda that can (1) summarize your most relevant experience and (2) "build a solid picture emphasizing how you *can* do the job" (p. 10). Once you have your points identified, practice communicating them fluently in 60 seconds or less.

3. Prepare a list of questions about the organization and the job. The employment interview should be a two-way street, where you size up the company the same way they are sizing you up. So you will probably have a number of specific questions to ask the interviewer. For example, "Can you describe a typical workday for the person in this position?" or "What is the biggest challenge in this job?" Make a list of your questions and take it with you to the interview. It can be difficult to come up with good questions on the spur of the moment, so you should prepare several questions in advance. One question we do not advise asking during the interview, however, is "How much money will I make?" Save salary, benefits, and vacation-time negotiations until after you have been offered the job.

4. Rehearse the interview. Several days before the interview, spend time outlining the job requirements and how your knowledge, skills, and experiences meet those requirements. Practice answering questions commonly asked in interviews.

INTERVIEWING The actual interview is your opportunity to sell yourself to the organization. Although interviews can be stressful, your preparation should give you the confidence you need to relax and communicate effectively. Believe it or not, the job interview is somewhat stressful for the interviewer as well. Most companies do not interview potential employees every day. Moreover, the majority of interviewers have little or no formal training in the interview process. Your goal is to make the interview a comfortable conversation for both of you.

Use these guidelines to help you have a successful interview.

1. Dress appropriately. You want to make a good first impression, so it is important to be well groomed and neatly dressed. Although "casual" or "business casual" is common in many workplaces, some organizations still expect employees to be more formally dressed. If you don't know the dress code for the organization, call the human resources department and ask.

2. Arrive on time. The interview is the organization's first exposure to your work behavior, so you don't want to be late. Find out how long it will take you to travel by making a dry run at least a day before. Plan to arrive 10 or 15 minutes before your appointment.

3. Bring supplies. Bring extra copies of your résumé, cover letter, business cards, and references, as well as the list of questions you plan to ask. You might also bring a portfolio of previous work you have done. You will also want to have paper and a pen so that you can make notes.

4. Use active listening. When we are anxious, we sometimes have trouble listening well. Work on paying attention to, understanding, and remembering what is asked. Remember that the interviewer will be aware of your nonverbal behavior, so be sure to make and keep eye contact as you listen.

5. Think before answering. If you have prepared for the interview, make sure that as you answer the interviewer's questions, you also tell your story. Take a moment to consider how your answers portray your skills and experiences.

6. Be enthusiastic. If you come across as bored or disinterested, the interviewer is likely to conclude that you would be an unmotivated employee.

7. Ask questions. As the interview is winding down, be sure to ask any questions you prepared that have not already been answered. You may also want to ask how well the interviewer believes your qualifications match the position, and what your strengths are.

8. Thank the interviewer and restate your interest in the position. As the interview comes to a close, shake the interviewer's hand and thank him or her for the opportunity. Finally, restate your interest in the position and desire to work on the company team.

FOLLOWING UP Once the interview is over, you can set yourself apart from the other applicants by following these important steps:

1. Send a thank-you note. It is appropriate to write a short note thanking the interviewer for the experience and again expressing your interest in the job.

2. Self-assess your performance. Take time to critique your performance. How well did you do? What can you do better next time?

3. Contact the interviewer for feedback. If you don't get the job, you might call the interviewer and ask for feedback. Be polite and indicate that you are only calling to get some help on your interviewing skills. Actively listen to the feedback, using questions and paraphrases to clarify what is being said. Be sure to thank the interviewer for helping you.

A-5 MEDIA INTERVIEWS

Today we live in a media-saturated environment in which any individual may be approached by a newsperson and asked to participate in an on-air interview. For example, the authors have a friend who became the object of media interest when the city council refused to grant him a zoning variance so that he could complete building a new home on his property. In the course of three days, his story became front-page news in his town, and reports about his situation made the local radio and TV news shows. You might be asked for an interview at public meetings, at the mall, or within the context of your work or community service. For example, you may be asked to share your knowledge of your organization's programs, events, or activities. Because media interviews are likely to be edited in some way before they are aired and because they reach a wide audience, there are specific strategies you should use to prepare for and participate in them.

A-5a Before the Interview

The members of the media work under very tight deadlines, so it is crucial that you respond immediately to media requests for an interview. When people are insensitive to media deadlines, they can end up looking like they have purposefully evaded the interview and have something to hide. When you speak with the media representative, clarify what the focus of the interview will be and how the information will be presented. At times, the entire interview will be presented; however, it is more likely that the interview will be edited or paraphrased and not all of your comments will be reported.

As you prepare for the interview, identify three or four **talking points**, that is, the central ideas you want to present as you answer questions during a media interview. For example, before our friend was interviewed by the local TV news anchor, he knew that he wanted to emphasize that he was a victim of others' mistakes: (1) he had hired a licensed architect to draw the plans; (2) the city inspectors had repeatedly approved earlier stages of the building process; (3) the city planning commission had voted unanimously to grant him the variance; and (4) he would be out half the cost of the house if he were forced to tear it down and rebuild. Consider how you will tailor your information to the specific audience in terms they can understand. Consider how you will respond to tough or hostile questions.

A-5b During the Interview

Media interviews call for a combination of interviewing, nonverbal communication, and public speaking skills (Boyd, 1999). Follow these strategies during a media interview:

1. Present appropriate nonverbal cues. Inexperienced interviewees can often look or sound tense or stiff. By standing up

> **talking points** the three or four central ideas you will present as you answer the questions asked during a media interview

during a phone interview, your voice will sound more energetic and authoritative. With on-camera interviews, when checking your notes, move your eyes but not your head. Keep a small smile when listening. Look at the interviewer, not into the camera.

2. Make clear and concise statements. It is important to speak slowly, to articulate clearly, and to avoid technical terms or jargon. Remember that the audience is not familiar with your area of expertise.

> **bridge** the transition you create in a media interview so that you can move from the interviewer's subject to the message you want to communicate

3. Realize that you are always "on the record." Say nothing as an aside or confidentially to a reporter. Do not say anything that you would not want quoted. If you do not know an answer, do not speculate, but indicate that the question is outside of your area of expertise. Do not ramble during the interviewer's periods of silence. Do not allow yourself to be rushed into an answer.

4. Learn how to bridge. Media consultant Joanna Krotz (2006) defines a **bridge** as a transition you create so that you can move from the interviewer's subject to the message you want to communicate. To do this, you first answer the direct question and then use a phrase such as "What's important to remember, however . . . ," "Let me put that in perspective . . . ," or "It's also important to know . . ." With careful preparation, specific communication strategies during the interview, and practice, one can skillfully deliver a message in any media interview format.

Chapter 1

Beebe, S., & Masterson, J. (2006). *Communicating in groups: Principles and practices* (8th ed.). Boston, MA: Pearson.

Berger, C. (1997). *Planning strategic interaction: Attaining goals through communicative action*. Mahwah, NJ: Lawrence Erlbaum.

Burgoon, J. K., Bonito, J. A., Ramirez, A., Jr., Dunbar, N. E., Kam, K., & Fisher, J. (2002). Testing the interactivity principle: Effects of mediation, propinquity, and verbal and nonverbal modalities in interpersonal interaction. *Journal of Communication, 52*, 657–677.

Burleson, B. R. (2009). Understanding the outcomes of supportive communication: A dual-process approach. *Journal of Social and Personal Relationships, 26*(1), 21–38.

College learning for the new global century. (2007). *A Report from the National Leadership Council for Liberal Education and America's Promise*. Washington, DC: Association of American Colleges and Universities.

Cupach, W. R. & Spitzberg, B. H. (Eds.). (2011). *The dark side of close relationships II*. New York, NY: Routledge.

Darling, A.L., & Dannels, D. P. (2003). Practicing engineers talk about the importance of talk: A report on the role of oral communication in the workplace. *Communication Education, 52*(1), 1–16.

Hansen, R. S., & Hansen, K. (n.d.). Top skills and values employers seek from job-seekers. Retrieved from Quintessential Careers Web site: http://www.quintcareers.com /job_skills_values.html

Hart Research Associates. (2010). Raising the bar: Employers' views on college learning in the wake of the economic downturn. Washington, DC: Association of American Colleges and Universities.

Hart Research Associates. (2006). How should colleges prepare students to succeed in today's global economy? Washington, DC: Association of American Colleges and Universities.

Hirokawa, R. Y., Cathcart, R. S., Samovar, L. A., & Henman, L. D. (Eds.). (2003). *Small group communication: Theory and practice: An anthology* (8th ed.). New York, NY: Oxford University Press, USA.

Kellerman, K. (1992). Communication: Inherently strategic and primarily automatic. *Communication Monographs, 59*(3), 288–300.

Knapp, M. L., & Daly, J. A. (2002). *Handbook of interpersonal communication*. Thousand Oaks, CA: Sage.

Littlejohn, S. W., & Foss, K. A. (2011). *Theories of human communication* (10th ed.). Long Grove, IL: Waveland Press.

McCroskey, J. C. (1977). Oral communication apprehension: A review of recent theory and research. *Human Communication Research, 4*(1), 78–96.

Millar, F. E. & Rogers, L. E. (1987). Relational dimensions of interpersonal dynamics. In M. E. Roloff & G. E. Miller (Eds.), *Interpersonal processes: New directions in communication research*. (pp. 117–139). Newbury Park, CA: Sage.

Pajares, F., Prestin, A., Chen, J., & Nabi, R. L. (2009). Social cognitive theory and media effects. In R. L. Nabi and M. B. Oliver (Eds.) *The SAGE handbook of media processes and effects* (pp. 283–297). Los Angeles, CA: Sage.

Richmond, V. P., & McCroskey, J. C. (1997). *Communication: Apprehension, avoidance, and effectiveness* (5th ed.). Scottsdale, AZ: Gorsuch Scarisbrick.

Samovar, L. A., Porter, R. E., & McDaniel, E. R. (2007). *Communication between cultures* (6th ed.). Belmont, CA: Thomson Wadsworth.

Samovar, L. A., Porter, R. E., & McDaniel, E. R. (2010). *Communication between cultures* (7th ed.). Belmont, CA: Thomson Wadsworth.

Spitzberg, B. H. (2000). A model of intercultural communication competence. In L. A. Samovar & R. E. Porter (Eds.), *Intercultural communication: A reader* (9th ed., pp. 375–387). Belmont, CA: Wadsworth.

Spitzberg, B. H. & Cupach, W. R. (Eds.). (2011). *The dark side of close relationships II*. New York, NY: Routledge.

Terkel, S. N., & Duval, R. S. (Eds.). (1999). *Encyclopedia of ethics*. New York, NY: Facts on File.

Humes, K. R., Jones, N. A., Ramirez, R.R. (2011, March). *Overview of race and Hispanic origin: 2010*. U. S. Census Bureau. Retrieved from http://www.census .gov/population/race/publications/

Young, M. (2003). Integrating communication skills into the marketing curriculum: A case study. *Journal of Marketing Education, 25*(1), 57–70.

Chapter 2

Aron, A. P., Mashek, D. J., & Aron, E. N. (2004). Closeness as including other in the self. In D. Mashek & A. Aron (Eds.), *Handbook of closeness and intimacy* (pp. 27–41). Mahwah, NJ: Lawrence Erlbaum.

Bandura, A. (1977). Self-efficacy: Toward a unifying theory of behavioral change. *Psychological Review, 84*(2), 191–215.

Baumeister, R. F. (2005). *The cultural animal: Human nature, meaning, and social life*. New York: Oxford University Press.

Becker, A. E. (2004). Television, disordered eating, and young women in Fiji: Negotiating body image and identity during rapid social change. *Culture, Medicine and Psychiatry, 28*(4), 533–559.

Becker, M., Vignoles. V. L., Owe, E., Easterbrook, M. J., Brown, R., Smith P. B., Bond, M. H., Regalia, C., Manzi, C., Brambilla, M., Aldhafri, S., Gonzalez, R., Carrasco, D., Paz Cadena, M., Lay, S., Schweiger Gallo, I., Torres, A., Camino, L., Ozgen, E., Guner, U. E., Yamako lu, N., Silveira Lemos, F. C., Trujillo E. V., Balanta, P., Macapagal, M, M. E. J., Cristina Ferreira, M., Herman, G., de Sauvage, I., Bourguignon, D., Wang, Q., Fulop, M., Harb, C., Chybicka, A., Mekonnen, K. H., Martin, M., Nizharadze, G., Gavreliuc, A., Buitendach, J., Valk, A., & Koller, S. H. (2014). Cultural bases for self-evaluation: Seeing oneself positively in different cultural contexts. *Personality and Social Psychology Bulletin*; DOI: 10.1177/0146167214522836

Bee, H., & Boyd, D. (2011). *The developing child* (13th ed.). Pearson Education.

Benet-Martinez, V., & Haritatos, J. (2005). Bicultural identity integration (BII): Components and psychosocial antecedents. *Journal of Personality, 73*(4), 1015–1049.

Berger, C.R., & Bradac, J.J. (1982). *Language and social knowledge*. London, England: Edward Arnold Publishers Ltd.

Biocca, F., & Harms, C. (2002). Defining and measuring social presence: Contribution to the Networked Minds theory and measure. In F.R. Gouveia & F. Biocca (Eds.), *Proceedings of the 5th International Workshop of Presence* (7–36).

Dovidio, J. F., & Gaertner. S. L. (2010). Intergroup bias. In S. T. Fiske, D. T. Gilbert, & G. Lindzey (Eds.), *The Handbook of social psychology* (5th ed., Vol. 2). New York: Wiley.

Downey, G., Freitas, A. L., Michaelis, B., & Khouri, H. (2004). The self-fulfilling prophecy in close relationships: Rejection sensitivity and rejection by romantic partners. In H. T. Reis & C. E. Rusbult (Eds.), *Close relationships* (pp. 153–174). New York, NY: Psychology Press.

Engel, B. (2005). *Breaking the cycle of abuse: How to move beyond your past to create an abuse-free future*. Hoboken, NJ: John Wiley and Sons.

Fiore, A. R. T. (2010). Self-presentation, interpersonal perception, and partner selection in computer-mediated relationship formation. *UC Berkeley: Information Management & Systems*. Retrieved from: https://escholarship.org/uc/item/0cd9r9ws

Gibson, J. J. (1966). *The senses considered as perceptual systems*. Boston, MA: Houghton Mifflin.

Guerrero, L. K., Anderson, P. A., & Afifi, W. A. (2007). *Close encounters: Communication in relationships* (2nd ed.). Los Angeles: Sage Publications.

Haiken, M. (2012, September 26). Lady Gaga puts bulimia and body image on the table in a big way. *Forbes*. Retrieved from http://www.forbes.com/sites/melaniehaiken/2012/09/26/lady-gaga-puts-bulimia-and-body-image-on-the-table-in-a-big-way.

Hewitt, John P. (2009). *Oxford handbook of positive psychology*. Oxford University Press.

Hinduja, S., & Patchin, J. W. (2010). Bullying, cyberbullying, and suicide. *Archives of Suicide Research, 14*(3), 206–221.

Littlejohn, S. W., & Foss, K. A. (2011). *Theories of human communication* (10th ed.). Long Grove, IL: Waveland Press.

Merton, R. K. (1968). *Social theory and social structure*. New York, NY: Free Press.

Mruk, C. J. (2006). *Self-esteem research, theory, and practice: Toward a positive psychology of self-esteem.* New York NY: Springer.

Mruk, C. J. (2013). *Self-esteem and positive psychology: research, theory, and practice* (4th ed.). New York: Springer.

Rayner, S. G. (2001). Aspects of the self as learner: Perception, concept, and esteem. In R. J. Riding & S. G. Rayner (Eds.), *Self-perception: International perspectives on individual differences* (Vol. 2). Westport, CT: Ablex.

Rose, P., & Kim, J. (2011). Self-monitoring, opinion leadership, and opinion seeking: A sociomotivational approach. *Current Psychology*, 30, 203–214.

Sampson, E. E. (1999). *Dealing with differences: An introduction to the social psychology of prejudice*. Fort Worth, TX: Harcourt Brace.

Shedletsky, L. J., & Aitken, J. E. (2004). *Human communication on the Internet*. Boston: Pearson.

Weiten, W., Dunn, D. S., & Hammer, E. Y. (2012) *Psychology applied to modern life: Adjustments in the 21st century.* Belmont, CA: Wadsworth.

Willis, J. and Todorov, A (2006). First impressions: Making up your mind after a 100-ms exposure to a face. *Psych Sci. 17*(7), 592–598.

Wood, J. T. (2007). *Gendered lives: Communication, gender, and culture* (7th ed.). Belmont, CA: Wadsworth.

Chapter 3

Andersen, P. A., Hecht, M. L., Hoobler, G. D., & Smallwood, M. (2003). Nonverbal communication across cultures. In W. B. Gudykunst (Ed.), *Cross-cultural and intercultural communication*. Thousand Oaks, CA: Sage.

Bornstein, M. H., & Bradley, R. H. (Eds.). (2003). *Socioeconomic status, parenting, and child development.* Mahwah, NJ: Lawrence Erlbaum Associates.

Chen, G., & Starosta, W. (1998). *Foundations of intercultural communication*. Boston, MA: Allyn and Bacon.

Desilver, D. (2013, June 7). World's Muslim population more widespread than you might think. *Pew Research Center*. Retrieved on September 25, 2014 at: http://www.pewresearch.org/fact-tank/2013/06/07/worlds-muslim-population-more-widespread-than-you-might-think/

Hall, E. T. (1976). *Beyond culture*. New York, NY: Random House.

Haviland, W. A. (1993). *Cultural anthropology*. Fort Worth, TX: Harcourt, Brace, Jovanovich.

Hofstede, G. (1998). *Masculinity and femininity: The taboo*. Thousand Oaks, CA: Sage.

Hofstede, G. (2000). Masculine and feminine cultures. In A. E. Kazdin (Ed.), *Encyclopedia of psychology* (vol. 5). Washington, DC: American Psychological Association.

Jackson, M. (Director). (2010). *Temple Grandin* [Motion picture]. USA: Home Box Office.

Jackson, R. L., II (Ed.). (2004). *African American communication and identities*. Thousand Oaks, CA: Sage.

Kim, M. (2005). Culture-based conversational constraints theory: Individual- and culture-level analyses. In W. B. Gudykunst (Ed.), *Theorizing about intercultural communication*, (pp. 93–117). Thousand Oaks, CA: Sage.

Kim, Y. Y. (2001). *Becoming intercultural: An integrative theory of communication and cross-cultural adaptation*. Thousand Oaks, CA: Sage.

Klyukanov, I. E. (2005). *Principles of intercultural communication*. New York, NY: Pearson.

Kraus, M. W., & Keltner, D. (2009). Signs of socioeconomic status: A thin-slicing approach. *Psychological Science, 20*(1), 99–106.

Luckmann, J. (1999). *Transcultural communication in nursing*. New York, NY: Delmar.

Lynch, D. J. (2013, December 11). Americans say dream fading as income gap hurts chances. *Bloomberg*. Retrieved on September 26, 2014 at: http://www.bloomberg.com/news/2013-12-11/americans-say-dream-fading-as-income-gap-hurts-chances.html

MacSwan, J. (2013). Code-switching and grammatical theory. In T. Bhatia and W. Ritchie *Handbook of multilingualism* (2nd ed.). Cambridge, Blackwell.

Neuliep, J. W. (2006). *Intercultural communication: A contextual approach* (3rd ed.). Thousand Oaks, CA: Sage.

Pew Research Center. (2007). *A portrait of "Generation Next": How young people view their lives, futures, and politics* (survey report). Retrieved from http://people-press.org/report/300/a-portrait-of-generation-next

Prensky, M. (2001). Digital natives, digital immigrants. *On the Horizon, 9*(5), 1–6.

Rhodes, G., Lie, H. C., Ewing, L., Evangelista, E., & Tanaka, J. W. (2010). Does perceived race affect discrimination and recognition of ambiguous- race faces? A test of the socio-cognitive hypothesis. *Journal of Experimental Psychology: Learning, Memory, and Cognition, 36*(1), 217–223. doi.org/10.1037/a0017680

Samovar, L. A., Porter, R. E., & McDaniel, E. R. (2012). *Communication between cultures* (8th ed.). Boston, MA: Wadsworth Cengage.

Schein, E. H. (2010). *Organizational culture and leadership*. (4th Ed.). San Francisco, CA: John Wiley and Sons.

Ting-Toomey, S., Yee-Jung, K. K., Shapiro, R. B., Garcia, W., Wright, T. J., & Oetzel, J. G. (2000). Ethnic/cultural identity salience and conflict styles in four U.S. ethnic groups. *International Journal of Intercultural Relations, 23*(1), 47–81.

Ting-Toomey, S., & Chung, L. C. (2012). *Understanding intercultural communication* (2nd ed.). New York: Oxford University Press.

United States Department of Commerce. (January 2010). Middle class in America. *Economics and Statistics Administration*. Office of the Vice President of the United States Middle Class Task Force. Washington, D. C. Retrieved on December 13, 2014 at http://www.commerce.gov/sites/default/files/documents/migrated/Middle%20Class%20Report.pdf

Wallis, C. (2006, March 27). The multitasking generation. *Time, 167*(13), pp. 48–55.

Wood, J. T. (2007). *Gendered lives: Communication, gender, and culture* (7th ed.). Belmont, CA: Wadsworth.

Chapter 4

Aronoff, M. and Rees-Miller, J. (Eds.). (2001). *The handbook of linguistics*. Oxford, UK: Blackwell.

Chaika, E. (2008). *Language: The social mirror* (4th ed.). Boston, MA: Heinle ELT/Cengage.

Cvetkovic, L. (2009, February 21) Serbian, Croatian, Bosnian, or Montenegrin, or "Just our language." *Radio Free Europe/Radio Liberty*. Retrieved from http://www.rferl.org/content/Serbian_Croatian_Bosnian_or_Montenegrin_Many_In_Balkans_Just_Call_It_Our_Language_/1497105.html

Grice, H. P. (1975). Logic and conversation. In P. Cole & J. L. Morgan (Eds.), *Syntax and semantics (Vol. 3)*. New York, NY: Academic Press.

Higginbotham, J. (2006). Languages and idiolects: Their language and ours. In E. Lepore & B.C. Smith (Eds.), *The Oxford handbook of philosophy of language*. Oxford, UK: Oxford University Press.

Korta, K. and Perry, J. (2008). Pragmatics. In E. N. Zalta (Ed.), *Stanford encyclopedia of philosophy (Fall 2008 Edition)*. Retrieved from http://plato.stanford.edu/archives/fall2008/entries/pragmatics/

Langer, E. J. & Moldoveanu, M. (2000). The construct of mindfulness. *Journal of Social Issues, 56*(1), 1–9.

Lewis, M. P. (Ed.). (2009). *Ethnologue: Languages of the world* (16th ed.). Dallas, TX: SIL International.

O'Grady, W., Archibald, J., Aronoff, M., & Rees-Miller, J. (2001). *Contemporary linguistics* (4th ed.). Boston, MA: Bedford/St. Martin's.

Slattery, K., Doremus, M., & Marcus, L. (2001). Shifts in public affairs reporting on the network evening news: A move toward the sensational. *Journal of Broadcasting & Electronic Media 45*(2), 295–298.

Ting-Toomey, S., & Chung, L. C. (2005). *Understanding intercultural communication*. Los Angeles, CA: Roxbury Publishing.

Wright, R. (2010). Chinese language facts. Retrieved from http://www.languagehelpers.com/languagefacts/chinese.html

Chapter 5

American Museum of Natural History. (1999). Exhibition highlights. *Body art: Marks of identity*. Retrieved from http://www.amnh.org/exhibitions/bodyart/exhibition_highlights.html

Australian Museum. (2009). Shaping. *Body art*. Retrieved from http://amonline.net.au/bodyart/shaping/

Axtell, R. E. (1998). *Gestures: The do's and taboos of body language around the world*. Hoboken, NJ: John Wiley and Sons.

Birdwhistell, R. (1970). *Kinesics and context*. Philadelphia, PA: University of Pennsylvania Press.

Burgoon, J. K., & Bacue, A. E. (2003). Nonverbal communication skills. In J. O. Greene & B. R. Burleson (Eds.), *Handbook of communication and social interaction skills* (pp. 179–220). Mahwah, NJ: Erlbaum.

Burgoon, J. K., Blair, J. P., & Strom, R. E. (2008). Cognitive biases and nonverbal cue availability in detecting deception. *Human Communication Research, 34*(4), 572–599.

Daft, R. L. & Lengel, R. H. (1984). Information richness: A new approach to managerial behavior and organizational design. In: Cummings, L.L. & Staw, B.M. (Eds.), *Research in organizational behavior 6*, (pp. 191–233). Homewood, IL: JAI Press.

Gudykunst, W. B., & Kim, Y. Y. (1997). *Communicating with strangers: An approach to intercultural communication*. New York, NY: McGraw-Hill.

Hall, E. T. (1968). Proxemics. *Current Anthropology, 9*(2,3), 83–108.

Jacobs, B. (2005, June). *Adolescents and self-cutting (self-harm): Information for parents* (Bringing Science to Your Life, Guide I-104). Retrieved from http://aces.nmsu.edu/pubs/_i/I-104.pdf

Knapp, M. L., Hall, J. A., & Horgan, T. G. (2014). *Nonverbal communication in human interaction*. (8th ed.). Boston, MA: Wadsworth, Cengage.

Littlejohn, S. W., & Foss, K. A. (Eds.). (2009). *Encyclopedia of communication theory*. (Vols. 1–2). Thousand Oaks, CA: Sage Publications, Inc. doi: http://dx.doi.org/10.4135/9781412959384

Martin, J. N., & Nakayama, T. K. (2012). *Intercultural communication in contexts* (6th ed.). New York, NY: McGraw-Hill Ryerson.

Mehrabian, A. (1972). *Nonverbal communication*. Chicago, IL: Aldine.

Neuliep, J. W. (2006). *Intercultural communication: A contextual approach* (3rd ed.). Thousand Oaks, CA: Sage.

Pearson, J. C., West, R. L., & Turner, L. H. (1995). *Gender & communication* (3rd ed.). Dubuque, IA: Brown & Benchmark.

Samovar, L. A., Porter, R. E., & McDaniel, E. R. (2012). *Communication between cultures* (8th ed.). Boston, MA: Wadsworth Cengage.

Santilli, V., & Miller, A. N. (2011). The effects of gender and power distance on nonverbal immediacy in symmetrical and asymmetrical power conditions: A cross-cultural study of classrooms and friendships. *Journal of International and Intercultural Communication, 4*(1), 3–22. DOI: 10.1080/17513057.2010.533787

Schurman, A. (n.d.). A brief and rich body piercing history. *Life 123*. Retrieved from http://www.life123.com/beauty/style/piercings/body-piercing-history.shtml

Walther, J. B., & Parks, M. R. (2002). Cues filtered out, cues filtered in: Computer-mediated communication and relationships. In M. C. Knapp & J. A. Daly (Eds.), *Handbook of interpersonal communication* (3rd ed.; pp. 529–563). Thousand Oaks, CA: Sage.

Watzlawick, P., Bavelas, J. B., & Jackson, D. D. (1967). *Pragmatics of human communication*. New York, NY: Norton.

Yuasa, M., Saito, K., & Mukawa, N. (2011). Brain activity when reading sentences and emoticons: An fMRI study of verbal and nonverbal communication. *Electronics and Communication in Japan, 94*(5), 17–24.

Chapter 6

Bodie, G. D., Cyr, K. S., Pence, M., Rold, M., & Honeycutt, J. (2012). Listening competence in initial interactions I: Distinguishing between what listening is and what listeners do. *International Journal of Listening, 26*(1), 1–28.

Burleson, B. R. (2010). Explaining recipient responses to supportive messages: Development and test of a dual-process theory. In S. W. Smith and S R. Wilson (Eds.) *New directions in interpersonal research*. (pp. 159–180). Thousand oaks, CA: Sage. Doi: http://dx.doi.org/10.4135/9781483349619.n8

Dunkel, P., & Pialorsi, F. (2005). *Advanced listening comprehension: Developing aural and notetaking skills*. Boston, MA: Thomson Heinle.

Gearhart, C. C., Denham, J. P., & Bodie, G. D. (2014). Listening as a goal-directed activity. *Western Journal of Communication, 78*(5), 668–684. Doi: 10.1080/10570314.2014.910888

Greenwald, G. (2011, Sept 8). Cheering for state-imposed death. *Salon*. Retrieved from http://www.salon.com/2011/09/08/death_17/

Harris, J. A. (2003). Learning to listen across cultural divides. *Listening Professional, 2*(1), 4–21.

Imhof, M. (2010). The cognitive psychology of listening. In A. S. Wolvin (Ed.), *Listening and human communication in the 21st century* (pp. 97–126). Boston: Blackwell.

International Listening Association (2003). *Listening factoid*. Retrieved from http://www.listen.org/pages/factoids/html

Janusik, L. A., & Wolvin, A. D. (2009). 24 hours in a day: A listening update to the time studies. *International Journal of Listening, 23*, 104–120. Doi: 10.1080/10904010903014442.

Kiewitz, C., Weaver, J. B., Brosius, H. B., & Weimann, G. (1997). Cultural differences in listening style preferences. *International Journal of Public Opinion Research, 9*(3), 233–247.

Mutz, D., Reeves, B., & Wise, K. (2003, May 27). *Exposure to mediated political conflict: Effects of civility of interaction on arousal and memory*. Paper presented at the annual meeting of the International Communication Association, San Diego, CA. Retrieved from http://www.allacademic.com/meta/p111574_index.html

Omdahl, B. L. (1995). *Cognitive appraisal, emotion, and empathy*. Mahwah, NJ: Erlbaum.

O'Shaughnessey, B. (2003). Active attending or a theory of mental action. *Consciousness and the world* (pp. 379–407). Oxford, UK: Oxford University Press.

Salisbury, J. R. & Chen, G. M. (2007). An examination of the relationship between conversational sensitivity and listening styles. *Intercultural Communication Studies, 16*(1) 251–262.

Stiff, J. B., Dillard, J. P., Somera, L., Kim, H., & Sleight, C. (1988). Empathy, communication and prosocial behavior. *Communication Monographs, 55*(2), 198–213.

Titsworth, S. B. (2004). Students' notetaking: The effects of teacher immediacy and clarity. *Communication Education, 53*(4), 305–320.

Watson, K. W., Barker, L. L., & Weaver, J. B., III (1995). The listening styles profile (LSP-16): Development and validation of an instrument to assess four listening styles. *International Journal of Listening, 9*(1), 1–13.

Weger Jr., H., Bell, G. C., Minel, E. M., & Robinson, M. C. (2014). The relative effectiveness of active listening in initial interactions. *International Journal of Listening, 28*(1), 13–31. Doi: 10.1080/10904018.2013.813234

Wolvin, A. D., & Coakley, C. G. (1996). *Listening*. Dubuque, IA: Wm. C. Brown.

Chapter 7

Alsever, J. (2007, March 11). In the computer dating game, room for a coach. *New York Times*. Retrieved from http://www.nytimes.com/2007/03/11/business/yourmoney/11dating.html

Altman, I., & Taylor, D. (1973). *Social penetration: The development of interpersonal relationships*. New York, NY: Holt.

Baxter, L. (1982). Strategies for ending relationships: Two studies. *Western Journal of Speech Communication, 46*(3), 223–241.

Baxter, L. A. (2011). *Voicing relationships: A dialogic perspective*. Thousand Oaks, CA: Sage.

Baxter, L. A., & Braithwaite, D. O. (2009). Relational dialectics theory, applied. In S. W. Smith & S. R. Wilson (Eds.), *New directions in interpersonal communication*. Sage.

Baxter, L. A., & Montgomery, B. M. (1996). *Relating: Dialogues and dialectics*. New York, NY: Guilford.

Baym, N. K. & Ledbetter, A. (2009). Tunes that bind? Predicting friendship strength in music-based social networks. *Information, Community, and Society, 12*(3) 408–427.

Beebe, S. A., Beebe, S. J., & Ivy, D. K. (2013). *Communication: Principles for a lifetime* (5th ed.). Upper Saddle River, NJ: Pearson.

Berger, C. (1987). Communicating under uncertainty. In M. Roloff & G. Miller (Eds.), *Interpersonal processes: New directions in communication research* (pp. 39–62). Newbury Park, CA: Sage.

Bowman, J. M. (2008). Gender role orientation and relational closeness: Self-disclosive behavior in same-sex male friendships. *Journal of Men's Studies, 16*(3), 316–330.

Brooks, M. (2011, February 14). How has Internet dating changed society? An insider's look. *Courtland Brooks.* Retrieved from http://internetdating.typepad.com /courtland_brooks/2011/02/how-has -internet-dating-changed-society.html

Bryner, J. (2011, November 4). You gotta have friends? Most have just 2 true pals. *Live Science.* Retrieved from http://vitals.msnbc .msn.com/_news/2011/11/04/8637894-you -gotta-have-friends-most-have-just-2-true -pals?lite

Burleson, B. R. (2003). Emotional support skills. In J. O. Green & B. R. Burleson (Eds.), *Handbook of communication and social interaction skills* (pp. 551–594). Mahwah, NJ: Erlbaum.

Burleson, B. R., & Goldsmith, D. J. (1998). How the comforting process works: Alleviating emotional distress through conversationally induced reappraisals. In P. A. Andersen & L. K. Guerrero (Eds.), *Handbook of communication and emotion: Research, theory, applications, and contexts* (pp. 248–280). San Diego, CA: Academic Press.

Clark, L.S. (1998). Dating on the net: Teens and the rise of "pure" relationships. In S. Jones (Ed.), *Cybersociety 2.0: Revisiting computer-mediated communication and community* (pp. 159–183). Thousand Oaks, CA: Sage.

Cupach, W. R., & Metts, S. (1986). Accounts of relational disclosure: A comparison of marital and non-marital relationships. *Communication Monographs, 53*(4), 319–321.

Dindia, K. (2003). Definitions and perspectives on relational maintenance communication. In D. J. Canary and M. Dainton (Eds.), *Maintaining relationships through communication.* Mahwah, NJ: Erlbaum.

Dindia, K. (2009). Sex differences in personal relationships. In H. Reis & S. Sprecher, (Eds.), *Encyclopedia of human relationships.* Thousand Oaks, CA: Sage.

Dindia, K., & Canary, D. J. (2006). (Eds.), *Sex differences and similarities in communication* (Second Edition). Mahwah, NJ: Erlbaum.

Duck, S. (1982). A topography of relationship disengagement and dissolution. In S. Duck (Ed.), *Personal relationships 4: Dissolving personal relationships* (pp. 1–30). New York, NY: Academic Press.

Duck, S. (1999). *Relating to others.* Philadelphia, PA: Open University Press.

Duck, S. (2007). *Human relationships* (4th ed.). Thousand Oaks, CA: Sage.

Duck, S. W., & McMahan, D. T. (2012). *The basics of communication: A relational perspective.* Thousand Oaks, CA: Sage.

Gershon, I. (2010). *The Breakup 2.0: Disconnecting over new media.* Ithaca, NY: Cornell University Press.

Giddens, A. (1993). *The transformation of intimacy.* Palo Alto, CA: Stanford University Press.

Gilbert, E., Karahalois, K. & Sandvig, C. (2008). The network in the garden: An empirical analysis of social media in rural life. Paper presented at the Computer Human Interaction Conference. Florence, Italy. Retrieved from http://social.cs .uiuc.edu/papers/pdfs/chi08-rural-gilbert .pdf

Golder, S. A., Wilkinson, D., & Huberman, B. A. (2007). Rhythms of social interactions: Messaging within a massive online network. In C. Steinfield, B. Pentland, M. Ackerman, & N. Contractor (Eds.), *Proceedings of the Third International Conference on Communities and Technologies* (pp. 41–66). London, UK: Springer.

Hatfield, E., & Rapson, R. L. (2006). Passionate love, sexual desire, and mate selection: Cross-cultural and historical perspectives. In P. Noller & J. A. Feeney (Eds.), *Close relationships: Functions, forms and processes* (pp. 227–243). Hove, UK: Psychology Press/Taylor & Francis.

Haythornthwaite, C. (2005). Strong, weak, and latent ties and the impact of new media. *Information Society, 8*(2) 385–401.

King, A. E., Austin-Oden, D., & Lohr, J. M. (2009). Browsing for love in all the wrong places: Does research show that Internet matchmaking is more successful than traditional dating? *Skeptic, 15*(1), 48–55. Retrieved from Infotrac.

Knapp, M. L., & Vangelisti, A. L. (2009). *Interpersonal communication and human relationships* (6th ed.). Upper Saddle River, NJ: Pearson.

Littlejohn, S. W., & Foss, K. A. (2011). *Theories of human communication* (10th ed.). Long Grove, IL: Waveland Press.

Luft, J. (1970). *Of human interaction.* Palo Alto, CA: National Press.

Lustig, M. W., & Koester, J. (2013). *Intercultural competence* (7th ed.). Upper Saddle River, NJ: Pearson.

McKenna, K. Y. A., Green, A. S., & Gleason, M. E. J. (2002). Relationship formation on the Internet: What's the big attraction. *Journal of Social Issues, 58*(1) 9–31.

McPherson, M., Smith-Lovin, L., & Brashears, M. E. (2006). Social isolation in America: Changes in core discussion networks over two decades. *American Sociological Review, 71*(3): 353–375.

Mesch G. & Talmud, I. (2006). The quality of online and offline relationships. *The Information Society, 22*(3), 137–148.

Moore, D. W. (2003, January 3). Family, health most important aspects of life. *Gallup.* Retrieved from http://www.gallup.com /poll/7504/family-health-most-important -aspects-life.aspx

Morman, M. T., & Floyd, K. (1999). Affection communication between fathers and young adult sons: Individual and relational-level correlates. *Communication Studies, 50*(4), 294–309.

Parks, M. R. (2007). *Personal relationships and personal networks.* Mahwah, NJ: Erlbaum.

Patterson, B. R., Bettini, L., & Nussbaum, J. F. (1993). The meaning of friendship across the life-span: Two studies. *Communication Quarterly, 41*(2), 145–160.

Peterson, C. (2006). *A primer in positive psychology.* New York, NY: Oxford.

Petronio, S. (2002). *Boundaries of privacy: Dialectics of disclosure.* Albany, NY: State University of New York Press.

Prager, K. J., & Buhrmester, D. (1998). Intimacy and need fulfillment in couple relationships. *Journal of Social and Personal Relationships, 15*(4), 435–469.

Rainie, L., Lenhart, A., Fox, S., Spooner, T. & Horrigan, J. (2000). Tracking online life: How women use the Internet to cultivate relationships with family and friends. Pew Internet and American Life Project. Retrieved from www.pewinternet.org /Reports/2000/Tracking-Online-Life.aspx

Rawlins, W. K. (1992). *Friendship matters: Communication, dialectics and the life course.* New York, NY: Aldine de Gruyter.

Rusbult, C. E., Olsen, N., Davis, J. L., & Hannon, P. A. (2004). Commitment and relationship maintenance mechanisms. In H. T. Reis & C. E. Rusbult (Eds.), *Key readings on close relationships* (pp. 287–304). Washington, DC: Taylor & Francis.

Sampter, W. (2003). Friendship interaction skills across the lifespan. In J. O. Greene & B. R. Burleson (Eds.), *Handbook of communication and social interaction skills* (pp. 637–684). Mahwah, NJ: Erlbaum.

Saramaki, J., Leicht, E. Al., Lopez, E., Roberts, S. G. B., Reed-Tsochas, R., & Dunbar, R. I. M. (2014). Persistence of social signatures in human communication. *PNAS 2014. 111*(3), 942–947. doi: 10.1073/ pnas.1308540110.

Swain, S. (1989). Covert intimacy in men's friendships: Closeness in men's friendships. In B. J. Risman & P. Schwartz (Eds.), *Gender in intimate relationships: A microstructural approach.* Belmont, CA: Wadsworth.

Taylor, D., & Altman, I. (1987). Communication in interpersonal relationships: Social penetration processes. In M. E. Roloff, & G. R. Miller (Eds.), *Interpersonal processes: New directions in communication research* (pp. 257–277). Newbury Park, CA: Sage.

Ting-Toomey, S. (2005) The matrix of face: An updated face-negotiation theory. In W.B. Gudykunst (Ed.), *Theorizing about intercultural communication* (pp. 71–92). Thousand Oaks, CA: Sage.

Walther, J. B. (1996). Computer-mediated communication: Impersonal, interpersonal, and hyperpersonal interaction. *Communication Research, 23*(1), 3–43.

Walther, J. B., & Parks, M. R. (2002). Cues filtered out, cues filtered in: Computer-mediated communication and relationships. In M. C. Knapp & J. A. Daly (Eds.), *Handbook of interpersonal communication* (3rd ed.; pp. 529–563). Thousand Oaks, CA: Sage.

Ward, C. C., & Tracy, T. J. G. (2004). Relation of shyness with aspects of online relationship involvement. *Journal of Social and Personal Relationships, 21*(5), 611–623.

Chapter 8

Alberti, R. E., & Emmons, M. L. (2008). *Your perfect right: Assertiveness and equality in your life and relationships* (9th ed.). Atascadero, CA: Impact Publishers.

Altman I. (1993). Dialectics, physical environments, and personal relationships. *Communication Monographs, 60*(1), 26–34.

Bilton. N. (2012, February 28). Apple loophole gives developers access to photos. *New York Times.* Retrieved from http://bits.blogs.nytimes.com/2012/02/28/tk-ios-gives-developers-access-to-photos-videos-location/

Brake, T., Walker, D. M., & Walker, T. (1995). *Doing business internationally: The guide to cross-cultural success.* New York, NY: Irwin.

Burleson, B. R. (2003). Emotional support skills. In J. O. Greene & B. R. Burleson (Eds.), *Handbook of communication and social interaction skills* (pp. 551–594). Mahwah, NJ: Erlbaum.

Cissna, K., & Seiberg, E. (1995). Patterns of interactional confirmation and disconfirmation. In M. V. Redmond (Ed.), *Interpersonal communication: Readings in theory and research.* Fort Worth, TX: Harcourt Brace.

Cupach, W. R., & Canary, D. J. (1997). *Competence in interpersonal conflict.* New York, NY: McGraw-Hill.

Dailey, R. M. (2006). Confirmation in parent-adolescent relationship and adolescent openness: Toward extending confirmation theory. *Communication Monographs, 73*(4), 434–458.

Dindia, K. (2000). Sex differences in self-disclosure, reciprocity of self-disclosure, and self-disclosure and liking: Three meta-analyses reviewed. In S. Petronio (Ed.), *Balancing the secrets of private disclosures* (pp. 21–36). Mahwah, NJ: Erlbaum.

Hample. D. (2003). Arguing skill. In J.O. Greene & B. R. Burleson (Eds.) *Handbook of communication and social interaction skills* (pp. 439–479). Mahwah, NJ: Lawrence Erlbaum.

Hendrick, S. S. (1981). Self-disclosure and marital satisfaction. *Journal of Personality and Social Psychology, 40*(6), 1150–1159.

Hess, N. H., & Hagen, E. H. (2006). Psychological adaptations for assessing gossip veracity. *Human Nature, 17*(3), 337–354.

Holt, J. L., & DeVore, C. J. (2005). Culture, gender, organizational role, and styles of conflict resolution: A meta-analysis. *International Journal of Intercultural Relations, 29*(2), 165–196.

Kleinman, S. (2007). *Displacing place: Mobile communication in the twenty-first century.* New York, NY: Peter Lang Publishing.

Petronio, S. (2013). Brief status report on communication privacy management theory. *Journal of Family Communication, 13*(1), 6–14.

Rancer, A. S., & Avtgis, T. A. (2006). *Argumentative and aggressive communication: Theory, research, and application.* Thousand Oaks, CA: Sage.

Roloff, M.E., & Ifert, D.E. (2000). Conflict management through avoidance: Withholding complaints, suppressing arguments, and declaring topics taboo. In S. Petronio (Ed.), *Balancing the secrets of private disclosures* (pp. 151–163). Mahwah, NJ: LEA.

Samovar, L. A., Porter, R. E., & McDaniel, E. R. (Eds.). (2012). *Intercultural communication: A reader* (13th ed.). Belmont, CA: Cengage.

Thomas, K. W. (1976). Conflict and conflict management. In M. D. Dunnette (Ed.). *Handbook of industrial and organizational psychology* (pp. 889–935). Chicago, IL: Rand McNally.

Thomas, K. W. (1992). Conflict and conflict management: Reflections and update. *Journal of Organizational Behavior, 13*(3), 265–274.

Thomas, K. W., & Kilmann, R. H. (1978). Comparison of four instruments measuring conflict behavior. *Psychological Reports, 42,* 1139–1145.

Ting-Toomey, S. (2006). Managing intercultural conflicts effectively. In L. A. Samovar & R. E. Porter (Eds.), *Intercultural communication: A reader* (11th ed.; pp. 366–377). Belmont, CA: Wadsworth.

Ting-Toomey, S., & Chung, L.C. (2012). *Understanding intercultural communication,* (2nd ed). New York: Oxford University Press.

Warren, C. (2011, June 16). 10 people who lost jobs over social media mistakes. *Mashable.* Retrieved from http://mashable.com/2011/06/16/weinergate-social-media-job-loss/

Wilmot, W., & Hocker, J. L. (2010). *Interpersonal conflict* (8th ed.). New York, NY: McGraw-Hill.

Chapter 9

Andres, H. P. (2002) A comparison of face-to-face and virtual software development teams. *Team Performance Management: An International Journal, 8*(1/2), 39–48.

Balgopal, P. R., Ephross, P. H., & Vassil, T. V. (1986). Self-help groups and professional helpers. *Small Group Research, 17*(2), 123–137.

Becker-Beck, U., Wintermantel, M., & Borg, A. (2005). Principles regulating interaction in teams practicing face-to-face communication versus teams practicing computer-mediated communication. *Small Group Research, 36,* 499–536.

Beebe, S. A., & Masterson, J. T. (2014). *Communicating in small groups: Principles and practices* (11th ed.). Uppersaddle River, NJ: Pearson.

Bordia, P., DiFonzo, N., & Chang, A. (1999). Rumor as group problem-solving: Development patterns in informal computer-mediated groups. *Small Group Research, 30*(1), 8–28.

Bradley, B. H., Postlethwaite, B. E., Klotz, A. C., Hamdani, M. R., & Brown, K. G. (2012). Reaping the benefits of task conflict in teams: The critical role of team psychological safety climate. *Journal of Applied Psychology, 97*(1), 151–158. http://dx.doi.org/10.1037/a0024200

Eisenberg, J. (2007). Group cohesiveness. In R. F. Baumeister & K. D. Vohs (Eds.), *Encyclopaedia of social psychology* (pp. 386–388). Thousand Oaks, CA: Sage.

Evans, C., & Dion, K. (1991). Group cohesion and performance: A meta-analysis. *Small Group Research, 22*(2), 175–186.

Gregoire, C. (2012, June 7). The hunger blogs: A secret world of teenage "thinspiration." *Huffington Post.* Retrieved from http://www.huffingtonpost.com/2012/02/08/thinspiration-blogs_n_1264459.html

Henman, L. D. (2003). Groups as systems: A functional perspective. In R. Y. Hirokawa, R. S. Cathcart, L. A. Samovar, & L. D. Henman (Eds.), *Small group communication theory and practice: An anthology* (8th ed., pp. 3–7). Los Angeles, CA: Roxbury.

Huang, W. W., Wei, K.-K., Watson, R. T. & Tan, B. C. Y. (2003). Supporting virtual team-building with a GSS: An empirical investigation. *Decision Support Systems, 34*(4), 359–367.

Janis, I. L. (1982). *Groupthink: Psychological studies of policy decisions and fiascoes.* Boston, MA: Houghton Mifflin.

Jiang, L., Bazarova, N. N., & Hancock, J. T. (2011). The disclosure-intimacy link in computer-mediated communication: An attributional extension of the hyperpersonal model. *Human Communication Research, 37*(1), 58–77.

Johnson, D., & Johnson, F. (2003). *Joining together: Group theory and group skills* (8th ed.). Boston, MA: Allyn & Bacon.

Katz, N., & Koenig, G. (2001). Sports teams as a model for workplace teams: Lessons and liabilities. *Academy of Management Executive, 15*(3), 56–67.

Katzenbach, J. R., & Smith, D. K. (2003). *The wisdom of teams: Creating the high-performance organization.* New York, NY: Harper Business Essentials.

LaFasto, F. M., & Larson, C. E. (2001). *When teams work best: 6,000 team members and leaders tell what it takes to succeed.* Thousand Oaks, CA: Sage.

Levine, J. M. (Ed.). (2013). *Group processes.* New York: Taylor and Francis.

Li, J., & Hambrick, D. C. (2005). Factional groups: A new vantage on demographic faultlines, conflict, and disintegration in work teams. *Academy of Management Journal, 48*(5), 794–813.

Midura, D. W., & Glover, D. R. (2005). *Essentials of team-building.* Champaign, IL: Human Kinetics.

Myers, S., & Anderson, C. A. (2008). *The fundamentals of small group communication.* Thousand Oaks, CA: SAGE.

Nussbaum, M., Singer, M., Rosas, R., Castillo, M., Flies, E., Lara, R., & Sommers, R. (1999). Decisions support system for conflict diagnosis in personnel selection. *Information and Management, 36*(1), 55–62.

Olson, J., & Teasley, S. (1996) Groupware in the wild: Lessons learned from a year of virtual collocation. In *Proceedings of the ACM Conference* (pp. 419–427). Denver, CO: Association for Computing Machinery.

Pascoe, C. J. (2008, January 22). Interview in Growing up online [Television series episode]. In D. Fanning. (Executive producer) *Frontline*. Boston, MA: WGBH. Retrieved from http://www.pbs.org/wgbh/pages/frontline/kidsonline/interviews/pascoe.html

Renz, M. A., & Greg, J. B. (2000). *Effective small group communication in theory and practice*. Boston, MA: Allyn & Bacon.

Sell, J., Lovaglia, M. J., Mannix, E. A., Samuelson, C. D., & Wilson, R. K. (2004). Investigating conflict, power, and status within and among groups. *Small Group Research, 35*(1), 44–72.

Shimanoff, M. (1992). Group interaction and communication rules. In R. Cathcart & L. Samovar (Eds.), *Small group communication: A reader*. Dubuque, IA: William C. Brown.

Timmerman, C. E., & Scott, C. R. (2006). Virtually working: Communicative and structural predictors of media use and key outcomes in virtual work teams. *Communication Monographs, 73*(1), 108–136.

Ting-Toomey, S., & Chung, L.C. (2012). *Understanding intercultural communication*, (2nd Ed.). New York: Oxford University Press.

Tuckman, B. W. (1965). Developmental sequence in small groups. *Psychological Bulletin, 63*(6), 384–399.

Valacich, J. S., George, J. F., Nonamaker, J. F., Jr., & Vogel, D. R. (1994). Idea generation in computer based groups: A new ending to an old story. *Organizational Behavior and Human Decision Processes, 57*(3), 448–467.

Wang, Z., Walther, J. B., & Hancock, J. T. (2009). Social identification and interpersonal communication in computer mediated communication: What you do versus who you are in virtual groups. *Human Communication Research, 35*(1), 59–85.

Warkentin, M. E., Sayeed, L., & Hightower, R. (1997) Virtual teams versus face-to-face teams: An exploratory study of a Web-based conference system. *Decision Sciences 28*(4), 957–996.

White, A. (2009). *From comfort zone to performance management*. Baisy-Thy, Belgium: White and MacLean.

Widmer, W. N., & Williams, J. M. (1991). Predicting cohesion in a coacting sport. *Small Group Research, 22*(4), 548–570.

Wilmot, W. W., & Hocker, J. L. (2007). *Interpersonal conflict*. New York, NY: McGraw-Hill.

Wilson, G. L. (2005). *Groups in context: Leadership and participation in small groups* (7th ed.). New York, NY: McGraw-Hill.

Chapter 10

Bailey, S. (2013, August 8). Just say no: How your meeting habit is harming you. *Forbes*. Retrieved on December 28, 2014 at: http://www.forbes.com/sites/sebastianbailey/2013/08/08/just-say-no-how-your-meeting-habit-is-harming-you/

de Wit, F. R. C., Greer, L. L., & Jehn, K. A. (2012). The paradox of intragroup conflict: A meta-analysis. *Journal of Applied Psychology, 97*(2), 360–390.

Duch, B. J., Groh, S. E., & Allen, D. E. (Eds.). (2001). *The power of problem-based learning*. Sterling, VA: Stylus.

Edens, K. M. (2000). Preparing problem solvers for the 21st century through problem-based learning. *College Teaching, 48*(2), 55–60.

Fairhurst, G. T. (2011). *The power of framing: Creating the language of leadership*. San Francisco, CA: John Wiley & Sons.

Frey, L., & Sunwulf. (2005). The communication perspective on group life. In S. A. Wheelen (Ed.)., *The handbook of group research and practice* (pp. 159–186). Thousand Oaks, CA: Sage.

Gardner, H. (2011). *Leading minds: An anatomy of leadership*. New York, NY: Basic Books.

Jensen, A. D., & Chilberg, J. C. (1991). *Small group communication: Theory and application*. Belmont, CA: Wadsworth.

Levi, D. (2014). *Group dynamics for teams* (4th ed.). Thousand Oaks, CA: Sage.

Levin, B. B. (Ed.). (2001). *Energizing teacher education and professional development with problem-based learning*. Alexandria, MN: Association for Supervision and Curriculum Development.

Martin, R. A., Kuiper, N. A., Olinger, J. L., & Dance, K. A. (1993). Humor, coping with stress, self-concept, and psychological well-being. *International Journal of Humor Research, 6*(1), 89–104.

Newman, H. (2007). "World of Warcraft" players: Let's slay together. *Detroit Free Press*. Retrieved from InfoTrac.

Northouse, P. G. (2013). *Leadership: Theory and practice* (6th ed.). Thousand Oaks, CA: Sage.

Seely Brown, J., & Hagel, J. (2009). How "World of War-craft" promotes innovation. *Businessweek Online*. Retrieved from Infotrac.

Snyder, B. (2004). Differing views cultivate better decisions. *Stanford Business*. Retrieved from http://www.gsb.stanford.edu/NEWS/bmag/sbsm0405/feature_workteams_gruenfeld.shtml

Weiten, W., Dunn, D. S., & Hammer, E. Y. (2011). *Psychology applied to modern life: Adjustment in the 21st century*. Boston, MA: Cengage Learning.

Williams, C. (2013). *Management* (7th ed.). Mason, OH: South-Western/Cengage Learning.

Young, K. S., Wood, J. T., Phillips, G. M., & Pedersen, D. J. (2007). *Group discussion: A practical guide to participation and leadership* (4th ed.). Long Grove, IL: Waveland Press.

Chapter 11

Berger, C. R., & Calabrese, R. J. (1975). Some exploration in initial interaction and beyond: Toward a developmental theory of communication. *Human Communication Research, 1*(2), 99–112.

Bitzer, L. F. (1968). The rhetorical situation. *Philosophy and Rhetoric, 1*(1), 1–14.

Callison, D. (2001). Concept mapping. *School Library Media Activities Monthly, 17*(10) 30–32.

Cohen, N. (2011, May 23) Wikipedia. *The New York Times*. Retrieved from http://topics.nytimes.com/top/news/business/companies/wikipedia/index.html

Durst, G. M. (1989, March 1). The manager as a developer. *Vital Speeches of the Day* (pp. 309–314).

Frances, P. (1994). Lies, damned lies . . . *American Demographics, 16*, 2.

Helm, B. (2005, December 14). Wikipedia: "A work in progress." *Business Week*. Retrieved from http: //www.businessweek.com/technology/content/dec2005/tc20051214_441708.htm?chan=db

Kirkpatrick, M. (2011, November 2). Wikipedia is a mess, wikipedians say: 1 in 20 articles bare of references. *ReadWriteWeb*. Retrieved from http://www.readwriteweb.com/archives/wikipedia_is_a_mess_wikipedians_say_1_in_20_articl.php

Knobloch, L. K., & McAninch, K. G. (2014). 13 Uncertainty management. In C. A. Berger (Ed.). *Interpersonal communication*, (pp. 297–319). Boston, MA: Walter de Gruyter.

Manguard, S. (2011, October 31). The monster under the rug. *The Signpost*. Retrieved from http://en.wikipedia.org/wiki/Wikipedia:Wikipedia_Signpost/2011-10-31/Opinion_essay

Nelson J. C. (2006). *Leadership*. Utah School Boards Association 83rd Annual Conference, Salt Lake City, Utah. Retrieved from http://www.ama-assn.org/ama/pub/category/15860.html

Chapter 12

Cossolotto, M. (2009, December). An urgent call to action for study abroad alumni to help reduce our global awareness deficit. *Vital Speeches*, pp. 564–568.

Fisher, W. (1987). *Human communication as narration: Toward a philosophy of reason, value, and action*. Columbia, SC: University of South Carolina Press.

Humes, J. C. (1988). *Standing ovation: How to be an effective speaker and communicator*. New York, NY: Harper and Row.

Jobs, S. (2005, June 15). You've got to find what you love. *Stanford University News*. Retrieved from http://news.stanford.edu/news/2005/june15/jobs-061505.html

Mackay, H. (July 2009). Changing the world: Your future is a work in progress. *Vital Speeches of the Day* (pp. 319–323).

Osteen, J. (2012). Best jokes of Joel Osteen. *Better Days TV*. Retrieved from http://www.betterdaystv.net/play.php?vid=247

Chapter 13

Booher, D. D. (2003). *Speak with confidence [electronic resources]: Powerful presentations that inform, inspire, and persuade*. New York, NY: McGraw-Hill.

Campbell, S. (2015). Presentation anxiety analysis: Comparing face-to-face presentations and webinars. *Journal of Case Studies in Education, 7*, 1–13.

Garcia-Retamero, R., & Cokely, E. T. (2013). Communicating health risks with visual aids. *Current Directions in Psychological Science, 22*(5), 392–399. Doi: 10.1177/0963721413491570

Guzman, M. (2009, April 16). A Seattle geek fest spreads its wings. *Seattle PI*. Retrieved from http://www.seattlepi.com/business/405192_IGNITE16.html

Hanke, J. (1998). The psychology of presentation visuals. *Presentations, 12*(5), 42–47.

Ignite Seattle. (n.d.). Retrieved from http://www.igniteseattle.com/

Ignite Seattle 7 is happening on 8/3. (2009). *Ignite*. Retrieved from http://ignite.oreilly.com/2009/07/ignite-seattle-7-is-happening-on-83.html

"What Is Ignite?" (n.d.). Ignite. Retrieved from http://igniteshow.com/howto

Chapter 14

Feldman, M. (2011, Sept 21). Report: Economists shut out of debt-ceiling debate. Media Matters. Retrieved from http://mediamatters.org/research/2011/09/21/report-economists-shut-out-of-debt-ceiling-deba/181620

Lanier, J. (2006). Digital Maoism: The hazards of the new online collectivism. *Edge The Third Culture*. Retrieved at: http://www.edge.org/3rd_culture/lanier06/lanier06_index.html

Lehman, C. M., & DuFrene, D. D. (2010). *Professional communications*. Cengage.

O'Connor, J. V. (2000). *FAQs #1*. Retrieved from http://www.cusscontrol.com/faqs.html

Rader, W. (2007). The online slang dictionary. Retrieved from http://www.ocf.berkeley.edu/~wrader/slang/b.html

Richards, I. A., & Ogden, C. K. (1923). *The meaning of meaning: A study of the influence of language upon thought and the science of symbolism*. Orlando, FL: Harcourt.

Rogers, L. (2013). *Visual supports for visual thinkers: Practical ideas for students with autism spectrum disorders and other special education needs*. London: Jessica Kingsley Publishers.

Saeid, J. I. (2003). *Semantics* (2nd ed.). Malden, MA: Blackwell Publishing Ltd.

Stewart, L. P., Cooper, P. J., Stewart, A. D., & Friedley, S. A. (2003). *Communication and gender* (3rd ed.). Boston, MA: Allyn & Bacon.

Treinen, K. P., & Warren, J. T. (2001). Antiracist pedagogy in the basic course: Teaching cultural communication as if whiteness matters. *Basic Communication Course Annual 13*, 46–75.

Witt, P., Wheeless, L., & Allen, M. (2004). A meta-analytical review of the relationship between teacher immediacy and student learning. *Communication Monographs, 71*(2), 184–207.

Chapter 15

Anderson, C. (2013). How to give a killer presentation. *Harvard Business Review, 91*(6), 121–125.

Ayres, J., & Hopf, T. S. (1990). The long-term effect of visualization in the classroom: A brief research report. *Communication Education, 39*(1), 75–78.

Ayres, J., Hopf, T. S., & Ayres, D. M. (1994). An examination of whether imaging ability enhances the effectiveness of an intervention designed to reduce speech anxiety. *Communication Education, 43*(3), 252–258.

Barron, J. (2011, August 26). With Hurricane Irene near, 370,000 in New York City get evacuation order. *New York Times*. Retrieved from http://www.nytimes.com/2011/08/27/nyregion/new-york-city-begins-evacuations-before-hurricane.html

Bates, B. (1992). *Communication and the sexes*. Prospect Heights, IL: Waveland Press.

Beatty, M. J., & Behnke, R. R. (1991). Effects of public speaking trait anxiety and intensity of speaking task on heart rate during performance. *Human Communication Research, 18*(2), 147–176.

Behnke, R. R., & Carlile, L. W. (1971). Heart rate as an index of speech anxiety. *Speech Monographs, 38*(1), 66.

Decker, B. (1992). *You've got to be believed to be heard*. New York, NY: St. Martin's Press.

Gardner, W. L. (2003). Perceptions of leader charisma, effectiveness, and integrity: Effects of exemplification, delivery, and ethical reputation. *Management Communication Quarterly, 16*(4), 502–527.

Hammer, D. P. (2000). Professional attitudes and behaviors: The "A's" and "B's" of professionalism. *American Journal of Pharmaceutical Education, 64*(4), 455–464.

Howlett, N., Pine, K. J., Cahill, N., Orakçıoğlu, İ., & Fletcher, B. C. (2015). Unbuttoned: The interaction between provocativeness of female work attire and occupational status. *Sex Roles, 72*(3–4), 105–116.

Kelly, L., Duran, R. L., & Stewart, J. (1990). Rhetoritherapy revisited: A test of its effectiveness as a treatment for communication problems. *Communication Education, 39*(3), 207–226.

Kelly, L., Phillips, G. M., & Keaten, J. A. (1995). *Teaching people to speak well: Training and remediation of communication reticence*. Cresskill, NJ: Hampton.

Levine, T., Asada, K. J. K., & Park, H. S. (2006). The lying chicken and the gaze avoidant egg: Eye contact, deception, and causal order. *Southern Communication Journal, 71*(4), 401–411.

Morgan, N. (2013, December 5). How to avoid disaster – Six rules for what to wear when giving a speech. *Forbes*. Retrieved from: http://www.forbes.com/sites/nickmorgan/2013/12/05/how-to-avoid-disaster-six-rules-for-what-to-wear-when-giving-a-speech/

Motley, M. (1997). COM therapy. In J. A. Daly, J. C. McCroskey, J. Ayres, T. Hopf, & D. M. Ayres (Eds.) *Avoiding communication: Shyness reticence, and communication apprehension* (2nd ed.). Cresskill, NJ: Hampton Press.

Phillips, G. M. (1977). Rhetoritherapy versus the medical model: Dealing with reticence. *Communication Education, 26*(1), 34–43.

Richmond, V. P., & McCroskey, J. C. (2000). *Communication: Apprehension, avoidance, and effectiveness* (5th ed.). Scottsdale, AZ: Gorsuch Scarisbrick.

Scott, P. (1997, January–February). Mind of a champion. *Natural Health, 27*, 99.

Sellnow, D. D., & Treinen, K. P. (2004). The role of gender in perceived speaker competence: An analysis of student peer critiques. *Communication Education, 53*(3), 286–296.

Towler, A. J. (2003). Effects of charismatic influence training on attitudes, behavior, and performance. *Personnel Psychology, 56*(2), 363–381.

Chapter 16

Baerwald, D. (n.d.). Narrative. Retrieved from North-shore School District Web site: http://ccweb.nor-shore.wednet.edu/writingcorner/narrative.html.

Goldberg, B. (2011, March 14). No liberal bias at NPR—just ask NPR. [Blog post] Retrieved from http://www.bernardgoldberg.com/no-liberal-bias-at-npr-just-ask-npr/

Michalko, M. (1998). A theory about genius. *The World and I, 13*(7), 292.

Moyers, B., & Winship M. (2011, March 25). What the right means when it calls NPR "liberal." *Salon*. Retrieved from http://www.salon.com/2011/03/25/moyers_winship_npr/

Ötzi, the ice man. (n.d.). *Dig: The archaeology magazine for kids*. Retrieved from http://www.digonsite.com/drdig/mummy/22.html.

Pew Research Center for the People & The Press. (2011, September 22). Press widely criticized, but trusted more than other information sources. [Press Release] Retrieved from http://www.people-press.org/2011/09/22/press-widely-criticized-but-trusted-more-than-other-institutions/

Chapter 17

Carter, B. (2008, October 31). Infomercial for Obama is big success in ratings. *New York Times*, p. A19.

Kennedy, G. A. (1999). *Classical rhetoric and its Christian and secular tradition from ancient to modern times* (2nd ed). Chapel Hill, NC: University of North Carolina Press.

Megan's Law. (n.d.). *Parents for Megan's Law*. Retrieved from http://www.parentsformmeganslaw.com/html/questions.lasso

Nabi, R. L. (2002). Discrete emotions and persuasion. In James P. Dillard and Michael Pfau (Eds.), *The persuasion handbook: Developments in theory and practice*. (pp. 291–299). Thousand Oaks, CA: Sage.

Perloff, R. M. (2010). *The dynamics of persuasion: Communication and attitudes in the 21st century* (4th ed.). New York, NY: Taylor & Francis.

Petri, H. L., & Govern, J. M. (2012). *Motivation: Theory, research, and application* (6th ed.). Belmont, CA: Wadsworth.

Petty, R. E., & Cacioppo, J. (1996). *Attitudes and persuasion: Classic and contemporary approaches*. Boulder, CO: Westview.

Sellnow, D., & Treinen, K. (2004). The role of gender and physical attractiveness in perceived speaker competence: An analysis of student peer critiques. *Communication Education, 53*(3) 286–296.

Solmsen, F. (Ed.). (1954). *The rhetoric and the poetics of Aristotle*. New York, NY: The Modern Library.

Timothy D. Naegele & Associates announces class action lawsuit against Guthy-Renker. (2002, June 26). *All Business*. Retrieved from http://www.allbusiness.com/crime-law/criminal-offenses-cybercrime/5968871-1.html

Toulmin, S. (1958). *The uses of argument.* Cambridge, UK: Cambridge University Press.

Van Eemeren, F. H., Garssen, B., Krabbe, E. C. W., Henkemans, A. F. S., Verheij, B., & Wagemans, J. H. M. (2014). *Handbook of argumentation theory.* New York: Springer.

Appendix

Beshara, T. (2006). *The job search solution.* New York, NY: AMACOM.

Betty, K. (2010, July 1). The math behind the networking claim. Retrieved from http://blog.jobfully.com/2010/07/the-math-behind-the-networking-claim/

Boyd, A. (1999). *How to handle media interviews.* London, UK: Mercury.

Employee Tenure in 2010. (2012, September 14). Bureau of labor statistics economic news release. U.S. Department of Labor, Washington, DC. Retrieved from http://www.bls.gov/news.release/tenure.nr0.htm

Farr, J. M. (2009). *Top 100 careers without a four-year degree: Your complete guidebook to major jobs in many fields.* Indianapolis, IN: JIST.

Graber, S. (2000). *The everything get-a-job book: From résumé writing to interviewing to finding tons of job openings.* Avon, MA: Adams Media.

Kaplan, R. M. (2002). *How to say it in your job search: Choice words, phrases, sentences and paragraphs for résumés, cover letters and interviews.* Paramus, NJ: Prentice-Hall.

Krotz, J. (2006). *6 tips for taking control in media interviews.* Retrieved from http://www.microsoft.com/smallbusiness/resources/management/leadership-training/6-tips-for-taking-control-in-media-interviews.aspx

Light, J. (2011, April, 4). For job seekers, company sites beat online job boards, social media. *Wall Street Journal.* Retrieved from http://online.wsj.com/article/SB10001424052748703806304576236731318345282.html

Ryan, R. (2000). *60 seconds & you're hired.* New York, NY: Penguin Books.

Slayter, M. E. (2006, January 14). Rehearse, rehearse, repeat: Have a rock-solid plan when preparing for an interview. *The Forum,* p. E3.

Taylor, J., & Hardy D. (2004). *Monster careers: How to land the job of your life.* New York, NY: Penguin Books.

Tengler, C. D., & Jablin, F. M. (1983). Effects of question type, orientation, and sequencing in the employment screening interview. *Communication Monographs, 50*(3), 261.

Yena, D. J. (2011). *Career directions: The path to your ideal career.* New York, NY: McGraw-Hill.

INDEX

Key terms are **boldface**. *Italicized* page numbers indicate material in figures, graphs, or tables.

A

abbreviations, 195
ableism, 28
abstract, 148
accent, 204–205
accommodating (lose–win), interpersonal conflict, 105
accountability, 116
accurate sources, 149
acoustic space, 62
acquaintances, 80–82
  guidelines, 81–82
acronyms, 6–7
action, 165
action-oriented listeners, 70
active listening, 71
  attending, 72
  evaluating, 74–76
  remembering, 74
  responding, 76
  understanding, 72–73
actual objects, 178
ad hominem, 252
adaptation phase, 202
adaptors, 58
adjourning, 118
Adobe Acrobat, 177
advertisements, 6, 253
Africa, 35
African Americans, 11, 59
age, 5, 48
age/generation, 34
ageism, 28
agenda, 126, 128
  for Internet course committee, *127*
aggressive communication style, 103
aids
  audio, 176, 179–181
  audiovisual, 176, 181
  presentational (*see* presentational aids)
  sensory, 181–182
  visual, 176, 178–179, *183*
alliteration, 197
alternative solutions, 106, 131
Altman, Irwin, 86
altruism, 41
Amazon.com, 192
ambiguity
  strategic, 102
  tolerating, 40

American Express, 252
American Indians, 36
American Psychological Association (APA), 168, *169*
analogy, 196
analyzers, 123
anecdotes, 152
anger, 254–255
animated delivery, 204
annotated bibliography, 152–153
anorexia nervosa, 115
Anthony, Katie, 170
anticipation phase, 202
antithesis, 197
antonym, 230
anxiety, 39
APA. *See* American Psychological Association
apathetic, 248
appeal to action, 167
appearance, physical, 26, 63–64, 205–206
Apple, 99
Arabic, 45
arguing from analogy, 250
arguing from causation, 250
arguing from example, 250
arguing from sign, 249
argument, 245
argumentation, 36
Aristotle, 209, 245
Armstrong, Neil, 197
articles, 147
articulation, 204
assertive communication style, 104
assertiveness, 36, 38
assonance, 197
assumed similarity, 26
asynchronous channels, 7
attending, 72
attention
  and selection, 16–17
attitude, 28, 30, 35, 39
attributions, 25
  dispositional, 25
  situational, 25
audience(s), 5
  analysis, 139–141
  tailoring propositions to, 247–248
  unexpected reactions, 215
audience adaptation, 139, 185

audience analysis, 139–141
  questions, *140, 141*
audience-based communication apprehension, 13
audience contact, 207
audience diversity, 141
audio aids, 176, 179–181. *See also* presentational aids
audiovisual aids, 176, 181. *See also* presentational aids
Australia, 35, 45
Austria, 37
authority, 149
authority positions, 38
automatic processing, 18
autonomy, 92
average group opinion method, 131
avoidance, uncertainty, 37
avoiding (lose–lose), interpersonal conflict, 105
avoiding stage, 89

B

Baby Boomers, 34
Bach, J. S., 228
back-up aids, 184
backgrounds
  lower-class, 34
  middle-class, 34
bar graph, 179, *181*
Bartlett's Familiar Quotations, 148
Basinger, Kim, 201
Belgium, 37
beliefs, 5, 11, 28, 30, 32, 35
bias, media, 234
bibliographic style, 168
Big Bang Theory, 110
biographies, 147
"blind" pane, 87
body art, 63
body movement, 59–60
body of speech, 156–163
  outlining, 161
body orientation, 59
body painting, 63
books, 147
Bosnia, 45
Bosnian, 45
The Brady Bunch, 109

brainstorming, 131, 143
breadth
    information shared, 86
    topic, 227
bright side messages, 12, *12*
bullying, 20
    cyberbullying, 20
Bureau of Labor Statistics, 149
Bush, George H. W., 71
BusinessWeek, 133

C

CA. *See* communication apprehension
Cacioppo, John, 245
Canada, 35, 38, 45
canned plan, 3, 11
Cantonese, 45
Carnegie, Dale, 75
CD/DVD players, 184
Central America, 35, 60
central route, 246
"chalk talks," 184
chalkboards, 183–184
channel(s), 6–7
    asynchronous, 7
    mediated, 26
    synchronous, 7
    technology-mediated, 7
chart, 178–179
chart, 178
China, 21, 39, 59
Chinese, 45
Christie, Chris, 210
chronemics, 36
chronemics (use of time), 62–63
chronological order, 160
Cicero, 209
circumscribing stage, 89
citation, 153–154, *169*
claim, 248
clincher, 167
Clinton, Bill, 71
Clooney, George, 228
closedness, 92
co-cultural and cultural considerations, 104
co-culture, 32
co-ownership, information, 100
code switch, 32
cognitive restructuring, 203, *203*
cognitive symptoms, public speaking
    apprehension, 201
cohesiveness, 115
collaborating (win–win), managing
    interpersonal conflict, 106
collaboration guidelines, 106
"collective intelligence," 192
collectivist cultures, 21, 35–36
color use, presentational aids, 183
comforting, 96
    guidelines, 97–98

committment, 125
common experiences, 191
common ground, 191
communication, 3
    barriers to effective intercultural,
        39–40
    characteristics of, 8–11
    and culture, 30–31
    effective, 13
    and ethics, 11–12
    face-to-face, 5, 6–7
    group, 108–120
    improvements plans, 14, *14*
    intercultural, 30
    interpersonal, 5
    intrapersonal, 5
    mass, 5–6
    messages vary in conscious thought, 11
    model of, 8
    nature of, 3–5
    and perception of others, 28
    process, 6–8
    public, 5, 6
    purpose, 9
    and self-perception, 23–25
    small-group, 5
    strategies, competent, 39–40
    unethical, 12
communication apprehension (CA),
    13–14
    codes, incompatible, 40
    improvement plan, sample, *14*
communication climate, 96
communication competence,
    13–14
    developing intercultural, 39–41
communication context, 4
communication orientation, 202
communication perspectives, 3–14
communication process, 6–8
    model of, 8
communication setting, 5–6
comparative advantages pattern,
    256
comparison and contrast, 230
comparisons, 152
compassion, 255
competent, 19
competing (win–lose), interpersonal
    conflict, 105–106
competition, 35
competitiveness, 38
complementary feedback, 11
comprehensive report, 132
compromising (partial lose–lose),
    interpersonal conflict, 106
computer conferences, *113*
computers, 184
concept mapping, 143–144
    endangered birds, *144*
concept, self-. *See* self-concept

conclusion, 166–168
concrete language, 48
conference calls, 8
confirming communication
    messages, 96
conflict
    culture and, 120
    interpersonal, 104–106
    management, 83
    and shared leadership, 125
    and virtual group, 120
confrontation phase, 202
Congressional Record, 149
connection, 92
connotation, 47
conscious processing, 18
consensual families, 109
consensus method, 132
consistency, forced, 27
constructed messages, 11
constructive criticism, 76, 101–102
content, critiquing, 77, *78*
content-oriented listeners, 70
content paraphrase, 72–73
context, 4–5, 36
    nonverbal message, 65
context-based communication
    apprehension, 13–14
continuum of communication
    channels, *8*
contrasts, 152
control, 110
conversational style, 203
cooperation, 35
creative information, 227–228
credentials, 146
credibility, 13, 166, 191, 253–254
criteria, 130
criteria satisfaction pattern, 256
critiquing, guidelines for, 77
Croatia, 45
Croatian, 45
cues
    nonverbal, 7
cultural and co-cultural
    considerations, 104
    influences on intimacy, 84–85
cultural context, 5
cultural diversity, 193
cultural groups, 5
cultural identity, 32
cultural norms, 20–21
culture(s), 11, 30, 31–35
    co-culture, 32
    collectivist, 21, 35
    and communication, 30–31
    and conflict, 120
    dominant, 31
    feminine, 38
    high-context, 36
    high power-distance, 37

high uncertainty-avoidance, 37
how they differ, 35–39
individualist, 21
individualistic, 35–36
long-term oriented, 39
low-context, 36
low power-distance, 37
low uncertainty-avoidance, 37
masculine, 38
monochronic, 36
polychronic, 36
short-term oriented, 38–39
culture-centered skills, 41
culture shock, 31
currency, 149
cyberbullying, 20, 103

D

Damon, Matt, 228
dark side messages, 12
  understanding, *12*
data-gathering methods, 140
Dating-Profile.com, 84
decision making, 131
decoding, 3, 6
deductive reasoning, 249
definition, 230
deliverables, 132
delivery, 203
  adapting while speaking,
    214–215
  analysis of, 215–216
  critiquing, 77, *78*
  methods, 208–211
  rehearsing and refining,
    211–214
  style, effective, 203–204
  use of body, 205–208
  use of voice, 204–205
demographic data, 140
demographics, 139
demonstration, 231
Denmark, 37
denotation, 47
depth
  information shared, 86
  topic, 227
derived credibility, 253
describing feelings, 100–101
description, 229–230
descriptive details, 48
desires and expectations, expressing,
    103–104
details, 195
  descriptive, 48
Dewey, John, 129
diagram, 178, *179*
dialectic, 92
dialect(s), 45
  in interpersonal relationship, 92–93

managing dialectical tensions, 93
dictionary, 47
difference or similarity, assumed, 39
digital media, 185
Digital Natives, 34
direct question, 164
direct strategy, privacy, 102–103
direct verbal style, 52
disability, 35
disclosure, 85–87
  effects on relationships, 99–100
  guidelines, 100–102
  intimacy and, 99–100
  managing, 98–103
  self-, 98, 100
**disconfirming communication
    messages,** 96
discrimination, 27
disengagement, 106
dispositional attribution, 25
distracting, nonverbal messages, 65
document camera, 184
dominant culture, 31–32
Douglass, Frederick, 235
drawings, 178
Drescher, Fran, 61
dual processing, 18
Duck, Steve, 87
DVD/CD players, 184

E

e-communication, 4
E-Cyrano.com, 84
e-mail, 4, 10, 26, 91, 113, 115, 126
ease, social, 13
East Asia, 41
"easy dark side" messages, 12, *12*
eating disorders, 115
EBSCO, 147
Edison, Thomas, 228
egocentricity, 41
either/or fallacy, 251
elaboration likelihood model
    (ELM), 245
elaborations, 152
Eliot, T. S., 228
ELM. *See* elaboration likelihood
    model
Elmo, 184
emblems, 58
emoticons, 6, 7, 56, 254
emotional support, 76, 83
  providing, 96–98
emotional symptoms, public speaking
    apprehension, 201
emotions, nonverbal communication
    and, 57
empathic responsiveness, 73
empathy, 73
  intercultural, 41

encoding, 3, 6
encyclopedias, 147
English, 45
Estée Lauder, 252
esteem. *See* self-esteem
ethical goals, healthy groups,
    114–115
ethical principles, 11–12
ethical use, audience data, 141
ethics, 11
  and communication, 11–12
ethnicity, 5, 33
ethnocentrism, 28, 39
ethos, 245
  rhetorical appeals to, 252–254
Europe, 35, 36, 60
evaluating, 74–76
examples, 151, 195
executive summary, 132
exigence, 138
expectations, 17
  and perception, *18*
expediters, 124
expert, 152
expert opinion method, 131
expert opinions, 151
expository speeches, 231–235, *233,*
    235
expressed struggle, 104–105
extemporaneous speeches,
    208–209
external noise, 7–8
eye contact (oculesics), 58–59,
    206–207

F

face, 97. *See also* saving face
face-to-face communication, 5, 6–7,
    88, 113
  and nonverbal messages, 56, 64
face-to-face groups, 113
Facebook, 24, 26, 34, 59, 82, 83, 91,
    113, 115, 181, 226
facial expression, 59, 207
"fact-checkers," 149
facts, 75
factual statements, 151
fair, 12
fallacies, 251
false cause, 251
familiar language, 48
familiar terms, 195
family, 19, 20, 109
  consensual, 109
  laissez-faire, 109
  pluralistic, 109
  protective, 109
Father Knows Best, 109
fear, 254
Federal Register, 148

CHAPTER REVIEW
Communication Perspectives

To help you succeed, we have designed a review card for each chapter.

KEY CONCEPTS

1-1
Describe the nature of communication. To transmit messages, we rely on personal experiences and those we have seen and heard about to create a ca... pull scripts th... others. How e... largely depen... context and s...

In this column, you'll find summary points that give an overview of important concepts.

1-2
Explain the communication process. The communication process is a set of three sub-processes (message production, message interpretation, and interaction coordination) intended to result in shared meaning. These sub-processes are affected by channel choice, whether using face-to-face communication or a method that has a technologically mediated form of communication (MC or CMC). They are also affected by interference or noise, which can be external, internal, and semantic.

Intrapersonal Communication | Interpersonal Communication

Small-Group Communication | Public Communication

THE HUFFINGTON POST

Mass Communication

ASYNCHRONOUS					SYNCHRONOUS
Bulk letters	Posted letters	Facebook	Interactive chat	Telephone	Skype
Posters	E-mail	Twitter			iChat
E-mail spam	Text messages	Other social media websites			Other video conferencing
LEAN					
LOW SOCIAL PRESENCE					HIGH SOCIAL PR

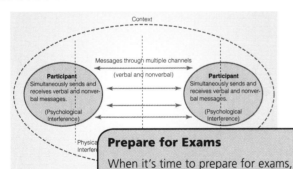

1-3
Identify the characterist... ...tion is guided by at least eight principles. First, communication has purpose. Second, communication is continuous. Third, communication is irreversible. Fourth, communication is situated. Fifth, communication is indexical and reflects the levels of trust, control, and intimacy in a relationship. Sixth, communication is learned.

KEY TERMS

1-1
communication the process through which we express, interpret, and coordinate messages with others

messages the verbal utterances, visual images, and nonverbal behaviors used to convey thoughts and feelings

encoding the process of putting our thoughts and feelings into words and nonverbal behaviors

decoding ... message

feedback ...

canned pl... us draws fro... worked for us... used numerous times in similar situations

script an actual text of what to say and do in a specific situation

communication context the physical, social, historical, psychological, and cultural situations that surround a communication event

physical context the location of a...

Here, you'll find the key terms and definitions in the order they appear in the chapter.

How to Use This Card:
1. Look over the card to preview the new concepts you'll be introduced to in the chapter.
2. Read your chapter to fully understand the material.
3. Go to class (and pay attention).
4. Review the card one more time to make sure you've registered the key concepts. Take the chapter self quiz to test your comprehension.
5. Don't forget, this card is only one of many COMM learning tools available to help you succeed in your communication class.

...characterized by the number of participants and the extent to which the interaction is formal or informal

intrapersonal communication the interactions that occur in our minds when we are talking to ourselves

interpersonal communication informal interaction between two people who have an identifiable relationship with each other

small-group communication three to 20 people who come together for the specific purpose of solving a problem or arriving at a decision

public communication one participant, the speaker, delivers a message to a group of more than 20 people

Prepare for Exams
When it's time to prepare for exams, use the card and the technique to the right to ensure successful study sessions.

WWW.CENGAGEBRAIN.COM

CHAPTER REVIEW 1

mass communication communication that is delivered by individuals and entities through mass media to large segments of the population at the same time

1-2

communication process a complex set of three different and interrelated activities intended to result in shared meaning

message production the steps you take when you encode a message

message interpretation the steps you take when you decode a message

interaction coordination the behavioral adjustments each participant makes in an attempt to create shared meaning

channel the route traveled by the message and the means of transportation

emoticons textual images that symbolize the sender's mood, emotion, or facial expressions

acronyms abbreviations that stand in for common phrases

media richness the amount and kinds of media transmitted via a particular channel

synchronicity the extent to which a channel allows for immediate feedback

interference (noise) any stimulus that interferes with the process of sharing meaning

physical noise any external sight or sound that detracts from a message

psychological noise thoughts and feelings we experience that compete with a sender's message for our attention

1-3

index a measure of the emotional temperature of our relationship at the time

trust the extent to which partners rely on, depend on, and have faith that their partners will not intentionally do anything to harm them

control the degree to which one participant in the communication encounter is perceived to be more dominant or powerful

complementary feedback a message that signals agreement about who is in control

symmetrical feedback a message that signals disagreement about who is in control

intimacy the degree of emotional closeness, acceptance, and disclosure in a relationship

spontaneous expressions messages spoken without much conscious thought

constructed messages messages that are formed carefully and thoughtfully when our known scripts are inadequate for the situation

culture a system of shared beliefs, values, symbols, and behaviors

1-4

ethics a set of moral principles that may be held by a society, a group, or an individual

bright side messages messages that are both ethical and appropriate

dark side messages messages that are not ethical and/or appropriate

---

Seventh, communication messages vary in conscious thought, meaning they may be spontaneous, scripted, or constructed. And eighth, communication is guided by cultural norms.

1-4
Assess messages using the principles of ethical communication.

Ethical standards do not tell us exactly what to do in any given situation, but they offer general principles that guide our behavior. There are five ethical principles to guide general communication: (1) be truthful and honest, (2) act with integrity, (3) behave fairly, (4) demonstrate respect, and (5) communicate responsibly. One way to evaluate and create ethical messages is to consider them on the bright side/dark side matrix.

1-5
Develop a personal communication improvement plan.

Competence in communication is achieved by a desire to improve (motivation), demonstrating knowledge, and practicing skills. Others also judge competence based on a person's credibility and social ease. Communication apprehension (CA) is detrimental to social ease, and can be classified into four types: traitlike CA, audience-based CA, situational CA, and context-based CA. There are four steps to create a communication improvement plan, which will manage CA to give the appearance of social ease: (1) identify the problem, (2) state the specific goal, (3) outline a specific procedure for reaching the goals, and (4) devise a method for measuring progress.

JOURNAL ASSIGNMENTS

> Every chapter has journaling activities for you to explore various aspects of communication.

A. FEEDBACK IN INTERPERSONAL COMMUNICATION

Keep a one-day log of all the feedback (verbal and nonverbal) you receive from others while you are communicating. Ask someone who knows you well to indicate the types of feedback you typically give them while they communicate with you. Analyze the similarities and differences in the feedback you give and receive.

B. COMPETENT COMMUNICATION

Identify an area of your life in which you feel, and others would agree, that you demonstrate communication competence. How are you personally motivated, personally knowledgeable, and what skills do you demonstrate in this area? Now identify an area in your life in which you feel you do not demonstrate communication competence. Are any of your skills, knowledge, and motivation from the first area transferable to this second area? What can you learn from your positive experience in the first area that could help you set goals for improvement in the second area?

1-5

communication competence the impression that communicative behavior is both appropriate and effective in a given situation

credibility a perception of a speaker's knowledge, trustworthiness, and warmth

social ease communicating without appearing to be anxious or nervous

communication apprehension the fear or anxiety associated with real or anticipated communication with others

KEY CONCEPTS

1-1
Describe the nature of communication. To transmit messages, we rely on personal experiences and those we have seen and heard about to create a canned plan, from which we pull scripts that guide our interactions with others. How each interaction proceeds is largely dependent on its communication context and setting.

1-2
Explain the communication process. The communication process is a set of three sub-processes (message production, message interpretation, and interaction coordination) intended to result in shared meaning. These sub-processes are affected by channel choice, whether using face-to-face communication or a method that has a technologically mediated form of communication (MC or CMC). They are also affected by interference or noise, which can be external, internal, and semantic.

Intrapersonal Communication

Interpersonal Communication

Small-Group Communication

Public Communication

Mass Communication

ASYNCHRONOUS					SYNCHRONOUS	
Bulk letters	Posted letters	Facebook	Interactive chat	Telephone	Skype	Face-to-Face
Posters	E-mail	Twitter			iChat	
E-mail spam	Text messages	Other social media websites			Other video conferencing	
LEAN						RICH
LOW SOCIAL PRESENCE						HIGH SOCIAL PRESENCE

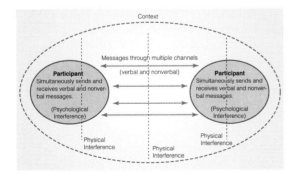

1-3
Identify the characteristics of communication. Our communication is guided by at least eight principles. First, communication has purpose. Second, communication is continuous. Third, communication is irreversible. Fourth, communication is situated. Fifth, communication is indexical and reflects the levels of trust, control, and intimacy in a relationship. Sixth, communication is learned.

KEY TERMS

1-1

communication the process through which we express, interpret, and coordinate messages with others

messages the verbal utterances, visual images, and nonverbal behaviors used to convey thoughts and feelings

encoding the process of putting our thoughts and feelings into words and nonverbal behaviors

decoding the process of interpreting another's message

feedback reactions and responses to messages

canned plan a "mental library" of scripts each of us draws from to create messages based on what worked for us in the past or that we have heard or used numerous times in similar situations

script an actual text of what to say and do in a specific situation

communication context the physical, social, historical, psychological, and cultural situations that surround a communication event

physical context the location of a communication encounter, the environmental conditions surrounding it (temperature, lighting, noise level), and the physical proximity of participants to each other

social context the nature of the relationship that exists between participants

historical context the background provided by previous communication episodes between the participants that influence understandings in the current encounter

psychological context the mood and feelings each person brings to a communication encounter

cultural context the beliefs, values, orientations, underlying assumptions, and rituals that belong to a specific culture

communication setting the different communication environments within which people interact, characterized by the number of participants and the extent to which the interaction is formal or informal

intrapersonal communication the interactions that occur in our minds when we are talking to ourselves

interpersonal communication informal interaction between two people who have an identifiable relationship with each other

small-group communication three to 20 people who come together for the specific purpose of solving a problem or arriving at a decision

public communication one participant, the speaker, delivers a message to a group of more than 20 people

mass communication communication that is delivered by individuals and entities through mass media to large segments of the population at the same time

1-2

communication process a complex set of three different and interrelated activities intended to result in shared meaning

message production the steps you take when you encode a message

message interpretation the steps you take when you decode a message

interaction coordination the behavioral adjustments each participant makes in an attempt to create shared meaning

channel the route traveled by the message and the means of transportation

emoticons textual images that symbolize the sender's mood, emotion, or facial expressions

acronyms abbreviations that stand in for common phrases

media richness the amount and kinds of media transmitted via a particular channel

synchronicity the extent to which a channel allows for immediate feedback

interference (noise) any stimulus that interferes with the process of sharing meaning

physical noise any external sight or sound that detracts from a message

psychological noise thoughts and feelings we experience that compete with a sender's message for our attention

1-3

index a measure of the emotional temperature of our relationship at the time

trust the extent to which partners rely on, depend on, and have faith that their partners will not intentionally do anything to harm them

control the degree to which one participant in the communication encounter is perceived to be more dominant or powerful

complementary feedback a message that signals agreement about who is in control

symmetrical feedback a message that signals disagreement about who is in control

intimacy the degree of emotional closeness, acceptance, and disclosure in a relationship

spontaneous expressions messages spoken without much conscious thought

constructed messages messages that are formed carefully and thoughtfully when our known scripts are inadequate for the situation

culture a system of shared beliefs, values, symbols, and behaviors

1-4

ethics a set of moral principles that may be held by a society, a group, or an individual

bright side messages messages that are both ethical and appropriate

dark side messages messages that are not ethical and/or appropriate

Seventh, communication messages vary in conscious thought, meaning they may be spontaneous, scripted, or constructed. And eighth, communication is guided by cultural norms.

1-4
Assess messages using the principles of ethical communication.
Ethical standards do not tell us exactly what to do in any given situation, but they offer general principles that guide our behavior. There are five ethical principles to guide general communication: (1) be truthful and honest, (2) act with integrity, (3) behave fairly, (4) demonstrate respect, and (5) communicate responsibly. One way to evaluate and create ethical messages is to consider them on the bright side/dark side matrix.

	Ethical	
	Bright side response: "Liz, it doesn't matter what I think. I can see that you really like how it looks and that makes me happy." *(This response is ethical and appropriate. It is both honest and respectful.)*	**Hard dark side response:** "Wow Liz, it's a dramatic change. I liked your hair long and I'd always admired the red highlights you had. But I'm sure it will grow on me." *(This response is honest but could hurt Liz's feelings and damage the relationship.)*
Appropriate		Inappropriate
	Easy dark side response: "It looks great." *(This response is dishonest but doesn't hurt Liz's feelings.)*	**Evil dark side response:** "It doesn't matter what you do to your hair, you're still fat and ugly." *(This response is unethical and inappropriate. It is hurtful and damaging to Liz's feelings and the relationship)*
	Unethical	

1-5
Develop a personal communication improvement plan.
Competence in communication is achieved by a desire to improve (motivation), demonstrating knowledge, and practicing skills. Others also judge competence based on a person's credibility and social ease. Communication apprehension (CA) is detrimental to social ease, and can be classified into four types: traitlike CA, audience-based CA, situational CA, and context-based CA. There are four steps to create a communication improvement plan, which will manage CA to give the appearance of social ease: (1) identify the problem, (2) state the specific goal, (3) outline a specific procedure for reaching the goals, and (4) devise a method for measuring progress.

JOURNAL ASSIGNMENTS

A. FEEDBACK IN INTERPERSONAL COMMUNICATION
Keep a one-day log of all the feedback (verbal and nonverbal) you receive from others while you are communicating. Ask someone who knows you well to indicate the types of feedback you typically give them while they communicate with you. Analyze the similarities and differences in the feedback you give and receive.

B. COMPETENT COMMUNICATION
Identify an area of your life in which you feel, and others would agree, that you demonstrate communication competence. How are you personally motivated, personally knowledgeable, and what skills do you demonstrate in this area? Now identify an area in your life in which you feel you do not demonstrate communication competence. Are any of your skills, knowledge, and motivation from the first area transferable to this second area? What can you learn from your positive experience in the first area that could help you set goals for improvement in the second area?

1-5

communication competence the impression that communicative behavior is both appropriate and effective in a given situation

credibility a perception of a speaker's knowledge, trustworthiness, and warmth

social ease communicating without appearing to be anxious or nervous

communication apprehension the fear or anxiety associated with real or anticipated communication with others

KEY CONCEPTS

2-1
Describe the perception process. Perception is the process of selectively attending and assigning meaning to information. Our perceptions are a result of our selection, organization, and interpretation of sensory information. We do so through dual processing.

2-2
Explain how self-perception is formed and maintained. Social perception consists of how we perceive ourselves and others. Perception of self consists of self-concept and self-esteem. Self-concept is the mental image we have about our skills, abilities, knowledge, competencies, and personality traits. Self-esteem is the value we place on the attributes of our self-concept.

2-3
Employ communication strategies to improve self-perceptions. Self-perception influences communication in terms of how we talk to ourselves, how we talk about ourselves with others, how we talk about others to ourselves, the way we present ourselves to others, and our ability to communicate competently with others.

2-4
Examine how we form perceptions of others. When we meet others, we strive to reduce uncertainty through communication. We begin by forming impressions based on physical appearance, assumptions about their personality, and assumed similarity. We also reduce uncertainty by making attributions that may help us predict how others will behave. Just as we make inaccurate and distorted perceptions of self, so do we make inaccurate assumptions about others based on selective perception, faulty attributions, forced consistency, and prejudice.

2-5
Employ strategies to improve perceptions of others. We can improve the accuracy of our perceptions of others and the messages they send by:
1. Questioning the accuracy of our perceptions.
2. Choosing to use conscious processing as we get to know them.
3. Seeking more information about our perceptions.
4. Realizing that our perceptions will change over time.
5. Practicing perception checking.

KEY TERMS

social perception who we believe ourselves and others to be

2-1
perception the process of selectively attending and assigning meaning to information

automatic processing a fast, top-down subconscious approach that draws on previous experience to make sense of what we are encountering

heuristics short-cut rules of thumb for understanding how to perceive something based on past experience with similar stimuli

conscious processing a slow, deliberative approach to perceiving where we examine and reflect about the stimuli

2-2
self-perception the overall view we have of ourselves, which includes both our self-concept and self-esteem

self-concept the perception we have of our skills, abilities, knowledge, competencies, and personality traits

self-esteem the evaluation we make about our personal worthiness based on our self-concept

ideal self-concept what we would like to be

independent self-perceptions perceptions based on the belief that traits and abilities are internal to the person and are universally applicable to all situations

interdependent self-perceptions perceptions based on the belief that traits and abilities are specific to a particular context or relationship

incongruence a gap between self-perception and reality

self-fulfilling prophecy an inaccurate perception of a skill, characteristic, or situation that leads to behaviors that perpetuate that false perception as true

2-3

self-talk the internal conversation we have with ourselves in our thoughts

social construction of self the phenomenon of sharing different aspects of our self-concept based on the situation and people involved

self-monitoring the internal process of being aware of how we are coming across to others and adjusting our behavior accordingly

2-4

uncertainty reduction communication theory that explains how individuals monitor their social environment to know more about themselves and others

impression formation processes we use to form perceptions of others

attributions reasons we give for our own and others' behavior

situational attribution attributing behavior to a cause that is beyond someone's control

dispositional attribution attributing behavior to a cause that is under someone's control

implicit personality theory the tendency to assume that two or more personality characteristics go together

assumed similarity assuming someone is similar to us in a variety of ways until we get information that contradicts this assumption

social presence the sense of being "there" with another person in a particular moment in time

selective perception the perceptual distortion that arises from paying attention only to what we expect to see or hear and ignoring what we don't expect

forced consistency the inaccurate attempt to make several perceptions about another person agree with each other

prejudice judging a person based on the characteristics of a group to which the person belongs without regard to how the person may vary from the group characteristic

stereotypes exaggerated or oversimplified generalizations used to describe a group

discrimination acting differently toward a person based on prejudice

racism, ethnocentrism, sexism, heterosexism, ageism, and ableism various form of prejudice in which members of one group believe that the behaviors and characteristics of their group are inherently superior to those of another group

2-5

perception check a message that reflects your understanding of the meaning of another person's behavior

JOURNAL ASSIGNMENTS

A. SELF AND OTHER PERCEPTIONS OF SELF

List ten words to describe how you perceive yourself. Include a variety of types of descriptors: roles, skills, physical attributes, personality characteristics, and so on. Have a family member, close friend, and acquaintance list ten words to describe how they perceive you. Analyze the differences and similarities between the lists.

B. HOW DID I GET THIS WAY?

Describe the five most significant situations, events, or experiences that have shaped your current self-concept. You may describe them through the written word or through pictures.

C. CULTURE AND SELF-ESTEEM

Imagine that you live in a culture that values age over youth and the group over the individual. Speculate about how your life would be different in this culture than it is now. If your culture emphasizes those values, imagine you live in a culture that values youth over age and the individual over the group.

D. SELF-MONITORING

Think back to a time when you were in a new situation. It could be your first day of high school or the first day of your first job. How did you use self-monitoring to help yourself feel more comfortable in this new situation? What feedback or cues did you receive to learn the "ground rules" of this new context? How did you apply this lesson to your future encounters?

KEY CONCEPTS

3-1

Define culture and the role of communication in it. Culture is the system of shared values, beliefs, attitudes, and norms that guides what is considered appropriate among an identifiable group of people. Intercultural communication involves interactions that occur between people whose cultures are so different that the communication between them is altered. Culture shock refers to the psychological discomfort people have when we attempt to adjust to a new cultural situation.

3-2

Explain the relationship between dominant and co-cultures. Both dominant and co-cultures exist in a society. A shared system of meaning exists within the dominant culture, but meanings can vary within co-cultures based on race, ethnicity, sex and gender, sexual orientation, religion, socioeconomic status, age/generation, and disability. Cultural identity is formed based on how closely we identify with the dominant culture and each of the co-cultural groups to which we belong.

3-3

Understand the seven dimensions in which cultures differ. Cultures are unique among a variety of dimensions. These include individualism/collectivism, context, chronemics, uncertainty avoidance, power distance, masculinity/femininity, and long-term/short-term orientation.

3-4

Describe the inherent barriers in intercultural communication and the methods to develop competent intercultural communication. To become interculturally competent, we need to acknowledge and overcome common intercultural communication barriers, which include anxiety, assumptions about differences and similarities, ethnocentrism, stereotyping, incompatible communication codes, and incompatible norms and values. We also need to employ the competent communication strategies of acquiring accurate knowledge, adopting an appropriate attitude, and developing culture-centered skills (e.g., listening, intercultural empathy, and flexibility).

KEY TERMS

3-1

culture the system of shared values, beliefs, attitudes, and norms that guides what is considered appropriate among an identifiable group of people

values the commonly accepted standards of what is considered right and wrong, good and evil, fair and unfair, etc.

ideal values values that members of a culture profess to hold

real values values that guide actual behavior

intercultural communication interactions that occur between people whose cultures are so different that the communication between them is altered

culture shock psychological discomfort when engaging in a new cultural situation

3-2

dominant culture the learned system of norms held by the majority group of empowered people in a society

co-culture a group consisting of a smaller number of people who hold common values, beliefs, attitudes, and customs that differ from those of the dominant culture

code switch altering linguistic and nonverbal patterns to conform to the dominant or co-culture

cultural identity the part of our self-concept that is based on how closely we associate with both the dominant culture and various co-cultures

ethnicity a classification of people based on combinations of shared characteristics such as nationality, geographic origin, language, religion, ancestral customs, and tradition

CHAPTER REVIEW 3

native language the language of one's ethnic heritage; typically the language learned at birth

sex biologically determined physical traits

gender the learned roles and communication patterns deemed "appropriate" for males and females in the dominant culture

religion a belief system with a set of rituals and ethical standards based on a common perception of what is sacred or holy

socioeconomic status (SES) the position of a person or family in the power hierarchy of a society based on income, education, and occupation

disability any physical, emotional, mental, or cognitive impairment that impacts how a person functions in society

3-3

individualistic cultures cultures that value personal rights and responsibilities, privacy, voicing one's opinion, freedom, innovation, and self-expression

collectivist cultures cultures that value community, collaboration, shared interests, harmony, the public good, and avoiding embarrassment

low-context cultures cultures in which speakers use words to convey most of the meaning; verbal messages are direct, specific, and detailed

high-context cultures cultures in which much of a speaker's message is understood from the context

chronemics the study of how the perception of time differs among cultures.

monochronic cultures cultures that view time as a series of small units that occur sequentially

polychronic cultures cultures that view time as a continuous flow

JOURNAL ASSIGNMENTS

A. INCOMPATIBLE COMMUNICATION CODES
Observe a group of people who seem to have a communication code with which you are unfamiliar. Perhaps they are speaking a different language, or perhaps they have certain "in-group" language behavior. How can you attempt to interpret the particular conversation you observe so as to avoid jumping to incorrect conclusions about the conversation?

B. CULTURAL NORM VIOLATION AND INTENTION
Have you ever intentionally violated a cultural norm described in this chapter? Describe the circumstance. Is it ever appropriate or effective to violate any of these norms?

C. CULTURAL IDENTITY
Think about your own family's cultural identity. How did you identify yourself growing up as a child: Did you see your family as a part of the dominant culture or from a co-culture? What values, attitudes, beliefs, and customs led you to this conclusion? Has your assessment changed now that you are an adult?

uncertainty avoidance the extent to which people desire to predict what is going to happen

low uncertainty-avoidance cultures cultures that tolerate uncertainty and are less driven to control unpredictable people, relationships, or events

high uncertainty-avoidance cultures cultures with a low tolerance for uncertainty and a high need to control unpredictable people, relationships, or events

power distance the extent to which members of a culture expect and accept that power will be equally or unequally shared

high power-distance cultures cultures that view unequal power distribution as normal

low power-distance cultures cultures in which members prefer power to be more equally distributed

masculine cultures cultures in which men and women are expected to adhere to traditional gender roles

feminine cultures cultures in which people assume a variety of roles and are valued for doing so regardless of sex

short-term oriented cultures cultures that tend to value static rewards in the here and now and emphasize quick results

long-term oriented cultures cultures that emphasize potential future rewards that will eventually be realized after slow and steady perseverance toward achieving a mutually acceptable result

3-4

ethnocentrism the belief that one's own culture is superior to others

nonparticipant observation learning about a culture or co-culture by watching as members interact with each other

participant observation learning about a culture or co-culture by living or working with people whose cultural assumptions are different from yours

altruism a display of genuine and unselfish concern for the welfare of others

egocentricity a selfish interest in one's own needs to the exclusion of everything else

intercultural empathy imaginatively placing yourself in another person's cultural world and attempting to experience what he or she is experiencing

flexibility the ability to adjust your communication to fit the other person and the situation

KEY CONCEPTS

4-1

Define a language, a dialect, and an idiolect. Although many different languages are spoken throughout the world, all of them share the same purposes and are based on the same fundamental principles. All are symbol systems used to communicate by labeling, comparing, and defining. And all are based on utterances bounded by silences. Verbal language consists of a symbol system that includes a lexicon, phonology, and syntax and grammar. Sharing meaning can be difficult because we may speak different languages, dialects, and idiolects.

4-2

List the characteristics of language. Language is arbitrary, abstract, and constantly changing. These characteristics add to the difficulty in sharing meaning. Attaching meaning to an arbitrary assortment of symbols requires a language community to agree on that meaning in order for understanding to occur. Even with shared meaning, each word is inherently abstract. In addition, language changes over time, with words taking on different meanings or losing meaning as society changes.

4-3

Compose effective verbal messages based on semantic, pragmatic, and sociolinguistic meanings. Since meanings are in people rather than the words themselves, verbal symbols convey semantic, pragmatic, and sociolinguistic meanings. Semantic meaning is derived from the words and how they are arranged into sentences. We can improve semantic meaning by using specific, concrete, and familiar words; descriptive details and examples; and linguistic sensitivity. Pragmatic meaning comes from understanding a message within the context of the conversation. We can improve pragmatic meaning by telling the truth, providing the right amount of information, relating what we say to the topic being discussed, acknowledging when we are violating one of these guidelines, and assuming the best first. Sociolinguistic meaning varies according to the norms of a particular culture or co-culture. We can improve sociolinguistic meaning by developing intercultural competence, practicing mindfulness, and respecting and adapting to the sociolinguistic practices of others.

KEY TERMS

4-1

utterance a complete unit of talk bounded by the speaker's literal or figurative silence

turn-taking the exchange of utterances

language a system of symbols used by people to communicate

lexicon the collection of words and expressions in a language

phonology the sounds used to pronounce words

syntax and grammar rules for combining words to form sentences and larger units of expression

language community all people who can speak or understand a particular language

dialect a unique form of a more general language spoken by a specific culture or co-culture

speech communities smaller groups that speak a common dialect

idiolect our own personal symbol system that includes our active vocabularies and our unique pronunciations, grammar, and syntax

4-2

words arbitrarily chosen symbols used to represent thoughts and feelings

4-3

semantic meaning meaning derived from the words themselves and how they are arranged into sentences

denotation the explicit meaning of a word found in the dictionary of a language community

CHAPTER REVIEW 4

connotation the implicit additional meaning we associate with a word

specific language precise words that clarify semantic meaning by narrowing what is understood from a general category to a particular item or group within it

concrete language words that clarify semantic meaning by appealing to the senses

linguistic sensitivity inclusive word choices that demonstrate respect for others

inclusive language use of words that do not apply only to one sex, race, or other group

pragmatic meaning understanding a message related to its conversational context

speech act the utterance of a verbal message and what it implies about how the listener should respond

sociolinguistic meaning meaning that varies according to the norms of a particular culture or co-culture

idioms expressions whose meanings are different from the literal meanings associated with the words used in them

direct verbal style language that openly states the speaker's intention in a straightforward and unambiguous way

indirect verbal style language that masks the speaker's true intentions in a roundabout and ambiguous way

mindfulness paying attention to what is happening at any given moment during a conversation

JOURNAL ASSIGNMENTS

A. ANALYZING LANGUAGE COMMUNITIES

Your textbook states that there are about 3,000 to 4,000 speech communities in the world. However, over 60 percent of these communities are speaking what is considered a threatened or endangered language, spoken by 10,000 or fewer people. What do you think are some of the consequences of so many languages becoming extinct? What would you do if your language was about to die out?

B. PRECISION AND LANGUAGE

Write a one-page story about an event that occurred during your first week of college. When you're done, rewrite the story using more precise words. Tell the two versions of the story to a friend and ask for feedback. Write about the feedback in your journal entry.

C. CONNOTATION

List your connotation for each of the following words: *assisted suicide, athlete, ballet dancer, censorship, CEO, criminal, date rape, domestic abuse, family values, government, feminist, illegal aliens, media, police officer, politically correct, soccer mom,* and *welfare*. Now look up each of these words in the dictionary. How do your connotative meanings differ from the denotative meanings of the words? Can you determine the source of your connotations? In other words, where did you get the connotations you have with these words?

D. CULTURAL AND GENDER DIFFERENCES

Discuss an experience you've had that involved either cultural or gender differences in verbal communication. Did these differences cause problems in the relationship(s) involved in this experience? How can verbal communication be improved to avoid difficulties that gender and cultural differences may bring?

KEY CONCEPTS

5-1
Identify characteristics of nonverbal communication. Nonverbal communication consists of all the messages that transcend spoken or written words. Nonverbal messages may emphasize, substitute for, or contradict a verbal message. They can regulate our conversations and project an image about who we are to others. Nonverbal communication is inevitable, multi-channeled, and ambiguous. It is also the primary way we convey our emotions.

5-2
Identify the different types of nonverbal communication. We communicate nonverbal messages through our bodies (gestures, eye contact, facial expression, posture, and touch), our voices (pitch, volume, rate, voice quality, intonation, and vocalized pauses), our use of space (personal space, territorial space, acoustic space, and artifacts), our use of time, and our physical appearance.

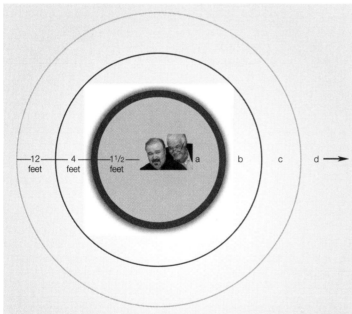

Zone a, **intimate distance**: spouses, significant others, family members, and others with whom we have an intimate relationship
Zone b, **personal distance**: friends
Zone c, **social distance**: business associates and acquaintances
Zone d, **public distance**: strangers

5-3
Employ strategies to improve your nonverbal communication. We can become more adept at sending nonverbal messages by consciously monitoring them, aligning them with our purpose, adapting them to the situation, and reducing or eliminating distracting nonverbal messages. We can improve our interpretation of nonverbal messages by remembering that the same nonverbal message can mean different things to different people, considering each in context, paying attention to nonverbal messages and their relationship to the verbal message, and performing a perception check.

KEY TERMS

nonverbal communication all the messages we send in ways that transcend spoken or written words

nonverbal messages cues we send with our body, voice, space, time, and appearance to support, modify, contradict, or even replace a verbal message

5-2

kinesics the interpretation of what and how body motions communicate

gestures movements of our hands, arms, and fingers to replace or accompany a verbal message

emblems gestures that substitute entirely for a word or words

illustrators gestures that clarify a verbal message

adaptors unconscious responses to physical or psychological needs

eye contact (oculesics) how and how much we look at others when communicating

facial expression arranging facial muscles to communicate emotions or provide feedback

posture how we position and move our body

body orientation how we position our body in relation to other people

body movement changing body position

haptics the interpretation of what and how touch communicates

paralanguage (vocalics) the voiced part of a spoken message that goes beyond the actual words

pitch the highness or lowness of vocal tone

volume the loudness or softness of vocal tone

rate the speed at which a person speaks

voice quality (timbre) the sound of a person's voice that distinguishes it from others

intonation the variety, melody, or inflection in one's voice

vocalized pauses extraneous sounds or words that interrupt fluent speech

proxemics the study of how space and distance communicate

personal space the distance we try to maintain when we interact with other people

territorial space the physical space over which we claim ownership

acoustic space the area over which your voice can be comfortably heard

physical appearance how we look to others

media richness how much and what kinds of information can be transmitted via a particular channel

JOURNAL ASSIGNMENTS

A. DISTRACTING MANNERISMS
Describe any distracting mannerisms that you may have. Ask someone who knows you well to provide input. Compare your perception with that of the person you asked. How aware of your nonverbal communication behaviors are you? What, if any, changes would you like to make?

B. TOUCH PREFERENCES AND PERSONAL SPACE
Are you a person who likes or dislikes being touched? Why? How do you communicate your preference to others? How does this correlate to personal space? Through observation, see if you can distinguish your preferred distance for intimate space. How does your preference for personal space and touch change when interacting with acquaintances, friends, and strangers?

C. ENVIRONMENT
How does your home, apartment, or dorm room communicate information about you? What is it saying right now? Why?

D. THE MULTI-CHANNELED NATURE OF NONVERBAL COMMUNICATION
For this assignment, select a popular syndicated talk show host who has both a radio and a TV or Internet broadcast. First listen to the host you chose speak on the radio. Then watch him or her on TV or the Internet. Pay attention to how you receive the message over the radio, when only paralanguage is available, versus when you watch the broadcast over a medium in which you can see facial expressions, eye contact, and other nonverbal channels. How is the message affected by the presence or absence of certain nonverbal channels? Do you interpret the message differently when you see it with paralanguage alone, or was the message the same when it was accompanied by other nonverbals?

KEY CONCEPTS

6-1

Define listening. People often believe that hearing and listening are the same thing, but they are not. Hearing is a physiological process, while listening is a cognitive process. Listening occurs only when we choose to attach meaning to what we hear. Listening is important for effective communication because we spend 50 percent or more of our communication time listening.

6-2

Identify the three challenges of listening. We must overcome three major challenges based on our personal listening style, listening apprehension, and processing approach to become effective listeners. Our listening style might be content-oriented, people-oriented, action-oriented, or time-oriented. Listening apprehension is the anxiety we feel when trying to listen effectively, which can interfere with our success. And our approach to listening may be unconscious and passive or conscious and active.

6-3

Practice the steps involved in active listening. The five steps in the active listening process are attending, the process of willfully perceiving selected sounds; understanding, the process of accurately decoding a message; remembering, the process of moving information from short-term to long-term memory; evaluating, the process of critically analyzing what you hear; and responding, the process of providing feedback.

Guideline	Example
1. Clearly state that your aim is to help.	I'd like to help you, what can I do?
2. Express acceptance or affection; do not condemn or criticize.	I understand that you just can't seem to accept this.
3. Demonstrate care, concern, and interest in the speaker's situation; do not give a lengthy recount of a similar situation.	What are you planning to do now? OR Gosh, tell me more! What happened then?
4. Indicate that you are available to listen and support the speaker without intruding.	I know that we've not been that close, but sometimes it helps to have someone to listen and I'd like to do that for you.
5. State that you are an ally.	I'm with you on this. OR Well, I'm on your side. This isn't right.
6. Acknowledge the speaker's feelings and situation, and express your sincere sympathy.	I'm so sorry to see you feeling so bad. I can see that you're devastated by what has happened.
7. Assure the speaker that his or her feelings are legitimate; do not tell the speaker how to feel or to ignore those feelings.	Hey, it's OK, man. With all that has happened to you, you have a right to be angry.
8. Use prompting comments to encourage elaboration.	Uh-huh, yeah. OR I see. How did you feel about that? OR Tell me more.

6-4
Employ strategies to respond effectively in different situations. Tk

KEY TERMS

6-1

listening the process of receiving, constructing meaning from, and responding to spoken and/or nonverbal messages

6-2

listening apprehension the anxiety felt about listening

listening style our favored and usually unconscious approach to listening

content-oriented listeners listeners who focus on and evaluate the facts and evidence

people-oriented listeners listeners who focus on the feelings their conversational partners may have about what they're saying

action-oriented listeners listeners who focus on the ultimate point the speaker is trying to make

time-oriented listeners listeners who prefer brief and hurried conversations and use nonverbal and verbal cues to signal that their partner needs to be more concise

passive listening the habitual and unconscious process of receiving messages

active listening the deliberate and conscious process of attending to, understanding, remembering, evaluating, and responding to messages

6-3

attending the process of willfully perceiving and focusing on a message

understanding the process of accurately interpreting a message

question an interrogative word, phrase, or sentence designed to get additional information or details

paraphrasing the process of putting your interpretation of a message into words

CHAPTER REVIEW 6

content paraphrase a paraphrase that focuses on the denotative meaning of the message

feelings paraphrase a paraphrase that emotions attached to the message

empathy the ability to identify with or vicariously experience another's feelings or attitudes

empathic responsiveness occurs when you experience an emotional response parallel to another person's actual or anticipated display of emotion

perspective taking occurs when you use everything you know about a sender and his or her circumstances to understand their feelings

sympathetic responsiveness is feeling concern, compassion, or sorrow for another's situation

remembering is being able to retain and recall information later

repetition saying something aloud or mentally rehearsing it two, three, or more times

mnemonic device associates a special word or very short statement with new and longer information

evaluating the process of critically analyzing a message

facts statements whose accuracy can be verified as true

inferences assertions based on the facts presented

responding the process of providing feedback

6-4

nonverbal feedback cues verbal and nonverbal signals used to indicate to the speaker that you are attending to and understanding the message

supportive responses create an environment that encourages another to talk about and make sense of a distressing situation

JOURNAL ASSIGNMENTS

A. LISTENING SELF-ANALYSIS

How would you evaluate your listening skills? Which of the five steps in the listening process causes the most difficulties for you? Are you consciously acting on all of the guidelines and suggested steps for the listening process? What will you do to improve your listening abilities?

B. CHILDREN & LISTENING

What special difficulties might children have with listening? Did you experience those difficulties as a child? If so, what helped you learn to listen more effectively?

C. LISTENING FOR UNDERSTANDING

How do you listen differently when you are listening for understanding versus when you are listening for pleasure? Use examples in your description.

D. ACTIVE LISTENING EXPERIMENT

Spend a full hour simply listening to a significant other. Practice all the active listening behaviors described in your text. Try to pay attention to your nonverbal behaviors and make them demonstrate active listening. See what happens when you limit your verbal reactions and only respond nonverbally during the conversation. Record the reaction and impact on the relationship.

KEY CONCEPTS

7-1
Identify the major types of relationships. Interpersonal communication helps us develop and maintain relationships. A healthy relationship is any mutually satisfying interaction with another person. There are three types of relationships. Acquaintances are people we know by name and talk with, but with whom our interactions are limited in quality and quantity. Friendships are marked by degrees of warmth and affection, trust, self-disclosure, commitment, and expectation that the relationships will endure. Close or intimate friends are those with whom we share a high degree of commitment, trust, interdependence, disclosure, and enjoyment.

7-2
Explain how disclosure and feedback affect relationships. A healthy relationship is marked by a balance of self-disclosure and feedback. Social penetration theory looks at the various kinds of self-disclosure used in relationships and uses the terms *breadth* and *width* to describe how much disclosure various topics have in a relationship. The Johari Window is a tool for analyzing disclosure balance and categorizing information based on whether it is or is not known by the self and others.

FIGURE 7.2 THE JOHARI WINDOW

	Known to self	Not known to self
Known to others	Open	Blind
Not known to others	Secret	Unknown

7-3
Examine levels of communication at various stages in relationships. Relationships go through a life cycle that includes building and developing, maintaining, and perhaps de-escalating and ending. In the first stage of beginning and developing a relationship, we try to get to know each other to reduce uncertainty, we develop feelings of relaxation and confirmation, and we experience greater levels of disclosure and support. There are various ways to maintain a relationship, including spending time together; merging social networks; doing unselfish acts; and exchanging affection, self-disclosure, favors, and support. When relationships start to deteriorate, we tend to recognize feelings of dissatisfaction, notice each other's faults, experience more conflict, discuss only safe topics, and spend less time together. Effective communicators consciously end relationships with direct, open, and honest communication rather than manipulation, withdrawal, or avoidance. Technology has impacted how we begin, form, maintain, and dissolve relationships and is continuing to change our interpersonal communication.

7-4
Examine how technology and social media influence interpersonal relationships. The Internet, social media, email, and text messaging are all examples of the *media multiplexity* that enable us to stay in touch with distant friends and family, as well as meet new people across any geographic span. While these tools have vastly broadened our opportunities for connection, they've also changed how we build and maintain our relationships. Friendships and even lasting romantic relationships can begin online through connections over

KEY TERMS

interpersonal communication all the interactions that occur between two people to help start, build, maintain, and sometimes end or redefine the relationship

interpersonal relationship a relationship that is defined by sets of expectations two people have for each other based on their previous interactions

healthy relationship a relationship in which the interactions are satisfying and beneficial to all those involved

7-1

acquaintances people we know by name and talk with when the opportunity arises, but with whom our interactions are largely impersonal

impersonal communication interchangeable polite chit-chat involving no or very little personal disclosure

saving face the process of attempting to maintain a positive self-image in a relational situation

friends people with whom we have voluntarily negotiated more personal relationships

intimates people with whom we share a high degree of interdependence, commitment, disclosure, understanding, affection, and trust

platonic relationship an intimate relationship in which the partners are not sexually attracted to each other or do not act on an attraction they feel

romantic relationship an intimate relationship in which the partners act on their sexual attraction

trust placing confidence in another in a way that almost always involves some risk

CHAPTER REVIEW 7

7-2

relationship life cycle moving back and forth among the relationship phases

disclosure the process of revealing confidential information

self-disclosure the confidential information we deliberately choose to share about ourselves

other-disclosure the confidential information shared about someone by a third party

social penetration theory describes the different kinds of self-disclosure we use in our relationships

Johari Window a tool for examining the relationship between disclosure and feedback in the relationship

7-3

relational maintenance communication strategies used to keep a relationship operating smoothly and satisfactorily

sacrifice putting one's needs or desires on hold to attend to the needs of one's partner or the relationship

circumscribing stage relationship stage during which communication decreases in both quantity and quality

stagnating stage relationship stage during which partners just go through the motions of interacting with each other routinely without enthusiasm or emotion

avoiding stage relationship stage during which partners create physical distance by making excuses not to do things with the other person in the relationship

terminating stage relationship stage in which partners no longer interact with each other

grave-dressing attempts to explain why a relationship failed

shared interests. By exchanging ideas in a virtual space, we can be unhindered by social boundaries such as race, class, and sex. Social media makes it easy to maintain existing relationships and communicate with friends and loved ones. Starting relationships online can be risky, as senders have a greater capacity to manage their self-presentation—an interaction known as *hyperpersonal communication*—and may not necessarily represent their true self.

7-5

Identify the sources of tension in relationships. In any relationship, there exist competing psychological tensions that are known as *relational dialectics*. The three most common are autonomy-connection, openness-closedness, and novelty-predictability. The autonomy-connection dialectic refers to the competing desires to do things independent of your partner or to link your actions with your partner. The openness-closedness dialectic refers to the tensions between sharing intimate ideas and maintaining privacy. The novelty-predictability dialectic is the tension between originality and consistency. In managing dialectics in relationships, it is helpful to talk openly with your partner about tensions and reach an agreement about how to manage them going forward.

JOURNAL ASSIGNMENTS

A. ELECTRONIC RELATIONSHIPS
Analyze a relationship that either began or was maintained via the Internet. Is the relationship different from those that allow you to interact face to face? What advice can you give for others in this same situation?

B. THE JOHARI WINDOW
The Johari Window is a good tool for analyzing the extent of disclosure and feedback in which you engage in your relationships. How would you assess your own Johari Window?

relationship transformation the process of changing a relationship from one level of intimacy to another

7-4

hyperpersonal communication online interaction in which senders have a greater capacity to strategically manage their self-presentation because nonverbal and relevant contextual cues are more limited

media multiplexity using more than one medium to maintain relationships

7-5

dialectic a tension between conflicting forces

relational dialectics the competing psychological tensions in a relationship

autonomy the desire to do things independent of one's partner

connection the desire to do things and make decisions with one's partner

openness the desire to share intimate ideas and feelings with one's partner

closedness the desire to maintain one's privacy in a relationship

novelty originality, freshness, and uniqueness in a relationship

predictability consistency, reliability, and dependability in a relationship

temporal selection the strategy of choosing one desire and ignoring its opposite for a while

topical segmentation the strategy of choosing certain topics with which to satisfy one dialectical tension and other topics for its opposite

neutralization the strategy of compromising between the desires of the two partners

reframing the strategy of changing one's perception about the level of tension

CHAPTER REVIEW 8

Interpersonal Communication

KEY CONCEPTS

8-1
Compose effective emotional support messages. Interpersonal relationships rely on communication and creating a communication climate. We should strive to create positive climates and use confirming communication messages to promote healthy relationships. Part of relationships involves comforting. Several skills can help us provide emotional support to others: clarifying supportive intentions, buffering face threats with politeness, encouraging understanding through other-centered messages, reframing the situation, and giving advice.

8-2
Practice direct and indirect strategies for managing privacy and disclosure. In any relationship, people will experience a tension between openness and privacy. Though people often move toward deeper disclosure as their relationships develop, this is not always the case. Privacy and disclosure decisions affect relationships in three major ways. They affect intimacy level, reciprocity expectations, and information co-ownership. Disclosure guidelines for sharing personal information, sharing feelings, and providing feedback are listed in this chapter's Concept Flowchart.

There are also a number of strategies for managing privacy. Indirect strategies include changing the subject, masking feelings, or telling a white lie. Establishing a personal boundary is a direct strategy to maintain privacy. You can establish personal boundaries by recognizing why you are choosing not to share the information, identifying your rule that guided the decision, and forming an "I"-centered message that briefly establishes a boundary.

8-3
Express your personal desires and expectations assertively.
People in relationships must negotiate different needs, desires, and expectations. We can communicate our needs, wants, and preferences by being passive, aggressive, passive-aggressive, or assertive. Our communication style impacts the communication climate and can be the deciding factor in how the relationship progresses or declines. Some cultures and co-cultural groups favor one communication style over another and may perceive other styles as rude; for this reason, it is important to be culturally aware of your communication partner.

8-4
Manage interpersonal conflict by using an appropriate conflict management style. Every relationship is marked by periods of interpersonal conflict, when the needs or ideas of one person are at odds with the needs or ideas of another. Conflicts can be resolved by avoiding, which creates a lose-lose situation; accommodating, which creates a lose-win situation; competing, which creates a win-lose situation; compromising, which creates a partial lose-lose situation; and collaborating, which creates a win-win situation.

FIGURE 8.1 CONFLICT MANAGEMENT STYLES

KEY TERMS

communication climate the overall emotional tone of your relationship

positive communication climate communication climate in which partners feel valued and supported

confirming communication messages messages that convey that we care about our partner

disconfirming communication messages messages that signal a lack of regard for our partner

8-1

comforting helping people feel better about themselves, their behavior, or their situation by creating a safe conversational space where they can express their feelings and work out a plan for the future

face the perception we want others to have of our worth

positive face needs the desire to be appreciated, liked, and honored

negative face needs the desire to be free from imposition and intrusion

other-centered messages comforting messages that encourage relational partners to talk about and elaborate on what happened and how they feel about it

reframe the situation offering ideas, observations, information, or alternative explanations that might help a relational partner understand a situation in a different light

give advice presenting relevant suggestions that a person can use to resolve a situation

8-2

privacy management theory maintaining confidential or secret information to enhance autonomy or minimize vulnerability

describing feelings naming the emotions you are feeling without judging them

praise describing the specific positive behaviors or accomplishments of another and the effect that behavior has on others

personal boundary The way we respond to others who expect disclosure of personal information or feelings we wish to keep private

8-3

passive communication style a communication style in which you do not express your personal preferences or defend your rights to others

aggressive communication style a communication style in which you belligerently or violently confront others with your preferences, feelings, needs, or rights with little regard for their preferences or rights

cyberbullying increasingly prevalent use of technology to convey verbally aggressive messages

passive-aggressive communication style a communication style in which you submit to others' demands and conceal your own preferences while indirectly expressing hostility toward them

assertive communication style a communication style in which you express your personal preferences and defend your rights to others while respecting their preferences and rights

8-4

interpersonal conflict an expressed struggle between two interdependent people who perceive incompatible goals, scarce resources, and interference from the other in achieving their goals

avoiding physically or psychologically removing yourself from the conflict

JOURNAL ASSIGNMENTS

A. PASSIVE, AGGRESSIVE, ASSERTIVE

You have probably heard someone being labeled as passive-aggressive in the past. Perhaps you were the one to use the expression. Perhaps you caught yourself saying, "He's passive-aggressive, isn't he?" Does this chapter change your understanding of this expression? If so, how has it changed? What do you think can be done to help those who have passive-aggressive tendencies to be more assertive?

B. WITHHOLDING FEELINGS

Is it ever in the best interest of an intimate relationship to withhold feelings permanently? Temporarily? Why or why not? Have you ever withheld information in an intimate relationship? Do you feel it was justified? Under what circumstances would you want someone else to withhold information from you?

C. FAMILY CRITICISM

Expressing criticism directly, in behavioral terms, is generally healthy for relationships. What additional factors affect family relationships? Consider the power dimensions of child-parent interactions.

D. UTILIZING CONFLICT MANAGEMENT STYLES

Discuss each type of conflict mentioned and give an example of a situation in which each of these may be the most appropriate. What steps will you take to ensure that you are using the right method during everyday interactions?

accommodating managing conflict by satisfying others' needs or accepting others' ideas while neglecting our own

competing satisfying our own needs with little or no concern for others' needs or for the harm it may do to our relationships

compromising managing conflict by giving up part of what you want to provide at least some satisfaction for both parties

collaborating managing conflict by fully addressing the needs and issues of each party and arriving at a solution that is mutually satisfying

KEY CONCEPTS

9-1
Identify different types of groups. A group is a collection of individuals varying from three to 20 members. There are various types of groups, such as families, social friendship groups, support groups, interest groups, service groups, work group teams, and virtual groups. Effective work groups develop team goals that meet four criteria: they are specific, serve a common purpose, are challenging, and are shared.

9-2
Analyze the characteristics of healthy groups. Healthy groups develop clearly defined and ethical goals, are interdependent, cohesive, work to establish and abide by norms, hold members accountable for group norms, and achieve synergy.

9-3
Understand how groups develop. Once groups have assembled, they tend to move through five stages of development: *forming*, getting people to feel valued and accepted so that they identify with the group; *storming*, clarifying goals while determining the role each member will have in the group power structure; *norming*, solidifying rules for behavior; *performing*, overcoming obstacles and meeting goals successfully; and *adjourning*, assigning meaning to what they have done and determining how to end or maintain interpersonal relations they have developed. Groups may also *transform* and continue to exist with a new goal instead of adjourning.

9-4
Describe the nature of conflict in groups. Conflict occurs both in interpersonal communication and group communication. Effective management of group conflict can actually make groups stronger rather than weakening them. The three types of group conflict are pseudo-conflict, issue-related group conflict, and personality-related group conflict. Just as with interpersonal communication, culture can affect conflict management skills. Virtual group conflict is more often unresolved than face-to-face group conflict, often because of the reduced ability to send and receive nonverbal messages.

KEY TERMS

9-1

group a collection of about three to 20 people who interact and attempt to influence each other to accomplish a common purpose

group communication all the verbal and nonverbal messages shared among members of the group

family a group of intimates who through their communication generate a sense of home and group identity, complete with strong ties of loyalty and emotion, and also experience a history and a future

social group a group consisting of friends who have a genuine concern about each other's welfare and enjoy spending time together

support group a group consisting of people who come together to provide encouragement, honest feedback, and a safe environment for expressing deeply personal feelings about a problem common to the members

interest group a group consisting of individuals who come together because they share a common concern, hobby, or activity

service group a group consisting of individuals who come together to perform hands-on charitable works or to raise money to help organizations that perform such work

work group team a collection of three or more people formed to solve a problem

heterogeneous group a group in which various demographics, levels of knowledge, attitudes, and interests are represented

homogeneous group a group in which members have a great deal of similarity

work group team goal a future state of affairs desired by enough members to motivate the group to work toward its achievement

virtual group a group whose members "meet" via technological media from different physical locations

virtual group communication communication that occurs in virtual groups

real time at the same time

netiquette etiquette rules users follow when communicating over computer networks

9-2

healthy group a group formed around a constructive purpose and characterized by ethical goals, interdependence, cohesiveness, productive norms, accountability, and synergy

interdependent group a group in which members rely on each other's skills and knowledge to accomplish the group goals

cohesiveness the force that brings group members closer together

team-building activities activities designed to build rapport and develop trust among members

norms expectations for the way group members are to behave while in the group

ground rules prescribed behaviors designed to help a group meet its goals and conduct its conversations

accountability group members being held responsible for adhering to the group norms and working toward the group's goal

synergy the multiplying force of a group working together that results in a combined effort greater than any of the parts

JOURNAL ASSIGNMENTS

A. COHESIVENESS IN GROUPS

Think of some of the groups in which you have experienced the most cohesiveness. What characteristics of cohesive groups listed in your textbook did these groups demonstrate? How did these characteristics contribute to group bonding? Now think of a group in which bonding did not occur. What element was missing from this group? How could that element have been introduced to make the group more cohesive?

B. FAMILY GROUPS

What are the rules (typically unwritten) for problem solving in your family group? Contrast these rules with the group problem-solving procedures described in your textbook.

9-3

forming the initial stage of group development characterized by orientation, testing, and dependence

storming the stage of group development characterized by conflict and power plays as members seek to have their ideas accepted and to find their place within the group's power structure

groupthink a deterioration of mental efficiency, reality testing, and moral judgment that results from in-group pressure to conform

norming the stage of group development during which the group solidifies its rules for behavior, resulting in greater trust and motivation to achieve the group goal

performing the stage of group development when the skills, knowledge, and abilities of all members are combined to overcome obstacles and meet goals successfully

adjourning the stage of group development in which members assign meaning to what they have done and determine how to end or maintain interpersonal relations they have developed

transforming the stage of group development that occurs when a group continues to exist with a new goal

9-4

pseudo-conflict conflict that occurs when group members who actually agree about something believe they disagree due to poor communication

issue-related group conflict conflict that occurs when two or more group members' goals, ideas, or opinions about the topic are incompatible

personality-related group conflict conflict that occurs when two or more group members become defensive because they feel like they are being attacked

KEY CONCEPTS

10-1

Understand how leadership functions in teams. Leadership is often thought of as a role fulfilled by an individual. However, recent thinking holds that leadership tasks are performed by many members of the group. Leadership, in this view, is a set of functions that can be performed by one, more than one, or all group members at various times. The leadership roles within a group can be divided into task, maintenance, and procedural roles. Task roles help the group acquire, process, or apply information. Maintenance roles help the group develop and maintain cohesion, commitment, and positive working relationships. Procedural roles are sets of communication behaviors that provide logistical support, keep the group focused on the task, and record the group's accomplishments and decisions. There are also five leadership roles that are shared among all members of the group that, when performed by all members, create a highly effective group. They are (1) being committed to the group goal, (2) keeping discussions on track, (3) completing individual assignments on time, (4) encouraging input from all members, and (5) managing conflict among members.

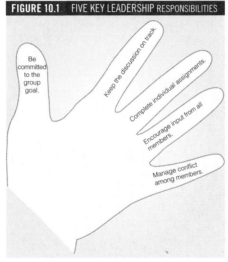

FIGURE 10.1 FIVE KEY LEADERSHIP RESPONSIBILITIES

Be committed to the group goal.

Keep the discussion on track.

Complete individual assignments.

Encourage input from all members.

Manage conflict among members.

10-2

Describe how to run effective meetings. Most managers and employees are required to attend meetings, and most of them feel that the majority of meetings are inefficient uses of time. To make group meetings effective and efficient, both the meeting leader and meeting participants should take certain actions before, during and after the meeting. By doing so, they can ensure that the meeting is an efficient and productive use of everyone's time.

10-3

List the six steps of systematic problem solving. A group that faces a problem can find a resolution either through a linear set of steps or a less-structured spiral pattern. In either case, the group must accomplish six tasks in order to find an optimal solution. First, it must identify and define the problem. Second, it must analyze the problem to find out as much about it as possible. Third, it must determine the criteria for judging the merits of proposed solutions. Fourth, it must identify alternative solutions. Fifth, it must evaluate the solutions and decide which solution should be used. Finally, the group will implement the agreed-upon solution.

10-4

Know the various methods for communicating group solutions. A group can communicate its decisions in a number of ways. Written formats, including a written brief or comprehensive report, involve the production of a written document. Oral formats, such as oral briefs, oral reports, symposiums,

KEY TERMS

10-1

leadership a process whereby an individual influences a group of individuals to achieve a common goal

formal leader a person designated or elected to facilitate the group process

informal emergent leaders members who help lead the group to achieve different leadership functions

shared leadership functions the sets of roles that group members perform to facilitate the work of the group and help maintain harmonious relationships between members

role a specific communication behavior that group members perform

task leadership roles sets of behaviors that help a group acquire, process, or apply information that contributes directly to completing a task or goal

maintenance leadership roles sets of behaviors that help a group develop and maintain cohesion, commitment, and positive working relationships

procedural leadership roles sets of behaviors that provide logistical support, keep the group focused on the task, and record the group's accomplishments and decisions

10-2

agenda an organized outline of the information and decision items that will be covered during a meeting

10-3

problem definition a formal written statement describing a problem

question of fact a question asked to determine what is true or to what extent something is true

question of value a question asked to determine or judge whether something is right, moral, good, or just

question of policy a question asked to determine what course of action should be taken or what rules should be adopted to solve a problem

criteria standards or measures used for judging the merits of proposed solutions

brainstorming an uncritical, non-evaluative process of generating possible solutions by being creative, suspending judgment, and combining or adapting ideas

decision making the process of choosing among alternatives

10-4

deliverables tangible or intangible products of work that must be provided to someone else

written brief a very short document that describes a problem, background, process, decision, and rationale so that a reader can quickly understand and evaluate a group's product

comprehensive report a written document that provides a detailed review of the problem-solving process used to arrive at a recommendation

executive summary a one-page synopsis of a comprehensive report

oral brief a summary of a written brief delivered to an audience by a group member

oral report a detailed review of a group's problem-solving process delivered to an audience by one or more group members

symposium a set of prepared oral reports delivered sequentially by group members before a gathering of people who are interested in the group's work

or panel discussions, involve a spoken presentation by an individual or group. Groups can also use virtual reports, such as remote access reports and streaming video, which involve the use of technology and have the advantage of providing simultaneous communication to multiple locations.

10-5
Evaluate group effectiveness using provided guidelines. Effective groups periodically evaluate how their interactions affect what they do and how the members interact with each other. One way to evaluate group dynamics is to describe how each member performed his or her specific tasks and how well his or her communication contributed to the cohesiveness, problem solving, and conflict resolution processes in the group. Evaluations of group presentations should incorporate an individual as well as a group component.

JOURNAL ASSIGNMENTS

A. CULTURE AND GROUPS
Many cultures value the group over the individual. If you have been raised in an individualistic culture, how would your typical day be different than if you lived in a collectivistic culture? How would your top three priorities change? If you have been raised in a collectivistic culture, what adjustments have you made or felt pressure to make living and interacting with people from individualistic cultures?

B. LEADERSHIP AND CHILDREN
Imagine you have been asked to teach a course on leadership to children. What topics would you include? Why?

C. HISTORY AND LEADERSHIP
Make a list of the world leaders you believe to be the greatest of all time. What leadership qualities do these leaders have in common? Was their style of leadership culturally determined, historically determined, or both? Explain.

D. GROUP ROLES
What roles do you take on in groups in which you participate? Do you tend to engage in task-oriented roles, maintenance roles or both? Pick a group situation and try assuming a different role than you would typically play, and see what happens. Write about your experience.

panel discussion a structured problem-solving discussion held by a group in front of an audience

remote access report (RAR) a computer-mediated audiovisual presentation of a group's process and outcome that others can receive electronically

streaming video a recording that is sent in compressed form over the Internet

10-5

group dynamics the way a group interacts to achieve its goal

KEY CONCEPTS

11-1

Determine a speech topic and goal that is appropriate for the rhetorical situation. To select an appropriate topic, you must understand the rhetorical situation, which encompasses you, the audience, and the occasion. By gathering and analyzing data about your audience members' information needs, you can more effectively select topics and develop your speech. Audience data should include demographic- and subject-related specifics. You can gather the data by conducting a survey, informally observing, questioning an audience representative, or by making educated guesses. It is important to use any data you collect in a respectful and ethical manner. Avoid marginalizing or stereotyping your audience. When selecting a topic, you will also want to understand the setting in which you will be speaking and the occasion.

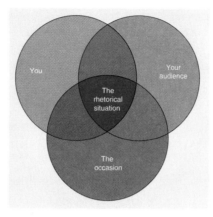

11-2

Locate and evaluate information sources. Subjects for speeches should come from areas that are of general interest to you. Then several more specific topics can be selected. Brainstorming is one way to generate many ideas for a speech topic, and using a concept map can help narrow that topic enough to cover in a single speech. Based on your audience and setting analyses, you can eliminate topics that would be inappropriate, and then select your personal favorite from among the topics that remain.

11-3

Identify and evaluate different types of evidence. Once you have a topic, you can move on to identify whether your general goal is to entertain, inform, or persuade. Then you can develop a specific goal—a single statement that identifies the exact response you want from your audience. Your specific goal should focus on just one main concept so your speech is easy for the audience to understand in one sitting.

Informative Goals

Increasing Understanding: I want my audience to understand the three basic forms of a mystery story.

Increasing Knowledge: I want my audience to learn how to light a fire without a match.

Increasing Appreciation: I want my audience to appreciate the intricacies of spiderweb designs.

Persuasive Goals

Reinforce Belief : I want my audience to maintain its belief in drug-free sports.

Change Belief: I want my audience to believe that SUVs are environmentally destructive.

Motivation to Act: I want my audience to join Amnesty International.

11-4

Record information and sources. The second action step of the speech preparation process is to gather and evaluate material to use in your speech. The three general sources for information include (1) your personal knowledge, experiences, and observations; (2) secondary source research; and (3) primary source

KEY TERMS

11-1

rhetorical situation a state in which you, the audience, and the occasion overlap

exigence the reason the speech needs to be given

audience analysis the study of the intended audience for your speech

audience adaptation the process of tailoring your speech to the needs, interests, and expectations of your audience

uncertainty reduction theory explains the processes we go through to get to know strangers

subject a broad area of knowledge

topic some specific aspect of a subject

demographics the statistical characteristics of a specific group of people

survey an examination of people to gather information about their ideas and opinions

marginalizing ignoring the values, needs, interests, and subject-specific knowledge of some audience members

stereotyping assuming all members of a group have similar knowledge levels, behaviors, or beliefs simply because they belong to that group

audience diversity the range of demographic characteristics and subject-specific differences represented in an audience

occasion the expected purpose and setting for the speech

11-2

concept mapping a visual means of exploring connections between a subject and related ideas

CHAPTER REVIEW 11

11-3

general goal the overall intent of the speech

specific goal a single statement of the exact response the speaker wants from the audience

11-4

secondary research the process of locating information about your topic that has been discovered by other people

primary research the process of conducting your own study in the real world

credentials your experiences or education that qualifies you to speak with authority on a subject

periodicals magazines and journals that appear at regular intervals

skimming rapidly viewing a work to determine what is covered and how

abstract a short paragraph summarizing the research findings

valid sources sources that report factual information that can be counted on to be true

accurate sources sources that present unbiased information that includes a balanced discussion of controversial ideas

reliable sources sources with a history of presenting accurate information

fieldwork observations a research method focused on careful observations of people or groups of people while immersed in their community

interview a planned, structured conversation where one person asks questions and another answers them

hypothesis an educated guess about a cause-and-effect relationship between two or more things

11-5

factual statements statements that can be verified

research. Before using information from a source, you will need to evaluate it using four criteria: authority, objectivity, currency, and relevance. If there is little information available on your topic, you may need to perform some primary research, which can be done through fieldwork observations, surveys, interviews, original artifact or document examinations, or experiments.

11-5

Cite sources effectively in your speeches. After your research is complete, you will need to identify the types of information you are using. These include factual statements (statistics and examples), expert opinions, and elaborations (anecdotes and narratives, comparisons and contrasts, and quotations). It is also important to draw information from a variety of cultural perspectives by seeking sources with different cultural orientations. As you review your sources, record the information accurately to provide accurate citations. Do so by creating an annotated bibliography and by recording information on research cards. It is important to cite your sources in your speech using oral footnotes, which will give credit to the source and protect you from accusations of plagiarism.

JOURNAL ASSIGNMENTS

A. POLITICAL CORRECTNESS

Ask three people of differing ages to define "political correctness." Compare and contrast their definitions with your own. Is there a difference between political correctness and using respectful language? How would you respond to an offensive speech? If we all avoided speech topics that might offend someone, would persuasion ever occur? Explain.

B. SUPPORTING EVIDENCE FOR EDITORIALS

Select an editorial or a letter to the editor from a national, local, or campus newspaper. (It's okay to use online newspapers.) Research the topic discussed in the editorial and locate material that either supports or contradicts the statements made in the editorial. Find an example of distorted facts on this topic. Discuss this example.

C. DIVERSE PERSPECTIVES IN SUPPORTIVE EVIDENCE

On the topic of parental rights, affirmative action, or same-sex marriage, find five different perspectives by consulting information from diverse groups.

statistics numerical facts

examples specific instances that illustrate or explain a general factual statement

expert opinions interpretations and judgments made by authorities in a particular subject area

expert a person who has mastered a specific subject, usually through long-term study

anecdotes brief, often amusing stories

narratives accounts, personal experiences, tales, or lengthier stories

comparisons illuminate a point by showing similarities

contrasts illuminate a point by highlighting difference

plagiarism the unethical act of representing a published author's work as your own

annotated bibliography a preliminary record of the relevant sources you find as you conduct your research

research cards individual cards or facsimiles that record one piece of relevant information for your speech

oral footnotes references to an original source, made at the point in the speech where information from that source is presented

KEY CONCEPTS

12-1

Develop your speech body using an appropriate main point pattern. Organizing is the process of selecting and structuring ideas that you will present in your speech; it is guided by your audience analysis. Once you have analyzed your audience, created a speech goal, and assembled a body of information on your topic, you are ready to identify the main ideas you wish to present in your speech and to craft them into a well-phrased thesis statement.

Once you have identified a thesis, you will prepare the body of the speech. The body of the speech is hierarchically ordered through the use of main points and subpoints. Once identified, main points and their related subpoints are written in complete sentences, which should be checked to make sure that they are clear, parallel in structure, meaningful, and limited in number to five or fewer. The sequential relationship between main point ideas and among subpoint ideas depends on the organizational pattern that is chosen. The three most basic organizational patterns are time, topic, and logical reasons order. You will want to choose an organizational pattern that best helps your audience understand and remember your main points. Main point sentences are written in outline form using the organizational pattern selected.

Subpoints support a main point with definitions, examples, statistics, personal experiences, stories, quotations, and so on. These subpoints also appear in the outline below the main point to which they belong. An organizational pattern will also be chosen for each set of subpoints.

Once the outline of the body is complete, transitions between the introduction and the body, between main points within the body, and between the body and the conclusion need to be devised so that the audience can easily follow the speech and identify each main point.

12-2

Create an effective speech introduction. The first step in completing the organization process is creating an introduction. The introduction should get the audience's attention, identify the relevance of the topic to the audience, establish speaker credibility, and state the thesis. Several strategies for getting attention are startling statements, questions (both rhetorical and direct questions), stories, jokes, personal references, quotations, action, and suspense. Relevance is key in maintaining audience attention, so establishing how the topic relates to the audience in the introduction will help get (and keep) audience attention. Credibility establishes why you are qualified to speak on your chosen topic. This also helps keep audience attention during the speech. Finally, stating the thesis in the introduction helps the audience understand what key points to listen for and what the speech will cover.

12-3

Construct an effective conclusion. The second step in completing the organization process is creating a conclusion to summarize the main points of the speech. In addition to a strong summary of key points, it is important to leave the audience with a vivid impression. This is done thorough a clincher, which often uses vivid imagery or an appeal to action to leave the audience with a strong impression of what the speech was about or needed them to accomplish.

KEY TERMS

12-1

organizing the process of arranging your speech material

organizational pattern a logical way to structure information that makes it easy for an audience to follow what is being said

time (sequential or chronological) order an organizational pattern that arranges the main points by a chronological sequence or by steps in a process

narrative order an organizational pattern that dramatizes the thesis using a story or series of stories that includes characters, settings, and a plot

topical order an organizational pattern that structures the main points using some logical relationship among them

logical reasons order an organizational pattern that structures the main points as reasons for accepting the thesis as desirable or true

thesis statement a one- or two-sentence summary of your speech that states your general and specific goals and previews the main points

speech outline a sequence representation of the sequential and hierarchical relationships between the ideas presented in a speech

subpoints statements that elaborate on a main point

supporting material developmental material you gathered through secondary and primary research

listener relevance link a piece of information that alerts listeners to why the main point is related to them or why they should care about the topic or point

transitions words, phrases, or sentences that show the relationship between or bridge ideas

CHAPTER REVIEW 12

section transition a complete sentence that shows the relationship between or bridges major parts of a speech

signposts short word or phrase transitions that connect pieces of supporting material to the main point or subpoint they address

12-2

startling statement a shocking expression or example used to arouse an audience's interest

questions requests for information that encourage an audience to think about something related to your topic

rhetorical question a question that doesn't require an overt response from an audience

direct question a question that demands an overt response from an audience

story an account of something that has happened or could happen

joke an anecdote or a piece of wordplay designed to be funny and make people laugh

personal reference a brief account of something that happened to you or a hypothetical situation that listeners can imagine themselves in

quotation a comment made by and attributed to someone other than the speaker

action an act designed to highlight and arouse interest in a topic

suspense wording your attention-getter so that it generates uncertainty and excites the audience

credibility the perception your audience has about your competence and character

12-3

clincher a one- or two-sentence statement that provides a sense of closure by driving home the importance of your speech in a memorable way

appeal to action describes the behavior you want your listeners to follow after they have heard your arguments

12-4

Compile a formal speech outline and reference list. The third step in the organization process is compiling a list of sources from the bibliographic information you recorded on your research note cards. Sourcing information is very important to avoid being accused of plagiarism and making sure that authors receive the credit for their ideas. Organize your source lists either alphabetically by author last name, which is appropriate for short lists, or by content category, with names listed alphabetically within each category. This second method is appropriate for long source lists. Source format will vary by professional discipline, but some common formats are MLA, APA, and the Chicago Manual of Style.

JOURNAL ASSIGNMENTS

A. CULTURE AND SPEECH ORGANIZATION

Many cultures use storytelling to structure public presentations. Can you provide examples of such speeches that you have heard? Why were they effective? With a multicultural audience, in which listeners represent many different backgrounds, how should the speaker organize his or her speech? What determines the most effective organizational structure: speaker, audience, topic, occasion, or a combination of these elements?

B. LISTENING TO SPEECHES

Go to a speech either on or off campus, on any subject. Write a few paragraphs about the speech, using the following questions as a guide:

1. What was the thesis, or central idea, of the speech?
2. What response was desired?
3. Did the speaker appeal to the needs, attitudes, and cultural values of the audience? Was the speech well organized?
4. What kind of introduction and conclusion did the speaker use?
5. What kind of supporting materials did the speaker use? How did he or she adapt this evidence to the audience?
6. Did language choices help the speaker reach the audience with his or her message? How?

C. PLAYING WITH ORGANIZATION?

If you were asked to give a speech on five random objects in your room, which organizational pattern would you choose? Pick the objects and indicate which pattern you think would be the most effective and why. What transitions would you use to move from your discussion of each object to another?

KEY CONCEPTS

13-1
Identify several reasons for incorporating presentational aids into your speech. Choosing the correct visual, audio, or audiovisual aid can enhance the message delivered in your speech. Presentational aids are useful when they help the audience understand and remember important information. People have various learning styles, and presentational aids appeal to different styles. It is important to remember, though, that aids should enhance the speech, not overwhelm it.

13-2
Describe the different types of presentational aids. The most common types of visual aids are objects, models, photographs, simple drawings and diagrams, maps, charts, and graphs. Audio aids include recordings of music, speeches, interviews, and environmental sounds. Audiovisual aids include clips from movies, television programs, commercials, and YouTube. Other sensory aids enhance the verbal message by focusing on taste, smell, or touch.

13-3
Choose appropriate presentational aids. Take time to evaluate the best type of visual aid by considering the following questions:
1. What are the most important ideas the audience needs to understand and remember?
2. Are there ideas that are complex or difficult to explain verbally but would be easy for members to understand visually?
3. How many visual aids are appropriate?
4. How large is the audience?
5. Is the necessary equipment readily available?
6. Is the time involved in making or getting the visual aid and/or equipment cost effective?

13-4
Prepare effective visual presentation aids.
1. Use printing or type size that can be seen easily by your entire audience.
2. Use a typeface that is easy to read and pleasing to the eye.
3. Use upper- and lowercase type.
4. Limit the reading done by the audience.
5. Include only items of information that you will emphasize in your speech.
6. Make sure information is laid out in a way that is aesthetically pleasing.
7. Add clip art where appropriate.
8. Use color strategically.
9. Customize visual aids created by others.

Presentational aids can be displayed via a flip chart or posterboard, a whiteboard or chalkboard, handouts, a document camera, a computer, a CD/DVD player, and/or an LCD projector. If you use electronic media, however, be sure to always prepare a back-up plan to account for potential equipment malfunctions.

KEY TERMS

presentational aid any visual, audio, audiovisual, or other sensory material used to enhance a verbal message

visual aids presentational aids that enhance a speech by allowing audience members to see what you are describing or explaining

audio aids presentational aids that enhance a verbal message through sound

audiovisual aids presentational aids that enhance a verbal message through a combination of sight and sound

13-2

actual objects inanimate or animate physical samples of the idea being communicated

model a three-dimensional scaled-down or scaled-up version of an actual object

diagram a type of drawing that shows how the whole relates to its parts

chart a graphic representation that distills a lot of information into an easily interpreted visual format

flow chart a chart that uses symbols and connecting lines to diagram the progression through a complicated process

organizational chart a chart that shows the structure of an organization in terms of rank and chain of command

pie chart a chart that shows the relationships among parts of a single unit

graph a diagram that presents numerical information

bar graph a graph that uses vertical or horizontal bars to show relationships between two or more variables

CHAPTER REVIEW 13

line graph a graph that indicates the changes in one or more variables over time

13-5

flip chart a large pad of paper mounted on an easel

handout material printed on sheets of paper to be distributed to an audience

JOURNAL ASSIGNMENTS

CHOOSING VISUAL AIDS

Choose a topic that is familiar to you and choose a potential audience. Using this information, determine how many different visual aids you can use for this presentation. Give a brief description of each potential visual aid and choose two you think will be the most effective.

KEY CONCEPTS

14-1

Explain how oral style differs from written style. Oral style is how we convey spoken messages. Because the context for spoken messages varies, oral style directly reflects the audience and should be adapted to fit. Oral style has four primary characteristics that differentiate it from written style.

1. Effective oral styles tend toward short sentences and familiar language
2. Effective oral styles feature plural personal pronouns (we, us, our)
3. Effective oral styles use descriptive words and phrases
4. Effective oral styles incorporate clear structural elements

14-2

Use appropriate language in your speeches. Appropriate language fosters verbal immediacy between you and your audience. In other words, you choose words that enhance a sense of connection with your listeners by demonstrating relevance, common ground, credibility, and linguistic sensitivity, and rehearsing in front of native speakers when speaking in a second language. Relevance attracts listeners by establishing timeliness, proximity, and personal impact for the audience. Establish common ground with the audience by using personal pronouns, asking rhetorical questions, and drawing from common experiences. Credibility involves describing formal education, special study, and personal skills, as well as sharing high-quality source material. Finally, audiences appreciate linguistic sensitivity, which is achieved by avoiding generic language, nonparallel language, offensive humor, profanity, and vulgarity.

14-3

Choose clear and specific language that helps the audience understand and remember your ideas. To ensure clarity, use specific language to give the audience a clearer view of what is in your mind. Familiar terms can help the audience understand unfamiliar concepts, so it is important to avoid using jargon or slang when talking to general audiences. Details and examples and limiting vocalized pauses also help the audience see your vision and keep their attention.

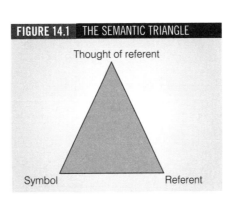

FIGURE 14.1 THE SEMANTIC TRIANGLE

Thought of referent

Symbol   Referent

14-4

Choose vivid language that helps the audience see and experience your ideas. To speak vividly, use language that appeals to the senses of seeing, hearing, tasting, smelling, and feeling, as well as rhetorical figures and structures of speech. Some examples include simile, metaphor, analogy, alliteration, assonance, onomatopoeia, personification, repetition, and antithesis.

KEY TERMS

14-1

oral style the manner in which one conveys messages through the spoken word

14-2

speaking appropriately using language that adapts to the needs, interests, knowledge, and attitudes of the audience

verbal immediacy language used to reduce the psychological distance between you and your audience

timeliness how the information can be used now

proximity information in relation to listeners' personal space

common ground the background, knowledge, attitudes, experiences, and philosophies a speaker shares with an audience

generic language words used that apply to one co-cultural group as though they represent everyone

nonparallel language words that are changed because of the sex, race, or other group characteristics of the individual

marking the addition of sex, race, age, or other group designations to a description

irrelevant association emphasizing one person's relationship to another when doing so is not necessary to make the point

14-3

speaking clearly using words that convey your meaning precisely

specific language words that narrow what is understood from a general category to a particular item or group within it

CHAPTER REVIEW 14

jargon the unique technical terminology of a trade or profession

slang informal, nonstandard vocabulary and definitions assigned to words by a social group or subculture

vocalized pauses unnecessary words interjected to fill moments of silence

14-4

vivid language words that are full of life

sensory language words that appeal to seeing, hearing, tasting, smelling, and feeling

rhetorical figures of speech language that makes striking comparisons between things that are not obviously alike

rhetorical structures of speech language that combines ideas in a particular way

simile a direct comparison of dissimilar things using the words *like* or as

metaphor an implied comparison between two unlike things, expressed without using *like* or as

analogy an extended metaphor

alliteration the repetition of consonant sounds at the beginning of words that are near one another

assonance the repetition of vowel sounds in a phrase or phrases

onomatopoeia the use of words that sound like the things they stand for

personification attributing human qualities to a concept or an inanimate object

repetition restating words, phrases, or sentences for emphasis

antithesis combining contrasting ideas in the same sentence

JOURNAL ASSIGNMENTS

TOPIC AND AUDIENCE
The text discusses how to build credibility through your audience's perception of your knowledge, trustworthiness, and personality. How does your desire to appear credible affect your topic selection? Make a list of topics and corresponding audiences for which you believe you could appear credible. Explain your strategy for building credibility.

KEY CONCEPTS

15-1
Employ strategies to effectively manage public speaking apprehension. As many as 76 percent of experienced public speakers experience some fear before speaking. The signs of speaking apprehension, or stage fright, vary from individual to individual. Symptoms can be cognitive, physical, or emotional. There are three phases of speech anxiety we experience in one speech: anticipation, confrontation, and adaptation. Five techniques can be effective for managing speech apprehension: communication orientation, visualization, systematic desensitization, cognitive restructuring, and public speaking skills training.

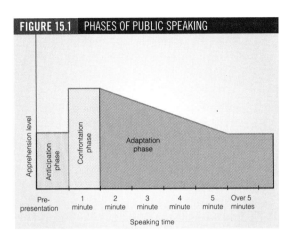

FIGURE 15.1 PHASES OF PUBLIC SPEAKING

15-2
Identify the characteristics of an effective delivery style. An effective delivery style is marked by a conversational style and an animated speaker. Speakers who use a conversational style make the audience feel that they are being talked with, not talked at. An animated speaker is lively and dynamic and able to convey passion.

15-3
Use your voice to convey effective delivery style. An effective use of voice depends on the sound of the voice, which is controlled by pitch, volume, rate, and quality. Articulation, accent, intelligibility, and vocal expressiveness also affect effectiveness.

15-4
Use your body to convey effective delivery style. In addition to voice, a speaker can make a speech more effective through body movements. Facial expressions, gestures, movement, eye contact, posture, poise, and appearance all contribute to the impression that a speaker leaves on an audience.

15-5
Select an appropriate delivery method for your speeches. Impromptu speeches occur most commonly during interviews and employment reviews. Scripted speeches can increase anxiety in the speaker if memorized and boredom in the audience if simply read from the paper unless the speaker makes a concerted effort to be conversational. Extemporaneous speeches are the most common. Because of the ability to research and practice a topic, speakers sound well-prepared but have enough leeway to modify the speech as needed based on audience reaction.

15-6
Engage in productive rehearsals. Effective delivery requires rehearsal. Experienced speakers schedule and conduct rehearsal sessions. Once outlines are

KEY TERMS

15-1

public speaking apprehension the level of fear you experience when anticipating or actually speaking to an audience

anticipation phase anxiety we experience before giving a speech

confrontation phase the surge of anxiety we experience when beginning to deliver a speech

adaptation phase the period during a speech when our anxiety gradually decreases

performance orientation believing we must impress a hypercritical audience with our knowledge and delivery

communication orientation seeing a speech situation as an opportunity to talk with a number of people about a topic that is important to the speaker and to them

visualization a method to reduce apprehension by developing a mental picture of yourself giving a masterful speech

systematic desensitization a method to reduce apprehension by gradually visualizing and then engaging in more frightening speaking events while remaining in a relaxed state

cognitive restructuring replacing anxiety-arousing negative self-talk with anxiety-reducing positive self-talk

public speaking skills training the systematic teaching of the skills associated with preparing and delivering an effective public speech, with the intention of improving speaking competence and thereby reducing public speaking apprehension

CHAPTER REVIEW 15

15-2

delivery how a message is communicated orally and visually through the use of voice and body

conversational style presenting a speech so that your audience feels you are talking with them

spontaneity a naturalness that seems unrehearsed and unmemorized

animated lively and dynamic

15-3

intelligible understandable

articulation using the tongue, palate, teeth, jaw movement, and lips to shape vocalized sounds that combine to produce a word

pronunciation the form and accent of various syllables of a word

accent the articulation, inflection, tone, and speech habits typical of the native speakers of a language

vocal expression the contrasts in pitch, volume, rate, and quality that affect the meaning an audience gets from the sentences you speak

monotone a voice in which the pitch, volume, and rate remain constant, with no word, idea, or sentence differing significantly from any other

pauses moments of silence strategically used to enhance meaning

15-4

poise graceful and controlled use of the body

audience contact when speaking to large audiences, create a sense of looking listeners in the eye even though you actually cannot

nonverbal immediacy communicating through body language that you are personable and likeable

motivated movement movement with a specific purpose

complete, effective speakers usually rehearse at least twice, often using speech notes on cards that include key phrases and words.

15-7
Adapt appropriately as you deliver your speech.
Be prepared to adapt to your audience and possibly change course as you give your speech.

15-8
Evaluate Speech Effectiveness.
Learn to evaluate the speeches you hear, focusing on content, organization, presentation, and adaptation.

8 days before	Select topic; begin research
7 days before	Continue research
6 days before	Outline body of speech
5 days before	Work on introduction and conclusion
4 days before	Finish outline; find additional material if needed; have all presentational aids completed
3 days before	First rehearsal session
2 days before	Second rehearsal session
1 day before	Third rehearsal section
Due Date	Deliver speech

JOURNAL ASSIGNMENTS

A. PRACTICING YOUR SPEECH
Follow the steps in your textbook on how to rehearse your speech (pp. 397–400). After you are done with your first practice session, reflect on your experience. Was your speech a lot longer or shorter than you expected it to be? Now listen to or watch your tape while you look through your complete outline. Did you leave out any important points? Did you talk too long on any one point? Were your note cards helpful? What do you notice about your delivery, pitch, rate of speech, and so on, that you are satisfied with? What would you like to improve?

B. ACCENTS
What stereotypes are associated with various accents within the United States? Why? How could an accent affect speech presentation? Have you ever been judged because of your accent? Is there a "standard" speaking style that would appeal to all U.S. English speakers? Why or why not?

C. COMMUNICATION APPREHENSION
Make a list of all the fears you have related to speech presentation. Order them on a continuum from least feared to most feared. Decide which fears are preventable and describe how they could be prevented. For the unpreventable fears, decide what you will do if they occur.

15-5

impromptu speech a speech that is delivered with only seconds or minutes of advance notice for preparation

scripted speech a speech that is prepared by creating a complete written manuscript and delivered by rote memory or by reading a written copy

extemporaneous speech a speech that is researched and planned ahead of time, although the exact wording is not scripted and will vary from presentation to presentation

15-6

rehearsing practicing the presentation of your speech aloud

speaking notes word or phrase outlines of your speech

KEY CONCEPTS

16-1
Identify the characteristics of effective informative speaking. The goal of an informative speech is to explain or describe facts, truths, and principles in a way that stimulates interest, facilitates understanding, and increases the likelihood that audiences will remember. In short, informative speeches are designed to educate an audience.

Effective informative speeches are intellectually stimulating, relevant, creative, memorable and address diverse learning styles. Informative speeches will be perceived as intellectually stimulating when the information is new and when it is explained in a way that excites interest. Using listener relevance links helps audiences understand how the speech relates to them. Informative speeches are creative when they produce new or original ideas or insights, many of which come from productive thinking. Informative speeches use emphasis to stimulate audience memory. Different people learn in different ways, and informative speeches address these different ways by rounding out the learning cycle and incorporating stimulus to four dimensions: the feeling dimension, the watching dimension, the thinking dimension, and the doing dimension.

16-2
Employ methods of informing in your speeches. We can inform by describing something, defining it, comparing and contrasting it with other things, narrating stories about it, or demonstrating it.

Description is used to create verbal pictures of objects, settings, or images discussed in your speech. Definition offers an explanation of something by identifying its meaning through classifying and differentiating it, explaining its derivation, explaining its use or function, or by using a synonym or antonym. Comparison and contrast demonstrates similarities and differences between your subject and other things. Narration explains something by recounting events. Narration can be presented in a first-, second-, or third-person voice. Demonstration shows how something is done, displays the stages of a process, or depicts how something works.

16-3
Create both process and expository informative speeches. Two of the most common types of informative speeches are process speeches, which demonstrate how something is done or made, and expository speeches, which provide carefully researched information about a complex topic. Expository speeches include speeches that explain a political, economic, social, religious, or ethical issue; forces of history; a theory, principle, or law; and a creative work.

KEY TERMS

informative speech a speech whose goal is to explain or describe facts, truths, and principles in a way that increases understanding

16-1
intellectually stimulating information that is new to audience members and piques interest

creative using information in a way that yields innovative ideas and insights

productive thinking contemplating something from a variety of perspectives

16-2
description method of informing used to create an accurate, vivid, verbal picture of an object, geographic feature, setting, person, event, or image

definition a method of informing that explains the meaning of something

synonym a word that has the same or similar meaning

antonym a word that has the opposite meaning

comparison and contrast a method of informing that explains something by focusing on how it is similar and different from other things

narration a method of informing that explains something by recounting events or stories

demonstration a method of informing that explains something by showing how it is done, by displaying the stages of a process, or by depicting how something works

16-3

process speech an informative speech that demonstrates how something is done, is made, or works.

expository speech an informative presentation that provides carefully researched, in-depth knowledge about a complex topic

JOURNAL ASSIGNMENTS

A. USING MEMORY AIDS
What are some ways you have used memory aids, such as mnemonics, in the past? What are some ways you could help apply some of these memory aids to remember key aspects of your informative speech?

B. INFORMATION VS. PERSUASION
Using examples from television and print advertisements, discuss how information can be persuasive. Compare and contrast persuasive and informative speaking.

C. FINDING CREATIVITY
Using your informative speech topic, develop several creative metaphors, memorable quotes, and descriptive narratives that can be used within the speech.

KEY CONCEPTS

17-1
Explain how people listen to and process persuasive messages. Persuasive speeches are designed to influence the beliefs and/or the behavior of audience members. They are designed to lead and convince listeners to agree, change their behavior, or take action. They do this with arguments that use logos, ethos, and pathos to connect with and inspire the audience to follow the speaker.

17-2
Tailor your persuasive speech goals as propositions aimed at your target audience. In preparing a persuasive speech, the speaker must choose a proposition (goal) that takes into account the audience's initial attitude. There are three types of propositions: propositions of fact, propositions of value, and propositions of policy. An audience may be opposed to the proposition, neutral (because they are uninformed, impartial, or apathetic), or in favor.

17-3
Employ rhetorical strategies of logos to support your persuasive proposition. Logical arguments follow a basic format with a claim, support, and a warrant. Four common types of logical arguments are sign, example, analogy, and causation. Speakers also need to check arguments so that they avoid five common fallacies.

17-4
Employ rhetorical strategies of ethos to support your persuasive proposition. No matter how good your speech might be, there will be some in the audience who will only pay peripheral attention. For these individuals, the most important cue of a speech is the speaker's credibility. This can be established by conveying good character, demonstrating empathy, and establishing competence and credibility.

17-5
Employ rhetorical strategies of pathos to support your persuasive proposition. Speakers can use emotional appeals to increase audience members' involvement with the proposition. Appeals to both negative and positive emotions can be effective.

17-6
Organize your persuasive speeches using an appropriate persuasive speech pattern. The reasons that support a proposition can be organized following one of seven patterns: the statement of reasons pattern, the comparative advantages pattern, the criteria satisfaction pattern, the refutative pattern, the problem–solution pattern, the problem–cause–solution pattern, and the motivated sequence pattern.

KEY TERMS

persuasion the process of influencing people's attitudes, beliefs, values, or behaviors

persuasive speech a speech attempting to influence the attitudes, values, beliefs, or behavior of others

17-1
rhetoric use of all available means of persuasion

argument articulating a position with the support of logos, ethos, and pathos

logos a persuasive strategy of constructing logical arguments supported with evidence and reasoning

ethos a persuasive strategy of highlighting competence, credibility, and good character

pathos a persuasive strategy of appealing to emotions

17-2
proposition a declarative sentence that clearly indicates the speaker's position on the topic

proposition of fact a statement designed to convince the audience that something did or did not occur, is or is not true, or will or will not occur

proposition of value a statement designed to convince the audience that something is good, fair, moral, sound, etc., or its opposite

proposition of policy a statement designed to convince the audience that a specific course of action should be taken

target audience the group of people a speaker most wants to persuade

incremental change an attempt to move an audience only a small degree in the speaker's direction

uninformed not knowing enough about a topic to have formed an opinion

neutral knowing the basics about a topic but still having no opinion about it

apathetic having no opinion because one is uninterested, unconcerned, or indifferent to a topic

CHAPTER REVIEW 17

17-3

claim (C) the conclusion the speaker wants the audience to agree with

support (S) evidence offered as grounds to accept the claim

warrant (W) the reasoning process that connects the support to the claim

inductive reasoning arriving at a general conclusion based on several pieces of evidence

deductive reasoning arguing that if something is true for everything in a certain class, then it is true for a given item in that class

syllogism the three-part form of deductive reasoning

arguing from sign supports a claim by citing information that signals the claim

arguing from example supports a claim by providing one or more individual examples

arguing from analogy supports a claim with a single comparable example that is significantly similar to the subject of the claim

arguing from causation supports a claim by citing evidence that shows one or more events always or almost always brings about, leads to, creates, or prevents another event or effect

fallacies flawed reasoning

hasty generalization a fallacy that presents a generalization that is either not supported with evidence or is supported with only one weak example

false cause a fallacy that occurs when the alleged cause fails to be related to, or to produce, the effect

either/or a fallacy that occurs when a speaker supports a claim by suggesting there are only two alternatives when, in fact, others exist

straw man a fallacy that occurs when a speaker weakens the opposing position by misrepresenting it in some way and then attacks that weaker (straw person) position

ad hominem a fallacy that occurs when one attacks the person making the argument, rather than the argument itself

17-4

goodwill the audience perception that the speaker understands, empathizes with, and is responsive to them

responsive showing that you care about the audience by acknowledging feedback

terminal credibility perception of a speaker's expertise at the end of the speech

initial credibility perception of a speaker's expertise at the beginning of the speech

derived credibility perception of a speaker's expertise during the speech

17-5

emotions buildup of action-specific energy

17-6

statement of reasons pattern used to confirm propositions of fact by presenting best-supported reasons in a meaningful order

comparative advantages pattern attempts to convince that something is of more value than something else

criteria satisfaction pattern seeks audience agreement on criteria that should be considered when they evaluate a particular proposition and then shows how the proposition satisfies those criteria

refutative pattern arranges main points according to opposing arguments and then both challenges them and bolsters your own

problem–solution pattern explains the nature of a particular problem and then proposes a solution

problem–cause–solution pattern demonstrates that there is a problem caused by specific things that can be alleviated with the proposed solution that addresses the causes

motivated sequence pattern a form of organization that combines the problem–solution pattern with explicit appeals designed to motivate the audience to act

A-1
Discuss how to form and order a series of questions for an interview. An effective interview protocol is marked by different types of questions. Primary questions are lead-in questions about one of the major topics of the interview. Secondary questions are follow-up questions designed to probe the answers given to primary questions. Open-ended questions are broad-based probes that allow the interviewee to provide perspectives, ideas, information, feelings, or opinions as he or she wishes. Closed-ended questions are narrowly focused and control what the interviewee can say, typically requiring short answers.

A-2
Discuss how to conduct information-gathering interviews. When you are interviewing for information, you will want to define the purpose, select the best person to interview, develop a protocol, and conduct the interview according to the protocol.

A-3
Examine how to conduct employment interviews. Employment interviews are a specific type of communication setting, with particular demands for both interviewer and interviewee. When you are interviewing prospective applicants for a job, structure your interview carefully to elicit maximal information about the candidate. Before the interview starts, become familiar with the data contained in the interviewee's application form, résumé, letters of recommendation, and test scores, if available. Be careful how you present yourself, do not waste time, do not ask questions that violate fair employment practice legislation, and give the applicant an opportunity to ask questions. At the end of the interview, explain to the applicant what will happen next in the process.

A-4
Discuss interview strategies for job-seekers. To get an interview, begin by taking the time to learn about the company and prepare an appropriate cover letter and résumé that are designed to motivate an employer to interview you. Electronic letters and résumés have become popular and need special preparation. For the interview itself, you should dress appropriately, be prompt, be alert, look directly at the interviewer, give yourself time to think before answering difficult questions, ask intelligent questions about the company and the job, and show enthusiasm for the position.

Before the Job Interview
1. Do your homework.
2. Based on your research, prepare a list of questions about the organization and the job.
3. Rehearse the interview.
4. Dress appropriately.
5. Plan to arrive on time.
6. Bring supplies.

During the Job Interview
1. Use active listening.
2. Think before answering.
3. Be enthusiastic.
4. Ask questions.
5. Avoid discussing salary and benefits.

After the Job Interview
1. Write a thank-you note.
2. Self-assess your performance.
3. Contact the interviewer for feedback.

interview a highly structured conversation in which one person asks questions and another person answers them

interview protocol the list of questions used to elicit desired information from the interviewee

primary questions introductory questions about each major interview topic

secondary questions follow-up questions that probe the interviewee to expand on the answers given to primary questions

open-ended questions broad-based queries that give the interviewee freedom about the specific information, opinions, or feelings that can be divulged

closed-ended questions narrowly focused questions that require very brief (one- or two-word) answers

neutral questions questions that do not direct a person's answer

leading questions questions that guide respondents toward providing certain types of information and imply that the interviewer prefers one answer over another

transcribe translate oral interview responses word for word into written form

job-seeker anyone who is looking for a job or considering a job change

APPENDIX IN REVIEW

visible job market easily accessible job opening announcements

hidden job market job openings that are not readily apparent and require alternative methods to locate

career fairs events that bring potential employers and applicants together to foster networking and create awareness about employment opportunities

employee referral programs in-house reward programs for employees who refer strong candidates to the company

networking the process of using developing or established relationships to make contacts regarding job openings

network the people you know, people you meet, and people who are known to the people you know

elevator speech a 60-second oral summary of the type of job you are seeking and your qualifications for it

résumé a summary sheet highlighting your related experience, educational background, skills, and accomplishments

cover letter a short, well-written letter or e-mail expressing your interest in a particular job and piquing curiosity about you as an applicant

chronological résumé a résumé that lists your job positions and accomplishments in reverse chronological order

functional résumé a résumé that focuses on highlighting the skills and experiences that qualify you for the position

employment interview a conversation or set of conversations between a job candidate and a representative or representatives of a hiring organization

talking points the three or four central ideas you will present as you answer the questions asked during a media interview

bridge the transition you create in a media interview so that you can move from the interviewer's subject to the message you want to communicate

A-5
Identify strategies for dealing with news media. To participate in media interviews, prepare by understanding the focus and format of the interview and considering the few main points you want to convey. During the media interview, you should present appropriate nonverbal cues, make clear and concise statements, realize that everything you say is on the record, and learn to use bridges as transitions to your message.

COMMUNICATING EMOTIONS NON-VERBALLY: ENCODING AND DECODING SKILL AND PRACTICE

THE ASSIGNMENT

Your instructor will write a simple sentence on the board that you will recite to your classmates while attempting to convey a particular emotion non-verbally. First, you will use only your voice; then you will use your voice and face; and finally you will use your voice, face, and body. The sentence could be as simple as "I had bacon and eggs for breakfast this morning."

1. To find out the emotion you will convey, draw a card from a stack offered by your instructor. Without letting your classmates see, turn the card over to read what emotion is written on the front. Some possible emotions include *anger, excitement, fear, joy, worry,* and *sadness.* Consider how you will use vocalics and kinesics to convey that emotion.
2. When your instructor calls on you, go to the front of the classroom and face the wall (so your classmates cannot see your face). Try to convey that emotion with only your voice while saying the sentence with your back to the class.
3. The class might make some guesses about the emotion you are conveying and give some reasons for their guesses. You should not tell them whether they are correct at this point.
4. Turn around to face your classmates and say the sentence again, this time trying to reinforce the emotion with your face and eyes.
5. The class might again make some guesses.
6. Repeat the sentence once more, this time using your voice, face, and body to convey the emotion.
7. The class might again make some guesses.
8. Tell them the emotion that was on the card and what you did with your voice, face, and body to convey it.
9. Your instructor may lead a discussion about what worked and didn't as well as how you could have made the emotional message more clear.

CRITICAL LISTENING

THE ASSIGNMENT

Find and attend a formal public presentation that is being given on campus or in your community. Your goal is to listen so that you remember and can critically evaluate what you have heard. Be sure to take notes and record the main ideas the speaker presents. After you have heard the speech, analyze what you heard. You can use the following questions to guide your initial thinking:

- What was the purpose of the speech? What was the speaker trying to explain to you or convince you about?
- Was it easy or difficult to identify the speaker's main ideas? What did you notice about how the speaker developed each point she or he made?
- Did the speaker use examples or tell stories to develop a point? If so, were these typical examples, or did the speaker choose examples that were unusual but seemed to prove the point?
- Did the speaker use statistics to back up what was said? If so, did the speaker tell you where the statistics came from? Did the statistics surprise you? If so, what would you have needed to hear that would have helped you accept them as accurate?
- Did the speaker do a good job? If so, why? If not, what should the speaker have done differently?

When you have finished your analysis, follow your instructor's directions. You may be asked to write a short essay about the speech or to present what you learned to the class.

PANEL DISCUSSION

THE ASSIGNMENT

Form a small group with three to five classmates. As a group, decide on a social issue or problem you would like to study in depth. Then select one group member to serve as moderator and the others as expert panelists. Members should do research to find out all they can about the issue, why it is a problem, and how it affects people and to what degree as well as potential ideas for solving it. The moderator's role is to come up with four to six good questions to ask the panelists. The panelists should prepare notes about the research they discovered.

On the day determined by the instructor, you will engage in a 15- to 20-minute panel discussion in front of your classmates. The moderator will guide the discussion by asking questions of the panelists as well as asking for questions from the class.

SUGGESTED FORMAT

1. Moderator thanks audience for coming and introduces the panelists and the topic.
2. Moderator asks panelists a series of questions, letting a different panelist respond first each time.
3. Moderator asks follow-up questions when appropriate.
4. Moderator asks for questions from the audience.
5. Moderator thanks the panelists and the audience members for participating.

A PERSUASIVE SPEECH

THE ASSIGNMENT

1. Follow the speech plan Action Steps to prepare a speech in which you change audience belief. Your instructor will announce the time limit and other parameters for this assignment.
2. Criteria for evaluation include all the general criteria of topic and purpose, content, organization, and presentation, but special emphasis will be placed on the primary persuasive criteria of how well the speech's specific goal was adapted to the audience's initial attitude toward the topic, the soundness of the reasons, the evidence cited in support of them, and the credibility of the arguments.
3. Use the Persuasive Speech Evaluation Checklist in Figure 16.4 to critique yourself as you practice your speech.
4. Prior to presenting your speech, prepare a complete sentence outline and source list (bibliography). If you have used Speech Builder Express to complete the Action Step activities online, you will be able to print out a copy of your completed outline and source list. Also prepare a written plan for adapting your speech to the audience. Your adaptation plan should address the following issues:

   - How does your goal adapt to whether your prevailing audience attitude is in favor, has no opinion, or is opposed?
   - What reasons will you use, and how will the organizational pattern you select fit your topic and audience?
   - How will you establish your credibility with this audience?
   - How will you motivate your audience?
   - How you will organize your reasons?